DATE DUE

OCT 27 1992	
NOV 9 1993	
MAY 1 0 1994	
MAY 1 6 1994	
NOV 2 2 1994	

BRODART, INC.   Cat. No. 23-221

ADMIRAL OF THE AMAZON

John Randolph Tucker

His Confederate Colleagues

and Peru

Contra Almirante Tucker?

Armada Peruana?

Fragta Indepia

ADMIRAL of the AMAZON

—+ +—

JOHN RANDOLPH TUCKER

His Confederate Colleagues, and Peru

+—+

DAVID P. WERLICH

University Press of Virginia
Charlottesville and London

THE UNIVERSITY PRESS OF VIRGINIA
Copyright © 1990 by the Rector and Visitors
of the University of Virginia

First published 1990

Library of Congress Cataloging-in-Publication Data
Werlich, David P., 1941–
    Admiral of the Amazon : John Randolph Tucker, his Confederate
colleagues and Peru / David P. Werlich.
        p.   cm.
    Includes bibliographical references.
    ISBN 0-8139-1270-9
    1. Tucker, John Randolph, 1812–1883.   2. Chile—History—War with
Spain, 1865–1866—Participation, American.   3. Amazon River—
Discovery and exploration.   4. Alto Amazonas (Peru)—History.
5. American Confederate voluntary exiles—Peru.   6. Explorers—Peru—
Biography.   7. Explorers—United States—Biography. 8. Peru.
Marina—Biography.   9. Confederate States of America. Navy—
Biography   I. Title.
F3447.T8W47   1990
985'.05'092—dc20
[B]   89-77279
                                                                        CIP

Printed in the United States of America

For My Mother

Contents

Illustrations

ILLUSTRATIONS

Nelson Berkeley Noland

Arturo Wertheman descends the Tambo

Original map by the Hydrographic Commission

Maps

Preface

COMMODORE JOHN RANDOLPH TUCKER shared the predicament of many Confederate naval officers after Appomattox. He was jobless and barred from resuming a career with his previous employer, the United States Navy. He was offered a post as a freight agent, but this landsman's duty held little attraction for a man who had been a mariner for almost four decades of his fifty-three years. Tucker seized a sudden opportunity to become a rear admiral in the Peruvian Navy. He commanded the combined fleets of Peru and Chile in a war against Spain and then served as president of the Hydrographic Commission of the Amazon, a Peruvian state agency. In this capacity the admiral and his handpicked team of former-Confederates spent seven adventurous but frustrating years in the jungle, charting the headwaters of the world's mightiest river for steam navigation.

When Tucker established the headquarters of his commission at Iquitos in 1867, that town was little more than a cluster of thatched huts on the bank of the Amazon River, accessible only by boat. The place still cannot be reached by road. But an international airport now serves this bustling city of nearly two hundred thousand persons, and oceangoing freighters from the Atlantic ascend the Amazon twenty-three hundred miles to this emporium for the Peruvian lumber and oil industries. Modern Iquitos is a monument to Peru's determination to develop and preserve its sovereignty over the almost two-thirds of the nation lying east of the Andes Mountains, in the Amazon Basin. The city fathers have honored the pioneers of eastern Peru, naming major Iquitos streets for the intrepid explorers Antonio Raimondi, Pedro Portillo, and Carlos Fermín Fizcarrald (the "Fizcarraldo" of the largely fanciful Werner Herzog film of that title). A large plaque in the city hall bears these same names and those of many other men who contributed to the progress of Amazonian Peru. Nothing in Iquitos, however, is named for the admiral, and probably few Iquiteños know who he was. In all the vast region he surveyed, there exists only one memorial to the explorer—a small encampment on the remote Nazarategui River called

Puerto Tucker. This place appears only on large-scale maps and as often as not is misspelled as "Puerto Tuker."

Throughout Peru only a few scholars know Tucker's story, and only in part. Although he commanded the nation's navy for eight months in wartime, the admiral's name never appeared in the published registers of that service. Chilean naval histories ignore him, and Tucker is not mentioned in the only substantial English-language study of Peru and Chile's war against Spain. Before his service in South America, Tucker had been a highly respected officer in the United States Navy and a key figure in the Confederate sea service. But North American historians have shown scant interest in him.

Admiral Tucker was little concerned about his place in history. The central files of the Confederate navy were destroyed in the final days of the war, forcing historians to rely heavily upon correspondence preserved by individual sailors and a handful of naval memoirs. Tucker left few documents from the Civil War, and in later years he was too modest or disinterested to record his reminiscences for posterity. Responding to a historian's inquiry in 1874, the admiral did write an autobiography—a sparse eighty-four words.[1]

Modern scholarship in Civil War naval history has required relatively little basic research on Tucker because historians have been able to draw upon a published biography. In 1888, five years after the admiral's death, his longtime friend and associate James Henry Rochelle wrote a *Life of Rear Admiral John Randolph Tucker*. This barebones, twenty-eight-thousand-word account was published posthumously in 1903. The author worked largely from memory, so the book has some errors. It also has many significant omissions. Rochelle wrote a century ago for contemporaries who well remembered the Civil War, and the book was a "labor of love," leading Rochelle to ignore or to minimize topics that might have detracted from his friend's reputation. "Admiral Tucker," he wrote, "possessed many of the qualities of a great commander," while in private life being a man "so gentle, generous and genial." The navy had "never produced a more thorough and accomplished sailor" or "a more honorable and gallant gentleman." In an article published two years earlier, Rochelle averred that he could not remember "a single instance" in which he had ever heard "a whisper of complaint against the professional or private conduct of John Randolph Tucker."[2]

The admiral, of course, did have enemies, and although Tucker was a highly skilled professional who accomplished much during a fascinating career, he was not, in historical perspective, a great man. But allowing for exaggeration, Rochelle's portrait of his friend was essentially correct. In an age when the adjective "gallant" was added almost habitually to the names of officers, Tucker deserved that description far more than most military men. In the language of that era, "gallant" had three meanings: it signified "gay, well-dressed, showy, splendid, magnificent," all qualities strongly exhibited by the young "Handsome Jack" Tucker. He was also "courtly, civil, polite and attentive to ladies." And many acquaintances thought him "brave, high spirited, courageous, heroic, magnanimous, fine, [and] noble."[3] Indeed, Tucker's associates admired him primarily for his attractive human qualities.

My biography of Admiral Tucker began two decades ago, when I stumbled across him while researching a history dissertation on Amazonian Peru. I read the reports of the Hydrographic Commission and became curious about its members—men with out-of-place names like Butt, McCorkle, Galt, Sparrow, Noland, Rochelle, and Tucker. A standard Peruvian reference satisfied me for the moment, identifying the admiral as a former "North American naval officer."[4] A decade later I cranked through the microfilmed dispatches of nineteenth-century United States diplomats in Lima, gathering material for a general history of Peru. In August 1866 the North American minister reported that "Admiral Tucker, ex of the U.S. Navy" had taken command of the allied fleet in the war against Spain.[5] My curiosity was immediately reborn. Advancing a few more frames of the film brought the discovery that Tucker was, more precisely, a Confederate exile. I was hooked. Since that moment of seduction, many persons and institutions have aided my research.

It is impossible to write a book of this size and complexity without considerable help. My research in Peru and Chile was made possible by a grant from the Johnson Fund of the American Philosophical Society and a fellowship from the Organization of American States. Additional financial support came from the Department of History, the College of Liberal Arts, and the Office of Research Development and Administration of Southern Illinois University at Carbondale. Daniel Irwin prepared the maps. Angela Calcaterra's expertise on the computer compensated for my ignorance of all but the basics of word processing.

I received much assistance from other institutions and individuals, including relatives of some of the book's characters, who generously shared their manuscripts, newspaper clippings, photographs, heirlooms, memories, and family traditions. These benefactors include John Randolph ("Josh") Tucker of Pensacola, Florida, and R. Douglas Tucker of Ellenboro, North Carolina, great-grandsons of Admiral Tucker; A. Royall Turpin and Mrs. David T. Ayers of Richmond, Virginia, and Mrs. Otto Aufranc of Wellesley Hills, Massachusetts, the admiral's great-grandnephew and great-grandnieces; Mrs. St. George Tucker Arnold of Oak Ridge, Tennessee, the widow of another Tucker great-grandnephew; Dr. Francis Land Galt's great-grandchildren,

Thomas R. Galt of Minneapolis, Minnesota, and Elizabeth A. Veselka of Englewood, Colorado, as well as their mother, Mrs. Stanier E. Mason of Atlantis, Florida; the late Mrs. William Churchill (Mary Bleecker) Noland, the sister-in-law of Nelson Berkeley Noland, and her son Nelson Berkeley ("Red") Noland of Colorado Springs, Colorado; Walter Raleigh Butt's great-grandnephew and great-grandniece, Marshall W. Butt, Jr., and Brooke Butt Maupin of Portsmouth, Virginia; the late Frederick Barreda Sherman of Mill Valley, California, the grandson of Federico L. Barreda; Ida Werthemann de Pérez Cornejo of Lima, Peru, the daughter of Arturo Wertheman; and Admiral Máximo Cisneros Sánchez, of Lima, a descendant of Luciano Benjamín Cisneros.

Several historians shared with me their documents, notes, and knowledge: James H. Bailey; George Mercer Brooke, Jr.; Norman C. Delaney; William D. Henderson; Jan M. Kermenic; Fernando Romero Pintado; José Valdizán Gamio; and Edward A. Wyatt IV.

All of the librarians and archivists who assisted me are too numerous to mention, but I wish to acknowledge the extraordinary service of several. First, the staff of the Morris Library of Southern Illinois University at Carbondale deserves special thanks. Within this group I am indebted to Social Studies Librarian James Fox, Documents Librarian Walter Stubbs, Curator of Special Collections David Koch, and, especially, Charles Holliday and Thomas Kilpatrick, who cheerfully secured an excessive number of interlibrary loans. Also generous with their time and knowledge were Edmund Berkeley, Jr., Curator of Manuscripts at the University of Virginia Library; Robert L. Byrd of the Manuscripts Department, William R. Perkins Library, Duke University; Margaret Cook, Curator of Manuscripts and Rare Books at the Earl Gregg Swem Library, College of William and Mary; William Cox of the Smithsonian Institution Archives; Carolyn A. Davis, Manuscript Librarian, George Arents Research Library, Syracuse University; William S. Dudley and Tamara Mosser Melia of the Historical Research Branch, Naval Historical Center, Washington; Ellen Emser, Archives Manager at the Old Dominion University Library; at the National Archives, in Washington, Rich Gould of the Diplomatic Branch and Charles Shaughnessy of the Old Army and Navy Branch; Allen W. Robbins of the Alexandria, Virginia, Library; Allen Stokes of the South Caroliniana Library, University of South Carolina; and Sandra Rouja of the Bermuda Archives in Hamilton.

At the Archivo Histórico Militar del Perú—Lima's friendliest archive—in the Center for Military History Studies, Director A. Elia Lazarte Ch. and her assistant María Luz Neyra Flores provided outstanding service. The Archive of the Naval Museum in Callao is among Peru's better-organized depositories. I spent many productive hours there assisted by the late museum director, Captain José Carlos Cosio, librarian Flor de María Cosio, and especially Iliana Vegas de Cáceres, the museum's outstanding archivist. My hostess at the Ministry of Foreign Relations, in Lima's Torre Tagle Palace, was Gladys García Paredes, the talented young diplomat in charge of the Archivo de Límites. While helping to obtain the documents I requested, she enriched my work there by posing important research questions I had not asked. Also generous with their expertise at the Foreign Ministry were Cristina López Albujar, of the general archive; map librarian Inés Vallejos de Pareja; and José Calixto Pomachagua, the official photographer. Admiral Federico Salmón de la Jara and his staff—especially librarian Esperanza Navarro Pantac—made profitable my visits to the Instituto de Estudios Histórico-Marítimos, in Lima. I also wish to thank Carmen Blossiers of the Sala de Investigaciones at the National Library of Peru, Vilma Fung and her staff in the History Section of the Archivo General de la Nación, and Director Cecilia Loli of Museo Antonio Raimondi—all in Lima; and Zoila Flores Arrué, Chief of the Municipal Library in Iquitos.

In Santiago, Chile, I was assisted by Javier González Echenique, Conservador of the Archivo Nacional, and his staff, especially archivist Miriam Reinoso. Chief Librarian Monserrat Pescador made me feel welcome at the Salón de los Fundadores of the National Library. Colonel Ernesto Videla Cifuentes, Undersecretary of Foreign Relations for Cultural Affairs and Information, secured photocopies of documents from the Foreign Ministry Archive in La Moneda. Admiral Fernando Navajos Irigoyen and Captain Peter Furniss Hodgkinson, naval attachés at the Chilean Embassy in Washington, also were very helpful.

United States diplomats who opened doors for me included Cultural Attaché Michael H. Morgan and his staff at the Lima embassy; Captain Lucian Martínez, the naval attaché of the same mission; and Cultural Attaché Guy Burton of the embassy in Santiago. I benefited from the friendly efficiency of the General Secretariat of the Organization of American States in Lima, including Director Antonio Lulli Avalos, Administrative Officer Rodolfo Ramos, and Julia Visquera, the fellowship officer. In Lima I enjoyed the special friendship of Luis José Diez-Canseco Núñez and his family, Ivo and Ursula Saric, John and Fina Withrow, and the Sala family of the Hotel Residencial Francia.

All of the above have my sincere thanks. I am most grateful, however, to my wife, Sandra, who participated in this project from the beginning and spent too many "vacations" working with me in libraries and archives.

ADMIRAL OF THE AMAZON

John Randolph Tucker

His Confederate Colleagues

and Peru

CHAPTER ONE

Handsome Jack

A NAVAL OFFICER. It is difficult, in retrospect, to imagine John Randolph Tucker as anything else. Both nature and nurture drew him to the sea and the profession of arms upon it. The future admiral was born on January 31, 1812, in Alexandria, Virginia, at that time part of the District of Columbia. His father, Captain John Tucker, was a substantial sea merchant who—like many of his numerous kinsmen— had migrated to the United States from Bermuda. Located about six hundred miles off the Virginia coast, these small islands, it was quipped, exported only onions, Easter lilies, and Tuckers.[1] From the colony's beginnings in the early seventeenth century, Bermudians had gained their livelihood from the sea. Using the native cedar of the islands, they built small sloops and brigs famed for their speed and durability. At any given time one-third of Bermuda's men were at sea, engaged in legitimate trade (usually between the British colonies on the North American mainland and the Caribbean), smuggling, or, in times of war, privateering. The typical Bermuda ship was manned by a skeleton crew consisting of her owner-captain, a younger white apprentice, and four black slaves who together performed all of the necessary tasks. Whether white or black, Bermudians were famed as magnificent seamen.[2]

The prolific Tuckers of Bermuda originated with Daniel Tucker of Milton, Kent County, England, the colony's tyrannical third governor (1616–18). Bermudians recorded the hot temper of this taskmaster in doggerel verse which quite possibly inspired an enduring American song. From "Old Dan Tucker" and his brother George, the family already had multiplied exponentially when, a half century later, St. George Tucker came to Bermuda from Northampton County and started a second clan which in its prominence soon overshadowed the original "petty Tuckers." His great-grandson St. George Tucker (1752–1827) migrated to Virginia, where he initiated a notable line of legal scholars and clergymen. In Bermuda and Virginia the Tuckers frequently intermarried and perpetuated favorite given names, creat-

1

ing a maddening tangle for genealogists. It seems likely, however, that the future admiral descended from the original branch of the family, steeped in Bermuda's seafaring tradition.[3]

Captain John Tucker (born 1764) owned at least one sloop and operated a ferry line in Hamilton harbor, Bermuda. But the colony's economy stagnated in the last years of the eighteenth century, so in June 1800 he emigrated with his second wife, Frances M. Dickinson Tucker, and two daughters to Alexandria, the bustling port on the south bank of the Potomac River. Here, with a younger kinsman, James H. Tucker, Captain Tucker opened a store on Fairfax Street, selling a large variety of goods "on very reasonable terms . . . by the quantity or by the piece." The partners also advertised "for freight or charter . . . the fast sailing Bermuda built sloop *Eliza*." Within a few years Captain Tucker became one of Alexandria's most successful merchants. In addition to a substantial house on the corner of Duke and St. Asaph streets, he owned several ships and their black crews, a store, and a number of warehouses, including some located along Tucker's Wharf.[4]

Frances Tucker died in 1806, and two years later the captain married twenty-three-year-old Susan Mary Ann Douglas Wallace, the recent widow of a Norfolk merchant. His new bride was the daughter of Dr. Charles and Susannah Randolph Douglas. A member of an old Scottish family, Dr. Douglas descended from at least three generations of British army officers. Colonel Charles Douglas, his grandfather, had been killed in 1741 leading a regiment of Royal Marines in an assault on Cartagena, Colombia. Himself a sometime Royal Navy surgeon, Dr. Douglas migrated to Virginia soon after the Revolutionary War. Susannah Randolph Douglas was one of the Virginia Randolphs who, like the Tuckers, were both prolific and prone to intermarriage. Sharing a common descent from William Randolph of Turkey Island and Mary Isham Randolph, this remarkable family gave the young republic many prominent figures. Like Admiral Tucker, some of the more notable Randolphs descended through the female line and bore different surnames, among them President Thomas Jefferson, Chief Justice John Marshall, and General Robert E. Lee.[5]

In addition to the future admiral, three other children of Captain John and Susan Tucker reached adulthood: Susan Jane (born 1810), Honoria Mary (1816), and Douglas Adam (1818).[6] Little is known about the sailor's childhood, except that he received his education in Alexandria, a town noted for its good schools. It seems likely, however, that the family's fortunes declined soon after his birth. The War of 1812 was a three-year disaster for American merchants, especially those of Alexandria. The British blockaded Chesapeake Bay, the port's outlet to the Atlantic, and in 1814 sacked the city's warehouses. Five years later at age fifty-six, John Tucker succumbed to a "painful illness," leaving a thirty-four-year-old widow and four young children.[7]

Although his eldest son was only seven years old at that time, Captain Tucker probably had instilled in the boy his own seafaring spirit. Residing in the city of Alexandria likely influenced the lad's decision to join the navy, an appropriate career for a young gentleman of reduced means. Alexandrians were very patriotic, taking great pride in their most famous son, George Washington. The town's role as a major port and its recent bitter experience at the hands of the Royal Navy enhanced public respect for the sea service. As a boy Tucker certainly watched the stately warships passing along the Potomac to and from the Washington Navy Yard, a few miles above his hometown. On June 1, 1826, the fourteen-year-old lad was appointed acting midshipman in the United States Navy. It was a profession, wrote his friend and biographer James Henry Rochelle, "for which he was by nature peculiarly adapted." Tucker "loved the sea and all that was connected with the life of a sailor."[8]

Youthful Indiscretions

In the years before the opening of the United States Naval Academy at Annapolis in 1846, apprentice officers like Tucker might briefly attend one of three small schools maintained by the navy or receive formal instruction from "professors" assigned to some larger ships. But most commonly they learned the ropes through practical experience at sea. According to navy regulations, "no particular duty" could be assigned to midshipmen; however, they were "promptly and faithfully to execute all the orders . . . from their commanding officer." One authority summarized the midshipman's job as "doing what he was told, and that [damned] quick." Tucker's training began on June 9, 1827, when he sailed from Boston aboard the frigate *Java*, bound for the Mediterranean.[9]

Considered the elite among the five regional forces regularly maintained by the navy, the Mediterranean Squadron was a choice assignment. But service in the Mediterranean also had its pitfalls for sailors. The most notorious of these was Port Mahon, on the Spanish island of Minorca, the base for the American fleet. Mahon "approximated the midshipman's idea of an earthly paradise," while presenting a disciplinary nightmare for ship and squadron commanders. The Mahonese, who whitewashed their town every Saturday afternoon, catered to sailors' vices whetted to their fullest during months at sea. The place had numerous taverns, gambling dens, and available women. Many a mariner appreciated the bittersweet lament

3

So of all the ports I have been in
Mahon is the best of them all
There's no other place that so quickly
Will prove a poor sailor's downfall.

Every liberty at Port Mahon seemed to bring a rash of court-martials—for brawling and dueling, for drunkenness and reckless horse racing through city streets, and especially for nonpayment of debts. At Mahon, as eighteen-year-old Tucker learned, "even midshipmen could borrow money and yet be prevented from paying the debt with the maintop bowline, which means not at all."[10] Funds for the squadron payroll reached Mahon at very irregular intervals, and sailors went unpaid for many months. Accommodating merchants extended them liberal credit without specifying the terms of repayment, and the debts of young midshipmen often accumulated faster than the pay—at $19 per month—credited to them in their ships' accounts. Upon taking command of the Mediterranean Squadron in 1830, Commodore James Biddle determined to put an end to the "disreputable practice" of "incurring debt on shore without the means or even the disposition to repay."[11]

On September 8, 1830, Tucker and five other midshipmen faced a court-martial for nonpayment of debts. The charges against Tucker included "unofficer-like and ungentlemanly conduct" and, more serious, "fraud" because he allegedly had incurred obligations "well knowing at the time that he did not have the means of satisfying said debts." The young officer owed about $200; he was due $86.57 in back pay. For three days the panel of officers heard testimony from Tucker's creditors—a victualler, a laundryman, two tavern keepers, a pair of tailors, a hatter, and a shoemaker. These men testified that the midshipman had violated no promises regarding his debts; several creditors had received partial payments from him. Tucker cross-examined each witness, repeatedly asking only one question: "Sir, did I intend to cheat you?" His creditors all replied in the negative. The young Virginian also questioned his immediate supervisor and the captain of his ship. These officers asserted that except for the problem of debts, Tucker always had been "attentive and correct on duty and unexceptionally correct off duty." In a written statement to the court, the midshipman described his conduct as "rash and inconsiderate" and declared that it caused him "indescribable regret and sorrow." Tucker had not intended to defraud the merchants, he explained, but had been a victim of "youthful indiscretions," for he was "unacquainted with the world." Noting the "proud feelings of honor" that he had "always cherished," he promised to satisfy his creditors, even if this required the embarrassment of asking his mother for money.

4

The panel announced its decision on September 10. The charge of fraud was "not proved," but the court found Tucker guilty of "unbecoming conduct." Describing itself as "lenient" because of Tucker's youth and "good character in other respects," the panel ordered that he be publicly rebuked in a reprimand to be read on board every ship of the squadron. He was to be assigned to port until all of his debts were canceled. Most important, Tucker could not take the examination for promotion to lieutenant until twelve months after the other midshipman of his "date," 1826.[12] This was a heavy penalty, for in the navy of that era, officers attained promotion solely by seniority; and because the service did not regularly retire senior officers, advancement came very slowly. After 1842, when the size of the officer corps was frozen, only the dismissal of wayward sailors, the resignation of disabled or impatient ones, and the deaths of wizened old captains afforded mobility for junior officers. The midshipman who completed his apprenticeship and passed his qualifying examination faced years of waiting as a passed midshipman (at $25 per month) until his turn came to fill a vacant lieutenancy. Only then would he earn a salary adequate to support a wife and family. Tucker's "youthful indiscretions" at Mahon cost him almost forty precious rungs on the promotion ladder.[13]

Tucker returned to the United States in the spring of 1831 and enjoyed one month's leave for each of his four years at sea. In September he requested assignment to the naval school at Norfolk, Virginia, to prepare for his examination. Navy Secretary Levi Woodbury, however, ordered him to the New York receiving ship (a combination recruiting office and barracks), with permission to attend the school there in his spare time. In early 1832 Tucker asked the secretary to review his court-martial and to permit him to take the forthcoming examination with the other midshipmen of 1826. But Woodbury could find "no sufficient reason" to reverse the decision made at Mahon. On May 1 of the following year, Tucker passed his oral qualifying exam at Baltimore and was warranted a passed midshipman to date from June 10, 1833. The examining board of senior officers—often quite subjective in their evaluations—ranked him twenty-third among the thirty-eight lads who qualified, most of whom had entered the service the year after Tucker.[14]

In October 1833 Tucker again petitioned the Navy Department to restore his lost seniority. Because his punishment had been for a specific offense, he "could not conceive" that the penalty was intended to "pursue" him "through every grade or rank in the Navy whilst life lasts," making him "perpetually junior" to men who had entered the service after him. Such an interpretation of his sentence would be "greatly injurious" to his "hopes and expectations," without which he "could neither feel pride or interest in the service." The young Virginian construed his intended punishment as a one-year delay in taking his examination, after which he would be ranked among the men who had qualified in 1832. If Woodbury was unable to reach a decision on the matter, suggested Tucker, the secretary might submit the case to the president. Irked by the midshipman's impertinence, Woodbury decisively refused to revise Tucker's status or to forward his petition to the commander in chief. But on December 6 the secretary authorized Tucker to address President Andrew Jackson directly, and the young officer wrote his appeal immediately. "Old Hickory" replied eight days later: he had examined Tucker's case and declined to make any change.[15]

Passed Midshipman Tucker reported on board the sloop *Erie* at Boston in June 1834 for service with the Brazil Squadron. His three-year cruise in the South Atlantic—calling at Rio de Janeiro, Montevideo, and Buenos Aires—was most satisfying. In October 1835 Tucker became acting master of the *Erie*, the officer directly charged with navigating the vessel. The following March, he received notice that President Jackson had again reviewed his court-martial and had placed Tucker at the bottom of the list of midshipmen of his original date. He advanced twenty-three positions on the navy roster. On September 1, 1836, Tucker became acting lieutenant on the *Erie*. And to crown this good fortune, the officer made three close friends among his shipmates—Alfred Taylor, from Alexandria's neighboring Fairfax County, who had entered the navy six months before Tucker, and two midshipmen making their first cruise, New Yorker John L. Worden and, most notably, Henry Augustus Wise.

Fifteen-year-old Midshipman Wise had been born at the Brooklyn Navy Yard but was a Yankee only by accident of birth. His father, navy Purser George S. Wise, was the scion of an old Virginia family. Orphaned at age five, Henry was raised on Craney Island, near Norfolk, in the home of his kinsman and guardian Henry Alexander Wise, a future governor of Virginia. Midshipman Wise had a literary flair and soon acquired a wealth of experience to fuel his talent. Under the pseudonym "Harry Gringo," Wise published *Los Gringos* in 1849, recounting his service with the Pacific Squadron during the war with Mexico. During the next decade and a half he published a children's book and three sea adventures, all under the same nom de plume, a nickname his friends often used for him.[16] In the sea stories, based loosely on fact, the narrator Gringo introduced the public to his shipmates. Wise garbled their names, but the characterizations were instantly recognizable within his circle of friends. John Randolph Tucker was Wise's most prominent hero.

By the time of his cruise on the *Erie*, the twenty-two-year-old Tucker had developed into a man of striking appearance and magnetic personality. His shipmates called him "Handsome Jack." He was "tall and erect in figure, with clearly cut features," wrote his future shipmate James Barron Hope. "His genial manners won him many friends whom the charm of his presence frequently drew around him." For young Midshipman Hope—and probably for Henry Wise, seven years Tucker's junior—the handsome lieutenant was "indeed a man to excite the imagination . . . of youth." He was "of commanding presence and manly beauty," a "personage in air, bearing, and address." Nevertheless, "his face was so frank, his eyes so honest, his generosity so open, his dignity so sweet and unaffected."[17]

It was on the "*Juniata*" (the *Erie*) that Harry Gringo, in *Tales for the Marines*, first "fell in company with a mate, as noble and handsome . . . as ever lived, named Jack Gracieux" (Graceful Jack), a "sweet-tempered" officer with "a mass of locks as glossy as jet." The narrator would "never forget the impression he made" at the time of their first introduction. As his former creditors at Port Mahon could attest, Handsome Jack Tucker dressed meticulously; but he was probably less of a dandy than Wise's caricature of him. Discovering that he had been the victim of a thieving washerwoman, Gracieux exclaimed to Gringo, "Split my canvas! half a dozen pairs of duck trousers gone, and as many fine shirts as ever were seen in New Spain. . . . Alas for my shirts! that is my greatest grief: I have a fondness for shirts, particularly linen ones, for there's a constitutional whiteness about linen which common dingy, yellow, plebeian cotton can never attain."[18] Wise and Tucker later sailed together in the Mediterranean, where an Italian nobleman habitually pronounced the Virginian's name as "Tokeker." So, in Wise's *Scampavias*, Gringo described his messmate "Jack Toker," explaining that "Gracieux was his right name, and the one he bore . . . in the first ship we sailed in." He was "the handsomest fellow you ever saw, and withal the most graceful figure," even though "having been fed considerably upon ham down in 'Old Virginny,' in his boyhood, he had run away a good deal into legs and arms." In cramped quarters, the legs of the lanky Toker "folded up like a two-foot rule."[19]

The *Erie* and Acting Lieutenant Tucker returned home in September 1837, and the navy honored his request for assignment to the *Java*, which now served as the receiving ship at Norfolk. On April 6 of the next year, Tucker obtained his long-awaited commission as a lieutenant. Two months later, on June 7, 1838, twenty-six-year-old Handsome Jack married eighteen-year-old Virginia Webb. A Norfolk native, the bride was the daughter of Harriett Davis Webb of Richmond and Master Commandant (Commander) Thomas Tarleton Webb. Also a Virginian and a thirty-year navy veteran, Webb commanded the *Java*.[20] During the next dozen years, the lieutenant's family responsibilities—in the Tucker tradition—grew rapidly, stretching thin his $1,500 annual salary. In May 1839 Virginia Tucker gave birth to John Tarleton Tucker, the first of nine children whose conceptions recorded their father's brief periods at home. A second son, christened Alfred Taylor (after Tucker's friend from the *Erie*), arrived in July 1841 but died the next year. Charles Douglas (named for Tucker's grandfather) was born in September 1842, followed by Virginia Fleming, who died before her first birthday. Harriet Reilly came in September 1847, Randolph in July 1849, and Tarleton Webb in February 1851, after whom there was a pause of five years.

The Tuckers' Norfolk household also included his grandmother Susannah Douglas, his mother, his maiden aunt Eliza Randolph Douglas, his two sisters, and two nephews. Susan Jane, Tucker's elder sister, had married navy Purser Andrew McDonald Jackson. When he died suddenly in 1840, the widow and her two young sons, Thomas Alphonse and Andrew St. George Jackson, were taken in by Lieutenant and Mrs. Tucker. Honoria ("Nora"), the officer's younger sister, also resided with him until her marriage in 1842 to their second cousin Joseph Williamson Randolph. The latter, who would become Virginia's foremost publisher of the Civil War era, admonished his bride-to-be not to plan a large wedding. "Your brother," he wrote, "has no money to spend unnecessarily"; yet he was "of such a generous nature" that if she permitted it, Tucker would "ruin himself in debt rather than not have things in style."[21]

Between March 1839 and August 1841, Lieutenant Tucker cruised with the Home Squadron on board the sloops *Warren* and *Levant*, sailing in the Caribbean and then shuttling in and out of ports from Florida to Maine. Next, he enjoyed an eighteen-month stint at home, serving in the Norfolk ordinary (where surplus vessels were mothballed) and on the receiving ship. In February 1843, however, the Navy Department ordered him to the sloop *St. Louis* for a "perilous voyage" to the East Indies.[22] During the next two and a half years, Tucker would sail around the world.

The *St. Louis* and the frigate *Brandywine*, her larger consort, departed Norfolk in May 1843 and took on supplies at Rio de Janeiro. Eleven days out of that port, bound for the Cape of Good Hope, a serious leak in Tucker's ship forced a return to Rio for repairs. In May 1844 the unescorted *St. Louis* ultimately reached Hong Kong where she joined a squadron supporting envoy Caleb Cushing, who negotiated the first commercial treaty between the United States and China. In the succeeding months Tucker and his shipmates cruised the Chinese coast, touching at several ports and riding out a typhoon. At Whampoa (near Canton) the *St. Louis* landed sailors and marines to suppress a riot which threatened American-owned property. Tucker's sloop resumed her solitary voyage in November 1844, calling at Manila, Batavia

(Djakarta), Australia, Tasmania, and New Zealand, where the vessel arrived in the midst of an uprising of Maori tribesmen. After carrying some 150 persons to safety, the *St. Louis* on April 3, 1845, began a voyage across the Pacific to Valparaíso, Chile, and then completed the long journey home by way of Cape Horn.

After expending his leave and a brief period "waiting orders," Tucker, who had been seriously ill during his recent cruise, requested posting at the Norfolk receiving ship "until required for more active service."[23] Two months earlier the United States had declared war against Mexico.

A Downright Fancy for the Navy

Lieutenant Tucker reported at Boston on March 3, 1847, for duty as executive officer of the *Stromboli*, Captain William S. Walker, commanding. One of several small merchantmen hastily acquired by the navy for use in the shallow rivers and ports of Gulf Coast Mexico, the *Stromboli* was designated a bomb brig because she carried a single 10-inch Columbiad gun which fired an explosive projectile, a relatively new weapon later called a shell gun. The vessel, with her seven officers and forty-two crewmen, left Boston on April 20 and arrived eight days later at Antón Lizardo, near Veracruz, the headquarters of Commodore Matthew C. Perry's squadron. As part of the general blockade of all Mexican ports, Perry stationed the *Stromboli* in front of Coatzacoalcos, down the coast from Veracruz, and ordered Captain Walker to destroy the small fort guarding the harbor. The vessel reached her destination on May 14, and in the darkness of the following morning Lieutenant Tucker led a scouting party on shore. Unexpectedly finding the fort deserted, the sailors made the most of their good fortune. They knocked the trunnions off the fourteen cannon there, so that the guns could not be remounted, and burned the gun carriages. During the next month, detachments from the *Stromboli* under Tucker and Lieutenant Louis C. Sartori methodically destroyed the fort itself and interdicted trade between Coatzacoalcos and the interior.[24]

On June 14 the *Stromboli* joined nine other ships under the personal command of Commodore Perry for an expedition against the city of Tabasco (Villahermosa), seventy-two miles upstream from the mouth of the Río Tabasco. The fleet, towing many surfboats and barges loaded with men and equipment, reached its destination two days later and landed almost twelve hundred sailors and marines. Lieutenant Tucker led a twenty-seven-man detachment from the *Stromboli* which fought their ship's gun on shore. After a brief artillery duel and a show of force by Perry's men, the outnumbered and dispirited enemy withdrew from the town. Already, however, Perry's sailors had encountered a foe far more dangerous than the Mexicans. Yellow fever ravaged the squadron that summer. The *Stromboli* returned to the mouth of the Tabasco River on June 25; the next day Captain Walker, stricken by the dreaded "yellow Jack," was removed to the USS *Raritan*. Thereafter, the *Stromboli* resumed her blockade of Coatzacoalcos under John Randolph Tucker, "lieutenant commanding." The fever continued to attack the men of the *Stromboli*, however, and on August 25 Tucker took his vessel back to Antón Lizardo. Only six of his men were fit for duty, and Tucker, too, was seriously ill. Although he had resisted the yellow fever, the young skipper was nearly incapacitated with a "disorder of the liver."[25]

This was a chronic problem for Tucker. It had delayed his first cruise as a midshipman and attacked him again during his voyage to Asia. As Harry Gringo noted, his "handsome friend Jack Gracieux . . . was always complaining of his gizzard." Over the years Tucker probably aggravated this condition through his heavy consumption of alcohol, a practice widespread in the navy then and now. In a letter to his sick friend Henry Wise, written in the persona of Jack Toker, Tucker admonished Gringo not to "neglect your tipple which, to one of your delicate constitution, might prove fatal; . . . let an old friend caution you against rash experiments. Recollect we are not as young as we were when we cruised together in [the] *Juniatta*—and the moister imbibed in the system during that happy cruise can not be allowed to evaporate without leaving our livers aground, whereas the most approved authority on the subject advise that they should be kept just afloat." On the advice of two naval surgeons and with Perry's permission, Tucker relinquished command of the *Stromboli* on September 13, 1847, and boarded the *Vixen* for the journey home.[26]

Tucker's first command had lasted less than three months. But during this brief period he established a reputation for maintaining a "smart ship." Under Captain Walker, discipline had been lax—the vessel's log recorded the punishment of only one mariner—and little maintenance work had been performed. Tucker kept his men busy and, in accordance with ancient naval practice, flogged sailors who broke the rules. On June 27, one day after the change in command, two crewmen each received six lashes with the cat-o'-nine-tails, "by orders of Captain Tucker," for neglect of duty and sleeping on watch. About once per week thereafter, six to twelve lashes were dispensed for the same infractions and a variety of others—disobedience, leaving the ship without permission, fighting, and, once, "for insolent conduct and making a noise." But the *Stromboli*'s young skipper offered the carrot as well as the stick; on August 1 Tucker mustered the crew to witness his promotion of two sailors. His men endured frequent inspections. They

10

exercised with the ship's gun and took target practice with carbines. Decks were cleaned, and the ship painted inside and out. Sailors refurbished the gig and "scrubbed hammocks, bedding and clothes."[27] After the United States Navy abolished the lash in 1850, Tucker adapted well to more humane methods of discipline. But sailors under his command in five navies would continue to be well acquainted with the paintbrush and scrub bucket.

By this point in his career, Tucker had won widespread respect for his professionalism. According to his friend Rochelle, "he could perform with his own hands the duties of every station on board a ship-of-war." He had a special interest in new naval technology, notably advances in ordnance and steam propulsion. Tucker was most admired, however, as a manager of men—for his "leadership qualities." Although a strict disciplinarian who demanded "prompt and unhesitating obedience to orders," Tucker "commanded the respect and confidence, as well as the good will, of his men." Lieutenant Tucker now had sufficient seniority to command a small ship. But his professional skills made him an ideal executive officer—the "second officer" on a vessel. This man, not the captain, usually managed the ship. A good executive officer was entirely familiar with his vessel and the function of each man on board. "By the Captain," noted sailor Herman Melville, "he is held responsible for every thing; . . . indeed, he is supposed to be omnipresent; down in the hold, and up aloft, at one and the same time."[28] A naval manual of the period explained that "there is no position so wearying, none so trying, none so much needing wisdom and good judgment, good temper and professional skill. In his general deportment [the executive officer] is supposed to represent the captain's wishes, and yet avoid any blunder the captain himself may make. He is the great *conservative* element in a ship-of-war. He stands between officers and themselves, between officers and men, and, as need be, between the captain and all the rest."[29] The executive officer was especially important on the flagship of a squadron because she set the standard for the other vessels under the commodore's command.

In April 1849 Commodore Foxhall A. Parker, under whom Tucker had served in the East Indies, learned that Tucker—again assigned to the Norfolk ordinary—was anxious for sea duty. Parker obtained his appointment as executive officer of the *Raritan*, the flagship of the Home Squadron. During this one-year cruise, primarily in the West Indies, the ship "was in splendid fighting order," recalled Robert D. Minor, a junior lieutenant on board. The crew was "well-disciplined and all hands happy and contented, and proud of their ship, with Tucker as the moving spirit of the whole."[30] After another brief posting on the receiving ship at Norfolk, Tucker reported in March 1852 as executive officer of the frigate *Cumberland*, flagship of Commodore Silas H.

11

Stringham's spit-and-polish Mediterranean Squadron. The scene of his first cruise a quarter century earlier, this was to be Tucker's last extended sea duty with the United States Navy. It was probably his most satisfying assignment, too, for his old friends John Worden and Henry Wise sailed with him.[31] In his book *Scampavias*, Gringo recorded his adventures with Toker in Spain and Italy, Greece and Turkey, Malta, Minorca, and other exotic places.

At a bathhouse in "Stamboul," the two mates encountered a "mahogany-colored, leather-faced object" wearing a "dark green turban . . . and a filthy caftan." In the crimson sash around his waist were "thrust three long pistols, a yataghan and an arabesque dagger." The "infidel," upon seeing the two sailors, "made a face as if he was sitting on a dead pig." Muttered Toker to his friend, "I say shipmate, . . . that fellow must be a Kurd, he looks so sour." Then, with a "villainous scowl," the Turk began drawing one of the flintlock weapons from his sash. Toker, however, quickly "laid his hand on his navy-revolver" and warned, "This is what we dogs call a six shooter, designed by Cadi Colt, and if you expose another inch of the ironmongery stuck about your filthy carcase, I'll make dog's meat of you." The "infidel" prudently backed down.

Throughout the voyage, the younger officers of the *Cumberland* boasted of myriad romantic encounters. But Gringo, like his friend Toker—with his "numerous progeny"—was now a married man. The two mates believed "that most of these conquests were myths," for neither sailor "had encountered so much as a wink, or a wave of a fan."[32] In time the mariners became homesick. "Harry, my lad," said Toker, "this would be pure . . . enjoyment if only we had those dear ones at home to enjoy all these pleasant scenes with us. This is the only drawback to the downright fancy I have for the navy. These long separations from those we love . . . often sadden me in my gayest moments. . . . Then again . . . the service has its charms, it is a gallant and honorable profession; promotion, though Tontine in its system, may come one of these days. If there ever came a war we have a chance for a gold chain or a wooden leg—fer you know, my boy, the spray and the prize money go aft." Gringo then interrupted Toker with his own discourse. "More than all . . . we yearn kindly toward our dear and true companions from boyhood to manhood; fellows with warm and generous hearts, . . . whom we . . . know to be as staunch and steadfast as the needle to the pole."

And Henry Wise acknowledged a special friendship, dedicating *Scampavias* to "John Randolph Tucker, of the Navy of the United States, who has been my tried friend, in storm and sunshine, for a full score of years, and who is as true a gentleman and gallant a sailor as ever trod the deck of a ship." The admiration was mutual. On October

18, 1856, fifteen months after the return of the *Cumberland*, Virginia Tucker gave birth to her eighth child. In navy artillery parlance the proud father announced the event to his friend. "It is a fine boy—XI pounder with a good crop of black hair. . . . As this is (positively) to be our last, I dedicate him to you by the name 'Harry Gringo Tucker.' What think you of it?"[33]

After Tucker returned home in 1855, the Navy Department gave him an important personnel assignment. He became commander of the *Pennsylvania*, the receiving ship at Norfolk. An old 120-gun ship of the line (the predecessor of the modern battleship), this vessel was the largest commissioned warship in the United States Navy and served as the barracks for hundreds of sailors. On October 8 of that year, after eighteen years in grade, Tucker was promoted to commander, the penultimate rank in the pre–Civil War navy. During his twenty-nine-year career, he had spent nearly eighteen years at sea, the duty most respected by naval officers. Although sixty-four commanders were senior to him, only eleven of these men had greater time afloat; twenty-eight of the navy's sixty-eight captains had less sea service than the fledgling commander. Including his earned leaves, Tucker had been "waiting orders" a total of three years and ten months; only three commanders had been unassigned for shorter periods.

During the next six years, however, Tucker remained almost permanently in Norfolk, where his family required special attention. On January 1, 1858, the Tuckers' ninth child, a son, arrived. It was probably a difficult birth; Virginia Tucker died ten days later, at age thirty-nine. According to Rochelle, the Tuckers' twenty-year marriage had been "most happy and harmonious." The last child of that union was christened Virginius. The loss of his wife drew Tucker even closer to his other "family"—his many navy friends and, especially, his subordinates on the receiving ship. There, the atmosphere of the officers' mess was more relaxed than on a warship at sea. For Tucker's young messmates of that period, recalled Midshipman Hope, service with him "was in itself a 'liberal education.'" He was a fine example for younger officers and a great storyteller. "But while simple and utterly without affectation no one ever felt that he could be approached with too great a familiarity, or looked upon without an ever-present feeling of respect."[34]

The secretary of the navy in April 1859 appointed Tucker to a five-member board of officers charged with investigating abuses in the navy yards at Norfolk, Washington, Philadelphia, New York, Boston, and Portsmouth, New Hampshire. Chaired by Captain Francis H. Gregory, this panel visited all six yards, interviewed many people, and on June 29, 1859, issued a long, comprehensive, and often scathing report. The board identified political patronage as the bane of the yards, with cronyism at its worst in New York and Philadelphia. The panel was least critical of the Washington Navy Yard, where Captain Franklin Buchanan had recently been appointed commandant. Tucker and his colleagues heaped praise upon that installation's experimental ordnance department, directed by Commander John A. B. Dahlgren, the brilliant inventor of the gun that bore his name. The board asked that he be spared the bureaucratic tedium of "useless forms" and that "any ideas he may suggest for the improvement of his department be carried out." The panel reserved some of its harshest words for the Norfolk yard—the navy's most important and Tucker's home base. Although virtually every officer there, "from the commandant down," testified that the yard "was in the highest state of discipline . . . and efficiency," the board had "ocular proof every day" that it was not.

The panel proposed many minor reforms and with no attempt at false modesty made a "few general recommendations" which its members believed would "relieve the navy yards of all the abuses that have so long existed in them." They urged the adoption of a merit system for civilian employees and their absolute subordination to naval officers. The team also recommended that yard commanders be appointed on the basis of demonstrated ability, rather than seniority alone. The Navy Department concurred with some of the board's proposals but not the more important ones. Secretary Isaac Toucey could not countenance the "subjection of the civil to the naval branch of the service," nor would he grant the power to appoint "master mechanics employed in the construction of ships . . . to those whose profession it is to navigate them." But soon the secretary replaced the commandant and executive officer at Norfolk and in May 1860 appointed Tucker ordnance officer there.[35]

North or South

In 1860 the sectional controversy between South and North—slave states and free—which had been brewing for some four decades and simmering since 1850, reached the boiling point with the election of President Abraham Lincoln, an outspoken enemy of slavery. On December 20, ten weeks before the new president's inauguration, the state of South Carolina issued an ordinance of secession and invited other Southern states to follow its lead. By February 1, 1861, Mississippi, Alabama, Georgia, Florida, Louisiana, and Texas also had left the Union. At Montgomery, Alabama, on February 8, delegates from these states formed the Confederate States of America, with Jefferson Davis as president. While the lame-duck administration of President James Buchanan temporized, armed forces from the secessionist states seized United States property within their boundaries, including the navy yard at Pensacola, Florida.

These early actions occurred without bloodshed. But at Charleston, South Carolina, the Union and nascent Confederacy confronted each other dramatically. Under Major Robert Anderson, all United States forces manning several installations in that port were gathered at Fort Sumter, an island stronghold commanding the entrance to the harbor. The state of South Carolina demanded the surrender of Sumter; both presidents Buchanan and Lincoln—inaugurated March 4, 1861— refused to yield. But neither North nor South wanted to fire the first shot that would bring civil war. Furthermore, Washington feared that any attempt to coerce the Deep South would result in the secession of the Upper South and the border states. On April 12, however, as the Lincoln administration prepared to resupply the besieged garrison in Charleston harbor, Confederate forces began the bombardment of Fort Sumter. On April 13, after forty hours of shelling, Major Anderson surrendered. Two days later, Lincoln issued a proclamation asking the states for seventy-five thousand militia to suppress the rebellion. This call to arms forced the remaining slave states to choose sides. Within little more than a month Arkansas, Tennessee, North Carolina, and Virginia also would leave the Union.

During the secession crisis many United States naval officers of Southern birth or affiliation resigned their commissions and entered the service of their home states or the Confederacy. Some of these men were ideologues who supported the constitutional doctrines of the secessionists or proslaverists willing to defend the South's "peculiar institution," the underlying cause of the sectional controversy. But many Southern officers were little concerned with these questions and agonized with divided loyalties—to the nation and to their region and home states. They were forced to make a fateful decision not faced by their northern comrades. Ultimately, many Southerners remained loyal to the Union; others, however, could not bear to take up arms against their families and neighbors. They sacrificed their careers and livelihoods to an uncertain future. Raphael Semmes, who had entered the navy the same year as Tucker, explained that it was especially difficult for mariners "who had been rocked together in the same storm, and had escaped perhaps the same shipwreck . . . to draw their swords against each other."[36]

Nowhere was the decision to secede more painful than in Virginia, the home of five of the country's presidents. That state made several attempts to avert civil war through mediation and compromise. But on April 17, two days after Lincoln's call for troops, the Virginia State Convention issued its ordinance of secession. On the same day that body instructed Governor John Letcher to "repel invasion and see that in all things the commonwealth take no detriment." To this end, the governor should immediately "invite all efficient and worthy Virginians . . . in the army and navy of the United States to retire therefrom, and to enter the service of Virginia," assigning to these men at least the same rank that they had held in the federal armed forces. During 1861, 367 Southern officers whose state affiliations are known left the United States Navy to "go South." Of these officers, 147 (40 percent) were natives or citizens of Virginia, and only 17 resigned before the secession of their state. Virginia's sailors, like the Old Dominion itself, were reluctant rebels.[37]

Commander Tucker left no written record of the period, and his friend Rochelle did not address Tucker's views concerning the secession crisis forthrightly. Tucker had been raised in a household that employed black bondsmen, and slaves manned his father's ships. Census data, however, indicate that Tucker himself did not own slaves during his navy years. Similarly, most of his family and friends were professional men, not planters, and they probably had no substantial, direct interest in the institution of slavery. Of the naval officers from the South, a large majority apparently opposed secession, and more than half remained in the United States Navy even after their states had left the Union. The best evidence suggests that Tucker, too, favored union, at least until Virginia seceded: on February 19, 1861—two weeks after the formation of the Confederacy—the commander's eldest son, John Tarleton Tucker, accepted a commission in the United States Navy.[38]

At the Norfolk Navy Yard tension had been building since the secession of South Carolina. Captain Charles S. McCauley, the loyal but, at age sixty-eight, ineffective officer who commanded the installation, had a staff composed primarily of Virginians, including his ordnance officer, Commander Tucker. Gideon Welles, Lincoln's navy secretary, instructed McCauley on April 10 to take no action that might provoke Virginia into secession or precipitate an attack on the yard by the citizens of Norfolk and its sister city, Portsmouth. However, the commandant was to defend the base and to protect the property under his care. In addition to a huge dry dock and many buildings, shops, munitions, and stores, Norfolk had perhaps three thousand pieces of artillery in its arsenal and ten warships in various states of disrepair. Six of these were unseaworthy old hulks; but three were sailing vessels of considerable utility, and the powerful, nearly new steam frigate *Merrimack* was probably more valuable than the other ships combined. On April 20, 1861, after McCauley's Southern subalterns had left their posts, loyal officers hastily and rashly attempted to destroy the yard and its contents to keep them out of enemy hands. The next day, Virginia forces entered the abandoned and still-smoldering installation and salvaged much valuable material, including almost all of the artillery. Within less than a year, the *Merrimack* would be repaired, modified, and fitted with iron plates. Recommissioned as the formidable CSS *Virginia*, she produced panic within the Lincoln administration.[39]

A Senate committee investigating the events at Norfolk attributed the loss of the yard to *"masked traitors"*—Tucker and the other Virginians on McCauley's staff—who "continued, nominally, in the service of the government only that they might more effectually compass their treasonable schemes." By their "base counsels" they persuaded the commandant "that peace and the security of the yard depended . . . upon doing nothing to further excite the already maddened public feeling, and upon allowing the government to lie still and be bound hand and foot, till it should be completely in the power of the insurgents." But Captain McCauley did not "remember or acknowledge the operation of such influences" upon his conduct. And the evidence, although incomplete, does not support the committee's harsh condemnations of Tucker and his fellow Southern officers at Norfolk. To a large degree they were scapegoats for errors made in the Navy Department, the bungling of their superior officers, and the "extraordinary circumstances" of that place and time.[40]

As early as February 1861 Captain McCauley had requested reinforcements for the Norfolk yard. He had only a few sailors and sixty marines to defend the place. But this appeal and later ones went largely unheeded in Washington. In late March, however, Secretary Welles ordered Captain Garrett Pendergrast and the heavily armed sloop *Cumberland* to Norfolk to help defend the navy base. On April 10 Welles instructed McCauley to prepare the *Merrimack*, which had faulty machinery, for escape to a Northern port. But, cautioned the secretary, "there should be no steps taken to give needless alarm" to the Virginians, whose state convention was considering secession. Welles dispatched Engineer in Chief Benjamin Isherwood to Norfolk to hasten work on the warship and Commander James Alden to take command of the vessel after her repair.[41]

On the morning of April 17—two days after Lincoln's call for troops from the states brought the secession crisis to a head in Virginia—Captain Pendergrast brought the *Cumberland*, which had been anchored a mile and a half below the base, into the yard proper, where her three hundred sailors might better defend the installation. The vessel also would be in position to bombard the cities of Norfolk and Portsmouth. The appearance of the *Cumberland* in the navy yard evoked angry demonstrations in both towns. That same day Isherwood and Alden informed McCauley that the repairs to the *Merrimack* had been completed. They requested permission to arm the vessel, fire the boilers, and depart immediately. The commandant, however, did not want to put the ship under steam until the next morning for fear of the reaction of the townspeople. Furthermore, McCauley believed that it was too early to decide whether the warship should seek safety or be used to defend the yard. But he gave Alden permission to arm the ship. According to Alden, ordnance officer Tucker "threw all kinds of obstacles in the way" of his getting the guns. McCauley soon countermanded his initial order to Alden because the arming of the *Merrimack* was "represented by the parties in the yard" as being provocative to local civilians.[42] That afternoon Captain Hiram Paulding arrived from Washington to assess the situation and explain Welles's concerns to the commandant, for whom Paulding carried new orders. "It may not be necessary," Welles wrote, "that [the *Merrimack*] should leave at this time, unless there is immediate danger pending." But guns should be immediately placed on board the vessel. McCauley, however, again was admonished to avoid "any sudden demonstration" that might endanger government property, which he was to "defend at any hazard."[43]

While Paulding conferred with McCauley, Commander Richard L. Page, the senior Virginian on duty in the yard, spoke to Welles's emissary on behalf of his fellow Southerners. Page, as Paulding recalled, explained that the Virginians "were painfully situated; that their families . . . were there; that there was very great excitement, and apprehensions were entertained of violence from the people outside of the yard." The Southern officers believed that the Virginia Convention would soon take the state out of the Union. Nevertheless, Page and the men he represented pledged to "stand by the commandant and defend the public property with their lives." At the same time Page "begged" Paulding to ask Welles to relieve them from duty at Norfolk. Paulding relayed this message to the navy secretary the next day and subsequently to the president. Lincoln directed Welles "to have those officers relieved and to send northern men there." Welles remembered Paulding's report in much the same way. The Virginian officers at Norfolk, he confided to his diary, wished "to be relieved from duty at the yard in anticipation of difficulty . . . with their kinsmen and neighbors." Paulding had told him that these officers were "patriotic, deprecated hostility, and were governed by honorable motives."[44]

On the morning of April 18, the *Merrimack*'s boilers were fired, but McCauley still had not decided whether to flee or to fight. The previous two nights, moreover, secessionists in Norfolk had sunk several vessels in the channel below the navy yard, and the commandant feared that the *Merrimack* might not be able to pass these obstructions. Engineer Isherwood, having completed his assignment, returned to Washington in disgust. That afternoon McCauley informed Commander Alden that he would retain the *Merrimack*, and Alden also left for the capital. The reports of Isherwood and Alden to Welles that afternoon and evening were disconcerting. To Alden the commandant "seemed stupefied, bewildered, and wholly unable to act." Isherwood thought McCauley was "under the influence of liquor and bad men."[45]

The situation at the yard became critical by the evening of April 18, when word reached both Washington and Norfolk that Virginia had seceded secretly the previous day. Federal authorities no longer feared that defensive preparations might provoke secession; that issue had been resolved. But could McCauley defend his base with the forces at his disposal? On the eighteenth, after learning of Virginia's secession, all of the Southern officers at the Norfolk yard had resigned. In accord with navy practice, Tucker's resignation, addressed to Welles, was endorsed and forwarded by McCauley.

> Sir.
> I respectfully tender to the President of the United States through you my resignation which I beg may be accepted as early as practicable.
>
> > I have the honor to be sir
> > your obedient Servant
> > John R. Tucker
> > Commander

The resignations of the other Southern officers at Norfolk, like Tucker's, did not contain explanations but only requested prompt acceptance, which would have given these men an "honorable discharge." But they were overtaken by events. All of these men ultimately were dismissed from the service as of the date of their resignations.[46]

In the morning of April 19, Virginia general William B. Taliaferro, dispatched from Richmond, took command of the Norfolk and Portsmouth militias. Soon the officers in the navy yard heard several trains arrive at the depot. Unconfirmed reports indicated that three thousand troops had come from the state capital and that hidden batteries were being readied on a nearby hill. Taliaferro, in reality, had only six hundred green "locals" and six small cannon. That night, however, secessionists captured Old Fort Norfolk, seizing eleven heavy guns and a large quantity of munitions. This action and an aborted attempt by Virginians to capture a navy tug in front of the yard convinced McCauley and others inside the installation that a powerful assault was imminent.[47]

By the afternoon of April 20, Tucker and the other Southern officers had left the Norfolk yard; indeed, most may have departed on the eighteenth. None of the men assigned to the yard left a record of their motives or actions during those critical days. However, Lieutenant Rochelle, on the *Cumberland*, recounted his experiences, which were likely similar to those of Tucker and the other Virginians posted on shore. Believing the state's secession imminent, Rochelle had written his resignation on the seventeenth, but he waited on the *Cumberland* for its acceptance. Probably on the nineteenth, a "false alarm" about an attack on the navy yard placed him in a very "painful position." He felt compelled to "obey the command" (it was, in fact, an "invitation") "of the Virginia Convention and leave the navy of the United States." But now it seemed likely that he would have to fire upon his fellow Virginians, the very thing that he had resigned his commission "to escape from doing." As long as he was "on duty . . . in the United States Navy," however, Rochelle "was fully determined to do that duty, and in case of necessity, would have stood to [his] guns." To extricate himself from this "embarrassing position," he and Surgeon Frederick Van Bibber, also a Virginian, asked Captain Pendergrast's permission to leave the ship, "in view of the delay in the acceptance of our resignations." After "some demur," the skipper assented, and the two Southerners left that day, "taking kind personal leave of all the officers on board."[48]

Lieutenant John S. Maury, another Virginian on the *Cumberland*, resigned on April 18. From Norfolk the following day, his mother, Frances B. Perry, eloquently explained the action of her son and the officers at the navy yard to her cousin Captain Samuel Barron. Maury, she wrote, had "always been a strong Union man . . . and opposed secession." But Lincoln's April 15 call for troops to quell the rebellion

> came like a desolating storm upon the people of this region, and aroused up feelings that seemed irresistible. It *then* became a question of North or South. It was no longer Union or Secession, but culminated like magic to one point, North or South. The strongest Union men felt constrained to go with the South. Every feeling of sympathy and affection was aroused and every one declared that honor and duty impelled them to one course. . . . The Cumberland . . . was brought up to Norfolk, her guns loaded and her heavy Battery pointed at our beloved town, the place of [Maury's] infancy and boyhood and *his HOME*, and the home of his Mother and her family, and of his wife and her family, and of *all* his nearest and dearest kindred. No human heart, no *American* heart can resist the influence of these sacred ties. His position was most painful and embarrassing. It was either *to fire on* his Home, and his Mother, wife and all that was dear to him on earth, or to resign his commission. . . . He went, in this step with a gallant galaxy— . . . Capts. Page, Sinclair, Robb, Roots, Tucker, Poindexter, Spottswood, etc. . . . *No Southern officer on duty in Norfolk*, could, under the circumstances, have done otherwise.

In Tucker's home on Fenchurch Street, well within range of the *Cumberland*'s guns, Virginia Tucker's aunt Louisa Webb looked after five of the commander's motherless children.[49]

Meanwhile, Welles had determined to send an expedition to Norfolk on the steamer *Pawnee* under the command of Captain Paulding, who was to replace McCauley as commandant. Paulding brought enough sailors to man the *Merrimack* and three other serviceable ships berthed there, along with a detachment of marines and a regiment of Massachusetts infantry to defend the yard. In addition, the *Pawnee* carried materials with which to destroy the installation should that become necessary. But in perhaps the navy's biggest blunder of the Civil War, the secretary did not telegraph McCauley that help was coming. As nightfall approached on April 20, the commandant decided that his position was untenable. He ordered the few remaining men under his command to disable the artillery and to scuttle all of the ships, including the *Merrimack*.[50]

The *Pawnee* reached Norfolk about three hours later. Water already had nearly filled the holds of the *Merrimack* and the other vessels. The expedition had not included divers to plug these ships or equipment to pump them out. Paulding quickly concurred with McCauley's appraisal that the yard could not be defended successfully. The officers originally assigned to take the ships to safety now were ordered to burn them to the waterline. This operation was accomplished efficiently under the direction of an officer from the Ordnance Bureau in Washington—Lieutenant Henry A. Wise.[51] For him, the voyage of the *Pawnee* to Norfolk must have been filled with apprehension. Would the next adventure of Gringo and Toker find the two mates shooting at each other? Happily, it did not.

The expedition finished its destructive business shortly before daybreak on April 21, and the *Pawnee*, towing the *Cumberland*, steamed out of Norfolk. Virginia forces immediately entered the yard and began salvage operations. Several of the officers who recently had abandoned their posts there assumed charge of the base. Commander Tucker, however, was not among them. He probably had taken his family to safety in Richmond where, a few days later, he tendered his services to the governor. Former commander Tucker, noted Rochelle, had abandoned a thirty-five-year career with "an established and illustrious navy to enter the service of a people who had neither ships nor sailors."[52]

Did Tucker and the other Southern officers at the Norfolk yard, like Rochelle on the *Cumberland*, receive permission to leave their posts? We do not know. These men, however, had sworn to defend the United States government; at some point Tucker and the others abandoned that charge and, soon, took up arms against the Union. These acts were treasonable. They became treason with the victory of North over South, when the Union reaped the legal and semantic spoils of war. But Tucker and most of his fellow "traitors" at Norfolk probably did not play a "treacherous" role in the loss of the yard. They candidly explained their position to Captain Paulding, and probably to Mc-

Cauley, and asked to be relieved from duty. The replacements ordered by President Lincoln reached Norfolk too late. It seems likely that their reluctance to undertake defensive measures at the yard was not based in a conspiracy to destroy the installation or to secure it for the Confederacy. Before April 18, when Virginia's secession became known, the Southern officers at Norfolk, like McCauley and the Lincoln administration, wanted to avoid any action that might precipitate hostilities or their state's withdrawal from the Union. Along with about 90 percent of the Virginians who resigned their navy commissions, Tucker and his comrades did not do so until the Old Dominion had asserted its independence. After resigning on April 18, the Southern officers at Norfolk quite literally refused to fire on their homes and families.

Other members of Tucker's family left the United States Navy soon after his resignation. Chief Engineer Thomas Alphonse Jackson, the nephew Tucker had raised, resigned on April 22. Three days later Third Assistant Engineer John Tarleton Tucker, the commander's son, relinquished the commission he had obtained two months earlier. Lieutenant William A. Webb, Tucker's brother-in-law, "went South" on May 17. But Tucker's family, like so many others, also was divided by the Civil War. Lieutenant James A. Greer—an Ohioan who had married Virginia Tucker's sister Mary—remained in the United States service, ultimately becoming a rear admiral. Commander (later, Rear Admiral) Alfred Taylor, the Virginian for whom Tucker had named his second son, also stayed with the Union, as did Harry Gringo. Henry Wise had many close friends who were strong Union men, including John Hay, Lincoln's private secretary. Most important, his father-in-law, who acted as a father to the orphaned Wise, was Edward Everett, the staunchly Unionist Massachusetts senator and former secretary of state. Everett had feared that Wise's strong attachment to the South would cause him to resign. But Gringo stayed with the Union, becoming an influential naval adviser to President Lincoln.[53]

CHAPTER TWO

Defending the James

URING THE FINAL TEN DAYS OF April 1861, the Commonwealth of
Virginia made hurried preparations to defend its newly proclaimed independence. To assist Governor John Letcher in military
affairs, the state convention on April 20 established the Advisory Council of Three, which included Commander Matthew Fontaine Maury, the
foremost American naval scientist of that era. This triumvirate recommended that command of Virginia's land and naval forces be tendered
to Colonel Robert E. Lee, late of the United States Army. Lee accepted
this charge on April 22. Five days later the convention officially created
the Virginia Navy. Although this service had an authorized strength of
two thousand men, it did not have a single warship to oppose the federal
navy. The Union, it seemed certain, would send its vessels up Virginia's
rivers, the highways linking the Atlantic with the heart of the state.
The James River was the most strategic of these waterways. From its
outlet in Chesapeake Bay, it led directly to Richmond, which soon
became the focal point of the Civil War. On April 25 Virginia provision-
ally joined the Confederacy, an act ratified by popular vote on May 23.
Six days later President Jefferson Davis arrived in Richmond, and
Virginia's capital became the seat of the national government as well.[1]

On April 22 John R. Tucker received his first order from Governor
Letcher: "You will conduct the defenses of the James River." The next
day he was instructed to examine several vessels seized on the James
by order of the governor and to retain those ships which he deemed
"absolutely necessary" for the defense of the state. He promptly recommended that the *Yorktown* and *Jamestown*, side-wheel steamers
belonging to the New York and Old Dominion Steamship Line, be
converted to war vessels. The officer proposed to remove the upper
passenger decks of both ships, "make some other like changes," and
mount batteries on them. He estimated that the conversion could be
accomplished in twelve days, if adequate manpower and materials were
available.[2]

Tucker had undetermined status within the Virginia forces during

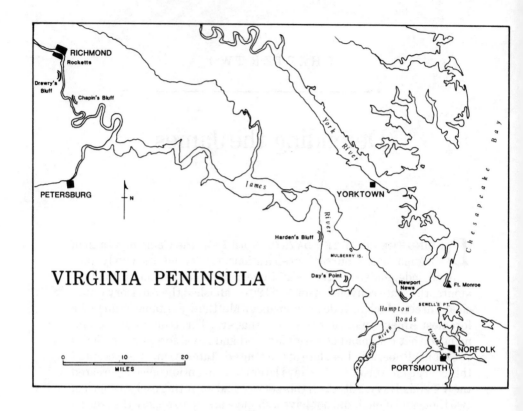

VIRGINIA PENINSULA

these early days of the war. His first communication from Letcher was addressed simply to "John R. Tucker, Virginia Navy." He was without rank in an organization that would not exist, legally, for another five days. As time passed and more officers abandoned the United States Navy for the Virginia service, state authorities assigned these men the same rank and relative order they had held in the "Old Navy." On May 2 Tucker was commissioned a commander in the Virginia Navy, the grade he maintained when the state transferred its naval forces to the Confederacy on June 19. He stood below thirteen captains, many of them aged and infirm, and sixteen other commanders. The Confederate navy had an abundance of senior officers but few ships or important shore assignments where they might be employed appropriately. While the mass resignation of Southern men and the great expansion of the federal fleet brought rapid advancement for Union officers during the war, promotion within the upper echelons of the Confederate navy would be very difficult. To circumvent rigid adherence to seniority and permit the advancement of younger, more aggressive officers, a law of April 21, 1862, made promotion also attainable through "gallant and meritorious conduct." Only by such means could the new ranks of rear admiral and admiral be won.[3]

24

We Will Be Happy to Meet You off Newport News

By mid-May most of Tucker's responsibilities for the defense of the James River had been assumed by Captain French Forrest, the new commandant of the Norfolk Navy Yard. So, on June 3 General Lee ordered Tucker to superintend work on the *Yorktown* and to take command of that vessel when conversion was completed. Tucker thought the steamer might be ready for combat by the first week of May, but a severe shortage of skilled workmen and materials rendered her serviceable only by the middle of August; several more months were required to make final modifications, obtain sufficient ammunition and other supplies, and enlist a full crew—about 150 men.

The conversion of the *Yorktown* was accomplished at Rocketts wharf, near Richmond. Carpenters removed the upper cabins and reinforced the deck so that the vessel could mount a respectable battery: ten 32-pounders in broadside along with one 10-inch shell gun and an 8-inch solid-shot gun pivoted, respectively, fore and aft. Initially rigged with sails to conserve coal, these later were removed so that the ship could slip undetected past Union forts on the lower James. To protect the machinery, 2-inch iron plates were fitted around the boilers and shields of 3¾ inches were placed in front and back of the engines—perhaps the earliest use of such armor in the Confederate navy. Lieutenant William H. Parker, tongue half-in-cheek, noted that Tucker's vessel was the South's "first iron clad." In honor of the American and Virginia patriot, Tucker rechristened his ship the *Patrick Henry*.[4] For several months, this vessel was the only credible Confederate warship on the James River. That the Navy Department entrusted the ship to Tucker, while many senior officers were stationed ashore, was a tribute to his professional reputation.

The long delay in preparing the *Patrick Henry* troubled Confederate navy secretary Stephen R. Mallory, for the Union quickly implemented its "Anaconda Plan" to strangle the South. Increasing numbers of Northern ships were sent to blockade rebel ports and to stop up navigable rivers; soon, combined operations by the federal army and navy would seize strategic points along the coast. Mallory hoped to get the *Patrick Henry* out to sea before the blockade became fully effective. There she could prey upon Yankee merchantmen and blockaders, capturing supplies and vessels sorely needed by the Confederates. Attacks on United States commerce might also divert warships from the blockade, making it easier for the South to export its cotton and to import the many manufactured goods required by the largely agrarian Confederacy. In the meantime, Mallory gambled that ironclad warships—constructed at home and overseas—could offset the North's great numerical advantage in ships and bust the Yankee blockade.[5]

On July 13, 1861, Mallory ordered Tucker to escape from the James as soon as possible and to make "an active cruise against the enemy," upon whom, "in accordance with the rules of Christian warfare," he was to inflict "the greatest injury in the shortest time." Trusting in Tucker's "good judgment," the secretary gave him great operational freedom but suggested that the relatively fast *Patrick Henry* could capture weaker vessels and elude more powerful opponents. Should Tucker be unable to reach the Atlantic, he was to cooperate with the army along the river.[6]

It would require several more weeks, however, to ready the *Patrick Henry* for sea duty. The vessel lacked several of her guns, sufficient ammunition, and coal; she needed sails, awnings, hammocks, and, probably, copper for her bottom. Tucker's compass was faulty, and he was very short of crewmen. To furnish the officers' quarters and mess, Tucker nearly stripped the *Jamestown*. Lieutenant Joseph N. Barney, that vessel's skipper, complained that he had "not a single carving knife or fork" and that Tucker had rejected his appeal to "disgorge" at least some of the cutlery.[7] While Tucker waited for his equipment and a full complement of sailors—who, like the *Jamestown*'s tableware, often were obtained irregularly from other commands—he established his headquarters at Mulberry Island, in the middle course of the James. Here, Tucker drilled his men, tested his ship, and held the *Patrick Henry* in readiness to assist General John B. Magruder, whose army was to defend the peninsula between the James and York rivers, east of Richmond.[8]

By September 13 Tucker still had not assembled a full crew or all of his equipment. But he decided to break the monotony of duty protecting Magruder's flank by testing his crew and armament and discovering the size and range of the enemy's guns. The *Patrick Henry* slipped downstream to Newport News, at the entrance to Hampton Roads—a large, open body of water where the James receives the flow of the Elizabeth and Nansemond rivers before reaching Chesapeake Bay, a short distance beyond. For about two hours the rebel steamer exchanged shots at long range with the much larger federal frigates *Savannah* and *Louisiana* as well as Union shore batteries. Most of the missiles fired by both sides fell harmlessly short. Tucker conducted a similar exercise on December 2, dueling several small gunboats at Newport News.[9]

During the month of October, Tucker witnessed the development of two important Confederate contributions to naval technology. In the first week of that month he observed Lieutenant John M. Brooke, the South's leading ordnance expert, conduct ballistic tests on iron plates. These soon would be used to transform the scuttled USS *Merrimack* into the armorclad CSS *Virginia*. The other innovation had a more immediate application—the destruction of the *Savannah* and other

Yankee ships at Newport News. Matthew F. Maury, the "Pathfinder of the Seas," was famed for his studies of navigation and hydrography. But after his resignation from the United States Navy, he devoted much of his time to the perfection of "torpedoes," that is, mines. In early July 1861 he had failed in his first experiment, an attempt to sink three Union vessels in Hampton Roads.

On October 10 Maury's assistant Lieutenant Robert D. Minor brought several "infernal machines" on board the *Patrick Henry* for another test. That night, dark and rainy, Tucker drifted his ship quietly down the James to a point less than two miles from the Yankee anchorage. Lowering the vessel's boats into the water, Minor and two of Tucker's young officers, Acting Master Thomas Dornin and Midshipman Alexander McComb Mason, along with crewmen armed with cutlasses, began the operation. They attached the mines at intervals of several feet to a chain which, kept afloat with buoys, was stretched across the river's channel. At a distance of about eight hundred yards from their targets, the team set the triggers of the explosive devices and cast them adrift. Soon, the frantic flashing of Union signal lights indicated that the Rebels had been discovered. Minor and his men hastened back to the *Patrick Henry*, which steamed to safety a short distance upstream. No explosion was heard, however, and a reconnaissance by Minor and Tucker in a rowboat the next day found the Northern fleet unscathed. The torpedo-loaded chain apparently had fouled before reaching the enemy.[10]

The new year arrived with the *Patrick Henry* still deficient in crew and armament, and Tucker's hopes for an offensive cruise faded. General Magruder anticipated a Union thrust up the James and York rivers toward Richmond, and on January 6, 1862, he ordered Tucker to "hold your command in readiness to repel attack, defending your position to the last." Tucker's "command" had been augmented on December 19, when Lieutenant Barney and the *Jamestown* (with two guns) had been ordered to report to him. Soon Tucker's flotilla added the tiny *Teaser*, a gunboat mounting a single cannon, under the command of Lieutenant William A. Webb, his brother-in-law. The James River Squadron already was something of a family enterprise. Assigned to the *Patrick Henry* were twenty-two-year-old Third Assistant Engineer John Tarleton Tucker and nineteen-year-old Charles Douglas Tucker, serving as his father's clerk.[11]

Because of the increased likelihood of a riverborne Union assault on Richmond, General Raleigh E. Colston in February solicited Tucker's opinion about the "practicability" of obstructing the James "at some point commanded by the guns of our forts." Tucker conferred with his officers and local pilots and responded with a detailed report, suggesting possible locations for barriers and the best method for constructing these. Although he identified several suitable points on the middle course of the river, Tucker urged that obstructions be placed higher upstream, where they would add "more to the safety of Richmond than perhaps all defenses hitherto suggested." To halt the enemy the obstruction should be "a series of piles, not less than three in a tier, or more than six, varied in angular position, and connected by heavy chains, . . . keeping them together, retained in position by heavy anchors. Simple tiers could be removed; a series of such difficulties would not be attempted, and, if attempted, would not be successful; . . . [because] ample time would be given to the forces afloat and adjacent batteries to operate against the [enemy's] labors." Tucker stressed that the barrier should have an opening large enough to accommodate ships sixty feet wide. Several expendable vessels should be loaded with stone and held in readiness to sink in this gap when necessary. Finally, Tucker advised that when the time came to close the river, "it will be advisable to plant several of Maury's submarine batteries [mines] beyond the barrier."[12] In less than three months, Tucker would find refuge behind such an obstruction at Drewry's Bluff.

As Union strength grew in Virginia waters, Confederate hopes for success increasingly rested upon the *Merrimack*. This vessel was being prepared for action as quickly as two-inch iron plates could be rolled in Richmond and bolted to the ship, in double layers, at Norfolk. The *Merrimack*, mounting ten guns, was launched on February 17, 1862, and recommissioned as the *Virginia*. One week later, Captain Franklin Buchanan assumed command of all naval forces in the James River and its tributaries and raised his pennant on the ironclad. A sixty-one-year-old Marylander who had entered the navy in 1815, he had been the first superintendent of the United States Naval Academy at Annapolis. He soon would prove to be the South's most aggressive senior officer. Mallory ordered Buchanan to attack the Union fleet in Hampton Roads; to conserve scarce ammunition, the secretary suggested that the *Virginia* ram her wooden adversaries. Authorities in Richmond hoped that he could force his way into Chesapeake Bay, proceed up the Potomac River, and bombard Washington. In his most sanguine moment, Mallory proposed that the ironclad might even attack New York City and "do more to achieve our immediate independence than . . . many campaigns."[13]

From Norfolk on March 3 Buchanan informed Tucker that he intended "to appear before the enemy off Newport News at daylight on Friday morning next [March 7]. You will, with the *Jamestown* and *Teaser*, be prepared to join me." The flag officer hoped to destroy the frigate *Congress* and sloop *Cumberland* and then to engage the smaller federal boats and shore batteries. Tucker was to use his "best exertions to injure and destroy the enemy." Buchanan, noted Lieutenant Parker, "could not have given the order to a better man," for Tucker was "the most chivalric and bravest of men." Tucker responded the following day: "The *Patrick Henry*, *Jamestown* and *Teaser* are ready and will be happy to meet you off Newport News."[14]

Bad weather delayed the attack one day, until March 8. At 11:00 A.M. Buchanan on the *Virginia*, accompanied by the *Raleigh* and *Beaufort* (converted tugs mounting one gun), left the Norfolk yard and steamed slowly down the Elizabeth River. About three hours later, the *Virginia* entered Hampton Roads and engaged the *Cumberland*. Within fifteen minutes, the ironclad had rammed her wooden adversary, which quickly sank. Next, Buchanan trained his guns on the *Congress*, and she soon was in flames. But the *Virginia* now became the target of the frigates *Roanoke*, *St. Lawrence*, and *Minnesota*, which had rushed from the mouth of the James to assist the *Congress*. At this critical moment Buchanan saw "that gallant officer, Commander John R. Tucker . . . standing down the James River under full steam, accompanied by the *Jamestown* and *Teaser*. They all came nobly into action."[15]

The previous evening, Tucker and the small squadron under his command had anchored off Day's Neck, just above the Union batteries at Newport News. Perched in their ship's rigging, Tucker's men could observe Hampton Roads and wait for the *Virginia* to emerge from the Elizabeth River. The officers of the *Patrick Henry* were finishing their dinner when the iron-skinned behemoth appeared. The drummer beat all hands to quarters, and Tucker ordered his vessels underway. "Never in my experience," recalled Midshipman William F. Clayton, "have I seen men more anxious for a fray than were those on the *Patrick Henry*."[16] With a "splendid gamecock appearance" the *Patrick Henry*, followed by the *Jamestown* and *Teaser*, approached the series of three Union batteries at Newport News, which mounted perhaps eighteen guns. Tucker anticipated that the Yankee artillerists expected him to pass their position at the farthest possible distance and that their guns would be trained on the opposite side of the channel. Therefore, he directed his ships close to the federal works, and the volleys from the first two redoubts passed over the flotilla. But the gunners at the final battery had corrected their aim, and they hit the *Patrick Henry* several times. One shot struck amid a gun crew, killing one sailor and wounding two others. Buchanan reported that the squadron's dash past Newport News was "miraculous, as they were under a galling fire of solid shot, grape and canister."[17]

Once inside the Hampton Roads "arena," the *Patrick Henry* came alongside the *Virginia* for instructions. Buchanan shouted to Tucker, "You have made a glorious run; use your own discretion, do the enemy all the harm you can, and sink before surrendering." The *Patrick*

Henry immediately "became engaged in the thick of the fight." Tucker's ship and her consorts were caught in a three-sided crossfire: from the batteries at Newport News, to the west; Yankee field artillery and sharpshooters, on the beach to the north; and to the east, from the forty-gun *Minnesota,* which had run aground. Remembered Rochelle, Tucker's executive officer that day, "whilst the forward guns were engaging one enemy, the after guns were firing at another." The *Minnesota's* skipper reported that fire from the *Patrick Henry* and *Jamestown* "did the most damage in killing and wounding men."[18]

Tucker also targeted the *Congress.* Already crippled by the *Virginia,* she had been purposefully grounded on a shoal at the north side of the channel so that the ironclad could not close to ram. But the *Patrick Henry* and *Jamestown,* noted the commander of the federal frigate, "approached us from the James River, firing with precision and doing us great damage." At about 4:30 P.M., the *Congress* surrendered, and Buchanan sent Lieutenant William H. Parker of the *Beaufort* along with the *Raleigh* to remove the crew and to burn the vessel. While the two gunboats were alongside the *Congress,* removing wounded sailors, Union field artillery and sharpshooters on shore opened fire, killing or wounding many men—in blue and gray—and forcing the Confederates to retreat. Next, Buchanan dispatched Lieutenant Minor in the *Virginia's* boat to destroy the prize; but he, too, encountered a hail of Yankee rifle fire and was seriously wounded before being rescued by the *Teaser.* The flag officer now signaled the *Patrick Henry* to burn the ship.[19]

Tucker had ceased firing at the *Congress* as soon as she had struck her colors and "steadily refused to let any gun be aimed at her," even though federal forces continued shooting at the rebel boats sent to take control of the prize. But in response to Buchanan's order, Tucker steamed as close to the *Congress* as his vessel's draft would permit and readied the ship's boats for action. At this point, the *Patrick Henry* came under fire from the shore and the grounded *Minnesota* to the east. Several shots hit the *Patrick Henry,* one rupturing a boiler. Steam filled the engine and fire rooms, scalding to death five sailors and driving the engineers topsides. The paddle wheels stopped. With the rebel vessel shrouded in a telltale cloud of vapor, the Union gunners intensified their fire. Although many of Tucker's sailors had been burned and the deck was a "sheet of steam," the crew continued to man their guns as the *Patrick Henry* drifted helplessly toward the enemy-held north shore. Fortunately, the *Jamestown* came alongside, threw a line to the crippled warrior, and towed her out of peril. The engineers soon had one engine functioning, and the *Patrick Henry* returned to action on half steam.[20]

In the meantime, the *Virginia* trained her guns on the *Congress* and fired red-hot shot into her. The Yankee frigate quickly ignited; she would sink that evening. As before, however, United States troops on shore now directed their guns at the Confederate flagship. Enraged at this breach in the rules of war, Buchanan came on deck with a rifle and returned the fire. A musket ball tore into his leg, and he was taken below. Nightfall soon ended the first day's combat at Hampton Roads, and the Confederate squadron anchored under the friendly guns of Sewell's Point on the south shore of the waterway. The rebel navy had scored a great victory. Two first-class Union warships had been destroyed; some three hundred Yankees had been killed or wounded. Eight Confederates, six of these from the *Patrick Henry*, had died, and nineteen suffered wounds.

The Southern officers at Sewell's Point got little rest that night. After attending to their casualties, they inspected their ships and repaired what damage they could. The excitement of the day's action, rekindled as they described it to their friends ashore, and the anticipation of the fight to come made sleep difficult.[21] Tucker, especially, must have been restless. What would the wounded Buchanan do? As the second-ranking officer, command of the squadron might be his on the morrow. Before sunrise on the ninth, Tucker conferred with Buchanan on the *Virginia*. "Old Buck" wanted to remain on board, as did the more seriously wounded Lieutenant Minor. But both men were in pain, and the ironclad had little room below deck for the casualties that she might suffer in the ensuing combat. So Buchanan and Minor reluctantly agreed to debark. According to Lieutenant Parker of the *Raleigh*, Buchanan was "sent to the Naval Hospital at Norfolk, . . . and command of the squadron devolved upon Captain John R. Tucker."

But the organization of the fleet was not so clear. Rochelle noted that "the command ought, in conformity with . . . naval usage, to have been formally transferred to . . . Tucker, . . . but this obviously proper course was not followed, and Flag Officer Buchanan's flag was kept flying on board the *Virginia*, though he . . . was not and could not be in command of that vessel, or the . . . squadron, being laid up in bed at the Norfolk Naval Hospital. Tucker did not assume command of the squadron, but simply continued to command the *Patrick Henry*."[22] Thus, on March 9, 1862, Lieutenant Catesby ap R. Jones, Buchanan's talented executive officer, commanded the *Virginia* in the first battle between ironclad ships.

At about eight o'clock that Sunday morning, the Confederate squadron steamed toward the *Minnesota*, still aground on the north side of Hampton Roads. Tucker's wooden vessels commenced the attack, but soon the Rebels saw a puff of smoke and then heard the report of two guns fired from a strange-looking black object alongside the federal frigate. "What could it be?" Rochelle asked himself. It was "a craft as the eyes of a seaman never looked upon before—an immense shingle floating on the water, with a gigantic cheese box rising from its center; no sails, no wheels, no smokestack, no guns."[23] The "cheesebox on a shingle," of course, was the ironclad USS *Monitor*, which had arrived fortuitously during the night. Lieutenant John L. Worden, Tucker's close friend since their voyage together on the *Erie* a quarter century earlier, commanded the experimental craft. Watching the combat from the shore was another veteran of that cruise and a mutual friend of Tucker and Worden, Lieutenant Henry A. Wise.

During their four-hour duel, the *Monitor* and the *Virginia* pounded each other—first at long range and then at very close quarters. Neither ironclad seriously damaged the other; but the *Monitor* gained a tactical victory, keeping the *Virginia* away from the nearly helpless *Minnesota*. The *Patrick Henry* fired an occasional shot at the *Monitor* from very long range, while the other wooden ships in the vicinity—Union and Confederate—watched the contest prudently from afar. Rochelle believed that no wooden ship could have survived fifteen minutes in an engagement at short range with either ironclad, an estimate Tucker almost tested. In the course of the battle, the *Virginia* grounded on a shoal. Jones raised his signal flags, but these were not clearly visible. The *Patrick Henry*'s signal officer mistakenly believed they said, "Disabled my propeller is." Tucker ordered the *Patrick Henry* and the *Jamestown* toward the *Virginia* to tow the ironclad to safety—a very grim prospect. But soon Jones freed his ship, and hearts beat easier on the *Patrick Henry*.[24]

The battle of Hampton Roads, which sounded the death knell for the age of wooden warships, ended shortly after noon. Worden, in the pilothouse of the "cheesebox," had been blinded when the concussion of an enemy shot drove carbon fragments from the powder-blackened walls of the turret into his eyes. Lieutenant Samuel Dana Greene, the *Monitor*'s twenty-one-year-old executive officer, assumed a strictly defensive position in front of the *Minnesota*. Meanwhile, the ebbing tide made Jones fear that his deep-drafted and difficult-to-manage monster might become dangerously grounded. He took the *Virginia* back to Sewell's Point. Both the Confederacy and the Union, employing different criteria, would claim that the combat of the ninth—essentially a draw—was a great victory for their own side. For his "gallant and meritorious conduct" at Hampton Roads, Captain Buchanan became the first Confederate admiral. Lieutenant Jones would be promoted to commander for his role in that engagement and the subsequent battle of Drewry's Bluff. To Tucker, as "senior officer present," fell the honor of presiding over the ceremony in which a congressional resolution of March 12 was read expressing thanks to Buchanan and his subordinates "for their unsurpassed gallantry."[25]

Major Drewry's Bluff

The action at Hampton Roads demonstrated to the Confederate officers that the ponderous *Virginia* could not make an extended sea voyage. Her engines were unreliable, and anything more than a moderate swell might swamp the ironclad. There would be no decisive attack on Washington or New York. But while the *Virginia* remained afloat, the water approaches to Norfolk and Richmond were closed to the United States Navy. The Union authorities, slow to recognize the limited offensive capabilities of the Confederate ironclad, also restricted the *Monitor* to a defensive role. On April 2 General George B. McClellan began landing a sixty-thousand-man army at Yorktown, on the peninsula between the James and York rivers. He planned to drive against Richmond, using Union vessels in the rivers to protect his flanks and transport men and supplies. But the *Virginia*, along with her consorts, interdicted the James, and the cautious McClellan feared that the Confederate squadron might steam past Fortress Monroe, the Union bastion at the mouth of the James, and attack his transports in the York River to the north. To guard against such a calamity, the *Monitor* anchored under the guns of Fortress Monroe. With primarily defensive assignments, both the Confederate and Union squadrons at Hampton Roads played cat-and-mouse.[26]

Captain Josiah Tattnall assumed command of the Confederate squadron, and on April 6 he and his officers formulated a daring plan to capture the *Monitor*. They would lure the federal vessel into another combat with the *Virginia*. While she was so occupied, Tucker would bring the wooden vessels alongside and board the Yankee ironclad. The attackers would cover the *Monitor*'s vents with wet blankets, forcing the hot gases back into the ship. They would throw a sail over the pilothouse, blinding the ironclad. Wedges would be driven between the turret and the deck, immobilizing the *Monitor*'s two guns. Finally, turpentine would be poured through the ventilators and ignited. After seizing the vessel, the Confederates proposed using her and the *Virginia* to destroy McClellan's base at Yorktown. But not even the capture of three Union transports in Hampton Roads sufficed to draw the *Monitor* into the rebel trap. Similarly, Tattnall refused to expose his ship to Union steamers specially fitted to ram the *Virginia*.[27]

On April 20, as the Union army advanced up the peninsula toward Richmond, Tucker received orders to take the *Patrick Henry, Jamestown, Teaser, Raleigh,* and *Beaufort* back up the James River and to cooperate with the defending Confederate army. The *Virginia*, standing alone in Hampton Roads, was to protect Tucker's rear. But by herself the rebel ironclad could not simultaneously bar the James and the Elizabeth River approach to Norfolk. For the moment the defense of Norfolk had priority, so Tucker prepared his squadron to protect the capital. Soon after arriving upstream, Tucker requested a conference with General Joseph E. Johnston, the commander of the Department of Virginia, to gain "a more thorough understanding" of Confederate strategy. He especially desired to know if the general wanted him "to act entirely on the defensive." During the next two weeks Tucker's squadron—placed directly under Johnston's orders in this emergency—was kept very busy transporting men and matériel and protecting the army's northern flank. On at least one occasion, the *Patrick Henry* dueled Yankee field artillery. While Flag Officer Tattnall, in Norfolk, threatened to resign because Tucker's squadron had been placed under the authority of Johnston, "a landsman, who can know nothing of the complicated nature of naval service," Tucker demonstrated his ability and willingness to cooperate with the army. General Johnston praised the commander's "intelligence and zeal."[28]

By April 28 it seemed unlikely that the Confederates could hold McClellan's army at bay on the lower peninsula, and Johnston planned a withdrawal toward Richmond. Tucker advised Mallory that "should the enemy send up iron vessels, or a large number of wooden men-of-war, our small force will be obliged to fall back." He wanted to know if any point on the James had been obstructed, so that his squadron could take up a position behind it. The secretary replied that the only obstructions were at Drewry's Bluff, a scant eight miles below Richmond. Tucker quickly inquired if this barricade had an opening large enough to admit his ships. If not, he might have to destroy them to prevent capture. Obviously concerned about the responsibility for such action, Tucker asked Mallory for instructions regarding "the final disposition" of his vessels. To his great relief, Tucker learned that a passage of one hundred feet would be provided in the barrier.[29]

With the abandonment of Norfolk expected at any time, Tucker on May 4 was ordered to take the *Patrick Henry* and *Jamestown* there to assist with the evacuation. The following night, the two ships, with their sails removed, slipped undetected past the Union guns at Newport News and reached Norfolk. In the darkness of May 6, the two steamers again sneaked under the nose of the enemy, towing up the James a brig loaded with guns and munitions and three gunboats that had been under construction at the navy yard. The most important of these was the ironclad ram *Richmond*. Tucker's mission was "a great success," wrote Lieutenant John Taylor Wood. Indeed, he saved the nucleus of the squadron that would defend Richmond until the close of the war.[30]

From his anchorage above Newport News on the morning of May 8, Tucker saw three Union steamers start upstream. One of these was the experimental *Galena*, the North's second ironclad. In less than an hour, that ship destroyed the Confederate battery at Day's Point. She then advanced to the works at Harden's Bluff, whose guns Tucker assumed would be silenced quickly. "Knowing the folly of [the *Patrick Henry's*] attempting to attack an iron vessel," he informed Mallory, "and being quite useless there," Tucker steamed upstream to assist in the completion of the obstruction at Drewry's Bluff. He warned that the *Galena* could "come up at any time and shell Richmond, and there is no force . . . to prevent it, except . . . an impassable barricade." On his way upstream, Tucker encountered Lieutenant William Sharp in the tiny *Beaufort*, which Mallory had sent from Richmond to halt the Yankees. Sharp's explanation of his mission "elicited a broad grin from everyone," remembered Midshipman Clayton, "from the captain to the powder boy." Tucker told Sharp, "Well, I hope you can do it; I am getting out of their way." The one-gun *Beaufort* quickly "fell in behind" the *Patrick Henry*. Tucker reached Drewry's Bluff before noon on May 8 and immediately requested a meeting with Commander Ebenezer Farrand, in charge of the naval batteries hastily being readied there. Tucker expressed himself "very anxious for the fate of Richmond" and advised that "no time be lost in making this point impassable."[31]

During the next week Tucker and the men of his squadron, along with an army artillery unit, worked feverishly to complete the defenses at Drewry's Bluff. With heights ranging from 80 to 110 feet, this steep-faced cliff overlooked the south bank of the river for a mile above and below the barricade, enabling its occupants to direct a deadly, plunging fire on an approaching enemy. Tucker took the *Patrick Henry* and his smaller vessels to safety upstream from the barrier. Then the *Jamestown* and several civilian craft were loaded with stone and sunk in the passageway. The sailors, meanwhile, dug gun emplacements into the brow of the bluff and reinforced them with logs. The *Jamestown's* two 6-inch guns and two similar pieces from the *Patrick Henry* along with the latter's 8-inch rifled pivot gun were hauled up the cliff and re-mounted on their naval carriages. On May 13 the crew of the *Virginia* joined Tucker's sailors. Three days earlier Captain Tattnall, who had supposed the evacuation of Norfolk to be several days distant, awoke to discover that the army had pulled out during the night. Hoping to retreat up the James, the flag officer lightened the *Virginia* as much as possible. But the pilots advised him that his ironclad still drew too much water. Rather than have her fall into Union hands, Tattnall destroyed his ship on May 11.[32]

With the *Virginia* no longer a menacing presence in Hampton Roads, the Union dispatched additional vessels up the James. The *Galena* and her two wooden companions, the *Aroostook* and *Port Royal*, were joined by the iron-hulled *Naugatuck* and the *Monitor*. The Federals hoped that this formidable force, under the brilliant Commander John Rodgers, might bombard Richmond into submission and allow the navy to snatch the prize away from McClellan's army. At about 7:30 A.M. on May 15, Rodgers led his fleet into action. He first brought the *Galena* into position with such an adept display of seamanship that he won the praise of the Confederate sailors on the bluff. The *Monitor* soon anchored abreast of the flagship, both about six hundred yards from the rebel guns. But even before the *Galena* had closed on the Confederate works, two shots had pierced her 3⅛-inch armor, killing one crewman and wounding five others. The *Naugatuck* and the two wooden gunboats remained about a half mile downstream. They were exposed to only four of the Southern cannon, but rebel sharpshooters hidden along the banks of the river constantly harassed them. After firing only sixteen times, the *Naugatuck*'s most powerful gun, a hundred-pounder, exploded. The *Aroostook* and *Port Royal* suffered very damaging hits, forcing them to retire from the engagement. After about two hours the *Monitor* advanced even closer to the Confederate batteries, but the small size of the vessel's gunports prevented elevating her twin cannon enough to fire on the emplacements high above. So, the *Monitor* backed away, reducing the impact of her 11-inch projectiles.

Unable to inflict much additional damage on the more distant Union vessels and the seemingly impervious *Monitor* (with eight inches of armor on her turret), the Southern gunners concentrated their fire on the *Galena*. This scrappy but lightly armored craft was hit about fifty times, and almost half of these shots perforated her shield. Shortly after 11:00 A.M., Rodgers withdrew from the combat. He had expended nearly all of his ammunition, firing 238 rounds. The *Galena* was in shambles; thirteen of her crew had been killed and eleven wounded. Among the thirteen Confederate dead and eight wounded was Midshipman Daniel Carroll, Tucker's aide, who was killed standing next to his commander. The battle of Hampton Roads had shown that wooden warships were no match for ironclads. The action at Drewry's Bluff indicated the defensive value of obstructions in narrow channels and the vulnerability of even armored ships, bravely fought, to the plunging fire of heavy guns. Reported Rodgers candidly, "we demonstrated that [the *Galena*] is not shotproof."[33]

Soon after the battle ended, President Davis and General Lee visited Drewry's Bluff to congratulate the victors. The ladies of Richmond sent wagonloads of "pies, cakes, turkeys, chickens, beef and mutton, with bread galore," remembered Clayton. "We forgot the taste of salt horse and hard tack." The Confederate Congress passed a resolution of thanks to all the officers and men who had fought in the contest for their "great and signal victory" and their display of "gallantry, courage and endurance." But in this engagement for which all were proclaimed heroes, each gun crew boasted that its contribution had been paramount. "The most effective gun on the bluff was the eight-inch solid shot gun of the *Patrick Henry*," asserted Rochelle. Knowing this weapon's great power, "Tucker gave it his personal supervision." Both Rochelle and Commander Farrand, in his official report, agreed that the last telling shot of the combat had come from Tucker's piece and entered one of the *Galena*'s ports. "Immediately the smoke rushed out," wrote Farrand, and "we gave three hearty cheers as she slipped her cables and moved down the river."[34]

Lieutenant Wood saw things differently. "The *Virginia*'s crew alone barred [Rodgers's] way to Richmond," he proclaimed. Boatswain Charles Hasker boasted that his 6-inch banded rifle, manned by men from the *Jamestown*, "did more damage to the *Galena* than all the rest of the guns on the bluff combined." Samuel A. Mann, an army artillery-man on top of the bluff, bristled at the claims of naval officers, especially Wood—"our web-footed brother." He insisted that gunners com-manded by Major Augustus H. Drewry, the owner of the bluff, had provided the margin of victory. Several days of rain before the battle had saturated the ground and made it unstable. "Capt. Tucker's naval gun . . . was disabled," wrote Mann. "Its casemate of heavy logs caved in on it which deprived us of their help until near the end of the fight."[35]

In the weeks after the battle, Tucker and the other sailors strengthened their batteries and mounted additional guns at nearby Chapin's Bluff. Commander Rodgers's squadron anchored downstream at City Point. The Union navy chiefs urged General McClellan to make a raid up the James; a few regiments of infantry, quickly deployed, might have taken Drewry's Bluff from the rear, enabling the navy to spearhead an assault by water and land against Richmond. But this was not done, and McClellan lost the initiative in the Seven Days battles on June 25–July 1. By August the federal forces along the James no longer posed a serious threat to the Confederate capital. On the twenty-fifth of that month, Commander Tucker received new orders: "Proceed to Charleston, S. Carolina and report to Capt. D. N. Ingraham . . . for command of . . . the *Chicora*." He departed for his new assignment five days later.[36]

CHAPTER THREE

Commodore in Gray

A MYSTERIOUS STRANGER registered at the Charleston Hotel on September 14, 1862. After his name in the guest book, he wrote his business address—"C.S.S. *Indian Chief*," the navy receiving ship in the harbor. Several curious onlookers examined the hotel register and, not knowing the meaning of the initials "C.S.S.," deduced that the newcomer was a visiting native American dignitary: he was "tall, majestic looking . . . with a bronzed, weather beaten countenance." The stranger, reported the *Charleston Daily Courier* gleefully, was "an officer of the Confederate Navy." Thus, quite likely, was Handsome Jack Tucker introduced to the people of Charleston, South Carolina. He had arrived in that city by September 9 to take command of the *Chicora*.[1] But his ship would not be serviceable for several more weeks, so her skipper probably established his headquarters on the receiving ship and found lodging ashore.

Genteel old Charleston was, after Richmond, the most coveted prize of the Civil War. Its role as a major Confederate port gave the city considerable strategic value. But Charleston had far greater symbolic importance. There, some three decades earlier, John C. Calhoun had enunciated the states'-rights doctrines now evoked to justify secession. In December 1860 the South Carolina State Convention, meeting in that city, began the parade of Southern states out of the Union. Soon the first shots of the Civil War echoed in Charleston harbor with the bombardment of Fort Sumter. For Southerners, Charleston was the "Cradle of the Confederacy," almost a shrine to be defended at any cost. To the North, however, the city was the odious "Nest of Rebellion," a font of heresy to be crushed and ostracized. Thus, the largest concentration of United States naval power assembled during the war was dedicated to the capture of "Rebellion Roads." The federal navy was held at bay, however, by powerful shore batteries, formidable obstructions, and several innovations—ironclad rams, mines, torpedo boats, and a submarine—which made Charleston the showcase of Confederate contributions to naval warfare.

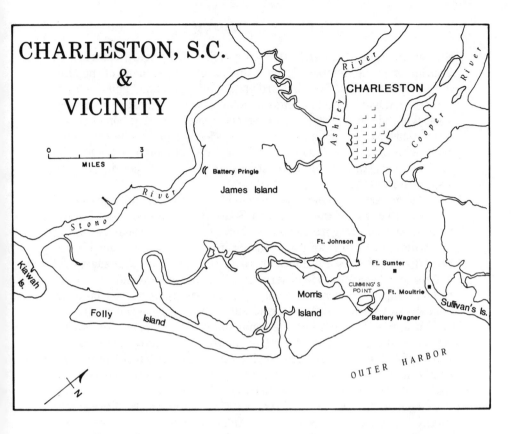

CHARLESTON, S.C.
&
VICINITY

MILES
0 ————— 3

Ashley River

CHARLESTON

Cooper River

((Battery Pringle

James Island

Stono River

Kiawah Is.

Ft. Johnson ▪

Ft. Sumter ▪

CUMMING'S POINT

Morris

Ft. Moultrie ▪

Island

Battery Wagner

Sullivan's Is.

Folly Island

OUTER HARBOR

N

Charleston sits at the tip of a tongue of land between the Ashley and Cooper rivers, which flow into a spacious basin in front of the city. Many creeks and inlets dissected the low, swampy ground astride the harbor into a maze of islands. The bay of Charleston resembled an hourglass, and the inner and outer harbor were pinched in the middle by a line of fortifications. On the north side of the port lay Sullivan's Island, with Fort Moultrie standing guard over the narrow ship channel between the outer and inner harbors. Guns on Morris Island defended the south side of the waterway. At the end of a sandbar extending from Morris Island into the center of the passageway, Fort Sumter defiantly dared intrusion. The outer harbor lay beyond the Moultrie–Sumter–Morris Island line, with a shallow bar at its entrance.

The man most closely identified with Civil War Charleston was a Louisiana Creole, General Pierre Gustave Toutant Beauregard. An outstanding military engineer, Beauregard commanded the Confederate forces during the initial bombardment of Fort Sumter in April 1861. In the succeeding two years he won fame and inspired great controversy for his roles in the Southern victory at the first battle of Manassas (Bull Run) in July 1861 and the defeat at Shiloh the following April.

Somewhat in disgrace after the latter fight, Beauregard returned to Charleston on September 15, 1862, and assumed command of the Military Department of North Carolina, South Carolina, and Georgia. Beauregard had a towering ego and a low opinion of most of his associates, whether in subordinate or superior positions. He hoped that a dramatic repulse of the anticipated Union assault on Charleston would restore his prestige and win him an important field command, where he might demonstrate the appropriateness of his favorite sobriquet—the "Napoleon in Gray."

The general cherished his place in history and carefully preserved his files. Because of the paucity of Southern naval documents, army records and Beauregard's memoirs became the major sources for reconstructing the story of the Confederate navy at Charleston.[2] Beauregard has received the lion's share of the credit for the successful defense of Charleston. He deserved it. But the general and some later historians gave scant recognition to the contributions of the Confederate navy at Charleston. In these accounts the Southern sailors (including Tucker, who would become commander of the Charleston Squadron) seem unaggressive and unimaginative, with Beauregard inspiring every offensive operation, coaxing his naval colleagues to adopt innovative technology.[3] It is difficult from the surviving record to determine with certainty the relationship between Tucker and Beauregard. But the image of Tucker as a timid spectator and hidebound traditionalist is totally inconsistent with the more fully documented periods of his career both before and after his service in Charleston. The sailor seems to have enjoyed amazingly amicable relations with the haughty and often rancorous soldier; Tucker emerged almost unscathed from Beauregard's memoirs. The two officers likely conferred, at least informally, on all matters of importance to the navy. Ever the diplomat, Tucker sought cooperation and avoided unnecessary conflict with the general, who fortunately had a relatively good grasp of naval strategy.

The Blood Tubs

The *Chicora* and her nearly identical twin the *Palmetto State*, flagship of Commodore Duncan N. Ingraham, were ironclad rams that looked very much like the *Virginia*. Nearly flat-bottomed, tapering to deadly points at either end, and plated with two inches of iron, their hulls sat low in the water, exposing little freeboard to enemy fire. A thick wooden casemate covered with four inches of iron, inclined at sixty-degree angles to deflect shot, sat atop the main deck of each gunboat. Inside the *Chicora*'s shield were four 32-pounder rifles, fired from broadside ports, and two 9-inch shell guns mounted on pivots, fore and aft. Although largely modeled after the *Virginia*, the Charleston gunboats were smaller than the prototype by about one-quarter. The *Chicora* was 150 feet long and 34 feet wide and drew 11 feet of water. The rams were designed for harbor defense, not sea service. Powered by small, unreliable engines taken from old tugboats, they could achieve speeds of six knots under ideal conditions. For the people of Charleston, familiar with the sleek lines of traditionally designed ships, the *Chicora* and *Palmetto State* were "blood tubs" and the "butt of . . . jokes and jibes." One newspaper noted their "grotesque ugliness."[4] Against wooden vessels at close quarters, however, the mailed gunboats could be as lethal as they were ugly.

In addition to their role in defending the harbor, almost everyone in Charleston assumed that the two rams, ready for action at the end of October 1862, would soon attack the Yankee blockading force. The latter consisted of about a dozen wooden vessels, mainly converted merchantmen, which would be no match for the rebel ironclads. If this squadron could be driven off, international law required that Washington give neutral nations sixty days' notice before enforcing the blockade anew. It was imperative that the attack occur before the arrival of several Union ironclads reportedly being rushed to completion for service off Charleston, but weeks passed in inactivity. Commodore Ingraham was reluctant to take the offensive. With the wisdom acquired during a half century in the navy, he doubted the seaworthiness of his awkward and underpowered gunboats in the rough winter water beyond the bar. Many junior officers, however, deemed him overly cautious and questioned his mettle.[5]

On Friday, January 30, the combination of weather and tides were propitious for the long-awaited raid. Shortly after midnight, the *Palmetto State*—with the commodore on board—and the *Chicora* passed Fort Sumter and reached the bar at the mouth of the outer harbor. Here they anchored, waiting for the moon to set and high tide to arrive, so that the heavy ships could pass out undetected into the Atlantic. At 4:30 that morning (Tucker's fifty-first birthday) the rams crossed the bar and began searching for their quarry in a thick haze. The *Palmetto State* went into action first, ramming and disabling the USS *Mercedita*, a converted merchant steamer anchored just outside the harbor. The federal skipper surrendered, but Ingraham procrastinated at length over the disposition of the prisoners. By the time he decided to release them on parole, most of the blockaders had fled beyond the range of his flagship.[6]

The *Chicora*, meanwhile, engaged several Union ships. At 5:30 A.M., reported Tucker, his vessel shot at a "schooner-rigged propeller," which caught fire and then disappeared. Next, the gunboat sent three shots into the *Keystone State*, a ten-gun side-wheeler, which also was set ablaze. Under Commander William E. LeRoy, the sailors of the *Keystone State* quickly extinguished the fire onboard and returned to the fray. LeRoy intended to ram his adversary, but when the Union vessel had closed to within five hundred yards, a shot from Tucker's ship exploded into the hull of the *Keystone State* and ruptured her boilers. Steam filled the engine room, forcing all hands topsides, while ten more blasts from the ram hit the paddle wheeler. The Union ship lost a quarter of her crew, twenty men dead and an equal number wounded.

As the *Chicora* came alongside, the *Keystone State* struck her colors in surrender; many Northern sailors rushed to the rail and extended their arms "in an imploring manner." Tucker ordered his gunners to cease firing and instructed Lieutenant George Bier and Engineer James Tomb to take charge of the prize. As the *Chicora*'s boat was being launched, the Rebels noticed that the *Keystone State*'s starboard wheel, on the far side of the ship, continued to turn. Suspecting that the Yankees were attempting to flee from the sluggish ironclad, the junior officers urged Tucker to resume firing. But he assumed—correctly, for the moment—that escaped steam prevented the Union engineers from shutting down their engines. Perhaps remembering his own experience at Hampton Roads, when the *Patrick Henry*'s boilers had been hit, he continued to hold his fire even though the *Keystone State* widened her distance from the gunboat by several hundred yards. Then the Union vessel raised her flag and resumed firing.

An outraged Tucker in his official report charged that the *Keystone State*'s commander "by his faithless act" had placed himself "beyond the pale of civilized and honorable warfare." Command of the Yankee steamer, in fact, had changed hands during the engagement. Believing his ship helpless and sinking, LeRoy ordered the flag hauled down. But soon he was confronted by his very agitated executive officer, who assumed responsibility for the vessel. With only one engine, initially operating solely on the accumulated vacuum, the *Keystone State* was able to outrun the *Chicora*. Within a short time, other Union steamers came to the rescue and towed both the *Mercedita* and the *Keystone State* to safety. After the fight with the *Keystone State*, the *Chicora* steamed six or seven miles farther out to sea and exchanged shots at long range with five more Union ships. Ingraham, however, decided to end the operation. The *Palmetto State* went back toward Charleston and signaled Tucker to follow. At about 8:00 A.M. the *Chicora* joined the *Palmetto State* off the Charleston bar, where they waited until 4:00 P.M., when high water permitted them to enter the harbor.[7]

As the rams steamed into the port, the guns of forts Sumter and Moultrie saluted them, and citizens on the wharves cheered loudly. "Not since the . . . fall of Fort Sumter," gushed the *Charleston Mer-*

cury, "has our community been as elated. . . . The gallant naval officers . . . have vindicated the reputation of our young navy in a style that will fairly take rank with the exploits of the *Merrimac.*" But euphoria over what Beauregard initially described as a "brilliant achievement" quickly became embarrassment. The early reports of the operation indicated that at least one ship, the *Mercedita,* and perhaps two others had been sunk; that several more had been damaged severely; and that all the Union vessels had dispersed. Beauregard and Ingraham hastily proclaimed the blockade lifted. Almost immediately, however, the Northern fleet returned; in a few days it became apparent that no Yankee ships had been lost. Nevertheless, the raid of the Charleston gunboats was the only time during the war in which Confederate ironclads successfully engaged the enemy on the open sea.[8]

Within two months of this modest victory, Rear Admiral Samuel F. Du Pont's South Atlantic Blockading Squadron was strengthened dramatically with the arrival of eight ironclad monitors and the recently commissioned *New Ironsides,* a potent armored frigate. From his base at Port Royal, about fifty miles south of Charleston, Du Pont threatened that city as well as Savannah, Georgia (twenty-five miles below Port Royal), and Wilmington, North Carolina, a major port some two hundred miles north of Charleston. In response to this crisis, President Davis in February 1863 dispatched his nephew and personal naval aide Lieutenant John Taylor Wood to inspect the defenses of Wilmington, Charleston, and Savannah. General Beauregard and the junior naval officers at Charleston probably corroborated for Wood earlier reports that "Old Ingle" lacked aggressiveness and had been indecisive during the raid of the previous month.

Upon his return to Richmond, Wood recommended that flag officers Josiah Tattnall at Savannah and Duncan Ingraham at Charleston be replaced by younger men. Secretary Mallory did so at the end of March. At the latter port Commodore Ingraham remained in charge of the station, supervising shore facilities and providing logistic support for the squadron. Commander Tucker became "flag officer, commanding afloat." The frail Ingraham, furthermore, often was absent from his post, leaving his junior colleague in command of the shore station, too. Tucker's promotion probably was recommended by Wood, who had served with him on the James River, and was supported within the squadron. Bemoaning service under Ingraham, Lieutenant Bier had written that Tucker was "one of the most energetic and capable officers in the service" and "ought to command" the squadron "with discretionary orders."[9]

The changes at Charleston and Savannah conformed to Mallory's long-held conviction that younger officers should hold the more important operational commands. In May 1863 Congress created the Provisional Navy of the Confederate States of America, ostensibly to exist only for the duration of the war. All officers retained their old rank and relative seniority in the "regular navy," but sea duty now was restricted to the men of this new organization. Mallory incorporated virtually all of the junior officers into the provisional service, some with increased rank. Only a few senior men, including Tucker, became part of the new corps. In January 1864 three commanders of the provisional navy were promoted to captain. The most junior of these was Tucker, who advanced some sixteen positions to become the Confederacy's seventh-ranking sea officer. With the grade of captain and command of a squadron, he was addressed as "Commodore."[10]

Torpedo on the Brain

Upon learning of the changes at Charleston, an officer at Mobile, Alabama, commented that "Tucker will have to do something at once or his head will go off too." Indeed, had his promotion come a few weeks earlier, the new flag officer might have been expected to "do something." But the January raid had demonstrated the limited offensive capabilities of the gunboats. The sea was "perfectly smooth," reported Ingraham, "and gave us no opportunity to test the sea qualities of the boats." It soon became apparent that "being low in the water and top heavy from the iron protecting the guns," the *Chicora* and *Palmetto State* "were not safe in a sea way." Even the eager Lieutenant Bier now admitted that they could not go ten miles beyond the bar.[11]

The deep draft of Tucker's slow ships and the overwhelming strength of Du Pont's reinforced squadron also discouraged offensive operations closer to shore. As the new flag officer hastily explained to Commander John K. Mitchell, in charge of the Bureau of Orders and Detail in Richmond, "The Ironsides and fourteen of the enemy's wooden vessels are off the bar—and three of their monitors are in the North Edisto River about fifteen miles from here—We can only cross the bar at high water [and] consequently must remain out twelve hours—in half that time the enemy could bring up his iron clads from the Edisto, and might prove rather too many guns for us. . . . I would like much to know what the Department think about it." Because of the South's great inferiority in ships and the difficulty in replacing or even repairing them, the defensively minded Confederate navy—from Secretary Mallory on down—was reluctant to risk their vessels in offensive operations, especially when the chances for success were slim.[12]

By the first week of April 1863, moreover, the major concern at Charleston had shifted from the blockade to the large Union assault force assembling off the southeastern coast. Confederate authorities at the South Carolina port had been preparing feverishly for a federal onslaught since the arrival of Beauregard the previous September. Tucker had participated in the first council of war, which analyzed the harbor's defenses,[13] and he likely continued to play a key role in strategic planning. The major elements in Charleston's defenses were heavy guns, obstructions, and mines. A man with considerable ordnance background in the "Old Navy," Tucker had kept abreast of recent advances in guns, ballistics, and armor. He was the only senior officer at Charleston with combat experience against ironclads—afloat at Hampton Roads and, more significantly now, from shore batteries at Drewry's Bluff. At the latter place he had witnessed the efficacy of obstructions in thwarting enemy ships. Finally, Tucker had been one of the first Confederate officers to employ torpedoes and, more than a year earlier, had recommended their use in conjunction with obstructions and shore batteries on the James River.

The stationary defenses at Charleston, even those seemingly within the proper realm of the navy, were prepared almost exclusively by army engineers; they had far greater resources. Beauregard mounted seventy-six cannon around the harbor, with the heaviest guns placed at forts Sumter and Moultrie. Buoys anchored in the channel at fixed ranges assisted the aim of the Confederate artillerymen. To impede the advance of Yankee ships and to permit a sustained fire against them, the engineers partially obstructed the passageway with piles and a boom of logs. But the Rebels placed more confidence in a barrier of heavy rope nets and a large number of mines. After crossing the bar into the outer harbor, approaching ships would pass over a huge electrical "torpedo"—three thousand pounds of powder in an old boiler anchored to the bottom and attached by insulated telegraph cable to a galvanic battery on shore. Between forts Sumter and Moultrie were three files of mechanical mines linked together by ropes and kept afloat with barrels. Inside the rope and wooden obstructions, many more contact mines were anchored below the water's surface. Battle plans formulated in December 1862—before Charleston's defenses had been completed and the Yankee ironclads had arrived—called for the rebel gunboats to engage the enemy head-on in the channel. By April 1863, however, the Confederates determined that Tucker's rams should be a secondary line of defense, held in readiness behind the obstructions between the Sumter-Moultrie gauntlet. As the enemy assembled for its assault, the channel would be entirely sealed or provided with only a small opening which Tucker's vessels must not reveal to the Union squadron.[14]

Admiral Du Pont's ironclad juggernaut crossed the Charleston bar on April 6, 1863. Consisting of the armor-belted, twenty-gun frigate *New Ironsides*, seven monitors (each mounting one 11-inch and one 15-

inch gun in her turret) and the experimental *Keokuk*, with guns mounted in stationary twin towers, the fleet spent the night anchored in the outer harbor beyond the effective range of the Confederate artillery. "The Hour at Hand," headlined the *Mercury* ominously the next morning. Indeed, at 1:30 that afternoon, the Yankees steamed up the channel toward Sumter and Moultrie. The resolute John Rodgers, whom Tucker had battled at Drewry's Bluff, led the way in the monitor *Weehawken*. Third in the order of battle was John L. Worden, of the *Montauk*, who also was facing his old friend Tucker in combat for a second time. The *New Ironsides*, Du Pont's flagship, held the fifth position, with the *Keokuk* in the rear.

At 2:50 the *Weehawken* came into range, and the Confederates welcomed her with concentrated fire. "The accuracy of the rebels was very great," reported Rodgers, who quickly guessed the secret of the enemy gunners. "As we passed a buoy all the guns opened at once." Many of the other federal commanders, however, feared that torpedoes were attached to these markers, a belief strengthened when an explosion near the *Weehawken* lifted her bow out of the water. Rodgers brought his ship close to the first line of obstructions, but they looked "so formidable" that he "thought it right not to entangle the vessel." He turned around and withdrew, after having been hit at least fifty-three times. The trailing ironclads suffered the same experience; they were badly battered by the Confederate guns before the nets, logs, and torpedoes forced their retreat. All the while, Yankee turrets jammed, their guns became disabled, and casualties mounted. The concussion of the rebel projectiles fractured bolt heads and metal fittings, which became flying shrapnel within the Union ships. Many shots pierced the federal armor. As billows of gun smoke reduced visibility, several collisions and near misses occurred, and the attacking commanders feared that their heavy ships might run aground. By 5:30 P.M. all of Du Pont's ironclads had steamed out of range.

For at least ten minutes during the battle, the *New Ironsides* had sat directly over the giant electrical mine, while Confederate engineers on shore frantically attempted to detonate the device. A wagon apparently had rolled over the exposed cable on the beach, severing the connection with the battery. This was Du Pont's only good fortune that day. His fleet had fired a scant 139 times, mainly at Fort Sumter, and caused only light damage. The Rebels had answered with 2,209 shots, almost a quarter of which found their mark. They hit the *Keokuk* ninety times, and nineteen shots had pierced her armor at or below the water-line. She sank the next morning. Five monitors required extensive repairs. Du Pont wanted to resume the assault the following day. But after a conference with his captains, the admiral concluded that "to renew the attack would convert failure into a disaster." Charleston, he warned, "could not be taken by a purely naval attack," an opinion unanimously shared by his skippers.[15]

During the Union assault, Tucker's ironclads had steamed in a circle behind the obstructions, ready to engage any enemy that might breach the barrier. None did, and not a shot was fired from either Confederate gunboat. Had Du Pont's vessels penetrated the inner harbor, however, the rebel sailors would have greeted them with a new weapon—the spar torpedo. Developed by Captain Francis D. Lee, Beauregard's chief engineer, this device was an egg-shaped copper vessel filled with gunpowder (about one hundred pounds in those mounted on the ironclads). Attached to the bow of the gunboats by an iron spar, the weapon could be lowered several feet below the water when approaching an enemy ship. On impact, chemical fuzes would break, detonating the charge. Lee had worked on this weapon for several months, perfecting it for use on a torpedo boat he had designed.

Tucker and some of the younger officers at Charleston became early supporters of the spar torpedo. But many mariners of both Civil War navies considered torpedoes of all kinds "uncivilized." Hoping to win approval from local navy men and "remove any objection arising out of the novelty of the device and the departure from long-established custom," Lee gave a practical demonstration in the harbor on March 13. With a spar torpedo mounted on a canoe, he sank an old hulk in "about twenty seconds." Lee reported that after witnessing the event, Charleston's naval officers "warmly approved . . . this terrible weapon of offense." Lieutenant William T. Glassell, of Tucker's *Chicora*, quickly proposed to attack the blockading squadron with six rowboats mounting spar torpedoes. But Ingraham (whom Glassell termed an "old granny") did not believe in "new fangled notions." Tucker, however, likely intervened, and on March 18 Ingraham permitted Glassell to attack the Yankees with a single small craft. The latter officer failed to get within striking distance of his target, the USS *Powhatan*. But by March 25, in anticipation of a full-scale assault by Du Pont's fleet, Lee was mounting spar torpedoes "on the iron-clads, together with every available steamer and small boat in the harbor."[16]

The flotilla of smaller craft was manned by the "Special Expedition," about sixty officers and men dispatched from Richmond under the command of Lieutenant William A. Webb, Tucker's brother-in-law. Initially organized to board and capture Union monitors—using essentially the same plan devised in April 1862 to take the original turret ship—this well-trained team and their torpedo-mounted boats would be positioned behind Fort Sumter to stop any enemy ship which might breach the obstructions. Webb had sufficient rowboats for his task, but he lacked small steamers to tow them into action. A few hours before Du Pont's attack, Tucker ordered him to "call upon . . . the firm of John

Fraser & Co." and inform the mercantile house that the navy required steamers to defend the harbor and that he "must and will have them." Tucker wanted this done "quietly and pleasantly if possible"; if not, Webb was to seize the vessels.[17]

Webb's torpedo team was not called upon for heroics against Du Pont's squadron that day. But Tucker and the other sailors soon developed "torpedo on the brain," and the spar torpedo quickly became the primary focus of Tucker's limited offensive efforts. For several days after Du Pont's attack, seven of the admiral's ironclads remained within the outer harbor. On April 10 Tucker, Webb, and Beauregard concurred in a plan which, if successful, would "shake Abolitiondom to [its] foundation." Under the cover of darkness six rowboats armed with spar torpedoes would assault, by twos, the three closest enemy ships. The next day, however, the officers decided that chances for success would be enhanced if all seven ironclads were attacked by three boats each. But two more days were required to assemble the additional boats and crews, and the monitors crossed the bar out into the Atlantic shortly before the raid was to begin.[18]

After leaving the outer harbor, some of Du Pont's monitors went to Port Royal for repairs, while the others anchored in the calm waters of the North Edisto River, some fifteen miles south of Charleston. The *New Ironsides* and a dozen wooden ships remained in front of the city, seaward of the outer bar. On April 13 General Beauregard proposed another ambitious operation, probably discussed earlier, and Tucker approved it with enthusiasm. On the first suitable night, four or five harbor steamers, each towing four rowboats armed with spar torpedoes, would cross the bar. Upon seeing the lights of the Union ships, the boats would cast off in pairs toward the wooden blockaders. Simultaneously, the *Chicora* and *Palmetto State* would steam directly at and sink the *New Ironsides*. The two gunboats then would finish the destruction or dispersal of the wooden ships and remain outside the harbor long enough to demonstrate for foreign consuls that the blockade indeed had been broken. However, Tucker's rams were not to "remain long enough to be overpowered by the return of the enemy's monitors."[19]

For the rowboats and the deep-drafted, unseaworthy rams to leave the harbor and to surprise the enemy in darkness, Tucker required a combination of relatively calm seas and nighttime high tides. Following "squally" weather on April 13 and winds that reached "hurricane" force the next day, Charleston experienced five days in which both high tides occurred during daylight hours. By April 21, when the weather and tides became propitious for the torpedo attack, five federal monitors had returned from Port Royal and anchored in the North Edisto. Nevertheless, Tucker hurriedly ordered an attack on the *Ironsides*, only to be thwarted by the breakdown of the *Chicora*'s boilers.[20]

Frustrated in his designs against the *New Ironsides*, Tucker now targeted the monitors in the Edisto. Under the command of Lieutenant William H. Parker, six boats fitted for spar torpedoes wended their way in darkness through the creeks and canals connecting Charleston's inner harbor with the Edisto. Parker reached his destination at about 2:00 A.M. on May 12. Halting in a creek within sight of the enemy, the raiders hid their boats and repaired to a nearby abandoned mansion for a "nap," as Parker called it. Unfortunately he (and probably others in the party) "got very drunk," affording one of the expedition's most knowledgeable sailors an opportunity to desert and to alert the enemy. The Federals positioned pickets to foil the attack and sent wooden gunboats to cut off a retreat by the Confederates. The expedition escaped by securing wagons that ignominiously hauled their "fleet" overland to safety. The turncoat sailor, meanwhile, gave the enemy valuable information about Confederate torpedo operations. Tucker would face an increasingly wary foe in the future.[21]

The foremost obstacle to torpedo attacks was the inadequacy of Tucker's delivery systems. The Yankees by now were not likely to be caught unawares by the awkward gunboats or even by smaller wooden steamers. They were too slow, too noisy and, lacking anthracite, burned bituminous coal that emitted thick black smoke and showers of sparks. Rowboats mounting spar torpedoes had limited range, and even brave crewmen understandably eased up on the oars as they neared the point of impact. After the failure of the North Edisto raid, the Federals increased the number of picket boats guarding their fleet at night.[22]

In October 1862 Captain Lee had proposed the construction of a steam "torpedo ram." Lightly armored, this craft would be much faster and more maneuverable than the ironclad gunboats, and she would be armed solely with the spar torpedo. Beauregard embraced the idea, asserting that this craft "would be worth several gunboats." After initially rejecting the proposal, Navy Secretary Mallory reluctantly agreed to provide an engine and other materials for the vessel. However, work on the project, performed by local contractors under Lee's supervision, proceeded very slowly. The experimental boat competed for scarce materials and skilled labor with two navy ironclads simultaneously under construction. Moreover, the ram was an army venture, and Mallory bristled at Beauregard's unfavorable contrasts between the torpedo vessel and the gunboats—the secretary's pet project.

In the months that followed, Beauregard became increasingly strident in his criticism of the navy's gunboats and unduly sanguine in his promotion of the army craft. The general emphasized the offensive limitations of Mallory's gunboats, particularly the short, 1½-mile range of their guns. The enemy ironclads, invulnerable above the waterline to shots fired beyond eight hundred yards, "should be attacked below the water," where their hulls were lightly protected. With a single torpedo ram, asserted Beauregard, he could raise the blockade "in less than one week." Mallory defended his gunboats, emphasizing that they had been designed for harbor defense and not offensive operations at sea. The rebel ironclads were not meant to fight at long range; and, as Beauregard himself acknowledged, the enemy monitors could resist any fire from more than eight hundred yards. Mallory, in turn, doubted the practicability of building a torpedo boat which could do the things Beauregard claimed. "It will always be in the power of the enemy," he wrote, "to anchor his ship and protect her against torpedo boats by means familiar to seamen and readily attainable."[23]

The dispute between Beauregard and Mallory put Tucker in an uncomfortable cross fire. An early advocate of both defensive and offensive torpedoes, Tucker probably embraced the concept of a torpedo boat. He may have been reluctant, however, to support Lee's project publicly, especially while the skeptical Ingraham commanded the Charleston Squadron. Furthermore, the Virginian probably did not want to endorse the Lee-Beauregard ram if this meant totally forsaking Mallory's gunboats. But the impotence of the *Chicora* and *Palmetto State* during Du Pont's attack on April 7 and the aborted torpedo operations of the following weeks apparently induced the new flag officer to board Beauregard's bandwagon. On April 22 Beauregard protested to Richmond that work on the Lee ram had come to a halt. Perhaps with some exaggeration, he asserted that Tucker declared "unhesitatingly that this one machine of war . . . would be more effective . . . than all the ironclads here afloat and building."[24] Unfortunately for Tucker and the Confederacy, time would prove both Beauregard and Mallory partially correct. The secretary's rams had severe offensive limitations—and so did the general's torpedo boats. The South was unable to obtain an invincible vessel, and the North ultimately rendered its ironclads nearly invulnerable to the torpedo craft that Tucker did acquire.

By mid-1863 Tucker was anxious to add torpedo boats to his squadron; however, he still apparently believed that under favorable conditions, his gunboats might attack the Yankee ironclads. Lieutenant Colonel Arthur Fremantle, of Her Majesty's Coldstream Guards, visited Charleston that June and had several conversations with Beauregard and Tucker. Both men, he wrote, expected "great things from a newly invented and extradiabolical torpedo ram." But the flag officer ("a very good fellow, and a perfect gentleman") expressed "great confidence" in his gunboats "during calm weather, and when not exposed to plunging fire." Tucker told the Englishman that "if it were not for certain reasons" which Fremantle did not reveal—probably the faulty engines of the gunboats—"he should not hesitate to attack even the present blockading squadron."[25] Within a few days, however, Tucker gained increased respect for the enemy ships.

Union and Confederate ironclads had not engaged each other since the duel between the *Monitor* and the *Virginia*. Tucker's gunboats were weaker than the Southern prototype. Although they had the same four-inch armor on their casemates (which were sandbagged, too), the rams mounted fewer guns, the largest firing a 9-inch projectile. The Federals' new *Passaic*-class monitors, however, were significant improvements over John Ericsson's first turret ship. Faster, larger, and more seaworthy, they had eleven inches of armor on their turrets (as opposed to eight inches on the original *Monitor*), and one of the twin 11-inch guns had been replaced by a new 15-inch weapon. William A. Webb, Tucker's daredevil brother-in-law, had the misfortune to test the improved monitors in the war's second battle between ironclads.

Promoted to commander, Webb in May 1862 became flag officer of the Savannah Squadron, which included the newly commissioned iron-hulled CSS *Atlanta*, the Confederacy's most potent warship. She had a four-inch armored casemate, like the other gunboats, but was bigger, faster, and capable of going to sea. Boasting that "the whole abolition fleet" had "no terror" for him, Webb on June 16 steamed the *Atlanta* down the Savannah River toward the ocean and two awaiting federal monitors. His deep-drafted flagship soon went aground, listing at an angle that would not allow her guns to be trained on the enemy. From three hundred yards away, Commander Rodgers fired the *Weehawken*'s huge 15-inch shell gun at the *Atlanta*'s casemate. The concussion from the first 350-pound explosive projectile incapacitated forty men inside. After receiving only four more deadly shots, Webb surrendered. He had not been able to demonstrate the efficacy of the *Atlanta*'s weapons, so the engagement with Rodgers's monitor was not a conclusive test. But the *Weehawken* clearly demonstrated the effectiveness of the big Yankee guns against Southern armor. The lesson learned that day probably was not lost upon Tucker. In the estimate of the leading authority on the subject, the Confederacy's best ironclad "was simply no match for one monitor."[26]

The Mariner and the Mechanic

Rear Admiral John Adolphus Bernard Dahlgren assumed command of the South Atlantic Blockading Squadron on July 6, 1863, replacing Admiral Du Pont, who had become embroiled in controversy over his failure to vanquish "Rebellion Roads." The son of a Swedish-born Philadelphia merchant, Dahlgren had entered the United States Navy in 1826, the same year as Tucker. The two men perhaps met for the first time in 1830, when both served as midshipmen in the Mediterranean. Thereafter, their careers followed very different paths before converging again at Charleston. While Tucker spent almost eighteen years at sea with the "Old Navy," gaining a reputation as an outstanding mariner and leader, Dahlgren won fame and some fortune as the nation's foremost ordnance expert. For his invention of the Dahlgren gun, Congress in 1851 awarded him the salary of the next higher rank. Before his posting at Charleston, however, Dahlgren had only a scant eight years of sea duty, and he had never been in combat. The personalities of the two men showed even greater contrast. Although a man of more than average intelligence, Tucker was admired most for his social traits—a good sense of humor, a genuine regard for other people, and a secure ego that facilitated cooperation with prima donnas like Beauregard. The taciturn Dahlgren was a stern and often unappreciative commander and a difficult colleague; he was conceited, self-righteous, spoiled—and utterly brilliant.

Dahlgren also was a staunch Unionist with an ever-deepening revulsion for Rebels, particularly former United States naval officers. In the early weeks of the war, Dahlgren had become an influential adviser and personal friend of the president. His promotion to the new rank of rear admiral ahead of several senior captains did not sit well with many of Dahlgren's colleagues, who called him "Mr. Lincoln's Admiral." To combat such sniping, Dahlgren had sought, unsuccessfully, the command of Du Pont's ironclad division in the attack on Charleston; later, he would expose himself repeatedly to enemy fire. The Lincoln administration and the Northern public expected much from the new squadron commander. The major obstacles to the capture of Charleston, explained the *New York World*, were "mechanical"— torpedoes, obstructions, and artillery—and required "a mechanic, not a mere sailor, to overcome them."[27] Dahlgren was the Union navy's best mechanic.

Four days after the change in command, Dahlgren joined General Quincy A. Gillmore in a combined operation against Morris Island, which fronted the ocean at the southern shore of the harbor entrance. Supported by the guns of the admiral's monitors, three thousand Union troops landed on the south shore and quickly drove a thousand Confederates northward into Battery Wagner, an extensive earthwork cutting across the narrow finger of sand hills that pointed at Fort Sumter. Except for an unsuccessful charge against the rebel redoubt the next day and another bloody repulse on July 18, the struggle was a siege operation that would continue for almost two months. The Union officers hoped to capture the island, mount artillery at Cummings Point, and pulverize Fort Sumter. Thereafter, Dahlgren could clear the obstructions in the ship channel, steam into the inner harbor, and shell Charleston into submission.[28]

While the federal monitors were decisive factors in the battle for Morris Island, Tucker's ironclads had a limited role in the contest. The commodore's two sluggish rams would be no match for Dahlgren's fleet. Beauregard agreed that the *Chicora* and *Palmetto State* should remain behind Sumter, to resist the repeated federal attacks on the fort and obstructions that began concurrently with the operation against Morris Island. The enemy vessels shelling Morris Island from the Atlantic were beyond the range of Tucker's guns, and shallow water landward of the island prevented his vessels from approaching close enough to fire effectively upon the Union soldiers besieging Battery Wagner. The flag officer, noted Beauregard, was "anxious to take an active part in the contest," but he "was compelled to remain passive . . . and admit his impotency to be of any assistance."[29]

Tucker's sailors, in fact, played a significant role in the battle for Morris Island. Manning small steamers and boats, they transported to the island supplies and fresh troops, who were rotated every three days. The mariners also operated against Union pickets and scouts who infiltrated the swamps and creeks around Morris Island, signaling the location of Confederate targets. Moreover, the commodore's squadron became increasingly important in the defense of Fort Sumter. Beginning on August 17 and continuing each day for one week, Dahlgren's monitors pounded the citadel, reducing it to rubble. Artillery could no longer be mounted there, so its guns were taken to Fort Moultrie, on the north side of the channel. Henceforth Confederate infantry, supported by the guns of Moultrie and Tucker's gunboats, would hold the prize. Each night the rebel rams and smaller boats armed with spar torpedoes stood guard off the fort, severely taxing Tucker's manpower.[30]

Tucker did not resign himself entirely to a defensive role. If his gunboats could not engage the enemy ships successfully, he might attack them with spar torpedoes. But he did not have sufficient sailors to man his gunboats, which were kept very busy, and to provide crews for the increasing number of boats needed to supply the garrison at Battery Wagner. Torpedo operations would require many additional men. While the commodore waited for reinforcements, he and other officers considered several desperate plans to attack Dahlgren's fleet. On July 12 Beauregard asked if the flag officer could destroy "all or part" of the Union ironclads in a major torpedo operation employing rowboats and harbor steamers. Tucker lacked the crews for such a large-scale assault. During the next week, however, Lieutenant Glassell and Engineer Tomb made five unsuccessful attempts to reach the Union monitors with torpedo-mounted rowboats. A plan to crash an explosive-laden fire ship into a cluster of federal monitors was supported by Tucker but rejected by Beauregard.[31]

Confederate hopes for a successful blow against Dahlgren's fleet increasingly focused upon three experimental craft designed specifically for torpedo warfare—a "cigar boat" under construction in Charleston, a "fish-boat" being sent from Mobile, and Captain Lee's long-awaited "steam torpedo ram," now christened the *Torch*. Only the latter could be put into service quickly. Launched on July 11, the *Torch* had an unreliable old engine and structural defects and leaked badly. Furthermore, the low-lying craft, which resembled a Confederate gunboat in miniature, could not support the armor specified in the original plan. Nevertheless, Captain James Carlin, a daring skipper of blockade runners, agreed to test the boat against the Yankees. If successful, he proposed to purchase the *Torch* and fight her as a privateer. The trading firm of John Fraser and Company offered prizes of $100,000 for the destruction of the *New Ironsides* and $50,000 for each federal monitor sunk. But after two failed attempts to sink the enemy blockaders on August 18 and 20, Carlin "most unhesitatingly" expressed his "condemnation of the vessel" for her designated role.[32]

On September 6 Confederate military authorities at Charleston determined that Morris Island could no longer be held, so the army commanders and Tucker planned its evacuation. That evening, Tucker's new flagship *Charleston* (designed like the other gunboats, but some thirty feet longer and mounting six guns) assumed a position off Cummings Point to cover the operation. Beginning at 9:00 P.M. and continuing for the next four hours, about forty small boats manned by sailors from the *Chicora* and *Palmetto State* ferried nine hundred weary soldiers from the beach to small steamers waiting in deeper water. The Federals captured the last three boats to leave the island; nevertheless, the operation was a major success. One of the evacuated army officers praised the "admirable discipline" of the sailors and the expert manner in which they performed their task. "Their boats kept abreast, with the length of an oar from gunwale to the blade separating them. The oars thus interlocked never touched or interfered with each other. As each detachment left, other boats grounded on the beach to receive their load, and thus silently and without confusion the embarkation was accomplished."[33]

Beauregard asserted that his decision to evacuate Morris Island rested on his belief that federal occupation of that place would not result in the capture of Charleston itself—"a barren victory to the enemy," he called it in his official report. He was correct. The city fell only after Union armies in the rear forced the Confederates to abandon the port. Charleston, the symbol of Southern defiance, remained in rebel hands for almost eighteen more months. But the South lost its strategic port. Union guns at Cummings Point now commanded the main channel through the outer harbor; there, Dahlgren's ironclads could anchor in relatively calm water, beyond the effective range of the remaining rebel batteries. With Morris Island bristling with Yankee guns and federal ships clogging the main waterway, the blockade of Charleston became much more effective. In addition, huge rifled guns mounted on the island regularly hurled two- and three-hundred-pound shells into the lower part of the city. "We live and move under a constant fire," wrote Tucker in January 1864. With projectiles exploding among the wharves at five-minute intervals, he had difficulty loading supplies on his gunboats and soon would have to find a new anchorage up the Cooper River.[34]

Although the Union had achieved its major strategic objective at Charleston—significantly tightening the blockade—Dahlgren and his superiors still dreamed of raising the Stars and Stripes over Fort Sumter and, perhaps, steaming up to the docks of the city. On September 7, only hours after the loss of Morris Island, Dahlgren demanded the surrender of Fort Sumter and the three hundred soldiers there. The Confederate commandant told him that he could have the citadel when he could take and hold it. For the preceding two weeks, in fact, the Yankees had planned and the Rebels had anticipated an amphibious assault on Sumter. From the wreck of the *Keokuk*, sunk during Du Pont's attack in April, the Southerners had recovered a signal book, and they soon captured an army signalman who helped them interpret it. On September 8 a signal officer on the *Chicora* intercepted messages indicating that a boat attack would be made that evening. Tucker relayed this information to the army, and the Confederates prepared to welcome the enemy.

About midnight, federal tugs towed thirty boats carrying some five hundred sailors and marines to within four hundred yards of the fort and cast them loose. As the first wave of raiders landed, the Confederate soldiers met them with a hail of musketry along with grenades, fireballs, and brickbats hurled down from the mountain of debris that Sumter had become. Rebel artillery at Fort Moultrie and other batteries on Sullivan's Island, sighted-in during the daylight, opened fire on the Federals. Meanwhile, the *Chicora* steamed out from behind the fort. She drove off the other Union boats and then turned her guns, loaded with grape and canister shot, on the stranded Yankees, who quickly surrendered. Northern losses totaled nearly 130 killed, wounded, and captured. For Dahlgren, who had asserted that a mere "corporal's guard" defended Sumter, the failure of this attack was an embarrassing disappointment.[35]

Lieutenant Glassell, Tucker's torpedo specialist, received a terse order from the flag officer on September 22, 1863: "You will assume command of the torpedo steamer 'David,' and . . . proceed to operate against the enemy's fleet, . . . destroying as many . . . vessels as possible." The *David*—so named because the diminutive boat's intended victims were Yankee Goliaths—was a cigar-shaped wooden craft 54 feet long. Tapered to points at both ends, the boat was 5½ feet in diameter amidships, where a 12-foot-long cockpit accommodated a crew of four. When manned and ballasted, the gray-painted boat sat very low in the water, with only her center section visible—like a turtle's back—about two feet above the waves. A small steam engine, vented through a funnel located behind the cockpit, burned smokeless anthracite coal and powered the *David* at speeds of seven knots or more in calm seas.

Just after dark on October 5, the *David* slipped almost silently from her berth in Charleston and steamed toward Dahlgren's fleet, lying in the outer harbor off Morris Island. In addition to Glassell, the craft carried three volunteers from the *Chicora:* pilot J. Walker Cannon, Fireman James Sullivan, and Acting First Assistant Engineer James Tomb, the intrepid veteran of Glassell's earlier unsuccessful torpedo attacks. Riding the last of the ebb tide, the cigar boat passed through the federal squadron and came abreast of the *New Ironsides.* At about 9:15 the *David* crashed her torpedo, with a sixty-pound charge, against the side of the armor-belted frigate. The explosion shook the heavy ship severely, knocking many sailors off their feet. A thick column of water shot about one hundred feet into the air and then fell on the deck of the *New Ironsides* and her tiny assailant. Glassell ordered Tomb to back away; but a piece of iron ballast, jarred loose by the shock of the blast, had lodged in the machinery, jamming it. Furthermore, a large amount of water had fallen into the *David*'s cockpit and down her smokestack, dowsing the fire under the boiler.

Believing his low-lying vessel about to sink, Glassell gave the order to abandon ship. The sailors took to the frigid water and, under a shower of small-arms fire, swam off in different directions. After several anxious minutes Tomb realized that the *David* was still afloat and had drifted some distance away from the federal ship. He swam back to the boat, where he found Cannon, who could not swim, clinging to the vessel's lifeline. The two men climbed aboard, cleared the machinery, fired the boiler, and brought the *David* back into the harbor. Although the *New Ironsides* suffered some structural damage, the vessel escaped destruction, probably because the *David*'s torpedo was too small and been exploded too shallow.

Admiral Dahlgren responded to the attack with a mixture of indignation, admiration, and consternation. Dahlgren warned Glassell and Sullivan, who were captured, that they probably would be hung for using a torpedo, "an engine of war not recognized by civilized nations." The threat did not loosen the tongue of the *David*'s skipper, who refused to give his captors any information; but Sullivan, "a frightened wretch," gave the admiral a "full statement." Both captured Confederates were sent to Union prisons. Dahlgren urged that Glassell not be exchanged "until some time has elapsed," for that officer would be "of great service to the enemy" in future torpedo attacks. More than a year would pass before Glassell was traded for Union prisoners. But for their "gallant and meritorious conduct," Glassell was promoted to commander, while Tomb advanced to chief engineer. Quite unusually, Tucker named Tomb (a staff officer, not in the line of command) skipper of the *David*.[36]

In a confidential report to the Navy Department, Dahlgren explained the significance of the new Confederate weapon. "Among the many inventions with which I have been familiar, I have seen none which have acted so perfectly at first trial. The secrecy, rapidity of movement, control of direction, and precise explosion indicate, I think, the introduction of the torpedo element as a means of certain warfare. It can be ignored no longer. If 60 pounds of powder, why not 600 pounds?"[37] Dahlgren quickly adopted very effective measures to defend against future torpedo attacks. He greatly increased the number of boats and small steamers on nightly picket duty and mounted huge calcium searchlights on several of his vessels. The ironclads and other major ships in the outer harbor were anchored amid a shield of less valuable craft, and after dark the Union vessels were also protected by heavy nets suspended from outrigger booms. For the remainder of the war off Charleston, Northern sailors would sleep during the day and stand to their guns at night. Union officers closely questioned prisoners, refugees, and Confederate deserters about Southern torpedo craft. The intelligence obtained was remarkably good. On January 7, 1864, two deserters from Tucker's squadron gave Dahlgren detailed and quite accurate descriptions of the *Torch*, the *David* and, most ominously, a novel "*Diver*." Ordering his captains to take additional precautions, the admiral explained that the latter vessel was "nearly submerged and can be entirely so."[38]

The *Diver* was the third in a series of submersible boats developed by a group of New Orleans businessmen. Using facilities provided by the army, they constructed the vessel in Mobile. The builders began with a cylindrical boiler twenty-five feet long and four feet in diameter, which they cut in half lengthwise. Welding one-foot-wide iron panels between the boiler halves, they produced a boat with an elliptical cross section. After a wedge-shaped nose and tail were added, the completed submarine was about forty feet long and resembled a fish. Separated by bulkheads from the crew's compartment amidships, the ends of the "fish boat" were ballast tanks. Seacocks admitted water to submerge, and pumps emptied the chambers to surface. Unable to devise a practical steam or battery-powered engine, the builders arranged the *Diver*'s "machinery" for hand power. An eight-man crew turned a crankshaft which passed through the vessel to a propeller located in front of the rudder. This "engine" could achieve speeds of up to four knots.

The *Diver* had two hatches, located at the front and rear of the crew's compartment, hinged to combings fitted with glass windows. The skipper, standing in the forward hatchway, steered the vessel, controlled the nose tank, and operated a pair of stabilizing "fins" on the sides of the submarine. The second officer, posted in the rear hatchway, operated the tail tank. The craft had a functional depth gauge, but the vessel's iron construction confounded the compass. Snorkels ("breathing tubes") devised for the *Diver* also did not function well, so the boat's "conning towers" had to be above the water and the hatches open to set a course and, periodically, to admit fresh air. When the boat was submerged, a candle provided light, and its flickering flame monitored the oxygen supply. After completing the *Diver* in July 1863, the owners tested her in Mobile Bay. Towing a torpedo some two hundred feet behind, the submarine dove under an old coal barge, pulled the explosive device into the side of the target, and sank it. For actual operations against the enemy, the boat's owners—who had registered her as a privateer—determined that Charleston was the best hunting ground.[39]

Tucker first learned about the "submarine iron boat" in an August 1, 1863, letter from Admiral Franklin Buchanan at Mobile, who was confident that the vessel could destroy "one or more" of Dahlgren's ironclads. With the federal squadron shelling Morris Island daily, Tucker and Beauregard immediately asked for the boat, which arrived by railroad in mid-August. The *Diver*'s initial crew at Charleston consisted of civilians from Mobile headed by James McClintock, the principal designer and part owner of the boat. Although well acquainted with the vessel, these men were unfamiliar with local waters, and McClintock seemed timid. After a week without an attack, Beauregard demanded that a naval officer be placed in command; when the owners refused, military authorities seized the submarine. Tucker named Lieutenant James Payne skipper of the *Diver*, and that officer enlisted a volunteer crew from the squadron. On August 30, one day after the change of command, the submarine was swamped when the steamer to which she was moored moved suddenly; the boat pitched violently to one side, and water rushed into the open hatches. Payne and his first officer escaped, but five sailors drowned.

Three weeks later, the *Diver* was raised and refitted by Horace L. Hunley, the boat's major investor, who brought a new crew from Mobile. Lieutenant George E. Dixon, an army engineer who had participated in the vessel's construction, became the new commander, and the boat apparently passed to Beauregard's control. Dixon and his submariners practiced daily with the craft, repeatedly diving under the

Charleston and the *Indian Chief* in the harbor. On October 15, while Dixon was absent from the city, the thirty-five-year-old Hunley put the boat through her paces. The submarine dove but did not resurface. After three weeks on the bottom, the *Diver* was raised once more, and the bodies of Hunley and eight crewmen were buried with honors.

Beauregard ordered the venture abandoned. But after pleading by Dixon, the general agreed to the recruitment of a third crew, once more from among Tucker's sailors. Amazingly, a new team of volunteers was found for the "peripatetic coffin," now appropriately rechristened *H. L. Hunley*. James Tomb, the *David*'s skipper, feared that the submarine's propeller might become fouled by the long rope used to tow her torpedo; so at his suggestion, Dixon mounted a spar torpedo on the *Hunley*.[40]

On the night of February 17, 1864, the *Hunley* made her historic attack. Because Dahlgren's ironclads, anchored in the outer harbor, had been made invulnerable, the Confederate submariners targeted the *Housatonic*, a new thirteen-gun wooden sloop posted some two miles out to sea. At about 8:45 the *Hunley*, probably operating on the surface of the water, crashed her spar torpedo into the rear quarter of the Union sloop. The explosion demolished the stern of the ship, quickly sinking her. All but five Northern sailors were rescued. The brave men of the *Hunley* were not so fortunate. For reasons that are still debated, the "fish boat" did not return. Tomb's advice may have been fatal, bringing the explosion too close to the vessel. The CSS *Hunley*, however, achieved a prominent place in naval history. Although the concept of a submarine boat was old and a few functioning models had been constructed earlier, the *Hunley* was the first submersible craft to sink a ship in combat.[41]

Dahlgren at first attributed the loss of the *Housatonic* to the *David* and warned Secretary Welles that "the whole line of blockade will be infested with these cheap, convenient, and formidable defenses, and we must guard at every point." The admiral ordered his commanders to "use their utmost vigilance—nothing else will serve." After dark in fair weather, all blockading vessels at anchor inside and, for the first time, outside the harbor were to be skirted with booms and nets, and all of their boats were to be kept on patrol. Ships not so shielded were to be under way constantly. As Dahlgren predicted, the partial success against the *New Ironsides* and the destruction of the *Housatonic* inspired Confederates in other ports to embrace the torpedo boat. In Charleston, meanwhile, the Confederates labored on a fleet of torpedo vessels. But a shortage of engines and skilled workmen delayed completion of the vessels, and Dahlgren's defensive measures frustrated the efforts of even the stealthy "Captain" Tomb.[42]

Hoping to catch the Yankees off guard, the engineer maneuvered his *David* through creeks and canals into the North Edisto River and in the early morning of March 6, 1864, attacked the *Memphis*, a wooden steamer mounting seven guns. He struck the side of his target twice, including one "splendid blow"; but his torpedo had a faulty fuze. On April 18 Tomb stalked the forty-eight-gun frigate *Wabash*, in front of Charleston. The Union sailors detected the *David* at a distance of 150 yards and opened fire with their big guns. The tenacious torpedoman continued to close on his target until a heavy swell nearly capsized his boat and forced the *David* to seek the calm waters of the harbor. Early in May, Tomb and his vessel joined three army torpedo craft on an ambitious but ill-fated expedition through interior waterways to attack enemy ships at Port Royal. This was the last offensive operation by Tomb and his torpedo boat. The *David*, however, frequently joined the rams standing guard off Fort Sumter. "It now keeps company with the gunboats," groused Beauregard.[43]

Sailors Unused to Marching

Throughout the dreary final months of the war at Charleston, Tucker's men continued to perform boat duty, transporting men and supplies to various batteries, laying mines, and patrolling the harbor at night. Increasingly, however, the sailors served on shore, manning heavy guns at several batteries. Many troops from Charleston were rushed to Virginia during the summer of 1864, and the army turned to Tucker for crucial reinforcements. The commodore organized about 150 of his men into the Charleston Naval Battalion. Under the command of Lieutenant James Rochelle and, later, Lieutenant William G. Dozier, this unit drilled as infantry. On July 3 these sailors and naval artillerists manning the guns at Fort Johnson, on James Island in Charleston's inner harbor, turned back a boat attack by some one thousand Yankees. The Charleston Naval Battalion continued to perform infantry duty until the evacuation of the city and received fulsome praise from army commanders.[44]

After September 1864 Tucker's rams rarely went so far out in the harbor as Fort Sumter; it had become apparent that the Yankees would not try to take the citadel. Instead, the rams regularly stood guard off Fort Johnson. Coal had become very scarce, and the gunboats increasingly inefficient in consuming it. The *Palmetto State*'s boilers were nearly inoperable; during the final months of the war this vessel was little more than a floating battery, being towed into position when needed. The other two gunboats, reported a deserter, "usually take advantage of the tide." They could "hardly make headway against it." The *Charleston*'s top speed had been reduced to four knots or less, while the *Chicora* required four hours to cover the three miles between her wharf and Fort Johnson.[45]

Admiral Dahlgren's hopes for taking Fort Sumter and razing Charleston were deflated in mid-1864, when several new ironclads that he wanted assigned to his command were sent instead to Mobile and the James River. Although he had seven monitors and, until June, the *New Ironsides*, the admiral and his senior officers believed that they could not attack with the certainty of success. Charleston's inner harbor now was strewn with torpedoes, including several huge electrical mines. A failed assault involving the loss of several monitors would have jeopardized the blockade and perhaps even Union control of Morris Island. Until the final weeks of the war, federal commanders believed that Tucker had no intention of taking the offensive; but the very existence of the Charleston Squadron required a fleet of Union ironclads to maintain the blockade. Frustrated in his desire to inflict further punishment on the "atrocious rebels" there, Dahlgren unsuccessfully requested transfer to a "more active post." During the closing months of the conflict, the Confederate commodore and the Yankee admiral faced each other impotently.[46]

In addition to professional frustration, the opposing naval commanders experienced personal tragedy. On March 1, 1864, the admiral's son Colonel Ulric Dahlgren—a brilliant twenty-three-year-old cavalry officer—was killed from ambush by irregular home guards while leading a column of troopers on a daring raid to free Union prisoners in Richmond. Documents found on his body indicated that he had planned to kill President Davis and his cabinet and to burn the Confederate capital. While the Confederates denounced Colonel Dahlgren as a war criminal, the young officer's superior blamed him for the failure of the operation. Tucker also bore a tragic burden. Four-year-old Harry Gringo Tucker died in January 1862; the commodore's only surviving daughter, sixteen-year-old Harriet, died the following November. On March 9, 1864—little more than a week after the death of Ulric Dahlgren—the blockade runner *Juno*, manned by volunteers from Tucker's command, ran out of Charleston bound for the Bahamas. The second day at sea, the ship encountered a severe gale, broke in two, and sank almost immediately. After five weeks of gnawing uncertainty, the flag officer learned that his twenty-two-year-old son, Acting Master Charles Douglas Tucker, was among the missing sailors. A few days later one of the disaster's two survivors informed the commodore that other men on the *Juno* might possibly have been rescued. Thereafter, Tucker's rekindled hope died slowly as the weeks passed without further news of his child.[47]

Tucker's Charleston Squadron was reputedly one of the more efficient and better disciplined units in the Confederate States Navy. This was due in part to the commodore's leadership, but Tucker also was more fortunate than most Southern flag officers in the men assigned to his command. All of his ship captains had two decades' experience or more in the United States Navy. Similarly, the executive officers of the gunboats and other key personnel were regular officers from the "Old Navy." Like the rebel sea service as a whole, however, Tucker's force was deficient in junior line officers—young lieutenants, masters, and midshipmen. The latter became especially scarce after mid-1863, when Secretary Mallory ordered many midshipmen to the new Confederate States Naval Academy, aboard the *Patrick Henry* at Richmond. To fill the void in the lower ranks, Mallory commissioned a large number of acting lieutenants and acting masters from civilian life. Some of these officers (like Tucker's son Charles, a former merchant mariner) had considerable experience at sea or familiarity with navy life. Tucker assigned less knowledgeable civilian appointees to posts appropriate to their abilities. Because of the faulty machinery provided for most Southern ironclads and the paucity of spare parts, the Confederate navy's greatest manpower deficiency was in competent engineers. Notwithstanding the many mechanical problems with his gunboats, Tucker's vessels broke down less often than those in other commands.[48]

The Confederates had a chronic shortage of able seamen. The South had relatively few sailors at the start of the war, and many of these men opted for more lucrative employment on blockade runners. The navy could not draft men, and the army often conscripted mariners who might have joined the sea service. During the Morris Island campaign, Tucker was desperately short of sailors. But after that crisis had passed, his manpower problem became less acute than that of other flag officers. As a major port, Charleston had a pool of local seamen, who formed the nucleus of Tucker's crews. Beauregard readily permitted his navy colleague to seek recruits from the ranks of the general's army. Long before Richmond, in desperation, seriously considered placing blacks in the army, Tucker's squadron had at least three black sailors, freemen serving on the *Chicora*.[49]

The commodore, recalled Engineer Tomb, "at all times was as considerate in the treatment of the men as of the officers." Until the final months of the war, his sailors received adequate rations and uniforms. The ironclads were extremely hot and wet inside, and their crews frequently suffered heat prostration. But Tucker adopted stringent measures to prevent the spread of yellow fever and other infectious diseases common in the city to the ships. Lieutenant Parker judged Tucker's vessels "the cleanest iron-clads . . . that ever floated" and noted that "the men took great pride in keeping them so." According to the same officer, the state of "drill at both the great guns and small arms was excellent, and the discipline perfect." Other men who served at Charleston also testified that Tucker continued to run a "smart ship."[50]

In Tomb's memoirs, however, the commodore seems less a martinet than a benevolent father from whom the engineer "received such generous treatment," even when he deserved reprimands. The *David*'s skipper related several incidents when he had erred and praised Tucker's tactful effectiveness in correcting him. For Tomb these examples showed "what goes to make a good officer." Tucker's subordinates responded with "a feeling of affection . . . stronger than respect and obedience." The commodore "was everything an officer should be to command the love, respect and confidence of the officers and men," asserted the engineer. "Up to the fall of Charleston, he retained it."[51]

General William T. Sherman completed his "march to the sea" on December 21, 1864, capturing Savannah, Georgia. A few days earlier, Commodore William W. Hunter had taken his lighter-drafted wooden vessels up the Savannah River to Augusta. Commander Thomas Brent, who stayed behind in the ironclad *Savannah*, had been ordered to cover the Confederate withdrawal from the city and then escape with his vessel to Charleston. But Brent could not get his gunboat past the Confederate obstructions in front of the port. He blew up the ironclad and took his men overland to join Tucker's command. On December 13, as the Yankees poised to storm Savannah, President Davis had telegraphed Beauregard, suggesting that should Dahlgren concentrate his vessels for an attack on the Georgia port, Tucker's squadron might "assume the offensive" and destroy the Union base at Port Royal. But with the capture of "Rebellion Roads" now in sight, the North would not loosen its grip on the long-coveted prize. That very day, Dahlgren instructed his commander off Charleston to keep "a vigilant eye" on Tucker's ironclads. The Rebels' position was "becoming desperate and they might be tempted by the least prospect of advantage to risk an attack." The admiral, however, assured Secretary Welles that Tucker's squadron had "no reasonable chance . . . if they venture out."[52]

By January 1865 the Yankee admiral had seven monitors in front of Charleston, and he would receive two more before the end of that month. His battle plan anticipated that Tucker's ironclads, in desperation, might attack any smaller number of monitors separated from the others; the admiral instructed his commanders to keep their vessels together. Dahlgren agreed with intelligence gained from Confederate deserters that Tucker, in the confusion of battle, would attempt to sink the Union ironclads with four torpedo boats reportedly operational. To guard against this, the federal warships would "scour the water" periodically with grapeshot. Dahlgren proposed to "draw [the gunboats] as low down this anchorage as they will come," to ensure the "capture of the whole by making retreat impossible."[53]

In the event that Tucker did not attack, Dahlgren still hoped for his moment of glory. The admiral ordered his monitors to reconnoiter the obstructions between forts Sumter and Moultrie. He might be able to remove these, steam into the inner harbor, and receive the city's surrender. On January 15, however, the *Passaic* ventured too close to Sumter and struck a mine. She sank in less than a half minute, with the loss of sixty-two lives. Dahlgren now concurred with Union army commanders that he should not endanger his remaining ironclads. For two long years the Union's most powerful squadron had stood in readiness off Charleston, only to watch the army march into the "Nest of Rebellion." Dahlgren's frustrations would be compounded when, on March 1, 1865, his flagship *Harvest Moon* struck a rebel mine and sank beneath his feet.[54]

Throughout the last gloomy weeks at Charleston, Tucker also seems to have hoped for a glorious finale. According to reports reaching England, Tucker planned to attack the enemy soon after his new flagship, *Columbia*, became available. This and two other ironclads nearing completion at Charleston, along with the possible addition of the *Savannah* to his squadron, would have significantly reduced Dahlgren's superiority. The scuttling of the *Savannah*, noted Engineer Tomb, "was severely felt" by the commodore. When it became apparent that two of the new gunboats could not be completed on time, all efforts were focused on the *Columbia*. Unlike his other ironclads, the *Columbia* probably had been designed to challenge the federal ships beyond Fort Sumter. She was 216 feet long and 51 feet in beam and, because of a shortened casemate, drew less water than the other rams. The vessel had six inches of armor, was pierced for six heavy guns, and had two excellent new engines. Dahlgren described her as "a remarkably fine, powerful vessel," a "really formidable customer," and a worthy opponent for one of his monitors. About January 12 the *Columbia* slipped away from her yard on Sullivan's Island. But because of the "ignorance, carelessness or treachery of her pilot," the vessel grounded on a sunken wreck. The Confederates labored frantically to lighten the ironclad so that she could be pulled free before the ebb tide; they lost the race. When the water level fell, the heavy ship's long keel snapped like a twig. The beleaguered Rebels had neither the resources nor the time to repair the vessel.[55]

Three days after this loss, Tucker received a telegram from President Davis. "The movements of Sherman render it important that you should, if practicable, attack the enemy's force off the harbor" and, "if successful, . . . destroy his depot" at Port Royal. It was enough to make a grown man cry. Tucker consulted with his ship captains and the army commander at Charleston and replied to the president: "It is decided impracticable to make the attack as proposed by you. I have but two iron-clads and they are with defective steam power. The enemy has six or seven monitors, besides several wooden vessels and heavy land batteries. In my opinion, the attack proposed would result in our capture or make it necessary to destroy the vessels, with all on board, to prevent their falling into the hands of the enemy. This sacrifice I am ready to make if it will advance the public interest." Davis apparently did not ask Tucker to make that sacrifice.[56]

Tucker's squadron, however, continued to bolster Charleston's defenses. During the last days of January and into February 1865, the commodore's ironclads prepared to meet a frontal assault by Dahlgren. If the Yankee monitors had been able to get past Fort Sumter, the *Charleston* and *Chicora*—with their stout rams and spar torpedoes— might have been moderately effective in the close quarters of the mine-choked inner harbor. On February 13 the rams repulsed another Union boat attack against Fort Johnson. Meanwhile, contingency plans were made to deal with Sherman. What would he do? If the Federals marched directly against Charleston, Tucker's gunboats would ascend the Cooper River as far as possible. From the stern of the *Charleston*, newly devised contact mines would be rolled into the river, to float downstream toward pursuing enemy vessels. But if Sherman's army marched behind the city, endangering its communications, Charleston would have to be evacuated. Then Tucker would have to choose between a desperate attack on the blockading monitors or the scuttling of his ships.[57]

On February 1 Sherman began moving northward from Savannah. Characteristically, he divided his sixty-thousand-man army into two columns, bewildering the vastly outnumbered Confederate defenders as to his intended target. By mid-month, Sherman threatened Charleston's rear from the south, while army transports—escorted by Dahlgren's fleet—made a feint at Bull's Bay, a short distance north of the city. To avoid the encirclement of his forces, Beauregard ordered Charleston abandoned.[58] The possibility of a final attack by Tucker—an unlikely option—was eliminated by stormy weather and heavy seas, which would have stymied his gunboats and swamped his torpedo craft.[59] After dark on February 17, as the army prepared to withdraw, Tucker's men destroyed the naval installations on shore along with the torpedo boats and other wooden vessels. Throughout the night, sailors carried gunpowder on board the ironclads—twenty tons on the *Charleston* alone. At daybreak on February 18, Lieutenant Robert Bowen set the rams on fire. Between 8:00 and 11:00 that morning—as Union forces began arriving in the city—the *Palmetto State*, then the *Chicora*, and finally the *Charleston* blew up in "tremendous clouds of smoke, . . . forming beautiful wreaths."[60]

The commodore's failure to make a final offensive blow had its critics, then and later. His friend Rochelle, who was present at the time, noted that Tucker's "judgment was excellent, and it was very rarely the case that he was mistaken as to what it was possible for the force at his disposal to accomplish." The flag officer was a brave man but not a foolish one. Especially after the loss of the *Columbia*, an assault on Dahlgren's vastly superior squadron had no chance of success and little to justify it militarily.[61] A suicidal attack at Charleston might have brought some glory to the navy of the Lost Cause. It might also have won Tucker a promotion to rear admiral. His men, however, would have paid a heavy price.

The commodore and his sailors withdrew from Charleston on the North Eastern Railroad, bound for Wilmington, North Carolina. Lieutenant Rochelle and some three hundred mariners from Charleston had reached that place several days earlier and were helping the army defend against a determined Union assault. At Florence, South Carolina—the junction with the Wilmington and Manchester Railroad, leading to the North Carolina port—Tucker announced his approach to army authorities and inquired, "Is Wilmington intact?" It was. The commodore transferred to the Wilmington line and proceeded to Whiteville, North Carolina, about fifty miles from his destination. Here, he learned that federal forces threatened the tracks ahead; Tucker telegraphed Wilmington for new instructions. General Braxton Bragg, commanding at Wilmington, was preparing to abandon the city on the following day, February 22. He advised Tucker to remain at Whiteville "to check any advance of the enemy if possible, and fall back before him for the protection of the Fayetteville arsenal." The commodore quickly responded, "I have 350 sailors unused to marching," and there was no rail connection with Fayetteville, some one hundred miles to the north. "I do not think [my] small force can check [the] enemy," he continued, "and propose leaving [by train] in any direction you think best." Nevertheless, Tucker and his sailors did march to Fayetteville where, on February 27, they were ordered to Richmond.[62]

CHAPTER FOUR

Sailor's Creek

IN EARLY MARCH 1865 Commodore Tucker and his sailors reached Richmond, the dreary capital of a much shrunken and nearly shattered nation. Except for the Confederate West, isolated beyond the Union-controlled Mississippi River, and a few pockets in the Gulf States and Georgia, the Confederacy consisted of southern Virginia and the interior of the Carolinas, where Sherman relentlessly pressed a much smaller Southern force, now commanded by General Joseph E. Johnston. Since June 1864, the Union army of General Ulysses S. Grant had invested General Robert E. Lee's Army of Northern Virginia in a semicircular line extending around the eastern edge of Richmond and the vital rail center of Petersburg, twenty-five miles to the south. With a numerical superiority of about two to one, Grant stretched Lee's defenses to the breaking point. The North had sealed every major Southern port and occupied vast areas of Dixie, crippling its economy. Lee's army, on half rations, was worn out. In the stark face of defeat, the morale of the Confederate government, armed forces, and people crumbled.

In mid-February, Raphael Semmes, recently promoted to rear admiral for his exploits on the commerce destroyer *Alabama*, had assumed command of the James River Squadron. Consisting of three ironclads and four wooden gunboats, this fleet was confined to the eight narrow miles of waterway between Richmond and the obstructions at Drewry's Bluff to the east. Tucker became "Flag Officer, Commanding Ashore," and his sailors (including some from Savannah and Wilmington) joined a few companies of Confederate marines manning the heavy guns at Drewry's Bluff and three or four other batteries nearby. While his web-footed artillerymen watched the river for the approach of the Union navy, Tucker drilled them as infantry in preparation for the war's final chapter.

Discipline and morale were especially difficult to maintain during these closing weeks of the conflict. On assuming command of the squadron, Semmes found his men "as much demoralized as the army." In fact, with the exception of the officers and a half-dozen mariners per ship—including some transfers from Tucker's command—the crews had been obtained from the land service. The men were poorly clothed and fed and confined to uncomfortable quarters aboard "little better than prison ships," they exhibited "great discontent and restlessness." A man of austere personality, the admiral did not gain the loyalty of his new subordinates, who deserted in droves. Although Tucker faced similar problems, they were of a lesser magnitude. His men, at least, could walk about in their batteries. The commodore's command also included larger numbers of navy and marine corps regulars, some with extended service under him at Charleston. Events soon would demonstrate that Tucker continued to enjoy the confidence and, it seems, even the affection of his men.[1]

Grant's army punctured the Confederate defenses near Petersburg on April 1, and Richmond became untenable. Lee ordered the capital evacuated the next day. In the evening of April 2, the president and his cabinet fled south by train for Danville, Virginia, ultimately joining Johnston's army in North Carolina. Semmes scuttled his ships and followed Davis southward. Lee's battered army retreated to the west, hoping to reach Lynchburg, Virginia, before the enemy could cut its railroad link to North Carolina and Johnston's forces. Alone among Richmond's defenders, Tucker was not informed of the evacuation. On a small, ragged scrap of coarse paper, the commodore penciled a note to General Lee, his fellow Alexandrian and distant relative. "I am without instructions as to what course to pursue. Have rec d no orders. Shall be happy to learn your wishes concerning this post and garrison."[2]

Lee did not reply, but the awesome explosions of Semmes's ironclads in the river below gave Tucker the signal to retreat. The commodore blew up his powder magazine and marched his men through Richmond, where they received two days' rations and ammunition for their Minié muskets. In the morning of the third, they set out toward the west to find Lee's retreating columns. Almost immediately swarms of mounted Yankees began harassing them. "Our men enjoyed fighting the cavalry," recalled Lieutenant Charles F. Sevier, one of Tucker's company commanders; the sailors took several trophy hats.[3] On April 5 Tucker reached General Richard S. Ewell's Sixth Corps at Amelia Court House, about thirty miles southwest of Richmond. Ewell attached the mariners to the division of General George Washington Custis Lee, the son of Robert E. Lee. This catchall command was not the stuff of generals' dreams. It included freshly uniformed government bureaucrats, ragtag Richmond militia, artillery units without cannon, and now sailors without ships.[4]

In the literature of the Appomattox campaign, Tucker's command has been variously labeled the Naval/Marine Battalion/Brigade, reflecting confusion about its composition and size. Estimates as high as two thousand men are gross exaggerations; Tucker's strength was probably four hundred or fewer effectives. His marines, under Captain John D. Simms, comprised one-quarter or less of the total. Tucker's designation as a navy flag officer equated with the army rank of brigadier general; hence his unit might be deemed a brigade. But the commodore's force was of battalion strength, about one-sixth the size of a full brigade. Quite understandably, however, those who soon would see the Naval Battalion in combat believed it to be a much larger force of seasoned marine infantry.[5]

In addition to Tucker, the Naval Battalion's senior officers included Commander Thomas T. Hunter (the former skipper of the *Chicora*), Lieutenant William G. Dozier, and two Confederate marine captains. Most of the remaining officers—about fifty of these can be identified—were younger lieutenants and, especially, masters and midshipmen.[6] Since his command of the *Stromboli* during the Mexican War, Tucker regularly had drilled his subordinates with small arms. At Charleston he had organized a naval battalion which, under Lieutenant Dozier, participated in several land engagements. Men from this unit probably marched with the commodore in these final days of the war. Present at the end, too, were Charles Cleaper, Joseph Johnson, and J. Heck—Tucker's three black sailors from the *Chicora*, the only Afro-American combat "soldiers" to participate in Lee's last campaign.[7]

Some contemporaries confused Tucker's battalion with the artillery units and, perhaps, some of the Richmond clerks in Custis Lee's division; like the sailors, they wore unusual uniforms. Many years later, Colonel William W. Blackford would claim to "remember the naval brigade particularly. The sailors did well enough on the march, but there were the fat old captains and commodores, who had never marched anywhere but on a quarter deck, . . . limping along puffing and blowing, and cursing everything black and blue." Fifty-three-year-old John R. Tucker, on horseback, was the only commodore on that march, and he was not fat. More likely, Tucker's appearance at that time colored the equally exaggerated recollections of General William Mahone, who remembered the Naval Battalion "armed with Cutlass' and navy revolvers, every man over six feet and [the] picture of perfect physical development."[8]

All participants in the retreat from Richmond agreed that it was a dreadful experience. The men were exhausted, nearly famished, and extremely tense. But "in all the discomfort and wretchedness of the retreat," noted Major Robert Stiles, the soldiers were "no little amused by the Naval Battalion." Tucker's sailors did not march "right" and "left" but to the "port" and "starboard." The army men soon dubbed them the "Aye, Ayes," because they responded "'aye,

aye' to every order, sometimes repeating the order itself, and adding, 'aye, aye, it is, sir!' "[9] The Army of Northern Virginia, now including the "Aye, Ayes," continued its westward retreat on April 6, closely pursued by the Union's Army of the Potomac. General Robert E. Lee rode with the vanguard of his force, the combined First and Third Corps of General James Longstreet, trailed by General Richard Anderson's Corps. Ewell's Sixth Corps, consisting of Custis Lee's and Joseph B. Kershaw's divisions, marched behind Anderson. The main Confederate wagon train followed, while General John B. Gordon's Second Corps served as the rear guard. During the day, however, the wagons and Gordon veered off the main road, and Ewell's men found themselves in the rear. Meanwhile, a breach developed between Longstreet and Anderson, ahead of Ewell. General Philip H. Sheridan's Yankee cavalry raced into this gap and secured a position blocking the line of retreat. The Union army's Second and Sixth Corps quickly closed on Ewell.

At about 3 P.M. Anderson encountered Sheridan's entrenched troopers. As the Confederates attempted to break through, Ewell's corps—some 3,600 men—prepared to halt about 10,000 Federals rapidly advancing behind them. The Rebels hastily assumed a position on a wooded hill overlooking the west bank of Little Sayler's Creek, a normally narrow stream swollen by recent rains. Named for the Sayler family, local landowners, the stream was referred to by contemporaries erroneously but appropriately as "Sailor's Creek." Ewell arrayed his men parallel to the stream, in a north-south line cutting across the road. Kershaw's division, mainly veteran infantry, were placed south of the road; Custis Lee's men extended the line to the north. Tucker's Naval Battalion formed the far right of Lee's position, just north of the road— essentially, the center of Ewell's entire corps. Unfortunately, the sailors also occupied the only open ground on the hill, with but a few scrub pines and waist-high weeds to conceal them from the enemy. From these heights the Rebels could see column after blue column form along the high ground on the opposite bank, about three hundred yards away.[10]

As Tucker positioned his command, one of Custis Lee's staff officers rode up and volunteered to assist the commodore in getting his mariners into formation. Tucker replied, "Young man, I understand how to talk to my people." There followed a "grand moral combination" of " 'right flank' and 'left flank,' 'starboard' and 'larboard,' 'aye, aye' and 'aye, aye'—until the battalion gradually settled down into place."[11] To Tucker—a man noted for his physical courage in earlier times—the events of the next hour probably were cathartic, purging the frustrations accumulated during his period in Charleston. Perhaps he now remembered his impotence in the face of overwhelming Union strength, the scuttling of his fleet, the explanations that—to landsmen—sounded like excuses. The complicated calculus of armor and guns, weak engines and bad coal, deep drafts and shallow shoals, weather, tides, and moonlight no longer concerned him. He needed only to stand and fight.

Shortly after 5 P.M. three or four Union batteries began softening Ewell's line from a deadly distance of four hundred yards. The Confederates had no artillery with which to answer. Captain McHenry Howard, of Lee's staff, described the barrage as "very rapid and severe," with the "shot sometimes plowing the ground, sometimes crashing through the trees, and not infrequently striking the line, killing two or more at once." Several veteran Confederates judged it the worst bombardment they had experienced during the war. In its exposed position, Tucker's battalion was especially vulnerable. The Union artillery, noted Sevier, "had a good line of fire and was knockin' our men out." With Sheridan's cavalry in the rear, the Confederates had no haven for their casualties. "The appeals of some of the poor fellows to their comrades and officers to put them in a place of safety were affecting," wrote Howard, "especially in the Naval Brigade where the sailors seemed to look up to their officers like children." He "vividly and painfully" remembered a scene "between a wounded man and the Commodore who spoke some words of sympathy to him." To inspire his men, Tucker remained on horseback, exposing himself to enemy fire, until one of the generals ordered him to dismount.[12]

After a half hour of terrible carnage, the Union infantry began wading across the river, shoulder deep in some places, with muskets held above their heads. Once on the west bank, the Yankees reformed their battle lines. "It was [the] grandest sight I ever witnessed," recalled Sevier. After an exchange of fire by opposing skirmish lines, the Northerners charged in force. Tucker's officers barked the appropriate naval command: "Prepare to repel boarders!" The Rebels held their fire until their foes were in easy range; then they discharged their weapons, taking a heavy toll among the Union men. Without orders, some of the artillerymen (and not Tucker's mariners, as often reported) countercharged, driving part of the federal line back into the creek. However, the Yankees regrouped and moved forward once more. Hoping to end the bloodshed, they waved white handkerchiefs, imploring the Confederates to surrender. But the fighting continued.[13]

Some of the fiercest hand-to-hand combat of the war ensued. Captain Tacitus Allen, in the artillery unit next to Tucker, "witnessed a scene, the like of which is seldom seen: men stood face to face and brained each other with clubbed rifles, and bayonetted each other on the ground." Major Stiles saw men "bite each others' throats and ears and noses, rolling around on the ground like wild beasts." At one point he noticed two officers fighting with swords over a stand of colors; the

Rebel "was a very athletic, powerful seaman," and his opponent quickly fell. Near the close of the battle, Captain Howard "noticed the naval brigade, which had been standing firm as a rock, apparently beginning to fall back but in a perfectly regular formation." Tucker told Howard that he had received orders to assume a new position in the rear. The army officer said that the commodore must be mistaken; there was no Confederate rear. "Very well," replied Tucker, "if you say so I will move back again." Howard said that he did not think this could be done. "Oh yes, I can," responded the commodore, "but it is very different from handling men on shipboard." To Howard's amazement, Tucker "faced them about" and under heavy fire "marched them back to their original position without a single skulker remaining behind." The soldier had "seldom, if ever, seen this done as well during the war."[14] Howard apparently was unfamiliar with the taut discipline on a warship in combat.

In the course of the battle Tucker's sailors and marines, swinging their cutlasses, repulsed three or four attacks, including a final cavalry charge. Both Northern and Southern witnesses heaped praise upon the Naval Battalion. A rebel prisoner brought to the rear at about the time that "Tucker was doing his best" overheard a Union courier bring "instructions to the Colonel commanding to 'hurry up, . . . those d——d rebels were giving them particular h—l.'" A Georgia sharpshooter fighting near the Naval Battalion asserted that "those marines fought like tigers and against odds of at least ten to one."[15] Union general Truman Seymour reported that "the Confederate Marine Battalion fought with peculiar obstinacy." In his official account, General J. Warren Keifer declared that "the rebel Marine Brigade fought with the most extraordinary courage." To Mrs. Keifer he wrote, "they fought better and longer than any other troops upon the field." Federal corps commander General Horatio Wright noted that his army "charged the enemy's position, carrying it handsomely, except at a point on our right of the road" defended by "the Marine Brigade and other troops" from Richmond. He "was never more astonished." Several years later, Wright told one of Tucker's officers that he could not understand the "obstinacy" of the Confederate center, "until he found that it had been held by sailors who did not know when they were whipped." The commodore jokingly reminisced that he had never been in a land battle before (he overlooked his experience at Tabasco) and supposed that "everything was going well."[16]

After about an hour of bitter fighting, a Union cavalry charge broke the Confederate line on Tucker's right and left. While the sailors continued to hold firm, the Federals swept behind them, capturing Ewell, Lee, Kershaw, and five other generals. Lieutenant Clarence L. Stanton, a naval officer assigned to Ewell's staff, informed Tucker that the corps and division commanders had surrendered and suggested that the Naval Battalion do the same. But the commodore led his men into a wooded ravine, where they took cover behind some fallen trees.[17] A Union lieutenant discovered them a short time later and reported their location to General Keifer. In disbelief, the general rode alone into the pines, where he encountered the Naval Battalion and mortal danger. The light was very dim now. The general, pretending he was a rebel officer, wheeled his horse around and commanded the Confederates to move "Forward!" Writing to his wife the next morning, Keifer described his narrow escape. "They did not recognize me as a 'Yankee' officer at first. They moved as I directed for about one hundred yards, before they recognized me. When the men brought down their pieces to shoot me, the muzzles of some . . . were not over four feet from me. Commodore Tucker who commanded the brigade knocked up the muzzles of the guns nearest to me and saved my life."[18]

Carrying a flag of truce, Keifer returned a few minutes later with Lieutenant Stanton who reconfirmed that Ewell had capitulated his entire command. Tucker finally ordered his stalwarts to lay down their arms. Rather than surrender their swords, most of the battalion's young officers broke them over their knees. Tucker, however, tendered his blade to Keifer. "I now have the sword of Commodore Tucker," the general informed his wife, "and hope some day to have the pleasure of returning it to him, with a suitable acknowledgement for his noble conduct." Keifer, who in later years became Speaker of the United States House of Representatives, kept his promise in 1878.[19]

As Keifer led Tucker's men out of the woods, the federal soldiers cheered the rebel sailors heartily. To Captain Howard a Union soldier "pointed out an officer in a naval uniform with wide gold lace on it" and asked who the man was. When Howard answered that he was a sailor, the Yankee's "jaw dropped and he said, 'good Heaven, have you gunboats way up here too?'" If the moment had been less serious, the Confederate officer might have replied, "we had them wherever there was a little dew on the grass."[20] Although part of General Anderson's Corps ultimately escaped through Sheridan's lines, the Army of Northern Virginia lost about one-third of its strength at Sayler's Creek. Further resistance became futile. On April 9, three days after the battle, General Robert E. Lee surrendered at Appomattox Court House. General Johnston capitulated to Sherman in North Carolina three weeks later. If the Confederacy had survived to fight another day, Tucker might have become the South's third admiral (along with Buchanan and Semmes) for his "gallant and meritorious conduct" at the battle of "Sailor's Creek." In the final major field engagement of the Civil War, Commodore John Randolph Tucker was the last of Lee's "generals" to surrender, and he did so with great style. But in the excitement attending the events at Appomattox, the public largely overlooked and then forgot Tucker and his "Aye, Ayes."[21]

Following their surrender, Tucker and the other senior officers of Ewell's corps were brought to the cavalry headquarters of General George A. Custer. "On account of the magnanimity of Commodore Tucker," noted Keifer, "I took great pains to have the officers treated in the most handsome style." The Confederate leaders were fed, and a Union army band serenaded them, alternately playing "The Bonnie Blue Flag" and "Dixie." The junior officers and men were brought to a "bull pen," where they, too, shared the rations of their captors. The next day, the wounded Rebels and their surgeons were taken to hospitals. They would be paroled along with Lee's army, surrendered at Appomattox.

The able-bodied Confederates captured at Sayler's Creek, however, were not included in the capitulation negotiated between Lee and Grant, nor in the similar agreement between Sherman and Johnston. Thus, while the South's highest-ranking military men and thousands of their subordinates went free, the Confederates from Sayler's Creek went to prison. The enlisted men were confined to several military stockades, while most of the junior officers were held at Johnson's Island, in Lake Erie. Ewell, Tucker, and six other general officers arrived at the Old Capitol Prison in Washington on April 14—the night President Lincoln was assassinated. The next day, a riotous mob outside the jail demanded that the Rebels be turned over to them. The army whisked Ewell and his companions off to Fort Warren, the military prison in Boston Harbor.[22] Immediately after their arrival, Ewell wrote to General Grant on behalf of himself, Tucker, and his other commanders. He expressed their "unqualified abhorrence and indignation" over the president's murder and deplored the tendency of the Northern public to "connect the South and Southern men with it." Ewell asserted, "we are not assassins, nor the allies of assassins," and would be "ashamed of our own people, were we not assured that they will reprobate this crime."[23]

General Grant apparently opposed the imprisonment of the Sayler's Creek captives, and General Robert E. Lee, at liberty in Richmond, made a plea on their behalf. He ingenuously (or in ignorance) explained that Tucker and his men, at least, should be treated leniently because "the Naval Battalion fell in the line of march of the army for subsistence and protection." General Keifer and others among Tucker's Northern friends petitioned for his release. Unfortunately, the magnanimous Lincoln had been succeeded by Andrew Johnson— the insecure and initially vindictive Tennessean—who believed that "treason must be made odious and traitors must be punished and impoverished."[24]

President Johnson issued a proclamation on May 29, 1865, offering amnesty and pardon to former Confederates who would take an oath of allegiance to the United States. Excluded from its benefits were fourteen classes of persons, including prisoners of war, Rebels with taxable property worth $20,000, Confederates from states that had not seceded from the Union, former United States naval officers who "went South," and all Confederate naval officers above the rank of lieutenant. However, members of these excepted categories were encouraged to petition the president for individual pardons. One day after Johnson's proclamation, Tucker addressed the president from Fort Warren.

> By your proclamation of the 29th instant, I am excluded from the amnesty therein contained. I most respectfully ask your favorable consideration of this, my application to be admitted to its benefits. I was a commander in the U.S. Navy, resigned on the 18th day of April, 1861, and was dismissed from that date. I am now a prisoner of war; was captured on the 6th day of April, 1865, at which time I held a commission of captain C. S. Navy and was styled commodore by courtesy. I have no property and was born in Alexandria, State of Virginia.[25]

Tucker's appeal for clemency and similar petitions from his high-ranking colleagues at Fort Warren were unsuccessful. Fortunately, the conditions of their confinement, never harsh, improved steadily as the weeks passed. The prisoners could walk about the parapets of the fort and watch the activity in the busy harbor, from which Tucker often had sailed in earlier days. They could send and receive brief letters and, ultimately, have visitors from the outside. The Sayler's Creek commanders formed their own mess—dubbed the "Handsome Company" by one of Tucker's female admirers—cooking and eating their meals together. The government provided adequate rations of meat and bread; beans, grits, and coffee were dispensed less frequently. From sutlers the prisoners purchased food, clothing, toiletries, and books; friends and relatives also sent these things and money. Complaining of the "very uniform . . . character" of the bland prison food, General Ewell entreated his wife to send ketchup.[26]

For Tucker the separation from his loved ones was the most painful aspect of prison life. "My friends," he appealed, "cannot confer on me a greater pleasure than to write." Many did. In mid-June, Charlotte Wise, Harry Gringo's wife, informed Tucker of her efforts to gain his release and her desire to visit him. The prisoner expressed "a thousand thanks" and sent his condolences on the recent death of her father, Senator Edward Everett. Thinking about the wartime deaths of his daughter and two sons, Tucker feared "to ask after my young friends your children"—"so many sad changes" might have occurred during the long lapse in their correspondence. The commodore, who signed himself, "as ever, your friend," asked Mrs. Wise to "remember me kindly" to her ill and absent husband. Henry Wise continued to cherish memories of happier times with Tucker; but Gringo and Toker probably did not renew their close friendship before Wise's death in 1868.[27]

The government began releasing Confederate military prisoners at a rapid rate in June 1865, with junior officers and those confined longest being freed first. On July 24 Tucker took an oath to "henceforth faithfully support, protect and defend the Constitution of the United States and the Union of States thereunder." He also signed his "parole of honor to be of good behavior and commit no act of hostility or perform any act either by word or deed prejudicial to the interests of the United States." He was released from Fort Warren that same day and received transportation home to Virginia.[28]

As a paroled prisoner of war, Tucker enjoyed an uncertain liberty. The government, conceivably, might later arrest and try him for treason or alleged war crimes. Furthermore, laws passed during the war deprived him of his civil rights and burdened him with numerous disabilities. He could not hold civil or military office at any level of government. It was not certain whether unpardoned Confederates might engage in professions requiring a license, buy and sell property, or make valid contracts—even for marriage. A presidential pardon could remove the threat of arrest and imprisonment. But even constitutional lawyers debated whether such an act would restore full civil and political rights. As President Johnson issued a series of general amnesties, excluding fewer classes of former Rebels, and granted thousands of individual pardons, Congress enacted a series of Reconstruction Acts and the Fourteenth Amendment to the United States Constitution which, among other objectives, sought to limit the president's amnesty powers.[29]

In this atmosphere of uncertainty, Tucker—who probably remained liable to prosecution until a general amnesty of 1868—looked for employment, a most discouraging prospect. Men like the commodore who had left the "Old Navy" in 1861 had given up more than their careers; they had lost a profession. Most naval officers believed themselves unsuited for civilian pursuits, an opinion shared by much of the public. Neither did they have the more marketable skills of Confederate army officers trained at the nation's foremost engineering school, West Point. The prostrate Southern economy had few sinecures for war heroes and an abundance of candidates—primarily from the army. Many former Confederates left the country.[30]

Shortly after his release from Fort Warren, Tucker wrote to Captain Andrew A. Harwood, the skipper of the *Cumberland* during Tucker's last cruise with the United States Navy, inquiring if an unpardoned Confederate might command a merchant vessel. Harwood sought opinions from the treasury and justice departments and informed his "shipmate and friend" that he was not barred from the civilian sea service. But the government's position soon changed. The *Richmond Daily Dispatch* protested that Confederate naval officers were "among the best sailors that ever trod the deck of a vessel" but could not "even take command of a schooner in the foreign trade." Tucker and several other officers joined a company formed by Dr. Henry Manore Price to colonize a 240,000-square-mile tract in the Orinoco Basin of Venezuela—a venture that came to naught. The commodore also sought, unsuccessfully, a commission in at least one foreign navy. In the spring of 1866, however, he accepted an offer from the Southern Express Company to be its agent in Raleigh, North Carolina.[31]

CHAPTER FIVE

Almirante Tucker

TUCKER WAS PREPARING to begin a new career in North Carolina when Nathaniel B. Wells sought him out in early May 1866, bringing an intriguing offer for employment in South America. During the 1860s the bumbling Spanish government of Queen Isabella II tried to cure a complex of domestic ills with a large infusion of international glory. Madrid adopted an aggressive foreign policy, especially in the Americas, where Spain aspired to a leadership role among its former colonies. At the behest of a faction in the Dominican Republic in 1861, the Spaniards reestablished a colonial regime in that Caribbean island nation. That same year Spanish warships joined those of Britain and France in a blockade of Mexico to collect debts; this action developed into a full-scale intervention by the French, who placed Austrian archduke Maximilian on a shaky Mexican throne. Despite disclaimers from Madrid, many Latin Americans believed that Spain wanted to restore its once-vast empire in the New World, lost four decades earlier.

Several American governments advocated a united republican front against the monarchical motherland. Popular manifestations of anti-Spanish sentiment occurred throughout the region, including an 1863 attack on immigrant Spanish farm workers in northern Peru. When local courts failed to punish the culprits and Lima rejected the demands of an abrasive Spanish diplomat, a powerful Spanish fleet seized the Chincha Islands. These bits of land, off Peru's south coast, were the principal source of guano, nitrogen-rich bird manure that provided the bulk of Lima's revenues. The Peruvian Navy was no match for the Spaniards, so the government of General Juan Antonio Pezet signed a treaty with Spain in early 1865, promising a large indemnity for the return of the Chinchas. The Europeans withdrew from the islands, but many Peruvians were outraged. A revolution began and gained widespread support as the movement's leaders promised to restore the national honor.

In Chile, Peru's neighbor to the south, a flurry of anti-Spanish demonstrations occurred. When the government in Santiago refused to

78

apologize for these or to permit the Spanish squadron to coal in Chilean ports, Spain proclaimed a blockade in September 1865. Chile responded, appropriately, with a declaration of war. In November the Peruvian revolutionaries toppled Pezet and installed Colonel Mariano Ignacio Prado with dictatorial powers. The new regime in Lima renounced the treaty with Spain and, on December 5, signed an agreement with Chile to war against their common foe. Bolivia and Ecuador soon joined this alliance, called the American Union, but these two weaker states contributed little to the military effort. Ultimately, John Randolph Tucker would command the allied fleet.[1]

The Awkward Alliance

At the outbreak of the war Spanish naval power in the Pacific—the 7,500-ton *Numancia* (one of the world's larger ironclads), five wooden frigates, and several smaller vessels—was quite superior to that of Chile and Peru. But Spain's task was highly problematic, and time was on the side of its adversaries. The Spaniards had to wage war thousands of miles from home, without a single friendly harbor on the West Coast of South America where they could repair their ships, rest their sailors, or take on coal and other supplies. Moreover, new allied warships nearing completion in British shipyards might tip the strategic balance. These vessels might attack ports in the Iberian Peninsula, raid Spain's major colonies (Cuba, Puerto Rico, and the Philippine Islands), or challenge the Spanish fleet in the Pacific. Chile and Peru also were arming merchantmen. These vessels and privateers licensed by the allies might prey upon Spanish commerce and disrupt the flow of supplies to the Pacific fleet. Thus, the queen's ministers hoped to secure an honorable peace through a quick, decisive victory.

Fortunately for Spain, word of Chile's declaration of war soon reached London. The British government invoked its neutrality laws and prevented the delivery of two warships being constructed for the Santiago government. But the regime in Lima postponed its formal entrance into the conflict until January 14, 1866. The delay enabled Peru to take possession of two ironclads in Great Britain, and a pair of new wooden corvettes arrived safely from France.[2] Meanwhile, Madrid had not achieved the dramatic triumph needed to extricate itself from this difficult war. Under the command of Capitán de Fragata (Commander) Juan Williams Rebolledo, Chile's two effective warships—the steam corvette *Esmeralda* and the armed transport *Maipú*—averted destruction by escaping from Valparaíso a few hours before the Spanish fleet arrived in strength. For two months Williams flitted in and out of minor ports, avoiding concentrated enemy power while waiting to pounce upon detached Spanish vessels. On November 26, 1865, while the *Esmeralda* was off Papudo, Williams learned that the Spanish gunboat *Covadonga*, on packet duty, was approaching. So that the Chileans might surprise the weaker but faster enemy ship, the *Esmeralda* put to sea flying the British flag and a distress signal. The trap succeeded. In less than a half hour the Chileans captured the *Covadonga*, increasing the size of their squadron by half. Williams received a hero's laurels and a promotion to *capitán de navío* (equivalent to captain in the United States Navy). The Spaniards, however, vowed to avenge this "cowardly" capture.[3]

In early December, as Peru prepared to enter the war, Lima dispatched its aging wooden steam frigates *Amazonas* and *Apurímac* south to Chiloé Island. Here, they rendezvoused with Williams's Chilean squadron and Peru's two French-built corvettes, the *América* and *Unión* (so named to celebrate the American Union alliance). On February 7, 1866, two heavy Spanish frigates attacked part of the allied fleet off Abtao Island, where the Latin American vessels were undergoing repairs. The two forces dueled at long range for more than an hour. Both sides incurred some damage, but the Spaniards probably suffered the worst in the exchange and withdrew. Although it had not been a decisive contest, the allies proclaimed a great morale-boosting victory.[4]

After the battle of Abtao, the allied fleet remained on the defensive in southern Chilean waters, awaiting the *Independencia* and *Huáscar*, Peru's new ironclads, which were expected from Britain at any time. The Spaniards, also anticipating the arrival of these potent vessels, sought to punish their foes and abandon the Pacific forthwith. After unsuccessfully attempting to draw the allied fleet into open combat, Admiral Casto Méndez Núñez determined to gain retribution by bombarding Valparaíso and Lima's contiguous port, Callao. In peacetime Valparaíso was the busiest port on the Pacific.Coast of the continent. It had a large foreign population and much foreign-owned property stored in the bonding warehouses of the Chilean government. Lacking the means for an adequate defense of the city, Chile's officials believed that Valparaíso could be protected best by leaving it defenseless. A Spanish attack on the unfortified port would invite condemnation by the "civilized world" and serious difficulties with nations whose citizens suffered personal or economic injury. Chile also believed—mistakenly— that the British and United States naval squadrons at Valparaíso would not permit the Spanish admiral to bombard the undefended harbor. On March 31, while Chilean authorities ordered that not a single gun be fired at the enemy, the Spanish fleet bombarded Valparaíso for three hours, destroying about $15 million in property.[5]

Two weeks later, Méndez Núñez departed for Callao. Unlike the Chileans, the Peruvians had been laboring feverishly to fortify their principal port. Fifty-two guns, including nine heavy new Blakelys and Armstrongs, had been mounted in masonry forts, sand batteries, and two armored turrets. In the harbor two improvised ironclads (a monitor and a Confederate-style casemated ram) along with three small wooden ships mounted an additional dozen guns. On May 2, 1866—the Dos de Mayo commemorated later as a Peruvian national holiday—Admiral Méndez's fleet of seven ships, carrying 245 guns, battled the defenders of Callao for almost five hours. Apprehensive of Peruvian torpedo defenses (directed by former officers of the United States and Confederate navies), Méndez Núñez kept his vessels at relatively long range, and many of their projectiles fell short of the mark. He inflicted only minor damage on the city he vowed would be reduced to ashes. Meanwhile, the Peruvian guns scored 185 hits on their enemies, seriously damaging several ships. On May 10, after completing urgent repairs, the Spaniards departed. Half of the fleet (including the most badly damaged vessels, accompanied by the *Numancia*) steamed for the Philippine Islands, while Méndez Núñez and the remainder of his ships made for Rio de Janeiro. While Spain abandoned the Pacific Coast, Peru and Chile were inspired to renew the contest, this time on the offensive.[6]

Notwithstanding the early successes of allied arms and frequent official pronouncements of fraternal solidarity, the partnership of Peru and Chile was awkward. The peoples of the two countries harbored deep-seated prejudices against each other that dated from the colonial epoch, when the powerful officials and merchants of Lima—a great viceregal capital of the Spanish Empire—dominated less-developed Chile and deprecated Chileans as provincials. During the Wars of Independence in the early 1820s, the government of liberated Chile dispatched a combined army-navy expedition which initiated the emancipation of Peru. In the four years of struggle required to break Spanish power there, relations between Chilean and Peruvian forces often were stormy, evoking Chilean complaints of ingratitude. As young republics, the two neighbors quickly became commercial competitors and rivals for political influence and military supremacy on the Pacific Coast of the continent. When a new confederation of Peru and Bolivia threatened to upset the regional balance of power in 1836, Chile went to war with its northern neighbors, defeated them three years later, and dissolved their union.[7]

As potential adversaries with hundreds of miles of nearly impassable desert separating their vital centers, Chile and Peru measured their relative strength, first and foremost, in naval power. In 1818 the Chileans had hired Thomas, Lord Cochrane (Admiral Horatio Nelson's youngest ship commander at Trafalgar), who brilliantly commanded the new nation's makeshift navy against the Spaniards. The Chilean

Navy maintained parity with the Peruvian Navy until the 1840s. Thereafter, frugal, civilian-dominated governments in Santiago neglected the sea service. By the early 1860s Chile still possessed a rich naval tradition, but the country had only one real warship and a few auxiliary craft. Meanwhile, huge revenues earned from guano exports after 1840 enabled Lima to acquire the most powerful fleet in Latin America. Among the nations of the region, Peru boasted the first vessels built expressly for war and the first steam warships.[8]

But navies consist of men as well as ships, and in its sailors Chile enjoyed a qualitative advantage over its northern rival. The Chilean Navy had a small corps of officers; in 1866 only thirty-eight men occupied the ranks from rear admiral through second lieutenant. The senior officers, several of whom had served under Cochrane, staffed administrative posts on shore, while the four ships then in commission were commanded by middle-aged mariners who averaged twenty years of service.[9] Most officers were graduates of the military academy or the naval school, founded in 1843. Many had gained valuable experience with foreign navies (especially that of Britain) or with the Chilean merchant marine—by far the largest in Latin America—which, together with the sizable fishing industry, also provided a pool of veteran seamen. Most important, the navy had benefited from the stability of the government in Santiago: after 1831, all Chilean presidents served two consecutive five-year terms; since 1851, all of these men had been civilians. Promotion within the navy had been a relatively slow but steady process based primarily upon seniority and merit, contributing to the discipline and morale of the service.[10]

By contrast, the Peruvian Navy in the mid-1860s had a bloated officer corps that numbered two rear admirals, twenty-six captains, nineteen commanders, and thirty-eight lieutenant commanders.[11] Peru's better officers were quite competent; several had considerable service with the merchant marine or foreign navies or had attended naval schools abroad. But many others had very little experience at sea.[12] Peru's naval school, established in the colonial era, closed its doors for a quarter century after independence and functioned only sporadically thereafter. Peru had more ships than Chile, but the often dilapidated condition of these and stringent operating budgets limited training cruises and even gunnery drill. While the service had an overabundance of senior officers, it had a severe shortage of junior line officers, engineers, petty officers, and able seamen.[13]

Peru's chronic political instability, moreover, had undermined the professionalism of the sea service, which in its institutional development was perhaps a generation behind the Chilean Navy. The nation's mariners had been participants—willing or reluctant—in many internal wars.[14] During these struggles, both the incumbent regimes (always dominated by army officers) and their revolutionary challengers demanded the adherence of the navy. When one side emerged victorious, its naval supporters received extraordinary promotions, while vanquished sailors were stricken from the register (generally to be reinstated a few years later). The revolutions that pitted officer against brother officer fostered strong personal animosities within the service and resulted in very irregular career patterns. In mid-1866 the commanders of Peru's four most modern warships possessed an average of only thirteen years' experience.

Unlike major maritime nations, Chile and Peru had little need to project their power beyond home waters; therefore, their mariners were relatively unfamiliar with distant seas. Allied officers were cognizant of recent advances in naval science, but most lacked practical experience with these innovations. Their last significant naval war had been fought against each other more than a quarter century earlier during the age of sail. Both Peru and Chile since had acquired steam warships, but their officers—like those of most navies—were unpracticed in the fleet tactics required by steam propulsion.[15] Similarly, the allied officers were inexperienced in handling ironclads and the heavy new guns and torpedoes designed to combat them.

The battles of Abtao and Callao, although trumpeted as great victories, had demonstrated allied deficiencies in ordnance and gunnery. In the first of these engagements, bad powder and faulty fuzes had reduced the effectiveness of their shell guns. At Callao the Peruvians exhibited poor marksmanship and wasted opportunities to sink several wooden ships because they directed most of their fire at the nearly impregnable ironclad Numancia. During the battle several Peruvian guns became disabled due to the inexperience of their crews. While Colonel Prado justly praised the heroism of the defenders, he ordered Minister Federico L. Barreda, in Washington, to hire a "professor of artillery."[16] Because of this inexperience, both Santiago and Lima contemplated hiring a foreign officer to command the allied fleet, an option provided in their treaty of alliance. But like Abraham Lincoln, who early in the Civil War considered placing a European general at the head of his faltering Union army, the allied governments feared wounding the pride of native officers.[17] In the end, however, personal conflicts and national rivalries would induce both Lima and Santiago to seek a foreign commander for their combined fleet.

Much of the turbulence within the Peruvian Navy at this time revolved around the stormy personality of Lizardo Montero, who had won his last promotion (to first lieutenant) through his key role in an 1856 revolution. A few days after Colonel Prado raised the standard of revolt against President Pezet in 1865, the thirty-three-year-old Montero, in command of the Lerzundi, joined the movement and quickly suborned the men of the *Túmbez*. Montero then surprised and captured the frigate *Amazonas* and the corvette *América*. Within a span of sixteen months, Montero was promoted to lieutenant commander, then commander, and, finally, captain. Although he had only fourteen years of naval service, Montero was appointed flag officer of the fleet, bypassing scores of senior men. Commodore Montero possessed considerable physical courage and great energy, but he was not well respected by his navy colleagues. The young officer was extremely vain and mercurial in temperament, and his personal ambition patently overshadowed his oft-proclaimed patriotism. Colonel Prado appreciated and rewarded Montero's support. But the dictator understood his limitations and soon came to doubt his political reliability: Montero's uncle was Colonel José Balta, Prado's major rival for leadership of the government. Probably to be rid of this controversial mariner, Prado dispatched Montero on an arms-buying mission to the United States in December 1865.[18]

The Chilean Navy was not so rent by personal animosities as that of Peru, but Chile's most prominent officer—Captain Juan Williams Rebolledo—was the source of much of the discord that soon developed between the allied squadrons. Born near Valparaíso in 1826 to one of Cochrane's British commanders and a Chilean mother, Williams was a twenty-three-year veteran of the navy and an officer of considerable professional attainment. But Williams's vanity rivaled that of Montero, while his low regard for others, including fellow officers, bordered on misanthropy. A stickler for discipline and professionalism, Williams held Peruvian officers in almost universal contempt, and he made little effort to conceal these feelings. At the same time, the superiority of Peru's ships fueled his jealousy.[19]

The treaty of alliance between Peru and Chile—signed on December 5, 1865, and ratified forty days later—stipulated that the fleets of the two nations were to combine and to obey the orders of the government in whose waters they were stationed. The senior officer of either squadron was to command the combined fleet; by mutual agreement, however, supreme command might be vested in the "national or foreign" officer deemed most competent. Because of the presence of the Spanish fleet in Chile's waters and the poor state of that nation's defenses, the partners understood that the allied navy initially would operate off the Chilean coast and, thus, under the instructions of the regime in Santiago. Both governments, however, wanted the supreme commander chosen from their own navy; his role would enhance their international prestige and also bring internal political rewards. Colonel Prado, especially, would have benefited from a successful naval campaign under Peruvian leadership, for the universal desire to punish Spain was the glue that held his increasingly controversial administration together. But the Chileans pressed hard to have their man, Captain Williams, appointed to supreme command, and Prado assented.[20]

The Peruvian frigates *Amazonas* and *Apurímac* departed Callao for Chile on December 3, 1865. According to Rafael Sotomayor, a Chilean official who accompanied the expedition, the vessels were short of officers, and those on board showed little interest in drilling their skeleton crews of largely inexperienced seamen. Several of the officers had been on opposite sides in the recent civil war, and frosty relations existed between Commander Benjamín Mariátegui, the senior officer and skipper of the *Apurímac*, and Acting Lieutenant Commander José Sánchez Lagomarsino of the *Amazonas*. Perhaps with some exaggeration Sotomayor informed his government of the "indiscipline" and "indolence" on board the vessels and attributed this state of "abandon" to the "inexperience or incompetence" of the Peruvian officers and their "absolute lack of military habits." It was a litany that Chilean officers would repeat many times in the months to come.

The two Peruvian frigates arrived at Ancud, the port of Chiloé Island, January 10 and 14. Friction immediately arose between their officers and Captain Williams, who was in port on the *Esmeralda*. The Chilean commander did not personally call upon Mariátegui, as protocol required, but sent a subordinate to welcome him, an action that the Peruvian chief attributed to the discourtesy exhibited by Williams on earlier visits to Peru. Williams was anxious to exercise supreme command of the combined fleet. He wanted to train Mariátegui's sailors and to assign Chilean officers and seamen to the undermanned Peruvian vessels. Mariátegui resisted these suggestions and rejected Williams's authority. The Peruvians had sailed from home before the treaty of alliance had been completed, and Mariátegui would not submit to Williams's orders until explicit instructions arrived from Lima. The two squadron commanders squabbled over repairs and provisions for the Peruvian ships, a controversy that would intensify as the weeks passed.[21] Peru's sailors wanted butter and sausage, not Chilean lard and jerked beef; the *aguardiente* (sugarcane brandy) ration was inadequate in quantity and quality. Williams complained that the Peruvians ate too much and consumed triple the spirits of his own sailors.[22]

On January 16 the combined fleet sailed in convoy from Ancud to the shipyard at nearby Abtao Island, at the head of the Chonos Archipelago whose treacherous channels wind southward to the Strait of Magellan. The *Amazonas* struck a submerged rock in the Chacao Channel and sank. The Peruvians blamed this disaster on the errors of a Chilean officer whom Williams had assigned to guide the frigate through the treacherous passage. The Chileans charged that Captain Sánchez Lagomarsino had rejected the advice of the Chilean pilot.[23] Recriminations over the loss of the *Amazonas* deepened the discord between the allied officers, and relations did not improve with the arrival on February 4 of the corvettes *América* and *Unión*, carrying Acting Captain Manuel Villar, who assumed command of the fleet's

Peruvian division. A man who had joined the navy six years before Williams's birth, Villar was uncomfortable serving under the abrasive Chilean supreme commander. And Williams's own jealousy soon was piqued. On February 7, while the Chilean officer was absent, Captain Villar commanded the allied fleet in the battle of Abtao.[24]

During the next month, the breach between Williams and the Peruvian officers became irreparable. On March 2 Manuel Ferreyros and Miguel Grau, the skippers of the *América* and *Unión*, and Commander Mariátegui, now serving as Villar's chief of staff, wrote to Williams formally protesting against his plan of organization. The Chilean flag officer summoned them to a meeting with his own officers and contemptuously tore their letter into little pieces. Six days later, in a sharply worded document, Williams demanded that Villar submit to his absolute authority, including the Chilean's prerogative as supreme commander to dictate the internal regimen of the Peruvian squadron, transfer personnel throughout the allied fleet, and raise his pennant on whatever vessel—Peruvian or Chilean—he selected as his flagship. The Peruvian commander responded acidly that neither the treaty of alliance nor Villar's instructions from Lima invested Williams with the power he claimed. On March 17 Williams asked to be relieved of command—officially for reasons of health. Privately, he informed the minister of marine that the hostile attitude of the Peruvian officers toward him had "closed the door" to the attainment of the order and harmony necessary to prosecute the war.[25]

The almost daily reports of discord within the allied fleet deeply troubled the governments in both Santiago and Lima. While entreating Williams to employ tact in his dealings with the Peruvian officers, the Chilean regime considered contracting a foreign officer who might command the respect and obedience of both squadrons. Lima had the same idea. On March 27, 1866, Peruvian foreign minister Toribio Pacheco instructed his minister to the United States to hire a "commodore."[26]

The Southern Yankees

Federico L. Barreda was a brilliant thirty-nine-year-old Peruvian businessman who during the 1850s amassed a large fortune through a variety of enterprises in the United States. He had served as Lima's envoy to Washington since 1860. In June 1862 Barreda approached John Ericsson about the acquisition of two monitors, vessels which had proved their worth only three months earlier at Hampton Roads. But the Lincoln administration, conserving the Union's resources for the struggle against the South, soon prohibited the export of war matériel. So Barreda sent his naval attaché to Great Britain to initiate the construction of the ironclads *Independencia* and *Huáscar*. In mid-1864 Minister Barreda went to Europe where, assuming the added duties of plenipotentiary to the courts at London and Paris, he secured the delivery of the two ironclads and purchased the French-built corvettes *América* and *Unión*. Foreign Minister Pacheco's instruction to find a commander for the allied fleet awaited him when he returned to Washington from London in the last week of April 1866.[27]

Barreda assumed that his man could be found within the Union navy. But he soon discovered that no suitable senior officer would abandon a long career with the United States for an uncertain future in the Peruvian service. The minister quickly turned to the register of the defunct Confederate States Navy. The new *comodoro* ideally should have earned high rank through many years of service. The job required substantial experience and professional expertise. But equally important, the politics of the appointment demanded a candidate of superior qualifications to justify the hiring of a foreigner and to encourage his acceptance by the Latin American officers. At the same time, the commodore should be young and vigorous enough to conduct a long and difficult campaign at sea. The officer should be familiar with the modern ships and ordnance recently acquired by the allies and yet be able to improvise and to make do with the limited resources of Peru and Chile. Finally, the ideal flag officer should be skilled at handling men—a diplomat who could evoke cooperation from the factious allied officers, a disciplinarian who could prepare inexperienced and often unruly men for combat, but also a leader sufficiently flexible to compromise when necessary.[28]

Barreda undertook this important assignment with his customary efficiency and conscientiousness. "It is not so easy to find a good commander of a squadron as a captain of a ship," he told Pacheco. "We have to be sure that we have a man who has proved himself." The minister likely sought the advice of Chilean "confidential agent" Benjamín Vicuña Mackenna, who was concluding his arms-buying mission to the United States. He had contacted several prominent former Confederates about possible commissions in the Chilean Navy and interviewed John Randolph Tucker in January. The unemployed commodore was anxious to "take command of any Chilean warship," but the opportunity passed when Vicuña proved unable to circumvent the neutrality laws and to put armed vessels to sea from United States ports. Barreda also made discreet inquiries at the Navy Department and Annapolis, contacted former Confederate political leaders, and sought advice from several officers of both the Northern and Southern navies. Among the latter, undoubtedly, was former commander Catesby ap R. Jones, the noted Confederate ordnance expert, who had fought the *Virginia* against the *Monitor*. Having earlier assisted Vicuña in the purchase of heavy guns and then consulted with Peruvian authorities concerning the defenses of Callao, Jones now became Barreda's agent and naval adviser. These sources recommended many officers, but the minister quickly narrowed his choice to a short list of candidates—Tucker, Commander Robert B. Pegram, and a third unidentified mariner—and dispatched his longtime agent Nathaniel B. Wells to Virginia to make contact with them.

On May 14 Wells returned to Washington with Tucker in tow. After a detailed discussion of the Peruvian post and Tucker's terms for accepting it, the former Confederate agreed to enter the service of the Lima government, provided that he could be released from his recent commitment with the Southern Express Company. Barreda informed his government that Tucker had an "excellent reputation in the South and the North," with "proven experience *on sea* and *land*." The minister briefly sketched the highlights of the sailor's wartime career—at Hampton Roads, Drewry's Bluff, and Charleston—and asserted that Tucker was noted for "intelligence, coolness, and valor," as well as "notable tenacity and boldness."

Tucker's contract with Barreda—a verbal agreement—stipulated that the Virginian would be commissioned a rear admiral (*contralmirante*) in the Peruvian Navy for the duration of the war with Spain and would receive an annual salary of $5,000, the same remuneration as a rear admiral in the United States Navy. Although the minister had been instructed to hire a *comodoro*, he artfully claimed that this courtesy title corresponded to the Peruvian rank of rear admiral, the grade Tucker probably requested. Barreda also exceeded his instructions by permitting Tucker to select three men personally known to him to comprise his staff. These officers were to receive commissions as *capitán de navío* (captain), *capitán de fragata* (commander), and *capitán de corbeta* (lieutenant commander), also at the compensation for those ranks in the federal navy. Tucker assembled his staff quickly, for he wanted to depart for Peru within one week's time. The men he selected were James Cooke, David McCorkle, and Walter Butt.[29] The Latin Americans, quite logically, would refer to this team as *los Yanquis del Sur* (the Yankees from the South), a label that certainly tickled Tucker and his colleagues.

James Wallace Cooke—Tucker's choice for his flag captain—was a North Carolinian who had entered the United States Navy in 1828, only two years after Tucker. They had served together on the *Warren* during a Caribbean cruise in 1839–41. Cooke had been one of the Confederacy's most aggressive and respected officers. Commanding a small gunboat in February 1862, he was severely wounded while tenaciously battling the Union expedition that captured Roanoke Island. After recovering his strength, he superintended the construction of the ironclad ram *Albemarle*, a herculean task accomplished in a cornfield on the banks of the North Carolina sounds. In a combined operation with the army, Cooke's vessel played the decisive role in the April 1864 capture of Plymouth, North Carolina. Two weeks later, Cooke participated in the unsuccessful assault on New Bern, in which the *Albemarle* simultaneously engaged four enemy ships. For his efforts Cooke became one of only two rebel mariners promoted to captain for "gallant and meritorious conduct." Unfortunately for Tucker, Cooke was unable to rescind a contract he recently had signed with the Southern Express Company.[30] His selection, however, reflected well upon Tucker's judgment.

David Porter McCorkle, Tucker's choice as his ordnance officer, came from a navy family. His father, Joseph Porter McCorkle, served many years as a Navy Department clerk. James Porter McCorkle, David's elder brother, followed in his father's footsteps, rising to chief clerk in the Bureau of Ordnance and Hydrography; after the secession of Virginia, James occupied the equivalent post in the Confederate navy. David McCorkle, like Tucker, was born in the District of Columbia (about 1822) but considered himself a Virginian. He entered the navy as an overage midshipman in 1841, a year when patronage ran amuck and produced 224 such appointments.[31]

Midshipman McCorkle spent his first five years with the Mediterranean and Brazil squadrons before his assignment in 1846 to the *Princeton*, Commodore Perry's flagship in the Gulf of Mexico. McCorkle's professional association with Tucker began at the battle of Tabasco, in which the midshipman manned a gun near Lieutenant Tucker's piece from the *Stromboli*. At the conclusion of the Mexican War, McCorkle attended the new United States Naval Academy at Annapolis, graduating in 1848. During the next dozen years, he became a "scientific" sailor. He served four years with the United States Coast Survey, mapping the harbors and waterways of the country—skills that later would serve him well in South America. In 1853 and 1854 McCorkle sailed on the *Vincennes*, along with his Annapolis classmate and budding naval scientist John M. Brooke, as a member of the navy's North Pacific and China Seas Exploring and Survey Expedition. Promoted to lieutenant in 1855, he received a coveted one-year assignment to Matthew Maury's Naval Observatory in Washington. In 1860, after a three-year cruise with the Pacific Squadron, McCorkle became an assistant to Commander John A. B. Dahlgren in the experimental ordnance department at the Washington Navy Yard. He made his final voyage, to Japan, with the United States Navy in 1861. Upon his return home, McCorkle refused the loyalty oath now required of all officers. He was dismissed from the service on May 17, 1861, ending a career of two decades.[32]

In the Confederate navy McCorkle formed part of a small but talented cadre of ordnance specialists that included his old friend John M. Brooke (chief of the Bureau of Ordnance and Hydrography), George and Robert Minor, and Catesby Jones. Initially assigned to Commander Tucker, McCorkle fitted the *Patrick Henry* with her armament. In the autumn of 1861, he was loaned to the army for ordnance service at Evansport, Virginia. The following February, McCorkle became the navy's ordnance officer at New Orleans. When Flag Officer David G. Farragut's Union fleet captured that city in April 1862, McCorkle alertly saved all of the precious machinery and stores under his care and transported them to Atlanta. Here he established the important ordnance works that he would command for the remainder of the war.[33]

Under the most trying circumstances—especially, severe shortages of labor and materials—McCorkle and his staff (including, for a while, Tucker's nephew Chief Engineer Thomas Alphonse Jackson) supplied munitions, gun carriages, and other matériel to Tucker at Charleston, to the Mobile and Savannah squadrons, and to the army as well. In June 1864, as General Sherman's army threatened Atlanta, McCorkle moved his establishment to Augusta, Georgia, and early the next year to Fayetteville, North Carolina. In late February 1865 he probably renewed his acquaintance with Commodore Tucker when the latter fell back to Fayetteville after the evacuation of Charleston. On May 9, 1865, after Johnston's surrender to Sherman, McCorkle was paroled.[34]

The few records that survive from McCorkle's ordnance factories indicate that he was a competent and energetic officer. A tall, powerfully built, ruggedly handsome man with a neatly trimmed mustache and goatee, McCorkle had a lively sense of humor, a salty vocabulary, and a no-nonsense, businesslike demeanor. He did not suffer fools easily. After the war McCorkle sought work ·in Richmond; he was willing to try anything except "cracking staves." But fierce competition raged over the few available jobs. McCorkle inquired about work in Mexico with his émigré friend General Walter H. Stevens. Everything in Richmond was "Yankee Yankee," he wrote; "any other country would be better than this." The next year McCorkle joined with Tucker in the stillborn Venezuelan colonization scheme of Dr. Henry M. Price.[35] The sudden opportunity to resume a career at sea was seized eagerly by Capitán de Fragata David Porter McCorkle, Armada Peruana.

Walter Raleigh Butt was the only member of Tucker's original team who would serve with the admiral throughout his time in South America. Born the son of a physician at Portsmouth, Virginia, on December 10, 1839, Butt was orphaned at an early age. He was raised by an uncle at Vancouver, in the Washington Territory. The West would continue to hold a special allure for him; but home was always the seafaring city of Portsmouth, where he had many relatives and friends, including members of prominent naval families. In September 1855 the fifteen-year-old lad received an appointment to the United States Naval Academy at Annapolis.

The academy's course was difficult and its discipline rigid; less than half of the 1855 appointees graduated. Butt's four adolescent years there were troubled. Sentimental, lonely, and prone to bouts of melancholy, the somewhat frail and baby-faced orphan was one of the smaller boys in his class. He masked feelings of inadequacy behind a prankish, smart-alecky exterior and sought the company of younger cadets. Butt was dismissed from the school in October 1856, only to be reinstated the next week. Until the beginning of his final semester, however, the cadet contemplated resigning his appointment and returning to Vancouver. Walter Butt graduated in June 1859 at the very bottom of his twenty-student class; only three of his classmates exceeded his ninety-nine demerits for that year.

Butt's graduating class included three future admirals, most notably the brilliant Alfred Thayer Mahan. Physically and scholastically unimpressive, Walter Butt—"that damned little Butt," Mahan called him—might soon have been forgotten by his classmates. However, Butt was a virtuoso violinist, and in later years all would remember the "Fiddler."[36] The man who emerged from the boy at Annapolis was of middling height (five feet seven inches) with a stocky frame, brown hair, and blue eyes. He had a keen aesthetic sense and relished all of life's pleasures. A close friend aptly described him as a man of "robust appreciation."[37] With an open, highly emotional personality, he was quick to make both friends and enemies.

After graduation, Midshipman Butt was ordered to the frigate *Constellation* for service with the squadron suppressing the slave trade off the African coast. Aside from summer training cruises while at Annapolis, this would be his only sea service with the United States Navy. When Butt's ship docked at Portsmouth, New Hampshire, in late September 1861, he learned that the mass resignation of Southern officers earlier that year had resulted in his promotion to lieutenant. He needed only to take the loyalty oath. Butt refused. On October 2 Secretary Welles ordered the young officer's imprisonment; three days later he was dismissed from the service by order of the president. "Had Butt been allowed to play the violin to Mr. Lincoln," speculated an Annapolis classmate, "he might have assuaged his hostility."[38]

Exchanged for a captured Union army captain in January 1862, Butt was commissioned a lieutenant in the Confederate navy and received orders to the CSS *Virginia* (ex-*Merrimack*), preparing at Norfolk. He commanded one of the famous ironclad's gun crews in the battle of Hampton Roads on March 8 and 9. Butt "fought his gun with activity," reported Captain Franklin Buchanan, "and during the action was gay and smiling." In one of the war's many ironies, the young officer found himself shooting at his Annapolis roommate, Lieutenant Samuel Dana Greene, who as executive officer of the *Monitor* succeeded to the command of the Union vessel after the blinding of Lieutenant Worden. "Buttsy," wrote Greene to his family, "was on board the Merrimac; little did we ever think at the Academy, we would be firing 150 lbs. shot at each other."[39] After the scuttling of the *Virginia* on May 11, Butt and his shipmates hastened to Drewry's Bluff where, with Commander Tucker of the *Patrick Henry*, they repulsed the attack of John Rodgers's Union flotilla four days later. Butt remained in the batteries of the upper James River until mid-August, when a persistent "low fever" forced him to take an extended leave.[40]

In March 1863 Navy Secretary Mallory ordered Butt to Europe for "special service." Among several officers slated for duty on warships being built for the Confederacy in England and France, Butt was to have become executive officer of the CSS *Texas*, one of two corvettes under construction at Nantes. Lieutenant Butt spent most of his fourteen months overseas in Paris, enjoying the duty immensely. One January evening in 1864 Assistant Paymaster Douglas French Forrest returned to his hotel room in "Gay Paree" to find Butt, along with three other young officers, itching for a party. "Butt played a little on the violin," recorded Forrest in his diary. "He is a capital performer."[41]

Union agents ultimately blocked delivery of the Nantes corvettes to the Rebels. Butt returned to the Confederacy and service with the James River Squadron (three ironclads and eight wooden gunboats) guarding the water route to Richmond. He briefly commanded the *Hampton* and then the *Nansemond*, small wooden steamers mounting two 8-inch guns. Under the orders of Flag Officer John K. Mitchell, on January 25, 1865, the squadron attempted to pass through federal obstructions below Drewry's Bluff and to attack General Grant's supply depot at City Point. The operation went badly. Several vessels ran aground, and three gunboats were lost. The *Nansemond*, however, succeeded in towing two other disabled ships to safety through concentrated fire from field artillery, mortars, stationary batteries, and swarms of sharpshooters. The hail of Minié balls, reported Butt, was "so severe" that a man could not show "himself above the hammock nettings to return the fire." He modestly attributed his success to his men and divine intervention.[42]

As Grant prepared to take Richmond on April 2, Rear Admiral Raphael Semmes, who had succeeded Mitchell in command of the James River Squadron, ordered Butt and his other skippers to destroy their vessels. After completing this dreary task, the Semmes Naval Brigade abandoned the Confederate capital by rail, following President Davis and his cabinet south to Danville, Virginia. The sailors then marched to Greensboro, North Carolina, where they were incorporated into General Joseph E. Johnston's Army of the Tennessee. A lawyer with punctilious regard for proper procedures, Semmes formally reorganized his command as an army unit. Thus, the rear admiral became a brigadier general. "Captain" Butt, a first lieutenant in the Confederate navy, became Captain Butt of the Confederate army and assistant adjutant general to Semmes. On April 28, after Johnston's capitulation to Sherman, Butt was paroled. He returned to the Portsmouth home of his brother, Dr. Holt Fairfield Butt, and tried to find a new career. However, the local economy was in shambles, and the area's largest employer—the United States Navy yard—would not hire former Confederates.[43] Like David McCorkle, Walter Butt did not hesitate to accept Tucker's offer of a Peruvian commission as *capitán de corbeta*.

Notice of the battle of Callao would not reach the United States until early June 1866. But anticipating a Spanish attack, Barreda ordered Tucker to arrange his affairs quickly and depart for South America without delay. When Captain Cooke proved unable to accept his commission, the envoy authorized Tucker to hire a substitute; but a suitable replacement could not be found on short notice. At the end of May 1866, Tucker, McCorkle, and Butt reached New York, where Barreda's financial agents, Barrie Brothers and Company, had made all of the arrangements for their journey. They were given tickets to Peru by way of Panama and $100 to cover incidental expenses. Best of all, the hungry "Rebs" received enlistment bonuses of three months' pay—$1,250 for Tucker, $700 for McCorkle, and $468.75 for Butt.[44]

Tucker and his staff—the first North American naval mission to Peru—left New York on June 1 aboard the mail steamer *Arizona*. At Panama, per Barreda's instructions, they were to ascertain if Callao was blockaded; if so, the Peruvian consul would arrange their journey to the open port nearest Lima. Tucker carried an order from Barreda (mustering all the authority of his formal diplomatic titles) to the "civil, military, and maritime authorities of Peru and its allies" to provide the travelers with "all necessary assistance." Tucker also bore a letter from Barreda to Foreign Minister Pacheco introducing "el Contralmirante de la Armada Nacional don Juan R. Tucker, . . . from whom I expect much." The Southern Yankees reached Callao without incident on June 15. Their arrival caused embarrassed surprise within the government. On May 21 the foreign minister had instructed Barreda to cancel his search for a commodore. This dispatch reached Washington after Tucker's departure. Furthermore, Barreda's letters to Pacheco concerning the Virginian's appointment would not arrive in Lima until a few days after the former Confederates. On the envoy's wayward correspondence a United States postal clerk had scratched, apologetically, "Missent to Boston."[45]

An Unknown Rebel

On April 17—three weeks after Barreda had been ordered to hire a commodore—José Pardo y Aliaga, Peru's minister to Santiago, approved a Chilean proposal to promote harmony within the allied fleet. The abrasive Captain Williams would be replaced as supreme commander by Manuel Blanco Encalada. A living monument to the Wars of Independence who held dual rank as a vice admiral in Chile's navy and a general in its army, Blanco had joined the Spanish Navy during the Napoleonic Wars. He tendered his sword to his homeland when it struck for independence. In 1817 he helped organize and bravely commanded Chile's first national squadron. With the arrival of Lord Cochrane the next year, Blanco relinquished his post and, with model self-abnegation, loyally served under the Scottish-born admiral. After Cochrane's departure in 1822, Blanco again became his nation's senior naval officer and briefly occupied the presidency of the republic. Blanco had commanded Chile's first expedition against the Peru-Bolivia Confederation in 1837. It was now hoped that the Peruvians would overlook this episode (a fiasco ending in the surrender of the general/admiral) and recall that for a short time during the fight for independence Blanco had also held a commission in the Peruvian Navy. The allies agreed that Blanco's name would be reinscribed in the navy register of Peru, giving their combined fleet a commander who belonged to both services.[46]

Although resolving the most immediate problem facing the allies, the appointment of Admiral Blanco was not entirely satisfactory. Peru, especially, desired to prosecute the war vigorously. The venerable Blanco had been semiretired for the last several of his seventy-six years; he was "deaf, old, and sickly" and unfamiliar with modern warfare at sea. The allied leaders understood, therefore, that the admiral would act as a patriarch, resolving squabbles among his children, while a younger officer would be the fleet's de facto commander. The Peruvians anticipated that the latter would be Capitán de Navío José M. Salcedo. A native-born Chilean who had emigrated to Peru at age nine, Salcedo had spent forty-five years in the Peruvian Navy and was one of that service's most respected officers. Salcedo had been dispatched to England to take command of the *Independencia* and *Huáscar*, and his return with the two ironclads was expected at any moment.[47]

The May 2 battle of Callao, however, produced new complications for the alliance. Although the Chilean government lauded the victory of its ally, this triumph and the resulting accolades inspired jealousy among some of Chile's mariners. Furthermore, the recent failure of the Chileans to resist the Spaniards at Valparaíso evoked criticism within the Peruvian service. The repulse of the Spaniards at Callao also increased the self-confidence of Peru's officers, while reports that their victory had been achieved by foreign mercenaries wounded their pride. When it became apparent that Méndez Núñez would not resume the offensive against the allies, the Lima government ordered Barreda to cease his search for a North American commodore. Under the circumstances, the Blanco-Salcedo command structure would suffice.[48]

Upon reaching Chile from Britain in early June, Salcedo found orders naming him commander of the Peruvian division of the allied fleet, replacing Manuel Villar. A few days later, however, Salcedo was called home to Lima to become director of marine, a desk job. During the voyage from Europe, Salcedo—a strict disciplinarian unjustly suspected by some Peruvians of harboring primary loyalties to Chile—had feuded bitterly with Commander Aurelio García y García, the skipper of the *Independencia*, and with the executive and other officers of his own *Huáscar*. The authorities in Peru feared a mutiny if Salcedo remained at the head of the squadron. For reasons of domestic politics, however, Lima replaced him with another problematic commander—Lizardo Montero. Famous for his "lucky star," the ambitious and influential Montero had returned fortuitously from his arms-buying mission in the United States only hours before the battle of Callao. His command of the harbor squadron that day enhanced his reputation with the public but not with his brother officers. "This ignorant and half-crazy lad," wrote Salcedo in disgust, "does not have a single good quality as a man"; the "bravery which some suppose he has, he does not have, as all his comrades know." The Peruvian squadron, reported navy bureaucrat Ricardo Palma, was becoming "a labyrinth where no man trusts another."[49]

Because of the renewed turmoil within the squadron, the Lima government viewed Tucker's unannounced arrival on June 15 as a stroke of good luck. And fortunately for the admiral, too, he carried copies of Barreda's errant dispatches, outlining the Virginian's distinguished background and the minister's diligent search for him. Tucker, McCorkle, and Butt were made comfortable at the Hotel Maury—one of South America's most luxurious establishments—and the next day the trio was welcomed with "marked courtesy" in a formal audience with President Prado and his cabinet. After this meeting General Pedro Bustamante, the minister of war and marine, along with his staff took the former Confederates to inspect the fortifications at Callao. Their party of twelve, with the Peruvians in dress uniforms, "mounted and giving full tilt through the streets . . . created quite a sensation." The sailors returned to the presidential residence that evening for an informal dinner with Colonel Prado, who gave them a tour of the sixteenth-century Palace of Pizarro. "The warmth of our reception," wrote Butt, "impressed us most favorably." The Peruvians were pleased, too. Pacheco pronounced the "president and all of us . . . very content with Tucker." Prado praised Barreda for anticipating the government's desires—it was as if the envoy in Washington had been attending cabinet meetings in Lima.[50]

But how would Peru's naval officers react to Tucker's appointment, and what would Prado tell his Chilean allies? On June 17 the dictator summoned Chilean envoy Marcial Martínez to the presidential palace. He candidly reviewed the events that resulted in Tucker's unexpected arrival and appealed for the minister's support in placing the Virginian at the head of the allied fleet. While praising Admiral Blanco as a great patriot, Prado emphasized that the aged and infirm Chilean mariner was unfamiliar with modern naval technology and could not "prosecute vigorously" a long, offensive war in "remote seas." The supreme chief then extolled Tucker's virtues. He was a "robust and healthy man, in the most vigorous part of life," who had earned a great reputation during the Civil War. The former Confederate was "brave," "daring," and "capable of facing the most dangerous undertakings." His knowledge of ironclads and other modern weapons could not be matched by any allied officer. Tucker possessed the "immense advantage of being perfectly familiar" with the coasts of many countries, where he also had acquaintances who could help him obtain supplies and repairs for his ships. Finally, the Spaniards would be "terrorized" upon learning that the allied fleet included "two ironclads and a North American admiral."

Minister Martínez—who had not been informed directly of Peru's search for a foreign flag officer—generally concurred with Prado's reasoning. From the first days of the alliance, the Chilean envoy had favored placing a British or North American officer at the head of the fleet. But Martínez was very sensitive to the political repercussions in Chile of replacing Blanco. He suggested that Tucker be named chief of the Peruvian division. Blanco would remain nominal supreme commander, while the *norteamericano* directed actual operations. After a decent interval, the aged Chilean mariner might resign, without embarrassment, for reasons of health. For the moment, however, Prado rejected this proposal.[51]

Martínez's tentative support for Tucker's appointment was based upon the assumption that the Virginian was indeed a meritorious officer. On June 21 the envoy sought independent information about the new *almirante* from Admiral George F. Pearson, who commanded the United States South Pacific Squadron, and from Captain Daniel B.

Ridgely, the commander of Pearson's flagship. The seventy-year-old Pearson probably knew Tucker only by reputation; the two men had not served together. But Ridgely had been Tucker's shipmate on the USS *Warren* a quarter century earlier. Ridgely also had been one of Admiral Dahlgren's senior officers during the blockade of Charleston, and he undoubtedly knew that Tucker commanded the enemy squadron there. Both Pearson and Ridgely, reported Martínez, hailed the former Confederate as "a sailor of the first order" and assured him that the allies could not have made a "better acquisition." After a personal interview with the Virginian, the envoy described the fifty-four-year-old Tucker as "a man of 45 to 48 years" who exhibited "tact, education, and congeniality." Chilean agents in the United States, meanwhile, sent similar appraisals to Santiago. Minister Francisco Solano Asta Buraga deemed the "distinguished commodore of the Confederates . . . very acceptable," and Confidential Agent Vicuña MacKenna attested to Tucker's "excellent reputation."[52]

Although the Chileans seemed amenable to placing Tucker at the head of the allied fleet and Captain Salcedo strongly supported his appointment, Peru's other naval officers were almost unanimous in their opposition to the Virginian. These men had "just whipped the Spaniards from Callao without foreign aid," explained Butt, "and they naturally . . . think [they] can repeat it." Peru's proud officers viewed Prado's plans for Tucker as a slap in the face. The supreme chief and his advisers at first underestimated the depth of opposition among their "little sailors," as Pacheco called them. By June 21, however, rumors that much of the officer corps might resign rather than serve under Tucker gave Prado second thoughts. He now proposed to follow Martínez's advice and to appoint the Virginian chief of the Peruvian squadron, while keeping Blanco as allied commander. But how would the volatile Montero react to his replacement, after only a few days in command, by a foreigner? In the end, the administration decided to retain Montero at the head of the Peruvian division and to name Tucker second-in-command of the allied fleet, without any official position within Peru's squadron. Lima hoped that Montero would resign voluntarily, making room for the new *almirante*, and that Blanco might step aside too.[53]

During the three weeks required to determine Tucker's status and to obtain Santiago's approval, the Southern Yankees visited military installations around Lima and conferred with Peruvian leaders. Language, however, was a frustrating obstacle. Tucker and McCorkle apparently understood little, if any, Spanish. In his Annapolis years Walter Butt had made a summer cruise to Spain and had studied the Spanish language; as with all of his academic work, however, he had done poorly. On June 20 Colonel Prado and Admiral Tucker attempted to have their first serious discussion of strategy. Through an aide, the young writer Ricardo Palma, the supreme chief ordered the Navy Department to provide him with a memorandum describing Peru's fleet and its armament. "Send me everything," he commanded, "with a naval officer who speaks English." None could be found that day. Or the next. "Send me Robertson—Delboy—or Espinoza of the *Túmbez*, the big Turk," demanded the exasperated dictator. Prado did not believe that an English-speaking officer "could be such a scarce fruit in the navy." Only on the fourth day did the president find an officer with the requisite linguistic skills.[54]

Peru still was celebrating the victory at Callao when Tucker and his companions arrived. In hotels, cafés, and private homes, proud citizens required little excuse to sing the national anthem, and the war was the main, animated topic of conversation. "It was impossible not to sympathize with them," noted Butt, "for their earnest enthusiasm seemed intense and their joy boundless." The Virginians attended a great victory ball in the hall of the Chamber of Deputies "one of the most brilliant" affairs that Butt had ever witnessed.

> The decorations of the ball-room displayed an aesthetic taste seldom equaled in our country. The galleries, which extended entirely around the hall, were supported by fluted columns, around which were entwined ribbons of lovely flowers. The flags of all nations save that of Spain adorned the walls. . . . Fountains of perfumed water cooled the atmosphere, and four or five military bands alternately played the dance music. . . . The scene . . . was magnificent; the gracefulness, wit, and vivacity for which the ladies of Lima are famed were displayed to a marked extent. . . . The general effect was much heightened by the brilliant court costumes of the diplomatic corps, and the rich uniforms of the officers.

As part of the festivities the North Americans also attended a bullfight ("not so brutal" as Butt expected), and the trio was entertained at numerous dinner parties. The table etiquette amused them. "When desiring to particularly honor a gentleman," recorded Butt, the ladies "presented him with some delicate morsel on their fork; after eating it, he returned the compliment in a similar manner." This practice, he assured his health-conscious readers, occurred (as it still does) "at the beginning of dinner, before the forks had been previously used." More quaint was the custom "to roll up bread pills whilst conversing." The Fiddler recalled "dignified old gentlemen with quite a pile . . . by the side of their plates." The ladies flirted with their "beaus, by tossing playfully a piece of bread at them," while the men retaliated in kind.[55]

Tucker's team and Jorge Mendiola, their assigned interpreter-secretary, departed for Valparaíso on July 12. In addition to his credentials as "second chief" of the allied fleet, the admiral carried secret orders naming him commander of the Peruvian division in the event of

Montero's resignation. Tucker understood that the officers of the squadron were unhappy about the presence of a foreign senior officer; reports to that effect had by now reached Lima. Benjamín Vicuña MacKenna, returning home from his mission in the United States, talked to the Virginian shortly before Tucker left the Peruvian capital. The *almirante*—a man of "the most honorable background, moderate, [and] prudent"—was prepared to resign immediately if the controversy surrounding him became overheated.[56] Neither he nor the officials in Lima, however, anticipated the fire storm he would encounter at the Chilean port.

On June 20 Colonel Prado had written to Commodore Montero on the *Huáscar* informing him that in accord with current plans, Tucker would replace Blanco as allied commander. Six days later, the supreme chief sent personal notes to Montero and captains Aurelio García y García of the *Independencia*, Manuel Ferreyros of the *América*, and Miguel Grau of the *Unión*. Addressing them all as "esteemed friend," the colonel now stated that the Virginian would become second chief of the allied fleet and successor to Blanco should that officer resign. The letters implied that Tucker would supplant Montero at the head of the Peruvian division. Hoping to gain acceptance for the new *almirante*, Prado inflated the former Confederate's biography, describing him as "no less than the second notability among the sailors of the Great Republic of the North, . . . who commanded the powerful squadron of the South" in the Civil War. "Mr. Tucker," declared the dictator, "is a complete gentleman, quiet and circumspect," with the "best good faith" and unlimited enthusiasm "for the cause we defend."[57]

Probably from Montero, Admiral Blanco learned about Prado's initial plan to have Tucker become supreme allied commander. The old Chilean sailor took sick leave on July 4, and Montero became acting chief of the combined fleet. Six days later Montero and the other Peruvian captains replied to Prado's informal notes in letters that crossed Tucker's path as he traveled southward on the mail steamer *Paita*. García y García condemned the appointment of a "pro-slaverist and unknown rebel" who could not even speak Spanish and urged the supreme chief to reconsider his action. Tucker, he wrote, would never be accepted by Peru's officers. Montero emotionally declared that he and all of his subordinates "reject with indignation the appointment . . . of this Mr. Tucker." Would Colonel Prado accept a "foreign general and adventurer" to head the army, asked the sailor rhetorically. The commodore suggested that the supreme chief would be the first to reject such an idea. Proclaiming his patriotism and loyalty to the regime, Montero asserted that he would defend Peru "in a launch, in whatever boat, but never under the orders of a Swiss"—i.e., a mercenary. The "ships of the alliance," he vowed, "will not pass to Tucker's control."[58]

The admiral and his party reached Valparaíso harbor on the morning of July 22. For Walter Butt the first sight of the Peruvian squadron probably produced strong feelings of déjà vu. Resting at anchor were the two Nantes-built corvettes originally slated for the Confederacy. The *Texas* (of which Butt was to have been the executive officer) was now the *América*, while the *Georgia* had become—Heaven forbid—the *Unión*. These twin vessels, purchased by Minister Barreda, each mounted a dozen 70-pounder rifled guns and were "beautifully modeled, . . . elegantly fitted up and could steam thirteen miles an hour." Tucker's memories were likely stirred too, for the *Independencia* closely resembled the *New Ironsides*, the federal flagship that had menaced Charleston during much of his tenure there. The Peruvian ironclad was a double-bottomed, two-thousand-ton, armor-belted frigate. Although the vessel's extremities were wooden, 4½-inch iron plates protected her sides. The *Independencia* carried fourteen rifled Armstrong guns—a dozen 70-pounders in broadside and a pair of 150-pounders on pivots, fore and aft.

Although only half the size of the *Independencia*, the *Huáscar* was the fleet's most potent vessel. Built by the Laird Brothers of Birkenhead, this state-of-the-art ship often has been described as a monitor. She was significantly different, however, from the Ericsson monitors of the Civil War. Designed by Captain Cowper Coles of the Royal Navy, the *Huáscar* (named for an Inca emperor) rode higher in the water, exposing some five feet of freeboard. Thus, she presented a larger target than the Union turret ships. But the Peruvian vessel was much more seaworthy and faster, too, making thirteen knots under ideal conditions. Of iron construction, the *Huáscar*'s sides were protected by 4½-inch armor, tapering to 2½ inches at the bow and stern. She had a double bottom and bulkheads that segmented the hull into four watertight compartments—features rendering the vessel less likely to sink if perforated. The ship's revolving turret, plated with five inches of iron, housed two huge 300-pounder Armstrong rifles, while a pair of 40-pounders were mounted on the quarterdeck. The allied fleet also included the twenty-eight-gun Peruvian frigate *Apurímac* and the Chilean corvette *Esmeralda* and gunboat *Covadonga* (mounting twenty and five guns, respectively), together with several armed transports and converted merchantmen. "It was quite a respectable, as well as a formidable, naval force," recalled Walter Butt proudly.[59]

Tucker was welcomed at Valparaíso by Peruvian minister José Pardo, a prominent man of letters, who had hurried from Santiago by special train. The embarrassed diplomat informed the *almirante* that the Peruvian officers would not permit him on board their ships. Tucker ("an excellent person," reported the envoy) tendered his resignation. But this did not resolve the minister's problem, for he had been ordered to secure the Virginian's position within the fleet. Tucker finally agreed to abide by the diplomat's wishes. Pardo lodged the three *norteamer-icanos* at the best hotel in Valparaíso, insisting that they "consider themselves guests of the nation" and that Tucker, "regardless of expense, maintain himself in a manner compatible with the dignity and importance of his position."[60]

During the next ten days, the former Confederates attended the theater and enjoyed "many pleasant entertainments," for "hospitality" was "one of the most prominent features" of Chilean society. Butt found the ladies "remarkable for their personal beauty and talent as musicians." José Pardo, meanwhile, conferred with Chilean officials and negotiated with the insubordinate Peruvian officers to find a solution to the impasse. Although President José Joaquín Pérez, his cabinet, and some of Chile's senior naval officers expressed themselves scandalized by the behavior of the Peruvian sailors, other Chilean mariners sympathized with them. "Franciscan subordination," muttered old Admiral Blanco repeatedly, "was a thing of the past century." Pardo ultimately reached a compromise with Montero. The commodore would take the entire Peruvian squadron back to Callao and place it directly under the orders of the Lima government.[61]

Colonel Prado, however, already had made other arrangements. Upon learning of the problem at Valparaíso, the supreme chief invested Premier and Finance Minister Manuel Pardo y Lavalle (the nephew of Lima's minister to Chile) with plenary powers to remove the insubordinate officers. With considerable difficulty the government found a handful of willing replacements; some were Pezet loyalists cashiered after Prado's victory. Premier Pardo, Navy Director Salcedo, and the new officers steamed for the Chilean port in the war transport *Callao*. Arriving soon after daybreak on August 3, the vessel fired a few blank rounds to awaken the port; then, with the presidential flag flying, the premier signaled the skippers of Peru's warships to come aboard. They did—and were immediately arrested. Manuel Pardo then repeated the procedure, summoning the squadron's executive and junior officers. The premier took thirty-nine mariners into custody.[62]

The officers from Lima took their assigned posts in the squadron and quickly informed Almirante Tucker (who had been named chief of the Peruvian division on July 23) that they awaited his orders. A protocol between Chilean foreign minister Alvaro Covarrubias and Peruvian envoy José Pardo, signed on August 13, formally appointed Tucker second chief of the allied fleet. The following day, citing poor health, Admiral Blanco submitted his resignation ("in disgust"), leaving Tucker in supreme command of the combined squadrons of Peru and Chile. Two days later, the admiral raised his broad pennant over the *Independencia* and received the salutes of the other ships in the harbor.[63]

A Colossal Undertaking

A secondary but very important objective of Premier Manuel Pardo's mission, after securing Tucker's position, was to obtain Santiago's agreement for an offensive against the Spaniards. Following the battle of Callao, three months earlier, the enemy ironclad *Numancia* and four wooden frigates (believed to have been seriously damaged) had crossed the Pacific to Spain's Philippine Islands. Admiral Méndez Núñez took his remaining four wooden frigates and several lesser vessels around Cape Horn, where severe storms battered them. The admiral distributed this force among the neutral ports of Montevideo, Uruguay, and Rio de Janeiro, Brazil. Méndez soon sent three of his frigates to Spain for repairs and awaited replacements from home. The Chileans were apprehensive of an early return of the enemy to the Pacific Coast and favored a relatively conservative strategy. The entire allied fleet should steam into the South Atlantic and attack the weakened enemy squadron. If Méndez obtained reinforcements and undertook a new expedition toward the Pacific, the allied vessels would be in a position to check the advancing enemy and might fall back to protect home ports.

The Peruvians thought that the Spanish admiral could not mount a major offensive, so far from home, before the end of the year and that an allied foray into the South Atlantic would be fruitless. Rather than engage the now vastly superior combined squadrons, the Spaniards would remain in the safety of neutral ports. The Peruvians also believed that the enemy had made a major strategic error in separating the powerful *Numancia* from the rest of the fleet, a blunder that the allies should exploit. Tucker undoubtedly had a major role in the formulation of Peru's strategy. Critics who deemed the Confederate commodore overly cautious for failing to attack the superior Union squadron off Charleston two years earlier would find no timidity in the plan of the Peruvian *almirante*.

The Peruvians wanted to attack the Spanish squadron in the Philippines, using the two ironclads, the *Unión* and the *América* (or one of these Peruvian corvettes and the Chilean *Esmeralda*), supported by a pair of transports. They hoped to surprise the enemy vessels (perhaps disarmed, while undergoing repairs in dry dock) and to capture or destroy them. Should Tucker not find the Spaniards, he would avert a barren expedition by bombarding Manila. This operation, from departure to return, would require an estimated five months. Thus, the *Independencia* and *Huáscar* would be in home waters before the likely arrival of any Spanish force from the Atlantic.

While the ironclad division attacked the Philippines, the remainder of the allied ships would cruise around Cape Horn. The fast converted merchantmen of the Chileans would raid Spanish commerce and interdict the flow of supplies to Méndez's force in Rio de Janeiro and Montevideo. The more heavily armed regular warships would seek an opportunity to engage dispersed elements of the enemy squadron. In the unlikely event that the Spaniards should attack in the Pacific before the return of the Philippine expedition, the Peruvians believed that the strengthened defenses of Valparaíso and Callao could inflict as much punishment as they received. The allied ironclads, upon returning from Asia, would encounter and defeat an exhausted and damaged enemy force.

The final portion of the Peruvian plan—a coup de grace most likely inspired by Colonel Prado—was contingent upon considerable good luck. If the wooden squadron could neutralize Méndez's force, if the Philippine expedition returned to combine with the allied vessels in the Atlantic, or if the allies could launch a third flotilla being purchased in the United States, they would attack Cuba and Puerto Rico. This operation, possibly in conjunction with internal uprisings and an allied invasion with an army dispatched by way of Panama, might secure the independence of Spain's two remaining colonies in the New World. For good measure, the allies might gain retribution for the bombardment of Valparaíso and Callao by shelling ports in Spain itself, before returning home.[64]

At a series of conferences in Santiago, Chile's civilian leaders and Captain Juan Williams Rebolledo pressed their position, while the Peruvian plan was championed by Manuel and José Pardo, supported by Tucker and Captain Salcedo. Ultimately, the Chileans gave their tentative concurrence to the Peruvian proposal. Before returning to Lima, Premier Pardo gave final instructions to his uncle José and the admiral. The two men were to seek a stronger Chilean commitment to Peru's strategy. In accord with the treaty of alliance, Tucker should obey the orders of the Santiago government—to a point. He might undertake minor naval operations desired by President Pérez. But the *almirante* was to conserve his resources for the Peruvian-backed offensive; he should not undertake a full-scale campaign to the South Atlantic without new instructions from Lima or, in an emergency, without the approval of José Pardo. The debate over strategy, however, was moot for the moment: the fleet was not prepared for any significant operation. All of the warships of both squadrons needed repair; the vessels lacked vital equipment and supplies, especially proper ammunition; the allied force was very short of both officers and men, and these had to be disciplined, trained, and organized into an effective force. It was "a colossal undertaking," asserted Butt without exaggeration.[65]

Immediately after assuming command of the fleet, Tucker thoroughly inspected his ships. He found them to be in much poorer condition than anticipated.[66] To avoid impoundment in neutral Britain, the *Independencia* had put to sea with an unpainted bottom; it was now badly fouled, greatly reducing her speed. The ironclad entered the Valparaíso dry dock for cleaning and painting, but on August 17 Tucker sent her to the larger facility at Callao, freeing the Chilean dock to receive the smaller warships. The admiral temporarily transferred his flag to the *Unión*. The old frigate *Apurímac*, with a broken main shaft and a leaky hull, was towed to Callao. The *Huáscar* was cleaned in the Valparaíso dry dock and was followed by the *América* and *Unión*. Severely pounded by storms in the Strait of Magellan, the twin corvettes needed extensive work. Both had damaged hulls; the *América* was taking on twenty inches of water per day. That vessel's sails were in shreds, and her engine was faulty, too. In addition to essential repairs, Tucker ordered modifications to the rigging of the *América* and *Huáscar* as well as to the machinery of the latter vessel. The Chilean *Esmeralda* and *Maipú* required new boilers, while the *Covadonga* needed sails.[67]

The limited dry-dock facilities and shortages of materials delayed major repairs to the fleet. But as the vessels waited their turn to enter the dock, Tucker put his mariners to work "scrubbing, cleaning, scrapping and painting." He equipped his vessels as completely as possible and put everything in working order. The admiral provided plans for condensers to desalinate seawater and a diagram for new galley stoves. The sailors refurbished gigs, mended sails and rigging, cut and painted new signal flags. Meanwhile, Tucker assembled supplies of food, clothing, medicines, and small arms.[68]

The fleet's armament was a special concern for the admiral. He ordered McCorkle to test the shells employed in the Peruvian squadron; at the battle of Abtao these projectiles had exploded prematurely, sometimes before leaving the gun muzzles. The former Confederate ordnance specialist immediately identified the problem—excessively long fuzes—for the South had experienced the same difficulty with detonators of similar design. Lima sent replacements, but these were too short; 60 percent of the shells tested did not burst at all. With specifications provided by McCorkle, the arsenal at Callao later rectified the problem. In the meantime, McCorkle and Captain José E. Gorostiaga, a Chilean ordnance officer, developed an adequate fuze of alternate design, which was manufactured in Chile. The fleet also was stocked with sufficient shells, solid shot, and armor-piercing bolts. For the latter, McCorkle supplied drawings of the projectile developed for the Confederacy by John M. Brooke.[69]

Under Tucker's command the Peruvian Navy probably became the world's first sea service to emphasize offensive torpedo warfare. He ordered huge spar torpedoes mounted on the *Independencia* and

Huáscar; the *Unión* and *América* were fitted to receive these devices when needed. The technology employed was Confederate. Tucker provided diagrams for the explosive devices themselves, carriers (*porta-torpedos*) to handle them safely, and spars that could be raised or lowered while the vessels mounting them were underway. The Peruvians were enthusiastic supporters of the new mode of warfare; they had embraced the "infernal machine" before the battle of Callao and now were building a fleet of torpedo boats for harbor defense. The Chileans, however, remained skeptical, and Tucker did not formally request the arming of their ships with torpedoes until five months after assuming command of the allied fleet.[70]

In addition to their own spar torpedoes, the four major vessels of the Peruvian squadron carried torpedo-mounted steam launches, which the admiral would send against enemy ships in the confusion of battle. This basic concept likely had been discussed during the Civil War by Confederate naval officers bottled up in several Southern ports; it was a logical solution to their major deficiency in offensive torpedo warfare— inadequate delivery systems. The specific technology and tactics adopted by Tucker, however, probably were developed by former commander Hunter Davidson, the successor to Matthew F. Maury at the head of the Confederate Submarine Battery Service. Davidson perfected electrical mines for the defense of the James River and became an avid proponent of offensive torpedoes, too. In April 1864 he attacked the frigate *Minnesota* at Hampton Roads in the torpedo launch *Squib*.[71]

In January 1866 Davidson and his partner Henry H. Doty—a shadowy figure who had recently obtained British patents for a system of retractable spar torpedoes—signed a contract in London with Chilean agent Ambrosio Rodríguez to purchase, equip, and provide a crew for the *Henrietta*, a fast iron-hulled steamer. They would take the vessel to Chilean waters and attack the Spanish squadron with three steam torpedo launches carried on board the mother ship. The partners were promised bounties of $100,000 for sinking the ironclad *Numancia* and half that amount for the destruction of each of Spain's wooden frigates. Rodríguez hoped that Davidson might "destroy the entire Spanish squadron in one month," giving Chile "revenge with much economy." The expedition encountered a series of problems, however, and the *Henrietta* did not reach Chile until July 24, 1866, three months after the Spaniards had departed. At Valparaíso, Davidson met Tucker, who had arrived two days earlier. The two former Confederates, who had served together with the James River Squadron in 1862, were close companions for the next month. Tucker requested that his "old shipmate" be commissioned a commander in the Peruvian Navy and assigned as flag captain of the *Independencia*. Describing Davidson as "the most experienced and practical 'Torpedo' officer in the United

States or Confederate Navies," the admiral asserted that his friend would be "highly useful as we contemplate using torpedoes in the squadron." Lima did not accede to Tucker's request but sent Davidson to the United States, where he would be available to command a potent ironclad being acquired there.[72]

The task of obtaining sufficient personnel and putting them into fighting trim was Tucker's foremost problem. Manuel Pardo had brought from Lima only a few officers to replace the insubordinate ones, and several weeks would pass before a full complement could be assembled. As news of Tucker's appointment appeared in United States newspapers, several former Confederates sought employment under him. The admiral would have liked to hire more of his "late naval friends." But such appointments would have caused further political embarrassment for the government; except for his appeal on behalf of Davidson, Tucker refrained from asking for them.[73]

Captain Salcedo, who took command of the *Huáscar* and the Peruvian division of the fleet, remained in Valparaíso only long enough to assist in the initial organization of the squadron. After his return to Lima on September 17, Captain José María García became chief of the Peruvian squadron. A twenty-three-year navy veteran who had been wounded at the battle of Callao, García doubled as skipper of the *Independencia*. Acting Captain Alejandro Muñoz assumed command of the *Huáscar*. An officer with two decades of experience (including some with the French Navy), Muñoz had been furloughed because of his support for the Pezet regime. Commander Juan Pardo de Zela, another twenty-year man, resumed charge of the *América*, which he had skippered on her maiden voyage from France. Command of the *Unión* changed hands three times, as additional officers arrived from Lima. That corvette's initial skipper was nineteen-year-veteran Lieutenant Commander Camilo Carrillo. Peru's foremost naval intellectual of his generation, Carrillo had converted the wooden steamer *Loa* to an armorclad ram and commanded the vessel against the Spaniards at Callao. Tucker later tabbed this talented mariner as executive officer of his flagship *Independencia*, and Lieutenant Commander Marcelo T. Proaño took over the *Unión*. Finally, Lieutenant Commander Juan G. Moore—a highly respected British-trained officer with a dozen years' service—became skipper of the *Unión*, while Proaño went to the *Huáscar* as second officer. Lieutenant commanders Nicolás Portal and Ulises Delboy served as executive officers of the *América* and *Unión*, respectively. It was a good, solid staff of senior officers. To the minister of war and marine, Tucker expressed his "pleasure and satisfaction . . . with the commanding and other officers now in the squadron" and requested that they "not be superseded."[74]

From his senior officers the admiral obtained the names of experienced junior men, and he asked for their assignment to the fleet. But Tucker apparently was unable to assemble an adequate corps of young line officers. On the *Unión*, noted Butt, the captain and executive officer "alone navigated the ship; and they placed but little confidence in their junior officers—which was a most fortunate thing." A large majority of the petty officers in both squadrons were foreigners, primarily from the British Isles, as were most of the engineers and their hands. Serving under contract, these key personnel demanded substantial pay raises at reenlistment time. The resulting wage differentials evoked frequent complaints from men of equal rank and constituted a nagging problem for Tucker. He advised General Bustamante, the minister of war and marine, that vessels in combat required at least three surgeons, but Lima could provide the admiral with only one physician per ship.[75] Experienced seamen also were very difficult to obtain. Sailors in Valparaíso, understandably, preferred service with Chile's 250-vessel merchant marine to the rigors and dangers of the wartime navy. A special recruiting office was opened in the Chilean port, and Tucker received some men from Callao. With enlistment bonuses of two months' pay, he assembled barely enough sailors to man the fleet. The admiral was well supplied with musicians, however. The *Independencia* boasted a nineteen-member band.[76]

Tucker's personal staff was headed by Commander McCorkle, who served as inspector general and chief ordnance officer. Lieutenant Commander Butt was assistant chief of staff and fleet signal officer. The admiral requested a bilingual lawyer to serve as his secretary, and Lima dispatched Emilio Bonifaz, the chief of the consular section of the Foreign Ministry. The Virginian loyally secured the appointment of his original interpreter-secretary, Jorge Mendiola, as auditor of the Peruvian squadron.[77] Tucker's staff also included an officer who may have been unique among Latin American navies of that day. The tantalizing documents are inconclusive; but to all appearances, "Presbyter" James F. Clark, the "contract English chaplain" of the *Independencia*, was Protestant. Probably hired in Britain by Salcedo at the request of that ironclad's large English contingent, Clark was among the handful of the squadron's original officers who served under Tucker.[78]

The admiral strove to win the loyalty and confidence of his Peruvian subalterns. As in his previous commands, he consulted with his officers, drawing upon their knowledge and experience. He commended them in correspondence with his superiors in Lima, and for at least one officer, Marcelo Proaño, he secured a long-overdue promotion. Tucker also defended the navy's institutional interests. When Minister of War and Marine Bustamante assigned three army colonels to the squadron's one-hundred-man infantry garrison, the *almirante* vigorously protested that these men, most awkwardly, ranked his ship commanders.

They were recalled. Tucker worked quietly to block a proposed transfer of the *Huáscar* to Chilean command, an option strongly opposed by Peru's mariners.[79]

On a subtler level, the admiral sought to overcome the prejudices and cultural differences that separated the Latin American officers and the Virginians. Walter Butt explained that service with the Peruvians required "much diplomacy" to avoid "offending their sensitivity and pride." He was "deeply impressed" by Tucker's "wonderful tact, . . . wisdom and moderation . . . displayed under the most trying circumstances." The admiral's "intelligent and just decisions" won him the "confidence and esteem" of many officers who served under him, and he even gained the begrudging respect of several "avowed enemies." Some officers who had strongly opposed the admiral's appointment admitted that the fleet "had never been in so good a condition for effective service" as during Tucker's tenure. The admiral always retained the Episcopal faith of his father (and that era's quasi-official religion in the United States Navy), but Tucker was likely very knowledgeable and tolerant of his hosts' religion: his mother and both sisters were converts to Roman Catholicism. During the Virginian's service in the allied fleet, his language took on an ecumenical flavor. "I pray to all the saints in the calendar for success," he wrote Minister Barreda in anticipation of a cruise against the enemy.[80]

The admiral's relations with the Chileans were awkward. He was anxious to begin organizing the fleet; soon after raising his flag on the *Independencia*, the Virginian asked José Pardo to make inquiries in Santiago about Tucker's "faculties" within the Chilean squadron. Chile's officials did not respond. They did not inform him officially of Admiral Blanco's resignation, nor did Santiago formally appoint him chief of the allied fleet. Although Chilean authorities addressed him as such, the admiral signed himself for two months as "second chief" or "acting chief" of the fleet. On September 14 Tucker put the matter directly to Minister of Marine Federico Errázuriz, asking him to "define the exact limit" in which the admiral should concern himself with "the minutiae and detail" of the Chilean vessels. The minister replied, belatedly and vaguely, that Tucker's authority included everything required "to maintain the personnel and matériel of the squadron in the best possible footing for service." Tucker promptly sent a copy of this letter to Commander Ramón Cabieses of the *Esmeralda*, the senior Chilean officer, instructing him to keep the *almirante* informed about "all affairs of the squadron that effect the public interest or that in your judgment I should know." Cabieses was to obey the signals of the flagship while at sea or in combat.[81]

Captain Juan Williams Rebolledo resumed command of the Chilean division on October 9. The new commodore, who already had participated in conferences with Tucker, had little respect for the *nortea-mericano*. In a mid-September letter dripping with sarcasm, Williams had told a friend that the Virginian had not yet ordered "any measure which reveals his vast and great professional (!) knowledge." To another correspondent Williams conceded that "Tucker may be a great sailor, but he is no organizing genius. If something has been accomplished in the Peruvian division, it is due to Salcedo." Relations between Tucker and Williams remained cool but correct. The two men generally concurred in strategies later adopted by the allies. Williams supported Tucker's request to arm Chile's vessels with torpedoes, claiming that the same idea had occurred to him before the former Confederate arrived. But the Chilean commodore obviously disdained serving under Peru's admiral. Tucker avoided interference with the internal affairs of the Chilean squadron, and when the allies undertook joint maneuvers, the haughty Williams remained on shore.[82]

As the fleet completed its repairs and received its personnel, Tucker began training his men for combat. He established a daily shipboard routine, exercising the sailors at the great guns and drilling them in the use of small arms. The crews practiced "loosing and furling sails, and reefing top sails," recorded Butt; "there were boat drills twice a week, and firing at a target at anchor and underway." About once each week, Tucker took the ships a few miles out to sea, where they spent the day performing "various evolutions of the line, frequently under sail alone."[83] On December 7 the Peruvian squadron and the Chilean *Maipú* began a dozen days of maneuvers off the Juan Fernández Islands, some six hundred miles west of Valparaíso. The admiral expressed his satisfaction with the performance of both ships and men.[84] The Peruvian vessels along with the *Esmeralda* returned to the same waters for three weeks of training in late January and early February 1867. During this cruise Tucker's torpedo-boat exercises and gunnery drills produced "very good results."[85]

While the admiral prepared for his immediate objective, a campaign against the Spaniards, he also instituted projects for the long-range development of the Peruvian Navy. He appointed McCorkle, Butt, Pardo de Zela, and the captain of the *Huáscar* (probably Muñoz) to a board charged with preparing a code of navy regulations, a complete system of signals (for day, night, and telegraph), an ordnance manual, and a handbook of fleet tactics for steam warships. These officers and subordinates chosen by them were ordered to begin their work without delay; when they were finished, Tucker would submit the results to Lima for approval and publication. The admiral recommended that copies of the forthcoming naval regulations and ordnance manual be provided to all officers on active duty.[86]

Tucker's panel apparently did not draft a new navy code to replace the one inherited from Spain; however, the board likely completed its other assignments. Modern English-language works on ordnance, signals, and fleet tactics were located, adapted to Peru's needs, and translated. Manuscript copies of these manuals soon circulated among the officers of the fleet.[87] The work on ordnance may not have been printed. But within a few years, the signal book was published,[88] and the treatise on naval tactics appeared in both Peruvian and Chilean editions.[89] The admiral recommended the establishment of a navy reserve, enrolling all of Peru's civilian mariners for possible service during national emergencies. He also suggested the formation of a navy signal corps, a recommendation soon approved by the government.[90]

To end the precarious dependence upon contract petty officers and able seamen, often foreigners, Tucker on October 25, 1866, proposed a "school of practical apprenticeship"; this ultimately would give Peru "a navy of its own." As outlined by the admiral, the school should be established on board a warship anchored at Callao. Up to eight hundred eighteen-year-olds would be enrolled for a three-year course to include academic subjects as well as naval training. After each graduation, products of the school would be assigned to the fleet for five years' service, while a freshman class of equal size filled their places. The *almirante* recommended that the school ship be officered by men "of experience, zeal and steadiness" and that the instructors "be selected from among the best and most loyal" sailors, for their "conduct and example" would "exercise an influence very lasting." Tucker believed that "discipline should be good and firm, without harshness." Well-behaved students who made adequate progress should be rewarded; incorrigible lads and those not making the grade should be sent home. Soon after Tucker's friend Manuel Pardo assumed the Peruvian presidency in 1872, he decreed the establishment of a school for naval apprentices on the frigate *Apurímac*, with a program very similar to that recommended by the admiral six years earlier.[91]

Rear Admiral John Randolph Tucker, Peruvian Navy, 1867. (Courtesy of John Randolph Tucker, Pensacola, Florida)

Engraving of an American frigate of the *Java* class. (Official U.S. Navy photograph)

Wash drawing of the CSS *Patrick Henry* by Clary Ray (ca. 1898). (Official U.S. Navy photograph)

R. G. Skerrett's 1901 drawing of the CSS *Palmetto State* shows the characteristic design of the Confederate rams. (Official U.S. Navy photograph)

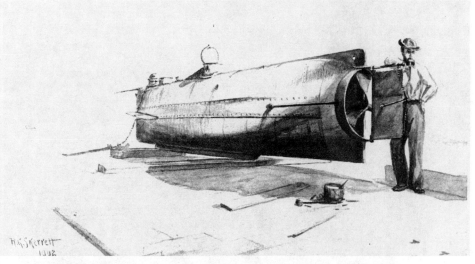

CSS *H. L. Hunley* shown in a 1902 drawing by R. G. Skerrett, after a painting in the Confederate Museum. (Official U.S. Navy photograph)

Lieutenant Walter Raleigh Butt, Confederate States Navy. (Official
U.S. Navy photograph)

Lithograph of the armored frigate *Independencia* in the F. L. Barreda Papers. (Courtesy of Special Collections, Morris Library, Southern Illinois University at Carbondale)

Ironclad *Huáscar*. (Courtesy of Instituto de Estudios Histórico-Marítimos del Perú)

Admiral Tucker's calling card. (Courtesy of A. Royall Turpin, Richmond, Virginia)

Plaza de Armas at Iquitos, ca. 1872. (From the Galt Diary folder, National Anthropological Archives. Smithsonian Institution photo no. 84-227)

Tucker and Butt at San Antonio de Acurucay, on the lower Ucayali, 1868. (Engraving in Antonio Raimondi, *El Perú*, vol. 3)

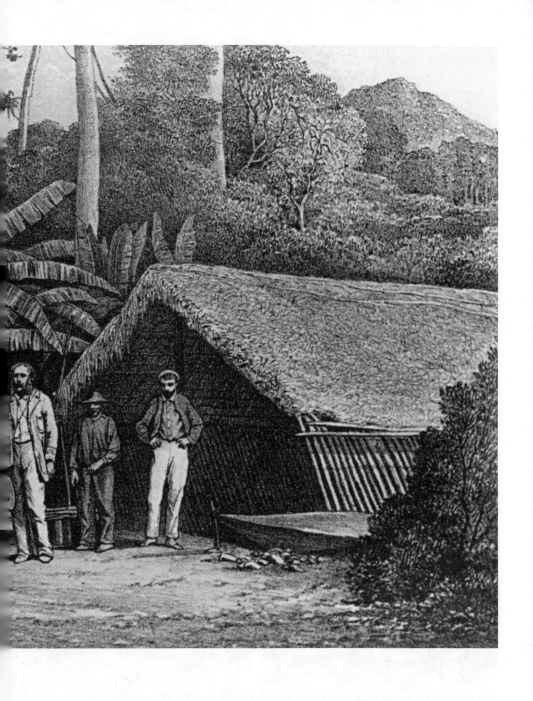

The Hydrographic Commission on the Ucayali River, 1868. Tucker stands third from the left, McCorkle is crouched in the center foreground, the chinless Wertheman is in the rear among Conibo Indians, and Butt stands on the far right, with the steamer *Napo* in the background. (From the Galt Diary folder, National Anthropological Archives. Smithsonian Institution photo no. 84-226)

Exploring steamer *Tambo* at the Pusey and Jones yard, Wilmington, Delaware, 1870. (Courtesy of Hagley Museum and Library)

Surgeon and Acting Paymaster Francis L. Galt

Surgeon and Acting Paymaster Francis Land Galt, Confederate States Navy. (Official U.S. Navy photograph)

COMMANDER JAMES H. ROCHELLE.
CONFEDERATE STATES NAVY.

Lieutenant James Henry Rochelle, Confederate States Navy. (Official U.S. Navy photograph)

"Flagship" of the Pichis expedition, 1873, painted by an unknown artist. (Courtesy of John Randolph Tucker, Pensacola, Florida)

"My home in Iquitos on the Amazon, 1874." (From the Galt Diary folder, National Anthropological Archives. Smithsonian Institution photo no. 84-228)

President Tucker of the Hydrographic Commission, ca.
1874. (Courtesy of A. Royall
Turpin, Richmond, Virginia)

Nelson Berkeley Noland, a
success at age forty. (Courtesy of Nelson B. Noland,
Colorado Springs, Colorado)

Arturo Wertheman descends the Tambo River, 1876. (Engraving in Arturo Wertheman, *Informe de la exploración de los ríos Perené y Tambo*)

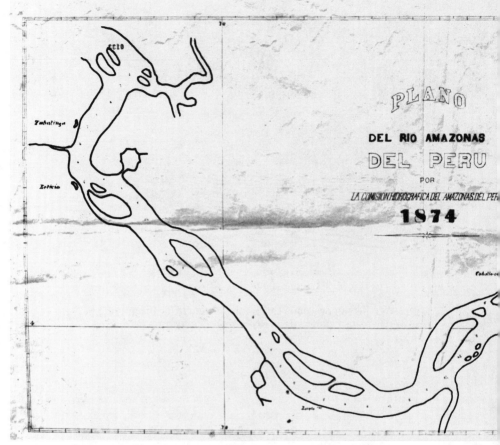

Enhanced photo of an original map (sheet 1 of the Amazon navigation series) by the Hydrographic Commission. (Courtesy of the Ministry of Foreign Relations, Torre Tagle Palace, Lima, Peru)

Pliego I

Latitud Sur
Longitud Este de Greenwich

CHAPTER SIX

Old Battles Rejoined

By THE END OF NOVEMBER 1866, Admiral Tucker was ready to
begin the long-awaited cruise against the enemy. He needed only
to take on full supplies of coal and provisions.[1] But Lima and Santiago
again differed over the proper course of action. Peru continued to press
its hesitant ally for a major naval campaign, beginning with a thrust at
the Philippines. As the end of the year drew nearer, however, the
impatient Peruvians became willing to embrace almost any offensive
operation, including Santiago's original proposal for a less ambitious
attack in the South Atlantic.[2] Chile's naval officers along with a sizable
element of the public and press still clamored for retribution against
Spain for the bombardment of Valparaíso.[3] But the influential merchants of that port feared the return of a greatly reinforced enemy fleet,
and the government shrank from the financial burdens and attendant
political costs of a large-scale war at sea. Madrid, meanwhile, indicated
its desire for a negotiated peace based upon the status quo, and offers of
mediation came from the United States and, jointly, from Britain and
France. Bound by treaty to a common course, the American Union
alliance began to unravel.

The Santiago government urged its ally to accept the Anglo-
French mediation proposal, entailing an immediate truce between the
belligerents. Lima desperately wanted to press the war further; and
should mediation become desirable, Peru preferred the plan sponsored
by the United States, which did not require an armistice.[4] Colonel
Prado insisted that an honorable peace demanded a final offensive blow
against the Spaniards. He still clung to his Quixotic dream of liberating
Cuba and increasingly looked to a successful war to bolster his eroding
political base at home. The aging generals who had dominated Peruvian
politics since independence had not accepted the presidency of the
upstart, forty-year-old Colonel Prado. Furthermore, the dictator's brilliant young "Cabinet of the Stars" championed reforms—a sweeping
reorganization of public finance, the pruning of the bloated state pen-
sion and pay rolls, and religious toleration—that angered powerful
interest groups.[5]

Prado sought to legitimize his regime through the election in October 1866 of a constituent assembly which named him provisional president the following February. The political campaign, however, intensified partisan spirit. While a rash of military revolts erupted in the provinces, Prado's civilian critics attacked the government from the pages of pamphlets and newspapers. Charges of irregularity in the negotiation of foreign loans and arms purchases brought the resignation of Premier and Finance Minister Manuel Pardo in November 1866, followed during the next six months by those of Foreign Minister Toribio Pacheco and envoy Federico L. Barreda, in Washington. Prado continued to exploit Peruvian nationalism and struggled to maintain the loyalty of the armed forces. But his appointment of Admiral Tucker and the protracted disciplinary proceedings against the naval officers who had refused to serve under Tucker became a running political sore.[6] The former Confederate, meanwhile, became the subject of a diplomatic imbroglio between Peru and the United States.

Death to Tucker!

Captain Lizardo Montero and the more than thirty other officers removed from the fleet at Valparaíso reached Callao on August 14, 1866. Held briefly under guard on the transport *Callao*, they soon were put ashore on San Lorenzo Island, just off the port. Their confinement was nominal; within two weeks, some of these men were seen walking the streets of Lima. Minister of War and Marine Bustamante indicted Montero and the others for insubordination, desertion in the face of the enemy, and treason and appointed a panel of senior army officers to render judgment in the case. But the court-martial required almost six months to reach a decision. In the meantime, recalled Walter Butt, friends of the accused officers waged a "vigorous attack" upon the Virginians in the press, alluding to them "in the most contemptuous terms." Because these journals circulated within the fleet at Valparaíso, the newspaper campaign was "especially disagreeable" and "subversive of discipline."[7]

At the end of September, Tucker, Butt, and two captains of the Peruvian squadron went to Santiago for meetings with officials and a gala presidential ball. At 1:30 A.M. on October 1, Captain Carlos Varea began a mutiny on the temporary flagship *Unión*. An army officer assigned to that ship's garrison, Varea—like Lizardo Montero—was a nephew of Colonel José Balta, President Prado's major rival. Varea hoped to seize the squadron, free his kinsman Montero and the other officers believed detained at Callao, and spearhead a decisive revolution against the government. The mutineers, including most of the soldiers and many sailors, launched their movement by cutting down Admiral Tucker's pennant and shouting "Long Live Montero! Death to the Yankees! Death to Tucker!" They quickly overpowered the ship's officers and placed most of the foreign sailors under guard; McCorkle was held at bayonet point in the admiral's cabin. At Varea's orders the engineers (mainly Englishmen) fired the boilers, but they left the valves open so that the vessel could not build adequate steam. The commotion on the *Unión* alerted the fleet's acting commander, Captain Alejandro Muñoz of the *Huáscar*. He quickly brought his potent ironclad alongside the wooden corvette and threatened to sink her if the rebels weighed anchor. Varea and forty-eight of his supporters lowered three boats into the water from the opposite side of their vessel and fled to shore. Chilean authorities apprehended them a few hours later.[8]

Upon learning of the mutiny, Tucker hurried back to Valparaíso. The admiral wanted to hang Varea—quickly. But under the modified Spanish naval code still employed by Peru, the squadron lacked sufficient senior officers to render a death sentence. Legal maneuvers and political pressures delayed the court-martial, and Varea, who was held on shore in Valparaíso, eventually escaped.[9] Although lacking concrete evidence of a broader conspiracy, the Prado regime charged that its political foes had instigated Varea's mutiny. The administration soon exiled to Chile Colonel Balta and several other high-ranking officers, including Peru's Great Man, Marshal Ramón Castilla. These arbitrary deportations provoked widespread disturbances in Peru and loud protests from democratically minded Chileans.[10]

The trial of Montero and his codefendants began in mid-December at the Callao naval arsenal; but riots outside the building by supporters of the "Four Aces" (as captains Montero, Grau, Ferreyros, and García y García came to be called) forced a change of venue to the frigate *Apurímac*, offshore. Linked to some of Peru's most influential families, the accused officers were defended by a brilliant team of lawyers. Luciano Benjamín Cisneros, the nation's foremost orator, represented Miguel Grau. José Antonio García y García, Peru's former chargé in Washington, spoke for his brother Aurelio.[11]

From every possible angle, the defense deftly parried the government's accusations. To the charge of insubordination they responded that their clients had not received valid, official orders to permit Tucker on their ships—only personal notes from Colonel Prado announcing the former Confederate's dispatch to Valparaíso and Lima's desire to have him named second chief of the allied fleet. Tucker had no post within the Peruvian squadron when he arrived at the Chilean port on July 22. He did not become second chief of the fleet until his appointment under the protocol of August 13. The Peruvian officers, argued their attorneys, had not deserted in the face of the enemy, nor had their actions delayed

113

offensive operations. Premier Pardo had removed them from command. At that time all Spanish warships were oceans away, and the allied fleet required time-consuming repairs before it could begin any cruise against the Spaniards.

Playing upon Peruvian nationalism, the defense turned the charge of treason against the government. The accused officers had committed no traitorous act; on the contrary, these men had defended the fatherland bravely at the battles of Abtao and Callao. Through its appointment of the mercenary Tucker, however, the Prado regime had sullied Peru's honor and humiliated its navy. In his indictment, General Bustamante had alluded briefly to the hiring of the former Confederate. He did not mention the embarrassing personal conflicts between the allied officers and within the Peruvian squadron that had prompted the original search for Tucker and the final decision to place him in command. Neither did the war minister specify the many professional attributes that recommended the admiral's appointment. Bustamante only asserted that the well-known bravery of Peru's officers, by itself, did not qualify them to "direct a powerful squadron," especially in "distant and dangerous expeditions." Therefore, it had been necessary "to entrust the squadron to a chief with proven experience."[12]

The defense attorneys retorted that Peru had several senior naval officers with the requisite qualifications to direct a campaign against the Spaniards.[13] José Antonio García y García, who presented the most extensive brief, took the argument one step further: he denigrated Tucker's career. To support his case García provided Spanish-language facsimiles of the entries for Tucker from the 1854 and 1856 United States Navy registers. Through judicious mistranslations he obfuscated the Virginian's nearly eighteen years of sea duty with the "Old Navy." He falsely indicated that Tucker had spent long periods inactive, "waiting orders." The huge ship of the line *Pennsylvania*, which Tucker commanded in 1856, became in the lawyer's translation a "pontoon" (a small supply ship). García wrongly suggested that Tucker had attained his rank through merit rather than seniority and that his grade of commander—the second highest in the United States Navy during that era—equated with that of "first lieutenant on our roster." But the Confederates, like all revolutionaries, asserted García, "lavished promotions, without standards or prudence, to attract adherents"; they "conferred upon [Tucker] the rank of commodore."

According to the lawyer, Tucker had not commanded a squadron or participated in a significant battle during his entire naval career. He had done nothing "to attract . . . the esteem of his country." The Virginian's record clearly demonstrated his professional "inferiority to many chiefs of our navy, who have made long and dangerous voyages, directed squadrons and battled bravely." Although David McCorkle had a decade more naval experience than Commodore Montero—the most senior of the accused officers—García claimed that the ordnance expert had not previously held a commission in any navy. The attorney similarly declared that Butt's name did not appear in the registers of the United States Navy; therefore, he might only have had experience with the "rebels of his country." After grotesquely distorting the service records of "this trinity unknown even in their own country," García abused the Peruvian officers who had consented to serve under Tucker. He accused Captain Salcedo of "shameless deficiencies" and charged that the replacement officers Salcedo had brought from Lima were "the least qualified of the . . . Peruvian Navy."[14]

The old army officers who heard the defense lawyers skillfully respond to the relatively weak prosecution were primarily political conservatives. They probably had little stomach for rendering an unpopular verdict in favor of the reformist and now tottering regime of Colonel Prado. The most prominent member of the panel—General José Rufino Echenique, a former president—had a son among the defendants. On February 7, 1867, a great banquet was held at the Hotel Maury to celebrate the anniversary of the battle of Abtao and the anticipated exoneration of Montero and his former subalterns. The affair was attended by some of the accused officers, many additional military men, members of Congress, and other prominent figures. The guests were feted with anti-Tucker toasts, speeches, and even poems. Three days later the court-martial found all of the accused officers innocent and ordered their restoration to active duty.[15]

A War of Salutes

From Valparaíso on October 16, 1866, Captain Fabius Maximus Stanly, skipper of the USS *Tuscarora*, wrote to Admiral George F. Pearson, the commander of the United States South Pacific Squadron, at Callao, with a complaint that Admiral Tucker had been discourteous toward him. The incident had occurred almost three months earlier, on July 22, the morning Tucker arrived in the Chilean port to join the allied fleet. Stanly—an "acquaintance" of Tucker in the "Old Navy" and one of Dahlgren's skippers at Charleston—made a visit to the Virginian on the mail steamer *Paita* soon after she had anchored. The United States officer approached Tucker "in the usual manner of respect," extending his hand and saying, "How do you do, Admiral Tucker, I am Commander Stanly of the *Tuscarora*." According to Stanly, the admiral "slowly extended his hand, but did not rise from his leaning posture, on a rail, nor take his foot down from a box." The visitor, he recounted, told the former Confederate that Commodore Montero would not acknowledge Tucker's position; Stanly offered to put the *Tuscarora*'s gig at the admiral's disposal. "I have taken my measures," the admiral reportedly told the officer. Tucker "never looked at me," wrote Stanly, so the latter "touched [his] cap and cleared out." The North American officer reported that in the weeks that followed, he acknowledged Tucker's rank with the "usual salutes" when passing him in boats. But Stanly warned Admiral Pearson that there was "some danger of collision" between the two men; should this happen, asserted Stanly, "Admiral Tucker will personally get the worst of it."[16]

For Pearson, Tucker's reported behavior toward Stanly was not only a personal slight but also a violation of the "well known and officerlike conduct" required between the naval officers of friendly nations. The Yankee admiral demanded that Tucker "make an immediate and satisfactory apology." If one was not forthcoming, Pearson would order his commanders not to salute any Peruvian warship or to make the customary courtesy calls upon Peruvian officers, including Tucker.[17]

The Virginian viewed the incident with Stanly quite differently. He insisted that the latter man's call upon him at Valparaíso was not an official visit to him as a Peruvian officer, requiring the observance of naval protocol. Tucker, wearing civilian dress, had not yet assumed any official position in the fleet; he was a "mere passenger" on a private vessel. The former Confederate stated that Stanly "offered . . . some advice," which the admiral declined, explaining that he had made all of his "arrangements." According to Tucker's friend Hunter Davidson, who met the Virginian at Valparaíso and discussed with him the Stanly encounter, the federal officer gave the admiral advice about resolving the impasse with Montero. Tucker had not yet consulted with the Peruvian minister, nor had he received any official communication regarding Montero. The admiral's position was "very delicate," requiring "coolness, firmness and tact." It would have been improper to "have exposed his intentions to the exaggeration and cavil of the public tongue." Stanly blundered by injecting himself abruptly in a matter which did not concern him and about which Tucker could not converse. Tucker repeatedly told the United States officer, "Thank you, my course is pretty clearly defined, sir."

Tucker asserted that he had "endeavored to treat Stanly with marked politeness." Davidson averred that "in all which defines and elevates the character, and in all the amenities of private life, the American navy had no superior to John R. Tucker"; the admiral was "incapable of treating . . . Stanly rudely." As the dispute aired in the North American press, Davidson claimed that naval officers who were acquainted with the "respective merits and demerits" of Stanly and Tucker would have no difficulty arriving at the truth in this controversy.[18] The conflicting accounts of the Tucker-Stanly fracas, in fact, cannot be resolved with certainty. But the admiral's former Confederate friend felt secure in appealing to the judgment of fellow officers because Tucker had a great reputation for decorum and Stanly was a notoriously dislikable person.

Although he had demonstrated great courage in the Mexican War, Fabius Stanly's thirty-five years in the navy had been stormy, with frequent reprimands that continued even during his current posting with the South Pacific Squadron. A boorish bully, intemperate in speech and action, Stanly was disobedient to superiors and tyrannical toward subordinates. A series of quarrels and physical altercations with fellow officers—Stanly attempted to badger one man into a duel—led to his court-martial in 1851. The panel that heard the case, including Lieutenant John A. B. Dahlgren, suspended him from the service for a year and, most unusually, expressed its "unqualified disapprobation" of the language Stanly had used in testifying before the court. Four years later the navy's "plucking board"—fifteen officers charged with removing from active duty men who were "mentally, physically or morally" unfit—furloughed Stanly on half pay. Through the intercession of his politically influential brother Edward, Stanly was restored to the service the following year. But his demeanor apparently did not improve. A navy wife who met Stanly in 1860 deemed him "very shrewd—very quick and witty, often cutting and sharp." With his "cross and snappish way," she thought, Stanly "would not be either a pleasant superior officer or sailing companion."[19]

Given Stanly's aberrant personality and Tucker's difficult situation, the admiral probably viewed that officer's sudden apparition on the *Paita* like a visit of the plague. But more germane to the dispute that followed was the fact that Fabius Stanly was a North Carolina Unionist; his equally unpleasant brother Edward had been Lincoln's hated military governor of that Confederate state. Tucker seems not to have harbored deep animosity toward former Northern colleagues; he called socially upon Admiral Pearson and Captain Ridgley in Lima. Like most Confederate officers, however, he scorned Southern men who had cast their lot with the Union—"sordid natures," Admiral Semmes called them, "capable of drawing their swords against their own firesides."[20]

To Stanly, Tucker's coolness toward him seemed a trifling matter at first; he joked about the episode to United States Minister Judson Kilpatrick in Santiago and indicated no intention of reporting it. During the ensuing weeks, however, several other incidents magnified the significance of the original encounter and exacerbated the conflict. One of Tucker's friends, reported Stanly, said that the admiral had treated the North Carolinian "rudely" because the latter should have "gone with the South in the war." During a dinner conversation Tucker indicated to Captain Ridgley that he had "no intercourse" with Stanly because that officer "was from the South and fought with the North." Ridgley responded that he, too, was a Southerner—from Kentucky. The admiral explained that Kentucky had not seceded, as did North Carolina. Stanly complained that soon after arriving in Valparaíso, Walter Butt had sent a calling card on board the *Tuscarora* to a former Annapolis classmate, William H. Barton; the inscription read "Lieut. of Confederate States Navy." Furthermore, "several gentlemen" had told Stanly that "those junior officers, late Confederates"—perhaps including Tucker's son Engineer John Tarleton Tucker and young Tucker's friend Lieutenant James Norris, now serving in the Chilean Navy—had been "loud in their abuse of our Navy and Government."[21]

The reports that Tucker had shunned Stanly on the basis of sectional loyalties, together with less substantial accounts about the conduct of the admiral's former Confederate associates, provoked the ire of United States officials. Pearson, who earlier had vouched for Tucker's fitness to command the allied squadron, now railed that the Peruvian officer rebuffed Stanly "because the latter was not guilty of the atrocious crime of violating his oath" to the United States at a time when the government "required the service of every good officer!" Such conduct, wrote the old Union admiral, could not "for a moment be tolerated by me."[22]

While Tucker continued to insist that he had not been rude to Stanly and that their dispute began as an unofficial matter, the admiral also complained about Stanly's subsequent behavior toward him. When Tucker formally raised his flag on the *Independencia* "under a salute," he had been "officially announced to the harbor as a Peruvian Admiral." According to protocol, he soon received courtesy calls from the commanders of the British and French warships at the Chilean port, which Tucker then returned. If Stanly had called upon him, asserted the admiral, the former's visit "would have been promptly" returned. "No private feelings," he wrote, "could ever prevent me from promptly responding to all and every official courtesy extended to me as a Peruvian officer." Tucker's later "absence of official intercourse" with the United States officer arose from Stanly's failure to extend the "usual compliments" at the pennant-raising ceremony or on other occasions requiring the exchange of traditional courtesies. Tucker's remarks to Ridgley about Stanly, asserted the admiral, concerned "social intercourse" and not "ceremonious visits." Tucker disavowed the statements reportedly made by his former Confederate friends. The Virginian suggested that the dispute over courtesies be submitted for adjudication to Commodore Richard A. Powell, the senior British officer along that coast, "or any other impartial naval officer."

Tucker would "abide by the result."

In a letter to Peruvian envoy Barreda in Washington, the admiral privately explained his views. He claimed "the right common to all gentlemen" to choose his "social friends." But Tucker, as a Peruvian officer, would do "all things appertaining" to his "official position." If he was "known only as a Peruvian officer," as he wanted, there would be "no cause of trouble in the future."[23]

Tucker's stance in the Stanly affair was perhaps technically correct; in the view of Minister Kilpatrick, the admiral had been "frigidly polite" during an unofficial visit by Stanly at a very difficult moment. Tucker did have the right to choose his own friends. But as Kilpatrick also pointed out, the admiral had been "extremely foolish under the circumstances."[24] The Virginian's renowned decorum had failed him. Tucker's duty as a Peruvian officer obligated him to avoid unnecessary conflict with the United States government. Perhaps he might have swallowed his personal disdain for Stanly and sent that officer a private note expressing gratitude for his offer of assistance. Or better, Tucker could have chosen to interpret Stanly's call as an official one and returned the visit officially, without any significance regarding the private relationship between the two men. Tucker should not have revealed his feelings about Stanly to Captain Ridgley, and the admiral should have admonished his Southern subordinates to refrain from Yankee baiting.

In the first round of diplomatic correspondence over the protracted "Tucker-Stanly Affair," Peru's deputy minister of foreign affairs expressed Colonel Prado's "profound concern" about the matter and informed United States Minister Alvin P. Hovey, in Lima, that the government was investigating the incident. For the moment, however, Lima hoped that the problem would be considered personal, not official; that it would not disturb the friendly relations between the United States and Peru; and that Pearson would refrain from suspending traditional naval courtesies. After receiving Tucker's explanation of the matter, the Prado administration supported the position of its admiral, paraphrasing his response to Stanly's charges. "With these explanations," wrote Foreign Minister Pacheco, Lima believed that "the affair" should "entirely disappear." But if not, Peru would welcome arbitration, as Tucker suggested, by Commodore Powell. Expressing his fear that Pearson might already have ordered a suspension of courtesies, the minister warned that Peruvian officers could not initiate salutes unless they were certain that these would be returned. At Hovey's urging Pearson did not order a suspension of naval courtesies. Because he soon would be relieved of his post, the old sailor left the resolution of the problem to the diplomats and to his replacement as commander of the South Pacific Squadron—Rear Admiral John Adolphus Bernard Dahlgren.[25]

While Tucker had a low regard for officers from secessionist states who had remained loyal to the Union, Dahlgren thoroughly detested Confederates of every stripe. Few men emerged from the Civil War harboring greater bitterness. After his return to Washington from Charleston in March 1865, Dahlgren attended to the grim task of recovering from a secret grave the body of his son, Colonel Ulric Dahlgren, killed during the controversial raid on Richmond one year earlier. After many false reports about its location, Dahlgren obtained the cadaver. He then discovered, in horror, that a thief had cut a finger from Ulric's body, to remove a ring. Thereafter, the grieving father poured his sorrow and venom into a lengthy memoir of his son. The admiral charged that like the naval officer's close friend President Lincoln, Ulric had been "assassinated." The admiral asserted that the documents allegedly found on Ulric's body indicating his intention to burn Richmond and kill the Confederacy's top civilian leaders were forgeries. But perhaps privately he feared they were genuine. The naval officer argued that the killing of President Davis and his cabinet would have been legitimate acts of war. The man who could have most convincingly defended Ulric's reputation, General Judson Kilpatrick, who had commanded the Richmond raid and now served as United States Minister to Chile, privately assured the admiral that the rebel accusations were untrue. But Kilpatrick's testimony at an official inquiry had been frustratingly inconclusive. The admiral hoped to get his defense of Ulric before the public quickly; several publishers, however, rejected the work as uncommercial.[26]

The failure to publish his manuscript was only one among a series of disappointments. The admiral had not been reassigned, as he thought his due, to command of the Washington Navy Yard. Then, on September 25, 1866, he learned that the Navy Department would order him to relieve Admiral Pearson in Lima. Dahlgren complained that he was unjustly ordered to sea, out of proper rotation; in any event, he preferred the Mediterranean or Brazil squadrons to that in the South Pacific. A widower, the admiral had married Madeleine Godard Vinton the previous year, and on September 15 she had given birth with great difficulty to twins. In spite of her delicate health and the frailness of her infants, Mrs. Dahlgren insisted that she live with her husband in Lima. The admiral requested permission for his wife to travel with him on navy vessels, but Secretary Gideon Welles denied his application. Dahlgren's wife and babies would have to make the difficult journey, including passage across the insalubrious Isthmus of Panama, by themselves.[27]

Dahlgren long had been contemptuous of Secretary Welles, but this sentiment now developed into a deep hatred. The "Old Sinner," wrote the admiral, had done him "the greatest injury in his power." A relatively weak and unassertive member of the Lincoln and Johnson governments, Welles shrank from conflict with the cabinet's dominant member, Secretary of State William H. Seward.[28] Perhaps Dahlgren relished the opportunity that his new assignment presented for causing the navy chief discomfort. The admiral soon would draw Welles into a confrontation with Seward about recognizing Tucker as a Peruvian officer, a matter certain to bring an international dispute. By raising the question, Dahlgren also may have hoped to force a change in his assignment—allowing him to stay home or to be given command of the Mediterranean or Brazil squadrons. Clearly, this is what should have been done.

Several of Tucker's former colleagues from the "Old Navy" had been gladdened by reports of his Peruvian commission; indeed, Yankee officers and officials from the Navy Department had recommended the Virginian to Minister Barreda. Washington had not protested the appointment of the former Confederate, and United States envoys in Peru and Chile sought to avoid controversy in the matter. Reporting on Tucker's arrival in Lima, General Hovey referred to him as "late of the United States Navy" and regarded his appointment as "highly politic." General Kilpatrick, in Santiago, did not mention the admiral's previous affiliations, while Admiral Pearson initially identified Tucker as "formerly of our Navy."[29]

But for Dahlgren, who had refused to recognize Tucker's official position at Charleston, the Virginian "was still . . . ex-Comdr. Tucker," an unpardoned rebel "under parole and liable still to trial" for treason. The Yankee admiral "could not even by a ceremonial acknowledge him as anything else." Soon after learning that he would relieve Pearson, Dahlgren made informal inquiries concerning Tucker's status within the Peruvian service. On October 12—a week before Stanly wrote his complaint against Tucker and more than a month before the first report of the incident reached Washington—Dahlgren officially addressed Welles concerning his relations with the former Confederate. Was the Union officer to recognize Tucker's position as a Peruvian admiral and to extend "the customary courtesies, just as if he had never been in the rebel service?"[30]

Welles forwarded Dahlgren's letter to the State Department and asked:

> When the government of Peru places in a position which by the comity of nations requires courtesy and respect, a criminal offender against our government and laws, are our naval officers to be subjected to the ignominy of saluting and paying honors to this offender? . . . Can a government [Peru] which disregards courtesy require courtesy from those to whom it is discourteous? Are our faithful and patriotic officers to be compelled to do honor and extend courtesies to a rebel deserter who was their subordinate until he became a criminal?[31]

Dahlgren and Welles had chosen a very bad time to complicate relations between Washington and Lima. A few days earlier Minister Barreda and Secretary Seward had an extended conversation about United States mediation of the war with Spain. The Peruvian envoy spoke of the allied governments' hopes for the creation of "a continental solidarity which might forever put an end to European intervention in America." Seward revealed that "a grand continental alliance" of American states had "for some time . . . preoccupied" the secretary too. Grand alliance or no, Seward wanted the United States rather than England and France to act as mediator, thus enhancing the influence of Washington and checking that of London and Paris in the Americas. Barreda expressed his belief that the allies soon would deliver an offensive blow to the Spaniards which would enable them to seek, through Washington's good offices, an honorable peace. A memorandum on the "Seward-Barreda Plan" was approved by President Johnson and his cabinet on October 9 and soon won the tentative approbation of the Lima government. Peru only needed the concurrence of its allies and the prerequisite attack against the enemy by Tucker's fleet.[32]

In response to Welles's inquiry, Seward questioned Barreda about Peru's employment of Tucker. The envoy replied with a virtuoso display of logic, flattery, seduction—and dissimulation. In seeking experienced foreign officers for service against Spain, explained the minister, preference had been given to "natives of the United States." The Peruvians, who had not "hesitated in showing their sympathy with the North" during the Civil War, wanted to employ Union navy officers, "patriotic and energetic men" who had "raised so high the reputation" of the United States. But Northern officers would not abandon the federal service. Barreda, of course, had recruited and hired Tucker in the United States. He told Seward, however, that Washington's neutrality laws would not permit Peru to seek naval officers in the northern republic, so Lima had to avail itself of "what was offered to us in our own territory." Peru "accepted the services of men, who having lost everything in this country, had migrated to ours in search of occupation." Lima believed that its actions conformed to Washington's policy of "forgiveness and magnanimity" toward former Confederates. These men had erred in their interpretation of the United States Constitution. But their "American birth and . . . republican antecedents," continued Barreda in a paraphrase of President James Monroe's famous doctrine, made the Southern officers preferable to "Europeans, whose education, former habits and previous political principles" would not "exert a healthful influence on our continent." In accepting Peruvian commissions, Tucker and his associates had become citizens of Peru. Their "previous nationality" and "their past—a political error" had "disappeared."[33]

A personal friend of Barreda, Seward was inclined to agree with the minister's position. According to Chilean envoy Asta Buraga, the secretary thought the Navy Department's stance "absurd." The issue of naval courtesies divided the cabinet. Dahlgren, meanwhile, pressed for official instructions concerning Tucker. Navy Assistant Secretary William Faxon informally told the admiral to "take no notice of the cuss" and promised that the department would support him. But Dahlgren did not obtain the explicit, written instructions he desired.[34]

About November 20, however, Admiral Pearson's report of the Tucker-Stanly affair reached Washington. Tucker's explanation of the incident would not arrive for several more days, and Barreda initially believed Stanly's account. Just when the minister thought he had resolved the problem of Tucker's appointment, the new controversy had arisen. "Tucker must have lost his head," lamented the diplomat to his foreign minister. "His pretext to slight" Stanly had been the North Carolinian's loyalty to the Union. Barreda astutely perceived that the controversy would become a personal matter for Tennessean Andrew Johnson: the president and Stanly, as Southern Unionists, were "in the same situation." On November 21 Welles authorized Dahlgren to waive, at the admiral's discretion, paragraph ninety-six of the *Navy Regulations*, pertaining to the required exchange of courtesies with foreign officers, in his relations with Tucker.[35]

Dahlgren reached Lima on December 23 and rented a suite for his family at the Hotel Maury; here he met General Hovey, who also lived there. The admiral tried to discuss the Tucker matter with the minister, but Hovey avoided the topic. Perhaps the envoy already had some unofficial notice of Dahlgren's intransigent attitude. Hovey's last communication from Secretary Seward, dated December 6, had indicated that the State Department supported Pearson's demand for an apology from Tucker. But the Virginian's response to Stanly's charges, Peru's explanation of the affair, and Hovey's own report on the matter had not yet reached Washington. The minister leaned toward accepting the position of his host government, and he hoped for the eventual concurrence of the State Department.[36]

Hovey and Dahlgren had their first extended discussion of the "Tucker matter" on January 4, 1867; during the next ten days they met again and exchanged letters clarifying their conflicting views. Given the background of the two men, the diplomat should have won the debate. Although a brevet major general of volunteers who had played a key role in the Union victory at Shiloh, Hovey was a "political general," appointed from Indiana. Trained in the law, he had been a delegate to his state's constitutional convention and had served on the Indiana Supreme Court. Dahlgren had no formal legal training, but the brilliant officer had a longtime interest in law. His dispute with Hovey, only the latest of several the admiral had experienced with United States diplomatic personnel, would inspire him to write a treatise on *Maritime International Law*—essentially a defense of his own actions. In this work the admiral argued that resident ministers had primary responsibility for representing the United States in foreign countries, but naval commanders were "independent . . . and in nowise subordinate to the Minister." Officers should confer with diplomats about international incidents but act on their "own responsibility" as they deem "expedient and proper."

With great force and considerable lucidity, Dahlgren told Hovey that Tucker was an unpardoned rebel, liable to trial for treason, and that his expatriation to Peru did not remove him from this liability. The Yankee admiral and his officers could not possibly exchange courtesies with "ex-commander Tucker"; to do so would indicate their exculpation of his treason and impinge upon the constitutional prerogatives of the president, who alone could grant clemency. For Dahlgren, Tucker's reported behavior toward Stanly—which formed the basis for Washington's authorization for the denial of courtesies—was a secondary consideration. Hovey rather meekly expressed his accord with the admiral's sentiments but argued that the sailor's conclusions were incorrect. Tucker had not been tried or convicted of treason; as long as the Virginian remained a Peruvian admiral he was "entitled to all the rights and courtesies of his position." In observing traditional protocol toward Tucker, Dahlgren would "not salute the *man* but the *officer*" of a friendly government.[37]

Hovey was "very adverse to collision" with Peru and wanted Dahlgren to wait for further instructions from Washington before ordering the suspension of courtesies. The stubborn sailor ignored the diplomat's counsel. He had made his decision in the matter on December 27, a week before his first conference with Hovey. On January 9 Dahlgren instructed Commander Egbert Thompson, preparing to depart for Valparaíso in the *Dacotah*, to deny courtesies to "all persons" who remained excluded from the presidential amnesty of May 29, 1865.[38] Thus, this order applied to McCorkle and Butt as well as Tucker and exceeded Dahlgren's authorization from Secretary Welles, which referred only to the commander of the Peruvian squadron.

Dahlgren perhaps had convinced himself that his attitude toward Tucker arose solely from considerations of national honor, not personal animosity. "In justice to myself," he told Hovey, "nothing will be more painful to me than to interfere . . . with the prospects or interests of one who like myself has tasted so bitterly of misfortune." The world was "wide enough for us both and it is in sorrow, not in anger that I speak as I have done, of an old Comrade." The Yankee admiral "would not add the least to his present trouble."[39] To Tucker's friends, however, Dahlgren's actions smacked of a mean-spirited vendetta.

Hunter Davidson noted that no former Confederate had yet been tried for treason and predicted (correctly) that none would face trial on that charge. Therefore, "the basis" for Dahlgren's action was "purely personal." Tucker and Dahlgren had commanded the opposing squadrons at Charleston. The Yankee admiral "did not assist in any way in taking" the port; "the glory went wholly to Sherman." The Union officer, continued Davidson, now was blind to his duty. "He only sees his enemy and attacks him with a dash, which, had it been exhibited at Charleston, would have rid him of Tucker ever after." Dahlgren, sneered the former Confederate, was "better suited to the ordnance department at Washington than the command of a squadron either at Charleston or Callao." After Dahlgren's death in 1870, his widow gave a more generous explanation of her husband's behavior. Although frustrated by his inability to capture Charleston and rankled by the attendant criticism, the circumstances surrounding the death of his "heroic son of bright promise . . . inflicted deep wounds in the heart of the patriot father never to be healed in life."[40]

Commander Thompson and the *Dacotah* reached Valparaíso on January 19, followed two days later by the USS *Pensacola* under Tucker's old friend John L. Worden, whom he twice had met in combat. According to protocol Tucker sent his card to both United States captains. Worden, who had arrived from the Atlantic, apparently was unaware of Dahlgren's order; the former skipper of the *Monitor* wrote Tucker a note saying that he would soon visit the Peruvian admiral. But Thompson communicated Dahlgren's instruction to Worden, and neither officer paid a personal call on Tucker, as required by naval etiquette. Similarly, the two United States vessels fired salutes to the British and Chilean warships in the harbor but not to the Peruvian flagship. On January 21 or 22 Tucker issued a general order to the Peruvian squadron withholding courtesies from United States vessels and their officers. That action, he informed Minister of War and Marine Bustamante, was "necessary for the dignity of the Peruvian flag." His order would remain in force "until further orders from the Government—or changed by circumstances."[41]

On February 4, after receiving Tucker's report on these events at Valparaíso, Peru formally protested the behavior of the United States officers. Their failure to salute Tucker, wrote Pacheco, was not merely a discourtesy to the admiral's person but also one to Peru, "whose colors he wears in his pennant," and Chile too, for Tucker represented both nations. Lima, warned the minister, "cannot permit this matter to continue, slighting as it is to the National Flag." Privately, the foreign minister informed Hovey that Tucker had suspended courtesies toward the United States Navy. Admiral Dahlgren was livid. He asked Hovey to inquire whether the Virginian had prior authorization for his order. "Mr. Tucker," noted the North American admiral, "seems to be succeeding very well in making his own quarrel that of the Peruvian Government."[42] Hovey probably held a similar view of Dahlgren's conduct.

Pacheco responded obliquely to Hovey's inquiry, indicating that the Peruvian commander had acted in accordance with a previously established policy. Tucker, he wrote, "was authorized to shape his conduct" by the behavior of the United States officers. But the Peruvian minister promised that "if courtesy be shown to our officers and ships, it will be immediately returned." Dahlgren protested that no courtesy had been withheld or would be denied to the "Peruvian flag" or "any *bona fide* Peruvian officers." But Tucker's "retaliatory measure . . . involves indiscriminately all the naval officers of the United States and the *bona fide* Peruvian naval officers who have no concern in the matter." He warned that the Peruvian admiral's salvo in the War of Salutes would "impress our government and people very unfavorably." For the moment, Dahlgren asked that Tucker's "offensive order" be revoked, pending a resolution by the two governments of the entire dispute concerning the former Confederate. But until that was accomplished, Dahlgren would not lift his own ban on courtesies toward Tucker, and he still demanded an apology for the Virginian's alleged slight of Captain Stanly.[43]

The escalating War of Salutes caused discomfort in both Lima and Washington. Barreda reported that the "accursed Tucker affair" was a political "nightmare" for Seward and his friends. President Johnson was being denounced increasingly for his pro-Southern policies; the House of Representatives soon would approve a resolution for his impeachment. On December 6 Seward told the Peruvian envoy that the navy had been overly zealous in regard to Tucker; the problem could be resolved if Peru would only "show something" to soothe Secretary Welles and the president. With the receipt in Washington a few days later of Peru's official report on the Tucker-Stanly dispute and an expression of "regret" that the incident had strained relation's between the two countries, Barreda hoped that the controversy had ended. The minister met with Seward several times in the days that followed, and the secretary did not mention Tucker.[44]

After being warned informally by Hovey of Dahlgren's intentions toward Tucker, Lima sought the support of its ally in Santiago. "I do not doubt that . . . Chile will be in accord with our contention," Pacheco wrote his envoy there, because the Peruvian admiral also commanded the Chilean squadron. Foreign Minister Alvaro Covarrubias, however, was reluctant to bring his government into the fray before consulting with General Kilpatrick, Washington's minister in Santiago. A diminutive but dashing Union calvary commander with great self-confidence, Kilpatrick was very pro-Chilean. Already he had privately expressed his concurrence with the Peruvian position in the Tucker-Stanly affair.[45]

On February 14 Kilpatrick, Covarrubias, and Peruvian envoy José Pardo conferred about the War of Salutes. The United States diplomat was appalled by Dahlgren's action and quickly sent protests to the admiral and Secretary Seward. "I am convinced," he wrote Dahlgren, "that the instructions which you have received from the Government and issued to your squadron, have been based upon an entirely erroneous impression at Washington," based upon the "misrepresentations of Captain Stanley." He asserted that "no one acquainted with the circumstances" could not believe that Stanly had "made an official matter out of . . . an entirely personal affair." Kilpatrick declared that he despised "an unpardoned and unrepentant rebel as much as any man living," but this was not the proper time "for the exercise of such feelings." The minister explained to Dahlgren that Washington recently had tendered its good offices to settle the present war; he believed the allies ready to accept this offer. "But under the present circumstances [they] of course cannot do so." Kilpatrick warned Seward that "unless this misunderstanding is rectified, . . . our relations on this coast may soon be involved in most embarrassing complications"—perhaps even the closing of allied ports to United States warships.[46]

Although the Tucker affair was becoming a diplomatic crisis and Hovey had gained the support of a vigorous ally in General Kilpatrick, the United States minister in Lima continued to shrink from an unpleasant showdown with the resolute Dahlgren. He indicated to the Peruvians his disagreement with the admiral—"very poor for a diplomatist," noted Dahlgren, who thought that Hovey "cottons" to Lima "more than he ought." The envoy confidentially suggested that Barreda use his influence to obtain a pardon for Tucker. Neither Lima nor Washington seemed aware that the "unrepentant rebel" had applied for amnesty in May 1865.[47]

Dahlgren rejected out of hand the forebodings of General Kilpatrick, whom he probably held in contempt for his failure to help exonerate the admiral's son Ulric. "As usual he goes off half-cocked," noted the sailor; Dahlgren extracted an opinion from Hovey that the minister in Santiago "exaggerated the matter very much." The sailor challenged Kilpatrick's contention that Peru had ordered its fortified ports to withhold salutes from United States warships and that Chile would issue similar instructions. But on George Washington's Birthday, February 22, the batteries at Callao "did not salute nor show an American color," and from Valparaíso came reports that the Chileans, too, had refrained from the usual show of courtesies on that day. To Secretary Welles the admiral admitted that Lima was "very sore" concerning the Tucker affair, but he insisted that the dispute was not detrimental to Washington's efforts toward mediation of the war with Spain.[48]

Hovey's initial report concerning Dahlgren's suspension of courtesies reached Washington in early February. Welles judged the controversy "troublesome" but "not of great moment." The navy secretary told Seward that George Washington "would not have extended courtesies to Benedict Arnold because Great Britain had given him a commission and uniform." For Federico Barreda, however, the dispute was very consequential and had "gotten ugly." Should Tucker be forced to relinquish command of the fleet, the proposed expedition against the Spaniards would be abandoned. "If Tucker does not move from Valparaíso," he wrote Colonel Prado, "it will be due to the United States." Barreda, who was preparing to resign his post, instructed Chargé A. B. Medina to present Peru's case forcefully to the secretary of state.

Seward again brought the Tucker issue before the cabinet on March 15. "No one stood by me," lamented Welles after the meeting. While President Johnson "listened patiently," Secretary of War Edwin M. Stanton urged that the Navy Department defer to the judgment of Seward and Attorney General Henry Stanberry, who supported the secretary of state. The president, after mulling over the question, "remarked that it was a matter which he did not like," but that Seward "seemed to consider it important." Most of the cabinet agreed. "The national honor," groused Welles, "seemed of little concern" to Seward "and never stood in the way of . . . expediency."[49]

In a dispatch to Hovey three days later, Seward praised Dahlgren's patriotic "sentiments," but the secretary recognized the absolute right of the allies to select "the agents to whom they will entrust their defence and the ensigns of national honor." Thus, the Navy Department would order Dahlgren to restore naval courtesies to Tucker, although he might still "decline personal and individual intercourse" with the Virginian. Welles informed his admiral that the Navy Department approved "the solicitude" he manifested toward "the respect due our flag." However, the Tucker matter was "the subject of a diplomatic correspondence in which neither this Department, nor an officer under its control, is called upon to take part." While squadron commanders should keep themselves informed on appropriate questions of international law, "when within reach, as you are, of a diplomatic representative" of the United States, a naval officer should "defer to his opinions and be guided by them." Washington, continued the secretary, could not "consistently dispute" Colonel Prado's contention that the Tucker-Stanly dispute was entirely personal. Furthermore, "after denying courtesies to Mr. Tucker," the United States could not "call upon that individual to apologize for discourtesy" toward Stanly. Therefore, President Johnson deemed it "expedient" that "paragraph 96 will in future be observed in your squadron."[50]

Duty and Honor

While Washington was arriving at a resolution to the War of Salutes, a series of events in Peru and Chile resulted in Tucker's resignation. Some mystery surrounds his action. In published accounts the admiral's close associates indicated that the cancellation of the campaign against the Spaniards weighed most heavily in his decision. "So great was our disappointment," recalled Walter Butt, "that we urged the President of Peru to accept our resignations."[51] Other sources attributed the resignation to the acquittal of the officers who had refused to serve under Tucker or to the mounting domestic discontent facing Colonel Prado, in part because of his appointment of the former Confederate.[52] Finally, several contemporaries indicated that the admiral's separation from the fleet resulted from the War of Salutes and the desire of the Prado administration and Tucker to prevent a further deterioration of relations between Washington and Lima.[53] Each of these factors, it seems, played some role in Tucker's decision, but which was paramount? The mystery is compounded by assertions that the admiral had offered to step down on two previous occasions—in July 1866 after his rejection by officers of the squadron and, again, at some unspecified date—and by the existence of two versions of his "final" resignation. Each of the latter documents bears a different date and offers a different explanation for his action.[54]

Tucker certainly desired to command in battle the force he had organized and trained, if only to justify the confidence placed in him by Peruvian authorities and to silence the critics of his appointment. He pressed Colonel Prado for an offensive. Had there remained a reasonable prospect for an expedition against the enemy, Tucker would have been very reluctant to relinquish his post, and Prado would have declined his resignation. In late January 1867, however, Santiago suspended plans for an offensive it had approved tentatively on the second of that month.[55] It was probably this decision which Butt remembered as causing the admiral such bitter disappointment. At this time, too, the War of Salutes escalated with the suspension of naval courtesies between the United States and Peru at Valparaíso. Tucker probably tendered his second resignation at this point.

Lima, however, now contemplated an expedition independent of its ally. Negotiations began for the separation of the two squadrons, returning operational control of the Peruvian vessels to authorities in Lima. On January 31 the fleet left port for ten days of maneuvers at the Juan Fernández Islands. According to his instructions, Tucker was to anchor at Coquimbo after this exercise and to await new orders from Peru. A small port some two hundred miles north of Valparaíso, Coquimbo made a good temporary base of operations. It shortened by one day communications with Lima; the movements of the squadron could be concealed more easily; and Tucker was unlikely to encounter United States naval officers there, thus avoiding an aggravation of the dispute over courtesies.[56]

An amicable agreement for the separation of the two squadrons could not be reached, so Tucker returned to Valparaíso on February 23. The news that greeted him was most distressing. During the previous three days, *El Mercurio* had published José A. García y García's defense of his brother Aurelio, one of Montero's codefendants—a document replete with slanders against the admiral. The same Santiago newspaper reported on the Abtao anniversary banquet in Lima, where so much anti-Tucker sentiment had been expressed. A few days later, word reached the Chilean port that Montero and his associates had been acquitted and ordered restored to active duty.[57]

In Peru, meanwhile, several new revolts against the Prado regime had flared in the provinces, and Tucker's enemies had found a new arena for attacks upon him. On February 27 Deputy Enrique Espinosa from Piura, the home department of Montero and several of his insubordinate colleagues, introduced a resolution in the recently assembled Constituent Congress calling upon the executive branch to cancel the admiral's contract. The congressman charged that Tucker had supported the Confederacy, created by "dissidents who sustained the principle of slavery" (abolished by Peru in 1855) and sought to destroy the federal Union which alone maintained "the American equilibrium with Europe." Espinosa's latter point implied that Washington's preoccupation with the Civil War had encouraged the French intervention in Mexico and Spanish aggression against Peru. Tucker's appointment, concluded the resolution, had separated from the navy "the most select part" of Peru's officer corps, men now exonerated by the court-martial. The resolution was referred to the Committee on War and Marine.[58]

During the early days of March, the vacillating Santiago regime indicated that Chile again might approve an offensive. By now, however, Colonel Prado had suffered great political damage—both domestic and international—because of the controversies surrounding Tucker. The acquittal of Montero, noted Admiral Dahlgren, had been "a hard blow" for the government. From Washington, Minister Barreda recommended that Prado secure Tucker's resignation when a convenient occasion presented itself. On March 14 the president responded that he had "taken [his] measures with the opportunity."[59] On that same day President Prado told Hovey confidentially that Tucker had tendered his resignation because of the War of Salutes. The colonel "spoke in high terms of the Admiral," reported the diplomat, and of Tucker's "generous conduct" in relieving the government of embarrassment. Prado indicated that the Virginian's resignation would be accepted, effective in early April. The president also mentioned that his administration was "much pressed" by its political enemies. Hovey believed that the domestic controversy attending Tucker's service by itself would have brought the same result.

The publication of Tucker's official letter of resignation in *El Progreso* on March 27 evoked surprise from Admiral Dahlgren. It was dated at Valparaíso on March 15, the day after Prado informed Hovey that the former Confederate already had resigned.[60] In this published document Tucker stated that he had tendered his resignation the previous July and that "recently" he again had offered to step down. Prado, however, "had the kindness" not to accept either resignation. Tucker now was resigning a third time because of the Espinosa resolution, which, "directed at me personally, compels me . . . to proceed in the action which my dignity requires." Because McCorkle and Butt had been employed under the terms of Tucker's contract, the admiral's resignation also included theirs. The Virginian expressed himself "extremely sad" at his separation from the officers of the Peruvian squadron because their relations with him had "always been of a most pleasant character." To Prado, for whom the admiral had "high respect," Tucker extended his "sincere thanks for the constant kindness and courtesy" shown to him.[61]

The discrepancies between Tucker's published resignation and Prado's conversation on the subject with Hovey suggested to Dahlgren that the letter had been composed according to an understanding between the Virginian and the government. This almost certainly was the case. Prado probably had written to Tucker about March 10 indicating his desire to accept Tucker's second proffered resignation—that of late January or early February. The president's note likely crossed paths with an informal letter the admiral addressed to Prado on March 17 tendering anew his resignation. The latter document was carried to Lima by Emilio Bonifaz, the admiral's secretary.[62] An accomplished lawyer and diplomat, Bonifaz probably had been authorized by Tucker to draft and sign for the admiral a formal resignation, phrased in terms deemed appropriate by the government. Thus, the document published in the newspapers—no manuscript copy has been located—probably was written by Bonifaz, in consultation with Prado and his advisers.

Although the failure of the Chileans to approve an expedition and pressure from what Hovey termed "the Montero faction" undoubtedly contributed to Prado's decision, the War of Salutes was likely the primary reason for removing the admiral from command. However, the administration did not wish to indicate that it had succumbed to pressure from Washington. Neither did Lima want to air publicly its dispute with Santiago. Attribution of Tucker's resignation to the exoneration of the insubordinate officers would have embarrassed both the admiral and the regime, suggesting a "defeat" at the hands of their enemies. Espinosa's resolution, therefore, was the most palatable explanation for the Virginian's action. Prado's critics had attacked him frequently for his arbitrary actions as dictator; the Espinosa resolution now provided Provisional President Prado an opportunity to show republican deference to the legislature.[63]

On March 22, probably after receiving Prado's note accepting his offer to step down, Tucker submitted his resignation as commander of the allied fleet to Chilean president Pérez. He vaguely noted that "the necessities" of the allies and the admiral's "own honor" compelled his action and referred Pérez to an enclosed copy of a letter Tucker had written to Prado that same day. "Circumstances relative to the country of my birth," the latter document stated, had "combined in such a manner against my intense desires" that the admiral's "duty and honor" required his resignation.[64] A close friend who later lived with Tucker explained that the admiral gave up his post because he was "fearful of complicating the relations . . . between the republics of the U.S. and those of the Pacific Coast" of South America. To Jefferson Davis, David McCorkle succinctly explained their separation from the Peruvian Navy: "We have been persecuted out of that service by the Yankees."[65]

Explaining his resignation to his sister in mid-April, Tucker indicated that the Espinosa resolution, "so personally offensive" to the admiral, had triggered his action. But the sailor's separation from the fleet had more fundamental causes.

> The opposition to *us*, has been active from the commencement and the pressure on the President has been immence. . . . The revolution now going on in the South of Peru, and the violent opposition existing in this country against foreigners, made it a necessity for him to yeald. Added to all that, the government in Washington objects to an *unpardoned rebel* holding so exalted a position, and informed Peru that my continuance as Admiral of their navy, would *interrupt* the friendly relations existing between the two countries. This with the affairs of Congress made it a point of honor, for me at once to resign.[66]

Admiral Dahlgren interpreted Tucker's resignation in the same way. When the Yankee sailor received Washington's order to observe formal naval courtesies toward the former Confederate, the acerbic Dahlgren deemed the decision "a shameless and outrageous backdown, and needless, too, for Tucker backed out first." Secretary Welles and his assistants in the Navy Department were "imbeciles," while Seward had "erred, as he always does when mere rules are applicable, and the decision must go beyond to the high sentiments of our nature." The secretary of state had instructed Hovey that he might inform the

Peruvians that Dahlgren would be ordered to restore official courtesies to Tucker. But because the *almirante* had resigned before these instructions reached Lima, Hovey did not formally apprise Lima of Washington's decision. Dahlgren did not have to salute Tucker. "Our flag," wrote the former, "happily escaped the indignity."[67]

The Peruvians also sought to salve their national honor. On April 20 Foreign Minister Simón G. Paredes instructed Chargé Medina in Washington to inform Seward unofficially that Tucker had resigned, eliminating the source of discord between the two nations. The envoy was to do this in an interview "not solicited expressly" for that purpose, and Medina was to give the official explanation for the admiral's resignation—the Espinosa resolution. The diplomat accomplished his mission and expressed his satisfaction that Peru had avoided a "precedent contrary to the dignity of the nation." But Medina lamented that Tucker had resigned before receiving the courtesies ordered by the Johnson administration, "which would have been a precedent in our favor."[68]

Tucker took formal leave of Chilean officials and Peruvian envoy José Pardo and departed from Valparaíso by mail steamer on March 25. He had arranged with the British and French naval commanders there that no guns be fired in his honor. Arriving at Lima on April 3, the admiral, McCorkle, and Butt were received by President Prado "in the same kindly manner as before."[69] Privately, Prado declared himself "very sad" over Tucker's separation from the fleet and thanked him for his "very important services to Peru and America" in the war with Spain. In officially accepting the resignation of the *almirante*, the president and Minister of War and Marine Bustamante wrote of their gratitude to Tucker and his two aides for their "dignified deportment and good services" to Peru. Although bitter about his forced resignation, Tucker believed that he had been "fully and honorably sustained . . . from the beginning to the end by the Presidents and Cabinets of both Peru & Chile, and by a large number of the best men in both countries."[70]

CHAPTER SEVEN

Commission in the Wilderness

AFTER EIGHT MONTHS in an important, highly paid position, fifty-five-year-old John Randolph Tucker again was an unemployed civilian, unsure of his future and concerned about the welfare of his three younger children. Nine-year-old Virginius was being raised in Norfolk by Harriet Webb Reilly, a sister of the boy's deceased mother. Randolph, aged seventeen, lived in Richmond. Cared for by Tucker's sister Nora and her husband, Joseph W. Randolph, during the Civil War, Randy now worked in a hotel owned by Oscar Cranz, the second husband of his aunt Delia Webb Cranz. Sixteen-year-old Tarleton resided with his aunt Susan Tucker Jackson Holt, a well-fixed District of Columbia matron, and recently had enrolled at Georgetown University. Tucker previously had hoped to bring his sons to South America but wisely postponed that step because of his uncertain employment. Now he counseled Randy to remain with Cranz and to "learn as much . . . about business" as he could. "What is to become of my poor dear son Tar," the admiral asked Nora; "my means of keeping him at college are at an end." Tucker wanted Tarleton to continue his studies for as long as the money he had provided would permit; "then my friends must . . . get him a place in some business establishment until I am perminently located, when I hope once more to get my children about me."

The former Confederate could not contemplate returning home "while the infernel *Radicals* control the destinies of the South." Fortunately, President Prado and the influential members of his old cabinet were the admiral's "warm friends," and they had "offered to do any thing in their power" for him. Tucker thought that he might try farming along the banks of the Amazon River. Such a venture, however, would be very experimental, and writing eleven days after his return from Chile, the admiral had not yet made a decision. But a few days later the president offered him a salaried post which would sustain him while he tried his luck as a jungle planter. On April 16, 1867, *El Nacional* reported that Admiral Tucker would head a scientific commission being formed to explore the Peruvian headwaters of the Amazon.[1]

The Highways of El Dorado

Peru does not conjure up images of vast jungles. When thinking about that country, foreigners usually envision the high Andes Mountains that transverse the nation's center, north to south, like a rugged backbone. Sailors approaching Peru from the Pacific see its narrow coastal plain, an extremely arid desert dotted by a score of oases where rivers flowing westward from the mountains permit irrigation. However, some 60 percent of the republic's half-million square miles—an area larger than Texas and about the size of France and the United Kingdom combined—lies east of the Andes, in the Amazon Basin. In the 1860s, before a series of territorial losses, Peru claimed 25 percent more land, with about three-quarters of the total area beyond the mountains.[2]

Called the Montaña (from the Spanish *monte*, or forest), Amazonian Peru is a lowland covered by dense tropical rain forest.[3] Life in the region always has centered on the rivers, which serve as highways through the jungle. The Amazon hydrographic system resembles a large tree lying on its side in the center of South America, with its wide trunk tapering inland from the Atlantic Coast and its many branches extending toward the Andes. The main stream originates as the Río Marañón, high in the mountains of central Peru. It flows northward through a deep gorge until it nears the border with Ecuador. Then it abruptly turns east through a gap in the cordilleras and descends toward the lowlands. At the Pongo de Manseriche (Gateway of the Parrots) the river bursts through the last of the outlying Andean ranges and begins an unimpeded journey to the Atlantic Ocean, some three thousand miles distant. From tributaries along the way, this mightiest of rivers collects one-eighth of the fresh water on the earth's surface.

A half-dozen significant rivers enter the Peruvian portion of the Marañón-Amazon from the north. Because these streams lead toward Ecuador, however, they are less important to Peru's transportation needs than the system's southern affluents. The Huallaga River, the first of the major southern tributaries, drains a long valley between the main Andean ranges and the jungle-covered Cordillera Azul, a lower outlying chain. Although navigable by canoe and small powerboats for much of its middle course, the Huallaga can be negotiated by sizable steamers for only the final 130 miles before its juncture with the Marañón. The Río Ucayali, about seventy miles east of the Huallaga, is Peru's most important tributary of the Marañón. Indeed, when the two rivers meet, the Marañón becomes the Amazon, according to Peruvian nomenclature. Large steamers can ascend the Ucayali for some one thousand miles; oceangoing vessels from the Atlantic call at the river port of Pucallpa, seven hundred miles upstream, the terminus of Peru's

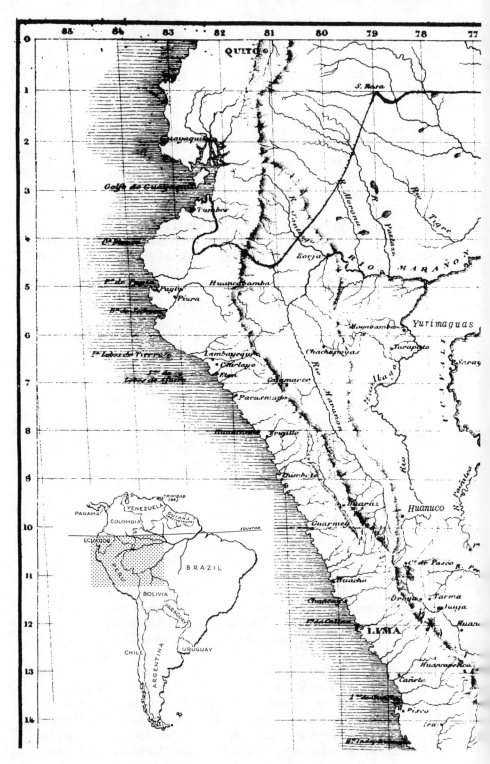

Peru, 1877. Longitude west of Paris. The insert shows modern boundaries. (Adapted from Antonio Raimondi's small "Mapa del Perú," in *El
Peru*, vol. 3)

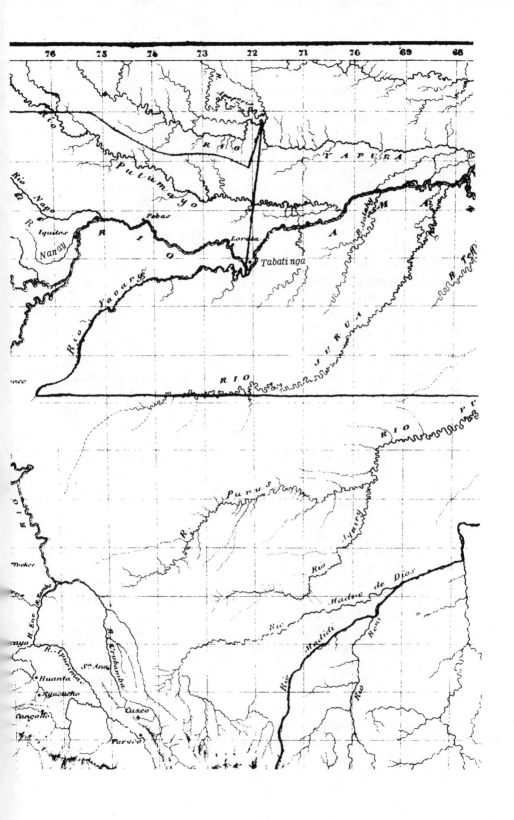

"transoceanic" highway from Lima. In Admiral Tucker's day, the Ucayali was of paramount interest to the government because that river and one of its western tributaries seemed likely to be the navigable waterway closest to the capital. Farther to the east, the Yavarí River marks part of the boundary between Peru and Brazil. In the far southeast, Peru's most remote corner, the Madre de Dios River flows eastward into Bolivia, joining the Beni and Madeira rivers (facts not fully ascertained in the 1860s) before discharging its waters into the middle course of the Amazon.

The Montaña has had an eerie fascination for Peruvians living to the west since ancient times. The Incas called the region Anti, the land of the sun-god Inti, who arose from his jungle home each morning to begin his daily westward journey across the sky. The gold washed from streams dissecting the forested eastern slopes of the Andes was said to be Inti's tears. From the jungle the native peoples of the highlands also obtained other precious items, including brilliant feathers, jaguar skins, honey, and coca, the cultivated source of cocaine. On several occasions Inca armies tried to conquer the eastern lowlands, but the imperial legions were thwarted by the hostile forces of nature and the often fierce jungle tribes. The civilized, Quechua-speaking highlanders called these people Chunchos (wild men), a term by which the lowland natives have been known ever since. According to pre-Columbian legends, wealthy kingdoms with fabulous cities lay hidden in the jungle. The most famous of these was ruled by the gilded king El Dorado; after bathing each morning, he was said to cover his still-wet body with gold dust, so that he "glistened like the sun." His name has been applied generically to other aureate phantoms that later lured the Spaniards and Peruvians into the forest in pursuit of easy riches. But El Dorado proved to be a most elusive quarry.

Soon after defeating the Inca armies in 1533, the *conquistador* Francisco Pizarro sent his lieutenants on a series of ill-fated expeditions into the Montaña. Gonzalo Pizarro, the conqueror's brother, headed the most famous of these. In search of a reported "Land of Cinnamon," he entered the jungle east of Quito, Ecuador. The explorers soon became lost, and their provisions failed. Pizarro sent a sixty-man scouting party under Francisco de Orellana to search for food. They embarked in a crude boat on the Coca River and soon entered the Río Napo, whose powerful current would not permit them to return upstream. So Orellana continued his voyage into the Amazon River, and seven months later, in August 1542, reached the Atlantic Ocean. During the next century, other expeditions repeated Orellana's adventure or made less ambitious explorations of the eastern rivers. In 1567 Juan Salinas de Loyola journeyed down the Marañón and ascended the Ucayali River for several hundred miles.

The Spaniards, meanwhile, established several settlements on the fringe of the Amazon Basin, gateway towns from which they tapped the natural wealth of the region. In the north of Peru, Moyobamba was built on the bank of the Río Mayo, a western tributary of the lower Huallaga which afforded relatively easy access to the jungle. Some four hundred miles up the Huallaga, the residents of Huánuco also exploited the resources of the forest. About seventy-five miles farther south, the town of Tarma stood at the head of the Chanchamayo Valley, drained by the headwaters of the Ucayali; Tarma served as another focal point for penetration of the Amazonian wilderness. During the next four centuries Moyobamba, Huánuco, and Tarma vied for government favor, as succeeding regimes in Lima sought to determine the best avenue into the eastern lowlands, an official designation which would bring prosperity to one of these towns.

While pioneers settled in the higher western valleys of the Montaña, missionaries ventured into the low country beyond. The *padres* tried to win Chuncho souls for their God and to protect the territories of their king from the Portuguese in Brazil. From their foothold on the Atlantic Coast, the latter followed the Amazon River upstream in a relentless effort to control the South American interior. The Society of Jesus in 1638 established a headquarters at Borja on the Marañón just below the Pongo de Manseriche. By the end of the century the Jesuits had gathered more than one hundred thousand Indians into seventy-five missions along the banks of the Marañón-Amazon and the lower portions of its tributaries. Franciscan friars from the monastery of Santa Rosa de Ocopa, near Tarma, dominated missionary activity in the central portion of the Montaña. In 1742 they were ministering to ten thousand Indian neophytes in forty missions located along the upper Huallaga, the Ucayali, and its headwaters. That year, however, an Indian from the highlands named Juan Santos appeared in the Chanchamayo Valley. Adopting the name Atahualpa, after the last Inca emperor, he led the Campa people in a rebellion against the Franciscans and Spanish colonial authorities. The missions in that area and the upper Ucayali were abandoned; thereafter, the Campas and some of their Indian neighbors tenaciously barred all intruders for almost a century and a half.

By the late eighteenth century most mission villages along the Marañón-Amazon, Huallaga, and lower Ucayali had become secularized. Many of their residents now spoke Quechua, the Inca tongue employed by the *padres* for proselytizing, or Spanish. Madrid had established the Commandancy General of Mainas to govern eastern Peru, and lay administrators largely replaced the missionaries. Traders from the west and Brazilian smugglers from the east regularly called at the Amazonian towns, bartering for salt fish, straw hats, fiber hammocks, and a myriad of products gathered in the forest. The more notable of these were rubber and bark from the cinchona tree, the source of quinine.

During Peru's War of Independence from Spain, 1820–24, and the politically chaotic two decades that followed, life in the Montaña's former mission towns retrogressed. Trails into the region deteriorated, most of the missionaries left, wild Indians repeatedly attacked peaceful villages, and local administrators went months without instructions or money from Lima. Republican Peru's hold over its Amazonian provinces became increasingly tenuous. The Brazilians—who simultaneously obtained their independence, from Portugal—established a relatively stable monarchy. They soon dominated the trade of eastern Peru and threatened Lima's sovereignty in the region. Peru's Spanish-speaking neighbors in Ecuador, Colombia, and Bolivia also disputed Lima's title to large portions of the Montaña, where colonial administrative boundaries had been ill-defined.

Beginning with the 1845 inauguration of Marshal Ramón Castilla, often considered Peru's greatest nineteenth-century president, the nation achieved increased stability and material progress, funded primarily by the prodigious sums earned from guano exports. Castilla gave special attention to the Montaña. He repaired trails into the region, promoted colonization, reestablished missions, built Fort San Ramón in the Chanchamayo Valley, and provided mail service and schools for some larger communities. The eastern lowlands became a separate province in 1853; eight years later this region was designated the Fluvial Department of Loreto, equal in status to Peru's other major political subdivisions. Most important, Castilla introduced steam navigation to the jungle waterways. In 1851 Peru and Brazil signed a treaty of commerce and fluvial navigation, promising a five-year subsidy to the first company, from either nation, that initiated steamer service on the Amazon. Two years later the first paddle wheeler, belonging to a Brazilian firm, reached Nauta, Peru's principal town in the lowlands, located on the north bank of the Amazon almost opposite the mouth of the Ucayali River. Peru purchased two steamers in the United States in 1854 to extend service beyond Nauta. But poorly constructed and badly maintained, these vessels (the *Tirado* and *Huallaga*) were useless hulks two years later. For many years thereafter, a strong prejudice against ships built in the United States existed among the people of that region.

In 1864 four new steamers—the five-hundred-ton *Morona* and *Pastaza*, destined for commercial traffic, and the sixty-ton exploring steamers *Napo* and *Putumayo*—were acquired in Great Britain. Meanwhile, a government commission had been sent to the Amazon River to select a headquarters for the new fleet, complete with repair shops and a navy post. This team rejected Nauta because silt from the discharge of the Ucayali formed bars in front of the town. In its stead, the commission chose the sleepy Indian village of Iquitos, sixty-nine miles farther downstream, on the left bank of the Amazon. While the prefect (chief executive) of Loreto resided in Moyobamba, the department's political capital, Iquitos became the commercial hub of the region and the home of the commandant general, the senior navy officer who commanded the steamer fleet and naval station. After years of resistance, the Brazilian Empire proclaimed the Amazon River an international waterway in 1867, opening it to the vessels of all nations. That same year Admiral Tucker's Hydrographic Commission of the Amazon arrived in Iquitos.

By this time most of the major rivers of eastern Peru had been navigated repeatedly by missionaries, traders, and explorers, including some notable scientists. The French Academy of Science sent a team of scholars to Peru in 1735 under the leadership of Charles-Marie de La Condamine, who later returned home by way of the Amazon River. The great German naturalist Alexander von Humboldt visited the Peruvian Montaña in 1802. With the coming of independence, foreign expeditions to the jungles of Peru became more frequent. Among the more important of these were the journey of British naval officers William Smyth and Frederick Lowe down the Amazon in 1834 and the reconnaissance of the French nobleman Francis, comte de Castelnau, a decade later. The Peruvian government also sent its own explorers to survey the region. The indefatigable Italian-born scientist Antonio Raimondi, whose life was devoted to studies of his adopted Peru, published a detailed account of Loreto in 1862.

In the United States, Matthew Fontaine Maury urged the navy to make a large-scale survey of the Amazon River and lambasted the exclusionary "Japanese policy" of the Brazilians, who would not permit the project. Refusing to be entirely thwarted, the United States did conduct a less ostentatious exploration in 1851, sending just two men into the Montaña. Lieutenant William Lewis Herndon, Maury's brother-in-law, and Passed Midshipman Lardner Gibbon began their adventure in Lima. After climbing the Andes together, Gibbon traveled south into Bolivia and reached the Amazon River by way of the Río Madeira, while Herndon descended the Huallaga River and continued his voyage down the Amazon. The delightful official report of the two officers, published by the United States Navy, quickly appeared in a commercial edition as well.[4] Shortly after Herndon's exploration, George Catlin, the famed painter of North American Indians, traveled through eastern Peru, making little-known sketches of the region and its peoples.[5]

Amazonian Peru also had been mapped repeatedly by the time that

Admiral Tucker and his team began their labors. Jesuit missionary Samuel Fritz drew the first credible map of the Marañón-Amazon in 1707. One year before Tucker's arrival in Iquitos, Prefect Benito Arana of Loreto headed a steamboat expedition up the Ucayali and its important western tributary the Río Pachitea. Members of that party sketched a crude navigation chart of those rivers—probably the first map of its kind for the region.[6] Nevertheless, the Peruvian government had a very imperfect knowledge of the eastern lowlands. Explorers had determined the elevations and geographical coordinates for a few points within the Montaña, but these measurements—made with crude instruments under very difficult conditions—were unreliable. Maps depicting Amazonian Peru in Mariano Felipe Paz Soldán's 1865 *Atlas geográfico del Perú* had great spatial distortions; many rivers were not shown; and the courses indicated for others were largely the product of guesswork. When Lieutenant Herndon made his journey through the region in 1851, the best available map had been drawn by the Franciscan Manuel Sobreviela in 1790, with a few minor corrections and additions made four decades later. Tucker carried the same map with him into the Montaña.[7]

Peru's basic long-term objectives in the eastern lowlands—the protection of its sovereignty and the economic development of the region—acquired a special urgency during the 1860s. The commandant general at Iquitos warned in early 1867 that the nation's Amazonian frontiers, with their sparse population, were "at the mercy of whomever wishes to invade our territory with a handful of armed men." Even while a mixed Peruvian-Brazilian commission surveyed part of their countries' mutual boundary along the Yavarí River, the Rio de Janeiro government strengthened its military position in the region. Given Brazil's "known absorbtionist tendencies," warned the *comandante,* Peru should not rely upon the "nobility and good faith" of its giant neighbor.[8] An admonition for vigilance against Brazilian designs headed the list of Lima's instruction to a new prefect of Loreto in 1868. Peruvian officials even feared that Spain might send warships up the Amazon River and attributed a series of Indian attacks in the region to the machinations of Spanish missionaries.[9]

By the mid-1860s the guano beds that provided the vast majority of Lima's revenues were being depleted rapidly, and Peru borrowed heavily against the bird manure that remained. Drawn once more under the spell of El Dorado, the nation's leaders looked to the supposed wealth of the Montaña—forest products, minerals, and fertile lands—to help rescue the treasury. The exploitation of these resources and their preservation against the designs of Peru's neighbors required a better knowledge of the region's geography and vastly improved transportation. The lowland rivers would have to be charted for the steamers servicing an expanding population and economy. The Montaña also needed more efficient links to the rest of Peru, arteries for the flow of colonists, commerce, and, in times of emergency, troops. Lima wanted to build a good road and, eventually, a railroad between the capital and the closest navigable point on the Amazon system. This monumental task required precise surveys, and not the unsystematic explorations characteristic of the past.[10]

Meanwhile, a bitter rivalry between the political authorities in Moyobamba and the naval officials in Iquitos had produced an exchange of accusations which likely undermined Lima's confidence in the honesty and competence of its representatives in the trans-Andean region.[11] Notwithstanding salary bonuses of 50 percent and double credit for time-in-service for military officers, the government had great difficulty finding good officials for Loreto and keeping them there. The region's uncomfortable and insalubrious climate, swarms of insects, lack of social diversions, and inflated prices for poor food and housing attracted few volunteers. The Amazonian provinces were developing a reputation as a dumping ground, a place of exile for public employees who had fallen from favor.[12]

A native of Huánuco, a major gateway to the Montaña, President Mariano Prado had a special interest in the development of Amazonian Peru. He also had great respect for Admiral Tucker's ability and integrity and desired to make continued use of his services. The political controversy surrounding the Virginian required that he be employed far from the capital, and quickly. Already considering themselves refugees, Tucker, McCorkle, and Butt preferred double exile in the Peruvian jungle to an uncertain future at home. Their needs and those of Peru converged once again.

The Exiles Exiled

President Prado established the Hydrographic Commission of the Amazon by a decree of May 25, 1867. This "scientific commission" was to explore and prepare hydrographic charts of the Amazon system within the limits of the republic, giving special attention to the Ucayali River and its tributaries. Tucker's annual compensation as president of the commission was set at thirty-two hundred *soles* (the *sol* was at par with the dollar); McCorkle and Butt were to receive sixteen hundred and twelve hundred *soles*, respectively—a reduction of 36 percent in the salaries previously paid Tucker and Butt and a 42 percent decrease for McCorkle. Although a civilian agency, the commission functioned like a military organization and reported to the minister of war and marine.

In the week after the establishment of the commission, the government added a secretary, a surgeon, and two engineers to Tucker's staff but for reasons of economy declined his request for a pair of natural scientists to study flora and fauna. Army Captain Timiteo Smith Buitrón, a member of President Prado's cavalry escort, was named secretary of the commission. This handsome twenty-seven-year-old Anglo-Peruvian had been born at Iquique on Peru's south coast, had received some of his education in Germany, and had lived ten years in England. Smith was fluent in both English and Spanish.[13] Twenty-six-year-old former army surgeon Santiago Távara requested service with the Hydrographic Commission for personal reasons. The previous August his younger brother, navy Ensign Juan Antonio Távara, and another ensign, Alberto West, had been murdered and reportedly eaten by the Cashibo Indians while exploring the Pachitea River. Dr. Távara wanted to visit the place where his brother had died and learn more about these "savages" who for centuries had rejected "with their arrows the Gospel and civilization."[14]

The admiral specifically requested the assignment of twenty-five-year-old Arturo Wertheman as chief engineer of the commission. Wertheman had been born at Mulhouse in the French province of Alsace but was educated in Switzerland, where he became a citizen. He served briefly under Ferdinand de Lesseps on the Suez Canal project and then traveled extensively in Africa before settling in California where railroad impresario Henry Meiggs recruited him for work in Chile. When he stopped over at Callao, however, Peruvian authorities persuaded Wertheman to join Peru's Corps of State Engineers. An organization with exacting standards, the corps gave the young Swiss its highest rank—first engineer. Fluent in five languages and a gifted musician, too, Wertheman could accomplish virtually every engineering task, "from mending a watch to building a road." In addition to his brilliance, Wertheman was noted for his unusual appearance. In childhood a kick from a horse had destroyed his lower jawbone. With penetrating dark eyes and a prominent nose, the engineer had a "bird-like face—running to a point at the beak."[15] First Assistant State Engineer Manuel Charon, a Franco-Peruvian, also joined Tucker's team. Trained in the United States, he was the son of Melchor Charon, the engineer who had installed Lima's gaslight system.[16]

In addition to the official members of the Comisión Hidrográfica, three others joined Tucker's party at the eleventh hour—President Prado's thirteen-year-old son Ensign Leoncio Prado; Tucker's eldest son, Jack (John Tarleton Tucker); and James A. Norris, a former lieutenant in the Confederate navy. Leoncio Prado was an intractable, high-spirited youth who already had experienced more adventure than most men encounter in a lifetime. After participating in his father's 1865 revolution against the Pezet regime, he was appointed a midshipman in the navy. The next year he fought in the battles of Abtao and Callao, before enrolling at Peru's military and naval school. Chafing under the strict discipline of the academy, Leoncio led a mutiny among the cadets, who barricaded themselves inside the school. After quashing the rebellion, President Prado determined to exile the boy to Loreto under the tutelage of Admiral Tucker.[17]

Benjamín Vicuña MacKenna had recruited Jack Tucker and Norris for service with the Chilean Navy in January 1866.[18] But the two sailors had become disillusioned with their assignments in Chile—young Tucker almost from the beginning. He had not received the rank he deemed commensurate with his experience in the Confederate navy and had been disappointed in his hope for ample prize money. The frustrated young naval engineer resigned his commission in November 1866 and together with Norris and a former Union navy engineer proposed a privateering venture which won the support of Henry Meiggs. Their plan almost certainly envisioned torpedo-boat attacks against the Spaniards, for in May 1867 they were joined by former chief engineer James H. Tomb, who had commanded the CSS *David* at Charleston. Unable to reach an agreement with Chilean authorities, Jack Tucker and Norris went to Lima in mid-June 1867, just in time to accompany the Hydrographic Commission into the Amazon Basin. The two men agreed to superintend the admiral's proposed plantation.[19]

The commission's departure from Lima, planned for June 1, was delayed for three weeks due to the last-minute addition of personnel and difficulties in obtaining equipment. The latter included surveying instruments and enough weapons to equip a small army—fourteen Spencer repeating rifles and revolvers for each member of the party. Although the expedition anticipated possible attacks by jungle Indians, the greatest danger was closer at hand. Bandit gangs infested the rugged road into the mountains, preying upon travelers and the pack-trains plying between the capital and the silver mines at Cerro de Pasco in the central Andes. Indeed, erroneous reports that highwaymen had murdered Tucker and much of his entourage would later bring great distress to the admiral's friends in the United States.[20]

At mid-morning on June 21, 1867, Admiral Tucker and his party of nine left Lima. The government had provided them with three months' pay, three hundred *soles* to cover expenses, four porters, eleven saddle animals, fourteen cargo mules, and a team of muleteers. The expedition followed the ancient road along the Rimac River westward into the Andes, a route frequently described—and cursed—in travel accounts of the period. Herndon's report, Tucker informed his son Randy, would give the folks in Virginia a "very correct impression of our trip." After two days' ride through the coastal lowlands, passing irrigated fields of sugarcane, the commission began climbing the mountains. On Sunday,

June 23, the party halted early at the village of Magdalena and observed the Sabbath as best they could. The men took target practice and then relaxed, listening to Butt play the violin, accompanied by Wertheman and Charon, who also brought musical instruments.

During the next six days the travelers climbed almost continuously, skirting a peak ominously called the Widow and crossing a pass at nearly sixteen thousand feet. The sparse mountain vegetation gave way to snow, the rarefied air of the high elevation caused headaches and nausea, and the cold winter winds (Peru's June is equivalent to December in the Northern Hemisphere) numbed their faces. On most nights they fortunately found lodging at haciendas, town halls, or the homes of local officials. But the expedition also braved the *tambos*, roadside inns that had sheltered travelers since at least the days of the Incas. Dr. Távara, who chronicled their journey in his diary, briefly noted that at one of these establishments he and his nine companions were "packed . . . like sardines" into a single nine-by-nine-foot room.[21] A German who earlier traveled the same route gave a more detailed account of a typical *tambo*, a "hut filthy beyond description."

> The beds consist of sheep-skins spread on the damp floor; and one bedchamber serves for the hostess ["a dirty old Indian woman"], her daughter, her grandchildren, and the travellers; an immense woolen . . . blanket being spread over the whole party. But woe to the unwary traveller who trusts himself in this dormitory! He soon finds himself surrounded by enemies from whose attacks it is impossible to escape; for the hut is infested with vermin. . . . Add to all this a stifling smoke, and all sorts of mephitic exhaltations, and troops of guinea-pigs who run about during the whole night, and gambol over the faces and bodies of the sleepers,—and it may readily be conceived how anxiously the traveller looks for the dawn of morning, when he may escape from the horrors of this miserable tambo.[22]

Tucker and his companions reached Cerro de Pasco, a bleak but bustling commercial and mining center, on June 29. After a four-day delay procuring fresh mules and a porter to replace one stricken with dysentery, they began their descent of the Andes and reached Huánuco "much fatigued" on July 5. Huánuco was a delightful old town of seven thousand people situated on the Río Huallaga, at that point a normally shallow, rapidly flowing stream. Nestled in a valley at an elevation of two thousand feet, its perpetually springlike climate permitted farmers to plant and harvest crops throughout the year. The Hydrographic Commission sojourned in these pleasant surroundings for several weeks to allow sufficient time for a steamer from Iquitos to reach their point of rendezvous in the jungle to the east. The half-dozen or so "better families" of Huánuco entertained Tucker's party graciously, and the town's rickety printing press devoted a special edition of the

Registro oficial to the commission. The visiting "dignitaries" toured the community's schools and hospital, where Doctor Távara volunteered his services. The engineers, meanwhile, prepared a map of the town and surveyed the local portion of the Huallaga for levees to control flash floods.[23]

For two centuries most travelers journeying to the Amazon River from Huánuco had followed trails extending northeastward to present-day Tingo María, the head of canoe navigation on the Huallaga, and then continued downstream to the Marañón. This point of embarkation, however, was several hundred miles above the limit for steam navigation. Therefore, Tucker had been ordered to explore a more rugged route, long known to missionaries and local residents, extending southeast of Huánuco to Pozuzo and Puerto Mairo, on the Palcazu River. This stream flows into the navigable Pachitea, a major tributary of the Ucayali; it was hoped that steamers might be able to negotiate the Palcazu itself. In early 1867 a survey team headed by naval engineer Luis Sandi examined the crude trail to Puerto Mairo. Three steamers from Iquitos, meanwhile, attempted to reach the same point by water. One vessel accomplished the task; but another was disabled, and a third was grounded, stranding their famished crews for many weeks.[24]

To avoid exhausting local food supplies along the trail, the Hydrographic Commission set out in two teams for Puerto Mairo (or Puerto Prado, as it was now diplomatically rechristened). McCorkle, Wertheman, Jack Tucker, and Norris departed from Huánuco on August 1 with instructions to map the route; the admiral and the remainder of the party followed on August 20. A few miles east of Huánuco the explorers entered the *ceja de la montaña*—the rugged "eyebrow of the forest"— where Amazonian jungle covers the steep mountain slopes. Along the trail Tucker met the explorer Antonio Raimondi, with whom he would establish a warm and productive friendship. The admiral's team required eight difficult days to travel the sixty miles between Huánuco and Pozuzo. They spent three weeks here as guests of a struggling colony of Tyrolese-German immigrants (with chaletlike houses built on stilts) established by the Peruvian government a decade earlier. At Pozuzo the Hydrographic Commission encountered Father Vicente Calvo, an intrepid explorer who served as prefect of the Franciscan Ocopa missions, and Major Ramón C. Herrera, of the Peruvian Army. In late June, Herrera and a troop of ten soldiers had been dispatched from Iquitos on the steamer *Morona* to pick up Tucker and his party. That vessel anchored at the confluence of the Ucayali and Pachitea rivers while Herrera and his men journeyed by canoe and foot to Pozuzo.[25]

At intervals of a few days in early September, the Hydrographic Commission set out in three teams for the Ucayali River. Walter Butt,

Manuel Charon, and Leoncio Prado departed first, taking canoes down the treacherous Río Pozuzo, which empties into the Palcazu near Puerto Mairo. The admiral instructed them to map the rivers ahead, as far as the Ucayali, and to determine the geographic coordinates for key points along their route. The second unit consisted of McCorkle, Wertheman, young Tucker, and Norris, who were charged with mapping the overland trail. Finally, the admiral, Dr. Távara, Captain Smith, Major Herrera, and Father Calvo (who accompanied them a short distance) comprised the rear guard. During the thirty-mile, six-day march to Puerto Mairo, frequent cloudbursts drenched the explorers; mosquitoes, fire ants, and other voracious insects attacked them incessantly. On the bank of the Río Palcazu, Tucker rendezvoused with McCorkle's team.

The commission spent a week at Puerto Mairo, a place with a few crude huts, waiting for the rest of their baggage to arrive from Pozuzo. They passed the time making scientific observations, hunting, and cleaning their instruments and firearms. Here, too, they acquired a troublesome new companion—John Reed, a demented Illinoisan who had been lost in the jungle for several weeks. The poor wretch, covered with ulcers, believed that the explorers wanted to kill him; he repeatedly attempted to escape until Tucker ordered him restrained for the journey to Iquitos. On September 18 the expedition boarded three *balsas* (large rafts protected by thatched canopies) and three canoes, and shoved off down the Palcazu. After a two-day voyage, they entered the Pachitea; five days and some two hundred miles later, they reached the Ucayali.

During their first day on the Pachitea River, a party of entirely naked Cashibos hailed the explorers from the left bank and gestured for them to come ashore. They did—after readying their guns—with Admiral Tucker in the lead. The commission presented the natives with axes, knives, mirrors, and colorful handkerchiefs, receiving in return some handicraft items and a monkey for their supper. Notwithstanding the fierce reputation of these Chunchos, Dr. Távara and his colleagues concluded that the Cashibos might become civilized through trade and good treatment. Two days later, the voyagers reached Chonta Island, where the Cashibos had murdered ensigns Távara and West. Earlier that year a punitive expedition had attacked a group of Indians near there, and the commission found the island deserted. With simple ceremony, Távara erected a cross in memory of his brother. On September 25 the expedition reached the mouth of the Pachitea and the waiting steamer *Morona*, Lieutenant Eduardo Raygada, commanding. After a week's voyage down the Ucayali and Amazon, Tucker and his party arrived at Iquitos, where they were greeted with enthusiasm.[26]

Iquitos stood atop a dark clay bluff, some sixty-five feet above the average water level, on the left bank of the Amazon, which flows northward at this point. The Nanay, a substantial river, enters the Amazon a short distance to the north; the smaller Río Itaya joins the Amazon at the southern edge of town. About two miles behind Iquitos the elongated Lake Morona (Moronacocha) occupies an ancient channel of the Itaya, which formerly emptied into the Nanay. Although still quite primitive, Iquitos had progressed considerably from the "miserable cluster of huts" encountered by the founding naval expedition in 1864. In the three succeeding years the population had increased from less than five hundred to about two thousand persons.

Covering an area of only 500 by 150 meters, Iquitos had three "streets" (little more than mud paths) running parallel to the Amazon and eight transverse ones extending inland from the river. The central plaza—today one of the more beautiful in Peru, with monuments, fountains, and a great variety of well-tended exotic plants—was adorned by a banana grove, providing both food and shade. The naval administration occupied the largest building on the square, with offices for the commandant general, his chief of staff (*mayor de órdenes*), the commissary, and Tucker's Hydrographic Commission. The structure's interior patio served as a temporary barracks for the "marine column," a garrison of eleven officers and fifty-one soldiers. Nearby stood the town hall, an arsenal, and a substantial though unfinished church.

Iquitos's more than thirty trading companies accounted for the bulk of Loreto's annual half-million-dollar international commerce via the Amazon River. The town also had several retail stores and artisan shops, three inns, two billiard parlors, and "many saloons." Unlike several other towns in Loreto, however, Iquitos did not have a public school; the wealthier families supported a private academy. The community had a crude hospital but found it nearly impossible to retain competent physicians. Similarly, the priest assigned to Iquitos also served several other congregations and often was absent from town.[27]

At the time of Tucker's arrival Iquitos was "full of life and high hopes," with fourteen houses under construction. A few major buildings—especially those around the plaza, which, in typical Latin American fashion, shared a common wall fronting the street—were constructed of brick, with tiled roofs and woodwork of finished boards. Other structures employed sun-dried adobe blocks. But most houses consisted of cane walls plastered with mud and whitewashed, occasionally with a pastel tint added to the lime-and-water mixture. Their palm-thatch roofs made Iquitos a tinderbox. Two years earlier a government warehouse and several other buildings on the Malecón, the street at the crest of the riverbank, had burned to the ground in a few seconds during Independence Day revelries.[28]

The naval factory, a complex of shops surrounding a large yard on

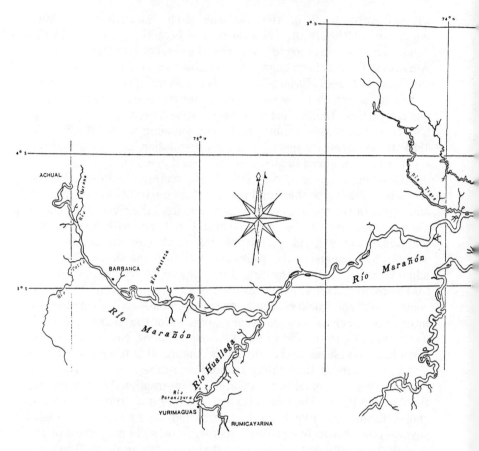

Plano de los Ríos Amazonas y Ucayali en el Perú, 1873. The top third of
Tucker's general map that showed all of the rivers surveyed by the Hydrographic Commission. Based on the Greenwich meridian, the original
map was five feet square and was drawn at a scale of ten miles to the

the southern edge of town, was the wonder of Iquitos. The machinery,
industrial materials, and naval stores for this facility had been carried
there in the old frigate *Arica* and brig *Próspero* (vessels memorialized
in principal Iquitos street names); the steamers *Pastaza* and *Morona*
had towed these sailing ships from the mouth of the Amazon. Carefully
laid out by Lieutenant Commander Camilo Carrillo, the Iquitos shops
were the most modern in Peru. A large building with probably the first
corrugated galvanized-iron roof in Loreto housed the sawmill. A miniature animal-powered railway carried timber through its large doorway
into a series of steam saws, which cut four thousand board feet of

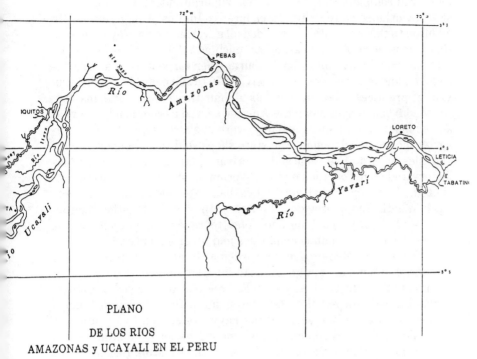

PLANO

DE LOS RIOS

AMAZONAS y UCAYALI EN EL PERU

Y DE SUS TRIBUTARIOS
POR
La Comisión Hidrográfica Del Amazonas
1873

inch; the sheets comprising the middle and bottom portions of the map
are lost. (Redrawn, with some detail omitted, from photos of the original in the *mapoteca* of the Ministry of Foreign Relations, Torre Tagle
Palace, Lima)

lumber per day. A carpentry shop was annexed to the mill. The adjacent foundry, boiler works, and machine shop were equipped with
modern furnaces, large forges, and an array of steam-powered ham-
mers, drills, lathes, and other tools. Work was progressing, slowly, on a
large iron floating dry dock anchored in front of the factory. This repair
facility, unfortunately, would sink and be lost before it could be put into
service. The government's brick and tile yard was located north of
town, where another primitive tramway carried clay from the riverbank to the works for shaping and firing in two large kilns.[29]

A Peruvian naval officer, the factory director, administered this

151

industrial complex. But the operating superintendent and most of the skilled workmen were British, men lured to Iquitos by high salaries. In addition to the navy rations provided all government employees posted there, master craftsmen earned as much as $150 per month ($10 less than an army lieutenant colonel); journeymen carpenters, masons, machinists, and other tradesmen received $70 to $90 monthly. Their Peruvian apprentices were paid at about half these rates. Indians conscripted from villages along the Amazon served as common laborers at $6 per month and, understandably, were in short supply.[30] To encourage economic development, the state shops sold their lumber, bricks, and tiles at cost. Fees charged to private parties for services at the factory and transportation on the government steamers also were subsidized. Therefore, local authorities had little independent income. Each month Lima provided Iquitos with a subsidy—the "contingent"—of twenty-two thousand *soles* to cover the payroll for the town's two hundred public employees and other expenses.[31]

The considerable progress recorded at Iquitos was largely due to its energetic commandant general, Acting Captain Federico Alzamora. A Lima native, thirty-eight years old when Tucker arrived in Iquitos, Alzamora had enjoyed the best and endured the worst assignments during his twenty-four years in the navy. He served five years as a naval aide in Peru's Washington and London legations; but he also spent three years at Nauta, the old naval base on the Amazon. Because of his jungle experience and knowledge of English—a prerequisite for supervising the British workmen—Alzamora had been named chief of staff to Admiral Ignacio Mariátegui who in 1864 had been charged with founding the Iquitos station. But Mariátegui did not venture beyond Pará, the bustling Brazilian port at the mouth of the Amazon. The heavy responsibility at Iquitos fell upon Acting Commandant General Alzamora. Lima then appointed Captain Francisco Carrasco to the top post in the jungle. The new *comandante* resided thirty-seven days at Iquitos—just long enough to be accused of misappropriating government funds. Finally, in January 1866 Alzamora was appointed to the job he had filled ad interim for two years.[32]

The Master of Manassas

Not the least among Alzamora's problems was Iquitos's chronic shortage of food. Nearby Indian communities maintained *chacras* (small gardens) but generally grew only enough crops to feed themselves. The soils of the region were poor, and the tasks of clearing land and controlling weeds laborious. The natives devoted their surplus energies to the collection of forest products, hunting and fishing, and the manufacture of handicrafts for export. Salt fish was abundant; Loreto typically sent some one hundred thousand pounds per year to Brazil. But even fresh fish (usually trapped or poisoned with rotenone in narrow channels) became a luxury during the annual floods, which inundated much of the lowland jungle from December to May. Game animals, at least those attractive to the palate, were relatively scarce; and among domestic varieties, only hogs did tolerably well. Iquitos imported many of its provisions from Brazil, Europe, and the United States. Common staples were very expensive and often unavailable at any price. Therefore, the navy maintained gardens near Lake Morona, where Arturo Wertheman soon cleared a *chacra*. Captain Alzamora and a few other prominent Iquiteños had farms along the Itaya River, just south of town.[33]

Soon after reaching Iquitos, Admiral Tucker, his son Jack, and James Norris began clearing their "plantation" (probably a few acres at most) on the Itaya, six miles by canoe from Iquitos. In conformity with Peruvian custom and Southern tradition, too, Tucker gave his farm a name. Alzamora, the admiral's neighbor, designated his place Abtao, in honor of the 1866 naval battle. Tucker called his plantation Manassas, after the Virginia battlefield (Bull Run, in Union accounts) where the Confederates had scored two major victories. Jack and Norris had direct charge of Manassas. The low-water planting season had passed by the time of their arrival at Iquitos, so the aspiring farmers began building a five-room house—probably a thatched-roof, wattle-and-daub structure on stilts—with a veranda surrounding it. Within a few months the admiral reported his "manor" to be "quite snug." With luck, he wrote son Randy, they soon would have a "good large country house . . . in the midst of orange and lemon trees," where the family could "again be all together under our own roof." But he would not send for his three younger children until the farm produced enough for their support "independent of other resources."

When the floodwaters subsided in April 1868, Jack and Norris planted sugarcane, coffee, tobacco, rice, and cotton. They quickly learned that farming in the Amazon Basin differed considerably from agriculture in Virginia. Although Iquitos enjoyed a "perpetual summer" and growth was "amazing," the weeds grew "as fast as plants." Jack ordered a plow and planned to "cultivate after the old style." Until that implement arrived, the planters hoped to obtain a "tollerable crop" with traditional Amazonian methods, using a pointed stick to poke holes in the soil for the insertion of seeds and cuttings. "Want of labor," predicted Tucker, would seriously hinder their experiment. In November the admiral returned from an expedition to find his Indian farmhand, José, losing a one-man battle with the jungle. Manassas had presented "many obstacles" to Jack and Norris, who abandoned Iquitos to "pursue [their] profession elsewhere." Although the admiral planted some seeds sent by his friends in Virginia, he now proposed to maintain the farm "at a very reduced scale" until he could live there and give it his "personal attention."[34] Tucker ultimately lost the third battle of Manassas.

Official duties occupied most of the admiral's time during his first year in the jungle. Upon reaching Iquitos in October 1867, he had found new orders from Lima. Without prejudice to his explorations but with "the greatest possible brevity," he was to supervise the construction of a fort on the Amazon at the Brazilian frontier.[35] The impetus for the project had come from Alzamora who in January had informed the government that the Brazilians were mounting fourteen guns in their old fort at Tabatinga, just across the border on the north bank of the river. In April, at Alzamora's request, Governor Benigno Bustamante of the frontier district cleared land and built a crude *tambo* at the Quebrada de San Antonio, a ravine marking the Peru-Brazil boundary at that point. Meanwhile, state engineer Maximiliano Siebert and naval engineer Luis Sandi selected a site for the fort.[36]

On October 16, two weeks after reaching Iquitos, Tucker ordered his engineer Manuel Charon to survey the environs of San Antonio, draft a plan for a twenty-gun fort, and begin work on the project. Charon (whose family had produced several notable French military engineers) rejected the location previously chosen and selected a new site atop a high bluff 1¼ miles farther upstream. From these heights, overlooking a relatively narrow, concave bend in the river, guns placed in two redoubts could command the Amazon for several miles in both directions and expose intruders to a deadly cross fire. Charon began clearing jungle from a one-mile strip along the river, employing forty Indians drafted from nearby villages. But half of his workers deserted before the arrival of twenty soldiers from Iquitos, who supplemented his labor force and prevented the escape of the other *peones*. To facilitate work on the project, Lima soon appointed Charon port captain at San Antonio in addition to his duties as engineer in chief. Within ten months he built a barracks for his men, a warehouse for supplies, a port office, and houses for himself and other officials. Meanwhile, two merchants, several families, and "some women" had formed the nucleus of a village alongside the government works. Progress on the fort itself, however, came slowly due to the shortage of workers.[37]

Admiral Tucker and his commission departed Iquitos on November 4 in the exploring steamer *Napo* to inspect Charon's fort and survey the rivers in the frontier region. The transport *Morona* accompanied them, carrying tools and building materials. On November 20, after reaching the fort, the commission members along with captains Ruperto Gutiérrez of the *Napo* and Eduardo Raygada of the *Morona* conferred about a name for the place. From the first days of his efforts

154

there, Charon had referred to the site as Puerto Leticia. The engineer's colleagues now concurred in that choice. Charon notified Alzamora of this decision and asked him to request the ratification of Lima.

The designation was rejected in the national capital. "This name Leticia," noted the director of marine, "has no significance whatsoever." He ordered that the post be called Ramón Castilla, in acknowledgment of the former president's great contributions to Amazonian Peru. But Charon persisted in addressing his correspondence from "Puerto Leticia." A presidential decree of May 15, 1868, officially christened the place General Castilla. Two months later First Assistant State Engineer Charon boldly confronted the chief executive on this important issue. The fort, indeed, had been designated General Castilla. The adjacent town, however, was Leticia. The latter name could not be dismissed as "insignificant," protested Charon, for it had been adopted through democratic procedures by the Hydrographic Commission to honor the "glorious deeds" of the Paraguayans in their current war with the Triple Alliance of Brazil, Argentina, and Uruguay—a struggle in which Peru sympathized with Paraguay. "The most notable" of these heroic acts, asserted the engineer, was "the defense of a fort which carries the name 'Leticia.'"[38]

But, of course, there was no Fort Leticia in Paraguay or elsewhere. And just as certainly, Leticia Smith, the sister of Hydrographic Commission secretary Timiteo Smith, was the prettiest unmarried woman in Iquitos. Manuel Charon courted her assiduously, and the smitten engineer's colleagues joined in his conspiracy to woo her. Miss Smith sang "with great sweetness" and very much reminded the Virginians of their "Southern girls."[39] Her name, moreover, had double significance for Tucker, McCorkle, and Butt. James Henry Rochelle, their old friend and future colleague on the commission, had a niece, Letitia Tyler Shands, famed for her beauty. As an exemplar of Southern womanhood and a granddaughter of former president John Tyler, she had been chosen to raise the new national flag over the first capitol of the Confederacy during the February 1861 inaugural ceremonies at Montgomery, Alabama.[40]

In the decades that followed, the designation Leticia prevailed over General Castilla, and the town became the capital of a large district bearing the same name. In the next century this remote Amazonian territory found its way into the headlines of the world's press. The cession of Leticia to Colombia sparked the overthrow of Peru's President Augusto B. Leguía in 1930. Two years later, armed civilians from Iquitos seized Leticia from its small Colombian garrison, and soon Peruvian army and navy units confronted Colombian forces in the region. A major war threatened until Peru again relinquished the area to its northern neighbor.[41] In the first battle of Leticia, however, two pretty young women—a Peruvian and a Virginian—were the victors, triumphing over the authorities in Lima.

After inspecting Charon's fort, the Hydrographic Commission explored the Yavarí River, which enters the Amazon from the south a few miles downstream from Leticia. An 1851 treaty established this stream as the boundary between Brazil and Peru, with such adjustments as might later be mutually acceptable. A mixed commission from the two governments had begun to survey the river, but its work had been suspended since November 1866, when Indians attacked the team, killing one man and wounding nine others. The results of Tucker's reconnaissance were disconcerting. The Peruvian government believed that the Yavarí had a nearly north-south course, as indicated in Paz Soldán's *Atlas*. The Hydrographic Commission confirmed other reports that it flowed east-northeast, nearly parallel to the Amazon for its final 220 miles. So that the problem might be rectified in future negotiations with Brazil, the admiral sent the minister of war and marine a preliminary map of the region, illustrating the "immense territory" lost to Peru by employing the Yavarí line.[42]

The Hydrographic Commission returned to Iquitos in December 1867 when the onset of the high-water season made surveys impractical. Tucker hoped to resume his work the following May. But the *Napo*, the little exploring steamer assigned to him, required extensive repairs that would not be completed until September.[43] Although the delay was frustrating, it afforded the commission an opportunity to determine the latitude and longitude of Iquitos, the key geographic coordinate upon which they would base their future surveys. The task was as difficult as it was important.

Since ancient times navigators had been able to ascertain their approximate location relative to the equator (expressed in degrees of north or south latitude) through observations of the sun. Under controlled conditions, the longitude of a place (its distance east or west of a well-known point—a prime meridian) could be determined by multiple astronomical observations with a telescope. But a practical method for reading longitudes by navigators and explorers dated only from the mid-eighteenth century. Based on the fixed relationship between longitudinal distance and time, this technique employed chronometers— very sensitive clocks with constant rates of error. Almanacs predicted the times and angles from which various celestial bodies could be viewed at Paris or Greenwich, England (or other places with observatories). By observing these same phenomena at local time, applying various mathematical corrections, and then comparing these data with those for the prime meridian, navigators and surveyors could determine their longitude.[44] But what was the local time?

The approximate longitude of Callao, Peru's major Pacific port, was known, and chronometers could be set accurately there. With the extension of telegraph lines from the coast over the Andes in the mid-1870s and the introduction of the wireless in the early twentieth century, it became rather easy to calculate local time—and with it, longitude—in Amazonian Peru, for electricity and radio waves travel at constant speeds. Before these developments, however, time had to be carried into eastern Peru with chronometers. When these clocks were transported over rugged Andean trails, severe jostling and great changes in air pressure significantly affected their accuracy—not only the time shown but also the rate of error. A discrepancy of only four seconds in time translated into a one-mile error in longitude; conversely, a variance of a single mile in the longitude of a place produced a four-second error in chronometers set for local time. A chronometer adjusted to an erroneous time at a longitude with an equal degree of variance doubled the rate of error for other longitudes determined from that base.[45]

In the 1860s time could be imported most accurately into Amazonian Peru from Brazil. Beginning with chronometers set at Rio de Janeiro (whose exact location was debated), the longitude and local time had been calculated for Tabatinga, some sixteen hundred miles to the west on the Peruvian frontier. In 1868 Arturo Wertheman repeatedly traveled on the government steamers between Tabatinga and Iquitos, rating his chronometers (several were used, as checks on each other) and calculating the distance between the two ports. The Swiss engineer also began a long series of astronomical observations at Iquitos to refine the data based on the Tabatinga meridian. The longitude he originally established for Iquitos was about seven miles east of the town's true location.[46]

In addition to the faulty coordinate for their base, the Hydrographic Commission faced extraordinary difficulties in their surveys. In the 1850s the United States Coast Survey (with which McCorkle had worked) measured the Atlantic Coast from Maine to Florida, with a total error of just eighteen inches. But the triangulations and other sophisticated techniques employed to achieve this amazing accuracy were not practical in the Amazonian jungles. The tall, unbroken wall of trees along the rivers reduced the visible horizon, severely limiting the choice of celestial bodies from which readings might be taken. Even solid ground for the placement of the theodolite (transit) was often difficult to find. Although the explorers protected their chronometers and other sensitive instruments in thick bundles of felt covered by waterproofed canvas, the high humidity of the rain forest quickly oxidized them. Finally, as Wertheman explained, the observer experienced "martyrdom" during the fifteen or twenty minutes required to make a reading. He was "obligated to concentrate his entire attention" while "thousands of mosquitoes or sandflies made good use of his immobility to mortify him atrociously."[47] Because of these inherent difficulties and the commission's misrecording of the key Nauta meridian,[48] the longitudes reported by Tucker's team during its early explorations had substantial errors—as much as thirty miles for points on the upper Ucayali. But these were corrected, and through repeated observations, the use of improved equipment, and acquired experience, the major coordinates determined by the commission during its later surveys would be surprisingly accurate.

On September 2, 1868, a few days after repairs to the *Napo* had been completed, the Hydrographic Commission began its first major exploration. Tucker hoped to ascend the Ucayali River to its source, the Río Tambo, and steam up that river to Fort San Ramón, the outpost guarding the approach to the Chanchamayo Valley. If this could be accomplished, the admiral would identify the navigable waterway closest to Lima and a link to the Atlantic markets for Tarma and the neighboring Jauja Valley. Commandant General Alzamora, who praised the "interest and enthusiasm which the commission brings for exploration," supplied Tucker with four months' provisions, ten rifles, a small cannon, and three thousand *soles* for expenses. In addition to its normal crew of a dozen men, the *Napo* carried photographer Alberto La Rose (shown as a gunner on the muster roll) who would "shoot" numerous photos during the expedition.[49]

After a brief stop at Nauta for minor repairs, the side-wheeler began wending her way slowly up the lower portion of the Ucayali. The men of the commission sketched the river's course, sounded its channel, and measured the current. During the frequent stops to cut firewood, the explorers made astronomical observations, determining for the first time the geographic coordinates for more than forty points along the waterway. In his diary of the voyage, Tucker recorded the limited agricultural potential of the low-lying riverbanks and the reaction of the Indians to the noisy *Napo*. They fled at the sight of the strange craft; but those on the west bank of the Ucayali, who were friendly toward white men, soon succumbed to their curiosity, timidly approaching the steamer whenever she touched land. The explorers gave them tools and money to cut firewood and to serve as pilots.

The expedition encountered no significant navigation hazards below the confluence of the Pachitea River, about halfway up the Ucayali. But beyond that point, where no steamer had yet ventured, the stream's mud bottom became rocky, the current grew much stronger, and frequent *mal pasos* (bad passes)—where shoals, massive boulders, and embedded trees obstructed the channel—tested the *Napo* and her crew. The greatest challenge came at the Devil's Whirlpool, a place christened by the French explorer Castelnau and, noted Tucker, "well worthy of the name." Swirling water locked the *Napo's* wheels and covered the bow of the little vessel—"a moment of great anxiety . . . and proportionate relief when it passed." Gradually the riverbanks became higher, and to the west the explorers could see the hills of the Gran Pajonal, a rolling area of forest dotted by patches of grassland. The air was cooler, and the commission was relieved from the constant torment of stinging insects. On the lower Ucayali sandflies—whose bites blackened exposed parts of the body—were the chief enemy during daylight. They followed their victims like "a smoke-cloud"; unceasing effort was required to keep them out of the mouth and nostrils. At night, while the flies slept, suicidal swarms of mosquitoes literally extinguished the fires in the *Napo's* lanterns.

On the upper Ucayali the commission found the Piro Indians, renowned as indomitable warriors. They were the "finest looking" natives that Tucker had yet seen, "being tall above the average" and having "complexions much lighter than the other tribes." The admiral hired Chief Benito Cayampay and six of his Piros to pilot the *Napo*. These new members of the expedition caused some uneasiness. "They go armed continually with their bows and arrows and war clubs," noted Tucker, "even when on board the steamer." The men of the commission believed that all of the Indians they encountered on the Ucayali could be civilized through peaceful trade and government gifts, especially of tools.

The expedition on October 15 reached the confluence of the Urubamba and Tambo rivers, which unite to form the Ucayali. After they traveled only six miles up the Tambo toward Chanchamayo, the powerful current and shallow bottom stymied them. The machinists built up one hundred pounds of steam, pressing the limit of safety for the *Napo's* boiler; but after ninety minutes of supreme effort, the little vessel had made no progress. Tucker ordered a retreat. Next, the commission ascended the Urubamba, a river that originates in the high Andes and flows near the ancient Inca capital of Cuzco before joining the Tambo from the south. The *Napo* climbed the stream for some thirty miles, grounding three times, before being stopped by shoals and strong currents. After making observations, the expedition retraced its thousand-mile voyage back to Iquitos, arriving on November 10, 1868. The failure to reach the Chanchamayo Valley greatly disappointed Tucker, but he believed that the Tambo River might be ascended by a steamer better suited for exploration.[50]

Soon after he first reached Iquitos in 1867, the admiral had informed Lima that the *Napo* was inadequate for his work, an opinion shared by Commandant Alzamora and other officers posted in Loreto. Rated at 60 tons burden, the craft was 100 feet long and 11 feet wide and drew a minimum 20 inches of water. A puny fifteen-horsepower engine turned her side wheels, and a moderate collision seemed likely to puncture her thin steel hull. The vessel could accommodate only a score of men and a few weeks' provisions. The steamer's inefficient engine consumed firewood at a rapid rate, but her bunkers could hold only a five-day supply, a great inconvenience. Notwithstanding the immensity of the jungle, accessible good-quality wood was scarce along the rivers, as were the men to cut it. For Tucker, the Ucayali expedition demonstrated the "absolute necessity" for a larger, specially built steamer of sturdy construction, relatively shallow draft, and ample power. He asked that he and one of his men be sent to the United States to superintend the construction of such a vessel, which he estimated would cost sixty thousand *soles*. If the order was given immediately, the admiral could accomplish this mission during the oncoming high-water season, when surveys were impractical, and return to challenge the Tambo River again in July 1869.[51]

Tucker did not address this appeal to the government of his friend Colonel Prado, but to a new administration adversely disposed toward the admiral because of his close association with the Prado regime. The insurrection against the latter, under way since late 1866, had steadily gained strength, especially after the exiled Marshal Ramón Castilla returned to Peru and assumed leadership of the movement. That old warrior died—literally in the saddle—before the final victory. But on January 5, 1868, Prado resigned the presidency; he sailed for Chile three days later. General Pedro Diez Canseco, Peru's second vice-president and a brother-in-law of Castilla, became provisional chief of state. A presidential election the next month was won by Colonel José Balta—the uncle of Tucker's old adversary Lizardo Montero. The new regime assumed power on August 2, 1868, a month before the Hydrographic Commission began its survey of the Ucayali.

Iquitos responded to the change of government in traditional fashion. Upon learning of Colonel Prado's overthrow, the local subprefect, an unpopular Ecuadorian-born partisan of the fallen president, fled the town. The next evening, a "spontaneous assembly" of Iquiteños expressed unanimous support for the revolution and selected a temporary subprefect. Commandant Alzamora wrote to the new minister of war and marine reporting these events and pledging his allegiance to the administration of "el Señor General, Second Vice-President of the Republic, don Pedro Diez Canseco, defender of the institutions and [constitutional] guarantees of the country." Alzamora also forwarded a manifesto of support signed by 121 persons, including Hydrographic Commission secretary Timiteo Smith and "Gualterio" R. Butt.[52]

The Fiddler perhaps did not realize that the document endorsed the replacement of both the despised subprefect and the regime of President Prado, the benefactor of the Hydrographic Commission.

Tucker's signature was notably absent from the manifesto. Peru's frequent changes of government, he wrote Randy, were "very unfortunate," retarding the nation's "advancement." With all of his friends removed from office in Lima, the admiral feared that the commission might be abolished. Indeed, decrees nullified, subject to review, all civil and military appointments as well as promotions granted by the Prado regime. But the "general impression" in Iquitos was that the admiral's work was too important to be interrupted.[53]

Although Tucker did not endorse the ouster of President Prado, he did participate in another common ritual attending changes of government: the admiral joined public employees throughout Peru who bombarded the new regime with advice and pleas for favors. On May 1, 1868, Tucker wrote to Provisional President Diez Canseco (whom he probably had met earlier in Lima), describing the commission's recent work and asking the temporary executive for support. Diez Canseco expressed satisfaction with the admiral's performance and pledged, within the limits of his power, to "protect" the commission.[54]

After José Balta's inauguration, the admiral sent Timiteo Smith to Lima with confidential letters for the new minister of war and marine, Colonel Juan Francisco Balta, the president's brother. In this and later correspondence, Tucker continued to press for his new exploring steamer. He also requested replacements for Dr. Santiago Távara (who had returned to Lima in early 1868) and David McCorkle. The latter man became very ill during the Ucayali expedition and resigned soon after returning to Iquitos. The admiral reported that a severe labor shortage was hindering construction of the fort at Leticia. He suggested two remedies: the immediate assignment of the post's full garrison to supplement the Indian workers or the dispatch of a large number of "Asiatics." About one hundred thousand indentured Chinese laborers were brought to Peru between 1850 and 1880. The admiral believed that these industrious people could provide a reliable labor pool for various public projects in Loreto and improve the "ruinous state" of agriculture there. Tucker urged that two new steamers, better suited for commerce, replace the *Morona* and *Pastaza* on the Marañón-Amazon and that the old vessels be employed on the Ucayali River, where he recommended the establishment of regular commercial service. The admiral also suggested administrative reforms at the Iquitos naval station, where Tucker's relations with Commandant General Alzamora had not been entirely harmonious. The admiral informed the war minister that Captain Smith, Tucker's messenger, could expound upon these problems "verbally and with great detail."[55]

Fortunately for Tucker, the Hydrographic Commission already had registered some notable achievements—the initiation of construction at Fort Castilla, the confirmation of the Yavarí boundary error, and an important survey of the Ucayali. The admiral's friends in Lima also worked on his behalf. In response to an appeal from Tucker, Manuel Pardo skillfully lobbied for the continuance of the commission. The former prime minister petitioned the war minister directly, while Pardo's friends at *El Nacional* and *El Comercio*, Lima's leading journals, editorialized favorably about the commission. The latter newspaper also published a preliminary version of Dr. Távara's diary of his journey to Iquitos. "Mr. Tucker," noted the surgeon in his preface, was "a distinguished . . . mariner" who viewed Peru as his "adopted country" and demonstrated great enthusiasm "for service to the republic."[56]

The campaign to save the commission faltered at first; the admiral's team was omitted from the budget approved in October 1868. But in January 1869 War Minister Balta ordered Tucker and Butt to the United States to obtain a new exploring steamer. He also authorized the admiral to hire replacements for Távara and McCorkle. The government's favorable decisions, the admiral informed his son, arose "not from any great love" for him but because of the "great interest manifested by all Peru" in the important work of the Hydrographic Commission. Whatever the regime's motives, the old sailor rejoiced that he soon would see his "dear children and relations." The admiral and Butt departed for the United States, by way of the Amazon, on March 15, 1869.[57]

Leoncio Prado, the lad who had traveled to Iquitos with Tucker in 1867, had been stranded by the revolution that toppled his father's government. In July 1868 the war minister ordered the fourteen-year-old navy ensign to the capital, so that he could join his exiled family in Chile. At Chachapoyas, en route to Lima, Leoncio learned from a newspaper about Tucker's mission to the United States. Hoping to accompany his former mentor and to further his education, Leoncio wrote to the admiral at Iquitos. "Tell my father in a letter," he asked awkwardly, "that school is very necessary for me." Tucker left Peru before young Prado's note arrived, but he probably did intercede later on the boy's behalf. In 1873 Leoncio and two of his brothers went to the United States to study engineering, a course that Tucker had recommended for his own son Tarleton. The Prado brothers pursued their studies in a city not especially noted for technical schools—Richmond, Virginia.[58]

CHAPTER EIGHT

Tribulations of the *Tambo*

TUCKER AND BUTT reached New York City in mid-April 1869. They spent a few days there making inquiries with local shipbuilders and then traveled to Washington for consultation with Colonel Manuel Freyre, Peru's minister resident, before joining their families in Virginia. After an absence of nearly three years, the two sailors must have felt as though they had returned from a long cruise. And like Tucker's "Old Navy" days, the admiral was laden with exotic gifts, including a woolen poncho and a magnificent chonta palm spear for brothers-in-law Oscar Cranz and Joe Randolph. Tucker ultimately had abundant time to visit his relatives and to renew old friendships. However, his initial "home leave" lasted only one week, for he was anxious to begin work on a "tip-top steamer."[1]

Peru's rigid and cumbersome financial regulations bedeviled Tucker throughout his association with that country. Instituted to check fraud, these procedures often caused gross inefficiency and exasperating delay, amply demonstrated during the admiral's mission. The republic's finances in the United States were managed by the firm of Hobson-Hurtado, based in New York and Lima, Peru's guano consignee for the northern republic. Under a state monopoly the company marketed the bird manure in the United States, retaining a commission for itself and placing the remaining proceeds in the government's account. The firm also funded the Washington legation and provided money for most other official transactions in the northern republic. Hobson-Hurtado could not make disbursements, however, without formal authorization from Lima.

On January 29, 1869, soon after ordering Tucker to the United States, Minister of War and Marine Juan Francisco Balta instructed the finance minister to have Hobson-Hurtado place sixty thousand *soles* at the admiral's disposition. The order was not issued. Although Tucker's instructions and those sent to Minister Freyre clearly stated that the guano agent would provide money for the admiral's work, Hobson-Hurtado could not act. It was merely an irksome oversight, thought the admiral, which would be resolved with the arrival of the mail from Lima in early May. But the order did not come. Freyre informed the foreign minister, who passed the word to Minister Balta, who reiterated his instruction to Finance Minister Nicolás de Piérola. Nevertheless, the Lima mail reached New York in early June without the necessary authorization. Freyre appealed once more to Lima, and Balta protested vigorously to Piérola in a ritual that would be repeated monthly until September.[2]

This bureaucratic bungling did not seriously hamper the admiral's mission at first. He and Butt established their headquarters in New York, and Freyre paid their monthly salaries from the legation's contingency fund. By July, however, the two men had not found a suitable shipbuilder in the New York area. They needed to visit shipyards scattered widely along the eastern seaboard but lacked the funds to pay for their travel. Tucker requested the ten-cents-per-mile allowance paid to United States government employees. Colonel Freyre deemed this reasonable, but the envoy could not draw upon his legation account for this purpose without the approval of Lima. August passed with the two sailors "almost inactive." In September, after a five-month delay, Lima properly authorized $55,000 in gold for the steamer and the mission's travel expenses. The latter item had required a presidential decree. Still, Hobson-Hurtado would not be instructed to pay salaries to Tucker and Butt until nearly the end of their mission. Month after month the two men received their pay from Freyre, almost exhausting his contingency fund.[3]

A Tip-Top Steamer

On October 13 Tucker signed a contract with Pusey and Jones Company of Wilmington, Delaware, for the construction of an exploring steamer to be christened *Tambo*, after the river she would try to conquer. Although the admiral had solicited bids from many firms, only Pusey and Jones would attempt to meet Tucker's exacting specifications. In 1854 the company had constructed the first iron sailing vessel in the United States. The firm obtained several United States Navy contracts during the Civil War, becoming one of the nation's largest ship works. As the American merchant marine entered a period of decline in the postwar years, Pusey and Jones began specializing in iron and steel steamers for Latin American rivers. In two decades they built more than one hundred such vessels for the American tropics, including thirty-seven destined for the Amazon Basin. Pusey and Jones remained competitive with the dominant British builders because of the firm's innovative technology. Employing metal of great strength that reduced the amount needed, their vessels had shallow drafts relative to their size and were very fuel-efficient.[4]

The *Tambo* contract provided for a nearly flat-bottomed twin paddle wheeler 135 feet long and 26 feet wide, with a hold 6½-feet deep (about 200 tons capacity). Fully loaded with six months' provisions and enough fuel for fifty hours' steaming, the vessel was, if possible, to draw only twenty inches of water. However, the steamer's "strength and durability" were not to be compromised by using material too light for her intended purpose. With a prow and a rudder both fore and aft (a "double-ender"), the *Tambo* would steam efficiently with either end ahead. Minister Balta had instructed Tucker to use only the best materials, and the admiral gladly complied. Because the borers that abound in tropical fresh water quickly ruin wooden boats, the framing and hull of the *Tambo* were to be entirely of wrought iron, the latter one-quarter inch thick. The hull was to have bulkheads front and back, dividing it into three watertight segments. The decking, also atop iron frames, was to be of 2-inch white pine, overlaid with 1½-inch boards "worked tight to keep out dirt."

The *Tambo* was to be powered at speeds of up to fifteen miles per hour by two high-pressure inclined engines (later rated at 127 horsepower), each having its own large locomotive boiler with double steam chests. The machinery—located on the main deck, amidships, to provide ventilation for the engine crew—would be arranged so that each engine drove one of the side wheels, independent of the other. The boilers, however, were to be linked; thus, steam from both systems could be fed to a single engine for added power in getting off shoals. The wheels would have iron frames and oak buckets. The quarters of the Hydrographic Commission were to be at the rear of the main deck, in a single suite. In addition to six staterooms with skylights, these accommodations would include a pantry, kitchen, dining room, parlor, bathroom, and water closet. Similar facilities for the vessel's officers were to be located up front. The contract specified a power ventilation system, providing fresh air to the living quarters, and a donkey pump, which would feed water to the kitchens, bathrooms, toilets, and fire hoses and could be used to empty the bilges, too. The *Tambo* was to be crowned by a hurricane deck of wood, covered by tin, and a pilothouse. All of the open spaces between decks were to be enclosed by copper-wire screens on hinged frames, which could be lifted open.

The vessel was to be fully equipped. Pusey and Jones promised a steam winch on the foredeck, a pair of ship's boats, and a metal 30-by-6-foot steam launch, whose side wheels could be readily hoisted out of the water. This smaller craft was to have a "movable shelter," enclosed with screens. The contract also included a full bunker of coal, spare parts, and complete sets of tools for the engineers, machinists, carpenter, blacksmith, and boilermaker; blocks and tackle, anchors, chains, and lines; bells, tanks, lanterns, and logs; an engine-room clock and scale; needles, thread, and bunting; a brass speaking trumpet, four telescopes, and a large compass with stand; a swinging barometer, one circle of reflection, three chronometers, two micrometers, two artificial horizons, nine thermometers, and a 100-foot measuring chain; and, lastly, "a complete set of furniture . . . including bedding, table furniture, crockery ware, etc." And the firm did not scrimp on that final "etc." The Hydrographic Commission's parlor would be appointed as comfortably as any gentlemen's club, with four overstuffed sofas of morocco leather, eight matching chairs, and a reed organ. A tip-top steamer, indeed.

Pusey and Jones promised to complete the *Tambo* by June 1, 1870. To protect Peru from the possible loss of the shallow-draft vessel in the stormy Caribbean, the firm would deliver her at Pará. Peru promised the builders $71,300 in greenbacks—about $55,000 in gold. Ten percent would be delivered upon ratification of the contract by Colonel Freyre, and 20 percent when the keel had been laid. Thereafter, installments of 10 percent would be paid upon completion of the hull and when the ship was launched. Tucker was to inspect the steamer after each of these steps and, if satisfied, to approve disbursements to the firm. After launching, the admiral was to give the vessel a trial and to identify any defects for the builder to correct. Upon delivery at Pará, Tucker again would inspect the *Tambo* before accepting her for Peru and authorizing payment of the final 50 percent of the contract price.[5]

Well aware of the scandals associated with naval contracts during the Civil War, Tucker thought that Pusey and Jones might have calculated their costs to include a "commission" for himself. After signing the contract, the admiral informed Colonel Freyre that he would try to obtain a 5 percent rebate—for the government. The firm, however, assured Tucker that it had "no expectation of making a profit" on the vessel but had taken the contract to "secure the patronage" of South American governments and companies. Colonel Freyre was delighted with the contract. The *Tambo*'s specifications, he wrote, not only conformed to the government's instructions but also fulfilled all of the requirements for her intended service. He considered the price "very reasonable," an opinion shared by Consul Juan Carlos Tracy, in New York. Admiral Tucker had "proceeded with intelligence and greatest interest," noted the minister, and could not have obtained the steamer "under better conditions." Freyre promptly ratified the agreement, and War Minister Balta approved on November 25.[6]

Pusey and Jones quickly began work on the *Tambo*, laying her keel in early November. Tucker and Butt rented rooms in Wilmington and constantly observed the project to insure the quality of materials and workmanship. In his regular progress reports the admiral invariably expressed himself as very pleased with the firm. In February 1870, as the vessel was about to receive her machinery, Tucker obtained the services of "an experienced mechanical engineer" to help him inspect the craft. This man—who received only travel expenses, paid from the admiral's own pocket—was almost certainly his nephew Thomas Alphonse Jackson, a former chief engineer of both the United States and Confederate navies.[7]

Pusey and Jones launched the *Tambo* in late March, and Tucker took his new steamer on a "very satisfactory trial trip down the river and bay" on May 24. He invited several United States Navy engineers to accompany him, and they "expressed admiration" for the machinery. But clearly, one of the vessel's features troubled the admiral. The builders had added two heavy longitudinal bulkheads, so the *Tambo* drew considerably more water than originally specified (later descriptions indicate that the steamer's draft was three feet or more). Although these braces could be removed to reduce the craft's weight, Pusey and Jones advised Tucker not to do so unless "absolutely necessary," as they added "so greatly" to the vessel's strength. The *Tambo* had been something of an experiment, and the firm was convinced that she was "as light as it is possible to make a boat of her size."[8] Tucker apparently concurred.

While the admiral waited for Hobson-Hurtado to disburse funds for the *Tambo*, he undertook some secondary tasks. On November 1, 1869, Tucker completed an extensive report requested by the war minister concerning commercial steamer service in Amazonian Peru. He again recommended that the *Pastaza* and *Morona* be replaced. These two vessels, which required major repairs, were unsuited to the role of commercial carriers. Designed like warships, they had limited cargo capacity and inadequate facilities for passengers. They compared very unfavorably with the steamers of the connecting Brazilian line and, noted the old sailor pointedly, were an embarrassment to their Peruvian officers. Properly repaired and modified, however, the *Morona* and *Pastaza* could provide many more years of useful service on the Ucayali. The admiral urged the minister to put two new eight-hundred-ton steamers, with cabin space for sixty passengers, on the Amazon and to extend the government's current service beyond Tabatinga to the mouth of the river. Tucker praised the craft built by Pusey and Jones expressly for South American waterways and enclosed a diagram and specifications for an appropriate model.[9]

Minister Freyre had been ordered to study rifles recently developed in the United States and to identify the best of these for use by Peru's cavalry. The colonel asked the admiral for assistance. On October 29 Tucker submitted a preliminary report on "breech loading military small arms." Noting the great importance of such basic procurement decisions, he urged Freyre to consult the technical studies of various military commissions in Europe and the United States, including one being prepared by a panel of army experts then meeting in St. Louis. The admiral explained that breechloaders all fell into two categories—single-shot weapons and repeaters—and succinctly described the advantages and shortcomings of each class. Among the guns he had been able to inspect, Tucker preferred the Remington and Roberts single-loaders and the repeaters made by Spencer and Winchester. Three weeks later Freyre was instructed to purchase one thousand rifles immediately. He bought the Winchester repeaters.[10]

The admiral also attended to personnel matters. At the time of his departure from Iquitos, Tucker had recommended that command of the new exploring steamer be given to Lieutenant Ruperto Gutiérrez, the young skipper of the *Napo* who had worked well with the Hydrographic Commission during the exploration of the Yavarí and Ucayali rivers. He urged that this officer be sent to the United States at an early date to observe the construction of the vessel; this would give him an "intimate understanding" of her operation, especially the steamer's novel high-pressure engines. But Lima assigned Lieutenant Eduardo Raygada, whose *Morona* was undergoing extensive repairs, to the *Tambo*, and he did not reach the United States until long after the craft had been launched. The *Tambo*, however, would have one crewman who was familiar with her machinery. With the approval of the government, Tucker recruited Pusey and Jones machinist José Manuel Pérez, who had worked on the vessel, for service in Amazonian Peru.[11]

Most important, the admiral found replacements on the commission for McCorkle and Távara. On January 3, 1870, he requested Lima's permission to hire James Henry Rochelle, "a well-educated and distinguished officer," for the post vacated by McCorkle. As a replacement for Dr. Távara, Tucker recommended Francis Land Galt, "a gentleman of much maritime experience" and "scientific attainments."[12] The admiral's brief characterization of Galt was quite apt: this sailor-scientist-gentleman was the most complex of Tucker's Amazonian associates.

Frank Galt had been born at Norfolk, Virginia, on December 13, 1833, the eldest son of Dr. John M. and Ann White Land Galt. Since emigrating from Scotland to Hampton and Williamsburg, Virginia, in the late seventeenth century, the Galt family had produced several distinguished physicians, including George Washington's chief surgeon at the battle of Yorktown.[13] Frank's father, however, was less successful. Although trained in medicine, he secured an appointment as a United States Army storekeeper in 1842. The elder Galt moved his family to Florida and then Augusta, Georgia, where he served in the arsenal. Francis Galt studied medicine in New York and then at the

University of Pennsylvania, the nation's foremost medical school. He received his medical doctorate in 1854, writing a thesis on typhoid fever. The next year, after postdoctoral studies, Galt was commissioned an assistant surgeon in the United States Navy. He made his first cruise with the Brazil Squadron, on the frigate *St. Lawrence*. Returning home in 1860, he passed the surgeon's examination and served briefly at the Norfolk naval hospital before shipping out on the *Pocahontas*, a vessel assigned to the Home Squadron.[14]

Galt loved the life of a navy doctor, and if his postwar attitudes reflect his opinions in 1861, he probably opposed secession. But on February 28, 1861, after Georgia had left the Union, his father resigned his post to enter the Confederate army. Frank's younger brother John also joined the Southern service. Dr. Galt tendered his resignation on March 16, and it was accepted three days later. On April 15 Francis Land Galt was commissioned a surgeon in the Confederate States Navy. Within a week Navy Secretary Stephen Mallory ordered Galt to report at New Orleans to Commander Raphael Semmes for duty on the CSS *Sumter*.[15] A converted merchantman mounting five guns, the *Sumter* was the first of many rebel cruisers that preyed upon the Yankees' seaborne commerce. These corsairs destroyed some 260 vessels, sent insurance rates soaring, and induced the transfer of more than one thousand American ships to foreign (primarily British) ownership. During the four-year Civil War, the tonnage of the United States merchant marine fell by three-quarters, a blow from which the industry never recovered.

The *Sumter* ran the Union blockade in front of New Orleans on June 30, 1861. During the next six months she prowled the Caribbean and the sea-lanes between the humps of Africa and Brazil, capturing eighteen merchant ships. The *Sumter's* men stripped these prizes of needed supplies and money and then burned them. They held the passengers and crews of their victims on board the raider until the prisoners could be put ashore safely. Short of coal and with worn-out boilers, the *Sumter* anchored at Gibraltar in January 1862, where she quickly came under the vigilance of a Union flotilla. Semmes and his officers abandoned their vessel and began journeying home by way of England and the Bahamas. At Nassau, however, Mallory ordered them back to Great Britain, where they would arrange a secret rendezvous with a new cruiser nearing completion at the Laird Brothers' yard at Birkenhead.

Designated by the builder with the serial number *290*, this vessel had been constructed expressly as a commerce destroyer—very fast, with commodious bunkers to permit a substantial cruising range. To skirt Britian's neutrality laws, the raider put to sea unarmed and manned by an English crew. In the Azores, Semmes and his men came on board, mounted eight guns, and on August 24, 1862, raised the Confederate flag over the CSS *Alabama*. The most famous and dreaded of the rebel cruisers, the *'Bama* first ravaged enemy shipping in the North Atlantic and Caribbean. In January 1863 she sank the Union gunboat *Hatteras* in a duel off Galveston, Texas, and resumed her depredations on Yankee commerce. The *Alabama* waylaid ships off the Cape of Good Hope and then cruised the East Indies. By June 1864, when the raider anchored at Cherbourg, France, for refurbishing, she had taken sixty-five prizes. In later years Francis Galt would denounce the Confederacy and its political leaders; but he always took pride in his service with Semmes on the *Alabama*, a vessel almost invariably condemned as a "pirate" in the North.

Within the great limits of that era's medical science, "Pills," as the sailors called Galt, was a skilled physician. During three years and some seventy-five thousand miles of cruising, primarily in tropical waters, the two corsairs on which he served did not lose a single sailor or prisoner to disease.[16] In January 1863 Semmes cashiered his troublesome paymaster. Thereafter, Galt, who inherited something of the storekeeper's ilk from his father, doubled as acting paymaster—handling supplies, the financial affairs of the ship, and records concerning prizes. He delegated many of his medical responsibilities to Assistant Surgeon David Llewellan. Galt's shipmate Lieutenant Arthur Sinclair testified that Frank was "as apt at figures as with his instruments and pills" and praised his expertise as a sailor, too. At a time of bitter controversy over the relative status of staff and line officers, Sinclair paid the physician the highest compliment within his purview. "Upon a pinch," he allowed, "Galt could have performed the duties of a line officer."[17]

Not yet twenty-eight years old when he joined the *Sumter*, Galt was "somewhat under middle size," with "black hair and eyes." Semmes characterized him as quiet, unassuming, intelligent, and cultured. Among the officers who served under him, the austere skipper felt most comfortable in the surgeon's company. In the adjectives of *Sumter-Alabama* scholar Edward Boykin, Galt seems merely a stereotype of the humane physician, "kindly, gentlemanly," and "lovable." He had those qualities—and much more. Filled with nervous energy, he could not bear to be idle. He was a compulsive compiler of lists, a voracious reader, and a talented writer, with an often cutting, sardonic wit. Ambitious for professional recognition matched by financial reward, Galt never achieved the success he craved. He was prone to bouts of self-pity. The physician had a special fondness for children. From one prize the *Alabama* seized David White, a seventeen-year-old black bondsman from the Union slave state of Delaware. Declaring the lad contraband of war, Semmes freed him and put him on the payroll as

Galt's steward. Lecturing Yankee hypocrites, the skipper moralized about the "affection which this boy conceived for Galt" and White's failure to avail himself of several opportunities to escape.[18]

On Sunday morning, June 19, 1864, Paymaster Galt put aside his ledgers and readied his surgical instruments as the *Alabama* steamed out of Cherbourg to challenge the USS *Kearsarge*, under Captain John A. Winslow, which had posted itself in front of the harbor. After an hour's duel at close range, many of the *Alabama*'s men were wounded, nine had died, and the vessel was sinking. Semmes surrendered and sent Galt, with a boatload of wounded sailors, to ask assistance from the Union ship. As the raider went under, the Confederates took to the water, where nine of them, including David White and Dr. Llewellan, drowned. Semmes and most of his officers were rescued by a private English yacht and some pilot boats, thus avoiding capture. Dr. Galt and most of the rebel sailors in Winslow's custody were released on parole.[19]

In July 1864 Galt returned to the Confederacy by way of Canada and a blockade runner which put him ashore at Wilmington, North Carolina. After a two-month leave at Lynchburg, Virginia, where his father was stationed, Galt requested assignment to the army, for service in the field. But the navy ordered him to Richmond. He became temporary fleet surgeon of the James River Squadron and then was transferred to the nearby naval batteries. In March 1865 he came under the command of Commodore Tucker. The two men probably had not met before, but Tucker likely had known Galt's family in Norfolk. The physician marched out of Richmond with the Naval Battalion on April 3 and served at the battle of Sayler's Creek. As a surgeon Galt did not suffer imprisonment after that engagement but was paroled with Lee's army at Appomattox.[20]

With the war behind him, Galt would have liked to start his own family, but not even a skilled physician enjoyed the necessary economic security in the prostrate South. "Trusting that the events of the last few years [had] not altogether obliterated former recollections," Galt sought employment through one of his professors at the University of Pennsylvania. The self-styled "ex-pirate of the rebellion" noted his service on the *Alabama* but now described himself as a "reconstructed Reb." He explained that "finding the practice of my profession in this country hardly capable to supporting even a bachelor—my escape from marriage was providential—I . . . inquire whether I can get anything to do in your city. My circumstances do not permit me to be nice in my choice, and I am therefore willing to go as a clerk in a store—a Drug establishment I would prefer—or to take a physician's position on board one of the ocean steamers sailing from any port."

But Galt's "circumstances" only worsened. He settled in Norfolk and supported himself primarily through odd jobs. He treated many patients, but very few who could pay him. His brother John had been killed in the war, and Galt's father—who now worked as a secretary for a railroad company—died in 1868, leaving Frank and one remaining brother to support their mother and two unmarried sisters. Early in 1869 the French sloop of war *Curieux* docked at Norfolk with no surgeon and a "virulent plague" of yellow fever ravaging her eighty-seven-man complement. Accompanied by a local priest, Galt went on board the dreaded "fever ship" and remained there until the crisis had passed. Several months later he received "an exquisite gold chronometer watch and chain," suitably inscribed, from the government of Napoleon III. Although it was worth at least $500, noted the local newspapers, Galt did "not like to show it" and took it from his pocket to check the time "as stealthily as if it was a cheap brass affair."[21]

In September 1869 Galt accepted a position teaching "natural philosophy, chemistry, natural history and botany" at the Norwood High School, near New Market, in Nelson County, Virginia. But Admiral Tucker soon invited him to join the Hydrographic Commission, and Galt accepted the post at "whatever the government wishes to pay." His contract, signed June 17, 1870, obligated him to serve three years at one hundred *soles* (about $96 in gold) per month. The guano agent in New York was to pay an allotment of thirty-two *soles* to Galt's mother, while the physician would receive the remainder in Peru. Although he agreed to render service at any government installation or ship near the Hydrographic Commission's field of operations, he was not to be detached from that organization. Galt was promised two months' pay in advance and passage to and from Peru.[22]

James Henry Rochelle, Tucker's second nominee for his reconstructed team, had been closely associated with him during the war and would become the admiral's biographer. Descended from French Huguenots who settled in Virginia in 1690, he had been born on November 1, 1826, at Jerusalem (now Courtland), Southampton County, in southeastern Virginia, to James and Martha Hines Rochelle. A lawyer and longtime clerk of the county court—as the chief county administrator was termed—the senior Rochelle died when his son was nine years old. The family, however, continued to enjoy powerful political connections. In 1838 Rochelle's sister Martha married John Tyler, Jr., the son of Virginia's former governor and current United States senator, who would succeed to the presidency three years later. In September 1841 President Tyler sent Mrs. Rochelle a warrant as acting midshipman in the United States Navy for her fourteen-year-old son James. The appointment had been unsolicited. The president thought that the navy—"the theatre where in the future, honour and renown are to be won"—would "suit a boy of his genius." But the widow Rochelle, who had lost several children in infancy, would not let loose of her youngest child. James did not report for duty until the final days of the Tyler administration in 1845, when he shipped on board the USS *Falmouth*, with the Home Squadron.

Rochelle enjoyed an extremely varied naval career. On the sloops *Falmouth* and *Decatur* he fought in the Mexican War, participating in the capture of Tuxpan and Tabasco. At the latter place he served with Midshipman David McCorkle and met, probably for the first time, Lieutenant John R. Tucker. In November 1847 he became a member of the first class of the new United States Naval Academy at Annapolis. After graduation eight months later, he passed his qualifying exam for promotion. Rochelle then spent nearly four years with the Mediterranean Squadron, until his transfer in 1853 to the storeship *South Hampton*, which joined Commodore Perry's historic expedition to Japan. Returning to the United States in 1855, he was promoted to lieutenant and assigned to the United States Coast Survey. For three years he charted New York harbor, Maine's Casco Bay, and the Florida Keys, experience that prepared him for service with Tucker's Hydrographic Commission. In 1859 Rochelle shipped on the *Southern Star* with the expedition sent to settle a dispute with Paraguayan dictator Carlos Antonio López. The next year found him, unluckily, on the steamer *Fulton*, which was destroyed in a hurricane off the Florida coast.[23]

An officer of the USS *Cumberland* at Norfolk when the secession crisis occurred, Rochelle resigned his commission on April 17, 1861, the day Virginia withdrew from the Union. A shipmate from his days with the Coast Survey remembered him as "a gallant fellow, a Virginian." Whenever his Northern colleagues mentioned the president's annual message, Rochelle would retort, "That is all very well, but wait until you read the message of the Governor of Virginia." The sailor never doubted that he owed primary loyalty to his state. The entire family later shunned Rochelle's famous first cousin who remained loyal to the Union, Major General George H. Thomas, "the Rock of Chicamagua." Intelligent, serious-minded, and gentlemanly, Rochelle had a dry sense of humor perfectly suited to his almost perpetually dour expression. His friends called him "Smiley."[24]

In the Virginia and Confederate navies Lieutenant Rochelle first commanded the tiny gunboat *Teaser* on the James River before his transfer in June 1861 to Tucker's *Patrick Henry*. As executive officer of that vessel, he fought in the battles of Hampton Roads and Drewry's Bluff. Rochelle remained on the James as skipper of the gunboat *Nansemond* until May 1863, when he took charge of the steamer *Stono* at Charleston. On the night of June 5 he attempted to run the blockade with a load of government cotton; but the federal fleet discovered him, and while attempting to regain the harbor, Rochelle lost his vessel on a shoal at its mouth. The Navy Department faulted the *Stono*'s pilot for the accident. Rochelle briefly resumed command of the *Nansemond* before returning to Charleston in September 1863 with some one hundred reinforcements for Tucker's squadron. He commanded the boat parties that performed various duties in the harbor and organized Tucker's Charleston Naval Battalion. Rochelle became skipper of the ironclad ram *Palmetto State* in April 1864. A few days before the evacuation of Charleston in February 1865, Rochelle took three hundred sailors to Wilmington, North Carolina, where they assisted in the army's unsuccessful defense of that port.

At the end of February, Rochelle became commandant of cadets at the Confederate States Naval Academy, on board the *Patrick Henry*, where Lieutenant William H. Parker served as superintendent. When Richmond was evacuated on April 2, the government entrusted the national treasury to the staff and students of the naval school. For three weeks they carried their trove (about a half-million dollars in gold and silver) on a circuitous trek through the Carolinas and Georgia, before transferring it to the army at Abbeville, South Carolina. Here, a few days later, Rochelle surrendered to federal authorities and was paroled.[25]

Former lieutenant Rochelle returned to Southampton County, where he was working a farm owned by his family when Tucker invited him to join the Hydrographic Commission. Minister Balta approved his appointment on May 4, 1870, but the authorization reached Washington after the admiral's departure for South America. In January 1871, after his return to Iquitos, Tucker again requested Rochelle's appointment to the commission. Lima assented, and on June 29 Rochelle signed a contract with Colonel Freyre for an indefinite period. He was to hold the same position that McCorkle had resigned and to receive the same compensation, 133.33 *soles* per month. Peru agreed to pay his travel expenses to Iquitos and, at the end of his service, passage to New York.[26]

In January 1870 Tucker had asked permission to purchase additional equipment and supplies for the *Tambo*, items not included in the agreement with Pusey and Jones. Authorization from Lima, however, had not arrived by the eve of the admiral's departure for Peru. So at Tucker's urging, Minister Freyre very uncharacteristically approved the purchase of items "absolutely necessary" for the explorations. On June 21 the admiral endorsed a detailed nine-page invoice for $10,600 worth of goods provided by marine outfitter Henry J. Davison of New York. The items listed included canned food (assorted meats, vegetables, soups, and 2,535 pounds of biscuit) sufficient to feed fifty men for six months; surveying instruments requested in a recent letter from Arturo Wertheman; painting and cleaning materials; hardware and hand tools; fishing equipment; photographic supplies; stationery and other secretarial needs; three Peruvian flags of various sizes; an iron seal for the "Comisión Hidrográfica del Amazonas"; two 12-pounder boat howitzers, with canister shot; twenty Remington carbines and an equal number of revolvers of the same make; two double-barreled shotguns; four Colt derringer pistols; and medical supplies. The latter items, undoubtedly specified by Dr. Galt, included surgical and dental instruments; bandages and syringes; adhesive plaster, epsom salts, and castor oil; and smallpox vaccine, quinine, and sundry other drugs. Ensconced inconspicuously among these tools of the healing art—for preventive medicine, no doubt—were forty gallons of "Best Rye Whiskey."[27]

Admiral Tucker, Walter Butt, Dr. Galt, and Lieutenant Raygada departed New York aboard the steamer *North America* on June 23, 1870. After coaling at Saint Thomas in the Danish Virgin Islands, they reached Pará on July 8. "I have never . . . left home with so much regret," Tucker told his sons. He felt "quite sad at being obliged a second time to exile" himself and wondered if it would be "for years or for ever." Fearing perhaps the latter, he closed, "Good by my dear boys—never do anything mean or dishonorable."[28]

Tambo *vs. Tambo*

The admiral and his companions did not travel to Brazil in the *Tambo* because the steamer's living quarters were disassembled and crammed with supplies and equipment; additional space had to be purchased on a second vessel to accommodate the overflow. While awaiting the arrival of the *Tambo* at Pará, they took rooms at the Hotel do Comercio and attended "several pleasant parties," where the sailors reverted to type. "We waltzed with the ladies," wrote Galt, "told them about eternal love" and "promised to come back to take them home with us." In private, however, the men agreed that they had not seen even one "pretty girl among the Brazilians." Notwithstanding these diversions, the delay in continuing their journey to Iquitos was exasperating. Tucker wanted to survey the Tambo River that year, but the favorable low-water season already was half passed. The *Tambo* reached Pará, with a crew provided by Pusey and Jones, on July 24, followed four days later by a sloop carrying additional supplies. Tucker examined his steamer, certified her undamaged, and transferred control of the vessel to Lieutenant Raygada. But an additional month was required to place everything on board and to ready the steamer for her voyage upriver. "They work so very slow here, have too many feast days," complained the admiral; "no country can ever be very great under such a system."[29]

At three o'clock in the morning of September 1, the *Tambo* got under way, with a crew dispatched from Iquitos. But the next day, after only thirty hours' steaming, the *Tambo*'s heavily laden launch—being towed by the mother ship—foundered, "owing to bad management," thought Galt. The line attached to the small craft quickly broke, and the vessel sank in forty-five feet of muddy, flowing water. A dozen days of searching, including efforts by a diver in an "armour suit," failed to locate the launch. Beyond the value of the craft itself, the loss was costly to the work of the commission, for Tucker needed the smaller vessel to reach areas where the *Tambo* could not go.[30] The remainder of the voyage passed without further major mishap. Tucker and his friends had "a gloriously wild time . . . among the alligators, turtles, . . . forests and magnificent scenery." They did some "pretty shooting at alligators and other 'varmits'" as the *Tambo* steamed "through a wilderness of waters" with "thousands of islands, monkeys, parrots, Indians and walls of forests—dipping their leaves into the very water itself." The "channel ways," wrote Galt, "seemed like . . . roads cut out from among the foliage." The steamer reached the frontier and touched briefly at Leticia on October 1. Although the Virginians had been saddened at leaving their families, the first sight of the Peruvian flag flying over the fort, recalled Galt, "made us feel that we had gotten among kinfolk again."

The exploring steamer anchored in front of Iquitos at 5:00 P.M. on October 4, and her passengers were given a tumultuous welcome by the entire town, including the cacophonous five-man municipal band, uniformed in red caps and white trousers. The throng quickly rushed on board what many proclaimed a floating "palace." In addition to "the prominent lights of the station," recorded Galt, "there was everybody else, from high to low—Big men and small boys, white people and black, dress and undress, Quichua and Castilian in every possible interesting diversity." The doctor was pleased "to notice the kind feelings which the people of Iquitos had observed towards the admiral and Capt. Butt."[31]

With the onset of the high-water season only six weeks away, Tucker made hurried preparations for an expedition to the Río Tambo. He obtained tools and trinkets for distribution among the Indians they would encounter. Commandant Alzamora assigned sixty-six men to the steamer, including Major Ramón Herrera and fifteen soldiers. But the commission itself was shorthanded. Tucker granted a personal leave to secretary Tim Smith, who had spent several months assisting Charon at Leticia. Walter Butt, whose Spanish had improved greatly, could assume his duties. Far more inconvenient was the loss of Arturo Wertheman.[32]

During Tucker's absence the Swiss engineer had explored the Río Marañón, as the Amazon is called above the confluence of the Ucayali.

In October 1869 he had participated in a remarkable feat: in the tiny steamer *Napo*, with young Lieutenant Manuel Melitón Carbajal at the wheel, Wertheman climbed the treacherous Pongo de Manseriche into the upper Marañón. That event electrified the officials and merchants of Chachapoyas. The capital of Amazonas Department—situated at the head of the Río Uctubamba, a southern tributary of the upper Marañón—Chachapoyas enjoyed what little prosperity it had because of its location on the rugged trail between Trujillo, on the Pacific Coast, and the navigable lower Marañón. The recent efforts to find a better, more southerly link to the eastern waterways threatened to doom Chachapoyas with isolation. Amazonas, therefore, secured the appointment of Wertheman as its department engineer, and he began surveys to establish a superior route between Chachapoyas and the navigable rivers. As a temporary replacement for Wertheman, Tucker enlisted engineer-architect Cristóbal Rosas. The former New York consul for Emperor Maximilian's Mexican government, Rosas was an inspector at the naval factory and also served as mayor of Iquitos.[33]

The entire population of Iquitos, filled with optimistic expectation, turned out at 11:00 A.M. on October 20 to wish the expedition bon voyage. Tucker and his colleagues endured the enthusiastic embraces of well-wishers, from Commandant Alzamora "down to the ale house keeper." After a brief stop at Nauta, the *Tambo* began her ascent of the Ucayali. That river, predicted the admiral, was destined to become "the great commercial center of all these regions," whose forests invited "the ax of the worker" bringing "progress and civilization."[34]

A short distance upstream the expedition added an important member, an old Italian trader named Romano, who contracted to provide firewood for the steamer.[35] A legendary figure on the Ucayali, Romano had been a member of the papal band in his youth, before going to London and Lima where he joined the Peruvian Army. While posted in Moyobamba, Romano quit the service and went to Sarayacu, the largest Indian mission on the Ucayali. Here he married an Indian woman and readily adapted to the ways of the natives. When among the Indians, Romano discarded his shoes and wore a *cushma*, the chemiselike gown used by many Amazonian tribes. With a swarthy, pock-marked face, dark eyes, and shoulder-length black hair, the Italian had "altogether . . . the appearance of a pirate" and business ethics to match. Romano induced the Indians to cut wood by threatening to inflict them with the dreaded smallpox, which recently had decimated many villages along the river.

Above all else, Romano continued to be an entertainer. On his accordion he played both sprightly Italian airs and mournful Indian melodies. He had "a smile and a tongue ready for every mind," including the scientific curiosity of Frank Galt. Romano brought the surgeon specimens of unusual flora and fauna and told him much about various Indian groups. Galt meticulously recorded all of this, often with sketches, in his diary-journal, two canvas-covered volumes sewn with "a sailor's handstitching." During one of their many stops to take on wood, the Italian took the physician to a Conibo Indian hut where Galt witnessed "the most degraded forms of human life," including a woman suckling her pet monkey. For Galt, still a novice to Amazonia, this sight lent credence to the comte de Castelnau's report about a native who had refused to sell a large monkey *"for it was her husband!!!"*[36]

As the *Tambo* steamed closer to the river of the same name, the conversation in the officers' mess turned increasingly to the fierce Campa Indians, who certainly would resist their passage to the Chanchamayo Valley. About twenty years earlier these tenacious warriors reportedly had mauled and turned back a canoe expedition of some two hundred soldiers. In May 1869 the Campas had driven off a heavily armed party attempting to build a road eastward from Fort San Ramón. The Virginians were told that the Campa religion required them to eat one white Christian annually. Galt suggested that the now portly Walter Butt would best satiate the savages if they had not " 'laid in' their Christian" for that year.

But the entire expedition—the Hydrographic Commission, the officers and crew of the *Tambo*, old Romano, and his team of native cutters, belonging to diverse tribes—took the Campa threat very seriously, and they placed little faith in their fifteen-man "marine column," a collection of poorly drilled Indians. Major Herrera, however, did inspire confidence. A mestizo from the Sierra with long experience in the jungle, that officer spoke several Amazonian dialects in addition to Quechua and Spanish. Galt was surprised to learn that this quiet, even-tempered man once had killed an Indian chief with his bare hands and that the major was currently under indictment for threatening to shoot the tyrannical subprefect of the Iquitos district. The physician judged Herrera "the most complete man for one of these expeditions," with a "perfect knowledge of how to manage the Indians, and full of resource" in supplying their party with game and fish. Through the major's expertise, the commission's canned foods were supplemented liberally with alligator, turtle, monkey, snake, badger, and other unusual fare, all prepared imaginatively by their cook "Johnny C," a "magnificent Chinaman."

In the evenings, after dinner, the leading men of the expedition gathered in the commission's "saloon" (parlor) to play cards and chess, swap stories, and provide their own music. In addition to Butt's violin and the vessel's melodeon, the *Tambo*'s ensemble included three or four accordions and various tin whistles, along with Andean panpipes and flutes. The villainous-looking Romano skillfully played classical arias on the accordion while accompanying himself with "a tolerable voice." They often invited the Indians, "a good natured set of fellows," to their parties. To "vary the entertainment," recalled Galt, one of the natives amused them "by swallowing smoke into his stomach and then emitting it with grunts." On another occasion, Butt performed a special concert for the Indian cutters, who "squatted on their haunches peering at the instrument, silent and wondering." Believing that he had found a most appreciative audience, the Fiddler volunteered to go live among them and play the violin whenever they liked. But the natives rejected his offer, explaining that the Virginian was a poor fisherman and that their women would "all get drunk listening to his music."[37]

The expedition climbed the lower Ucayali without difficulty, except for the often stifling heat and clouds of mosquitoes that made "dressing and bathing . . . truly painful" tasks. On the higher portion of the river, however, the current became stronger and the island-strewn channels more treacherous. The *Tambo* ran aground on December 1 and required several hours to get free. Some of the Indian cutters deserted, but these soon were replaced by a team of Piros under Chief Benito Cayampay, who had assisted the commission during its first visit, on the *Napo*. Shortly after noon, on December 6, the explorers entered the Río Tambo, firing a howitzer to celebrate the event. But two days later, after traveling only a few miles against currents twice the strength of those of the Ucayali, the *Tambo* was thrown on a rocky beach. She thrashed her wheels, while all hands heaved on the anchor chains in a futile effort to pull the vessel free. With the rainy season due to begin, they hoped for high water to lift the steamer loose. The river, however, kept falling. Tucker and his companions were stranded more than three weeks at what they christened "Port Sal Si Puedes" (escape if you can).

The scenery was magnificent, with the wild river, dense forest, and mist-shrouded Andes visible in the background. The air was cooler, and the insects mercifully were less persistent. But the frustration of their captivity built with each passing day, and the men developed acute cabin fever. "Shut up with the same party" and "having pretty well exhausted each other's minds," noted Galt, "the character who says a good thing, . . . or an aptly put quotation" was deemed a "public benefactor." As Christmas approached the Virginians sank into a despondent mood, "six thousand miles away from all the smiles of the young" and the pleasant "scenes of our birthland."

Christmas Eve found the crew and some of the officers "being drunk generally" and determined to forget their misfortune, "tumbling overboard, . . . waltzing up against the machinery," and "singing ghastly notes." The next evening the revelers moved into the commission's parlor, and Galt retreated to his stateroom early. He vividly recorded the sight that greeted him the next day.

> The morning after the feast opened mistily on the hills, on the river and in the eyes and heads of a good many worthy people called the "Cabin Mess." The saloon looked as though a gale . . . had circulated in it disturbing plates with and without soup, glasses with and without toddies, persons and things every where from the table to the sofa, from the sofa to the deck. . . . Old [Chief] Benito . . . was . . . trying to get up and not very certain whether he had to do it by getting on his head or his feet. Romano, with his head hanging from the sofa, formed a pleasingly balanced portrait. . . . Cigar stumps and cigarette paper floundered about in the wreck, and a long silence told how the evening before had been enjoyed. One by one they gradually strolled into a waking condition, and peered with eyes looking like burning holes into the fresh morning air uncertain of their identity and location.

At the breakfast table each man "repented in silence, and a calm resolve to be disgusted with ones self." The doctor concluded that the government had misnamed the Hydrographic Commission; it should have been called the "*Hydrophobic Commission.*"[38]

On January 3, 1871, the river suddenly rose; the *Tambo* built up steam and crawled off the rocks, bringing "unadulterated . . . joy . . . and hearty cheers from all on board." The expedition spent the next two days anchored a few miles upstream, loading the 17,000 sticks of wood cut while they had been stranded. But after going a short distance on January 6, the *Tambo* again ran aground, on a bar in the middle of the river. The frustrated Tucker ordered a reconnaissance by canoe. Two of Romano's Indians who had been farther upstream many years earlier thought the river ahead passable, but old accounts of the Franciscan missionaries cast doubts about this. To provide for their current exigency, the expedition had purchased a large dugout canoe and fitted it, native-style, with a palm-thatch "cabin" at the back for protection against the sun, rain, and Campa arrows.

At noon the next day the Hydrographic Commission, Major Herrera and four soldiers, and Chief Benito and five Piros shoved off. They carried provisions for three days and an arsenal of rifles, pistols, and shotguns. Perhaps to avoid appearing too deliciously Christian in Campa country, Galt and another member of the commission donned *cushmas* purchased from Romano; the surgeon found the cool, loose-fitting garment "extremely serviceable." The explorers poled their way some six miles upriver the first day—the current was too swift for paddles—before bedding down in improvised shelters.[39]

The next afternoon the party reached the mouth of what seemed a substantial river, "its water beautifully clear, like pure green crystal," flowing from the high mountains to their left. The commission thought it to be the Río Ene, which unites with the Perené to form the Tambo. But the explorers almost certainly had not traveled far enough to have reached the Ene. Tucker estimated that the river they had come upon

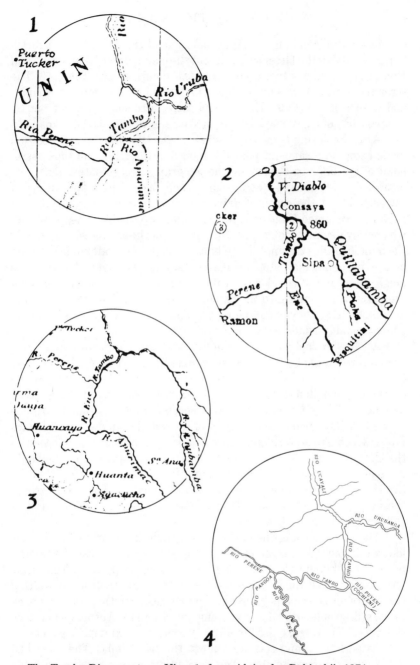

The Tambo River system. View 1, from Alejandro Babinski's 1874
"Mapa del Perú" (the Ene is mislabeled "Apurimac"). View 2, from
James Orton's map "The Marañón and Its Tributaries, 1875." View 3,
from Antonio Raimondi's 1877 small "Mapa del Peru." View 4 shows
the true configuration of the river system as explored and mapped by
Arturo Wertheman in 1876.

(he mistakenly called it the Apurímac) joined the Tambo about forty-five miles above the latter's mouth, but the confluence of the Perené and Ene is about eighty-two miles from the mouth of the Tambo.[40] The stream in question was more likely the Puyeni, also called the Anapati and the Cochiene (False Ene, in Quechua), a conclusion borne out by comparisons of early maps based on Tucker's work with later maps.

After exploring some three miles up the tributary, the expedition made camp on a sandspit near the mouth of the river and took astronomical readings to determine the geographic coordinates. Dr. Galt, meanwhile, attended to badly sunburned faces with applications of "sweet oil." At the crack of dawn the next morning, January 9, the explorers resumed their voyage, struggling up the main watercourse, which they deemed the Perené. Staying out of the strongest currents in the middle of the stream, they tediously poled their craft along the base of the perpendicular stone walls containing the river. From these heights an enemy could have rained stones and arrows down upon them; but the Campas, to the explorers' great relief, were not waiting in ambush. Had they in fact penetrated into the Perené, Tucker's small party probably would have sustained casualties.

At three o'clock, after traveling about eight miles, the commission encountered a shallow bed of rocks extending across the river. The canoe had to be pulled over this obstacle, which Tucker judged the extreme upper limit for steam navigation. Continuing on for another half hour, the explorers reached a second, more formidable rapids formed by huge boulders; the rush of the water sounded like Niagara Falls, which the admiral and Butt had visited during their mission to the United States. As in the previous two days, a pair of thatched huts were erected—one for the soldiers and Piro Indians and the other for the Hydrographic Commission and Major Herrera. The latter group, thoroughly exhausted, "laid down all five . . . in a row like good little children, and slept, oh so well."

The next morning the party turned their canoe around and "shot like an arrow" downstream. They stopped at the mouth of the supposed Ene, hoping to get a second reading of its position from solar observations. But the weather was too stormy; after fruitlessly waiting two hours for the clouds to break, the men resumed their journey back to the still-grounded *Tambo*, reaching her after a total of seven hours on the river. The water, quite fortuitously, rose the next day. The steamer extricated herself and retreated down the Río Tambo. The river had defeated its namesake-ship. The expedition, especially the extreme exposure to the jungle environment during the canoe reconnaissance, had taken its toll on the fifty-nine-year-old Tucker. "My health is not as good as it used to be," he informed Randy. "I cannot be taking those liberties with myself," for unlike "good wine," the admiral did not "improve with age."[41]

A Very Unkind and Jealous Feeling

Deeply disappointed by his failure to reach the Chanchamayo Valley by way of the Tambo, Admiral Tucker still hoped to provide some positive news for the authorities in Lima. As the expedition descended the upper Ucayali on January 13, he asked Captain Raygada to take them up the Pachitea River, so that the commission might explore a more northerly route to Chanchamayo. Raygada refused. He first protested that the season was too far advanced for the steamer to make the voyage safely and that damage to one of the vessel's wheels, incurred during the initial trip from Pará, required immediate repair. Tucker deemed these problems insignificant; but he proposed that the *Tambo* anchor at the mouth of the Pachitea, while the commission ascended the river by canoe. The skipper now asserted that he had been ordered to convey the commission to the Río Tambo, instructions Raygada interpreted as precluding the exploration of any other river. Earlier, during their outward voyage, the skipper had suggested that Tucker immediately explore one of the southern tributaries of the Marañón if the Tambo proved to be impassable. Galt, and probably the admiral too, believed that Raygada and the other officers of the *Tambo* were merely anxious to return home.[42]

Relations between the Hydrographic Commission and Raygada probably had been uneasy long before this expedition. A member of an old navy family, Raygada had come out to Iquitos with Alzamora in 1864 and played a key role in several early explorations. Before his departure for the United States in March 1869, Tucker had recommended him for command of one of the new steamers that the admiral urged the government to buy. But Raygada had not been the Virginian's choice for skipper of the *Tambo*. During Raygada's sojourn in the United States, the admiral seems to have treated the Peruvian officer congenially and quite likely made him a personal loan. The lieutenant's modest salary did not go far in the northern republic ("where everything" was "so dear"), and he had pawned his watch. As the date of their return to Peru approached, Raygada—who styled himself as "always your affectionate subaltern and friend"—asked the admiral for $100 to redeem his timepiece.[43] Raygada initially seemed pleased with the *Tambo*. He praised her to a friend in a letter later published in a Lima newspaper. Once back in Peru, however, the skipper began criticizing his vessel. Perhaps the hostile comments regarding her from Raygada's friends in Iquitos contributed to his reservations. Perhaps he blamed the steamer for his own inadequacies—the Virginians were unimpressed with his seamanship. His actual experience operating the craft also may have produced an honest change of opinion.[44]

The *Tambo* proved to be marginally underpowered and required skill to obtain maximum efficiency from her novel engines. The flatness of the vessel's bottom rendered her difficult to handle. During the voyage up the Ucayali, Galt—who at that time may not have been privy to Tucker's innermost opinions regarding the craft—noted the *Tambo's* shortcomings. "As far as her power is concerned," he wrote, "she is a failure." Although "contracted to go at the rate of 13 knots, she has never under the most favorable circumstances gone over ten." The vessel's passage of the Devil's Whirlpool showed "the great ease" with which the *Tambo* was affected by the current and the "great necessity for skill at the helm." He feared that "the slightest mistake helping out the force of the currents here, may endanger her very seriously." The physician-sailor concluded, however, that Raygada and some of the other officers, with their "Latin jealous disposition," exaggerated these deficiencies. The surgeon expressed "one consolation" regarding the craft. She was "Yankee built," and he had "no objection to all the anathemas which may be passed on her on that account"; it was "a gentle reminder of the 'late unpleasantness.'"

But Galt soon came to the *Tambo's* defense, and so did Tucker, for his "tip-top steamer" became the target of increasingly strident attacks and the focus of a bitter struggle between the commission and the officials at Iquitos. Although the admiral apparently admitted the steamer's shortcomings privately to friends and top officials in Lima, he probably understated them. And as the *Tambo's* detractors became more extreme, so did her defenders. When unfavorable comments about the vessel appeared in the Moyobamba newspaper *Fraternidad*, Walter Butt prepared to challenge its editor to a duel.[45]

Reporting to the minister of war about the recent expedition, Tucker expressed himself "completely satisfied with the qualities of the exploring steamer *Tambo*." He was not pleased with Lieutenant Raygada, however, and asked that orders be issued placing the steamer completely under the admiral's control. Raygada, in his report to Chief of Staff Enrique Espinar, explained his refusal to explore the Pachitea, emphasizing the restrictive nature of the skipper's original instructions. Raygada also contradicted Tucker's appraisal of the steamer, which he deemed underpowered and cumbersome. He concluded, sarcastically, that the expedition had been a waste of time, confirming only what missionaries had known for more than a century—that the Tambo River was impassable.[46] Commandant General Alzamora supported Raygada in his conflict with Tucker. In forwarding Raygada's report to Lima, Alzamora made no mention of the lieutenant's insubordination; in the same mail, moreover, the *comandante* strongly recommended a promotion for that officer, whom he earlier had praised, pointedly, as the "true explorer of the Ucayali" and other rivers of Loreto. Alzamora repeated the skipper's assertions that the *Tambo* was "unsuited" for exploration and added that the vessel required extensive repairs.[47]

Raygada may have been a cat's-paw in Alzamora's own long-brewing dispute with Tucker. At the time of the commission's creation, President Prado had promised that the admiral would have a steamer placed at his disposition and that he would be independent of the naval authorities at Iquitos, reporting directly to the minister of war and marine. Alzamora was instructed to provide "all of the assistance and facilities which . . . Sr. Tucker solicits" for his work.[48] Probably from the beginning, Alzamora and the other officers at Iquitos had not welcomed the establishment of the commission. They believed that assignment to Loreto, a very unpleasant place to live and work, stunted their careers, notwithstanding the double-time-in-grade credited to their service records.[49] In the absence of a war in the region, their primary opportunity to obtain recognition for their sacrifices and to win promotion lay in the field of exploration. The intrusion of the Hydrographic Commission condemned them to a secondary role in that important task. The foreign composition of this new agency, moreover, implied that Peruvian officers and specifically those posted at Iquitos were not competent to perform this duty.

The Peruvian officers protested against the Virginians' independence and high salaries. The latter complaint was more emotional than rational. Given their former rank and experience, Tucker and his colleagues were not overpaid; and because the Peruvian sailors received a 50 percent bonus not enjoyed by the commission, there was no appreciable gap in actual compensation.[50] But the differential in base pay probably contributed to the belief at Iquitos that Lima unduly favored the foreigners. The arrival of Tucker's "floating palace," where the commission members presumably would live in relative comfort, certainly reinforced this perception.

A personal conflict over turf was perhaps inevitable between Alzamora and Tucker—the thirty-eight-year-old acting captain and the fifty-six-year-old former rear admiral. For the *comandante* the establishment of the Hydrographic Commission, independent of his authority, was a blow to his well-earned prestige. Tucker, of course, had been a naval officer long before Alzamora was born, and his values had been molded in an institution where rank was the "dearest object on earth to an officer." The old sailor could not tolerate any intimation that he was subordinate to Alzamora.[51] Even before Tucker's mission to the United States, several disagreements had strained the relationship between the admiral and the commandant general; and a marked decline in Alzamora's cooperativeness seems to have occurred after the overthrow of the admiral's benefactor, President Prado, in January 1868. But both men remained correct in their professional and personal dealings with each other.

In his dispatches to Lima, Alzamora asserted that Peru's eastern rivers had been explored repeatedly in the past and, thus, that

Tucker's work was redundant. At the same time, somewhat inconsistently, the *comandante* claimed that his own men could perform the duties of the Hydrographic Commission. These views were not shared in the capital. In March 1870, while serving as acting minister of war and marine, geographer Mariano Felipe Paz Soldán reprimanded Alzamora because explorations conducted by his officers had provided only general information about the "configuration, depth, and currents" of rivers; the sailors had not made "the astronomical observations indispensable to determine the geographic locations of the most notable points." These omissions reflected poorly upon the "ability and fitness" of the commandant's subordinates. Alzamora bitterly replied that thorough surveys required very expensive instruments such as those lavished upon Tucker's team but denied to the *comandante*'s officers.[52]

Time and again in his reports to Lima, Alzamora stressed the independence of the commission and the *comandante*'s ignorance of its work because Tucker reported directly to the minister. The admiral likely apprised the commandant informally about his expeditions. In any event, the captains of the steamers conveying the commission submitted reports to Alzamora's chief of staff that contained essentially the same information found in Tucker's dispatches, including the geographic data. In his report of the first expedition to the Tambo River in 1868, the admiral had given latitudes and longitudes for only a few key places; but the commission supplied Lieutenant Gutiérrez with all of their coordinates, which he presented in his own report.[53]

After Tucker's return from the United States in October 1870, the struggle between Alzamora and the admiral was waged indirectly over the admiral's "tip-top steamer"—her serviceability and Tucker's use of the craft. The faulty construction of the United States–built *Tirado* and *Huallaga*, Peru's first river steamers, had given North American vessels a poor reputation all along the Amazon. By 1870, however, the success of four iron Pusey and Jones steamers operated by the Brazilian state of Pará had converted the skeptics on the lower part of the river. Soon after the *Tambo* reached Iquitos, several of the officers and engineers there expressed reservations about the innovative vessel. Her design and high-pressure engines differed significantly from the familiar British-built steamers. With hull and framing of wrought iron, rather than rolled metal, the *Tambo*'s finish was rough, and her boiler plates were only half the thickness of those found in the other vessels at that station. Alzamora, meanwhile, asked Lima for instructions about the new craft's disposition. On December 19 Minister Balta responded that the *Tambo* was to be under the admiral's control during expeditions. However, Alzamora would have authority over the vessel when she was not so employed.[54]

On January 31, 1871, one week after his return from the Río Tambo, Tucker informed Alzamora of his desire to explore the Pachitea at the onset of the low-water season in April. He requested repairs to the *Tambo*'s damaged wheel and asked that the steamer and her officers be placed under his orders. The *comandante* responded that according to the factory superintendent the vessel required extensive repairs to both wheels and a "complete overhaul" of her machinery. This work could be accomplished in four weeks, after which Alzamora would facilitate the admiral's proposed expedition.[55]

During the next month several disagreeable incidents thoroughly soured the Virginians' attitude toward their Peruvian colleagues. Paymaster Leopoldo Alzamora of the *Tambo*, a brother of the commandant general, presented the North Americans with a bill for their share of the officers' mess during the recent expedition. It was much larger than they anticipated. Although they did not openly challenge Alzamora, Galt—a former paymaster himself, who watched such things closely—felt certain that they had been cheated. A few days later, Paymaster Alzamora found a pretext for stopping the food allowance that the commission, like all public employees in Iquitos, had heretofore received. Even their friend Major Herrera, thought Galt, turned against them, spreading a "falsehood" about Tucker and Butt's behavior (perhaps their drinking habits) during the recent expedition.[56]

Meanwhile, the new directive from Lima concerning the status of the *Tambo* had arrived. Notwithstanding the fact that the indispensable "complete overhaul" of the vessel's machinery had yet to begin, the *comandante* ordered the steamer on an errand to Borja, the outpost at the foot of the Pongo de Manseriche on the hazardous upper course of the Marañón. The Hydrographic Commission reluctantly found lodging on shore. They were not to enjoy the comforts of their "floating palace" except when on expeditions. Even as the Peruvians delivered these bureaucratic blows to the commission, they remained outwardly cordial. Their habitual Latin American courtesy (often overly formal and effusive by North American standards—even those of "genteel" Southerners) convinced the Virginians that their hosts were hypocrites. "They salute a bitter enemy with the same delight that they will a friend," wrote Galt. Unable to identify the commission's opponents with certainty, the surgeon's suspicions bordered on paranoia. The "treachery . . . shown by some of the officials," he noted, had sufficed "to disgust us with the whole surroundings of our present position."[57]

On March 5 Tucker wrote a letter of resignation for himself and Butt; however, the document was postdated to the sixteenth of that month—the day after muster—probably to ensure payment of their salaries to that date. The admiral explained that the directive of December 19 "withdrawing the *Tambo*" from his control, "together with the manifest bad feeling and opposition to the Commission as foreigners," rendered him "powerless to satisfactorally prosecute the object" of his mission. He thanked the government for its "uniform kindness and courtesy" and requested that he and Butt be given travel expenses to the United States along with the three months' severance pay (at their original rates) promised them when they entered the Peruvian service in 1866.[58]

At the same time Tucker explained his action to his friend Manuel Pardo, now the mayor of Lima. When the commission had been established, he wrote, "it was with the full understanding of the President" that the admiral would have a steamer under his orders, "entirely separate from the authorities" in Iquitos. But War Minister Balta now had put the *Tambo*, a vessel "built expressly" for the commission's work, "under the direction of the Commander General." Alzamora, "at his pleasure," could deny Tucker use of the vessel; "in other words," bristled the admiral, "placing me *almost* under his control." The old sailor could not "for a moment submit" to this. Tucker also noted the "very unkind and jealous feeling existing against the Commission principally because we [are] foreigners." The officials at Iquitos exhibited this "in their fondness for writing and saying disagreeable things" about the Virginians. "Self respect," concluded the admiral, "obliges me to resign." Because Pardo was familiar with Tucker's 1866 verbal contract with Minister Barreda, the admiral asked his friend's assistance in securing their severance pay and passage money. He also made a special plea on behalf of Galt, who had two more years to serve under his contract. The physician, he explained, "will be in an unpleasant position" after the departure of his colleagues. Galt wanted reassignment to one of the government railroads being built by Henry Meiggs.[59]

On April 19 Commandant Alzamora, who had not been told of Tucker's resignation, informed the admiral that all essential repairs to the *Tambo* had been completed; the *comandante* awaited Tucker's request to ready the vessel for the Pachitea expedition. The admiral declined to receive the steamer, explaining that he was awaiting new instructions from the capital. Alzamora quickly denounced the Hydrographic Commission and its "idle" craft in a letter to Minister Balta.[60] Tucker had not received responses to his report on the Tambo River expedition or his resignation when, on May 6, Alzamora opened a new campaign against the exploring steamer. At the request of the *Tambo's* chief engineer and after hearing "alarming reports" from other sources, the commandant appointed a junta to examine the vessel. This board's report, issued four days later, declared that the *Tambo's* boiler plates were dangerously thin. Although Pusey and Jones had rated the boilers safe for eighty pounds of steam, the panel recommended that the vessel build no more than twenty pounds of pressure—less than was required to stem the current of even the relatively sluggish Amazon. Therefore, Alzamora ordered the *Tambo* withdrawn from service until new boilers from overseas could be installed.[61]

The admiral anticipated that he would soon leave the Peruvian service. Nevertheless, he responded angrily to the survey report in letters to Minister Balta and, again, to Manuel Pardo. He emphasized the solid reputation and proven experience of Pusey and Jones and recounted his own diligence in superintending the *Tambo*'s construction. The admiral emphasized that the North American engineers who had taken her some five thousand miles from Wilmington to Pará and then another two thousand miles up the Amazon to Iquitos experienced no trouble with the boilers. The steamer had been thoroughly tested during the two-thousand-mile expedition to and from the Tambo River and her recent nine-hundred-mile journey to Borja and back. Tucker "would not hesitate for a moment to start on another or a dozen expeditions" in the vessel. The old sailor attributed the *Tambo*'s condemnation to the hostility of the Peruvian officers at Iquitos along with the ignorance and jealousy toward American technology of the English "elves" at the naval factory, who had caviled about the steamer since her arrival. Alzamora's junta, he noted, had consisted of the *Tambo*'s chief engineer, José Díaz, an Ecuadorian trained in London; James Rae, the new Scottish superintendent of the factory, who was entirely unfamiliar with the steamer; and the British machinist John Smalls. The latter man had told one of the Virginians that he completely disagreed with the board's other two members. For Tucker the "little circumspection" exhibited in the panel's report demonstrated "that the boat had been condemned before [the junta] was convened." In justice to his own reputation and that of the builders, the admiral asked that a new mixed board of English and North American engineers reexamine the boilers.[62]

The reports of Tucker's recent conflicts in Loreto angered War Minister Balta. He condemned Raygada's insubordination and reiterated that the *Tambo* was to be under the admiral's complete control during explorations. Balta sternly ordered Alzamora to remove all impediments to the work of the commission. Tucker's resignation caused the minister "surprise and sorrow." He insisted that the directive of December 19, about which the admiral complained, had placed the *Tambo* at Tucker's entire disposition for the work of the commission and dependent on the Iquitos station only for support services. Balta was determined that no person employed by the government be treated as a "foreigner." He stressed the importance of the commission, praised the admiral's work, and rejected his resignation.[63] Balta ordered Alzamora to place the *Tambo* at the admiral's disposition. If the commission had been the victim of antiforeign prejudice, the *coman-*

dante was to punish those responsible. After learning about the boiler dispute, the minister instructed Alzamora to form, with Tucker's concurrence, a new survey board of British and North American machinists to reinspect the power plant. The minister later allowed that the admiral might even reject the findings of this new junta and have the *Tambo* put back into service under his own responsibility. To soften the blow of these adverse decisions, Balta credited Alzamora with patriotic good intentions but emphasized that the national interest required the rapid conclusion of Tucker's surveys.[64]

The commandant reacted bitterly to these developments, charging that Tucker had made "gratuitous accusations" against him. The *Tambo*, he claimed, had been at the admiral's disposition up to the day of her condemnation by the junta. The commandant had taken special care not to "offend this gentleman, to the extreme that it seemed that I was at his orders." He denied the existence of antiforeign prejudice and urged the government to accept Tucker's resignation, for the "so-called Hydrographic Commission" was "not needed to explore rivers . . . already explored." Such surveys, in any event, could be made competently and at much less expense by the men of his command, who as Peruvians were "naturally called to do these tasks." In the four years of its existence, concluded the *comandante*, Tucker's team had "not done anything beneficial for the nation."[65]

On July 4 Tucker learned that his resignation had been rejected and that the *Tambo* was to be entirely under his control. He immediately asked Alzamora to ready the steamer for the long-delayed survey of the Pachitea. But the commandant replied that the vessel needed sundry repairs, not previously identified, that would require two months' work. Balta's specific instructions concerning the boiler dispute had not yet reached Iquitos, and Alzamora on July 12 reiterated that the steamer could not be used until she received a new power plant. The *Tambo* would be moored indefinitely. The next day Tucker informed the commandant that he was going to Lima. Appointing Walter Butt acting president of the commission, the admiral left Iquitos on July 17.[66]

Traveling by way of the Amazon River and the Isthmus of Panama, Tucker reached the capital on the last day of August. Four days later he addressed a long letter to the minister of war and marine. In this and a supplementary memorandum of September 21, the admiral reviewed his problems in Loreto. Experience had convinced him that the Hydrographic Commission would be unable to discharge its duties efficiently "unless the whole plan is changed," making Tucker and his team "entirely separate from the station" except for supplies and repairs. The admiral wanted absolute control over the *Tambo* as well as a new steam launch he needed for scouting smaller streams. The commanding officers of these vessels should be directly responsible to him, and "competent Americans" should be in charge of their machinery. The admiral also wanted two "topographical engineers" from the United States to fill the posts vacated by Wertheman and Charon.

Tucker urged that operating funds for the commission be placed under the control of the *Tambo*'s paymaster, who also would be subject to the admiral's orders. Because funding from Lima for the Iquitos station had become irregular, Tucker wanted authority to issue drafts against Peru's accounts in London and New York, instruments readily accepted by Amazonian merchants. Similarly, he wanted authority to request supplies and equipment from Peru's overseas financial agents. The admiral asserted that the "enormous" expense of living on the Amazon did not permit his subordinates to "live free from debt on their present allowance." Therefore, he asked that his men receive the same half-salary bonus paid to other public employees in Loreto.[67]

In his negotiations with the government, Tucker enjoyed considerable leverage, even beyond that accruing from the recent rejection of his resignation. One month earlier José Allende, an old general, had been named minister of war and marine. The transition probably enhanced the influence of the senior naval official within the ministry, Director of Marine Alejandro Muñoz; he had been skipper of the *Huáscar* during the admiral's command of the allied fleet. Furthermore, Tucker's friend Manuel Pardo recently had been nominated for the presidency, and he seemed to be the leading candidate for that post. Finally, the very influential Henry Meiggs, who held the admiral in "high regard," was making rapid progress on a railroad linking Callao with La Oroya in the central Andes. A Lima newspaper explained that the new Central Railroad would facilitate the development of Amazonian Peru, a vast area of "unsurpassed value and richness." This region was currently being surveyed by Admiral Tucker, "a gentleman of large experience, great learning, indefatigable energy, and well-tried abilities."[68]

In November, Minister Allende acceded to most of Tucker's requests. The admiral's team and its steamers were to be "completely independent" of the commandant at Iquitos, who would render "all aid" to the commission. Tucker would have entire control of the officers and crews of the *Tambo*. The insubordinate Lieutenant Raygada would be replaced as skipper of that vessel, and the admiral was to report any future disciplinary problems directly to Lima. Tucker did not receive financial autonomy, but the Iquitos commissary would be instructed to place at his disposal monthly, with "entire exactitude," the money required for the explorers' salaries and operating expenses. General Allende promised to request a half-salary bonus for Tucker's associates in his next budget proposal. Most important, the admiral was ordered to the United States where he would obtain a new steam launch and all the equipment needed for his work. He was to hire two civil engineers for the commission and three machinists for the exploring steamers. The latter men also would sit on the mixed board that would reexamine the *Tambo*'s boilers.[69]

"Old Tuck," recorded Galt triumphantly, "still keeps ahead of the opposition—another of the many proofs of the power of integrity in a servant of the government." The admiral departed for New York on November 22, 1871.[70]

CHAPTER NINE

Perils of the Pichis

ADMIRAL TUCKER arrived at New York in mid-December 1871 and soon began his search for new members of the Hydrographic Commission and a builder for the steam launch. By the third week of January he had signed a contract with Pusey and Jones, the Wilmington, Delaware, firm that had constructed the *Tambo*. Perhaps this choice was, in part, a final slap at the critics of the admiral's "tip-top steamer"; but he soon had reason to express his own dissatisfaction with the company. After waiting three months for the government to provide the funds needed to begin the project, Pusey and Jones "humbugged" Tucker with numerous delays. The launch would not be completed until the end of August 1872.[1]

Tambo Wawa

For about $10,000 Pusey and Jones built a flat-bottomed, side-wheeled launch of thirty-five tons capacity. Some 60 feet long and 12 feet wide, with a 5-foot hold, the vessel drew about 30 inches of water. The hull, constructed of 3/16-inch iron, had three watertight compartments. A single high-pressure engine, rated at sixteen horsepower, permitted a cruising speed of about six miles per hour. The "cabin," located at the rear of a single deck, was an iron-framed canvas shelter. Tucker christened the vessel *Mairo* after a stream in the Pachitea river system.[2] To the Quechua-speaking Indians of Loreto, however, the launch would look like the *Tambo* in miniature. They called her the *Tambo Wawa*— *Tambo's Baby*.[3]

Tucker divided his time in the United States superintending the construction of the launch, visiting his family in Virginia, recruiting men, and obtaining supplies for the commission (he had been given $2,000 dollars for that purpose). As the steamer neared completion, the admiral again obtained the services of his nephew 'Fonce Jackson to inspect the *Mairo*, "a beautiful little craft" that gave "great satisfac-

193

tion." To service the engines of the *Tambo* and *Mairo*, Tucker hired three machinists employed by Pusey and Jones, John W. Durfey, David W. Bain, and W. Dodds, who enlisted as first, second, and third engineers, respectively, in the Peruvian Navy. They accompanied the *Mairo*, which was shipped disassembled from Wilmington in early September 1872.[4]

The two civil engineers Tucker hired for the Hydrographic Commission signed three-year contracts at 1,440 *soles* (about $1,400) per year, salaries comparable to those paid United States government engineers.[5] Thomas Wing Sparrow, the senior man, had been born at Alexandria, Virginia, early in 1841, among ten children of Dr. William and Frances Greenleaf Ingraham Sparrow. A distinguished Episcopal clergyman and educator, the Reverend Dr. Sparrow had been a founder and executive vice president of Kenyon College in Gambier, Ohio. In 1840 he joined the faculty of the Theological Seminary in Virginia, at Alexandria, where he soon became dean, a post he would occupy until his death in 1874. Dr. Sparrow was a strict disciplinarian (a "tyrant," according to one of his Kenyon students) and, apparently, a rather humorless and ascetic man.[6] His son Thomas, like many other "ministers' kids," was a reverse image—a worldly, blunt, and often boastful extrovert with a lively sense of humor.

Thomas Sparrow graduated from the Episcopal High School in Alexandria and entered the civil engineering program at the University of Virginia in 1858. After the secession of his state in April 1861, he enlisted as a private in former governor Henry Wise's Fifty-Ninth Regiment of the Virginia Army ("Wise's Legion"). But a difficult campaign against Union forces in the mountains of western Virginia dampened the "delicate" Sparrow's initial enthusiasm for military life. Through the influence of his uncle Senator Edward Sparrow of Louisiana (the wealthiest man in the Confederate Congress), Sparrow was appointed a Confederate treasury agent in March 1862. As the shrunken Confederacy neared collapse in late February 1865, Sparrow again entered the army, rising from private to sergeant major in Battery B, Twelfth Battalion, Virginia Light Artillery, which was attached to General Richard Anderson's Corps. He may have been captured, along with Commodore Tucker, at the battle of Sayler's Creek. During the next half-dozen years, Sparrow gained considerable engineering experience in Pennsylvania.[7]

Tucker's second recruit was Nelson Berkeley Noland. Born on September 19, 1846, in Hanover County, Virginia, near Richmond, Nelson was the son of Callender St. George and Mary Edmonia Berkeley Noland. Callender Noland had spent two decades in the United States Navy before resigning his lieutenant's commission in 1854; thereafter, he managed Edgewood and Airwell, two estates owned by his wife, a member of a prominent Virginia family. With the secession of Virginia, the elder Noland was commissioned a lieutenant colonel of volunteers and commanded an artillery post on Mulberry Island in the James River. Volunteers from Noland's battery served under his friend Commander Tucker on the CSS *Patrick Henry* at the battle of Hampton Roads.[8]

In July 1863 Nelson Noland enrolled in the engineering course at the Virginia Military Institute, the "West Point of the Confederacy." When the Union army of General Franz Sigel moved down the Shenandoah Valley toward Staunton in May 1864, Confederate general John C. Breckinridge appealed for reinforcements from VMI, in nearby Lexington. On the fifteenth of that month, Noland and 246 other VMI cadets participated in a still-commemorated charge that turned back the Federals at the battle of New Market. The following month, however, Union forces occupied Lexington. Noland attended classes at VMI's temporary quarters in Richmond until the capture of that city in April 1865.

Returning to the VMI campus at Lexington in 1868, Noland graduated two years later. He was employed as a rodman with a surveying crew on the Chesapeake and Ohio Railroad when Tucker invited him to join the Hydrographic Commission in January 1872. A friend urged him to take the post "more for the love of adventure than the hope of reward." The experience gained would be very valuable, and Noland might later obtain one of the "splendid oppennings" for engineers on Peru's railroad projects. Nelson's parents were apprehensive about the salubrity of Amazonian Peru. But his mother thought it a good opportunity "to see something of the world," while Callender Noland told his son that "Admiral Tucker is a man I admire greatly and you will find him a good friend."[9]

At age twenty-five, Noland still retained a good deal of youthful innocence and naïveté. He was ambitious, self-confident, and highly opinionated, denouncing Yankees, "niggers," and, later, Peruvians with equal vehemence. "I know I have never done any thing yet in the way of making money," he told his mother, "but I have a sound constitution, and industry, *and a firm determination to do something*." He also was "glad to be out of the sight of the detestable Yanks." Noland rendezvoused with Tucker and Sparrow in New York on August 19. The youngster thought the thirty-one-year-old Sparrow "a very nice man and a good Eng[ineer]" from whom he expected to learn much. He was "a shrewd fellow," who was going to Peru "simply to make money." The two engineers were "both alike in that particular." Tucker's energy, perseverance, and generosity favorably impressed Noland. The admiral told Nelson to save his one-month salary advance until they reached Saint Thomas, in the Virgin Islands, with its duty-free bargains. Should Noland ever need money, Tucker would "share all he had" with him. A few days later Nelson wrote that the admiral "improves *if possible* on acquaintance."[10]

The trio departed New York on the mail steamer *South America* in the morning of August 23. Tucker, Noland thought, "minds leaving civilization very much," and parting with his family "goes very hard with him." But Sparrow, "a rare bird," seemed relieved by the prospect. "His wife," noted Noland, "was dead only 8 months when he was married [again], and I have never heard him mention his second one yet, though we have the same state room." The young engineer relished his first ocean voyage—the prodigious amounts of food provided and the odd assortment of passengers, including a circus troop and "two Yankee girls with plenty of money." Nelson judged the latter "not bad looking, but the most ridiculous fools I ever saw." After a stop at Saint Thomas, where they purchased clothing, cigars, and bay rum, the party reached Pará on September 7, 1872.[11]

Tucker obtained lodging in the last spare room of his friend Colonel José M. Ríos, the Peruvian consul, while the two engineers found quarters at the French-owned Hotel do Comercio overlooking the Amazon. Although it was the best establishment in town, the lizards and roaches sharing their room were "enormous." For one month they awaited the arrival of the steamer *Burnett*, carrying the *Mairo*. Sparrow and Noland whiled away the time "swinging in our hammocks and smoking a box of Havana cigars" that the admiral had given them. For diversion the engineers fashioned peashooters and expended a bag of buckshot sniping at buzzards from their window. "Even the Ad[miral]," reported Noland, took "a pull now and then." There was plenty of time, too, for spinning pipe dreams. After two years' service with the Hydrographic Commission, Noland and Sparrow hoped "to have the government very pleased with us" and to get "some influencial man (probably the Admiral) to take an advantageous Govmt. Contract (*Railroad*)." The two young tycoons would do the surveys and supervise the construction work, and "make a fortune." Tucker sometimes joined in these idle reveries, joking that "he must hurry and make his" money, for he did not have "much time left to enjoy it."

In early October, Sparrow and Noland almost lost the opportunity to make their "pile." Yellow fever struck both men. After rejecting the services of reputedly the best physician in town—a black Brazilian—Tucker found them an English doctor who prescribed "plasters and drugs." The admiral, wrote Noland, "was just as *kind* and *true* as steal, would come around and stay for hours." Noland had given the "pledge" to his abstemious grandmother; but Tucker now recommended that Nelson "take a little wine" with his water; the admiral prescribed it "as a physician." Noland believed "in going 'whol hog' when you start," and Dr. Tucker's prescription soon prevailed over Grandma's proscription.[12]

The *Mairo* reached Pará on October 4; and Sparrow, Noland, the three machinists, and a team of Pusey and Jones workmen began assembling the craft. By mid-November all was ready for the trip upriver. But on the eve of their departure, Machinist Dodds, who had left the group "in perfect health" three hours earlier, returned to the launch and exclaimed "For God's sake let me lie down for I have the fever." Tucker put him in the hospital where, on December 3, he died. Dodds's colleagues buried him early the next morning and then started for Iquitos with a ten-man Portuguese crew hired by the admiral.

They were on the river only a few days when their cook was stricken with smallpox. Tucker placed the highly contagious man down in the hold, on top of the supplies. At Manaus, the major Brazilian port at the junction of the Amazon and the Río Negro, the admiral persuaded local authorities to admit the sick man to the hospital. After they fumigated the *Mairo* and got under way again, a second crewman came down with the dreaded pox. He too was put below and soon expired. "So great was the stench," wrote Noland, that only with great difficulty could they induce the crewmen to carry the corpse on deck, where "a black oose ran out of him." At the launch's next stop for wood, four men deserted. Then another sailor became ill; before he could be restrained below, the delirious man jumped overboard and drowned. Tucker again fumigated his vessel. Now woefully shorthanded, the admiral appointed Sparrow "first officer" and Noland "second officer" of the boat. Until their arrival at Iquitos eight days later, the two men alternated, every four hours, at the *Mairo*'s wheel. For Noland the journey entailed "as hard manual labor as I ever did in my life." Tucker quipped that Nelson had been spared the smallpox because he "did not have the time." However, all of the Virginians aboard broke out in a rash; Dr. Galt later diagnosed it as variola, a less virulent version of the pox.

The *Mairo* reached Iquitos in the evening of January 21, 1873. Rochelle, Galt, and Butt were "overjoyed at seeing the admiral," and Noland, too, was pleased with his new associates. Rochelle and Galt were "model gentlemen"; although "Capt. Butt" did not fall within that exemplary category, the young engineer liked him "very much also." He reserved his highest praise, however, for Tucker, "one of the most remarkable men I ever saw and one of the truest." The admiral was "a great man in this country, though they don't half appreciate him." Noland thought himself "peculiarly fortunate to have gotten with such gentlemen as compose this commission."[13]

During Tucker's eighteen-month absence, the remnants of the Hydrographic Commission in Iquitos had endured the monotony of relative inactivity. Use of the still-condemned *Tambo* was denied them. Butt and Galt volunteered to make an arduous canoe reconnaissance of the Río Tigre, a northern affluent of the Marañón. The admiral's instructions to Rochelle, however, did not countenance any official expedition until his return with the resources needed for a thorough survey, and the Iquitos treasury lacked money for the two men to make the unofficial exploration authorized by Rochelle. Thus, the Virginians busied themselves as best they could, preparing charts of the rivers previously explored, repairing instruments, attending to their correspondence, and sundry other tasks.

In addition to treating the ailments of his colleagues and other Iquitos residents (often charity patients), Dr. Galt maintained a regular reading program, especially in works pertaining to Peru and the Amazon Basin. Four times each day he conducted systematic observations of the weather, recording temperature, rainfall, barometric pressure, and unusual atmospheric phenomena. He sent his meteorological journal to Lima quarterly and provided copies to the Smithsonian Institution in Washington. The physician also prepared reports on climate, geography, soils, agriculture, and sanitary conditions; these indicated that Loreto was a more attractive place to live than most outsiders believed. Rochelle forwarded Galt's studies to Lima, suggesting that they might assist the government in attracting immigrants. Several of the surgeon's essays appeared in the Lima press and, later, in prestigious British and North American periodicals.

Rochelle, too, disseminated knowledge acquired by the commission. He submitted a report on "Geographical Positions in the Valley of the Amazon" to the Royal Geographical Society in London. Noting that all existing maps of Amazonian Peru were "traced most inaccurately," Rochelle sent similar data to his former colleague John M. Brooke, now a professor of geography at the Virginia Military Institute. Rochelle and his fellow Virginians on the commission, he told Brooke, hoped "to render some service to Peru, since it is not permitted to us to render any to our own country or state."[14]

Rumors reaching Iquitos in mid-1871 indicated that Henry Meiggs, "from his high regard" for "old Admiral Tucker," was personally financing a preliminary survey for a road or railroad between the highlands and the Ucayali river system. In June 1872 these reports were substantiated with the arrival of a letter from Ernesto Malinowski, the impresario's chief engineer. Using the best data available, the Polish immigrant had prepared a map, which he enclosed, of the region between Lima and the Ucayali. Starting from the Chanchamayo Valley, he proposed to employ a pair of hot-air balloons to carry him over the rock-choked Perené River and to identify the best overland route to the Pichis or Palcazu rivers, tributaries of the Pachitea. Malinowski promised to report his findings to Tucker and expected to receive similar information from the admiral, so that they could "calculate . . . the time and place of our juncture, which will be a great day."

Rochelle responded with enthusiasm. He sent Meiggs the geographic coordinates of several possible eastern termini for routes from Lima and asked how the Hydrographic Commission might "best cooperate" with his ambitious project. Although he noted the great economic benefit that Andean and Amazonian Peru would enjoy from opening new avenues to outside markets, he emphasized the strategic value of such links. Rochelle warned that the power which controlled the major lowland rivers, "the only highways of this part of the country, must be the masters of Eastern Peru." Arteries to transport "men, arms, and munitions of war . . . with rapidity and ease" between Lima and the Amazon River were a "military necessity."[15]

The Virginians had a great deal of leisure time, but little money with which to enjoy it. During Tucker's absence, the flow of funds from Lima nearly stopped, and Iquitos residents lived on whatever credit they could obtain from local merchants. Galt earned a little ready cash treating some of the town's wealthier families. "I sent out some medical bills for collection today," confided the physician to his diary. This "first experiment at professional exaction on the Marañón" was quite successful, netting him ten *soles*. He would "do very well, provided they are sick more frequently." With much of the town reduced to "misery and poverty," however, Commandant Alzamora feared a rebellion.[16]

The penury of Iquitos added to the tension occasioned by Peru's protracted election campaign. In mid-October 1871 partisans of Tucker's friend Manuel Pardo triumphed in the contest for presidential electors. This choice was confirmed the following May, when the electors cast their ballots and the country selected new members of Congress. Although Pardo was the popular choice, the Balta regime and much of Peru's military establishment opposed him because his Civilista party campaigned against the dominance of the nation's uniformed politicians and proposed to cut the military budget. It seemed quite possible that President José Balta would impose a candidate more favorable to the soldiers or continue in office beyond his constitutional term.

Pardo enjoyed strong support in Iquitos (Galt cynically commented that the local Civilistas favored "civil as opposed to military misrule"). Many Iquiteños suspected that the Balta administration was withholding their subsidy for partisan reasons. Rumors of political conspiracies in the capital were echoed on the banks of the Amazon. Chief of Staff Enrique Espinar and other officers loyal to Balta were said to be plotting against Commandant Alzamora, who was thought to favor Pardo. Because of the ties between Tucker and Pardo, the Hydrographic Commission was suspected of "revolutionary tendencies" in the other direction. Indeed, former commission secretary Timiteo Smith, "a great advocate of Pardo," sounded out the Virginians regarding a possible revolution. But the former Confederates had had their fill of rebellion. Although they hoped for Pardo's victory, Galt and the others were content "to take merely a sporting interest in the affair."

In July 1872 Congress assembled to ratify the choice of the electoral college, and Balta decided to abide by the decision of his countrymen. But Colonel Tomás Gutiérrez, the minister of war and marine, seized and imprisoned Balta. Supported by his four brothers, also army colonels, Gutiérrez proclaimed himself president. Peru's navy and much of the army, however, opposed the coup, as did the citizens of Lima, who demonstrated their anger in the streets. When President Balta's captors panicked and murdered him, the popular fury could not be contained. Urban mobs slaughtered the Gutiérrez brothers and hung their mutilated corpses from the spires of the cathedral. On August 2 Manuel Pardo was installed as president with a reinforced popular mandate. Isolated Iquitos did not learn of the bloodshed in the capital until after it was over. But on September 20 the jungle outpost observed a day of official mourning for the slain president. The *Tambo's* two howitzers, the only large guns in town, were fired every thirty minutes in Balta's honor.[17]

Apo Tucker

Admiral Tucker now had a friend in a very high place. Experience soon would demonstrate, however, that President Pardo's ability to assist the Hydrographic Commission was limited by the intractability of Peru's bureaucracy, the isolation of Iquitos, and the nation's disastrous financial condition. By 1872 virtually all of Lima's guano revenues had been mortgaged to service the huge foreign debt, incurred primarily for railroad construction. The government's domestic expenditures were double the treasury's income from other sources. The budget crisis deepened with the onset of an international economic recession soon after Pardo's inauguration. The new regime cut spending sharply and raised taxes, but Peru continued to teeter at the brink of bankruptcy. The government lived hand-to-mouth, and Iquitos occupied an unfavorable niche in the fiscal food chain.

The Pardo administration made several personnel changes in Loreto that initially appeared to benefit the Hydrographic Commission. Even before his return to Iquitos, Tucker had secured the replacement of Eduardo Raygada, the insubordinate skipper of the *Tambo*, with First Lieutenant Fidel Cater, reputedly the most skilled sailor posted in Loreto. But Cater had commanded the commercial steamer *Morona*, an assignment affording "a good opportunity to make money." With government salaries many months in arrears, such ventures, wrote Galt, were "about the only thing these poor . . . fellows desire out here." Cater's strong protests soon secured his transfer to the *Pastaza*, another commercial vessel. Acting Lieutenant Commander Carlos Gustavo Donayre became the *Tambo*'s skipper, while young Acting Second Lieutenant Ismael Meza was given charge of the *Mairo*. Neither man seemed enthusiastic about their new assignments. "The honor of being explorers," thought Galt, was "something they cannot . . . see the glory of."[18]

Tucker also obtained a new secretary for the commission. Captain Timiteo Smith, who originally held that post, took a leave of absence in late 1871 and resigned the next year, becoming a prominent Iquitos merchant. Engineer Cristóbal Rosas handled the agency's correspondence until March 1872, when he was ordered to Leticia in relief of Manuel Charon, who had been elected to Congress as a deputy from Loreto.[19] The multitalented (Louis) Maurice Mesnier, fluent in several languages, became Tucker's translator-scribe at a salary of sixty-eight *soles* per month. Of French and Portuguese ancestry, Mesnier was likely a United States citizen—perhaps part of the sizable Portuguese-American community recently established at Pará. Smith had recruited Mesnier at that Brazilian port to clerk in his store, and the linguist soon assumed additional duties as municipal secretary of Iquitos. A great lothario (Galt called him the "Gypsy of Iquitos"), Mesnier also became the surgeon's favorite chess partner. He was best known, however, as the "Piano Man." A gifted musician, Mesnier drew large crowds nightly at the Builders' Arms, Iquitos's most popular saloon.[20]

Of greatest import to the Hydrographic Commission, the Pardo administration honored Captain Alzamora's previous requests for reassignment, and his replacement reached Iquitos the day after Tucker arrived in the *Mairo*. Upon first meeting Alzamora two years earlier, Galt had described him as a "man of much more than ordinary elegance of bearing and address," the most "distinguished person" he had met on the Amazon. Despite the *comandante*'s opposition to the commission, the physician still praised him as "a gentleman of unusual calmness of nature," whose "courtesy toward us . . . disarms the grudge which against a vulgar man would be more irritating."[21]

Acting Captain Enrique Carreño, the new commandant general, was a thirty-nine-year-old Lima native who had built a commendable record during his twenty-two-year naval career. A graduate of Peru's military academy where he later taught, Carreño had spent two years as a midshipman with the Royal Navy. He fulfilled several important assignments in Great Britain and the United States and served from

1862 to 1864 on the commission that selected Iquitos as the site of the new naval station. A Pezet loyalist during the 1865 revolution, he was furloughed after the victory of Colonel Prado. In July 1867, however, the new regime reinstated Carreño and gave him a very delicate assignment. In the guise of a Colombian merchant, he went to Manila and gathered intelligence on Spanish defenses. But the Spaniards discovered his mission and nearly executed him as a spy. After six months of incarceration he was exchanged as a prisoner of war.

A "black-bearded, sharp-featured, bilious-looking subject," the new commandant seemed to Galt "a fit character for Blue Beard." Unlike Alzamora, Carreño was a "nervous sort of character, . . . more irritating and with less tact in managing people." Carreño had been a vocal critic of Tucker's employment by Peru. Initially, however, the surgeon was optimistic. "Altogether," the *comandante's* record showed him "to be a man of some force of character." After spending several days on a ship with Carreño in 1865, Chilean historian Benjamín Vicuña Mackenna (famed for a candor that embroiled him in numerous lawsuits) provided a much different appraisal. Carreño was "a being in which were marked in a most strong and repulsive manner . . . all of the possible deformities of the spirit." These were "revealed in each one of the features of his cameloid physiognomy: his glossy eyes," his mouth "prominent like that of a dromedary," and his nose, curved like "the beak of the birds of prey."[22] True to Vicuña's analysis, Carreño soon disabused the Hydrographic Commission of their initial good impressions.

In his first official communication with the new commandant general, Tucker asked that the exploring steamers be readied for an expedition to the Pachitea River. He also requested that Carreño appoint a mixed board of British and North American machinists to reexamine the *Tambo's* boilers, as War Minister Balta had ordered in July 1871. If the *Tambo* could not be made serviceable quickly, the admiral wanted the *Napo* assigned to him. The new panel consisted of two English mechanics, W. G. Edmonds and Alfred Warforne, and the two men hired by Tucker, Durfey and Bain, with Chief of Staff Enrique Espinar as presiding officer. After the inspection on January 25, Edmonds began the discussion, observing that the boilers "were not in a perfect state"; he thought the ends were weak "but could be made entirely safe" by placing these vessels in an upright position. The other members concurred. Durfey noted that some boiler tubes required repair, a view the others also shared. "With the repairs indicated," concluded the panel unanimously, the *Tambo* could safely build seventy-five pounds of pressure. Tucker informed General Miguel Medina, Pardo's minister of war and marine, that the dispute which had stymied the commission's work for twenty months had been resolved. With a few "insignificant repairs," the *Tambo* would be ready for service by March 1.[23]

But now the old dispute over Tucker's control of the steamers resurfaced. On February 13, after learning that the *Mairo* was ready for service, Tucker asked that the vessel's skipper be placed under his orders and that the admiral be given a copy of these instructions. Carreño refused, explaining that his files contained no directive from Lima authorizing such power for the admiral. Tucker promptly provided the *comandante* with War Minister Allende's letter of November 15, 1871, which stated that the officers of the exploring steamers were to be under the admiral's direct control. Carreño now ordered the skippers of the *Mairo* and *Tambo* to obey Tucker's commands; but he did so under his own authority, thus rejecting Tucker's assertion of independence. Furthermore, Carreño's instructions provided detailed procedures for protesting the admiral's orders.[24]

"With much sadness," Tucker informed Minister Medina of the new controversy and asked him to impart "clear and decisive orders" to Carreño. The commandant general, meanwhile, defended his actions to the authorities in Lima and volunteered "some points about the history" of the Hydrographic Commission. The diatribe that followed was based, in part, on a December 31, 1872, letter from Alzamora to the minister of war—a denunciation so harsh that the former *comandante* was reprimanded for his language. Carreño asserted that since 1867, Peru had lavished 160,000 *soles* on Tucker and his colleagues for salaries, equipment, and "weakly constructed" vessels. The admiral's team had provided no benefits to the nation, desiring only "to collect their salaries and nothing more." Since 1871, while Tucker dallied in the United States, his subordinates in Iquitos had been "loitering and enjoying their high salaries." The tasks assigned to the *norteamericanos*, concluded Carreño, could be performed by the naval officers of his command "with better results than those obtained up to today by the onerous and useless Tucker commission."[25]

After consulting with President Pardo about the latest round of wrangling in Iquitos, Minister Medina praised Carreño's patriotism and diligence; but he sided with Tucker and defended the commission's record. Although Peruvian officers had explored many rivers in the Montaña, explained Medina, these expeditions had not obtained the technical data to map the area adequately or to prepare navigation charts. Nor did Peru have sufficient native officers with the training required for these important tasks. Therefore, the Hydrographic Commission would continue its work, entirely independent of the commandant general; the *Tambo* and *Mairo* were to be under Tucker's control; and Carreño was to give the commission his full cooperation.[26]

Tucker was very anxious to explore the Pachitea system while the rivers were still rising; should his steamers run aground, the swelling of the waters would lift them free. On February 20 the *Mairo*, with Walter Butt and Nelson Noland on board, departed from Iquitos. The admiral ordered Lieutenant Meza to follow Butt's instructions while proceeding to the mouth of the Pachitea. The *Mairo* was to wait there for the arrival of the *Tambo*, which Tucker hoped would follow within a short time. En route, Meza was to have firewood cut and stacked for the larger steamer. Tucker instructed Butt and Noland to make all the observations needed for the preparation of charts. After many stops to cut wood, the *Tambo Wawa* reached her destination on March 22. The men of this advance party made a clearing on shore, erected temporary shelters, and awaited the mother vessel. It would be nearly two months before the *Tambo* joined them at what they called Port Patience.[27]

Back at Iquitos work on the *Tambo* progressed with "vigorous delay." Galt suspected that Carreño wanted to prevent the vessel's departure until at least mid-March, when the overland mail from Lima would reach Iquitos, perhaps with orders detrimental to Tucker. On March 18 the *Tambo*, with her boilers newly arranged, made a test run in front of the town. But some vital machinery had been left out of the vessel—Galt thought it sabotage. The steamer became disabled, lost an anchor, and nearly grounded. By April 4, however, the *Tambo* was ready, and she departed with Tucker, Rochelle, Galt, Sparrow, and Mesnier. The admiral again had obtained the services of the "indispensable" Major Ramón Herrera, who commanded ten Indian soldiers.[28]

The voyage to the mouth of the Río Pachitea required forty days. The Ucayali now was in full flood; and with its low banks inundated for several miles behind the river, the Indians had moved their villages inland. The *Mairo*'s crew had struggled to obtain sufficient firewood for their own vessel and could not stockpile fuel for the larger steamer. Thus, the *Tambo* made frequent stops while her sailors, in waist-high water, laboriously cut wood. Swarms of mosquitoes and sandflies attacked them incessantly, and each blow of their axes brought a shower of biting red ants from the branches above. Many of these stalwarts were stricken by fever and developed painful ulcers on their legs. By the end of their journey, the men of the *Tambo* appreciated the local proverb that the lower Ucayali was "only fit as a place of banishment for a man who has killed his mother."[29]

To the joyous relief of the *Mairo*'s party, the *Tambo* reached Port Patience on May 13. Already, however, the level of the Pachitea had begun to fall at a rate of ten inches per day. Tucker could not risk grounding his steamers in the unknown channels ahead, a disaster that might leave them stranded until the water rose again in October. Therefore he obtained six dugout canoes for the expedition. These craft were 30 to 35 feet long and 3 feet wide, with thatched shelters covering their rear third. Pedro and Clemente, local Conibo Indian chiefs befriended by Tucker during his earlier voyages, provided twenty-four oarsmen for this flotilla. For these new members of the expedition, the admiral was a "great chief"—"Apo Tucker," they called him.

Drawing forty-five days' rations from the *Tambo*, the explorers began their ascent of the Pachitea on May 19. In the rear of each canoe sat an old Conibo helmsman (*popero*), "all knots, scars and bruises," who steered the craft with a paddle and acted as coxswain. An "active young Indian" served as *puntero* (point man) of the vessel, keeping a close watch for obstacles and communicating with the helmsman through whistles and hand signals. The "order of battle" placed Tucker's canoe in the lead. From its rear flew a small Peruvian flag to show the "savages to what country they belong," explained Noland. His and Sparrow's canoe followed the "flagship," trailed by the boat carrying Rochelle and Butt. The succeeding two craft contained the expedition's provisions, while Dr. Galt and Mesnier, in the last canoe, served as the rear guard, to prevent their supplies from "running away." The Conibo boatmen did not relish the almost certain prospect of encounters with their traditional enemies, the fierce Cashibos and Campas.

For the first few days, the expedition paddled its way uneventfully up the winding river, through a "dense, dark archway of boughs, festooned with enormous flowering creepers." At night they camped on islands or pebbly promontories that afforded them a few yards of unobstructed vision and an open field of fire against attacking Indians. After supper (usually coffee, salt fish, rice, and such game as they were able to take during the day), the men retired to thatched lean-tos where they slept on the ground under mosquito nets. Major Herrera's soldiers stood guard. To avoid attracting the Cashibos, they dispensed with the periodic cries of "Sentinel, alert!" normally used to keep each other awake. With the crack of dawn each morning, the explorers broke camp, took their ration of grog, and got under way again. At mid-morning they stopped briefly for a breakfast of the same fare ingested the previous evening. During the day's journey the engineers sketched the course of the river and measured its depth and current.[30] At well-defined landmarks, Rochelle supervised readings of longitude, latitude, and elevation. Dr. Galt continued his meteorological observations, recording the data in his journal.[31]

In the early afternoon of May 24, the commission had its first brush with the Cashibos. The expedition's scout, a Brazilian Indian named Malafia, was alone in his small canoe a short distance ahead of the others when he heard the hum of bowstrings. The expert woodsman instinctively fired his shotgun to warn the others and jumped into the river to protect himself from the ensuing hail of projectiles. Four arrows struck around him, one grazing his arm and another passing through his dugout, over an inch thick. The main body of the expedition hurried to Malafia's rescue, with their rifles and pistols at the ready. But the attackers quickly disappeared into the jungle.

That evening the party camped at a place called Warm Water or

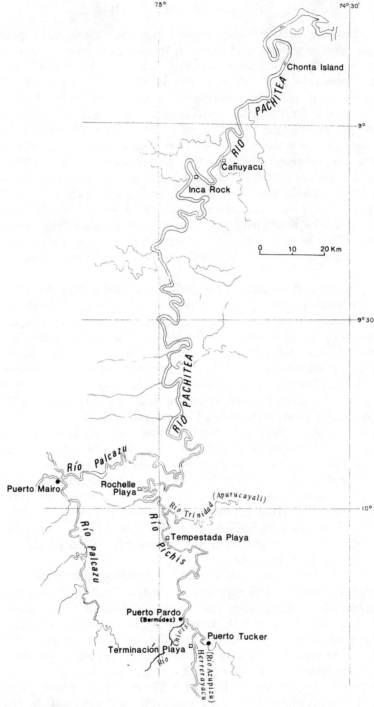

Exploration of the Pachitea and Pichis rivers, 1873

Warm River (Cañu-yacu) by the Indians—a site designated "Baths" on modern maps—where they enjoyed thermal sulfur springs that registered 113 degrees Fahrenheit. During the next day's journey, the river cut through a range of flat-topped hills, the San Carlos "Mountains." Here, wrote Noland,

> walls of colored sandstone rise to the height of one hundred feet and more, with every degree of inclination— some rising so beautifully straight and with such regular faces that you could hardly convince yourself that the hand of man had not been concerned in it; others with a gentle, regular slope from the water, like the front of some old fortress; others lean out over the water, presenting perfectly-formed Gothic arches and niches of every size, ornamented with beautiful basins, supplied with sparkling water from miniature cataracts above. Now and then a stream comes gushing out from a narrow gorge as dark as midnight; and over the whole face of this superb picture is hung, in graceful folds, a gorgeous lace-work of flowering vines and richest tropical foliage.

The commission stopped for breakfast in this cathedral of nature and discovered that the cliff face behind them was covered with glyphs. The carved representations of the sun and llamas suggested that the place had been visited by ancient explorers from the Andes. Tucker and his companions called it Inca Rock.[32]

On May 30, as their canoes approached a large island, a group of unarmed Cashibos called out to the expedition and made gestures of friendship. Tucker ordered his men ashore, and soon they were surrounded by a score of natives, the men "perfectly naked" and the women wearing only "a covering of bark about the loins." Noland judged them "the most miserable devils I ever saw"; their language sounded like "the ravings of a man shot in the brain." The natives gave them sugarcane and plantains, while the visitors reciprocated with knives, fishhooks, and some old clothing. Most of the Indians quickly hid the gifts they had received and returned with empty hands outstretched again. One old man amused the commission with his first essay at donning trousers, "floundering about with only one breeches-leg on, and the other tied around his neck in imitation of a cravat."

As the expedition shoved off and rounded the island, they came upon a large party of Cashibos with bows and arrows in hand. The soldiers in the two supply canoes attempted to trade fishhooks for a pair of bows; the natives took the hooks but would not part with their weapons, which the guards now tore from their hands. Some of the Cashibos then attempted to drag the canoes ashore while others opened fire with arrows. The explorers answered with volleys from their Remingtons. Tucker's party believed that the Indians, ignorant of firearms, thought the strangers to be unarmed and easy objects of capture. For a long time after this clash, the expedition heard the natives beating on hollowed logs—to assemble their people, thought Noland, for another attack.

The commission on June 4 reached the confluence of the Pichis and Palcazu rivers, which unite to form the Pachitea. They made camp and for two days took repeated astronomical readings to fix accurately the location of this important site. The land here, reported Tucker, was relatively high and "very desirable . . . for a town or settlement." A planter from the Ucayali who had accompanied the expedition departed up the Palcazu, bound for Lima, and the explorers entrusted him with their mail. "Having in view the prosperity and advancement of this part of . . . the Republic," Tucker requested that War Minister Medina forward through regular channels a joint application by himself and Rochelle to purchase ten square leagues (about thirty square miles) of land "at the point where the Pichis and Palcazu unite." The two men hoped to "demonstrate in this manner . . . tangible proof" of their faith "in the future grandeur of these limitless regions." The government apparently did not approve the sale of this tract, today the locale of Puerto Victoria.

The Hydrographic Commission began its ascent of the Pichis River on June 6. The region through which they would pass had been closed to outsiders since the great Campa uprising of Juan Santos Atahualpa 130 years earlier. The prospect of deadly encounters with these resolute warriors especially frightened the Conibo oarsmen, and they became increasingly unnerved as the expedition pushed deeper into Campa territory. To ward off enemy arrows, the Conibos painted their faces with a blue stripe running across their mouths, from ear to ear. For the commission members the perils of the Pichis would be partially offset by the honor of naming key points in this uncharted wilderness.

During the first night on the Pichis, eight Conibos deserted, fleeing downstream. Fortunately, they took the expedition's smallest canoe and only enough supplies for their own needs. Because of reduced manpower, however, Tucker had to abandon another boat. In a "council of war," the commission and Herrera agreed that they could no longer trust the remaining Conibos and that the major's soldiers—themselves Amazonian Indians—might also desert. Each night thereafter, the younger Virginians would stand guard. On June 7 the explorers reached the first significant navigation hazard on the Pichis, a shallow gravel bar extending across the swiftly flowing river. Beyond this point, christened Rochelle Beach, only canoes or powerful shallow-draft launches could pass. The next day, Trinity Sunday, the commission discovered a large stream entering the Pichis from the east. Shown as the Apurucayali on modern maps, Tucker's team appropriately named it the Río Trinidad. On the tenth the expedition, which had been advancing about a dozen miles daily, halted for a day due to the serious illness of one man. A violent storm pounded their camp, felling large trees all around them. The explorers dubbed the spot Tempest Beach.

The Andes now came ever closer into view, their forested slopes appearing dark green or blue through the hazy atmosphere. With increased elevation, the river cut more deeply into the rocky landscape, shoals became more numerous, and the night air was chilly. The explorers saw frequent signs of the Campas, passing their gardens, beached rafts, and empty villages with fires still smoking. The intruders often heard drums in the forest, perhaps calling warriors for an attack.[33] On the afternoon of June 13, the commission reached a fork in the river, where they took up quarters in two vacant Campa huts. The next morning, after leaving gifts to mollify their absent hosts, the explorers pushed up the western branch of the stream. Three hours later a rapids halted their heavily laden canoes, some four miles upstream. The explorers called this point Termination Beach and the river itself Herrera-yacu, in honor of the major. In later years, the Herrera-yacu often was thought to be the Río Chivis; but it was probably the Azupizu River, which unites with the Río Nazarategui to form the Pichis.[34] After determining the geographic coordinates, Tucker and his colleagues returned to the mouth of the Herrera-Yacu and bedded down in the previous night's lodgings, where they found their gifts untouched. They spent the next day there, making repeated observations.

At dawn on June 15, the admiral ordered the expedition up the eastern branch of the Pichis, shown as the Nazarategui on today's maps. The Conibos protested strongly against going deeper into Campa country; when this failed to dissuade Apo Tucker, the Indians feigned illness. "They discover very suddenly," recorded Noland in his journal, "that they have ailments of various kinds, pleading sore hands and feet from exposure to sun and water, though they have known nothing else all their lives." Nevertheless, the explorers climbed the river for eleven miles, struggling through three rapids before reaching a fourth, impassable barrier at 10:00 A.M. They made camp and carefully established the position of this point—1,041 miles from Iquitos and about 190 miles from the Pacific Coast—which they designated Puerto Tucker.[35]

The next morning the commission began its journey downstream, covering in one day the distance traveled in three during the ascent of the Pichis. By the early afternoon of the seventeenth, they had reached the mouth of the Río Trinidad. Again ignoring the remonstrances of the Conibos, Tucker ordered the party up this tributary where, after a difficult two-hour struggle, they camped for the night. Daylight brought the discovery that five more Indian boatmen had fled, this time without provisions, on a raft. Now desperately shorthanded, the commission had to abandon their survey of the Trinidad. They turned around and reached the junction of the Pichis and Palcazu that evening.

By this time, most of the explorers were experiencing the intermittent chills and fever of malaria as well as other illnesses. But the admiral was determined to ascend the Palcazu River and to fix the position of Puerto Mairo, the terminus of the trail he had taken from Huánuco in 1867. The next morning, June 19, Tucker induced sufficient Conibo "volunteers" to man a pair of canoes and set off again, leaving Dr. Galt and Mesnier behind to care for three of their sickest comrades. The admiral accomplished his mission and returned five days later to find Galt and Mesnier locked in combat. They had improvised a chess set, using a box top and men carved from charcoal. The physician assumed the role of Germany, while his opponent represented France, and they "refought old battles."

The expedition commenced its five-day voyage down the Pachitea on June 24. The relative monotony of the return trip was broken, the next afternoon, by another Cashibo ambush. The supply canoe—at the rear of the line and manned only by Conibos—received a fusillade of arrows. They called out to Galt and Mesnier in the next boat, who dispersed the attackers with rifle fire. At noon on June 28, 1873, after a forty-one-day, four-hundred-mile journey by canoe, the commission reached the *Tambo* and *Mairo*, anchored at the mouth of the Pachitea.[36] All of the party now had symptoms of malaria, some also had intestinal disorders, and Tucker was pained with rheumatism. The admiral's health had "suffered much from the exposure and hardships" of the voyage, he informed his sons. "I held my own as well as sixty winters could, but it was as much as I could do." The experience convinced the old sailor that he "must think about going on the retired list." But Tucker was gratified in the belief that the expedition would be "important to the future of Peru."[37]

The weary explorers relished the comforts of the *Tambo*—"the best boat on the river," Noland told his mother. "I wish you could hear the music we have." Captain Butt, "a remarkable violinist," knew "all the operas by heart from A to Z," and Mesnier was "equally proficient" on the vessel's "parlor organ." During the journey back to Iquitos, they also were entertained by the wild creatures that the crew of the steamers had added to the normal complement of domestic animals, creating a "menagerie of monkeys, parrots, macaws, chickens, turtles, pigs and Lord only knows what else." The commission soon acquired a young jaguar which promptly killed two chickens and a turkey. Because of his "chronic case of appetite, like a good 'reb,'" they called him Dixie.[38]

Back at Iquitos, two weeks later, Tucker informed Lima about the results of the expedition. In the season of high water, small steamers of sixteen-inch draft could ascend to Puerto Tucker. Throughout the year, vessels drawing eighteen inches of water could reach a "point just below the mouth of the Herrera-yacu," marked by an anchor on the preliminary chart forwarded with the admiral's report. Tucker diplomatically designated the latter place Port Pardo and recommended it as the terminus of a road or railroad from the Andes.[39] President Pardo judged the results of Tucker's latest survey "very satisfactory." *El Comercio*, Lima's leading newspaper, praised the admiral effusively. "No one has carried out works so important as those . . . of Tucker and his companions." They deserved the "thanks of the nation" for the great "sacrifices and the abnegations which are indispensable for . . . exploration in the Amazon jungles."[40]

Final Touches

With the Pichis expedition Tucker had located the navigable point on the eastern river system closest to Lima, and the conclusion of his assignment was now in sight. He needed only to survey the Marañón-Amazon and its remaining uncharted tributaries. If the commission could accomplish this task before the onset of low water in December, they would require only a few more months in Iquitos to prepare their navigation charts. Three days after his return from the Pichis, Tucker asked Commandant Carreño to ready the steamers and to assemble five months' provisions for the commission's anticipated departure on August 15. But repairs to the *Tambo*'s woodwork and a dearth of supplies in Iquitos (where only thirty days' provisions could be spared) delayed the admiral's labors for more than a month.[41]

For this race with the falling rivers, the admiral divided his command into two teams. The *Tambo*, carrying Tucker, Rochelle, Sparrow, Galt, and Mesnier, steamed out of Iquitos on September 18 bound for the Yavarí River, the boundary with Brazil. The commission had charted its course for some 220 miles in 1867, and a new Peruvian-Brazilian boundary commission presently was engaged in a meticulous survey of the river. Tucker, however, hoped to obtain precise coordinates for the junction of the Yavarí and Amazon to serve as a basis for the commission's other observations. They reached their destination after a voyage of eleven days and made camp on a small island in the center of the Yavarí just above its mouth—probably the Isla de Islandia. For two days the commission made repeated observations, determining to within one second (a one-hundred-foot margin) the longitude and latitude of this important point. On September 29 the *Tambo* began a slow ascent of the Amazon, arriving at Iquitos on October 12. En route to and from the Yavarí, the commission had made observations at intermediate points along the river. Sparrow sketched the course of the waterway, marking its main channel, while his colleagues measured depths and currents.[42]

Meanwhile, Butt and Noland in the *Mairo* had commenced surveys of the Nanay and Itaya rivers, whose mouths bracket Iquitos. In addition to obtaining data for navigation charts, Tucker instructed this team to evaluate the agricultural potential of these districts. Farms established there might provide food for the expanding population of Iquitos. Beginning on September 18, Acting Second Lieutenant Carlos LaTorre, the *Mairo*'s new skipper, guided the launch up the Nanay, passing the confluence of the Pinto-yacu—the Paint River, whose yellowish water gives the Nanay its characteristic color. After eight days and some 195 miles, they reached an impassable palisade of tree trunks embedded in the channel. Although the Nanay's banks were high enough to permit planting along much of its course, the expedition noticed few gardens. The local Indians devoted most of their energies to fishing, catching the abundant turtles, and gathering wild rubber. The survey of the Itaya produced discouraging results. Soon after entering the river on October 13, the *Mairo* encountered a series of snags. A logjam only thirty-eight miles upstream halted the launch three days later. The explorers found a few gardens cultivated near the mouth of the river, but the area beyond was too low for planting and nearly devoid of population.[43]

In mid-October the entire Hydrographic Commission reassembled in Iquitos, where a continued shortage of provisions delayed their surveys for another two weeks. At the end of the month the *Tambo* and *Mairo* departed with a scant forty-five days' rations. The rivers now were falling rapidly, threatening to halt Tucker's final labors for at least six months. Thus, he ordered the *Mairo* to proceed quickly to the Río Potro, a small southern affluent of the Marañón. After surveying that stream, Butt and Noland were to explore the Morona, Pastaza, and Tigre rivers, major northern tributaries of the Marañón. Meanwhile, the admiral and his team in the *Tambo* would chart the Marañón proper and the lower, navigable portion of the Río Huallaga. The *Tambo*'s party had the easier task, for Peru's commercial steamers regularly serviced the waterways they would survey, and Arturo Wertheman recently had determined the geographic positions of many points along their banks. Tucker needed only to verify Wertheman's coordinates and to obtain data for navigation charts. The *Mairo*'s team would explore rivers where no steamer had yet ventured and determine for the first time the coordinates for important points in these regions.[44]

On November 8, after an eleven-day voyage, the *Mairo* reached the Potro River, the proposed terminus of a road to Chachapoyas, beyond the mountains to the southwest. For two days the launch battled the river, with its strong currents, narrow bends, and numerous obstructions until, forty-eight miles upstream, the little steamer could go no farther. Returning to the mouth of the Potro and ascending the Marañón for some fifteen miles, the *Mairo* entered the Río Morona. Along its banks lived the hostile Capahuana people (a branch of the Jívaro) who, noted Butt, were famed for "shrinking the heads of their victims to diminutive proportions." Although the Morona was quite deep, its powerful current, tight curves, and many palisades made navigation treacherous. Two days and only thirty-seven miles upstream, Butt and Lieutenant LaTorre agreed that they had reached the limit of safe navigation.

The *Mairo* proceeded from the Morona to the Pastaza, a river almost as broad at its mouth as the Marañón. But the Pastaza was very shallow, with numerous bars. The light-drafted launch grounded several times and turned back after negotiating only seven miles of the stream. Three days downriver from the Pastaza, the *Mairo* reached the Río Tigre, "wide and deep in all seasons of the year." The explorers spent six days climbing 111 miles up the waterway. Butt deemed the Tigre the richest in natural resources of any northern tributary of the Marañón, abounding in rubber, wax, copal, sarsaparilla, and the copaiba tree, which yields a medicinal oil. He also noted tar oozing from the petroleum deposits that a century later would bring a bonanza in the upper reaches of the rivers surveyed by the *Mairo* on that expedition. By November 29 the team had nearly exhausted their provisions. From the appearance of the river, Butt estimated the limit of steam navigation to be about a dozen miles ahead. After establishing the geographic coordinates, the men of the *Mairo* began their journey home, anchoring in front of Iquitos on December 4.[45]

Admiral Tucker and his companions on the *Tambo* left Iquitos on October 28 and slowly steamed up the Marañón, charting the river and making astronomical observations at all important places. On November 20 they reached Point Achual, at the entrance to an archipelago a few miles below the head of steam navigation at Borja. But the river was now too low to hazard a passage; the final portion of the Marañón would have to be surveyed later. The *Tambo* backtracked to the Huallaga River, the westernmost of the Marañón's major southern affluents. The commission surveyed the Huallaga for 169 miles to Rumicayarina (near Shucushuyacu)—some 40 miles above Yurimaguas, the highest point served by Peru's commercial steamers. Anchoring at Iquitos on December 6, the *Tambo* completed her final voyage with the Hydrographic Commission.[46]

During the next ten days Tucker and his colleagues worked intensely on the report of their final surveys. The admiral wanted to take it to Lima on the steamer that would leave Iquitos at mid-month. After returning from the Pichis expedition in July, Tucker had requested orders to the capital, where he would discuss the final work of the commission—the publication of its maps. President Pardo summoned him to Lima on September 18. Now in broken health and feeling the results of advancing age, the admiral was anxious to return home.[47] He also relished the prospect of leaving Loreto, for his last months there had been very unpleasant. Commandant Carreño had vented his hostility toward the Hydrographic Commission by attacking the skippers of the exploring steamers. He removed Lieutenant Meza from command of the *Mairo* and apparently dragooned Lieutenant Commander Donayre, the *Tambo*'s captain, into open opposition toward the commission.[48] The *comandante* also had launched a new campaign against the admiral's "tip-top steamer."

In early August, as Tucker waited anxiously to begin his final surveys, Carreño ordered factory superintendent Rae to inspect the *Tambo*. Rae found the steamer's machinery to be in good condition, but much of her long-neglected woodwork, especially the paddle-wheel housings, was in a "very advanced state of deterioration." Nevertheless, Machinist Durfey estimated that all essential repairs could be completed within ten days. Rae's report did not satisfy the commandant. He ordered a full, formal survey of the vessel and selected a junta hostile to the commission. This panel judged the steamer's hull and engine to be "in a perfect state"; but the examiners (like those in 1871) deemed the boilers "very thin" and, therefore, "extremely weak." The board also noted the craft's bent auxiliary rudder (damaged three years earlier) and the deteriorated woodwork. The junta concluded, sweepingly and inconsistently, that the *Tambo* appeared "weak in its construction"; only major modifications, "correcting its design," could render the steamer serviceable for "some years more."

The board delayed writing its report for several days, until Tucker had departed for the Yavarí River. Carreño forwarded the document to Lima along with his own estimate that the indispensable repairs to the *Tambo* would require eight months of constant labor. He volunteered that Tucker's team would be very expensive to maintain during this extended period of inactivity and requested instructions "concerning the permanence" of the Hydrographic Commission in Loreto.[49] The authorities in Lima rejected the latest attack on the exploring steamer, informing the *comandante* (in Rochelle's words) that they were "perfectly acquainted with everything relating" to the vessel and "did not wish to hear anything more about her defects." Once Tucker had left the region, Carreño allowed the *Tambo* to rot at her moorings.[50]

On December 16, 1873, Tucker named Rochelle acting president of the Hydrographic Commission in Loreto. He formally thanked Carreño for his "consideration" and offered to perform "with pleasure" errands for the *comandante* in Lima. The next day the admiral departed from Iquitos for the final time. He took the Peruvian steamer *Morona*—which had first carried him to Iquitos six years earlier—to Tabatinga. From there a Brazilian vessel took him to Pará, where he caught a steamer bound for Rio de Janeiro. The old sailor had last visited the Brazilian capital three decades earlier, during his voyage home from the East Indies. The city had changed much since that time, he told Randy, "but the grand scenery" remained the same. The admiral's removal from the Amazon already had brought an improvement in his health; he was "decidedly re-gaining" his weight. But Tucker's reminiscences about Rio also evoked some sadness. "I am afraid my dear Ran I am getting old—a thing which I very much dislike." After a journey on a "fine large English steamer" through the Strait of Magellan, the admiral reached Lima on March 3, 1874.[51]

CHAPTER TEN

Poker Flat, Peru

MODERN IQUITEÑOS proudly proclaim their attractive, bustling city the "Pearl of the Amazon." But persons familiar with the rustic settlement of the 1860s and 1870s frequently described it in reference to better-known places. As an ambitious commercial center on the bank of a great river, it was touted as the "St. Louis" of Peru by local promoters. The naval shops, with their scores of British mechanics, evoked comparisons with Birmingham, England. Negative analogies also were common. For British engineer-naturalist Frederick J. Stevenson, Iquitos was a "little Hell upon Earth," where in 1867 he had "spent five of the most disagreeable and unhappy days" of his life. The public morals of Iquitos gained it notoriety as the "Sodom of the Amazon." Indeed, the vice-ridden outpost reminded Nelson Noland of the setting for Bret Harte's popular short story "The Outcasts of Poker Flat."

The young engineer might have identified several other similarities between Iquitos and Harte's fictional California mining town. Both were crude, isolated frontier communities, far removed from the restraining influences of established society. Iquitos, like Poker Flat, was peopled by an eccentric assortment of humanity, including many castoffs and adventurers hoping to "make their strike." A score of nationalities were represented among the town's residents, about three thousand persons by 1872. The population was disproportionately male and young adult. About half of the inhabitants were Indians; the remainder consisted of whites and mestizos, with a sprinkling of blacks and Chinese. Although overwhelmingly Catholic in religion, the polyglot community also had Protestants and Jews. Probably fewer than one townsman in five could read and write.[1]

Iquitos also was a boomtown, destined to experience periods of considerable prosperity interspersed with epochs of numbing poverty. The rubber boom of the late nineteenth and early twentieth centuries would produce Iquitos's most extravagant golden age. A second scramble for rubber along with quinine and barbasco (rotenone), a natural insecticide, brought a smaller economic resurgence during World War

216

II. Since 1970, Iquitos has benefited from the new petroleum industry of Amazonian Peru. Admiral Tucker and his colleagues witnessed Iquitos's very first boom, based on government largess. Although Loreto's exports—already including substantial quantities of wild rubber—expanded throughout the residence of the Hydrographic Commission, the twenty-two-thousand-*sol* monthly subsidy from Lima was the mainstay of the local economy. The government's payroll quickly found its way into the pockets of Iquitos's merchants, artisans, landlords, and saloon keepers. Beginning in July 1871, however, the flow of funds from the capital became irregular; and it would become increasingly so during the stay of the Virginians. What little money reached the post, at infrequent intervals, went to Peru's creditors at Pará for materials and freight and to the British contract workmen at the factory. When not paid, the latter became sullen, refused to work, and threatened to file claims through their government. But even the English mechanics did not receive their wages regularly after July 1872.[2]

Iquitos survived by virtue of its "remarkable credit system," explained Noland. "Without showing a cent of money," anything could be purchased, "from a box of matches to a house." Tucker and his associates fortunately enjoyed cordial relations with many Iquitos merchants, especially Timiteo Smith, the former secretary of the Hydrographic Commission. With an inheritance from his father, Smith formed a partnership with Alexander B. Johnston, a Scotch merchant. This business alliance was reinforced by marriage. Smith's sister—the lovely Leticia—married Johnston, while Tim Smith wed Johnston's sister Cecilia. Smith and Johnston purchased the first private steamer in Amazonian Peru, the *Cecilia*, and quickly became the most successful of Iquitos's merchants.[3] Less well connected residents of Iquitos, however, often suffered the indignity of begging for credit. As salaries fell further into arrears, many merchants went bankrupt; Iquitos's already high prices soared. Public employees who left Loreto could only settle their accounts with instruments from the commissary that creditors accepted at discounts of 25 percent or more. Those unwilling to absorb such losses were stranded in the frontier settlement, hoping that the next steamer would bring money from Lima. But the funds did not arrive, and Iquitos became "filled with dissatisfied adventurers."[4]

The economic woes of Iquitos were compounded on August 27, 1872, by the town's second major fire in seven years. The conflagration began at 10:00 A.M. in the house of Juana Espinosa on the north edge of town. A strong breeze from the northeast carried sparks to the thatched roof of the church, on the Plaza de Armas. From there the fire jumped to the nearby naval complex, destroying the offices of the captain general, chief of staff, commissary, and port captain and the barracks of the marine column. The blaze then spread down Putumayo Street, consuming several business establishments and private homes. The one small water pump in Iquitos could not halt the blaze, so the authorities ordered the thatched roofs removed from nearby buildings. For four hours the entire population of Iquitos fought the flames, but they were losing the battle until a providential shift in the wind saved the town.[5]

With the morale of Iquitos already sapped by poverty and fire, two more plagues struck the town in 1873: a smallpox epidemic, which frightened away nearby Indian farmers, making food "unavailable at any price," and Comandante Enrique Carreño. Soon after replacing Alzamora in January 1873, Carreño launched a sweeping "moralization" campaign.[6] Viewed as a place of banishment for officials who had fallen from favor, the Department of Loreto and in particular Iquitos had a reputation for corruption in every branch of government—administrative, judicial, ecclesiastic, and military.

The concept of official misconduct was not well defined a century ago. And the phenomenon was not confined to poorer countries, as the plethora of political scandals in the post-Civil War United States attests. In Peru, however, the problem was endemic, deeply rooted in the practices of Spanish colonialism, including a tradition of inadequate government salaries, which often compelled public employees to supplement their regular income. The government anticipated that officials would devote much of their time to secondary occupations and tolerated, within varying limits, conflicts of interest and petty bribery. Reports of official corruption in Loreto were perhaps somewhat overdrawn. Dr. Galt described the officials of Iquitos as "the greatest scandal mongers and intriguers" he had ever known, with a propensity toward gossip "as obtains in all small towns." But allowing for exaggeration, official malfeasance in Loreto was patent, even by contemporary Peruvian standards. It was also entirely understandable. To high-priced, isolated Loreto—"almost outside the action of the government," where "abuses can be committed with impunity"—Lima dispatched many incompetent and incorrigible officials and then failed to pay them.[7]

Galt recorded almost every variety of misconduct. Lecherous prefects and subprefects exacted sexual favors from poor women and their children. These officials profited from their control over levies of conscript Indian labor, assigning them to their own private businesses. They jailed citizens who protested against these and other abuses of power. The surgeon marveled at the "utter inability of these Spanish Peruvians to comprehend what is meant by Republican liberty"; the officials of Loreto employed "as despotic a mode of action as could obtain in Turkey."[8]

The treasurers and government contractors at Moyobamba, who forwarded the contingent to Iquitos, substituted debased Bolivian or Chilean money for the sound Peruvian *soles* they received from the capital. In 1872 the treasurer absconded with the long-awaited subsidy from Lima. Judges, too, were said to be corrupt and incompetent; those at the lowest level, complained one prefect, "could scarcely sign their own name." Even churchmen—public officials in Peru—were frequent subjects of scandal, from the bishop of Moyobamba, who was accused of extortion, to the unchaste "soliciting confessors" of Iquitos and other towns in the district.[9]

The disciplinary problems among common sailors at Iquitos probably did not differ much from those at naval stations around the world. These men behaved badly. But scandalous conduct within the officer corps appears to have been excessive. The official correspondence was replete with charges of chronic drunkenness, fighting, sexual assaults, and insubordination among commissioned officers; even so, the minister of war and marine scolded Alzamora for "covering up" many breaches of conduct among his subalterns. The steamer captains were merchants in uniform, transporting their goods on government vessels without paying freight charges. Commissary officials embezzled funds and stole public property. Reports of speculation, misappropriation, and blatant conflicts of interest tainted the records of the highest-ranking officers. Commandant Alzamora—himself the target of such accusations—frequently appealed to the capital for honest and competent subordinates. Carreño complained that after nine years of Alzamora's administration, the new *comandante* had inherited a "corrupted department, . . . a theater of orgies, . . . where dignity is drunk and honor played with." Carreño assumed the post with assurances that Lima would replace most of the officers at Iquitos. But the minister of war and marine reneged on his promise, explaining that he lacked sufficient officers to man the nation's warships. He instructed Carreño to reform his existing staff "with the most severe discipline."[10]

Carreño launched his purge with enthusiasm. He expressed his lack of confidence in Captain F. Enrique Espinar, the station's capable and experienced chief of staff, and secured his replacement. The commandant jailed the chief commissary along with other employees of that department, the naval factory, and arsenal. He sent several officers to Lima under arrest. The steamer captains were "lashed without mercy for their speculations." After four months the *comandante* reported that, through the fear of his "raised arm," Iquitos had improved "500 percent in morality." To be sure, many of his victims deserved punishment; but Carreño carried his campaign to extremes, severely chastising subordinates for minor infractions or their failure to comply with unreasonable orders. "With great want of judgment and good faith," noted Galt, the commandant "alienated his own officers and the [government] employees so that the place is in a perpetual row." The "general system of bad feeling" along with "poverty and smallpox" threatened Iquitos with "complete ruin."[11] Within the next four years the town's population would be reduced by half.

Three months after his arrival in Iquitos, Carreño began a litany of petitions for his own transfer. But the self-congratulatory reports of his accomplishments in Loreto may have convinced Lima that he was irreplaceable. At the beginning of his third year in the jungle, the desperate *comandante* "took the liberty" to list by name suitable candidates for his job. "It is not just," he implored, that some officers "should enjoy the pleasures of the capital and be paid up to the day," while others were "indefinitely posted in savage country without resources of any kind," where they were "devoured by plagues of mosquitoes." If no other post was available, Carreño would "prefer a thousand times *la indefinida*" (furlough at reduced pay).[12]

In October 1876 former chief of staff Espinar would return to Iquitos, in relief of Carreño. After inspecting the station, the new *comandante* charged that Carreño "had not proceeded with legality" and that his actions had "not been in accord with his official correspondence." Although Carreño had reported steady progress in replacing the offices lost in the 1872 fire, he had devoted most of Iquitos's meager resources to the construction of his own house. The steamers were in "a lamentable state," the naval factory was almost silent, and the fortress at Leticia had been abandoned to the jungle. Discipline had been "scandalously relaxed." The young employees from the Ministry of Finance who, at Carreño's request, had replaced the naval commissaries, were incompetent and corrupt, trained in "the Machiavellian school of Señor Carreño." The latter's "exaggerated severity and rectitude, . . . as well as his integrity," were in "complete doubt." Lamented Espinar, "All is ruin, . . . all is disorder."[13]

The Sodom of the Amazon

Visitors to early Iquitos were shocked by the prevalence of public drunkenness, concubinage, and other vices among its inhabitants. "Sodom would shine alongside of Iquitos in point of morality and temperance," asserted Professor James Orton. Dr. Galt, a seasoned world traveler, deemed the morals of the Marañón "probably the worst on the globe." The problem was not confined to the town's Peruvian residents; the place was distinguished for "the utter immorality . . . of all nations and races, foreign and aboriginal."

Only a handful of men—the senior Peruvian officers, a few of the

Englishmen at the naval shops, and some of the merchants—brought their wives to Iquitos. Orton estimated that the settlement had only a dozen lawful marriages. But fifty or more public officials and an equal number of British workmen maintained "housekeepers," as they were politely described. Indeed, the English mechanics claimed that they had to take mistresses to "get their washing and cooking done." Although "not received into the society of the few better families," noted Galt, these women had a "semi-recognized position" and were "acknowledged by those keeping them and others without any gainsaying." Soon after his arrival in Iquitos, Galt confided to his diary that the concubines were "often quite faithful." But after more time in the city, he struck out the word "often" and substituted "rarely." Three decades later a Loreto prefect would explain that matrimony "inspires fear and . . . almost repugnance" among the common women of Loreto. "Free love, transitory union . . . while harmony lasts and the ties of affection are not broken, . . . this is what they seek and accept." Simple prostitution was also widespread and venereal disease rampant. One official report on Loreto warned that "sexual pleasures have killed more men than drunkenness."[14]

Many of Iquitos's concubines were mestizas (*cholas* was the term most commonly used) from Moyobamba, the department capital, where the admixture of Spaniard and local Indian had produced offspring of a predominantly European appearance. The Moyobambinos boasted that "no stranger ever passed" by their city; "all became captivated by the pretty girls." A Yankee visitor who escaped the trap reported that "marriage is a thing hardly worth notice, and only a few old fogies trouble themselves about it." But Moyobamba was "filled with young women, considered pretty, who are not backward in singing and dancing, and rendering themselves agreeable." Women from Moyobamba— founded three centuries before the rise of Iquitos—implanted the customs of their town in settlements throughout Loreto, where the *cholas* typically wore "simple pink or light blue frocks, trimmed with a bit of lace or ribbons." They had "dark lustrous eyes" and "dark hair . . . secured behind by a ribbon," from which their tresses fell "loose down the back. A few pinks and rosebuds half encircle the head like a broken wreath." Galt described them as "sometimes a pretty animal—fond of trinkets, sleep, voluptuousness and ignorance." A less-inhibited North American later praised their "queenly carriage," with "back and shoulders wonderfully erect, head held high, Bali-like breasts thrust forward." And to lonely "exiles"—be they from Lima, from Europe, or from the United States—the Loretanas looked more attractive with each passing month.[15]

"Drunkenness," reported Dr. Galt, was the "endemic disease" in Iquitos, and chronic intoxication was more universal there than in any other place he had visited. Every store in town sold liquor—imported cognac, beer, and wines to more affluent residents; rum, *cachaza* (a cruder sugarcane distillate), and fermented maize or manioc beverages (*chicha* and *masato*) to the common people. Most Loretanos imbibed heavily; the habit began in childhood among the lower classes, as did the universal use of tobacco by both sexes. Alcoholism was most acute among the foreign community, especially the English mechanics, who seemed "to go to the bad pretty fast, the most of them going home broken down physically and morally, or dying here of delirium tremens." Three Yankee tradesmen employed at the naval shops also were as "idle and drunken as could be wished."[16]

Thoughtful observers attributed Iquitos's intemperance to the "lack of society and the restraining influences of home," aggravated by short workdays and high salaries. Galt could not imagine "a set of employees in the world" who did "as little work for so much money." Most government offices conducted business from eleven to three o'clock. The working hours at the naval shops extended from six in the morning to three in the afternoon on weekdays and a half day on Saturday, relatively short hours for that era. The men of Iquitos spent "their spare money and time in drinking and lounging about the beer shops," playing billiards and "gambling with cards and dice." They were "the most persevering players," noted a traveler, "playing all day and a great part of the night."[17]

Sunday in Iquitos was "a day of drunkenness," as were the many civil and religious holidays. With parades, band concerts, cockfights, and fireworks displays, the revelry lasted several days during major fiestas, the most unrestrained of which was Carnival (Mardi Gras) when, Noland reported, there was

no respect paid to rank, sex, or condition. The door of the highest official in the place can be broken open, and he dragged out and painted all over, and obliged to laugh at it, too. . . . Try to imagine a dirty village of three thousand inhabitants, three-fourths of whom are cholos, mulattoes, Chinese, and Indians, with a fair sprinkling of the lowest class of English workmen; imagine them all desperate from receiving no money; imagine an order . . . giving them holiday and absolute license for four days, and you may then . . . have an inkling of what transpires on such occasions. . . . During this reign of liquor and absence of law, the streets are incessantly paraded by gangs of yelling men and women, who throw, at every one they meet, balls of mud, and skins filled with paint, and all kinds of horrid-smelling things. . . . You would see a Captain in the Peruvian Navy start down the street to his breakfast, looking . . . as neat as a pin, and a dozen women would break from the crowd; and while some would be smearing his face with red, white and blue paint, others would be throwing flour over him from top to toe. . . . His shirt-collar is . . . pulled aside, to make way for a handful of soft, black mud, from the street; and, at the same time, he feels his pockets being filled with the same article.

A state of abandon prevailed during all holidays except Good Friday, when the people of Iquitos dressed in black, stayed in their homes, and abstained from liquor and sex. "All are supposed to be virtuous for one day," commented Galt acidly, "as a sort of reminder of what devils they are at other times."[18]

The people of Loreto had a passion for music and dancing. Iquitos's small elite favored the piano and violin; the lower classes preferred the accordion and especially the concertina, on which the *cholas* played *tristes*, the traditional laments of the Andes. To Noland these melodies were "the sweetest, saddest, and most weird, imaginable." For dancing the musicians played sprightly airs to accompany the creole waltz and faster-paced *chilena* and *zamacueca*. The latter, according to Galt, was a "graceful expression of motion when genteelly danced, but being a species of 'can-can'" could be "made as lascivious as the company may choose." And in Iquitos it was most often "a flirtation with the body."

Iquitos had at least one dance party (or "fandango," as the *gringos* usually called them) every night. "They are indulged in and enjoyed by all classes, and the passion for them is remarkable," wrote Noland. Seventy years later the young United States vice-consul and his wife, Hank and Dot Kelly, would still find dancing "the one unfailing source of energy and joy" in Iquitos, "the great, fraternal bond of all classes and nationalities." To initiate a fandango in the 1870s, the host merely purchased some liquor, threw open the doors of his house, and had a musician sound a few notes on the concertina. Besides this instrument or some other to carry the melody, a proper band only needed a large crate (dry-goods boxes were favored) to serve as a drum. The "high shrill" voices of the women along with clapping hands and feet of the "wall-flowers" of both sexes completed the ensemble. "Any passerby," wrote Noland, could join the party and stay until the liquor was gone.[19]

At fandangos throughout Loreto, noted traveler Joseph Beal Steere, the women believed "it their right and duty to choose their partners for the dance, a custom that would be scarcely allowable even in countries where women's rights are better recognized." But Steere soon forgot this unusual behavior as he observed the *zamacueca* at a lower-class dance in Moyobamba. While "two boys at the dry-goods box pounded themselves red in the face," "barefoot couples made the dust fly" and "quick and quicker flew." He explained that the handkerchief was "a most necessary article with both parties, and upon its proper use depends much of the grace of the dancer. With it the young man beckons on his partner and now floats it around her head as they whirl about each other and now stoops as if he would sweep the dust from her bare feet, she sometimes using her handkerchief as a shield to keep off his advances, and sometimes urging him on to greater endeavors."

Frederick Stevenson attended a formal ball among Iquitos's elite at Commandant Alzamora's quarters on Independence Day, 1867.

While "flourishing handkerchiefs" in one hand, the men held their coattails in the other. The women pranced about, "some of them pretty and graceful, but most of them far too fat for violent exercise in the hot stuffy little room, and visibly suffering from excessive perspiration." The scene had not changed much at a dance three-quarters of a century later. "The women's flimsy dresses were plastered to their bodies in soggy intimacy," wrote Consul Kelly, "accentuating the contour of breast and thigh. . . . The men sweated through their shirts and white coats so that the starch oozed from the fabric and was slimy to the touch, while the dye from their partners' dresses left rainbow patterns on their white sleeves and other points of contact."[20]

Nearly every household in Iquitos, including that of the Hydrographic Commission, maintained a small menagerie of Amazonian fauna—jaguar kittens, monkeys, and especially parrots. Throughout the day these birds shouted out names, recited the alphabet, and cursed or sang parts of the Mass, according to the predilections of the owners they mimicked. A clinging monkey was Walter Butt's constant companion.[21]

The Outcasts

The numerous impediments to the explorations of the Hydrographic Commission condemned Admiral Tucker and his fellow Virginians to endure long periods of discomfort, temptation, and ultimately boredom in Iquitos. Except for a few weeks in early 1871 when they lived on board the anchored *Tambo*, they shared rented houses. These crude dwellings of mud-plastered canes and thatched roofs did little more than provide shelter from moderate storms; during the rainy season's torrents they often flooded, bringing in "sloths, rats, lizards," and "a snake or two." Nor did the Virginians master "the art of keeping our neighbors' chickens and pigs out of the house," noted Galt, "and a stray dog or so now and then gets into the bread basket."

Mosquitoes were a constant torment, especially during the rainy season, when the poorly drained town became an immense "frog pond." On some evenings the men could not sit still long enough to read, play a game of cards, or write a letter. "I don't mind a half dozen biting at once," explained Noland; "it is only when they come by the thousands." After only a few days in Iquitos, Galt reported that "the exposed parts of our bodies are beginning to look like red hot nutmeg graters." Sleep was possible only with a mosquito bar, and "no thin netting like that used at home will do for the mosquitoes of the Amazon," reported one Yankee visitor. Only "sheeting and calico" stopped them, but the heavy fabric kept "out the air as well as the pests, so that one must choose between being suffocated and being eaten alive." While their quarters did not keep out invaders, the poorly ventilated structures retained heat; the thermometer in Galt's room occasionally registered 102 degrees. The hottest weather corresponded with the rainiest months, making the physician feel like "clothes look after a hard day's parboiling." He was "afraid to . . . walk about for fear that all the flesh [would] fall away from the bone" and imagined himself "an escaped joint of beef from some soup tureen."[22]

All government employees in the jungle outpost were entitled to navy rations—fixed quantities of specific foods that were mandated by bureaucrats in Lima but often unavailable in Iquitos. Therefore the men of the Hydrographic Commission each received forty-nine *centavos* (a half-dollar) per day in lieu of the official ration and fended for themselves. Dietary staples included imported rice and local yucca and plantains, along with the small green limes and red or yellow peppers served with every meal. Fresh or salted fish and excellent pork were usually available. But this fare soon became monotonous, and the alternatives were unattractive. Beef—imported live from the Andean districts or Brazil—was expensive and of poor quality, as was the rare sheep, "thin and warm" with "ragged wool hanging down in shreds" as if the poor beast had "been trying to pull it all off to get cool." The locally grown chicken was a "tasteless brute." Indians supplied the Iquitos market with monkey, iguana, and an abundance of turtles, "most abominable, . . . tasteless and sickening," declared the doctor. Walter Butt, whose stomach Galt described as "a double-plated, boiler-iron machine," sometimes received canned lobster from home. He prepared the delicacy with large quantities of "mustard and red pepper infusion"; when the surgeon ate some "in sheer despair," he experienced "more torment than can be conceived."

The physician doubled as Hydrographic Commission cook for a few weeks in 1871. But he was repelled by "the detestable fact of knowing what we have to eat hours before hand" and soon found a "party of Celestials" who relieved him of the unpleasant duty. Still, the meals catered by the Chinese were "infamously insipid and choking." As money became scarce, the Virginians found more vegetables and less meat or fish in the perennial *sopa seca,* a stewlike concoction. This dish, complained Galt, was laced with bones "just the size to produce a 'cross berth'" in the throat; his companions often looked "rather apoplectic at the table," much to his "professional anxiety."[23]

Life in Iquitos did have its pleasanter moments. The commission's favorite haunt was a combination café and billiard parlor overlooking the river run by Madam Gil, a good-natured 250-pounder from France. The place had lace curtains and arbor-covered tables outside "where an hour" could be "whiled away with great pleasure," drinking wine, watching the moon on the river, and reminiscing about "old times, old cruises, old mess mates." Livelier entertainment could be found at the Builders' Arms, Iquitos's most popular saloon, owned by an English Jew named Myers, where Maurice Mesnier regularly performed on a "half-cracked piano."[24] Iquitos also had a Masonic lodge, to which most of the Peruvian officers and probably Rochelle belonged, and a room suitable for an occasional play, patronized primarily by the English-speaking community. For a while the small elite maintained a literary society, which circulated books among its members. On Saturdays a local printer published a satirical newspaper—a lampoon appropriately entitled *El Mosquito*.[25]

The Virginia gentlemen especially relished the company of Iquitos's few "refined women" and the conversation of any female who could speak English. Even the arrival of the Cockney wife of a British mechanic cheered Dr. Galt. She was "decidedly fine looking" but complained much of the mosquitoes making her "hitch so orrid." In addition to the men of the Hydrographic Commission, Iquitos's "genteel society" included a few of the leading merchant families, especially the Smiths and Johnstons, along with the senior Peruvian officers and their wives. Indeed, the Virginians and their Latin colleagues tried to maintain cordial social intercourse even when their professional relations were stormy. On Sundays this small coterie would assemble in one member's home or on board the *Tambo* for polite conversation and music provided by the guests. The repertoire ranged from classics to popular pieces, including "The Old Rebel," "Tenting Tonight," and the very appropriate "Shoo Fly! (Don't bother me!)."[26]

At 8:00 P.M. on March 28, 1874, Iquitos staged its most ambitious social event, a benefit concert for the Cuban independence movement. Ticket sales raised $625 for the cause, and a thousand dollars' worth of liquor was sold—all on credit. Rochelle supposed "there was $10 in cash amongst the whole audience." Announced with a crudely printed handbill, the gala featured the small municipal band's heroic attempt at no less than three "symphonies for orchestra," along with performances by the town's leading amateur musicians. Dr. Galt provided vignettes of the artists. Señora Carreño, the commandant's wife, was "a native of Rome, Italy; pretty when well rouged, 'fair, fat and forty.'" Señora Leticia Johnston was "a pleasant lady" who sang "with great sweetness"; unfortunately, she brought her "three children who cry like the——." Vocalist Tim Smith was an "extremely handsome man, and a brave, fine fellow." Walter Butt, of course, was "one of the best amateur" violinists that the physician had ever heard, and Maurice Mesnier, "a fine performer on the piano." However, the elegantly dressed J. M. da Silva, the town's Portuguese tailor, was "altogether a dog" on the flute.[27]

The monotony of Iquitos also was relieved by occasional visitors, many of these more eccentric than the residents. Mr. LaMotte—a very English merchant, complete with a bulldog—sojourned there briefly. He had "travelled much abroad," noted Galt, "evidently in the vanguard of a sheriff's investigation." The questionable dealings of John Houxwell, another British trader who resided in the downstream village of Pebas, were definitely established: Peruvian authorities seized a shipment of surplus United States Army cavalry lances he was selling to hostile Indians of the Napo River.[28] In early 1871 a party of French "communists"—refugees from the Paris uprising of the previous year—passed through town en route to an agricultural colony at Yurimaguas founded earlier by Enrique, vicomte Onffroy de Thoron. This émigré French monarchist styled himself "Emir of Lebanon by general acclamation in 1840, former Commander in Chief of the Maronites, and Chief of Staff Major General of the Turco-Maronite Army under the Grand Vizier Izzet-Mehemet-Pacha, Viceroy of Syria and Egypt." The viscount's linguistic studies convinced him that King Solomon had navigated the Amazon River and that the ancient lands of the Old Testament were located in the Department of Loreto. He placed the Garden of Eden somewhere on the Ucayali River,[29] where God certainly had created the mosquitoes and sandflies after the fall of Adam.

A few reputable scientists also called at Iquitos and enjoyed the hospitality of the Hydrographic Commission. The twenty-nine-year-old naturalist Joseph Steere arrived there in late January 1872 on his around-the-world expedition collecting specimens for the University of Michigan museum. Galt proclaimed him a "live Yankee, . . . a great, brawny, good-natured 6-2½ footer." Rochelle provided the visitor with geographic data obtained by the commission; Galt gave him an abstract of his meteorological studies; and "Captain Butt," reported the grateful Steere, "contented himself with running about the town to find me a room, and to procure letters of introduction to aid me on my trip across the mountains."[30]

The men of the commission initially planned to snub Professor James Orton, the prominent natural scientist and travel writer from New York. In the first edition of his popular *Andes and the Amazon*, Orton briefly mentioned passing, in late 1867, a steamer carrying Admiral Tucker, whom he identified as "the rebel" (a "rather gratuitous impudence," thought Galt). Upon his return to Iquitos in August 1873, however, Orton did not wait for formal introductions or invitations but immediately sought out the admiral, even before calling on Commandant General Carreño. This compliment and Orton's good humor quickly assuaged the hostility of the Virginians. Still, the commission diarist could not resist some literary retribution: the scientist was "the most thorough specimen of unmitigated ugliness." Galt was certain that Orton recently had been "chosen professor at that female college Vassar" because of the "impossibility" of his "being too fascinating to the fair Yankee girls there." The third edition of the professor's travelogue would delete the offensive characterization of the admiral[31] and include much information provided by the Hydrographic Commission.

With each passing month and especially as their work neared completion, the expatriate Virginians found fewer satisfying diversions and became increasingly homesick. "Minutes" had become "what years used to be," as Galt contemplated the "daily nothingness of life in Iquitos." The less poetic Noland simply proclaimed the place "dreadfully dull." A day did not pass without the physician thinking of the Shenandoah Valley. "Are the lands [still] as good, the fields as green, the cattle as fat?" Galt asked James Cloyd. He missed his friend's children, and with only Peruvian tykes to talk with, the surgeon feared that he was losing some of his "love language in English." The "life of an exile" had become a "gnawing cancer."[32]

Nevertheless, when Galt's original contract expired in June 1873, he agreed to stay on for an indefinite period. Four months earlier a barefoot robber had taken his cash savings of 92 *soles;* all that remained for his three years' labor was the 159 *soles* due him in back pay. He could not "bear to return home" with so little money and "no particular prospect" for employment. With a strong plea from Tucker, the government agreed to raise his salary from 100 to 160 *soles* per month— slightly more than the going rate for physicians in Iquitos. The other members of the commission, of course, were delighted by Galt's decision, for his departure would have been "a dreadful loss." But with 50 *soles* of his new wage being withheld for his mother, and salaries in Iquitos now two years in arrears, the physician could only express despair. "Again I linger in the lap of the old prostitute called Hope."[33]

For Galt and most of the other commission members, Peru had always been a place of temporary exile where they might rebuild their fortunes. However, Tucker initially hoped to find a new home on the Amazon and to establish his family there. That dream quickly collapsed along with his house at Manassas. One Sunday, two years after the admiral's son Jack had returned to the United States, Tucker took Galt out to his erstwhile plantation for a picnic. The garden was now a "confused wilderness" of fruit trees and jungle growth. The house was rotting away, its "windows and doors invaded by vines." The old sailor took his guest inside and, as he "passed here and there," pointed out "where the table stood, that 'there was Jack's bed'; 'there was my room,' and 'here stood the pantry.'" This "inventory . . . of past hopes," wrote the physician, "seemed sad in the crumbling ruin that had been his home."

Admiral Tucker thought about his family "every night" as he

smoked his pipe and was "very anxious" that his sons "should turn out well." Hard work and study, he counseled Randy, would bring him success in the business world. But he also wanted the teenager to become "a polished gentleman." He urged him to "read up in the poetic literature of the age" and to learn to "dance gracefully." For the latter, the "most agreeable" method was "to get some young ladies to give you lessons." "Cultivate the society of ladies of refinement," he admonished, "and if *possible*, do not know any others." With his own children far away, Tucker referred to young Nelson Noland as his "adopted son."[34]

Service in Peru took a heavy toll, physical and financial, on all the commission's members. Walter Butt paid the highest price for his experience on the Amazon. His salary of only one hundred *soles* per month was the lowest of the team, and he endured life in the jungle longer than any of his colleagues—about six years. The extended periods of inactivity in Iquitos were especially monotonous for Butt, with few official duties to occupy his time. Tucker and Rochelle attended to their administrative chores; Galt treated his patients and conducted meteorological studies; Sparrow and Noland worked on their charts. Butt retreated into the underside of Iquitos society, to the saloons and fandangos, where his fluency in Spanish and skill on the violin gained him easy access. Butt, noted Noland, "makes me his mentor, and gives me as much as I can do sometimes to take care of him." An old acquaintance from the United States Navy who encountered Butt during this period reported that "his habits . . . had become very bad." Other members of the commission—even "Old Tuck"—might occasionally have sought out the charms of Iquitos's "dusky venuses"; such information, of course, was not revealed in their letters home. Walter Butt, however, was apparently the only man in the group to take a mistress— a striking Indian woman named Estefanía.[35]

To escape the boredom of Iquitos, Butt in February 1872 began an ill-fated journey to Pará to meet Tucker, who was expected to arrive soon from the United States with the *Mairo*. The Fiddler made the voyage as captain of the *Cecilia*, with owner Timiteo Smith on board. Under circumstances that remain unknown, the steamer was lost off the Brazilian river port of Obidos.[36] The unlucky skipper eventually reached Pará, where he lived in the house of the Peruvian consul. In July—some six weeks before Tucker reached Brazil—Butt exhausted his funds and returned to Iquitos. Although his services had not been required in Iquitos and Butt received proper authorization for his mission from Rochelle, Commandant General Alzamora refused to approve Butt's pay for the period. The dispute was not resolved until July 1873. In December, Butt discovered that his name had been inadvertently omitted from the national budget for 1874. Comandante Carreño struck him from the payroll again until the error was corrected in May.[37] None of the commission members collected any salary during this period. Walter Butt, however, lived with the added anxiety that he might never be paid for his travails.

For the homesick Virginians life in Iquitos—with its hardships, frustrations, and exasperations—served as a balm in healing old wounds from the Civil War. One of them told Steere that "at such a distance from home, political differences fade out, so that all can see how great and good our country is compared with such an abomination as this." The traveler from Michigan left "with the conviction that it would be hard to find more loyal or warm hearted Americans." During his visit to Lima late in 1871, Tucker made friends with the United States minister, Judge Thomas Settle, a Unionist from North Carolina. "The old Admiral seemed to have somewhat doffed his Confederate antecedents," commented Galt, and showed "a returning harmony quite pleasant and childlike."

Dr. Galt continued to disdain the "braggard, hurrah style of Yankeeism," but he was even more critical of his own region and especially bitter toward its former leaders. "Travelling," he explained, "may possibly make a man too much of a cosmopolitan to be a good patriot, but . . . does make him able to reason more correctly about human affairs." Although he expected to "catch it," Galt revealed his innermost thoughts to his friend Cloyd.

> I believe that the . . . Yankee is a much wiser, much more powerful, much more self-governing man of reason than our volatile, excitable, unstable, and easily destroyed Southerner—and the former is to be the ruling power of our land—and bring about a general education and more advanced type of common sense civilization than we of the South who ruined ourselves in fighting for the worst cause that ever was— slavery. Thank heaven there's no more such craziness as "Secession" to take place. The U. States is now an Empire respected over the whole planet, and will not permit such crazy children as [secessionist leader Robert] Toombs, and such a set of sky rockets to deluge their land in useless slaughter of the good and true again. I'm done with the poetic idea of Southerners forever. . . . What a pack of fools we all were to support such a narrow minded concern as Jeff Davis' government. . . . To see that . . . the most honored of the land were during the fight the most speculating, . . . makes me somewhat harsh toward my section. I don't believe in the races which inhabit hot countries; they never get out of childhood.[38]

An Alabama-Amazon Melodrama

As the leading members of the small North American community in Iquitos, the men of the Hydrographic Commission were gracious hosts to infrequent visitors from the United States and felt an obligation to assist their countrymen who occasionally found themselves in distress. In November 1867, soon after reaching the Amazon, David Porter McCorkle wrote to the United States consul in Pará seeking passage home for John Verdin, a "lunatic" from Illinois whom the commission had encountered at Leticia. "Although not being recognized as a citizen of the United States by that Government," noted the former Confederate, "the cause of humanity," compelled him to write. "John's sufferings and miserable state ought to enlist the sympathies of all of his countrymen."[39] Six years later the commission became involved in a tragic story combining all the elements of a maudlin nineteenth-century melodrama: highly sympathetic, helpless victims, a nasty villain, and a noble hero—Frank Galt.

About 1867 William Henry Dowd, a thirty-one-year-old carpenter from Mobile, Alabama, migrated to Brazil with his wife, Anne Elizabeth, and their two children. Dowd first worked in Pará but later moved up the Amazon to Santarem, where a sizable group of former Confederates had established an agricultural colony. This venture failed, however, and the family returned to Pará, where Mrs. Dowd died. In 1870, while bringing the *Tambo* up the Amazon to Iquitos, Tucker hired Dowd to serve as ship's carpenter. On this voyage Dr. Galt met the Dowd children—seven-year-old Lorena and William Henry, Jr., aged three.[40] The former surgeon of the CSS *Alabama* felt a special kinship with the two young Alabamians.

The elder Dowd practiced his trade in Iquitos where—in Galt's narrative—he soon "fell into dissipated habits, neglected his own and his children's interests." The carpenter placed Lorena and little William in various homes, trusting the "casual kindness of his acquaintances." Dowd's best friend was John Parker, a "plain and simple" British workman, with a good reputation "for generosity and honesty." He cared for the Dowd children on several occasions. The father, meanwhile, "gradually proceeded from bad to worse, got much in debt, especially to a liquor seller, an Italian named Cristoval Marques." Ultimately, Dowd put his children in the saloonkeeper's charge, perhaps—as Galt had heard—as "mortgages for the father's debts."

In mid-1873 Dowd and Parker took some trade goods to Jéberos, an Indian village in the hinterland of the lower Huallaga River, where the carpenter "abandoned himself to the extreme of dissipation from which he died." Although barely literate, Parker touchingly chronicled his friend's final days in a document which, after he translated it aloud into Spanish, was signed by village leaders.

Certiffigate

That   William Dowds was born 1836

 Fell sick in Jeveros Agust 10th 1873. Through drink and taking Cola [i.e., coca], brought on fits had them night and day. Was speachless some days, received a deale of attencion from the Town, lost all appite—on the 5th of September, all he could take was grogg, up to the 15th of September and then he vometed Blood and could not take anything but a few drops of Woater, up to his death, Died Wensday the 16th of September 2 P.M. 1873.

The scool mises Dona Lorenza Vasquez made his Buriell gown, and Don Gavino Harnandez suplied me with men and candalls and grogg; the bells was rung and with the healp of the Clarck, I maniged to put him in the ground desent; 5:30 P.M. on the same day of his death.

His ding word ware John Parker I want you to read me the Bible, I want you to take charge of my two children give them a little education, and then some kind of trade untill they can look after them selves; I owe you about Eighty or ninety Dollars; and some other peoples as well, and they, they likewise owe me You must get my tools They are in different houses the largest part are in Don Retavio Masias House I owe him a few Dollars, but he has not paid me for my weark, in your house there is a small Beadstead and my tool chest with out loocks or loocked, and without tools.

Owe old Matias I think that is all

This is signed by the magastrate of the town and by other witness.

Jose Ma. Llerena

Fgo. Jose Ma. Chavez[41]

On October 16, 1873, after learning of Dowd's death, Rochelle petitioned the United States consul at Pará for passage money to return the Dowd children to Mobile. Galt wrote to his old commander, Admiral Raphael Semmes, who lived in that city, asking him to inquire about the orphans' relatives. In the meantime the physician sought to remove the children from Marques's "low" establishment. John Parker agreed to take the boy, and a "respectable English family" offered to care for the little girl. But the saloonkeeper refused to surrender the children. He claimed that Dowd owed him money and—falsely—that he had boarded the orphans for two years, for which he demanded compensation. The Italian, in fact, employed his young charges "as servants," and they had been "pitiable objects to every one from their ragged and miserable condition." Little William fled from the Italian's abuse, but Marques recaptured him. Galt quickly brought the matter before the subprefect, Lieutenant Colonel La Hoz, who sent the physician to Elías Babilonia, the well-named local judge of the first instance. The latter insisted that he could not intervene in the case without reference to a higher court and expressed his personal opinion that the children should remain with Marques. The surgeon put the issue before the Iquitos city council; they referred it to a committee, where it was ignored.

On October 27 Dr. Galt wrote to Francis Thomas, the United States minister in Lima, who brought the case before the Peruvian government. The minister of war and marine ordered Commandant

General Carreño to obtain the release of the orphans and to turn them over to Galt. The *comandante* expressed his sympathy for the waifs. Marques's establishment, he told the physician, was "little removed from a house of prostitution," where "the orphan girl . . . would soon be ruined." Carreño promised to deliver the children promptly to Galt, who bought them new clothing so that they would be properly dressed when placed in their foster homes. But in the face of Marques's continued intransigence, Carreño failed to carry out his orders from Lima. Galt again appealed to Minister Thomas on behalf of his "homeless prodigees." He feared that the officials in Iquitos might "humbug" him for months. Believing it most politic not to appear "too eager against the local authorities," Galt had Peruvian friends make informal inquiries about the status of the children.[42]

The issue became quite controversial in Iquitos. Child stealing was an old institution in Loreto. A common practice among warring Indian tribes (especially the Conibos of the Ucayali), it was adopted by many Spanish-speaking residents as a convenient solution to the "servant problem." They rationalized the traffic as a beneficial, "civilizing" experience for their victims, generally Indians or lower-class mestizo children. The particular question of the Dowd orphans, noted Galt, "has very much taken the form of favor or disfavor according to race—though the most enlightened and best people of the Spanish [Peruvian] community look on the conduct of the Italian as most scandalous." The English and North Americans were "very much incensed about this deliberate kidnaping."[43]

After he reached Lima in March 1874, Admiral Tucker appealed on behalf of the orphans to Minister Thomas and probably to President Pardo as well. The Dowd children's condition was "most deplorable," he asserted; they would be "ruined" if not "speedily removed from the bad influence and example that now surround them." On July 4, 1874, the minister of war and marine again ordered Carreño to do everything in his power to rescue the Dowds. Fortunately for the orphans, the minister of government issued the same instructions to the new subprefect of the Bajo Amazonas district—Captain Timiteo Smith. He liberated the children by force and took them to Dr. Galt, who brought them home to the United States.[44]

Against the Devil Himself

Following Admiral Tucker's departure for Lima in December 1873, Rochelle and the explorers who remained in Iquitos worked incessantly on their navigation charts. They were "stagnating here in this hole," Noland told his mother, and were anxious to go home. The dispatch of the steamer *Pastaza* to Borja for a cargo of limestone on March 21, 1874, provided an opportunity for Sparrow and Noland to complete the survey of the Río Marañón, which had been thwarted by low water the previous November. Rochelle instructed the engineers to verify data previously obtained for that portion of the river between Iquitos and the mouth of the Morona River. Beyond that point they were to draw the river's course, measure distances, and make soundings. At Borja— the head of steam navigation—they would also determine the elevation. The one-month voyage was "most delightful," wrote Noland. Borja proved to be the "prettiest spot" the engineer had yet visited, "just in front of a narrow mountain-gorge, through which rush the contracted waters of the mighty Amazon," accompanied by a "current of cool air."[45]

By April 30 the commission had finished drafting virtually all of its maps. The navigation charts were drawn at a scale of two miles per inch on thirty-two sheets measuring 30 inches long by 15 inches wide. The charts of the Amazon-Marañón for the 848 miles between the mouth of the Yavarí River and Borja required ten sheets and also showed the navigable portions of the Itaya and Pastaza rivers, 45 and 7 miles, respectively. The plan of the Ucayali River for its entire 885-mile course covered nine sheets and included 24 miles of the Urubamba and 53 miles of the Tambo rivers. Two sheets each were required to chart the navigable portions of the rivers Yavarí (220 miles, to the confluence of the Yacarana and Yavarasino rivers); Nanay (160 miles); Tigre (111 miles); and Huallaga (169 miles, to Rumicayarina). On single sheets the Hydrographic Commission plotted the courses of the Pichis for 85 miles to Puerto Tucker (and also showed 5 miles of the Herrera-yacu and 4 miles of the Trinidad); the Palcazu (37 miles to Puerto Mairo); the Pachitea (191 miles); the Morona (37 miles); and the Potro (64 miles).

These detailed charts were cumulated on two sheets, also 30 by 15 inches, at a scale of fifteen miles to the inch. The map of the Peruvian Amazon and its tributaries included 1,661 miles of that system; the plan of the Ucayali and its affluents covered 1,284 miles. Finally, all of the commission's labors—2,945 miles of surveys—were summarized in a "Plano General" of the hydrographic system of Amazonian Peru, a 5-foot-square map, with a scale of ten miles per inch. As an afterthought, the commission also prepared a map of Iquitos.[46]

Their charts completed, Rochelle and his subordinates anxiously awaited the mail from Lima, where Admiral Tucker had arrived on March 3. The old sailor's final visit to the capital was a welcome contrast to the unpleasantness he had endured in Iquitos. President Pardo honored him with an informal dinner at the Palace of Pizarro, along with his friends Ernesto Malinowski, Antonio Raimondi, and Captain Juan Pardo de Zela. With his prestige still high at the center of power, old acquaintances sought his assistance. Manuel Charon—Tucker's former engineer, who was now a deputy in Congress—solicited the admiral's participation in a venture to establish European colonists on the Amazon River downstream from Iquitos. Although the admiral apparently rejected this project, he likely supported Arturo Wertheman's proposal to reexplore the Tambo River in canoes by way of the Chanchamayo Valley.[47]

Tucker laid out his own plan for completing the final task of the Hydrographic Commission—the publication of its maps. He proposed returning to the United States by way of England, which would enable him to compare both the costs and quality of printing in the two countries. The admiral asked that his colleagues in Iquitos be ordered to meet him in New York with the charts and records of their explorations. Tucker would retain the services of those members he deemed necessary and discharge the others. He asked for direct control over sufficient funds to pay their salaries and expenses in New York and authority to contract with "one of the best engravers" for the plates necessary to publish an atlas of navigation charts and, separately, the general map of the Peruvian Amazon region. "The members of the commission," he appealed, "all feel a great desire that the result of their years of labour should be presented to the government in a style that cannot fail to be acceptable to the country."

The government partially acceded to Tucker's plan. A supreme decree of April 23, 1874, and orders issued to the admiral on May 5 suspended the labors of the Hydrographic Commission in Loreto. Tucker was to proceed directly to New York (the treasury lacked funds for a stop in England) and to obtain estimates for the cost of publishing his maps. The commission members in Iquitos were to receive from the local commissary all of the pay due them plus a bonus of an additional month's salary. They were to be given passage to New York, where they would report to Tucker. He would retain the services of two men and cancel the contracts of the others, "thanking them in the name of the Government." While on duty in New York, the admiral and his two aides would receive their salaries from Peru's guano agents, Hobson-Hurtado and Company.[48]

The admiral left Peru for the final time in mid-May 1874. His journey had been delayed for several weeks because the national treasury lacked sufficient funds to pay his passage to New York. Ultimately, he obtained one thousand paper *soles*, which he exchanged for a paltry forty-five United States gold dollars. Tucker covered part of his travel expenses from his own pocket.[49] Fortunately, the admiral's personal finances were in a much better condition than those of his colleagues in Iquitos. His posting in the United States to construct the *Mairo* in 1872 had enabled him to collected his salary regularly from the guano consignees, while his subordinates in Peru went unpaid. Now, the government located enough silver—2,232.15 *soles* from the customs house at Callao—to cover his back pay through March 1874 and reimbursement for his travel expenses between Iquitos and Lima.[50] Throughout his years in Peru, the admiral's relatively high salary had provided a surplus, which he may have invested with Iquitos merchants; and he served as an unfailing source of interest-free loans to his hard-pressed friends.[51]

On October 25, 1873, Tucker had forwarded to the minister of war and marine a petition from his subordinates asking for their back pay. Anticipating that the commission would finish its tasks in Loreto by the following March, Tucker requested that sufficient funds to cover their salaries and travel expenses—an estimated 17,500 *soles*—be sent to Iquitos with strict instructions that this money not be diverted to any other purpose. Citing the troubled "political as well as financial circumstances of the country," the minister of war apologized for the failure to pay the commission with regularity and assured them that Lima was diligently addressing the problem. He ordered Carreño to settle the accounts of the Virginians with the first money that entered his treasury. The *comandante*, however, protested that these few foreigners should not be paid unless all of the public employees in Iquitos received their salaries. "Justice," he asserted, "consists of equality."[52]

Rochelle and his companions in Iquitos frequently discussed the problem of their arrears. Noland concluded, with undue optimism, that their money was "perfectly safe." Although the country's finances were in a "dreadful condition," the Virginians were members of a commission that was "known abroad." If it was discovered that Peru had hired a team of foreign explorers "and then could not pay them the miserable little sum [of] 20 or 25 thousand soles . . . she would be ruined." There was also a "great rivalry between all these little South American republics," continued the engineer. Although the Peruvians "have no honor, and scruple at nothing," they had "a *tremendous lot of pride*, and a very wholesome dread of the U.S. which will make them pay us." Tucker was less sanguine. The officials in Lima suggested that the debts owed the commission be liquidated by Hobson-Hurtado in New York. But remembering his own financial exasperations during his missions to the United States, the admiral feared that such an arrangement would create a bureaucratic maze in which his friends' wages would be lost. Peru's New York consulate recently had failed to pay the allotments due Galt's mother and machinist Durfey's wife. Therefore, Tucker insisted that the commission be paid before leaving Iquitos.[53]

In mid-July 1874 documents concerning the future of the Hydrographic Commission—the supreme decree of April 23, instructions of the same date to Rochelle and Carreño, and copies of the May 5 order to

Tucker—reached Iquitos. Under a careful inventory, Rochelle and his team were to surrender all of the government property in their possession except for the maps and other data pertaining to their surveys, which they would deliver to Tucker in New York. Carreño was ordered to liquidate the payroll accounts of the Virginians, give them a one-month bonus, and cover their travel expenses to the United States.[54] The *comandante* instructed his commissary to disburse the funds. But, of course, the strongbox was empty. Carreño claimed that he was unable to borrow enough money even to pay the commission's passage to New York. The commissary, meanwhile, balked at providing official accounts of the members' arrears so that they might obtain their own loans.[55]

The correspondence from Lima, read in its entirety, unmistakably conveyed the government's intentions. But a poorly constructed sentence in the instructions to the *comandante* left him an opportunity to vent his longtime hostility toward the commission and, perhaps, to hold them hostage until the government sent a subsidy to Iquitos. The minister of war explained to Carreño that he had enclosed a copy of the *decreto supremo* of April 23, "for your knowledge and to the end that all of the members of the commission be furnished their passage to N. York and that they be paid by the commissary the wages due them, and an extraordinary one prior to their departure, considering from that moment their contracts canceled."[56]

Quite obviously, their contracts were supposed to remain in force until the men departed Iquitos; indeed, the supreme decree ordered Admiral Tucker to discharge them in New York. But Carreño interpreted "that moment" when their contracts were to be canceled as the April 23 date of the dissolution decree. The *comandante* stopped the commission's pay and ration allowance as of June 30. Through an equally perverse interpretation of the budget law, Carreño next determined that only the two engineers had been entitled to the rations they had received since December 16, 1873; the food allowance credited to the others after that date would be deducted from their back pay. Finally, Carreño decided that, notwithstanding the orders from Lima, travel expenses to New York might be provided only to those commission members whose contracts contained this provision. Thus, Mesnier was not entitled to passage; and Butt, whose contract was verbal, almost certainly would be denied transportation too.[57]

The Virginians were unaware of their grave predicament until Rochelle on July 15 submitted the monthly muster and pay rolls to the *comandante* for his inspection. Carreño returned them with neither endorsement nor comment. Rochelle asked for an explanation and enclosed copies of the dispatches he had received from Lima. Addressing Rochelle as the "former Acting President of the Hydrographic Commission," the commander general asserted that he already had copies of these documents, which he had obeyed precisely.[58] Rochelle sent the rejected personnel rolls directly to Lima and on July 31 explained his impasse with Carreño to the minister of war and marine, enclosing copies of the pertinent correspondence. "You will see," he wrote, "that the commander general does not recognize me as acting president of the Hydrographic Commission, and neither myself or the other members . . . as employed in the service of the republic. If this is so," he continued, "I have no right to order these individuals to go to New York and present themselves to the president of the Hydrographic Commission, nor have I the right to order them to carry the plans and data to comply with the supreme decree [of April 23]." In strict compliance with his instructions, however, Rochelle had ordered his subordinates to the United States. They would leave Iquitos as soon as they could obtain passage money, from the commissary or on their own account. He asked that arrangements be made for the guano agents to pay their arrears in New York.

Under the same date, Rochelle forwarded through the minister a long petition to President Pardo, signed by the members of the commission. "We did not come to Peru in the character or spirit of adventurers," they asserted, "but with a desire to comply with our duty." They had done "everything possible to promote the government's objectives," in spite of the "persistent and prolonged opposition" of the local authorities. The men thanked the president for his "invariable friendship" and asked his assistance in resolving their current problems.[59] General Nicolás Freire, the minister of war and marine, was at first incredulous and then outraged at the news from Iquitos. Carreño had placed Tucker's team "in a most unjust situation, without wages, without means of transportation, and without rations." He had damaged "the good name of the republic." The minister ordered Carreño to comply immediately with his orders regarding the commission. If his treasury lacked the funds, the *comandante* was to "find a way," as he had done "in other times." Unfortunately, word of the commission's plight did not reach Lima until mid-September, and another two months would pass before Freire's new directives arrived in Iquitos.[60]

Rochelle was at a loss to understand Carreño's behavior; the commission members had had no recent difficulty with him. On August 16, however, commission secretary Maurice Mesnier compromised their already difficult position. James Rae, the superintendent of the naval factory, with whom Mesnier had been at odds for some time, told Carreño that the secretary had made an insulting comment about the commander's wife. In the presence of the *comandante*, Mesnier challenged Rae's veracity. A fight ensued. Mesnier injured Rae "a good deal, throwing him down several times." In the course of this altercation Carreño "struck Maurice with a brick." Witnesses differed as to whether Mesnier also assaulted the commandant general. "Knowing the revengeful nature" of the men involved, Rochelle feared for the worst. But Mesnier resigned his post the next day and fled from Iquitos, taking with him a rifle belonging to the government.[61]

By this time the commission's affairs were becoming desperate. The merchants with whom they had enjoyed the best credit were absent from town. One had gone to Lima in an effort to collect some of the debt owed him by the government; another was in Moyobamba, waiting to intercept any contingent bound for Iquitos. Timiteo Smith, now the subprefect of Loreto Department, had been summoned to Moyobamba to suppress a revolt of the local gendarmes, who had ousted the prefect. In any event, the commercial success of Smith and his partner Johnston in penurious Iquitos had brought them only a severe shortage of ready cash. The Virginians tried to borrow money for their daily support from other businessmen but could not obtain any, even at discounts of 50 percent. "Surely the devil himself is working against us," Rochelle wrote Tucker, "but it is the part of strong men to defeat the old boy and I believe we can do it in the end."[62]

Thoroughly disgusted by their unpleasant circumstances, the Virginians now rarely left their rooms and only conversed among themselves. "If it were possible for an Anglo-Saxon to have a *remote conception* of the Spanish American character," Noland told his mother, she might understand their delay in leaving Iquitos. But the men of the commission "all intend to be home some of these times and when 5 Americans determine upon a thing . . . all the Half Breeds in all the *Bogus governments* of S[outh] A[merica]" could not stop them.

An opportunity to escape Iquitos suddenly presented itself with the appointment of Colonel José M. Ríos as the new prefect of Loreto. The longtime Peruvian consul in Pará, Ríos had been friendly toward the men of the commission; they now sent him an effusive congratulatory letter. It apparently won them a strategic ally. With Ríos's approval, Rochelle, Sparrow, and Noland persuaded Carreño to give them letters of credit against the prefect's treasury in Moyobamba; they sold these instruments to merchants at discounts of 20 and 25 percent. The 1,330 *soles* obtained in this transaction barely covered their debts in Iquitos and their passage home. Carreño informed the minister of war that he had consented to this unusual arrangement because of his "vehement desire" to comply with the government's wishes; he had done so "with sadness," however, because the three men incurred substantial losses to the "claws of the merchants."[63]

On September 18 Rochelle, Sparrow, and Noland departed Iquitos on the steamer *Morona*. But near Caballococha, a tantalizing half day's journey above Tabatinga where they were to connect with the Brazilian steamer for Pará, the vessel went solidly aground. They were stranded there for about a month. At the end of October, however, the trio reached Pará, where they boarded the steamer *Ontario* for New York.[64]

Butt and Galt remained behind in Iquitos, hoping that funds might reach the local treasury and enable them to avoid the losses incurred by their colleagues. Butt's finances were especially precarious. After two long suspensions from the payroll, his debts were probably heavy and his accounts with the commissary hopelessly tangled, making it extremely difficult to borrow money to fulfill his obligations and to pay his passage home. Before leaving Iquitos, Tucker had instructed Rochelle to collect some of the money due the admiral and to loan Butt two hundred *soles*. Rochelle, however, could not obtain any of Tucker's funds.[65] Butt's personal affairs were also complicated. His mistress had recently given birth to a child. Because she was not looking after the baby, Butt had placed it in the care of an English woman. Deeply troubled during his final months in Iquitos, he seems to have lived in a state of perpetual intoxication which isolated him even from his fellow Virginians. "Poor Butt is very far gone and ought to leave this place at any sacrifice," wrote a friend, "but it is very doubtful whether he will be able to get off."[66]

Although Galt, too, was in failing health and needed a "change in climate as soon as possible," he had stayed behind to care for his unfortunate colleague. Furthermore, the physician hoped for a successful conclusion to his year-long struggle to rescue the Dowd children. At the end of September, Galt obtained custody of the two orphans. Meanwhile, the merchant Paul Mourraille, a friend of the commission, returned from Lima and agreed to "manage Butt's affair." In the end, the Hydrographic Commission's two stragglers also had to borrow money, at a 25 percent discount. Galt, Butt, and the Dowd children departed Iquitos on October 24, 1874.[67]

CHAPTER ELEVEN

High and Dry

ADMIRAL TUCKER reached New York City on June 7, 1874, and
telegraphed the good news to his family. He wanted to leave
immediately for Virginia. But "being on duty," the old sailor deemed "it
a point of honor" to start his "business affairs first." A notice concerning the admiral's mission appeared in the *New York Herald* on June 11
and quickly brought inquiries from several firms interested in bidding
on the map project. Tucker gave them his specifications and hurried
home.[1]

In a Handsome Style

Before the end of the month, W. Spaythe and Company had submitted a
proposal which suited the admiral's taste. The large chart of the Peruvian Amazon region, showing all the rivers explored by the Hydrographic Commission, would be published as a wall map measuring 54 by
60 inches, "of the very best style and finish known to the trade, . . .
bound, varnished, and the rollers first class." Thirty-five other maps
and charts would be published in an atlas with pages measuring 18 by 33
inches. The volume would employ paper weighing 150 pounds to the
500-sheet ream—a stock, noted the publisher, "three times the weight
and thickness" of that theretofore used in folio-sized atlases. The maps
would be engraved on stone plates, with "forest trees" filling the spaces
between the rivers. The front matter and thirty-five pages of Spanish
text accompanying the maps would be set in letterpress. Of the 100
atlases in the first printing, 80 would be bound in half morocco and 20 in
full leather, with "gilt sides and edges." The covers would be lettered in
gold and stamped with Peru's coat of arms.

Spaythe agreed to provide the first 100 wall maps and atlases for
$3,850 and a second printing of the same number for an additional
$1,375, provided that the order for the latter was received within
ninety days after completion of the initial run. One-third of the contract

price was to be paid at the beginning of the project, with the balance due on completion. Tucker urged Minister of War Freire and President Pardo to accept Spaythe's proposal. The admiral had carefully examined the firm's work and the specified materials, and he assured Pardo that the results of the commission's labors would be presented in a "handsome style" and at a cost "so much less" than he had expected.

The publisher had made its bid on the basis of Tucker's specifications and copies of a few charts that the admiral had brought to New York. Anticipating that additions and alterations might have to be made later (as the government, indeed, would order), Tucker asked for a contingency fund of $1,000. He also requested $400 for the rent of an office during the eight months he estimated would be needed to complete his mission along with a $3 per diem for himself and each of his two aides. "The expense of living in New York," wrote the admiral, where "a simple room and board" at the New York Hotel cost him $5 per day, would not permit the commission members to "live here like gentlemen" at their "small rate of pay." Finally, Tucker emphasized that the publication of the maps could not begin until the arrival of his colleagues from Iquitos and urged that they be sent to New York immediately.[2]

In September, Freire acceded to all of the admiral's wishes. Tucker was to order two hundred maps and atlases and to send copies directly from New York to scores of persons and organizations around the world listed by the minister. The admiral would be provided with $6,775, the entire amount he had requested. Instead of a per diem, the commission members would receive a bonus of $90 per month while on duty in the United States. In response to reports that Tucker's colleagues were still delayed in Iquitos, the minister had again sent orders that they be paid and dispatched to New York without further delay.

Rochelle, Sparrow, and Noland arrived in New York on November 20, 1874, followed by Galt and Butt one month later. Because they all had left Iquitos without their back wages, travel allowance, and the one-month separation bonus due them, General Freire had been asked to arrange for the liquidation of their accounts by Hobson-Hurtado Company in New York. But the necessary order had not yet arrived from Lima. Fortunately for Rochelle and Sparrow, Tucker had chosen them to assist him with the publication of the maps; Hobson-Hurtado promptly paid their salary and bonus for the month of December. Noland, Butt, and Galt returned to the United States without employment and with little more than the clothes on their backs. Tucker loaned Noland $100 to cover his travel to Virginia, and he may have assisted the others, too.[3]

After enduring years of discomfort and boredom in the Amazon Basin, the return to "civilization" was exhilarating. Galt had a "jolly time" in New York during Christmas week, relishing the "splendour of the stores" and "staring at the thousand and one pretty things in the windows." "Being elbowed by the crowd," he wrote, was "something so young and fresh to my blasted vision—I felt almost a boy again." Stopping at Philadelphia during his journey southward, he visited his former professors at the University of Pennsylvania and donated a collection of Amazonian rocks to the Academy of Natural Sciences. Some of its learned members questioned the physician with "fatiguing closeness," but Galt "got the better of them" concerning the geography of the Amazon, about which they were "charmingly ignorant." As his train rolled through Virginia toward his Lynchburg home, he noted "quite a progress . . . in the improved size and appearance of the villages"; he even enjoyed watching the "semi barbarous tobacco chewers . . . bedaub themselves with saliva tinted with the nepenthe of American taste." By early January, Galt was "busily employed" with his mother and sister "answering questions and telling traveller's stories." Walter Butt, whom the doctor saw briefly in Portsmouth, was "looking well and cursing Peru."

Rochelle celebrated his homecoming in "full feather," purchasing a "gushing" $55 suit and a "huge gold watch chain" which he was "very fond of twisting in his fingers." Sparrow joined his wife and son at Fort Hamilton, overlooking New York harbor. Its commander, General George W. Getty (probably a relative or family friend), gave him carte blanche. "This is a bully place," he told Noland, with "a fine billiard table . . . at my disposal" and "a splendid pair of horses in the General's stable which I air to a sleigh every day or so."[4]

Tucker, Rochelle, and Sparrow continued to receive their pay with regularity from Hobson-Hurtado. But the money for the map project did not arrive from Lima. Each month the admiral urged Minister Freire to expedite the funds; and each month the minister apologized for the delay, bemoaning the barren state of the treasury. Tucker appealed directly to President Pardo and railroad impresario Henry Meiggs—whose projects would be aided by the commission's maps— but to no avail. Without reason for remaining in New York, the admiral and Rochelle went to their Virginia homes sometime in late 1875, leaving Sparrow behind to receive the fortnightly mail from Lima.[5]

Peru's financial condition, already precarious when Tucker left the country in mid-1874, had become desperate by 1876. The nation's guano resources, mortgaged to service the towering foreign debt, were nearly exhausted. Unable to obtain new loans abroad, Peru suspended its international payments on January 1, 1876. The republic was formally bankrupt. Within the country, huge emissions of paper money fed a dizzying inflationary spiral. Notwithstanding deep cuts in the domestic budget, revenues fell eight million *soles* short of expenditures. Peru was experiencing "a state of poverty without example," wrote Captain

243

Juan Pardo de Zela to his friend Tucker. "We have been under the necessity of performing miracles to live." In his July 1876 memorial to Congress, Minister of War and Marine Freire reported that wages in Iquitos were now five years in arrears. Even the men assigned to Peru's warships in the Pacific had not been paid in nine months, and the sailors were "almost naked." Nevertheless, Freire urged that money be found to publish Tucker's maps. These already had "cost the nation much, . . . and it would be sad if all of this were lost."[6]

Former president Mariano Ignacio Prado was installed for another term in the Palace of Pizarro on August 2, 1876. His treasury minister soon suspended all government payments until the new administration could review the nation's finances and reorder its priorities. On October 31 Hobson-Hurtado refused to pay the wages due Tucker, Rochelle, and Sparrow. The admiral addressed inquiries to Lima in mid-November, and on January 3, 1877, General Pedro Bustamante—the new minister of war and marine, who had occupied the same post when Tucker first entered the Peruvian service—wrote an astonishing reply. The government assumed that the admiral had had sufficient time to complete the publication of his maps. No funds were available for the project, and the commission had not been included in the appropriation bill for the next biennium. "I think the Peruvians are anxious to get rid of us," wrote Rochelle to Tucker. "I suppose our status now is that of a 'Commission for the Publication of the Maps of the Peruvian Amazon and its Tributaries, without any Pay.' . . . Our life with these Peruvians is one eternal squabble and justice is never done us."[7]

Tucker quickly set the record straight. In letters of February 10 and 19 to President Prado and General Bustamante he explained that the maps had not been published because the government had not provided the necessary funds. The admiral placed his resignation and those of Rochelle and Sparrow at the government's option. The president and minister responded on March 13. A decree of that date terminated the Hydrographic Commission. Tucker was instructed to deliver, under inventory, the charts and other property of Peru to the Peruvian minister in Washington, Colonel Manuel Freyre. Lima, in turn, would issue orders to pay all of the money owed to the members of the commission, including wages due Tucker, Rochelle, and Sparrow for the period between October 1, 1876, and April 15, 1877, the date on which their resignations were to become effective. President Prado addressed Tucker as "Esteemed Friend" and explained that "grave economic difficulties" made the dissolution of the commission necessary. But neither the president nor his minister expressed gratitude for their services.[8]

"I do not think we have been well treated," Rochelle told Tucker; "they do not even thank us at parting." He urged the admiral not to surrender the charts until the commission had been paid. But Tucker dutifully complied with these final instructions from Lima. He shipped the iron seal of the Comisión Hidrográfica del Amazonas directly to Colonel Freyre in Washington. The maps had been deposited for safe-keeping at the Peruvian consulate in New York City when Tucker went home to Petersburg in 1876. Now, Rochelle sent Consul Juan Carlos Tracy the key to the map case and an inventory of its contents, along with a receipt for property previously delivered by the commission to Commandant General Carreño in Iquitos. On November 13 Tracy gave the case of maps to Ricardo Alvarez Calderón, Freyre's assistant, who signed a detailed inventory. Alvarez delivered them to Freyre at the Washington legation that same day.[9]

Tucker and Rochelle feared that they would never "receive a cent of pay" from Peru, but they were equally apprehensive about the fate of their maps. The admiral pleaded that the Peruvian government "not delay in having published under the supervision of some competent person the charts and maps," because they would "give credit to the commission and serve the interests of the entire world." Without success Rochelle urged that arrangements be made for their publication by the Royal Geographical Society in London or the Brazilian government. "After all the difficulties, dangers and hardships we encountered during our explorations," he noted, "it is too bad that the . . . important and interesting result of our labors should be hid . . . in the archives of some wretched bureau in Lima" where, Rochelle was certain, the maps would be lost. In the months that followed, frequent news of political unrest in Peru kindled hopes that Manuel Pardo might return to power and provide funds for the map project. Tucker again appealed to Meiggs for help. "Perhaps old Meiggs will be so alive to his own interests," speculated Rochelle on October 7, 1877, "as to have the commission revived with sufficient means to complete its work." But the railroad builder had died the previous week, and Pardo would be assassinated eleven months later. Early in 1878 Rochelle suggested that Tucker ask President Prado to reactivate the Hydrographic Commission; he and the admiral would be its only members, serving "without pay until they could afford it."[10]

Tucker and other members of the Hydrographic Commission had been petitioning the Lima authorities for their back pay since at least October 1873. Each plea brought assurances that these arrears soon would be settled and orders for the commandant general in Iquitos to pay the Virginians from his treasury—which, of course, was empty. Soon after the admiral's colleagues reached New York, Tucker again asked that his friends be paid and forwarded documents from the commissary in Iquitos certifying the amount of back wages due them. In January 1875 the minister of war and marine disingenuously instructed the finance minister to order Hobson-Hurtado to pay the wages due the commission after obtaining the money from the Loreto contingent—a subsidy that had not been paid in years. Hobson-Hurtado did not receive the necessary funds, and the bureaucratic merry-go-round continued. Admiral Tucker protested to Lima on April 14, 1875; Minister Freire in early August directed the minister of finance to order payment through the New York financial agents, again debiting the Loreto budget. The required authorization did not reach Hobson-Hurtado. Tucker addressed a personal letter to President Pardo about the matter, but without success.[11]

In March 1877, when the Hydrographic Commission was terminated, both President Prado and his war minister pledged to pay the amounts due Tucker and his friends. The admiral urged Lima to satisfy this "debt of honor" repeatedly acknowledged by the government. These wages were due for "arduous services" surveying rivers, including some which "had never been explored before by civilized men" and whose banks were "inhabited by hostile savages." But the money was not forthcoming. On two more occasions Tucker wrote personal letters to both the minister of war and the president. These went unanswered, as did a joint petition by Rochelle, Galt, and Noland to President Prado.[12]

The amounts justly due the members of the Hydrographic Commission cannot be determined with certainty. Walter Butt's payroll account remained confused; the Peruvians asserted that he had been paid in full at the time he left Iquitos.[13] But Tucker, who always had been careful about his financial responsibilities, appealed for wages still owed his colleague. Conversely, the admiral declined to submit the claims of his subordinates for shortages in the amounts allowed for their passage home and losses they incurred discounting government certificates to obtain cash in Iquitos. In his last official dispatch Tucker informed the minister of war and marine that Peru owed the commission back pay totaling 11,959.17 *soles* (about $11,500). Of this amount, Tucker was due 1,961.63 *soles;* Rochelle, 2,906; Sparrow, 2,563.26; Noland, 2,742.30; Galt, 1,060; Butt, 512.16; and Maurice Mesnier, who had not returned to the United States with the other explorers, 213.82 *soles.*[14]

While Tucker, Rochelle, and Sparrow continued drawing their current salaries in New York, they confined their appeals for back pay to Peruvian authorities. But those commission members whose services ended upon their return home asked for the assistance of the United States government soon after they encountered delay in collecting their money. In November 1875 Galt and Noland asked Richard Gibbs, the United States minister in Lima, to make informal inquiries. The foreign minister mistakenly told Gibbs that Hobson-Hurtado recently had paid the wages due all the Virginians except Noland, whose money awaited him in New York. Several months passed before the truth was known: the aforesaid payments were to Tucker, Rochelle, and Sparrow for current wages; Hobson-Hurtado had no instructions to pay the others.[15]

Noland vented his rage to his father. He had been "deceived time after time by complimentary letters." Nelson speculated that President Manuel Pardo might be among the scores of world dignitaries who would visit the United States for the centennial celebration in July 1876. "I don't see why Admiral Tucker can't see [Pardo] and if he is quite the man the Admiral thinks him . . . he ought to make a resolution or give some slight bounty (as governments never pay interest) as remuneration for the losses we have sustained." The engineer suggested that the commission hire a lawyer to "interview the Grand Humbug . . . and threaten to publish him in all the papers." He thought it "would be rather wounding to his pride to be shown up in his propper light to the assembled representatives of Europe." For his part, Noland would be satisfied "to interview him with a load of bird shot and call the account squared."[16]

President Pardo did not come to the United States, however, so Noland and Galt followed Tucker's advice to "keep things stirred up all around." They wrote again to Minister Gibbs in Lima, who in July 1876 prodded the foreign minister once more. The next January, after Hobson-Hurtado stopped paying their current wages, Rochelle and Sparrow joined Noland and Galt in a series of petitions to Gibbs. The Peruvian officials, explained Rochelle, "would have forgotten or neglected the whole matter if it had not been brought to their notice in a manner they are unable to ignore." In April 1877 when Tucker surrendered his maps to the Peruvian authorities, both he and Rochelle asked Minister Manuel Freyre for assistance in obtaining their pay. But the envoy asserted that he had nothing to do with finances and suggested that the Virginians retain a lawyer in Lima. "Whenever you touch the money question," Rochelle told Tucker, "you make a Peruvian shrink." In such matters, "all reliability of the Peruvians seems gone, and even the highest and best of them are not to be depended on." Rochelle was determined to press Lima, vowing "they will be d——d glad to get rid of old Smiley."[17]

Gibbs, in the meantime, informed the Virginians that his informal efforts had not produced results, and he could not present their claims officially without authorization from Washington. Sparrow, therefore, hired claims attorney Cazenove G. Lee, who requested the formal intercession of the State Department. On October 31, 1877, Secretary of State William Evarts authorized Gibbs to make an official reclamation against Peru. The secretary explained that the United States government did not "as a rule interfere" in breach-of-contract suits, directing claimants to seek relief in the courts of the country where the agreement was to be fulfilled. But Sparrow's contract was "directly with the Government of Peru," which might not "hold itself amenable to the suits of private individuals in its own tribunals." If so, Sparrow would be "without legal remedy"; therefore his case "may properly be held to form an exception to . . . the general rule."[18] To Sparrow's initial claim the United States later added those of Noland, Rochelle, Galt, Butt, and Mesnier.

For almost three years Gibbs repeatedly prodded the Peruvian foreign minister regarding the Hydrographic Commission claims. On November 8, 1878, President Prado signed a resolution for Hobson-Hurtado to pay 11,447.63 *soles* to the Virginians in monthly installments until Peru's debt to them had been liquidated. For this purpose, the republic's financial agents were to use funds previously allocated for Colonel Manuel Freyre, the minister in Washington, who had died recently. Gibbs informed Evarts of his hard-won success on January 22, 1879, and the secretary passed the good news to the claimants. After more than four years of wrangling, Hobson-Hurtado finally received an order from Lima to pay the commission. But in mid-April 1879 the firm refused to disburse the money.[19] The republic's account was empty, and Lima's finances seemed unlikely to improve: on the third day of that month, Chile had declared war on Peru.

On October 2, 1877, Captain Antonio de la Haza, Peru's director of marine, had written to Tucker on President Prado's behalf. He noted the "estrangement" felt by the president because Tucker, "to whom the Peruvian Government . . . dispensed so many considerations," had made "an official reclamation" to the State Department. Although other members of the commission had appealed to United States officials, the admiral had taken no such action. In July 1878 Gibbs would ask Foreign Minister Manuel Yrigoyen to pay "certain citizens of the United States" formerly employed on the Hydrographic Commission. Probably drawing upon Navy Department records, Yrigoyen promised payment as soon as the government could determine the amounts owed the members of the commission, whom he listed. In a dispatch to Evarts, enclosing Yrigoyen's note, Gibbs commented that "the honorable minister has included the name of J. R. Tucker. This is an error, as I did not mention that name in any of the notes passed."

Throughout the long struggle to obtain the money due the commission, the admiral had directed his appeals only to Peruvian authorities and a few influential friends in Lima; one strongly worded letter to President Prado found its way into the *South Pacific Times*, published in Callao.[20] Holding himself partially responsible for his friends' predicament, Tucker was concerned primarily about their arrears, and he probably felt relieved when the State Department took up their cause. Unlike his colleagues, the admiral was not owed wages for work performed in the jungle but only for the period between October 1, 1876, and April 15, 1877. This was not "hard-earned-money," for he had spent most of that time in Petersburg. Perhaps because of a lingering antagonism toward the federal government or, more likely, a residual loyalty to Peru, the admiral could not bring himself to request the intervention of the United States on his own behalf.

Save, Lord, or We Perish

The men of the Hydrographic Commission anticipated that upon their return home, the back wages due them would amount to a sizable nest egg. They would make up for time lost in the Amazon and get on with their lives. For Noland, Butt, and Galt—discharged from the Peruvian service in December 1874—their arrears would provide a cushion until they could find suitable employment; perhaps they would have sufficient financial security to start families. After learning about the wedding of a well-situated friend, Noland had told his mother, "I don't know any thing I like to see more than . . . a marriage of that kind, and nothing I detest more than a notice of poor people's getting spliced, and the consequent drudgery to both parties, particularly the woman." But neither money nor jobs awaited them. Two years later, Tucker, Rochelle, and Sparrow found themselves in the same unpleasant circumstance. It was a bad time to be unemployed. Virginia's economy had not yet recovered from the Civil War, and the United States as a whole experienced a severe recession between 1873 and 1878. Three years after leaving Peru, Galt related the commission's experiences to his old shipmate John M. Kell. The explorers had returned home "somewhat in broken health" and "badly swindled by the government we served. . . . Of course none of our party have married, respect for the [opposite] sex and want of it for our fitness as heads of families being partially the causes."[21]

Unable to find work in Virginia, Nelson Noland went to Colorado in 1875. The ambitious young man initially was "forced to manual labor in the mines" because he could not find employment as an engineer. But soon Noland was hired to survey a wagon road across the mountains. After surviving the fevers of Amazonian tropics, he now suffered frostbite trudging on snowshoes over waist-deep snow in the high Rocky Mountains. Within a year, he found work opening a mine for the Boston Silver Company at Sts. John in Summit County and doing a variety of tasks for other employers in his few spare hours. Noland also served as a deputy United States mineral surveyor in that district and tried his own luck as a prospector. After seven profitable years in Colorado, he returned to Virginia and briefly worked as a civil engineer with the Richmond, Fredericksburg and Potomac Railroad. In 1883 the thirty-seven-year-old bachelor married Elizabeth Mayo, of Ashland, Virginia; she died a few months after their wedding. Following this tragedy, Noland settled at Edgewood, one of his family's estates in Hanover County. In addition to farming, he developed nearby waterpower resources and invested shrewdly in real estate. He likely became the wealthiest veteran of the Hydrographic Commission. Nelson Berkeley Noland died at his farm on March 2, 1913, at age sixty-seven.[22]

Thomas Sparrow, too, could not find steady work after the dissolution of the Hydrographic Commission and drifted into a series of temporary jobs. One of these took him back to the Amazon Basin. Probably using his family's Ohio political connections (which included incumbent president Rutherford B. Hayes) and obfuscating his own Confederate service, the engineer became a consultant to a United States naval survey of the lower Amazon and Madeira rivers undertaken to facilitate the construction of the ill-fated Madeira-Mamoré Railroad. The expedition, headed by Commander Thomas O. Selfridge, Jr., left Norfolk on the USS *Enterprise* in early May 1878. Despite mechanical breakdowns on the mother ship and its steam launch, the explorers completed their mission in canoes and returned to the United States some five months later. Selfridge's party included several naval officers experienced in hydrographic surveys. But they entrusted Tucker's veteran engineer with most of the expedition's astronomical observations, and he also plotted the courses of the rivers. These tasks "required the most unceasing watchfulness," noted Selfridge, "for a single error would throw out all the remaining work of the day." Sparrow was "deserving of great credit for the painstaking fidelity with which he kept up his work" and his "untiring . . . efforts" to make the survey "both reliable and complete." For a year or so after the return of the *Enterprise*, the navy employed Sparrow as a draftsman in its Washington hydrographic office, where he prepared the expedition's maps. About 1880 he began a thirty-year career as a civil engineer and draftsman for the Southern Railway Company at Knoxville, Tennessee, and Washington, D.C. He retired to Staunton, Virginia. On October 1, 1915, while visiting a son in Jacksonville, Florida, Thomas Wing Sparrow died at age seventy-four.[23]

Sparrow and Noland, the civilian veterans of the Hydrographic Commission, successfully made the transition back to life in the United States. The adjustment was far more difficult for their sailor friends. "Perhaps no biography of a class of men," speculated Galt, "would be more interesting—probably sadly so—than that of the old . . . officers who resigned" from the United States Navy to support the Confederacy. Many of these men "had a fearful pilgrimage" after the Civil War. Tucker and the other former naval officers of the commission were in many ways representative of these "pilgrims." They not only had lost secure jobs in the United States Navy; they also had sacrificed their professions and a treasured way of life. These old salts recoiled at the suggestions of ill-informed civilians that their naval training and experience suited them for careers in the merchant marine.[24] They were seafaring warriors. Moreover, an important and lasting legacy of the Confederate navy had been the dramatic diminution of the United States merchant fleet. The civil sea service, ironically, had few places available for unemployed Rebels. Like Tucker and his team, a small number of former Confederate sailors enlisted in foreign navies. But most of these mariners ultimately found themselves "high and dry."

They took considerable interest in various proposals that would have given them some form of government assistance. Dr. Galt lobbied his congressman on a plan to appoint former naval officers to consular posts and a bill to expand the army by employing Southern officers. The physician hoped to become a regimental surgeon. The older officers closely followed an initiative to provide pensions for Mexican War veterans. Their fondest dream, however, was reinstatement in the United States Navy. Each national election, especially in years with a presidential contest, sparked a glimmer of hope for government favor, especially in the event of a victory by the Democrats. But disappointment invariably followed the inauguration of each new administration.[25] In October 1875 the state of Virginia honored Tucker by appointing him a marshal for the official unveiling of a statue of Stonewall Jackson on the Capitol grounds in Richmond. Representing the Confederate navy, the admiral rode beside General Joseph E. Johnston. The two old comrades-in-arms, noted a witness, "made a pair of which any country might well be proud." But while nurturing the cult of the Lost Cause, the state government failed to render meaningful assistance to the former Confederates. The old sailors felt a special bitterness toward Virginia officials and other leaders of the "New South."[26]

Any federal benefits that might have been made available to former Confederates would have been limited to men who had been pardoned. By the end of 1868 all former Rebels had received amnesty from prosecution for treason, and many individual Southerners had obtained full pardons. But the Fourteenth Amendment to the Constitution, adopted in that year, barred from federal or state employment former officials who had taken an oath to defend the United States Constitution and then participated in the rebellion. This group included all commissioned naval officers who "went South." A more inclusive law of 1873 barred from pensions anyone "who in any manner voluntarily engaged in, or aided or abetted, the late rebellion." A universal pardon bill which would have removed all political disabilities failed passage in 1876. So, proscribed Southerners continued their individual appeals to Congress which, by a two-thirds vote of both houses, could grant clemency. Through this process Walter Butt and Francis Galt were pardoned in 1880; James Rochelle applied for a pardon in 1888 but died before it could be granted.[27] Tucker and David Porter McCorkle did not ask for clemency.

Walter Butt was the only sailor among the former members of the Hydrographic Commission to resume a career at sea. Unable to find proper work in Portsmouth, he went to California in September 1875, where the San Francisco–based Pacific Mail Steamship Company hired him as third officer of the *City of San Francisco*. The firm apparently hoped that this vessel would attract Southern patrons. Its captain was James I. Waddell, the former skipper of the famous Confederate raider *Shenandoah;* William H. Parker, the former superintendent of the Confederate States Naval Academy, served as its executive officer. On the morning of May 16, 1877, the steamer was five days out of Panama, bound for San Francisco. Butt emerged from the galley shortly after breakfast and quickly realized that the vessel was dangerously close to Tartar Shoal, a submarine hazard some seventy-five miles south of Acapulco. He warned Waddell, but the captain imprudently continued on course. At 9:18 rocks hidden some three to five fathoms below the waves tore a gaping hole in the hull. The officers managed to bring the sinking ship to within three miles of the shore before it was lost. In this crisis Butt coolly took charge of the ship's boats and life rafts; although many of these capsized in the rough surf near the beach, all 252 passengers and crewmen survived. At an inquiry to determine responsibility for the accident, Butt tailored his testimony to protect Waddell, who repaid him with ingratitude.[28]

Butt had "detested the merchant service" from the start. And having already survived the loss of one vessel, the steamer *Cecilia*, on the Amazon, he now lost his nerve. "The shock was a great one to me," he wrote. "I thereafter determined never to go to sea again." He worked briefly with a surveying party in California and then became a manager of the large Belle View Ranch, seven miles from Bakersfield. The former sailor enjoyed the hard outdoors work—riding horseback many miles each day—and occasional hunting expeditions into the mountains. Although he had grown reluctant to play the violin in public, "a committee of ladies" could still persuade him "to perform in concert for the benefit of the Episcopal Church." The absence from his family, however, often made him "badly afflicted with the blues . . . and very lonesome indeed." In 1885 Butt decided to go home. He went to San Francisco, arranged for his passage to Portsmouth, and was making a farewell visit to a friend when on April 26 he collapsed and died at age forty-five. Butt may have suffered from intermittent fevers even before his service in Peru, and he was stricken badly by the "Kern County Fever," a local form of ague, soon after he began ranching. As his old classmate Admiral Mahan noted, however, the Fiddler's years in the Amazon probably had taken a heavy toll, too. "Certainly he died before his time."[29]

Dr. Galt, of course, had his profession to fall back on after his return from Peru. But physicians of a century ago enjoyed neither the prestige nor the economic security of today's medical practitioners. The surgeon wanted a salaried position. Moreover, the former naval officer found civilian society disagreeable. The representatives of "Virginia chivalry," he groused, were a "cross between the Gascon and the bankrupt." Galt applied for medical service in the armed forces of Turkey and Egypt and received an offer from the latter. But, as he wrote Noland, "I fear that my Mamma will not let me go out of her sight for some time." He merely mentioned the word "Egypt," and "her eloquent face denounced the suggestion" with a power stronger than words. After Galt's brother died in October 1877, the physician became the sole support of his mother and an unmarried sister; overseas employment became an increasingly elusive dream. Without success he sought appointments as surgeon at the Virginia Military Institute and as quarantine officer at the port of Norfolk.[30]

For a while Galt continued his scientific writing. He revised his "Medical Notes on the Upper Amazon" for the third edition of Orton's *Andes and the Amazon* and established an ultimately frustrating relationship with the Smithsonian Institution. Soon after his return from Peru, Galt sent an abstract of his meteorological journal to Joseph Henry, the superintendent of the institution. Although he claimed no "scientific expertness in such matters," the physician hoped that this record of his meticulous weather observations as well as a lexicon of Amazonian Indian languages that he had compiled might be "worthy of remuneration or publication." Although the Smithsonian could not offer payment, Henry expressed interest in publishing Galt's studies and asked him to submit them for review. The institution's philologist reported favorably on the lexicon—a list of common English words with their equivalents in highland Quechua, the Quechua dialect spoken in Amazonian Peru, and in several other lowland tongues.[31]

The Smithsonian did not publish Galt's meteorological work. Henry entrusted the lexicon to Major John Wesley Powell, the famous explorer and director of the Bureau of Ethnology, who "misplaced" the manuscript. He returned the piece, unpublished, to the irate author eleven years later. However, Galt's ethnographic notes accompanying his linguistic study probably led the Smithsonian to solicit his article on "The Indians of Peru," which appeared in the institution's *Annual*

Report for 1877.[32] Informative, sensible, and exhibiting a degree of scientific restraint uncommon in contemporary works about South American Indians, this short piece was one of the first creditable ethnographies of Amazonian Peru to be published in the United States. For a few years after his return to Virginia, the physician also worked sporadically on a "sketch" of the Hydrographic Commission. The project was "a sort of mental 'blue pill' to get rid of biliousness," and Galt probably did not submit this "sickening record" for publication. Friends urged him to contribute to that era's often polemical outpouring of Civil War literature. But the surgeon, noted a local newspaper, "never indulges in war talk." He seems to have broken this public silence only in a glowing review of his friend John McIntosh Kell's *Recollections* and in a letter to the Baltimore *Sun* challenging a spurious account of the CSS *Alabama*'s career.[33]

In 1876 Galt moved from Lynchburg to Loudoun County in northern Virginia and settled into the "not very agreeable or lucrative role of country doctor." With a practice which included many charity cases, he was "making expenses and nothing more," reported Rochelle. Meanwhile he joined the "can't get away club." Rural physicians, he explained, were "very much hobbled as to social enjoyment outside of their bailiwick." He soon looked old beyond his years, once being mistaken for a neighbor in his seventies, and became "acutely sensible of the flight of time." In spite of continued dissatisfaction with his situation, he lost "pretty much all the ambition and hopes of earlier years." By 1880 Galt still was "very much embarrassed" by Peru's failure to pay him. Nevertheless in June of that year, the forty-seven-year-old physician married Lucy Harrison Randolph, a woman eighteen years his junior. The couple had a son and daughter.[34]

David Porter McCorkle—who had left the Peruvian service in early 1869 and returned to Virginia in broken health—was the most pitiable member of Tucker's team. In the sparse documentation concerning his later years, this once powerfully built officer with an almost swaggering self-confidence seems reduced to a fragile, pathetic relic of the Lost Cause. Although a skilled engineer with considerable experience as an industrial manager during the Civil War, McCorkle could not establish a new career. He remained on a "taut bowline" after resigning from the Hydrographic Commission. Between 1874 and 1879 McCorkle served as a vice-president of the Army of Northern Virginia Association, an organization of Confederate veterans. He "thought a good deal about ironclads" and passed his time corresponding with Confederate navy colleagues. He maintained a roster of 144 surviving officers who had left the "Old Navy" for the Southern service and noted where they would have ranked on the current United States list: "Now from Hollins down to Jno H. Parker, 36 . . . would be Rear Admirals; . . .

9 would be Commodores; . . . 32 . . . Captains; . . . 56 . . . Commanders; . . . 11 . . . Lieuts Commander."

On his roll of lost opportunities, McCorkle would have been a captain, at an annual salary of as much as $4,500. But in 1877 he was a none-too-successful, occasional agent for Eagle Wing propellers and had an "arrangement" doing odd jobs for the Virginia Iron and Steel Company at Buffalo Gap near Staunton. As McCorkle explained to his former shipmate John M. Brooke, he was "leading a very quiet life" in a "bachelor's Hole" provided by that firm. "My mess bill [is] furnished, but I do not receive any pay. . . . It is a hard battle to fight," he wrote, and the fear that he might "have to be buried by charity" haunted him. Four years later he reportedly was employed as an engineer with a railroad in New Orleans. McCorkle died, back at Staunton, in 1882 at about age sixty.[35]

Advancing age and poor health handicapped Tucker and Rochelle as they searched for employment. For at least three years after their return to the United States, both men frequently experienced recurrent fevers. "This confounded Malarial fever of the Amazon gives me a twinge now and then," Tucker told his son. He "could well dispense with the reminder." Rochelle complained that "the Tropics follow us wherever we go." It was "almost a heartless task to fight such an obstinate disease." The "malarial poison" reduced their tolerance for cold weather, especially during their stay in New York. Both men suffered from rheumatism, too. For the two "Amazon birds" even the relatively mild Virginia winters made their "thoughts turn to the ever green tropics."[36]

Even while Tucker and Rochelle continued drawing their salary in New York, the desperate finances of the Lima government made them anxious about the future. Rochelle, to his later regret, rejected a "lucrative offer" from Argentina to join Hunter Davidson there as a hydrographer and torpedo specialist. In November 1876, after their pay stopped, Rochelle asked the admiral, "How would you like to try a year or two with the Turks . . . or the Egyptians? It would never do for us to be poor amidst the loud and nasty chivalry of Tom Jefferson's democracy." Tucker feared that his useful years had passed, but his friend assured him that "men, so long as they retain all their faculties," were never "too old to command fleets and armies." Rochelle proposed that they "up anchor for the golden horn . . . and spend a few years in crossing swords with the Russian bear." Perhaps Galt and Tucker's nephew 'Fonce Jackson might join them. This quartet "would make a jolly party of free lances."[37]

The international tensions monitored by Tucker and Rochelle in the press erupted into the Russo-Turkish War during April 1877. The admiral already had addressed a preliminary inquiry to the Turkish minister in Washington, who forwarded it to his government. The two sailors hoped to become purchasing agents for war matériel or ordnance inspectors. The Turks reportedly had obtained much damaged weaponry in recent months; Rochelle thought that "the employment of honest and competent inspectors would have saved hundreds of thousands of dollars." However, no offer came from Constantinople, and the failure of England and France to support the Turks altered the complexion of the war. It was not to be "free Europe against . . . despotic Russia"; instead, the struggle was assuming "a religious character, Christian against Mohometan." The two Virginians, asserted Rochelle, "could not very well accept active service against the Christians."[38]

They still hoped to find work "in some foreign service." Rochelle could not "bear to remain idle here." It was "a great pity," he told Tucker, that they could not "get some employment in which we could make, in a few years, enough to make us independent of the world. . . . As we grow older we realize how hard a fate it is to be without adequate pecuniary means. In our time and country grey hairs are not honored but ridiculed unless accompanied by wealth. . . . It would kill either you or I to be condemned to remain high and dry amid the sneers and jeers of an ungrateful people."[39] Unless the admiral had resigned himself "to remain in Petersburg and poor," Rochelle urged that he go to Lima and, if necessary, Santiago. "Chile, as well as Peru," he wrote, was obligated to Tucker "for services rendered in time of war." The Peruvian Congress recently approved a plan to introduce one hundred thousand European colonists into the Amazon region, and Rochelle thought his friend well suited to the post of immigration commissioner. Perhaps Lima might appoint the admiral Peruvian consul at Baltimore, or even for the entire eastern seaboard south of the Potomac River. But the two men remained high and dry. They probably saw each other for the last time during the autumn of 1876, when they vacationed at White Sulphur Springs in West Virginia. The two old sailors hiked along the Blue Ridge and enjoyed themselves flirting with numerous widows.[40]

Rochelle fortunately had inherited a modest farm with a "comfortable home" near Courtland in Southampton County, Virginia. "I have taken to short waisted coats and broad brimmed hats," he wrote the admiral, "and if you were to meet me on Sycamore Street you would know me to be a Granger and a man who owned a cow." He supported himself through farming, though not very aggressively. "According to my observation," he told Tucker, "those farmers do best who work two horses only, and let out the rest of their land." Rochelle also served as honorary commander of the Southampton Camp of Confederate Veterans, corresponded with his old friends, and indulged his avocation as a historian. He published brief pieces in the *Army and Navy Journal* and an article in the *Southern Historical Society Papers* before ultimately undertaking his biography of Admiral Tucker. After a one-day illness, James Henry Rochelle died at his home on March 31, 1889. He was sixty-two years old.[41]

Admiral Tucker was sixty-five years old when he began his involuntary retirement in 1877. None of his children had established themselves sufficiently to provide him a home in his old age. But the admiral had enough resources to purchase a two-story house at 22 Hinton Street in Petersburg. He lived there with the recently widowed Thomas Alphonse Jackson, the nephew Tucker had raised, and Jackson's young daughter Saintie (Mary St. George Tucker Jackson).[42] Although Tucker's health improved during his final years, the old mariner rarely left his home. He passed his time serenely—reading, receiving frequent visitors, and satisfying on a modest scale his yen for farming. "He planted trees, and hedges, and vines, and flowers, and had a vegetable garden," noted his former messmate James Barron Hope, who spent a summer's day with the admiral in 1882. But Tucker's garden was obviously that of a sailor, with "a quarter deck walk under a spreading tree." His hair and whiskers, "trimmed *a l'Anglaise*," had turned "snow white," and there was now "a little drawing up of his tall figure." But the admiral still retained "the old flash in his eyes."

After supper on June 12, 1883, the seventy-one-year-old mariner sat under a grape-covered arbor in his garden, chatting with his nephew and some old friends. A few minutes before eight o'clock, the admiral excused himself with a joke about needing a "carriage with outriders" and stood up to go into his house. His heart stopped. "Death was instantaneous," reported his physician somewhat indelicately, "as if a bullet had been fired into his brain."

Tucker had given instructions concerning his funeral, and his family respected his desire for simplicity. The service at St. Paul's Episcopal Church in Petersburg on June 14 consisted of a brief reading from the Gospel of St. Matthew (8:23–27). ". . . And behold, there arose a great storm on the sea, so that the boat was being swamped by the waves. . . ." The mourners then sang Reginald Heber's "Mariner's Hymn," based on that passage.

> When through the torn sail the wild tempest is streaming,
> When o'er the dark wave the red lightning is gleaming,
>   Nor hope lends a ray the poor seaman to cherish,
>   We fly to our Maker—"Save, Lord, or we perish!"

Accompanied by family members, the admiral's remains were taken by railroad to Norfolk that same day. There several old Confederate comrades served as pallbearers, and local militia units formed a guard of honor, escorting the coffin to Cedar Grove Cemetery. The admiral's body was interred beside that of his wife.

In addition to the house on Hinton Street, Tucker's personal estate included home furnishings and garden tools worth $90. He also left a $5,000 bond—the interest from which probably had satisfied his modest needs—$192 in silver, a half-dozen IOUs totaling $994.36, and a claim against the Peruvian government for 1,961.63 *soles*. Friends who had talked with the old mariner during his final days believed that he harbored no bitterness.[43] He had lived a full span of years, incredibly rich in experience and friendship. He seemed not to have regretted any of the major decisions that had shaped his life—even his enlistment in the Peruvian service. Notwithstanding the many frustrations of that association, Peru had given him honors beyond the reach of all but a few naval officers: command of a fleet in wartime and the title of admiral— the initial word engraved on his tombstone, today somewhat askew, at Cedar Grove.

At the time of Tucker's death, the bloody War of the Pacific between Peru and Chile was drawing to a close. The men of the Hydrographic Commission followed the conflict with interest, if only because the outcome might affect the collection of their back wages. For Tucker, McCorkle, and Butt, however, that preeminently naval struggle probably held an eerie fascination. They knew many of the men and ships on both sides. The contest, furthermore, demonstrated the evolution of naval technologies—notably torpedoes, big guns, and heavy armor— that they had helped to pioneer during the Civil War and, later, played a significant role in transferring to the South American belligerents. The War of the Pacific also demonstrated the timelessness of warfare at sea as human drama.

On May 21, 1879, the Peruvian ironclads *Huáscar* and *Independencia* (Tucker's former flagship) attacked the Chilean *Esmeralda* and *Covadonga*, wooden relics of the war with Spain blockading the port of Iquique. The *Huáscar* rammed and sank the *Esmeralda*, sending Captain Arturo Pratt to his death and apotheosis as Chile's foremost naval hero. Pratt had been a young second lieutenant under Tucker's command a dozen years earlier. The tiny *Covadonga* lured the *Independencia* into shallow water, where it grounded and was later salvaged by the Chileans. Peru now had only one seagoing ironclad, the nearly obsolete *Huáscar*. Chile's formidable new armored cruisers *Almirante Cochrane* and *Almirante Blanco Encalada* trapped the turreted frigate off Point Angamos on October 9, 1879. After ninety minutes of frightful carnage, the Chileans triumphed in the world's first major combat between armored vessels on the high seas. The *Huáscar*'s Admiral Miguel Grau—Peru's most revered naval hero, who died early in the engagement—had been the young skipper of the *Unión* who refused to serve under Tucker in 1866. Dr. Santiago Távara, the Hydrographic Commission's first surgeon, also won laurels at Angamos. Although seriously wounded himself, the physician heroically attended his injured shipmates. He became the highest ranking medical officer of the Peruvian Navy. Surgeon Major Távara died at Lima on August 22, 1897, in his fifty-sixth year. [44]

The battle of Angamos opened the sea-lanes to Peru, and Lima fell to the Chilean Army in January 1881. Peru's military reverses already had produced political chaos. President Mariano Ignacio Prado, a hero of the war with Spain a dozen years earlier, had abandoned the country in December 1879, ostensibly to seek arms overseas. The nation rejected his lame rationalization. Nicolás de Piérola seized power and, after the loss of Lima, took the remnants of his army into the Andean highlands to continue the now hopeless struggle. Soon the Peruvian presidency was claimed by three men—including Admiral Lizardo Montero, Tucker's old adversary. In October 1883 Peru and Chile signed the Treaty of Ancón which, when ratified the next year, ended the war. Peru surrendered its southernmost coastal department (mineral-rich Tarapacá) and consented to Chilean occupation of two neighboring departments.

Leoncio Prado, the lad who journeyed to Iquitos with Tucker in 1867, partially atoned for his father's ignoble flight during the war. Sent to Richmond in 1873 to study engineering, perhaps at the admiral's suggestion, he went the next year to Cuba, which was fighting its Ten Years' War for independence. He joined the insurgent army and quickly rose to the rank of colonel. In 1876 Prado and ten companions seized the Spanish steamer *Moctezuma* at Kingston, Jamaica, hoping to use it for transporting Peruvian weapons to Cuba. But Spanish warships trapped the vessel in a Nicaraguan port and soon the Cuban insurgency ended. Leoncio Prado was en route to the Philippines, where he planned to foment another revolution against Spain, when the outbreak of the War of the Pacific brought him home. Appointed a colonel in the Peruvian Army, he fought tenaciously in numerous engagements. But on July 10, 1883, while commanding a guerrilla army in the Andes, he was seriously wounded at the battle of Huamachuco. The Chileans captured the thirty-year-old officer two days later and executed him by firing squad. Leoncio Prado is a major national hero. A large province in the Amazonian portion of his native Huánuco Department bears his name. [45]

The "indispensable" Major Ramón C. Herrera, who accompanied the Hydrographic Commission on its two most important expeditions, also served with distinction in the War of the Pacific. Unlike many men from Loreto who died in that struggle, Herrera returned to Iquitos. He was murdered there by a neighbor on June 3, 1884. The designation "Herrera-yacu" that Admiral Tucker and his colleagues gave a tributary of the Pichis River in his honor no longer appears on Peruvian maps. Timiteo Smith, the young army officer who served as Tucker's secretary and later was subprefect of the Iquitos district, also survived the war. After thirty years of service, he retired as an acting colonel in 1895. Smith died at Lima on June 19, 1900, in his sixtieth year.[46]

Peru Is Not Paying

Peru's early military reverses in the war with Chile and the chaos within the Lima government eliminated any chance that the Hydrographic Commission might collect its debt while the conflict continued. In 1880 Rochelle wrote to General Prado, "the refugee executive," who had fled to New York. The former president admitted the legitimacy of the commission's claim but "saw no present prospect" of payment. Prado explained that he had been the explorers' "friend in Peru" but could not help them now. "I suspect," noted Galt, "his fleeing his country in the face of the enemy had pretty well destroyed his influence there." Another erstwhile friend, Peruvian consul Juan Carlos Tracy in New York, ignored their letters. Galt and Rochelle privately appealed to the State Department, which advised them to delay action on their claims. "Under the circumstances," wrote Galt, "I do not know that we can do anything."[47]

The Chilean occupation of defeated Peru ended in August 1884, bringing some prospect that Lima might be able to pay its debts. Cazenove G. Lee, the attorney who already represented Sparrow and Noland, now added Rochelle and Galt to his list of clients, apparently charging each man a contingency fee of 20 percent of the amount he might collect. Lee presented their case to the State Department, and in April 1885 Secretary of State Thomas F. Bayard instructed the United States minister in Lima to use his "good offices" on behalf of the Virginians. Bayard and Minister Charles W. Buck, who petitioned the Peruvian foreign minister on September 16, 1885, put the most generous interpretation on the forbearance of the commission members. These "considerate claimants," they wrote, had been "patiently waiting" many years for a "fair and just settlement" and had "refrained from pressing the claims" during the war. Buck's note went unanswered as a civil war wracked Peru and toppled the government in December 1885.[48]

The Hydrographic Commission claims dispute lay dormant for the next three years, until Lima unwittingly injected new life into the case. With its guano resources exhausted and its nitrate deposits lost to Chile, Peru increasingly looked to the trans-Andean jungles as a source of wealth. In 1880 that region's wild rubber industry began to grow dramatically. The Booth Company, whose steamers connected Liverpool with the Brazilian river port of Manaus, wanted to extend service to

Iquitos, while W. R. Grace and Company also proposed to put steamers on the rivers of eastern Peru. Henry Meiggs's dream of extending the railroad system into the eastern lowlands received new consideration, and Lima launched a major effort to lure European immigrants into the Amazonian region. All of these projects would benefit from the maps and charts of the Hydrographic Commission. But most important, in April 1888 Peru and Ecuador completed an agreement to submit their Amazonian territorial dispute to arbitration by the king of Spain, and Lima appointed a committee to assemble documents supportive of Peru's case.[49] Tucker's maps would have been of major importance. The Peruvian government, however, could not locate them.

On May 25, 1888, the minister of foreign relations urgently instructed Félix C. Zegarra, his envoy in Washington, to search for the maps. The diplomat scoured the legation archives without success. Then he addressed a letter to Tucker in Petersburg; one of the admiral's relatives forwarded it to James Rochelle. The latter informed Zegarra that Tucker was dead and that Peru owed back wages to the Hydrographic Commission. The envoy attributed his government's "apparent indifference and oblivion" toward the explorers to his nation's "trials" of the previous decade. "In Peru," he told Rochelle, "they have almost forgotten the Hydrographic Commission." Zegarra advised him to "stir up the memory of your companions" among the authorities in Lima and offered his "personal assistance" in bringing the issue before the government. The minister, however, revealed his primary objective in a series of emphatic questions: Who were Tucker's heirs and where did they live? Did Tucker surrender his maps to Minister Freyre, as ordered in 1877? Did Rochelle have a receipt for these? Did the former members of the commission or Tucker's family have any maps or other documents of the commission? Rochelle's assistance in securing the maps for Peru, wrote Zegarra pointedly, would "clear the way" for a "speedy and favorable resolution" of the pay dispute.[50]

A month later Zegarra reported on the results of his inquiries. He believed that Tucker had surrendered the maps; Manuel Freyre probably had sent them to Lima. The admiral's son Randolph, however, had many of the commission's documents. In the event that the maps could not be located, Rochelle volunteered to use these records to prepare a report for the Peruvian government.[51] Zegarra's willingness to assist the claimants waned markedly after he discovered that they did not have the maps. The envoy apparently deemed Rochelle's proffered report not worth the cost of paying the former explorers, who deluged him with letters. Responding to Rochelle, Noland, and Galt, the minister now explained that he had "privately" informed his government about the debt question and could "do nothing else." They should "appoint an attorney at Lima" to represent them.[52]

The commission members exchanged correspondence regarding the proper strategy for pressing their claim anew. They agreed that a Peruvian lawyer would demand the greater portion of the debt for collecting it. The Virginians had not heard from Cazenove Lee in several years and probably believed that he could render no assistance commensurate with the fee he would exact. Nelson Noland suggested that the explorers themselves write a well-documented account of their claim, have their congressmen endorse it, and send the statement to the State Department. The Peruvians "in no case will pay if they think they can well keep from it," he told Rochelle. "I have no faith in their honor or law. But I think we might touch their pride, at least it would be disagreeable to their lofty hidalgo notions, to think that the U.S. government knew that they could not pay a little debt of a few thousand dollars."

Noland's plan, however, probably would have alerted Cazenove Lee to their new initiative. If the effort succeeded, he would demand 20 percent of the proceeds. Therefore, the Virginians again opted to explore informal channels. Galt sent a statement of the commission's claim to prominent Kentucky lawyer A. E. Richards, an acquaintance of the physician. Richards forwarded the document to his close friend Charles Buck, the United States minister in Lima. Buck explained that he had unsuccessfully presented the claim to Peru in 1885 and that the government still was unable to meet even its payroll with regularity. He saw no hope that the commission might be paid in the foreseeable future. An equally pessimistic appraisal came from Juan Carlos Tracy, who had quit his consular post some two years earlier. "Countries like individuals," he wrote, "cannot pay when they have not the wherewithal."[53]

The death of James Rochelle at the end of March 1889 brought into the case a new and persistent advocate—attorney William G. Shands of Courtland, Virginia. The husband of Rochelle's niece Letitia, Shands became administrator of the deceased sailor's estate. In July 1889 the lawyer requested assistance from the State Department, which instructed Minister John Hicks in Lima to place the issue before the Peruvian government once again. The envoy's inquiries at the foreign ministry brought a promise that the claim would be investigated; if it was validated, funds to cancel the debt might be included in the forthcoming budget request to Congress. Hicks had some hope of success, "unless a revolution upsets everything, a contingency not entirely improbable." The foreign minister determined that the claim was legitimate and in October 1890 asked Congress to appropriate money for it. But the legislators went home without considering the matter. Shands continued to press Washington, and Hicks again dunned the Peruvians in 1891. "This is no ordinary claim," he told Foreign Minister Juan F.

Elmore, "but a debt of honor" whose payment was demanded by "justice and equity." Once more Congress ignored the claim.

Before the opening of the 1892 legislative session, Hicks probed the limits of diplomatic rhetoric with an almost impassioned appeal to Elmore. The money, he wrote, was due "worthy men" who had "periled their lives" in the service of Peru. Several of the explorers had since died, "leaving as an inheritance to their families this still unsatisfied claim." The foreign minister again submitted the matter to Congress. But now the ministers of England, France, Germany, Spain, and Italy made a joint petition on behalf of their citizens, and Hicks feared that the European claimants might be favored at the expense of the Hydrographic Commission. The envoy's apprehension proved to be unfounded. As the congressional session neared adjournment, Hicks informed Washington that "the Peruvian Government is not paying any of its creditors."[54]

This latest failure to squeeze blood from the Peruvian turnip discouraged even the tenacious Shands. He let the matter rest for almost three years, until a death in the family, which apparently complicated the affairs of the Rochelle estate, gave new impetus toward a resolution of the Hydrographic Commission claim. In June 1895 Shands again asked the State Department for assistance, and envoy James A. McKenzie placed the matter before Peruvian foreign minister Manuel Candamo the next month.[55] Meanwhile, the attorney wrote to other Hydrographic Commission claimants asking to represent them as well. To Randolph Tucker, the admiral's son, Shands asserted that he already had devoted much time to the case while pressing his "uncle" James's claim. He suggested that there was "but little chance" of collecting the debt and that success would require considerable effort and expense. Therefore, Shands wanted half of the amount collected. Tucker's heirs quickly accepted the lawyer's terms, as did Galt and Noland.[56]

Shands was not entirely candid with his new clients. The State Department long ago had aggregated into a single claim the debts owed to the individual members of the commission. The attorney's representation of the other claimants, therefore, required little additional work on his part. Indeed, he would be grossly negligent in his responsibilities toward the Tucker family. The lawyer's work on behalf of the Rochelle estate—in which Shands had a personal interest—had benefited the other claimants, and they in justice owed him some compensation. But his expenses do not appear to have been great, and his effort consisted primarily of directing periodic inquiries to Washington. Nor were the prospects of success so bleak as to justify a 50 percent commission. In recent years various European powers had sent warships or had threatened to employ force to collect debts and to resolve other disputes with several Latin American nations. The United States, too, demonstrated an increased willingness to employ armed force in the region. As Nelson Noland suggested with characteristic acerbity, "It strikes me that the policy of civilized governments in regard to these little thievery S. American states is undergoing a change, and that this is a propitious time" to press for a settlement. Within Peru itself the nation's two major political parties, heretofore bitter enemies, had united in launching a broadly based revolution which in March 1895 toppled a ten-year military dictatorship. The new civilian regime in Lima seemed more likely to be mindful of the republic's international financial obligations. Furthermore, Shands had recruited influential allies in Washington. Former secretary of state Evarts agreed to make inquiries concerning the claim, and Virginia senator John W. Daniel, the attorney's "warm personal friend," also promised assistance.[57]

On January 16, 1896, Daniel secured a resolution placing before the Senate the voluminous diplomatic correspondence pertaining to the protracted Hydrographic Commission claim. Twenty days later Peruvian foreign minister Ricardo Ortiz de Zevallos informed United States minister McKenzie that the budget to take effect on March 1 would include a fund from which Peru would begin to extinguish several foreign debts. He asked for a meeting with the North American envoy to negotiate a settlement on behalf of the Virginians.[58]

The previous July, McKenzie had calculated that the original debt acknowledged in 1878 by Peru, 11,447 silver *soles*, had grown after seventeen years at 6 percent simple interest to 23,124 *soles*. A more bankerly diplomat might have compounded the interest annually and presented the Peruvians with a bill for nearly 31,000 *soles*. The determination of the amount due the claimants was complicated by the devaluation of Peru's currency. At the time that Peru had incurred most of the debt, the *sol* was almost at par with the dollar; it now had fallen to about half that value. In his meeting with the North American envoy, Foreign Minister Ortiz explained that "the great poverty of Peru" and the straitened finances of the government would not permit payment of the entire debt. He offered 20,000 *soles* in settlement of the claim. At the current rate of exchange, this was about 85 percent of the sum originally owed; but if the principal had been expressed in dollars with accrued interest compounded annually, the offer was only about one-third of the amount now due. Nevertheless, McKenzie deemed Peru's proposition "the best solution of this matter that may be hoped for at an early date." Secretary of State Richard Olney forwarded the Peruvian proposal to Shands, who on March 24, 1896, assented to it.[59]

Shands, however, did not have sufficient authority to approve a settlement on behalf of all his clients (who might have rejected Lima's offer) or to receive in their names the proceeds of any agreement (enabling him to subtract his fee). Therefore, on March 30—six days after he had approved Peru's terms—the lawyer wrote to Randolph Tucker. He casually noted that he had not heard from Tucker recently and wanted to apprise him about the status of his claim. Shands asserted that he had been steadily at work on the case and continued to incur considerable expense. He hoped "some of these days to get Peru [to] pay a part if not all of the claim. I have succeeded in getting the [Peruvian] govmt. [to] take the matter up for consideration." He asked Tucker to have executed two powers of attorney, the forms for which he enclosed with his letter. Eight days later—April Fools' Day—the administrator of Admiral Tucker's estate, his nephew Norman V. Randolph, signed the documents and sent them to the shyster. At about the same time, and probably under similar circumstances, Shands also became the representative of Walter Butt's estate.[60]

As matters stood, Nelson Noland would net—after Shands's commission—$1,165 for his three years' labor in the Amazon jungle. Shands anticipated about $3,600 for his services. But the State Department had an unpleasant surprise for the attorney. On April 13, 1896, Secretary Olney informed Shands that the department had received a letter from "Cazenove G. Lee, Esquire, . . . attorney for Thomas W. Sparrow and others, members of the Hydrographic Commission, accepting the [Peruvian] settlement in that capacity." After a decade of inactivity on the case, Lee now had come forward, wielding old contracts with Sparrow, Noland, Galt, and—worst of all—Rochelle. He soon produced powers of attorney from Sparrow (who had not signed an agreement with Shands) and Galt. The surgeon was not satisfied with the settlement and certainly preferred Lee's 20 percent fee to a 50 percent split with Shands. "I have *never* heard from Lee in my life," wrote the distraught country lawyer. "I do not propose to let a Washington claim agent who . . . may have long years ago, done a little work on the matter . . . come in and get the pay." Shands was especially livid about Lee's claim against Rochelle's share of the settlement. But Lee succeeded in having the State Department withhold the amount due the Rochelle estate, forcing Shands ultimately to reach an agreement with him.[61]

Peru's settlement of the Hydrographic Commission claim provided for the payment of half of the twenty thousand *soles* in 1896 and the remainder during the following year. The first year's remissions came in two drafts of five thousand *soles*. During 1897 Peru remitted the remainder of the money in irregular installments, delivering the final check, for one thousand *soles*, to the United States legation in Lima on December 31. The Hydrographic Commission case, noted John Bassett Moore in his classic *Digest of International Law*, was something of a landmark. For the first time the United States government had interceded in a civil contract dispute between its citizens and a foreign government. It had done so on the grounds of simple justice.[62]

Unfortunately, justice was not entirely served. On September 25, 1896, State Department solicitor Walter E. Faison issued his report on the appropriate distribution of the settlement among the various claimants. He did not have the original documents concerning the debt. Therefore, the solicitor based his findings on Peru's agreement of November 8, 1878, to pay 11,447 *soles* to the commission. Faison was unaware that Peru had arrived at this amount by subtracting Walter Butt's 512-*sol* claim (whose validity Lima had challenged) from the 11,959 *soles* which Admiral Tucker, on April 14, 1877, had asserted was due the commission. Faison meticulously factored each member's original claim into his share of the final settlement and converted the *soles* into United States currency, right down to the penny. However, in the final distribution Walter Butt's estate received $492.60; Tucker's family got nothing. The admiral's share (about $1,660) was distributed among the other claimants.

Tucker had never asked for assistance from United States officials in Lima or Washington, and Shands in his "representation" of the admiral's estate had not even mentioned his name. In determining whom to pay and how much, Faison had poured over the diplomatic correspondence and found Foreign Minister Manuel Yrigoyen's July 22, 1878, note to United States envoy Richard Gibbs, listing by name each member of the Hydrographic Commission, including Tucker. But in forwarding this document to Washington, Gibbs had explained that the inclusion of Tucker had been an error, for the envoy had not mentioned that name in any of his correspondence with the foreign ministry. Faison also found Cazenove G. Lee's letter to the department in October 1877 presenting Sparrow's claim. The attorney stated that Sparrow had entered into a contract with Peru, signed "*by its Agent, Mr. Tucker.*" The solicitor concluded that "Mr. Tucker was evidently acting as an agent for the Peruvian Government. . . . But it does not appear that he was a member of the Hydrographic Commission." Tucker's heirs, therefore, were denied their share of the settlement, and the documents do not indicate that the injustice was corrected.[63]

CHAPTER TWELVE

Tucker's Tin Can

FOREIGN MINISTER Enrique de la Riva-Agüero in July 1897 instructed envoy Víctor Eguiguren in Washington to make a new search for the maps and other works of the Hydrographic Commission of the Amazon. Based upon a few scraps of information and a large amount of supposition, Riva-Agüero produced a plausible but erroneous account of the fate of these materials. During the course of Tucker's service in the Amazon, wrote the minister, the admiral had sent to Lima only "partial reports," containing little more than "travel itineraries and data of secondary importance."

> The final, complete report . . . of the Hydrographic Commission and the maps . . . were not delivered by Mr. Tucker. Neither did the latter comply with his duty to deliver the books and papers of the commission. . . . It appears that the reason Mr. Tucker behaved in this manner was founded in the inopportune termination of his commission and because he was owed some wages. On two different occasions the government of Peru . . . sought to obtain these documents, but Admiral Tucker died without delivering them, excusing himself with the debt Peru owed to him.

Now that Peru had nearly liquidated its debt to the commission, Riva-Agüero believed that Minister Eguiguren, with the assistance of the State Department, could obtain these maps and documents from Tucker's heirs or the survivors of the admiral's team.[1]

Eguiguren sent a paraphrase of the foreign minister's note to the State Department, which forwarded it to the attorneys for the claimants. The bitter Shands ignored the department's request for cooperation. Cazenove Lee, however, contacted Galt.[2] Peru's contention that Tucker had not fulfilled his obligations greatly troubled the physician. He was determined that the "Govt. of Peru shall have nothing to remark" about the admiral's conduct. Galt quickly went to Washington for a conference with Eguiguren. The diplomat indicated that Peru now wished to publish Tucker's maps and studies and "spoke very pleasantly about . . . the commission's duty" to help find them. The publication of these materials, suggested Eguiguren, would not only benefit Peru; it also would add to the admiral's stature as an explorer and enhance the scientific reputation of his entire team. Although the surgeon believed that Tucker had not retained the maps, he offered to make inquiries regarding them.

In his effort to relieve the admiral "from all criticism," Galt wrote to Tucker's heirs, asking them to make a thorough search for the works desired by the Peruvians and any correspondence pertaining to these items. He also contacted Noland and Sparrow who, along with himself, were the only North American survivors of the Hydrographic Commission (Eguiguren reported that Maurice Mesnier was dead). Noland could provide no information. Galt and Sparrow prepared statements of their recollections regarding the maps. The surgeon testified that after arriving in New York from Peru in December 1874, he had gone to Consul Tracy's office to inquire about his pay. Tracy showed him the case containing the maps, which Tucker had left in the consulate for safekeeping. The container was probably the same "tin can," measuring three feet in length and two inches in diameter, that Tucker had ordered from the Iquitos naval factory in December 1873 to protect his precious charts. Neither Tucker nor any of his associates, wrote Galt, had ever indicated that the admiral retained the maps or other property of Peru.

Sparrow, of course, could provide the most detailed information regarding maps; but the passage of twenty years had clouded his memory. The engineer's sworn affidavit recounted Tucker's efforts to publish the maps and the failure of Peru to fund the project. As the commission prepared to disband, in May 1876, Sparrow thought, the engineer had spent several days in Tucker's New York room "revising and arranging the maps, notes and our studies." He "numbered and marked" the maps, "indicating the points of connection; and properly rolled, they were put in a long cylindrical tin case, with a hinged cap and a lock." The "books and notes" of the commission were "wrapped in coarse brown paper, and the package strongly tied" and labeled "Notes on the Studies made by the Hydrographic Commission of the Upper Amazon."[3]

Randolph Tucker's search of his father's papers produced correspondence indicating that the maps had been turned over to Consul Tracy (Minister Manuel Freyre's actual receipt for the charts was among Rochelle's papers) and tracings of four maps. The latter included the first two sections of the ten-sheet navigation chart of the Amazon-Marañón, dated 1874; an undated chart showing the confluence of the Ucayali and Pachitea rivers (probably one segment of the nine-sheet Ucayali navigation series); and a single sheet showing the northernmost portion of the commission's 1873 general map of the "Amazon and Ucayali Rivers in Peru and Their Tributaries." Tucker probably had brought these copies to New York in 1874 as specimens for the engravers.

The "books and notes" that Sparrow recalled wrapping two decades earlier may have been merely the copybook of the Hydrographic Commission. Eguiguren retrieved this important record from the consulate in New York. In his biography of Admiral Tucker—at that time still an unpublished manuscript—Rochelle wrote that he, Sparrow, and Tucker "had the charts and plans, with explanatory notes" ready for the publisher. These "notes" may have been the text to accompany the maps; perhaps they went into the tin case with the charts, as Galt suggested. Tucker and his team probably had not prepared a final report at the time that they left New York in frustration. They likely intended to assemble such a document later from the earlier reports of their various surveys. This account, according to naturalist and travel writer James Orton, was to have included Rochelle's geographic and hydrographic tables, Galt's meteorological and medical studies, and probably a general essay on the economic potential of Amazonian Peru. Copies of these documents along with fragmentary notes in Tucker's hand pertaining to agriculture and colonization were among the admiral's papers and those of Rochelle, the man who would have prepared the report.[4]

After a three-month investigation, Eguiguren informed the foreign minister of his conviction "that Mr. Tucker and his companions kept back nothing." He shipped the commission's copybook to Lima but delayed sending the four map tracings until he could have duplicates made. Because these were all that remained of the commission's cartographic work, the diplomat did not want to hazard their being lost en route to Peru. The two sheets of the Amazon navigation chart and the portion of the general map showing the Amazon-Marañón and the lower portions of its tributaries between 2° and 5° south latitude are housed today in the *mapoteca* of the Peruvian Foreign Ministry; the chart of the Ucayali-Pachitea confluence is missing.[5]

What had happened to the "tin can" with the commission's maps? Minister Manuel Freyre almost certainly sent it to Peru in November 1877. In the margin of that envoy's dispatch enclosing an inventory of the maps is an endorsement by a Foreign Ministry official dated Lima, January 3, 1878: "Transcribe with a copy of the enclosure to Sr. Raymondi, indicating to him that the maps can be found in the Ministry of Marine."[6] As Rochelle predicted more than a century ago, the maps may be lost in some "dusty" Peruvian archive. However, a diligent search did not locate them. Captain Fernando Romero, the distinguished naval historian whose research on the Hydrographic Commission spans more than a half century, also has not found this cartographic trove.[7]

The maps probably were a casualty of the War of the Pacific. "It is a very lamentable truth," wrote Captain Eduardo Raygada in 1896, that the works of the commission "have been lost." He had been unable to find the maps or even the reports of the Hydrographic Commission in Lima's naval archives. Raygada speculated, quite logically, that these materials were the victims of "the disorder and disturbance and even the destruction of documents, . . . in the state offices, during the occupation of this capital by the Chilean Army."[8] In addition to government archives, the Chileans had sacked the national library and sent its books and manuscripts to Santiago. But the Hydrographic Commission maps apparently did not find their way into those Chilean depositories where they should have been placed.[9] Perhaps Tucker's charts, in a tubular tin coffin, rest in a watery grave. Arturo Wertheman reported that seventy-two of his maps were seized from government offices during the occupation; these were lost in the shipwreck of the Chilean steamer *Valdivia* in July 1884.[10]

Fortunately, much of the Hydrographic Commission's work—perhaps the more important portion of their labors—was not lost. The navigation charts did disappear. But the anarchic rivers of the Peruvian Amazon system—constantly cutting new courses, rearranging the shoals beneath their murky surfaces, and choking their channels with debris—soon would have rendered these aids obsolete. Only with frequent revision would the charts have adequately served the navigation of the rivers. In the opening years of the twentieth century, a new generation of Peruvian naval officers, well trained for hydrographic surveys, remapped the rivers originally charted by Tucker and his team.[11]

The Hydrographic Commission, nevertheless, did contribute significantly to the geographic knowledge of Amazonian Peru. Tucker and his associates accomplished their primary mission: they located the navigable point on the eastern river system closest to Lima. Although proponents of competing routes continued to debate the issue for many years, government surveys between 1889 and 1892 confirmed Tucker's belief that the Pichis River was the optimum eastern terminus for an artery between the capital and the jungle. In 1893, regularly scheduled traffic began on the Pichis Trail; it would remain the primary overland route between Lima and the Department of Loreto for almost a half century. From the Amazonian gateway town of Tarma, linked to the capital by road and railroad, horses and mules descended the trail into the Chanchamayo Valley, veered north to the Río Azupizu (the commission's Herrera-yacu), and followed its course to the head of steam navigation on the Pichis. Here, travelers rendezvoused with launches from Iquitos. Originally designated Puerto Pardo by the Hydrographic Commission, this point of embarkation was rechristened Puerto Bermúdez to honor the incumbent president.[12]

During their seven years in the jungle the Hydrographic Commission established the longitudes and latitudes of scores of places; for the more important of these points, they also determined elevations and magnetic variations of the compass. These data—especially after the early erroneous coordinates for the Ucayali River had been corrected— are surprisingly consistent with modern readings obtained by radio waves and other advanced techniques. The commission reported this information to the government and fellow explorers and insured its preservation and dissemination through publication in Great Britain and the United States as well as Peru. Other surveyors and cartographers would employ these data in their work.[13]

And the commission's own cartographic labors were not entirely lost. The charts that disappeared after 1877 were the culmination of a mapping program which began when Tucker and his friends departed from Lima for the Amazon Basin a decade earlier. For each major river explored, the commission prepared a chart, most commonly on a single sheet at a scale of fifteen miles to the inch. They updated these frequently as their own surveys progressed and with the receipt of new information from other explorers. The large general map of the "Amazon and Ucayali Rivers in Peru and Their Tributaries," showing all of the region surveyed, was a compendium of these individual charts, drawn on a scale one-third larger. The large-scale (two-inch-to-the-mile) navigation charts evolved in a similar manner. A five-sheet map of the Yavarí River had been prepared before 1870; preliminary versions of the Amazon and Ucayali navigation series quite likely existed too.

The explorers willingly provided copies of these maps, at least those contained on single sheets, to state agencies and appropriate individuals. Explaining that the government desired "to extend information regarding . . . navigation," Rochelle authorized a tracing of the "small chart" of the Ucayali for use on the steamer *Cecilia*, which was about to begin a trading expedition up that river in May 1872. Tucker gave Captain Carreño a copy of that same map the following February as the *comandante* prepared to institute commercial service on the Ucayali with the government steamer *Napo*. Charts of the Amazon-Marañón may have been used on the national steamers that plied between Tabatinga and Yurimaguas. The Peruvian members of the joint Peru-Brazil boundary commission almost certainly had Tucker's maps of the Yavarí River. The Hydrographic Commission's geographic coordinates and perhaps copies of its maps also reached Henry Meiggs, the railroad builder.[14]

The commission and Arturo Wertheman continued their collaboration after 1870, when that brilliant engineer left Tucker's team to work for the Department of Amazonas. Although this relationship was some-times strained, the explorers shared equipment and, especially, infor-mation. The Hydrographic Commission and the Swiss immigrant jointly provided the technical foundation for the modern cartography of Amazonian Peru. Wertheman had prepared Tucker's early maps; copies of these and later commission charts were likely among the large cartographic collection he lost during the war. The results of the admi-ral's surveys also were provided on a regular basis to his friend Antonio Raimondi.[15]

Foreign Minister Riva-Agüero's assertion in 1897 that Tucker had not sent copies of his maps to the Ministry of War and Marine was patently untrue. After each of its expeditions, the commission sent charts of the rivers surveyed to the Ministry of War and Marine, which further disseminated them. Thus, when Rochelle sent two maps to Lima at the end of 1873, War Minister Freire ordered them "sent to the Junta Central de Ingenieros so that they can produce copies, one for its Geography Section and the other to remit to Sr. Raimondi."[16]

Alejandro Babinski, a Polish-born, Paris-trained engineer and car-tographer, headed the geography section of Peru's Central Board of Engineers. This forgotten hero of Peruvian cartography had been charged with the preparation of a new national map based on a variety of recent sources, especially works by railroad and government sur-veyors. He planned to publish an oversize atlas to replace Mariano Felipe Paz Soldán's 1865 volume. In addition to plates depicting each of Peru's departments, this collection would include maps of the entire course of the Amazon River to the Atlantic Ocean. Of special value for this part of the project was a large-scale, ten-sheet series drawn by Wertheman, showing all of the Marañón-Amazon. A map of the Ucayali River (which the engineer had explored as a member of the Hydro-graphic Commission in 1868) was an integral part of Wertheman's set.[17]

In July 1874 Babinski prepared to publish a smaller-scale map to serve the nation's needs until the atlas might appear. In addition to Wertheman's maps, Babinski had five charts made by the Hydro-graphic Commission on which to base the Amazonian portion of his new national map. Two of Tucker's works—an 1870 version of the Ucayali chart and a "Plan of the Roads from Lima to the Amazon (1871)"[18]— had been superseded by three more recent ones: a "Plano de los Ríos Marañón, Ucayali y Pachitea (1873)," probably an intermediate version of the commission's general map; an undated "Plano del Río Ucayali"; and a "Plano del Río Amazonas," also without a date.

Babinski's assembled maps were of a bewildering variety of pro-jections, sizes, and scales. Some were based on the longitude of Paris; others (like the maps of Wertheman and the Hydrographic Commission) employed the Greenwich prime meridian. But from this cartographic potpourri, Babinski produced the *Mapa del Perú, hecho según los documentos del Archivo de la Junta Central de Ingenieros*. Based on the meridian of Paris, drawn at a scale of 1:4,000,000, and measuring 41 by 72 centimeters (about 26 by 16 inches), it was appended to the 1874 *Memoria* of the Junta Central de Ingenieros.[19] With the exception of Peru's remote southeastern corner and the as yet unscrambled Tambo River system, Babinski's map provided the first essentially accurate cartographic representation of Amazonian Peru. Gone were the guesswork squiggles that had indicated many eastern waterways on earlier maps. The major rivers of the northeast appear much as they do on today's maps.

The Amazonian portion of the *mapa* was a composite of Wertheman's charts and those of the Hydrographic Commission. Employing essentially the same data, there were probably few substantive differences between them. Perhaps Tucker's maps more faithfully depicted the sinuous meanders of the Ucayali. Wertheman's charts likely were superior for the Marañón-Huallaga region, which he had repeatedly explored.[20] The three most recent commission charts, however, were of varying scales; and because of constant revisions, they had minor disagreements with each other. The results of Tucker's surveys, of course, were scheduled to be published in the admiral's own atlas. Therefore, Babinski relied heavily on Wertheman's more coherent series (which also was a key to the compiler's proposed atlas) for delineating the Marañón-Amazon and Ucayali rivers. The Pachitea system, the Río Yavarí, and the courses of the Nanay and Tigre rivers apparently followed Tucker's maps.

The third edition of James Orton's *Andes and the Amazon*, published in 1876, included a map entitled "The Marañon and Its Tributaries, 1875." Orton explained that it was the result of the "generous contributions most courteously furnished" by the Hydrographic Commission. Probably based upon a hasty, partial tracing of the commission's general chart during Orton's one-day visit to Iquitos in August 1873, the map also included data on altitudes and magnetic variations along with information on the depth, width, and currents of rivers that Rochelle had furnished the author at that time. A revised version of this information along with geographic coordinates appeared in tabular form as an appendix to the book.[21]

German cartographer Herman Habenicht published in 1879 a quite attractive though badly flawed map showing the portion of Amazonian Peru west of Iquitos. Although he employed several sources, Habenicht prominently acknowledged his reliance on the surveys made by the Hydrographic Commission between 1868 and 1873.[22] In plotting the Ucayali River, unfortunately, Habenicht combined the faulty coordinates from Tucker's 1868 exploration with the highly detailed maps in "Paul Marcoy's" beautifully illustrated *Travels in South America,* published in 1869. Marcoy was Laurent Saint-Cricq, a French-born Cuzco artist and writer who accompanied the comte de Castelnau's expedition down the Urubamba and Ucayali in 1845. Saint-Cricq's maps had little scientific merit. But he showed the Ucayali with convincingly bold meanders; and because the date of his journey was not mentioned, readers assumed that the maps were based on a recent and careful survey.[23] The most curious result of Habenicht's gullibility was a pronounced eastward bulge at the head of the Ucayali River. This aberration, in fact, is the lower portion of the Urubamba River; the stream labeled "Tambo" is apparently the Sepa River, a tributary of the Urubamba.

Between 1874 and 1879 Antonio Raimondi published his monumental three-volume *Perú,* a treasury of the great naturalist's quarter century of exploration and geographical research. The final volume of this classic summarized the reports of Admiral Tucker's surveys and made available to a large audience the commission's technical data, with the faulty early longitudes for the Ucayali River now corrected by Rochelle. The third volume also included Raimondi's small *Mapa del Perú,* dated 1877.[24] The Amazonian portion of this map, based largely on the work of the Hydrographic Commission and Arturo Wertheman, seems almost a replica of Babinski's 1874 map, which employed the same sources.

Alejandro Babinski never published his proposed atlas. But Raimondi produced a mammoth thirty-seven-sheet *Mapa del Perú,* published between 1883 and 1900. Most modern Peruvian maps descend from this masterpiece. Although based largely upon geographic coordinates obtained by other explorers, the large Raimondi map is notable for its richness of detail and beautiful representations of topography, features derived from the scientist's own exhaustive travels. The map incorporated much information from the surveys of the Hydrographic Commission, including the positions of many places in Amazonian Peru, the courses of the major rivers, and the limits of steam navigation on these waterways. In addition to Tucker's reports, Raimondi (like Babinski) almost certainly employed copies of the admiral's maps at some point in his work.[25] Like a genetic inheritance, modern Peruvian maps exhibit characteristics of their cartographic ancestors—including the "lost" charts of Tucker's Hydrographic Commission.

Raimondi had published or prepared for the engraver only the first eleven of his plates before he died in 1890. The remainder of the project was completed under the supervision of his assistant Manuel Charon.[26] One of the original engineers of the Hydrographic Commission, Charon later served as Loreto's representative in the Chamber of Deputies and in the late 1870s explored the Chanchamayo region for colonization. He died at Lima in 1900. Architect-engineer Manuel Rosas, who succeeded Charon on the Hydrographic Commission, also died at the national capital, in 1880.[27]

Raimondi's large map for the first time showed the rivers of southeastern Peru with some accuracy, and it also depicted the true configuration of the Tambo River system. In November 1876 Arturo Wertheman had untangled the mysteries of the Tambo and its headwaters in a remarkable expedition. From Puerto Wertheman at the foot of the Chanchamayo Valley, he rafted through showers of Campa arrows down the Perené and Tambo rivers into the Ucayali. The explorer believed, optimistically, that shallow-draft steamers from the latter stream could reach an obstruction some eleven miles above the junction of the Perené and Ene rivers.[28]

About 1878 Wertheman ended his service as engineer for the Department of Amazonas. Under the most difficult circumstances he had surveyed several routes from Chachapoyas, the department capital, to navigable points on the Amazon system and had determined the geographic coordinates for scores of towns in that region. In addition, the engineer supervised numerous public works in Chachapoyas, including construction of a high school and the grading of the town's principal streets. He accomplished the latter task employing hidebound local workmen who spurned the picks, shovels, and wheelbarrows he had brought from Lima. Wertheman also made the first scholarly investigations at Cuelap, a major archaeological site a few miles south of Chachapoyas.[29]

Between 1882 and 1884 Wertheman studied new mining and metallurgical technology in Mexico and then introduced these modern methods to Peru as superintendent of the Tarica silver mine in Ancash department. There, in 1899, this wizard startled his neighbors with Peru's first automobile—a French-built, steam-powered car which had been carried, disassembled, by mules into the Andes. A few years later he pioneered the use of motor trucks in the Peruvian mining industry. In 1904 the Swiss immigrant became a consulting engineer in Lima, where he raised the large family resulting from his two marriages to Peruvian women. A founder of Peru's Society of Engineers and the Geographical Society of Lima, Wertheman published articles on a wide variety of subjects in several Peruvian and European scientific journals. The last surviving member of the Hydrographic Commission, Arturo Wertheman died in Lima on March 24, 1921, at the age of seventy-nine. This pioneer in so many fields was highly honored at the time of his death.[30] He is all but forgotten today. Puerto Wertheman no longer appears on the nation's maps, he is not included in any of Peru's collective biographies, and not even in Chachapoyas is there a street named for him.

Francis Land Galt practiced medicine in Upperville, Virginia, until poor health forced his retirement at age seventy-seven. This sailor-scientist, noted a local newspaper, rode horseback around Loudoun County as though he had "never . . . served on board a war vessel." But even as an old man, he always walked "as if he had his uniform on." Galt died at Woodside, his country home, on November 17, 1915, at age eighty-three. He was the second-to-the-last surviving officer of the CSS *Alabama* and the final North American member of the Hydrographic Commission of the Amazon.[31]

Martha ("Mattie") Rochelle Tyler was a middle-aged spinster. Unlike her heralded sister Letitia, she was a plain-looking woman and the brunt of jokes by adolescent boys. She took pride in her independence, however. As a granddaughter of former president John Tyler, she could claim some manner of federal employment, whether the occupant of the White House be Republican or Democrat. In 1899 she left a clerical job in Washington to become postmistress at Courtland, Virginia, her hometown. Mattie moved into the house left by her favorite uncle, James Henry Rochelle. While going through his papers one day, she found a manuscript entitled "Life of Rear Admiral John Randolph Tucker." Describing it as a "labor of love," Rochelle had completed the work eight months before his death in 1889. But Civil War memoirs and biographies, so popular a few years earlier, had become far less attractive to publishers. Mattie offered the manuscript to the Neale Publishing Company of Washington, which specialized in such works. That firm, however, required a subvention of $480, as much money as Mattie earned in a year. Then, almost miraculously, she received a check for just about that amount. It was her share of Peru's settlement with the Rochelle estate. "Old Smiley's" wages, a quarter century overdue, paid for the publication of this tribute to his friend in 1903.[32]

ABBREVIATIONS
NOTES
BIBLIOGRAPHY
INDEX

Abbreviations

AGMREP   Archivo General del Ministerio de Relaciones Exteriores del Perú
AGNP   Archivo General de la Nación (Perú)
AHMP   Archivo Histórico-Militares del Perú
AMNP   Archivo del Museo Naval del Perú
AMRECh   Archivo del Ministerio de Relaciones Exteriores de Chile
ANCh   Archivo Nacional de Chile
CDL   Carlos Larrabure i Correa, comp. and ed., *Colección de leyes, decretos, resoluciones, i otros documentos oficiales referentes al Departamento de Loreto, formado de orden supremo.*
CGEA   Comandancia General de la Escuadra Aliada
CGL   Comandante General del Departamento Fluvial de Loreto
CHA   Comisión Hidrográfica del [en el; del Perú en] Amazonas
CHAlc   Perú, Comisión Hidrográfica del Amazonas, Exploraciones en el Amazonas y sus tributarios, 1870–1874: Libro copiador de la correspondencia de la Comisión Hidrográfica del Amazonas.
DAB   *Dictionary of American Biography.*
DANFS   United States Navy Department, Naval History Division, *Dictionary of American Naval Fighting Ships.*
DeP   *Diccionario enciclopédico del Perú.*
DFL   Departamento Fluvial de Loreto
DhbbCh   *Diccionario histórico, biográfico, y bibliográfico de Chile.*
DML   Departamento de Marina de Loreto
GBFOGC   Great Britain, Foreign Office, General Correspondence
lc   libro copiador (copybook)
MGM   Ministro de Guerra y Marina
MM   Ministerio de Marina
MRE   Ministerio de Relaciones Exteriores
MREP   Ministerio de Relaciones Exteriores (Perú)
NAUS   National Archives (United States)
NHCUS   Naval Historical Center (United States)
ODU   Old Dominion University
ORA   United States War Department, *The War of the Rebellion: A Compilation of the Official Records of the Union and Confederate Armies.*
ORN   United States Navy Department, Office of Naval Records and Library, *Official Records of the Union and Confederate Navies in the War of the Rebellion.*

ABBREVIATIONS

PROUK   Public Record Office (United Kingdom)
RG   Record Group. (Note: microcopy and roll numbers are cited as M143/4 or T52/3.)
USDS   United States Department of State
ZB   Biography (File)

Notes

Preface

1. Tucker to H. Storm, Dec. 6, 1874, Storm Papers.

2. Rochelle, *Tucker*, 18, 80; Rochelle, "Steamship 'Patrick Henry,'" 134 n. 1.

3. Webster, *American Dictionary*, 491.

4. Basadre, *Historia* 4:1464.

5. Hovey to Seward, Aug. 31, Nov. 14, 1866, USDS, Despatches from Peru, T52/21, RG 59, NAUS.

Chapter One: Handsome Jack

1. Rochelle, *Tucker*, is the only substantial biography of the admiral and has been the major source for briefer sketches, of which the more significant are William M. Robinson, Jr., *DAB*, s.v. "Tucker, John Randolph, 1812–1883," and two articles by Núñez, "Almirante Tucker en el Perú" and "Viajeros de tierra adentro." Woodie L. Tucker, Richmond, provided the quip about Bermuda exports.

2. Kerr, *Bermuda and the American Revolution*, 3, 57–58; Wilkinson, *Bermuda in the Old Empire*, 17–18, 23–24.

3. Kerr, *Bermuda and the American Revolution*, 13–14, 17; Terry Tucker, *Bermuda*, 59, 84–85, 94–95; Wilkinson, *The Adventurers of Bermuda*, 87, 100–113; Kennedy, *Isle of Devils*, 105, 125, 264. Extensive genealogical notes are in the Tucker Papers, Pensacola.

4. Wilkinson, *Bermuda from Sail to Steam* 1:23, 204, 2:707; genealogy notes, Tucker Papers, Pensacola; Edwards, "Abstracts of Reports of Aliens," 113; *Alexandria Times and District of Columbia Daily Advertiser*, June 27, 19, 1800. Manuscript insurance records at the Alexandria Library include policies obtained by Captain Tucker in 1810 for two warehouses valued at $4,700. During that same year, the captain employed two slaves as domestics in his household (Veloz, "Butcher, Baker, Candlestick Maker," s.v. "Tucker, John").

5. Genealogy notes, Tucker Papers, Pensacola; Rochelle, *Tucker*, 20; Dalton, *English Army Lists, 1661–1714* 6:376.

6. Genealogy notes, Tucker Papers, Pensacola. As a young man, Douglas Adam Tucker moved to Montrose, Henry County, Mo., where he married Maria Elizabeth Brounough, also a native Virginian, and raised six children on a moderate-sized farm (Population Schedules of the Eighth Census of the U.S., 1860, M653/622, p. 891, RG 29, NAUS).

7. Rochelle, *Tucker*, 20; Morgan, "Education," 89–102; Sharrer, "Commerce and Industry," 16–27; Powell, *History of Old Alexandria*, 224–25, 253–57; *Alexandria Gazette and Daily Advertiser*, Nov. 9, 1819.

8. Rochelle, *Tucker*, 20. Although a citizen of the District of Columbia, Tucker was appointed from Indiana, probably through social ties or a political swap with a senator from that state. See the detailed, six-page synopsis of Tucker's career, based on an extensive search of Navy Department archives, in the John Randolph Tucker folder, ZB File, NHCUS.

9. Benjamin, *Naval Academy*, 105–6, 109; Langley, *Social Reform*, 22; Lewis, *Buchanan*, 18.

10. Rochelle, *Tucker*, 20; Valle, *Rocks and Shoals*, 46, 85–87; Benjamin, *Naval Academy*, 74–76.

11. Benjamin, *Naval Academy*, 74, 104; Biddle to Navy Secretary, Sept. 8, 1830, Navy Captains' Letters, M125/152, RG 45, NAUS.

12. Biddle to Navy Secretary, Sept. 16, 1830, Navy Captains' Letters, M125/152, RG 45, NAUS; Records of the General Courts Martial and Courts of Inquiry of the Navy Department, M273/24, case no. 523, RG 125, NAUS.

13. Benjamin, *Naval Academy*, 103–5; Langley, *Social Reform*, 22–25; Valle, *Rocks and Shoals*, 13. Tucker's relative rank was determined from U.S. Navy, *Register, 1834*, 46–48.

14. Career synopsis, Tucker folder, ZB File, NHCUS; Woodbury to Tucker, Feb. 9, 1833, Navy Letters to Officers, M149/20, p. 260, RG 45, NAUS. Benjamin, *Naval Academy*, 114–16, and F. Williams, *Maury*, 87–88, discuss the examinations.

15. Career synopsis, Tucker folder, ZB File, NHCUS; Tucker to Woodbury, Oct. 10, 1833, Navy Letters from Officers, M148/89, p. 65, RG 45, NAUS; Woodbury to Tucker, Dec. 6, 14, 1833, Navy Letters to Officers, M149/20, pp. 293, 301, ibid.

16. Career synopsis, Tucker folder, ZB File, NHCUS; Logbook of the USS *Erie*, June 24, 1834–Dec. 17, 1835, Records of the Bureau of Naval Personnel, RG 24, NAUS; Muster Roll of the USS *Erie*, June 1834, 2:116, Records of the Office of the Secretary of the Navy, 1776–1913, RG 45, NAUS; "Taylor, Alfred," *National Cyclopaedia of American Biography* 4:220–21; *DAB*, s.vv. "Worden, John L.," and "Wise, Henry Augustus."

17. Rochelle, *Tucker*, 80; *Petersburg Index-Appeal*, June 13, 16, 1883.

18. Wise, *Tales for the Marines*, 16, 56, 355–56.

19. Riddick to Wise, July 5, 1866, Wise Letters, New York; Wise, *Scampavias*, 143, 147.

20. Career synopsis, Tucker folder, ZB File, NHCUS; "Webb Family," 330; *Appleton's Cyclopaedia*, s.v. "Webb, Thomas T."

21. Genealogy notes, Tucker Papers, Pensacola; Population Schedules of the Seventh Census of the U.S., 1850, M432/964, RG 29, NAUS; career synopsis, Tucker folder, ZB File, NHCUS; Strohm, "J. W. Randolph"; J. W. Randolph to Honoria Tucker, Oct. 2, 1842, Randolph Papers.

22. Career synopsis, Tucker folder, ZB File, NHCUS; Logbook of the USS *Warren*, Feb. 13, 1839–Feb. 18, 1841, and Logbook of the USS *Levant*, Sept. 2, 1839–April 21, 1841, RG 24, NAUS; J. W. Randolph to Honoria Tucker Randolph, Apr. 23, 1843, Randolph Papers.

23. Career synopsis, Tucker folder, ZB File, NHCUS; Logbook of the USS *St. Louis*, Feb. 27, 1843–June 12, 1844, RG 24, NAUS; Parker to Navy Secretary, Oct. 31, 1843, June 12, July 13, 1844, Aug. 9, 1845, McKeever to Parker, Oct. 13, 1844, May 17, 1845, East India Squadron, Com. F. A. Parker, Feb. 27, 1843, to Sept. 28, 1845, Squadron Letters, RG 45, NAUS.

24. Career synopsis, Tucker folder, ZB File, NHCUS; *DANFS* 4:657–58; Logbook of the US Bomb Vessel *Stromboli*, RG 24, NAUS; Perry to Mason, May 24, 1847, Home Squadron, Commo. M. C. Perry's Cruise, Mar. 15–July 19, 1847, Squadron Letters, RG 45, NAUS.

25. *Stromboli* Logbook, RG 24, NAUS; Bauer, *Surfboats*, 114–22, 125; Perry to Mason, Aug. 27, 29, 1847, Rice to Perry, Sept. 7, 1847 (enclosed with Perry to Mason, Sept. 11, 1847), Home Squadron, Commodore M. C. Perry's Cruise, July 19, 1847, to December 31, 1847, Squadron Letters, RG 45, NAUS.

26. Career synopsis, Tucker folder, ZB File, NHCUS; Wise, *Tales for the Marines*, 214; Valle, *Rocks and Shoals*, 85; Toker to Lt. Scampavias, Oct. 12, 1856, Wise Papers, Washington, D.C.;

Stromboli Logbook, RG 24, NAUS; Perry to Tucker, Sept. 8, 1847, Tucker to Perry, Sept. 9, 1847, Home Squadron, Commodore M. C. Perry's Cruise, July 19, 1847, to Dec. 31, 1847, Squadron Letters, RG 45, NAUS.

27. *Stromboli* Logbook, RG 24, NAUS.

28. Rochelle, *Tucker*, 20, 80, 21; Delaney, *Kell*, 115; Melville, *White-Jacket*, 24.

29. Roe, *Naval Duties and Discipline*, as quoted in Delaney, *Kell*, 115.

30. Career synopsis, Tucker folder, ZB File, NHCUS; Parker to Navy Secretary, Apr. 6, 1849, Home Squadron, Com. Parker's Cruise, April 5, 1849, to Jan. 23, 1851, Squadron Letters, RG 45, NAUS; Robert D. Minor, undated "Notes" (probably the draft of a letter to a newspaper editor, concerning Tucker's commission in the Peruvian Navy), section 34, Minor Family Papers.

31. Career synopsis, Tucker folder, ZB File, NHCUS; Logbook of the US Frigate *Cumberland*, vols. 10–11, April 28, 1852–July 5, 1855, RG 24, NAUS.

32. Wise, *Scampavias*, 261–63, 32, 148. After the excerpt containing Gringo's assertion of their fidelity appeared in *Putnam's Magazine*, Tucker wrote Wise that "Mrs. Tucker pays you and I the compliment to say she has no doubt we were bad enough, and . . . not as innocent as you make it appear" (Toker to Lt. Scampavias, Oct. 12, 1856, Wise Papers, Washington, D.C.).

33. Wise, *Scampavias*, 150–51, and dedication page; Tucker to Wise, Oct. 23, 1856, Wise Papers, Washington, D.C.

34. Career synopsis, Tucker folder, ZB File, NHCUS; U.S. Navy, *Register, 1856*, 102, 18–25; Genealogy notes, Tucker Papers, Pensacola; Rochelle, *Tucker*, 21; *Petersburg Index-Appeal*, June 16, 1883.

35. U.S. House, *Board of Naval Officers Ordered to Examine the Navy Yards*, 1–11, 42, 45, 74–77, 30–31; U.S. House, *Letter from the Secretary of the Navy, Transmitting Evidence Taken by the Board of Navy Officers Investigating the Navy Yards*, 1–2; career synopsis, Tucker folder, ZB File, NHCUS.

36. Dudley, *Going South;* Scharf, *Confederate Navy*, 32–33; Semmes,

Memoirs, 73; see also F. Williams, *Maury*, 348–64.

37. Scharf, *Confederate Navy*, 38–39; Virginia, *State Convention of 1861* 4:273–85; statistics on resignations calculated from Dudley, *Going South*, 35–55.

38. Rochelle, *Tucker*, 22; Veloz, "Butcher, Baker, Candlestick Maker," s.v. "Tucker, John"; Genealogy notes, Tucker Papers, Pensacola; Scharf, *Confederate Navy*, 32–33; Callahan, *List of Officers of the Navy*, 552.

39. Long, "Gosport Affair," 155–72.

40. U.S. Senate, *Circumstances at Norfolk*, 11–12; Niven, *Welles*, 339–45; Long, "Gosport Affair," 171–72.

41. U.S. Senate, *Circumstances at Norfolk*, 1–15, 37–50; Long, "Gosport Affair," 155–59; Welles, *Diary* 1:42–44.

42. U.S. Senate, *Circumstances at Norfolk*, 37–39, 77–78, 103–4, 110–11; "Narrative of the Destruction of the Norfolk Navy Yard," *ORN*, 1st ser., 1:305.

43. Welles to McCauley, Apr. 16, 1861, *ORN*, 1st ser., 4:277–78.

44. "Narrative of the Destruction of the Norfolk Navy Yard," *ORN*, 1st ser., 4:305; U.S. Senate, *Circumstances at Norfolk*, 26; Welles, *Diary* 1:46.

45. U.S. Senate, *Circumstances at Norfolk*, 77–79, 103–5; Welles, *Diary* 1:44–45.

46. Tucker to Welles, Apr. 18, 1861, Resignations and Dismissals of Officers from the U.S. Navy, 1861, p. 134, RG 45, NAUS. The resignations of the other officers assigned to the yard are in the same volume. Dudley, *Going South*, 4, 34–55.

47. Long, "Gosport Affair," 165–67; Taliaferro to Governor, Apr. 23, 1861, *ORN*, 1st ser., 1:306–9.

48. Rochelle to Scharf, Jan. 3, 1887, James H. Rochelle folder, ZB File, NHCUS.

49. Perry to Barron, Apr. 19, 1861, Samuel Barron Papers; Population Schedules of the Eighth Census of the U.S., 1860, M653/1366, p. 262, RG 29, NAUS.

50. Niven, *Welles*, 343–45; McCauley to Welles, Apr. 25, 1861, *ORN*, 1st ser., 1:288–89.

51. Paulding to Welles, Apr. 23,

1861, *ORN*, 1st ser., 1:288–91; Long, "Gosport Affair," 167–70. For Wise's account, see U.S. Senate, *Circumstances at Norfolk*, 50–55.

52. Long, "Gosport Affair," 169–70; Sinclair to Mallory, Apr. 22, 1861, Taliaferro to Governor, Apr. 23, 1861, *ORN*, 1st ser., 1:306, 308–9; Rochelle, *Tucker*, 22.

53. Dudley, *Going South*, 38, 52, 53; Callahan, *List of Officers*, 552; *DAB*, s.vv. "Greer, James A." and "Wise, Henry Augustus"; "Taylor, Alfred," *National Cyclopaedia of American Biography* 4:221; Frothingham, *Everett*, 418–21; Paullin, "Lincoln and the Navy," 37–38.

Chapter Two: Defending the James

1. Virginia, *Convention of 1861* 4:283, 305–6, 311, 328, 366–67, 559–60; F. Williams, *Maury*, 365–72.

2. Letcher to Tucker, Apr. 22, 1861, Munford to Tucker, Apr. 23, 1861, *ORN*, 1st ser., 5:797; Tucker to Maury, Apr. 23, 1861, Gratz Collection.

3. Virginia, *Advisory Council*, 40; C.S. Navy, *Register to January 1, 1863;* Wells, *Confederate Navy Organization*, 28–29; Scharf, *Confederate Navy*, 33–34.

4. Barron to Tucker, June 3, 1861, Clark to Tucker, July 23, 1861, *ORN*, 1st ser., 5:797, 6:711; Rochelle, *Tucker*, 25–26; Parker, *Recollections*, 208.

5. Still, "Confederate Naval Strategy," 330–43; Anderson, *By Sea and by River*, 3–17; Spencer, *Confederate Navy in Europe*, 1–4.

6. Mallory to Tucker, July 13, 1861, *ORN*, 1st ser., 5:812–13.

7. Forrest to S. S. Lee, July 16, 1861, Welles to Goldsborough, Sept. 24, 1861, ibid., 6:709, 250; Tucker to Barron, July 23, Aug. 7, 22, 1861, Jones to Barron, Aug. 14, 1861, Barney to Barron, Aug. 22, 1861, Barron Papers.

8. Rochelle, *Tucker*, 28–30; Parker, *Recollections*, 209; Jones to Barron, Aug. 14, 1861, Barron Papers; Magruder to Noland, Sept. 5, 1861, *ORN*, 1st ser., 6:723.

9. Hull to Stringham, Sept. 13, 1861, Murray to Stringham, Sept. 20, 1861, Tucker to Mallory, Dec. 2, 1861, Smith to Goldsborough, Dec. 2, 7, 1861, *ORN*, 1st ser., 6:208–10, 457–59; Clayton, *Narrative*, 17.

10. Brooke, *Brooke*, 240–41; R. Minor to Maury, Oct. 11, 1861, *ORN*, 1st ser., 6:304a–304b; Perry, *Infernal Machines*, 8–11.

11. Magruder to Tucker, Jan. 6, 1862, Mallory to Tucker, Dec. 19, 1861, *ORN*, 1st ser., 6:754, 752; "Muster Roll, C.S.S. *Patrick Henry*, July–September, 1861," *ORN*, 2d ser., 1:299.

12. Colston to Tucker, Feb. 23, 1862, Tucker to Colston, Feb. 23, 1862, *ORN*, 1st ser., 6:774–76.

13. Tordich, "Franklin Buchanan"; Still, *Iron Afloat*, 5–25; W. C. Davis, *Duel between Ironclads*, 8–13, 26–41; Mallory to Buchanan, Feb. 24, Mar. 7, 1862, *ORN*, 1st ser., 6:776–77, 780–81.

14. Lewis, *Buchanan*, 180–81; Parker, *Recollections*, 253; Tucker to Buchanan, Mar. 4, 1862, *ORN*, 1st ser., 6:779–80.

15. W. C. Davis, *Duel between Ironclads*, 76–104; Still, *Iron Afloat*, 25–32; Buchanan to Mallory, Mar. 27, 1862, *ORN*, 1st ser., 7:44.

16. Rochelle, *Tucker*, 30–31; Rochelle to Tucker, Jan. 30, 1865, *ORN*, 1st ser., 7:51–52; Clayton, *Narrative*, 23–26.

17. Rochelle, *Tucker*, 31–32; Robert D. Minor, "Notes," sec. 34, Minor Family Papers; Buchanan to Mallory, Mar. 27, 1862, *ORN*, 1st ser., 7:44.

18. Clayton, *Narrative*, 26; Rochelle to Tucker, Jan. 30, 1865, Van Brunt to Welles, Mar. 10, 1862, *ORN*, 1st ser., 7:52, 11.

19. W. C. Davis, *Duel between Ironclads*, 97–103; Still, *Iron Afloat*, 30–32; Pendergrast to Marston, Mar. 9, 1862, *ORN*, 1st ser., 7:23.

20. Rochelle, *Tucker*, 33–35; Rochelle to Tucker Jan. 30, 1865, *ORN*, 1st ser., 7:52–53; Clayton, "Battle of Hampton Roads," 456–57.

21. W. C. Davis, *Duel between Ironclads*, 103–7; Rochelle to Tucker, Jan. 30,

1865, *ORN*, 1st ser., 7:52–53; Clayton, *Narrative*, 28.

22. Buchanan to Mallory, Mar. 7, 1862, *ORN*, 1st ser., 7:46; Parker, *Recollections*, 260–61; Rochelle, *Tucker*, 36–37.

23. "Report of the Commander of the Gassendi" and Rochelle to Tucker, Jan. 30, 1865, *ORN*, 1st ser., 7:72, 53.

24. W. C. Davis, *Duel between Ironclads*, 116–37; Rochelle, *Tucker*, 37–38; Clayton, "Battle of Hampton Roads," 457; Rochelle, "Steamship 'Patrick Henry,'" 135 n. 3.

25. W. C. Davis, *Duel between Ironclads*, 136–37; Still, *Iron Afloat*, 34–36; "Resolution of Thanks to Buchanan" and Buchanan, [general order], Mar. 21, 1862, *ORN*, 1st ser., 7:56, 57. A second congressional resolution, of Apr. 16, 1862, specifically thanked "the officers and crews of the *Patrick Henry, Jamestown, Teaser*, and other vessels engaged" at Hampton Roads.

26. Still, *Iron Afloat*, 34–39; W. C. Davis, *Duel between Ironclads*, 146–51.

27. Tattnall, "General Order," *ORN*, 1st ser., 7:759–60; Clayton, "Battle of Hampton Roads," 457; W. C. Davis, *Duel between Ironclads*, 148–52. A small diagram of the proposed operation, labeled on the back "'Monitor,' April 11, 1862," is among the Tucker Papers, Pensacola.

28. Tattnall to Tucker, Apr. 20, 1862, Tattnall to Mallory, Apr. 21, 1862, Tucker to Mallory, Apr. 21, 1862, Tucker to Johnston, Apr. 25, 1862, Hunt to Tucker, Apr. 27, 1862, Brent to Tucker, Apr. 27, 1862, Johnston to Tucker, Apr. 28, 1862, Tattnall to Mallory, Apr. 29, 1862, *ORN*, 1st ser., 7: 768, 769–70, 771, 774–75, 775–76, 776–77; Clayton, *Narrative*, 36–37; Johnston to Tattnall, Apr. 28, 1862, *ORN*, 2d ser., 1:633.

29. Tucker to Mallory, Apr. 28, 1862, Mallory to Tucker, Apr. 30, 1862, Tucker to commander at Drewry's Bluff, May 2, 1862, Tucker to Mallory, May 2, 1862, C. T. Mason to Tucker, May 4, 1862, *ORN*, 1st ser., 7:776, 778, 781, 784.

30. Barney to Tucker, May 4, 1862, Tucker to Mallory, May 8, 1862, ibid., 7:784, 786–87; J. T. Wood to wife, May 7, 1862, Wood Papers.

31. Tucker to Mallory, May 8, 1862, *ORN*, 1st ser., 7:786–87; Clayton, *Narrative*, 37; Tucker to Farrand, May 8, 1862, C. T. Mason Papers.

32. Rochelle, *Tucker*, 40–41; Robinson, "Drewry's Bluff," 167–75; Still, *Iron Afloat*, 39–40; W. C. Davis, *Duel between Ironclads*, 153–55.

33. Robinson, "Drewry's Bluff," 172–75; Shingleton, *Wood*, 46–51; R. Johnson, *Rodgers*, 194, 202–4; Rochelle, *Tucker*, 43; Farrand to Mallory, May 15, 1862, Rodgers to Goldsborough, May 16, 1862, Jeffers to Rodgers, May 16, 1862, *ORN*, 1st ser., 7:369–70, 357, 362.

34. Mann, "Recollections," 15; Clayton, *Narrative*, 40; Rochelle, *Tucker*, 43; "Joint Resolution of Thanks" and Farrand to Mallory, May 15, 1862, *ORN*, 1st ser., 7:370.

35. Wood, "First Fight," 711; Parker, *Recollections*, 279–80; Mann, "Recollections," 1–2, 13, 16. Mann's views were shared by his commander; see Drewry, "Drewry's Bluff Fight."

36. Rochelle, *Tucker*, 43–44; Robinson, "Drewry's Bluff," 175; Wood to wife, July 5, 1862, Wood Papers; Shingleton, *Wood*, 52–60; F. Forrest to Tucker, Aug. 25, 1862, Tucker folder, ZB File, NHCUS; Wood to Jones, Aug. 30, 1862, *ORN*, 2d ser., 2:256.

Chapter Three: Commodore in Gray

1. *Charleston Daily Courier*, Sept. 16, 1862; Tucker to Pemberton, Sept. 9, 1862, manuscript collection, Gilpin Library.

2. T. Williams, *Beauregard*, 164–66, 172–73, 304–18, and passim.

3. See, for example, Lockhart, "Confederate Squadron," 257, 270–72, 274.

4. Still, *Iron Afloat*, 93–105, 115; *DANSF* 2:508; *Charleston Mercury*, Oct. 9, 1862, quoting the *New York Herald*; *Charleston Daily Courier*, Feb. 2, 1863.

5. Still, *Iron Afloat*, 112–13; Burton, *Siege of Charleston*, 126.

6. Still, *Iron Afloat*, 117–20.

7. Ibid., 121–23; Tucker to Ingraham, Jan. 31, 1863 (with enclosed statement of Bier, Glassell, and Shelby), and "Report of Casualties," *ORN*, 1st ser., 13:619–20, 582–83; *Richmond Daily Dispatch*, Feb. 6, 1863.

8. Still, *Iron Afloat*, 124–25; *Charleston Mercury*, Feb. 2, 10, 1863; McBride, *Ironclads*, 106.

9. *Charleston Daily Courier*, Feb. 10, Mar. 31, 1863; Bier to George, Feb. 10, Jan. 29, 1863, Navy Area File, M625/414, RG 45, NAUS; Reminiscences Books 5–6, Memoranda to Book 5, pp. 2–3, Beauregard Papers; Lockhart, "Confederate Squadron," 268–70; Shingleton, *Wood*, 69–72.

10. Wells, *Confederate Navy Organization*, 29–31; Durkin, *Mallory*, 147–48; C.S. Navy, *Register to January 1, 1864*, 4–5.

11. J. B. Grimball to Mama, Apr. 7, 1863, Grimball Papers; Ingraham to Mallory, Feb. 2, 1863, *ORN*, 1st ser., 13:618; Chew Reminiscences, 20; Bier to George, Mar. 8, 1863, George H. Bier folder, ZB File, NHCUS.

12. Tucker to J. K. Mitchell, Apr. 1, 1863, Mitchell Papers; Wells, *Confederate Navy Organization*, 151; Rochelle, *Tucker*, 48–49; Lockhart, "Confederate Squadron," 269–70.

13. The minutes of the meeting are in *ORN*, 1st ser., 13:808–10.

14. Perry, *Infernal Machines*, 49–51; Tomb, "Last Obstructions," 98–99; T. Williams, *Beauregard*, 167–68, 175; Beauregard, "Defense of Charleston," 421–24; Ripley, [circular], Dec. 26, 1862, *ORA*, 1st ser., 14:734; Parker, *Recollections*, 309.

15. Du Pont to Welles, Apr. 8, 15, 1863, Du Pont, "Order of Battle," Apr. 4, 1863, Rodgers to Du Pont, Apr. 8, 1863, *ORN*, 1st ser., 14:3, 5–8, 8–9, 11–13; *Charleston Mercury*, Apr. 7, 1863; Perry, *Infernal Machines*, 51–52; Burton, *Siege of Charleston*, 136–40.

16. Parker, *Recollections*, 308–10; Perry, *Infernal Machines*, 63–73; Tomb, "Last Obstructions," 98–99; Tomb,

"Submarines and Torpedo Boats," 168–69; Glassell, "Torpedo Service," 113–16; Lee to Jordan, Feb. 27, Mar. 13, 19, 25, 1863, *ORA*, 1st ser., 14:791, 820–21, 837, 843–44.

17. Scharf, *Confederate Navy*, 687–89; Tucker to Webb, Apr. 7, 1863, *ORN*, 1st ser., 13:825–26.

18. Beauregard to Webb, Apr. 11, 1863, Beauregard to Orr and Barnwell, Apr. 12, 1863, *ORA*, 1st ser., 14:895, 898; Parker, *Recollections*, 313–16.

19. Tucker to Mitchell, Apr. 1, 1863, Mitchell Papers; Parker, *Recollections*, 316; Roman, *Beauregard* 2:79; Beauregard to Tucker, Apr. 13, 1863, *ORN*, 1st ser., 14:688–89.

20. Du Pont to wife, Apr. 10, 13–14, 1863, Du Pont, *Letters* 3:18, 22; Drayton to Du Pont, Apr. 20, 1863, Du Pont to Welles, May 1, 1863, Tucker to Dozier, Apr. 21, 1863, *ORN*, 1st ser., 14:154–55, 167, 692; "Port Calendar," *Charleston Daily Courier*, Apr. 13, 20, 1863; A. Beauregard to Tucker, Apr. 21, 1863, P. Beauregard to Tucker, Apr. 23, 1863, *ORA*, 1st ser., 14:904–5, 908.

21. Parker, *Recollections*, 316–21; Tucker to Dozier, May 8, 1863, Ammen to Rodgers, May 12, 1863, *ORN*, 1st ser., 14:694, 188–89; Du Pont to wife, May 12–13, 1863, Du Pont, *Letters* 3:109.

22. Tomb, "Submarines and Torpedo Boats," 168–69; Glassell, "Torpedo Service," 113–16.

23. Beauregard to Pickens, Oct. 8, Nov. 8, 1862, Beauregard to Cooper, Oct. 13, 1862, Beauregard to Mallory, Oct. 31, 1862, Lee to Jordan, Nov. 8, 1862, Beauregard to Miles, May 2, 1863, Beauregard, "Remarks Relative to Gunboats," Nov. 14, 1863, *ORA*, 1st ser., 14:631–32, 672–73, 636–37, 661, 671–72, 923–24, 28 (pt. 2): 503–4; Mallory to Miles, Dec. 19, 1863, *ORN*, 1st ser., 15:699–701.

24. Beauregard to Cooper, Apr. 22, 1863, *ORA*, 1st ser., 14:906–7.

25. Fremantle, *Diary*, 151, 152, 158.

26. Webber, *Monitors*, 10; Webb to Mallory, June 10, 1863, *ORN*, 1st ser., 14:710–11; Still, *Iron Afloat*, 129–38.

27. Allison, "John A. Dahlgren: Innovator in Uniform"; M. Dahlgren, *J. A.*

Dahlgren; MacCartney, *Lincoln's Admirals,* 144–71; career synopsis, J. A. Dahlgren folder, ZB File, NHCUS; V. Jones, *Civil War at Sea* 3:6–7; *New York World,* as quoted in the *Charleston Daily Courier,* July 10, 1863.

28. Burton, *Siege of Charleston,* 151–82; V. Jones, *Civil War at Sea* 3:3–38.

29. Beauregard to Tucker, July 12, 27, 1863, *ORN,* 1st ser., 14:725, 736; Reminiscences, Book 11, Memorandum to Book 11, p. 10, Beauregard Papers; Roman, *Beauregard* 2:98.

30. Scharf, *Confederate Navy,* 696–97; A. T. Smythe to Aunt Janey, Aug. 8, 25, Sept. 2, 1863, Smythe to Mother, Aug. 30, Sept. 2, 1863, pp. 95, 102–3, 111, 105, 109, Smythe Papers; Jordan to Ripley, Aug. 4, 1863, Beauregard to Tucker, Aug. 24, 1863, *ORA,* 1st ser., 28 (pt. 2): 258, 305; Ripley to Jordan, Aug. 21, Sept. 22, 1863, *ORN,* 1st ser., 14:737–45, 750–63.

31. Tucker to Mallory, July 18, 19, 1863, Mallory to Davis, July 24, 1863, *ORA,* 4th ser., 2:664, 662–63; Beauregard to Cooper, Aug. 25, 1863, *ORA,* 1st ser., 28 (pt. 2): 305; Beauregard to Tucker, July 12, 18, 1863, Ripley to Jordan, July 23, 1863, Beauregard, [conference notes], July 28, 1863, *ORN,* 1st ser., 14:725, 728, 734–35; Tomb, "Submarines and Torpedo Boats," 168–69.

32. Lee to Jordan, July 11, 1863, Lee to A. Beauregard, July 25, 1863, Wagner to Beauregard, Aug. 13, 1863, *ORA,* 1st ser., 28 (pt. 2): 191, 229–30, 280; "Information from Deserters," Jan. 7, 8, 1864, Beauregard to Carlin, Aug. 20, 1863, Carlin to Beauregard, Aug. 22, 1863, *ORN,* 1st ser., 15:231, 14:498–500.

33. Jordan [memorandum], Sept. 7, 1863, Beauregard, "Special Orders No. 176," Sept. 6, 1863; Ripley to Jordan, Sept. 22, 1863, *ORA,* 1st ser., 28 (pt. 1): 102, 104–5, 401–2; Scharf, *Confederate Navy,* 698–99.

34. Beauregard to Cooper, Sept. 18, 1863, *ORA,* 1st ser., 28 (pt. 1): 91; Dahlgren to Lincoln, Jan. 23, 1864, *ORN,* 1st ser., 15:252; Anderson, *By Sea and by River,* 227; T. Williams, *Beauregard,* 191; Tucker to Mitchell, Jan. 14, 1864, Mitchell Papers.

35. The official reports are in *ORN,* 1st ser., 14:606–40. See also Smythe to Mother, Sept. 9, 1863, p. 119, Smythe Papers; Scharf, *Confederate Navy,* 699–700; Clayton, *Narrative,* 76–77; Burton, *Siege of Charleston,* 194–97; MacCartney, *Lincoln's Admirals,* 158–61.

36. Official documents concerning the *David* and its attack on the *New Ironsides, ORN,* 1st ser., 15:10–21; Tomb Memoirs, 34–38, 41 (unless the manuscript is indicated, page references are to the typescript copy of the Tomb Memoirs); Tomb, "Submarines and Torpedo Boats"; Tomb, "Confederate Torpedo Boats"; Tomb, "First Steam Torpedo Boat"; Glassell, "Torpedo Service"; Sass, *"Little David"*; Smythe to Joe, Oct. 4, 1863, Smythe to Mother, Oct. 6, 1863, pp. 138, 145, Smythe Papers.

37. Dahlgren to Fox, Oct. 7, 1863, *ORN,* 1st ser., 15:13–15.

38. Dahlgren to Rowan, Oct. 18, 1863, Feb. 19, 1864, Dahlgren to commanders of ironclads, Jan. 12, 1864, Dahlgren to Welles, Jan. 13, 1864, "Order of Dahlgren," Feb. 19, 1864, "Information from Deserters," Jan. 7–8, 1864, "Order Enjoining Precautions," Jan. 7, 1864, ibid., 15:50, 338, 227–33, 237, 238–39, 330–31, 226–27.

39. Useful though conflicting accounts of the *Diver (Hunley)* include Perry, *Infernal Machines,* 90–108; Burton, *Siege of Charleston,* 227–41; V. Jones, *Civil War at Sea* 3:114–30; *DANFS* 2:531–32.

40. Lewis, *Buchanan,* 212; Burton, *Siege of Charleston,* 229–32; Tomb, "Submarines and Torpedo Boats," 169.

41. The official reports of the *Hunley* attack are in *ORN,* 1st ser., 15:327–38.

42. Dahlgren to Welles, Feb. 19, 1864, "Order of Dahlgren," Feb. 19, 1864, Dahlgren to Rowan, Feb. 19, 1864, ibid., 15:329–30, 330–31, 338; Burton, *Siege of Charleston,* 223–26.

43. Tomb Memoirs, 41–44; Tomb, "Submarines and Torpedo Boats," 168; "Torpedo attack upon the Memphis" and DeCamp to Rowan, Apr. 9, 1864, *ORN,* 1st ser., 15:356–59, 405; Beauregard to Whiting, Mar. 31, 1864, Book file, Reminiscences, Charleston, Book E, Beauregard Papers.

44. Scharf, *Confederate Navy*, 701–4; Rochelle to Scharf, Jan. 3, 1887, Rochelle folder, ZB File, NHCUS; Tucker to Rochelle, June 15, 1864, Tucker, General Order, June 29, 1864, Rochelle Papers; Gray to Echols, Apr. 2, 1864, Stringfellow to Tucker, June 20, 1864, Tucker to Dozier, Aug. 26, 1864, *ORN*, 1st ser., 16:423, 15:744, 766; Gilchrist to Ripley, Oct. 19, 1864, Jones to Tucker, May 18, 1864, *ORA*, 1st ser., 35 (pt. 2): 640, 489; Jones to Cooper, Aug. 22, 1864, ibid. (pt. 1), 126.

45. Beauregard to Tucker, Jan. 13, 1864, *ORA*, 1st ser., 35 (pt. 1): 523; Schimmelfennig to Dahlgren, July 22, 1864, and "Examination of Harris," Sept. 7, 1864, *ORN*, 1st ser., 15:577–78, 677–78.

46. Dahlgren to Welles, May 14 (with enclosures), Sept. 5, 25, 1864, *ORN*, 1st ser., 15:430–33, 661–62, 688–89.

47. V. Jones, *Eight Hours*, 32, 91, 114, 116; genealogy notes, Tucker Papers, Pensacola; unidentified newspaper announcement of Harriet's death, Ayers Collection; Price, "Four from Bristol," 253; Tomb Memoirs, 39–40; *Charleston Mercury*, Apr. 14, 15, 1864.

48. Parker, *Recollections*, 288–89; Rochelle, *Tucker*, 50–51; Still, *Iron Afloat*, 101–4, 114, 219; Wells, *Confederate Navy Organization*, 32, 107–17.

49. Wells, *Confederate Navy Organization*, 33–34; Still, *Iron Afloat*, 114; Ingraham to Mallory, July 20, 1863, *ORA*, 4th ser., 2:664; Beauregard, "Special Order No. 92," Apr. 2, 1864, Navy Area File, M625/414, RG 45, NAUS; La Bree, *Campfires*, 266–67.

50. Tomb Memoirs, 31; Parker, *Recollections*, 288–89; Smythe to Aunt Janey, Aug. 25, 1863, p. 102, Smythe Papers; Lockhart, "Confederate Squadron," 262; La Bree, *Campfires*, 267; Rochelle, *Tucker*, 50–51; Chew Reminiscences, 20; Sevier Questionnaire, item 46.

51. Tomb Memoirs, manuscript, p. 102, and typescript, pp. 63–65, 31.

52. Still, *Iron Afloat*, 214–18; Davis to Beauregard, Dec. 13, 1864, in Davis, *Letters* 6:415; Dahlgren to Scott, Dec. 13, 1864, Dahlgren to Welles, Dec. 29, 1864, *ORN*, 1st ser., 16:130, 151.

53. Smythe to Miss Lou, Jan. 22, 1865, p. 378, Smythe Papers; Dahlgren to Schimmelfennig, Dec. 20, 1864, "Memorandum of Instructions," Dec. 31, 1864, Dahlgren to Welles, Jan. 15, 1865, *ORN*, 1st ser., 16:152–54, 174.

54. Dahlgren to Welles, Jan. 16, Mar. 1, 1865, *ORN*, 1st ser., 16:171–75, 282–83.

55. Bulloch to Page, Feb. 14, 1865, and "Extract from Diary of Dahlgren," ibid., 3:739, 16:372; Tomb Memoirs, 54 (Tomb confused the *Savannah* and the *Atlanta*); *DANFS* 2:510; Smythe to Miss Lou, Jan. 22, 1865, p. 378, Smythe Papers; Rochelle to Scharf, Jan. 12, 1887, Rochelle folder, ZB File, NHCUS.

56. Davis to Tucker, Jan. 15, 1865, Tucker to Davis, Jan. 18, 1865, *ORA*, 1st ser., 47 (pt. 2): 1014, 1022. See also Schauffler to Schimmelfennig, Jan. 29, 1865, ibid. (pt. 1), 1016–17.

57. Smythe to Aunt Janey, Feb. 13, 1865, p. 391, Smythe Papers; Hardee to Tucker, Feb. 11, 1865, *ORA*, 1st ser., 47 (pt. 2): 1159; "Examination of Wood," Mar. 28, 1865, *ORN*, 1st ser., 16:418.

58. Burton, *Siege of Charleston*, 312–22.

59. Dahlgren to Gilmore, Feb. 14, 1865, Dahlgren to Scott, Feb. 17, 1865, Dahlgren to Welles, Feb. 22, 1865, *ORN*, 1st ser., 16:243, 248, 264–66.

60. Still, *Iron Afloat*, 219–20; Scharf, *Confederate Navy*, 706; *Charleston Daily Courier*, Feb. 20, 1865.

61. Cowley, *Lawyer's Life*, 151–52; Wells, *Confederate Navy Organization*, 150–52; Rochelle, *Tucker*, 80. Still, *Iron Afloat*, 219, apparently concurs with Tucker's decision; Lockhart, "Confederate Squadron," 273, asserts that any attack by Tucker after the loss of the *Columbia* would have been "doomed to failure."

62. Rochelle, *Tucker*, 51–52; Rochelle to Scharf, Jan. 3, 1887, Rochelle folder, ZB File, NHCUS; Tucker to Bragg, Feb. 19, 1865, Tucker to Hoke, Feb. 21, 1865, Bragg to Tucker, Feb. 21, 1865, Tucker to Bragg, Feb. 21, 1865, Tucker to Bragg or Hoke, Feb. 27, 1865, *ORA*, 1st ser., 47 (pt. 2): 1227, 1243, 1289; Rochelle, *Tucker*, 52–53; Sinclair, *Two Years on the* Alabama, 295.

Chapter Four: Sailor's Creek

1. Semmes, *Memoirs*, 802–4; Scharf, *Confederate Navy*, 745.

2. Tucker to R. E. Lee, [Apr.] 2, 1865, Correspondence file, Lee Papers; see also Rochelle, *Tucker*, 53.

3. Rochelle, *Tucker*, 53; Sevier Questionnaire, item 46; Howard, *Recollections*, 373; Mahone, "Road to Appomattox," 7.

4. The best account of the Battle of Sayler's Creek and related events is the unpaginated Calkins, *Thirty-Six Hours before Appomattox*. See also "Report of General G. W. C. Lee," 256; Howard, *Recollections*, 372–73; Rodick, *Appomattox*, 55–56.

5. Howard, *Recollections*, 373; Mahone, "Road to Appomattox," 7; B. Johnson, "Battle of Sailor's Creek," 538; Donnelly, *Confederate States Marine Corps*, 42–45; Wells, *Confederate Navy Organization*, 19; J. Stiles, "Navy at Sailor's Creek," 252.

6. The officers captured at Sayler's Creek are listed in the *New York Herald*, Apr. 9, 1865. Not enumerated there are sailors and marines paroled at Appomattox, who included wounded men and surgeons from Tucker's force, sailors and marines who escaped capture on Apr. 6, and probably some mariners unattached to Tucker's battalion; their names appear in the *Appomattox Roster*, 3, 4, 110, 312, 449–50, 457, 458–60.

7. La Bree, *Campfires*, 266–67, places three blacks on board the *Chicora* but identifies only a "Charlie Cleaper." The one extant muster roll for that vessel (*ORN*, 2d ser., 1:284) lists a "John Cleaper, Landsman." The *Appomattox Roster*, 460, shows "Chas. Cleapor," Johnson, and Heck as "Privates Attached to the Naval Brigade"; after each man's name is the notation "(col'd)." The only other blacks identified in the *Appomattox Roster* are eight Georgia cooks and musicians and eight teamsters (226, 487).

8. Howard, *Recollections*, 388; Blackford, *War Years*, 283; *Norfolk Landmark*, June 16, 1883; Mahone, "Road to Appomattox," 7.

9. R. Stiles, *Four Years under Marse Robert*, 329.

10. Calkins, *Thirty-Six Hours before Appomattox;* W. C. Davis, "The Campaign to Appomattox," 15–22; Rodick, *Appomattox*, 56–59.

11. R. Stiles, *Four Years under Marse Robert*, 329.

12. Calkins, *Thirty-Six Hours before Appomattox;* Howard, *Recollections*, 380–84; Sevier Questionnaire, item 46; Stevens, "Battle of Sailor's Creek," 445, 448; Basinger, "Crutchfield's Artillery," 39; *Norfolk Landmark*, June 16, 1883.

13. Calkins, *Thirty-Six Hours before Appomattox;* Sevier Questionnaire, item 46; Rodick, *Appomattox*, 62; R. Stiles, *Four Years under Marse Robert*, 330–33; Basinger, "Crutchfield's Artillery," 40; Blake, "Artillery at Sailor's Creek," 213–14; Howard, *Recollections*, 382, 388.

14. Schaff, *Sunset of the Confederacy*, 107; Allen Memoirs, 28; R. Stiles, *Four Years under Marse Robert*, 333; Howard, *Recollections*, 384.

15. Sevier Questionnaire, item 46; Gilman, "Concerning Battle at Sailor's Creek," 451; Sanford, letter to "Inquiries and Answers," 170.

16. Seymour to Whittelsey, Apr. 15, 1865, Keifer to Tracy, Apr. 18, 1865, Wright to Ruggles, Apr. 29, 1865, *ORA*, 1st ser., 46 (pt. 1): 980, 998, 906; Keifer to Mrs. Keifer, Apr. 7, 1865, Keifer Papers; Scharf, *Confederate Navy*, 749; Parker, *Recollections*, 354.

17. Scharf, *Confederate Navy*, 749; Donnelly, *Confederate States Marine Corps*, 44; Calkins, *Thirty-Six Hours before Appomattox*.

18. Keifer, *Slavery* 2:210–11; Keifer to Mrs. Keifer, Apr. 7, 1865, Keifer Papers.

19. Keifer, *Slavery* 2:210–11; Keifer to Mrs. Keifer, Apr. 7, 1865, Keifer Papers. Tucker recalled that Keifer wanted the commodore to retain his sword; but this would not be allowed while he was in custody, so Tucker entrusted it to Keifer (Keifer to Tucker, Jan. 12, 1878, Tucker to Keifer, [Jan. 14, 1878], Tucker to Congressman John Randolph Tucker, Jan. 14, 1878, Tucker Papers, Pensacola). The sword surrendered by Tucker and re-

turned by Keifer (the sailor's U.S. Navy sword) is now in the possession of Mrs. St. George Tucker Arnold of Oak Ridge, Tenn.

20. Scharf, *Confederate Navy*, 749; Parker, *Recollections*, 354; Howard, *Recollections*, 386–87.

21. Calkins, *Thirty-Six Hours before Appomattox;* Keifer to Mrs. Keifer, Apr. 9, 1865, Keifer Papers; Watson, "Fighting at Sailor's Creek," 448–52.

22. Calkins, *Thirty-Six Hours before Appomattox;* Howard, *Recollections*, 386, 390–94; Keifer to Mrs. Keifer, Apr. 7, 1865, Keifer Papers; Sevier Questionnaire, item 46; "Battle of Sailor's Creek: Part Taken by Savannah Guards," 252.

23. Ewell to Grant, Apr. 16, 1865, *ORA*, 1st ser., 46 (pt. 3): 787; McLain, "Prison Conditions in Fort Warren," 266–67, 294.

24. Lee to Grant, Apr. 25, 1865, *ORA*, 1st ser., 46 (pt. 3): 1013; Keifer, *Slavery* 2:211; Stampp, *Era of Reconstruction*, 51; Dorris, *Pardon and Amnesty*, 86–102.

25. Dorris, *Pardon and Amnesty*, 35, 111–12; Tucker to Johnson, May 30, 1865, Tucker folder, ZB File, NHCUS. Tucker likely had very little savings in negotiable currency. Among the Tucker Papers, Pensacola, are a $1,000 Confederate government bond and another of the same amount issued by the state of

North Carolina—both, of course, worthless.

26. Dorris, *Pardon and Amnesty*, 161–66; McLain, "Prison Conditions in Fort Warren," 283, 305–6; Tucker to Mrs. Wise, June 17, 1865, Wise Letters; [A. W. Lattie?] to Tucker, Nov. 5, [1865], folder 32, Tucker Papers, ODU; Ewell, *Letters*, 134–43.

27. Tucker to Mrs. Wise, June 17, 1865, Riddick to Wise, June 24, July 5, 1866, Lansdale to Wise, July 24, 1867, Wise Letters.

28. McLain, "Prison Conditions in Fort Warren," 298–99; Dorris, *Pardon and Amnesty*, 111, 154–55, 158. Copies of Tucker's oath and parole are in the Tucker folder, ZB File, NHCUS.

29. Dorris, *Pardon and Amnesty*, 115–17, 127, 172, 320–21, 330.

30. West to Tucker, Dec. 6, 1865, folder 25, Tucker Papers, ODU; Dorris, *Pardon and Amnesty*, 115–19, 172; Semmes, *Memoirs*, 72; Karsten, *Naval Aristocracy*, 26; Sutherland, "Exiles, Emigrants, and Sojourners," 237–56.

31. Tucker to Harwood, Aug. 19, 1865, Tucker folder, ZB File, NHCUS; McCullock to Harwood, Aug. 11, 1865, copy, folder 29, Tucker Papers, ODU; *Richmond Daily Dispatch*, May 23, 1866; Hanna and Hanna, *Confederate Exiles in Venezuela*, 25, 43; Merli, "Alternative to Appomattox," 210–19; Rochelle, *Tucker*, 54.

Chapter Five: Almirante Tucker

1. The only extensive study of the war in English is W. Columbus Davis, *Last Conquistadores*, which ends its coverage before Tucker's arrival in Peru. Following traditional Latin American scholarship, Davis attributes Spain's actions to territorial ambitions. More convincing (and adopted here) is the revisionist interpretation in Cortada, *Spain and the American Civil War.*

2. W. Columbus Davis, *Last Conquistadores*, 216, 232, 268; Romero Pintado, *Historia marítima, 1850–1870* 2:48–50, 490–91, 546–47; Wagner de Reyna, *Relaciones diplomáticas*, 311.

3. W. Columbus Davis, *Last Con-*

quistadores, 249–55; López Urrutia, *Marina de Chile*, 206–15.

4. Valdizán Gamio, *Tradiciones navales*, 173–77; W. Columbus Davis, *Last Conquistadores*, 271–72.

5. W. Columbus Davis, *Last Conquistadores*, 291–310; R. Johnson, *Rodgers*, 284–93; López Urrutia, *Marina de Chile*, 219–23.

6. Romero Pintado, *Historia marítima, 1850–70* 2:596–697; Valdizán Gamio, *Tradiciones navales*, 191–224; W. Columbus Davis, *Last Conquistadores*, 311–21.

7. Werlich, *Peru*, 71–72; Wagner de

Reyna, *Relaciones diplomáticas*, 314–17; Burr, *By Reason or Force*, 21–57.

8. López Urrutia, *Marina de Chile*, 61–132, 187–200; Basadre, *Historia* 2:786–87, 957.

9. See the "Lista de oficiales" appended to Chile, *Memoria de Marina, 1866*.

10. This prosopography of the officer corps is based upon sketches of about one-third of these men in the *DhbbCh*. Romero Pintado, *Historia marítima, 1850–70* 1:351–64, analyzes the Chilean naval tradition, contrasting it with that of Peru.

11. Perú, *Memoria de guerra y marina, 1868*, app. 11. In the numbers given here, I have combined the effective and acting ("graduado") ranks.

12. Biographies of a dozen prominent officers of the period are in the *DeP*. Romero Pintado, *Historia marítima, 1850–70* 2: chaps. 7 and 8, discusses in depth naval organization and personnel. Captain Romero's account occasionally differs in detail and emphasis from the treatment given here.

13. See the assessment by Williams Rebolledo ("Observaciones acerca de las fuerzas navales de Perú") in Varas Velásquez, "Cartas y documentos sobre el conflicto hispano-peruano," 205–9.

14. Basadre, *Historia* 2:690, 3:1098, 1130–34, 1154, 1185–86, 4:1552; Romero Pintado, *Historia marítima, 1850–70* 2: chap. 11.

15. Brodie, *Sea Power*, 17.

16. López Urrutia, *Marina de Chile*, 218; Romero Pintado, *Historia marítima, 1850–70* 2:568–69, 644–51; Rodgers to Welles, May 10, 1866, in *New York Times*, May 23, 1866; *Times* (London), June 14, 1866; Prado to Barreda, May 27, 1866, Barreda Papers.

17. Martínez to Covarrubias, June 19, 1866, Comunicaciones dirigidas al MRE de Chile: Perú, 1865–1866, vol. 85, AMRECh; Pacheco to Barreda, Mar. 21, 1866, Barreda Papers.

18. Basadre, *Historia* 3:1130, 4:1552, 1562; Wagner de Reyna, *Relaciones diplomáticas*, 170, 184–85; Vicuña MacKenna, *Diez meses* 1:72–74. The "Escafalón general de la armada nacional" appended to Perú, *Memoria de marina,*

1876, provides a detailed record of the promotions of Montero and his colleagues.

19. Encina, *Historia de Chile* 2:1429–30; Vicuña MacKenna to Covarrubias, July 26, 1866, Misión confidencial, vol. 127, MRE, ANCh; Wagner de Reyna, *Relaciones diplomáticas*, 188–89, 208; Solar to Varas, Jan. 16, 1866, in Varas Velásquez, "Guerra entre Chile-Perú y España," 539–40.

20. Wagner de Reyna, *Relaciones diplomáticas*, 200–216.

21. Ibid., 288; Sotomayor, "Viaje de los buques," 27–42; Williams to Ministro de Marina, Jan. 13, 1866, Escuadra Aliada, 1865–1870, vol. 230, MM, ANCh.

22. Williams to Ministro de Marina, Feb. 14, Mar. 14, Apr. 29, May 2, 1866, Escuadra Aliada, 1865–1870, vol. 230, MM, ANCh.

23. Williams Rebolledo, *Guerra del Pacífico*, 78–82; Sotomayor, "Viaje de los buques," 36–41; Wagner de Reyna, *Relaciones diplomáticas*, 288.

24. Wagner de Reyna, *Relaciones diplomáticas*, 289; *DeP*, s.v. "Villar, Manuel."

25. Williams Rebolledo, *Guerra del Pacífico*, 149–57; Grau, Ferreyros, and Mariátegui to Williams, Mar. 2, 1866, in H. Williams, *Williams Rebolledo*, 49–50; Williams to Villar, Mar. 8, 1866, Villar to Williams, Mar. 9, 1866, Williams to Ministro de Marina (nos. 227 and 232), Mar. 17, 1866, Escuadra Aliada, 1865–1870, vol. 230, MM, ANCh.

26. Errázuriz to Williams, Feb. 6, Mar. 24, 1866, in H. Williams, *Williams Rebolledo*, 55, 52; Gálvez to Villar, Apr. 11, 1866, Correspondencia de la Marina, 1865–66, lc L101, p. 131, AHMP; Pacheco to Barreda, Mar. 13, 21, 27, 1866, Barreda Papers.

27. Sherman, *Guadalquivir to Golden Gate*, esp. 159, 167, 173–74; Barreda, *Ministro del Perú*, fasc. 1 (pt. 2) and 10.

28. Barreda to Pacheco, Apr. 30, May 18, June 30, 1866, lc de las comunicaciones entre el MREP y su legación en los Estados Unidos de América entre los años 1863 y 1866, vol. 68A, AGMREP.

29. Barreda to Pacheco, May 1, 1866, Barreda Papers, 5:465v; Barreda to Pacheco, Apr. 20, May 10, 18, 24, June

20, 1866, lc de las comunicaciones entre el MREP y su legación en los Estados Unidos de América entre los años 1863 y 1866, vol. 68A, AGMREP; Vicuña Mac-Kenna, *Diez meses* 1:326–31; H. Jones, *Captain Roger Jones and Descendants*, 271–74; entry for N. B. Wells, Apr. 30 [1866], Libro de cuentas de la Legación del Perú en los Estados Unidos de América para los años 1866 y 1867, vol. 98A, AGMREP; Vicuña MacKenna to Covarrubias, Apr. 30, 1866, Misión confidencial, vol. 127, MRE, ANCh.

30. Scharf, *Confederate Navy*, 408–9; Logbook of the USS *Warren*, Feb. 13, 1839–Feb. 18, 1841, RG 24, NAUS; Still, *Iron Afloat*, 152–65; Barreda to Pacheco, May 31, 1866, lc de las comunicaciones entre el MREP y su legación en los Estados Unidos de América entre los años 1863 y 1866, vol. 68A, AGMREP.

31. U.S. House, *Navy Clerks Employed during 1827;* U.S. Navy, *Register, 1860*, 16; Brooke, *Brooke*, 9; Mc-Corkle to Tyler, Oct. 1, 1841, David P. McCorkle folder, ZB File, NHCUS. Wells, *Confederate Navy Organization*, 47, identifies James as Joseph McCorkle.

32. U.S. Navy, *Registers*, 1841–61; Taylor, *Broad Pennant*, 400–401; Benjamin, *Naval Academy*, 426–28; Brooke, *Brooke*, 76; Dudley, *Going South*, 40.

33. U.S. Navy, *Register of the Confederate Navy*, 121; Brooke, *Brooke*, 240; McCorkle to R. D. Minor, Oct. 17, 1861, Minor Family Papers; Mallory to Benjamin, Jan. 23, 1862, G. Minor to Mallory, Aug. 15, 1862, Brooke to Mallory, Nov. 25, 1863, Mallory to Mitchell, Feb. 24, 1862, *ORN*, 2d ser., 2:135, 250, 548, 1:466; Mallory, Special Order No. 27, Feb. 3, 1862, Mallory to McCorkle, Feb. 15, 1862, McCorkle folder, ZB File, NHCUS.

34. U.S. Navy, *Register of the Confederate Navy*, 121; Brooke, *Brooke*, 281; Durkin, *Mallory*, 298–300; McCorkle to Brooke, May 7, 1864, *ORA*, 4th ser., 3:522; Brooke to Mallory, Nov. 4, 1864, *ORN*, 2d ser., 2:755–56.

35. Beers, *Archives of the Confederate States*, 374; McCorkle to Walter Stevens, Oct. 24, 1865, Virginia Miscellaneous Papers; *Richmond Daily Dispatch*, May 23, 1866.

36. Stewart, *Norfolk County*, 499–

500; conversations with M. W. Butt, Jr., Portsmouth, Va.; career synopsis, W. R. Butt folder, ZB File, NHCUS; W. R. Butt alumnus file, U.S. Naval Academy Archives; U.S. Naval Academy, *Annual Register, 1859*, 7; Seager, *Mahan*, 22–23, 29, 609; Callahan, *List of Officers of the Navy*, 624–25; Mahan to Ashe, Dec. 19, 1858, Jan. 9, Feb. 7, 1859, Apr. 12, 1903, in Mahan, *Letters* 1:38, 51, 56–57, 3:54. A photo of Midshipman Butt is in the Butt Collection.

37. Travis, Abstract of the Names and Descriptions of Persons to Whom Passports Have Been Issued, July 1 to Dec. 31, 1872, USDS, Consular Despatches, Para, T478/3, RG 59, NAUS; F. Galt Diary, 2:29.

38. Career synopsis, Butt folder, ZB File, NHCUS; Ashe, "Memories of Annapolis," 204.

39. Career synopsis, Butt folder, ZB File, NHCUS; Huger to Goldsborough, Jan. 15, 1862, Marston to Huger, Jan. 18, 1862, *ORA*, 2d ser., 3:201; Buchanan to Mallory, Mar. 27, 1862, *ORA*, 1st ser., 9:11; Green [i.e., Greene], *Eye-Witness Account*, 6.

40. Career synopsis, Butt folder, ZB File, NHCUS; Wood to wife, Aug. 14, 1862, Wood Papers.

41. Career synopsis, Butt folder, ZB File, NHCUS; Barron to Sinclair, Nov. 10, 1863, with enclosure, *ORN*, 2d ser., 2:516; Forrest, *Odyssey in Gray*, 92, 113.

42. Career synopsis, Butt folder, ZB File, NHCUS; Mitchell to Lee, Nov. 18, 1864, Mitchell to Butt, Dec. 1, 1864, Mitchell to Mallory, Feb. 13, 1865, Butt to Mitchell, Jan. 26, 1865, *ORN*, 1st ser., 11:766, 772, 669–73, 681–82.

43. Career synopsis, Butt folder, ZB File, NHCUS; Semmes, *Memoirs*, 803, 818–19; Semmes, "Admiral on Horseback," 129–50; M. Butt, *Portsmouth*, 24.

44. Barreda to Pacheco, May 24, 30, 31, 1866, lc de las comunicaciones entre el MREP y su legación en los Estados Unidos de América entre los años 1863 y 1866, vol. 68A, AGMREP; Barreda to Barrie Brothers, May 23, 1866, lc de las comunicaciones entre Perú y su legación en los EE UU de América correspondiente a los años 1862–1866, vol. 62A, AGMREP; entry for payment to Tucker, May 31, 1866, Barreda Papers, 6:100v.

45. Basadre, *Historia* 4:1626; Butt to Fairfield, June 27, 1866, Butt Collection; Barreda to Tucker, May 24, 1866, Barreda to Las autoridades, May 24, 1866, lc de las comunicaciones entre Perú y su legación en los EE UU de América correspondiente a los años 1862–1866, vol. 62A, AGMREP; Barreda to Pacheco, May 24, June 20, 1866, lc de las comunicaciones entre el MREP y su legación en los Estados Unidos de América entre los años 1863 y 1866, vol. 68A, AGMREP; Pacheco to Barreda, June 21, 1866, Barreda Papers.

46. Pacheco to José Pardo, June 20, 1866, Comunicaciones de la cancillería peruana a la Legación del Perú en Chile entre los años 1866 y 1878, vol. 89A, AGMREP; *DhbbCh* 2:216–19; Wagner de Reyna, *Relaciones diplomáticas*, 290–91.

47. Balmaceda to Williams, June 14, 1866, in H. Williams, *Williams Rebolledo*, 67–68; Salcedo to Varas, Dec. 1, 1865, in Varas Velásquez, "Guerra entre Chile-Perú y España," 527–28; Wagner de Reyna, *Relaciones diplomáticas*, 292–93.

48. Thomson to Clarendon, May 16, 1866, FO 16/140, GBFOGC, Chile, PROUK; Pacheco to Barreda, May 27, 1866, Barreda Papers; García y García, *Defenza de Capitán García*, 6–8; Vicuña MacKenna to Covarrubias, July 26, 1866, Misión confidencial, vol. 127, MRE, ANCh.

49. Espinoza to Salcedo, June 6, 1866, Correspondencia de la Marina, 1865–1866, lc L101, pp. 185–86, AHMP; Melo, *Marina del Perú* 2:40–45; Pacheco to Barreda, May 27, June 13, 1866, Barreda Papers; Vicuña MacKenna, *Diez meses* 1:73; Salcedo to Varas, June 23, 1866, in Varas Velásquez, "Guerra entre Chile-Perú y España," 543–44; Palma to Alzamora, July 7, 1866, in Palma, *Epistolario* 1:37.

50. W. Butts [i.e., Butt], "American Officers," 147–49; Butt to Fairfield, June 27, 1866, Butt Collection; Pacheco to Barreda, June 21, 27, 1866, Prado to Barreda, June 21, 1866, Barreda Papers.

51. Martínez to Covarrubias, June 19, 21, 1866, Comunicaciones dirigidas al MRE de Chile: Perú, 1865–1866, vol. 85, AMRECh.

52. Martínez to Covarrubias, June 21, 1866, ibid.; Logbook of the USS *Warren*, Feb. 13, 1839–Feb. 18, 1841, RG 24, NAUS; Asta Buraga to Covarrubias, May 30, 1866, Legación de Chile en los Estados Unidos de N. América, 1866–1867, vol. 134, MRE, ANCh; Vicuña MacKenna to Covarrubias, June 10, 1866, Misión confidencial, vol. 127, MRE, ANCh.

53. Butt to Fairfield, June 27, 1866, Butt Collection; Martínez to Covarrubias, June 21, 25, July 3, 1866, Comunicaciones dirigidas al MRE de Chile: Perú, 1865–1866, vol. 85, AMRECh; Pacheco to Barreda, June 21, 27, July 13, 21, 1866, Barreda Papers.

54. Butt to Fairfield, June 27, 1866, Butt Collection; Registro de los despachos desde el 27 de febrero de 1866.

55. Butts, "American Officers," 148–50.

56. MGM to Ministro de Relaciones Exteriores, July 12, 1866, segundo semestre [1866], lc I48, AHMP; Bustamante to Tucker, July 12, 1866, Cisneros Sánchez Collection; Bustamante to Montero, July 12, 1866, Correspondencia de la Marina, 1865–1866, lc L101, p. 235, AHMP; Vicuña MacKenna to Covarrubias, July 12, 1866, Misión confidencial, vol. 127, MRE, ANCh.

57. Montero to Prado, July 10, 1866 (enclosed with Pacheco to Barreda, July 27, 1866), Barreda Papers; Prado to García y García, June 26, 1866, in García y García, *Defenza de Capitán García*, app. 3.

58. Blanco to Ministro de Marina, July 4, 1866, Blanco to Montero, July 4, 1866, Escuadra Aliada, 1865–1870, vol. 230, MM, ANCh; García y García to Prado, July 10, 1866, in García y García, *Defenza de Capitán García*, app. 4; Montero to Prado, July 10, 1866 (copy enclosed with Pacheco to Barreda, July 27, 1866), J. Pardo to Pacheco, July 18, 1866 (copy enclosed with Pacheco to Barreda, Aug. 13, 1866), Barreda Papers.

59. Tucker to Randy, Sept. 3, 1866, Tucker Papers, Pensacola; Butts, "American Officers," 147–48, 151; Romero Pintado, *Historia marítima, 1850–70* 2:268–316; Barreda, *Ministro del Perú*, fasc. 10; *DANFS* 2:574; Chile, *Memoria de*

Marina, 1866, 11–13; Vargas Caballero, "Adquisiciones navales," 84–91.

60. J. Pardo to Pacheco, July 25, 1866 (copy enclosed with Pacheco to Barreda, Aug. 13, 1866), Barreda Papers; Wagner de Reyna, *Relaciones diplomáticas*, 293–94; Butts, "American Officers," 151.

61. J. Pardo to Tucker, Aug. 18, 1866, Tucker-Randolph Correspondence; Butts, "American Officers," 151; J. Pardo to Pacheco, July 25, Aug. 3, 1866 (copies enclosed with Pacheco to Barreda, Aug. 13, 1866), Barreda Papers; Lira Urqueta, "Guerra con España," 165; Montero to J. Pardo, Aug. 2, 1866 (two letters), J. Pardo to Montero, Aug. 2, 1866, in *El Mercurio* (Valparaíso), Aug. 3, 1866; Wagner de Reyna, *Relaciones diplomáticas*, 294–98.

62. J. Pardo to Pacheco, Aug. 3, 1866 (copy enclosed with Pacheco to Barreda, Aug. 13, 1866), Barreda Papers; Registro de los despachos, 253–55; Melo, *Marina del Perú* 2:50; Butts, "American Officers," 151.

63. Butts, "American Officers," 151; Bustamante to Tucker, July 23, 1866, Cisneros Sánchez Collection; Pardo-Covarrubias protocol, Aug. 13, 1866, folder 7, Tucker Papers, ODU; Pinto to Blanco, Aug. 25, 1866, Correspondencia de los ministros de estado y demás autoridades, 1866, vol. 237, MM, ANCh; *El Mercurio*, Aug. 18, 28, 1866; Thomson to Hammond, Oct. 16, 1866, FO 16/141, GBFOGC, Chile, PROUK; Tucker to Randy, Sept. 3, 1866, Tucker Papers, Pensacola.

64. Manuel Pardo to Tucker, Aug. 17, 1866, M. Pardo to J. Pardo, Aug. 17, 1866, Correspondencia general y consular de la Legación del Perú en Chile hacía Lima en 1866, legajo 5–4, año 1866, AGMREP; see also Thomson to Clarendon, Aug. 16, 27, 1866, FO 16/141 and 223, GBFOGC, Chile, PROUK; Barreda to Pacheco, June 9, July 9, Aug. 9, 18, 1866, lc de las comunicaciones entre el MREP y su legación en los Estados Unidos de América entre los años 1863 y 1866, vol. 68A, AGMREP; Pacheco to Barreda, July 13, 21, 27, Aug. 27, Sept. 13, Nov. 2, 1866, Prado to Barreda, July 21, Aug. 9, 1866, Barreda Papers.

65. M. Pardo to Tucker, Aug. 17, 1866, M. Pardo to J. Pardo, Aug. 17, 1866, Correspondencia general y consular de la Legación del Perú en Chile hacía Lima en 1866, legajo 5–4, año 1866, AGMREP; Butts, "American Officers," 151.

66. Butts, "American Officers," 151; Salcedo to M. Pardo, Aug. 6, 1866, Werlich Collection; Tucker to Bustamante, Sept. 2, 1866, Corbeta "Unión," CGEA, AMNP.

67. Melo, *Marina del Perú* 2:45–47; Tucker to Bustamante, Aug. 25, Sept. 24, Oct. 17, 1866, Corbeta "América," CGEA, AMNP; Tucker to M. Pardo, Sept. 16, 1866, J. Pardo de Zela to M. Pardo, Oct. 10, 1866, Werlich Collection; Pacheco to Barreda, Sept. 21, 1866, Barreda Papers; Bustamante to Tucker, Oct. 25, Dec. 11, 1866, Dirección de Marina, 1866–1867, lc 126, AMNP; Registro de los despachos, 278–81, 283, 288–89; Chile, *Memoria de Marina, 1866*, 6, 15; *El Mercurio*, Aug. 9, 18, Oct. 18, 24, 1866.

68. Butts, "American Officers," 152; Tucker to Bustamante, Sept. 16 (and enclosures), Oct. 8 (and enclosure), Oct. 15, Oct. 25 (and enclosures), 1866, Corbeta "Unión," CGEA, AMNP; Tucker to Bustamante, Sept. 24, 1866, Corbeta "América," CGEA, Bustamante to Tucker, Oct. 20, 1866, Dirección de Marina, 1866–1867, lc 126, AMNP; Fragata blindada "Independencia," Copias de pedidos, requisitions 14, 16, 20–23, 26.

69. Butts, "American Officers," 152; McCorkle to Tucker, Aug. 23, 1866 (enclosed with Tucker to Bustamante, Aug. 25, 1866), Tucker to Bustamante, Sept. 15, 16, 1866, McCorkle to Tucker, Oct. 6, 1866 (enclosed with Tucker to Bustamante, Oct. 8, 1866), Corbeta "Unión," CGEA, AMNP; Tucker to Errázuriz, Oct. 2, Nov. 6, 1866, MM, Escuadra Aliada, 1865–1870, vol. 230, MM, ANCh; *El Mercurio*, Oct. 6, 1866.

70. Butts, "American Officers," 152; Tucker to M. Pardo, Sept. 2, 1866, Werlich Collection; Fragata blindada "Independencia," Copias de pedidos, requisitions 14, 24–26; Registro de los despachos, pp. 255, 288–89; resolución suprema no. 1181, Nov. 14, 1866, Resoluciones supremas desde el 22–11–1865 hasta 1867, lc C40, AHMP; Tucker to Errázuriz, Jan. 26, 1867; Williams to

NOTES

Errázuriz, Jan. 29, 1867, MM, Escuadra Aliada, 1865–1870, vol. 230, MM, ANCh.

71. U.S. Navy, *Register of the Confederate Navy*, 46; Perry, *Infernal Machines*, 16–18, 110–12, 125–28, 192–93; Davidson, "Electrical Torpedoes"; Davidson, "Electrical Submarine Mine"; career synopsis, Hunter Davidson folder, ZB File, NHCUS.

72. E. R. F., "Torpedoes," 472; U.S. House, *H. H. Doty;* Rodríguez to Antonio Varas, Dec. 17, 1865, Jan. 1, 1866 (with enclosed contract between Rodríguez and Doty), in Varas Velásquez, "Guerra entre Chile-Perú y España," 531, 534–38 (Doty's name is printed "Doby"); Doty to Ministro de Marina, July 24, 1866, in Chile, *Memoria de Marina, 1866,* 76–80; Tucker to Manuel Pardo, Sept. 2, 1866 (two letters), Werlich Collection; Pacheco to Barreda, Sept. 27, 1866, Barreda Papers.

73. Tucker to Barreda, Nov. 10, 1866, Tucker to M. Pardo, Sept. 2, 1866 (two letters), Werlich Collection.

74. *El Mercurio* (supplement), Aug. 4, 1866; Melo, *Marina del Perú* 2:50–51; Bustamante to Tucker, Oct. 12, 1866, Dirección de Marina, 1866–1867, lc 126, AMNP; Muñoz to Bustamante, Oct. 14, 1866, Ordenes generales de la Armada, Callao—octubre, AMNP; "Escafalón general de la armada nacional," appended to Perú, *Memoria de Marina, 1876; DeP,* s.vv. "Carrillo, Camilo," and "Moore, Juan G."; Tucker to Bustamante, Sept. 16, 1866, Corbeta "Unión," CGEA, AMNP.

75. Tucker to M. Pardo, Sept. 16, 1866, Werlich Collection; Butts, "American Officers," 151; Tucker to Bustamante, Sept. 17, Oct. 25, 1866, Corbeta "Unión," CGEA, AMNP; Elcorrobarrutia to Tucker, Sept. 26, 1866, Dirección de Marina, 1866–1867, lc 126, AMNP; Tucker to Pacheco, Nov. 8, 1866, Corbeta "América," CGEA, AMNP; J. M. García to Tucker, Nov. 9, 1866 (enclosed with Tucker to Pacheco [no. 67], Nov. 9, 1866), García to Tucker, Nov. 9, 1866 (enclosed with Tucker to Pacheco [no. 69], Nov. 9, 1866), Fragata "Independencia," CGEA, AMNP.

76. Chile, *Memoria de Marina, 1866,* 39–41; Bustamante to Tucker, Oct. 25, 1866, Dirección de Marina, 1866–1867, lc 126, AMNP; Errázuriz to

Tucker, Oct. 5, 1866, Ministerio de Marina, Correspondencia de los ministros de estado y demás autoridades, 1866, vol. 237, MM, ANCh; Tucker to Bustamante, Oct. 17, 1866, Corbeta "Unión," CGEA, AMNP; revista de comisario [*Independencia*], Nov. 15, 1866, Listas de revista (marina), cuaderno no. 8, 0.1866.4, AHMP.

77. Tucker to Bustamante, Aug. 25, 1866, Escuadra Aliada, Comandancia General de la Escuadra, AMNP; Bustamante to Ministro de Hacienda, Sept. 10, 1866, Ministerio de Guerra y Marina, oficios remitidos, OL479–546, Archivo de Hacienda, AGNP; Tucker to Bustamante, undated (asking Mendiola's appointment), Corbeta "Unión," AMNP.

78. "Relación de oficiales," enclosed with Pardo de Zela to Salcedo, Aug. 5, 1866, Cisneros Sánchez Collection; Elcorrobarrutia to Comandante General del Departamento Marítimo del Callao, Oct. 13, 1866, Toma de razón de resoluciones supremas, decretos, montepíos, nombramientos, 1865–1872, lc 191, AMNP; Bustamante to Tucker, Nov. 29, 1866, Dirección de Marina, 1866–1867, lc 126, AMNP.

79. Tucker to M. Pardo, Sept. 16, 1866, Pardo de Zela to M. Pardo, Oct. 10, 1866, Werlich Collection; Tucker to Bustamante, Sept. 16, 1866, Elcorrobarrutia to Tucker, Sept. 26, 1866, Dirección de Marina, 1866–1867, lc 126, AMNP; Tucker to Pacheco (nos. 65 and 66), Nov. 8, 1866, Escuadra Aliada, Comandancia General de la Escuadra, AMNP.

80. Butts, "American Officers," 151–52; Karsten, *Naval Aristocracy,* 73–74; communications from Mrs. David Ayers and Mrs. Otto Aufranc, descendants, respectively, of Tucker's sisters Honoria and Susan; obituary of the admiral's mother from an unidentified newspaper in the Ayers Collection; Tucker to Barreda, Nov. 10, 1866, Barreda Papers.

81. J. Pardo to Tucker, Aug. 18, 1866, Tucker-Randolph Correspondence; Tucker to Errázuriz, Sept. 14, 1866, MM, Escuadra Aliada, 1865–1870, vol. 230, MM, ANCh; Errázuriz to Tucker, Sept. 25, 1866, Correspondencia de los ministros de estado y demás autoridades, 1866, vol. 237, MM, ANCh; Tucker to Cabieses, Sept. 27, 1866 (copy enclosed

with Tucker to Bustamante, Oct. 3, 1866), Corbeta "Unión," CGEA, AMNP.

82. Errázuriz to Tucker, Oct. 9, 1866, Correspondencia de los ministros de estado y demás autoridades, 1866, vol. 237, MM, ANCh; Williams to Recabarren, Sept. 17, 1866, Williams to Márquez de la Plata, Sept. 19, 1866, in H. Williams, *Williams Rebolledo*, 70, 71–72; Williams to Errázuriz, Jan. 29, 1867, Escuadra Aliada, 1865–1870, vol. 230, MM, ANCh; J. R. Lira to Errázuriz, Feb. 25, 1867, Comandantes de buques de guerra: Esmeralda, Maipú, Independencia, Maule, y Valdivia, 1852–1866, vol. 118, MM, ANCh.

83. Butts, "American Officers," 152; Pacheco to Barreda, Nov. 2, 1866, Barreda Papers; *El Mercurio*, Nov. 23, 28, 1866. A report by the *Maipú*'s captain describing a typical one-day training exercise is extracted in Lira to Errázuriz, Nov. 27, 1866, Correspondencia de la Comandancia General de Marina (anexo), 1860–1868, vol. 171, MM, ANCh.

84. Tucker to Bustamante, Dec. 18, 1866, Corbeta "América," CGEA, AMNP; Lira to Errázuriz, Dec. 21, 1866, Correspondencia de la Comandancia General de Marina (anexo), 1860–1868, vol. 171, MM, ANCh.

85. Tucker to Errázuriz, Jan. 24, Feb. 23, 1867, Escuadra Aliada, 1865–1870, vol. 230, MM, ANCh; Lira to Errázuriz, Feb. 25, 1867, Comandantes de buques de guerra, vol. 118, MM, ANCh.

86. Tucker to Bustamante, Sept. 15, 1866, Tucker to McCorkle, Butt, and the captains of the *América* and *Huáscar*, Oct. 7, 1866 (copy enclosed with Tucker to Bustamante, undated), Corbeta "Unión," CGEA, AMNP.

87. Tucker to Bustamante, Oct. 25, 1866, Corbeta "Unión," CGEA, AMNP; Butts, "American Officers," 152.

88. Camilo Carrillo and Juan Pardo de Zela, *Plan de señales para el uso de la marina peruana arreglado por los Capitanes de Navíos graduados . . . y mandado observar por supremo decreto de 12 de diciembre de 1871*, 2 vols. (Lima, 1872), cited in Basadre, *Bases documentales* 1:419.

89. F. Parker, *Táctica naval;* the Chilean version is *Táctica de escuadras*.

90. Rochelle, *Tucker*, 59; Elcorrobarrutia to Tucker, Sept. 26, 1866, Dirección de Marina, 1866–1867, lc 126, AMNP.

91. Tucker to Bustamante, Oct. 25, 1866, Corbeta "Unión," CGEA, AMNP; "Reglamento para la escuela de marineros," in San Cristóval, *Pardo y Lavalle*, 445–55.

Chapter Six: Old Battles Rejoined

1. Tucker to Barreda, Nov. 10, 1866, Prado to Barreda, Nov. 26, 1866, Barreda Papers; Thomson to Stanley, Nov. 16, 1866, FO 16/141, GBFOGC, Chile, PROUK; Lira to Errázuriz, Dec. 7, 1866, Correspondencia de la Comandancia General de Marina (anexo), 1860–1868, vol. 171, MM, ANCh.

2. Prado to Barreda, Nov. 14, 1866, Pacheco to Barreda, Nov. 21, 27, 1866, Pacheco to Barreda, Dec. 13 [i.e., Jan. 13], 1867, Barreda Papers; Prado to Tucker, Jan. 26, 1867, folder 8, Tucker Papers, ODU; J. Pardo to Pacheco, Jan. 5, 9, 23, 1867, Correspondencia de la legación peruana en Chile y el MREP en 1867, tomo 4A, 1867, AGMREP.

3. Thomson to Stanley, Nov. 1, Dec. 2, 1866, FO 16/141, GBFOGC, Chile,

PROUK; *El Mercurio*, Oct. 17, 18, 1866, Jan. 1, 4, 7, 9, 1867.

4. Thomson to Stanley, Oct. 9, Nov. 1, Dec. 16, 1866, FO 16/141, GBFOGC, Chile, PROUK; *El Mercurio*, Oct. 24, 1866; Pacheco to Barreda, Nov. 27, 1866, Jan. 27, Feb. 13, 1867, Barreda Papers; J. Pardo to Pacheco, Jan. 16, 23, Feb. 6, 1867, Correspondencia de la legación peruana en Chile y el MREP en 1867, tomo 4A, 1867, AGMREP; Wagner de Reyna, *Relaciones diplomáticas*, 217–52.

5. Vicuña MacKenna to Covarrubias, July 26, 1866, Misión confidencial, vol. 127, MRE, ANCh; Prado to Barreda, Aug. 9, 13, 1866; Basadre, *Historia* 4:1571, 1623, 1631–33, 1636–37, 1653–54.

6. Tejeda to Barreda, Oct. 13, 1866,

Pacheco to Barreda, Oct. 15, 1866, Feb. 13, 1867, Barreda Papers; Basadre, *Historia* 4:1613, 1637–38, 1646–50, 1664.

7. Martínez to Covarrubias, Aug. 20, 22, Sept. 1, 1866, Ajentes de Chile en Perú, 1866, vol. 88, AMRECh; Bustamante to Torrico, Aug. 17, 1866, Torrico, "Conclusión fiscal," Oct. 5, 1866, in García y García, *Defenza del Capitán García*, apps. 5 and 15; Melo, *Marina del Perú* 2:50; Basadre, *Historia* 4:1626; Butts, "American Officers," 154.

8. Lira to Errázuriz, Oct. 2, 1866, Correspondencia de la Comandancia General de Marina (II), 1866, vol. 236, MM, ANCh; Butts, "American Officers," 154; *El Araucano* (Santiago), Oct. 4, 1866; *El Nacional*, Oct. 11, 20, 1866.

9. *El Mercurio*, Oct. 3, Dec. 28, 1866; Tucker to Bustamante, Oct. 10, 25, 1866, Corbeta "Unión," CGEA, AMNP; Pardo de Zela to M. Pardo, Oct. 10, 1866, Werlich Collection; Bustamante to Tucker, Oct. 11 (two letters), 25, 1866, Feb. 1, 1867, Dirección de Marina, 1866–1867, lc 126, AMNP; Butts, "American Officers," 154.

10. *El Nacional*, Oct. 11, 1866; Prado to Barreda, Oct. 12, 21, 28, Nov. 26, 1866, Pacheco to Barreda, Oct. 15, 1866, Barreda Papers; Thomson to Stanley, Nov. 29, 1866, FO 16/141, GBFOGC, Chile, PROUK.

11. *El Mercurio*, Jan. 3, 1867; Basadre, *Historia* 4:1626.

12. Bustamante to Torrico, Aug. 17, 1866, in García y García, *Defenza del Capitán García*, app. 5, and pp. 6–8, 24–28, 31–32.

13. Ibid., 5, 6, 12. García's defense of his brother was published in *El Mercurio*, Feb. 20–21, 1867; the same newspaper printed Luis Mesones's brief for Montero on Feb. 16 and Manuel Ortiz de Zevallos's defense of Ferreyros on Feb. 18, 1867.

14. García y García, *Defenza del Capitán García*, 10–12, 15, and apps. 1 and 2.

15. Echenique, *Memorias* 1:282–83, 370 n. 21; *El Mercurio*, Feb. 22, 1867.

16. Stanly to Pearson, Oct. 16, 1866 (enclosed with Hovey to Seward, Nov. 4, 1866), USDS, Despatches from Peru, T52/21, RG 59, NAUS.

17. Pearson to Hovey, Oct. 25, 1866, Pac. and S. Pac. Sq., Pearson, 1866, Squadron Letters, RG 45, NAUS.

18. Tucker to Pacheco, Nov. 8, 1866 (enclosed with Tucker to Barreda, Nov. 10, 1866), Barreda Papers; [Hunter] D[avidson] to the *New York World*, undated clipping with Davidson to R. D. Minor, July 3, 1867, Minor Family Papers.

19. Career synopsis, Fabius Stanly folder, ZB File, NHCUS; *Naval Encyclopedia*, 771–72; Pearson to Welles, Oct. 27, 1866, Pac. and S. Pac. Sq., Pearson, 1866, Squadron Letters, RG 45, NAUS; Dahlgren to Welles, Feb. 20, 1867, S. Pac. Sq., Dahlgren, 1866–67, ibid.; U.S. House, *Court-Martial of Fabius Stanly;* Dobbin to Shubrick et al., June 20, 1855, Shubrick to Dobbin, July 26, 1855 (with enclosures), in U.S. Navy, *Report of the Secretary* [1855], 32–35, 40; Blanche Kell to N. C. Munroe [1860], Kell Papers.

20. Tucker to Pacheco, Nov. 8, 1866 (enclosed with Tucker to Barreda, Nov. 10, 1866), Barreda Papers; Semmes, *Memoirs*, 72.

21. Kilpatrick to Dahlgren, Feb. 15, 1867 (enclosed with Kilpatrick to Seward, Feb. 16, 1867), USDS, Despatches from Chile, M10/24, RG 59, NAUS; Stanly to Pearson, Oct. 16, 1866 (enclosed with Hovey to Seward, Nov. 14, 1866), USDS, Despatches from Peru, T52/21, ibid.

22. Pearson to Hovey, Oct. 25, 1866, Pac. and S. Pac. Sq., Pearson, 1866, Squadron Letters, RG 45, NAUS.

23. Tucker to Barreda, Nov. 10, 1866, and enclosed Tucker to Pacheco, Nov. 8, 1866, Barreda Papers.

24. Kilpatrick to Dahlgren, Feb. 15, 1867 (enclosed with Kilpatrick to Seward, Feb. 16, 1867), USDS, Despatches from Chile, M10/24, RG 59, NAUS.

25. Barrenechea to Hovey, Oct. 27, 1866 (enclosed with Hovey to Seward, Nov. 14, 1866), Pacheco to Hovey, Nov. 23, 1866, and Hovey to Pacheco, Nov. 26, 1866 (both enclosed with Hovey to Seward, Nov. 28, 1866), USDS, Despatches from Peru, T52/21, RG 59, NAUS; Pearson to Welles, Aug. 27, 1866, Pac. and S. Pac. Sq., Pearson, 1866, Squadron Letters, RG 45, NAUS.

26. J. Dahlgren, *U. Dahlgren*, esp.

204–66; J. Dahlgren Diary, Oct. 16, 30, Nov. 5, 1866. V. Jones, *Eight Hours*, 136–41, and Riggs, "Dahlgren Papers Reconsidered," 658–68, argue convincingly that the controversial documents were bona fide.

27. J. Dahlgren Diary, Sept. 27, 29, Oct. 5, Nov. 8, 1866; M. Dahlgren, *J. A. Dahlgren*, 619–28.

28. J. Dahlgren Diary, Oct. 12, Nov. 15, 1866.

29. Hovey to Seward, Aug. 21, 1866, Mar. 22, 1867, USDS, Despatches from Peru, T52/21, RG 59, NAUS; Kilpatrick to Seward, Oct. 2, 1866, USDS, Despatches from Chile, M10/24, ibid.; Pearson to Welles, Aug. 21, 1866, Pac. and S. Pac. Sq., Pearson, 1866, Squadron Letters, RG 45, NAUS.

30. J. Dahlgren Diary, Jan. 10, 1867; Dahlgren to Welles, Oct. 12, 1866, letter book no. 1, box 17, General Correspondence Letter Books, South Pacific Squadron, September 1866–April 1868, J. Dahlgren Papers, Library of Congress. At Charleston, Dahlgren addressed Confederate army officials when he needed to communicate with the enemy; see *ORN*, 1st ser., 14:421–27.

31. Welles to Seward, Oct. 18, 1866, Navy Letters to the President and Executive Agencies, M472/11, RG 45, NAUS.

32. "Memorandum of a Conversation between Mr. Seward and Mr. Barreda," USDS, Notes from Peruvian Legation, T802/3, RG 59, NAUS; Cortada, "Diplomatic Rivalry," 54–55; Barrenechea to Barreda, Nov. 13, 1866, Prado to Barreda, Nov. 14, 1866, Barreda Papers.

33. Barreda to Seward, Oct. 26, 1866, Notes from Peruvian Legation, T802/3, USDS, RG 59, NAUS.

34. Asta Buraga to Covarrubias, Oct. 31, 1866, Legación de Chile en los Estados Unidos de N. América, 1866–1867, vol. 134, MRE, ANCh; J. Dahlgren Diary, Nov. 15, 22, 1866.

35. J. Dahlgren Diary, Nov. 22, 1866; Barreda to Pacheco, Nov. 30, 1866, Barreda Papers, 6:203r–205r; Welles to Dahlgren, Nov. 21, 1866, Navy Letters to Officers, M149/84, RG 45, NAUS.

36. J. Dahlgren Diary, Dec. 1, 23, 25, 1866, Jan. 2, 8, 1867; Hovey to Dahlgren, Jan. 9, 1867 (enclosed with Hovey to Seward, Jan. 14, 1867), USDS, Des-patches from Peru, T52/21, RG 59, NAUS.

37. Hovey to Dahlgren, Jan. 9, 1867, Dahlgren to Hovey, Jan. 11, 1867 (enclosed with Hovey to Seward, Jan. 14, 1867), USDS, Despatches from Peru, T52/21, RG 59, NAUS; *DAB*, s.v. "Hovey, Alvin Peterson"; J. Dahlgren, *Maritime International Law*, 11, 120; J. Dahlgren Diary, Jan. 8, 13, 1867.

38. J. Dahlgren Diary, Jan. 8, 9, 1867; Dahlgren to Welles, Dec. 27, 1866, S. Pac. Sq., Dahlgren, 1866–67, Squadron Letters, RG 45, NAUS; Dahlgren to Welles, Jan. 11, 1867, letter book no. 1, box 17, General Correspondence Letter Books, South Pacific Squadron, September 1866–April 1868, J. Dahlgren Papers, Library of Congress. Dahlgren's actual order to Thompson has not been located; that quoted was an identical instruction to Cmdr. Pendergrast on Jan. 14, 1867, Copy of Letters and Genl. Orders, from Sept. 28, 1866, to Mar. 1, 1867, J. Dahlgren Papers, Library of Congress.

39. Dahlgren to Hovey, Jan. 11, 1867 (enclosed with Hovey to Seward, Jan. 14, 1867), USDS, Despatches from Peru, T52/21, RG 59, NAUS.

40. D[avidson] to the *New York World*, clipping enclosed with Davidson to R. D. Minor, July 13, 1867, Minor Family Papers; M. Dahlgren, "Biographical Sketch of the Author," in J. Dahlgren, *Maritime International Law*, 18.

41. Tucker to Bustamante, Jan. 24, 1867, Tucker Papers, Pensacola; J. Pardo to Pacheco, Feb. 2, 1867, Correspondencia de la legación peruana en Chile y el MREP en 1867, tomo 4A, año 1867, AGMREP; J. Dahlgren Diary, Feb. 3, 5, 1867.

42. Pacheco to Hovey, Feb. 4, 1867, Dahlgren to Hovey, Feb. 8, 1867 (enclosed with Hovey to Seward, Feb. 22, 1867), USDS, Despatches from Peru, T52/21, RG 59, NAUS; J. Dahlgren Diary, Feb. 5, 6, 7, 1867.

43. Hovey to Pacheco, Feb. 8, 1867, Pacheco to Hovey, Feb. 8, 1867, Dahlgren to Hovey, Feb. 16, 1867 (all three enclosed with Hovey to Seward, Feb. 22, 1867), USDS, Despatches from Peru, T52/21, RG 59, NAUS. A new breach of

etiquette reported by Dahlgren probably was unintentioned.

44. Barreda to Pacheco (private), Dec. 9, 1866, Jan. 19, 1867, Barreda Papers, 6:235v, 441v; Barreda to Pacheco, Dec. 9, 1866, Oficios de la Legación del Perú en los Estados Unidos de América dirigidos a Lima, 1866, segundo semestre, carpeta 5–3, AGMREP.

45. Pacheco to J. Pardo, Jan. 19, 1867, Comunicaciones de la cancillería peruana a la Legación del Perú en Chile entre los años 1866 y 1878, tomo 89A, AGMREP; J. Pardo to Pacheco, Feb. 2, 1867, Correspondencia de la legación peruana en Chile y el MREP en 1867, tomo 4A, AGMREP; *DAB*, s.v. "Kilpatrick, Hugh Judson"; Vicuña MacKenna to Covarrubias, Dec. 20, 1865, Misión confidencial, vol. 127, MRE, ANCh.

46. J. Pardo to Pacheco, Feb. 15, 1867, Correspondencia de la legación peruana en Chile y el MREP en 1867, tomo 4A, AGMREP; Kilpatrick to Seward, Feb. 16, 1867, and enclosed Kilpatrick to Dahlgren, Feb. 15, 1867, USDS, Despatches from Chile, M10/24, RG 59, NAUS.

47. J. Dahlgren Diary, Feb. 12, 18, 1867; Pacheco to Barreda, [Jan. 13, 1867], Barreda Papers.

48. V. Jones, *Eight Hours*, 128–29; J. Dahlgren Diary, Feb. 22, 24, 1867; Dahlgren to Welles, Feb. 26, 1867, Dahlgren to Kilpatrick, Mar. 5, 1867, S. Pac. Sq., Dahlgren, 1866–67, Squadron Letters, RG 45, NAUS; *El Mercurio*, Feb. 23, 1867.

49. Welles, *Diary* 3:37, 66, 71; Welles to Seward, Feb. 9, 1867, Navy Letters to the President and Executive Agencies, M472/11, RG 45, NAUS; Barreda to Prado, Feb. 19, 1867, Barreda to A. B. Medina, Mar. 6, 1867, Barreda Papers, 6:573r, 609v–607v.

50. Seward to Hovey, Mar. 18, 1867, USDS, Diplomatic Instructions, M77/31, RG 59, NAUS; Welles to Dahlgren, Mar. 18, 25, 1867, J. Dahlgren Letter Book, 1867, New York Public Library.

51. Rochelle, *Tucker*, 60; Távara, *Viaje de Lima a Iquitos*, 4; Butts, "American Officers," 154.

52. *El Mercurio*, Mar. 30, Apr. 3, 1867; Thomson to Stanley, Mar. 25, 1867,

FO 16/149A, GBFOGC, Chile, PROUK; J. Dahlgren Diary, Mar. 16, 1867.

53. See Wagner de Reyna, *Relaciones diplomáticas*, 303; M. Dahlgren, *J.A. Dahlgren*, 630.

54. Butts, "American Officers," 154; Tucker to Prado, Mar. 15, 1867, in *El Mercurio*, Apr. 12, 1867. No manuscript copy of the latter, the official resignation accepted by President Prado, has been located. The other version is Tucker to Prado, Mar. 22, 1867 (enclosed with Tucker to Pérez, Mar. 22, 1867), Escuadra Aliada, 1865–1870, vol. 230, MM, ANCh.

55. Prado to Tucker, Jan. 26, 1867, folder 8, Tucker Papers, ODU; J. Pardo to Pacheco, Jan. 16, 23, Feb. 1, 1867, Correspondencia de la legación peruana en Chile y el MREP en 1867, tomo 4A, 1867, AGMREP; Wagner de Reyna, *Relaciones diplomáticas*, 302.

56. J. Pardo to Pacheco, Feb. 1, 6, 1867, Correspondencia de la legación peruana en Chile y el MREP en 1867, tomo 4A, 1867, AGMREP; *El Mercurio*, Feb. 25, 1867.

57. Tucker to Minister of Marine, Feb. 23, 1867, Escuadra Aliada, 1865–1870, vol. 230, MM, ANCh; *El Mercurio*, Feb. 20–23, 1867, and an undated "February [1867] supplement" to the same newspaper.

58. Prado to Barreda, Feb. 21, 1867, Barreda Papers; Palma, *Semblanzas*, 47; Perú, Congreso Constituyente de 1867, *Diario de los debates* 1:41.

59. J. Pardo to Ministro de Relaciones Exteriores, Mar. 2, 11, 1867, Correspondencia de la legación peruana en Chile y el MREP en 1867, tomo 4A, 1867, AGMREP; J. Dahlgren Diary, Feb. 12, 1867; Prado to Barreda, Mar. 14, 1867, Barreda Papers.

60. Hovey to Seward, Mar. 22, 1867, USDS, Despatches from Peru, T52/21, RG 59, NAUS; J. Dahlgren Diary, Mar. 16, 27, 1867.

61. Tucker to Prado, Mar. 15, 1867, in *El Mercurio*, Apr. 12, 1867.

62. J. Dahlgren Diary, Mar. 27, 1867; Prado to Tucker, Mar. 26, 1867, folder 8, Tucker Papers, ODU.

63. Prado to Barreda, Feb. 21, 1867, Barreda Papers.

64. Tucker to Pérez, Mar. 22, 1867, and enclosed Tucker to Prado, Mar. 22, 1867, Escuadra Aliada, 1865–1870, vol. 230, MM, ANCh.

65. Galt Diary, 2:6; McCorkle to Davis, June 12, 1867, Davis Papers.

66. Tucker to Sister [Honoria], Apr. 14, 1867, Tucker Papers, Pensacola.

67. J. Dahlgren Diary, Apr. 2, and [May 2?], 1867; Seward to Hovey, Mar. 18, 1867, USDS, Diplomatic Instructions, M77/31, RG 59, NAUS; J. Dahlgren, *Maritime International Law*, 125.

68. Paredes to Medina, Apr. 20, 1867, Comunicaciones cursadas entre la Legación del Perú en los Estados Unidos de América y la cancillería peruana en 1866 y 1867, tomo 107A, años 1866–1880, AGMREP; Medina to Paredes, May 20, 1867, Oficios de la Legación del Perú en los Estados Unidos de América dirigidos a Lima, 1866 [*sic*], segundo semestre, carpeta 5–3, AGMREP.

69. Tucker to Sister [Honoria], Apr. 14, 1867, Tucker Papers, Pensacola; J. Pardo to Tucker, Mar. 29, 1867, Powell to Tucker, Mar. 20 [1867], folders 8, 17, Tucker Papers, ODU; Butts, "American Officers," 154.

70. Prado to Tucker, Mar. 26, 1867, Bustamante to Tucker, Apr. 2, 1867, folder 8, Tucker Papers, ODU; resolución suprema no. 1740, Apr. 2, 1867, Resoluciones supremas desde el 22–11–65 hasta 1867, lc C40, AHMP; Tucker to Sister [Honoria], Apr. 14, 1867, Tucker Papers, Pensacola.

Chapter Seven: Commission in the Wilderness

1. Tucker to Randy, Sept. 3, 1866, July 28, 1867, Tucker to Sister [Honoria], Apr. 14, 1867, Tucker Papers, Pensacola; J. Dahlgren Diary, Apr. 24, 1867.

2. Paz Soldán, *Atlas*, 31, gives the area of Peru as 1,605,742 sq. km. (619,816 sq. mi.).

3. The following survey of Amazonian Peru is based primarily on Werlich, "Peruvian Montaña." See also Romero Pintado, *Historia marítima, 1850–70* 3:21–65 about the history of exploration there.

4. Dozier, "Path Finder of the Amazon," 554–67.

5. Catlin, *Episodes*, 56–71. The editor apparently confused Peru's Pampa del Sacramento (the region between the Ucayali and Huallaga rivers) with the Argentine Pampas; consequently, several Peruvian illustrations are misplaced within this volume.

6. The Arana expedition map, "Carta de navegación de los ríos Ucayali y Pachitea, realizada en los años 1866 y 1867," is reproduced in Romero Pintado, *Historia marítima, 1850–70* 3:186–194. Romero (3:185) believes it to have been drawn by Lt. Eduardo Raygada, who commanded the steamer *Morona* during that voyage. But Arana himself reported that it was prepared by the officers of the expedition and Father Vicente Calvo, who accompanied them (Arana to MGM, Mar. 11, 1867, in Arana, *De Lima al Amazonas vía Mayro*, 21).

7. The Tucker Papers, ODU, folder 42, has a copy of this map detached from Herndon, *Valley of the Amazon*.

8. Alzamora to Director de Marina, Jan. 25, 1867, Comandancia General de Loreto, Departamento de Marina, situación del departamento, AMNP.

9. The Nov. 4, 1868, instructions to the prefect are copied in an endorsement to J. Lino Olaria to Ministro de Gobierno, Sept. 30, 1869, Prefectura de Loreto, 1869, OL496–1129, Archivo de Hacienda, AGNP; Gálvez to CGL, Feb. 5, 1866, Correspondencia de la Marina, 1865–66, lc L101, AHMP; *El Mercurio*, December 1866 supplement.

10. Werlich, "Peruvian Montaña," 340–41; Raimondi, *Apuntes sobre Loreto*, 97–109, 122–29, 136–41; Paz Soldán to CGL, Mar. 24, 1870, DFL, 1868–1872, lc 127, AMNP.

11. In response to an attack against Commandant General Alzamora signed "The Truth" and published in Moyobamba, the *comandante*'s secretary, F. Fernández, published *El progreso del apostadero de Iquitos*, defending Alzamora and pillorying the officials at Moyobamba. Viewing such reports with "profound displeasure," Prado ordered

an investigation. See MGM to CGL, May 24, 1866, Correspondencia de la Marina, 1865–1866, lc L101, AHMP.

12. CGL to Director de Marina, Jan. 25, 1867, Comandancia General de Loreto, Departamento de Loreto, situación del departamento, AMNP; CGL (Carreño) to MGM, Jan. 29, 1873, Comandancia General del DFL, DML, AMNP; Fernández, *Progreso de Iquitos*, 29–30.

13. Prado, decreto supremo, May 25, 1867, Decretos supremos, mayo, 0.1867.1, AHMP; Távara, *Viaje de Lima a Iquitos*, 3–4; J. Dahlgren Diary, Feb. 14, 1867; Galt Diary, 2:193, 204, and "The performers are," in the folder accompanying the Galt Diary; see also the personnel records in Timiteo Smith, Expediente personal, Expedientes personales, letra S, Archivo Central del Ministerio de Guerra, Lima.

14. Távara, *Viaje de Lima a Iquitos*, 3; Mould Távara, *Távara;* Valdizán Gamio, *Tradiciones navales*, 141–47.

15. Elcorrobarrutia to Tucker, June 8, 1867, Dirección de Marina, 1866–1867, lc 126, AMNP; Ida Werthemann de Pérez Cornejo to Werlich, Sept. 2, Dec. 10, 1985; *La crónica* (Lima), Mar. 27, 1921, and unidentified newspaper clippings in the Werthemann Collection; Galt Diary, 2:159. In Peru, Wertheman hispanicized his name with a single final *n*. Lima's Museo Antonio Raimondi has a photo portrait.

16. Elcorrobarrutia to Tucker, May 29, June 3, 1867, Dirección de Marina, 1866–1867, lc 126, AMNP; Orton, *Andes and Amazon*, 233 (unless otherwise indicated, all references are to the 3d edition); Herrera, *Leyendas y tradiciones de Loreto*, 324; Regal, *Castilla constructor*, 28–30.

17. Pavletich, *Prado*, 29–53; M. I. Prado to Tucker, July 22, 1867, folder 8, Tucker Papers, ODU.

18. Vicuña originally hired young Tucker in December 1865 to inspect ships he hoped to acquire in the United States. Norris was a nephew of Cuban exile leader Juan Manuel Macías, who conspired with Vicuña to liberate the Spanish island colony. A native Georgian and a graduate of the Confederate States Naval Academy, Lt. Norris had served under Tucker at Charleston and was wounded at Sayler's Creek (Vicuña MacKenna to Covarrubias, Jan. 30, 1866, Misión confidencial, vol. 127, MRE, ANCh; U.S. Navy, *Register of the Confederate Navy*, 141).

19. Vicuña MacKenna to Covarrubias, July 12, 1866, Misión confidencial, vol. 127, MRE, ANCh; Lira to Ministro de Marina, Nov. 9, 1866, Correspondencia de la Comandancia General de Marina (II), 1866, vol. 236, MM, ANCh; Fish to Williamson, Jan. 8, 1877, USDS, Diplomatic Instructions, M77/36, RG 59, NAUS; Meiggs to J. H. Tomb, May 23, 1867, Tomb Papers; Tucker to Randy, June 19, 1867, Tucker Papers, Pensacola.

20. Elcorrobarrutia to Tucker, May 27, June 8, 1867, Dirección de Marina, 1866–1867, lc 126, AMNP; Távara, *Viaje de Lima a Iquitos*, 5–6; Lansdale to Wise, July 24, 1867, Wise Letters.

21. Távara, *Viaje de Lima a Iquitos*, 5–8; Elcorrobarrutia to Tucker, June 8, 1867 (two letters), Dirección de Marina, 1866–1867, lc 126, AMNP; Prado, resolución suprema no. 259, June 8, 1867, Resoluciones supremas desde el 22–11–1865 hasta 1867, lc C40, AHMP; Tucker to Ran, July 28, 1867, Tucker Papers, Pensacola.

22. Tschudi, *Travels in Peru*, 193.

23. Távara, *Viaje de Lima a Iquitos*, 8–15; Werlich, "Peruvian Montaña," 154–55; Prado to Tucker, July 22, 1867, folder 8, Tucker Papers, ODU.

24. Werlich, "Peruvian Montaña," 208, 235, 237, 280–83; Raygada to CGL, Feb. 16, 1867, in Raygada, *Departamento de Loreto*, 13–27; Dávila to Ministro de Gobierno, Mar. 25, 1867 (with enclosures), Prefectura de la Provincia Litoral de Huánuco, 0.1867.3, AHMP; Sandi to Director de Guerra y Marina, May 2, 1866 (enclosed with Sandi to Comandante General de Marina, May 24, 1868), Correspondencia general, 0.1868.8, AHMP.

25. Saavedra to MGM, June 14, 1867, Ministerio de Gobierno, junio, 0.1867.1, AHMP; Távara, *Viaje de Lima a Iquitos*, 16–23; CGL to Raygada, June 22, 1867, Raygada to CGL, Oct. 4, 1867, in Raygada, *Departamento de Loreto*, 10–12, 27–33; Werlich, "Peruvian Montaña," 328–37.

NOTES

26. Távara, *Viaje de Lima a Iquitos*, 23–36; Raygada to Mayor de Ordenes, Feb. 16, 1867, Raygada to CGL, Oct. 4, 1867, in Raygada, *Departamento de Loreto*, 17–18, 31–33.

27. Távara, *Viaje de Lima a Iquitos*, 44–46, 80; Orton, *Andes and Amazon*, 380; Fernández, *Progreso de Iquitos*, 10–11, 22–23; Mattos, *Diccionário de Loreto*, 88–89; Charon, *Estado comercial*, 33; CGL to Director de Marina, Jan. 25, 1867, Comandancia General de Loreto, Departamento de Marina, situación del departamento, AMNP; CGL to Director de Marina, Dec. 3, 1867, Comandancia General del DFL, diciembre, 0.1867.4, AHMP; Rosas, Extracto de las noticias . . . para la formación de la estadística de la república, copy inserted in Galt Diary, 2: facing p. 198.

28. Távara, *Viaje de Lima a Iquitos*, 45; Orton, *Andes and Amazon*, 380; Fernández, *Progreso de Iquitos*, 10–11; Tavares Bastos, *Valle do Amazonas*, 204; Valdizán Gamio, *Tradiciones navales*, 126–34.

29. Fernández, *Progreso de Iquitos*, 23–27; Orton, *Andes and Amazon*, 380–81; CGL to Director de Marina, Jan. 25, 1867, Comandancia General de Loreto, Departamento de Marina, situación del departamento, AMNP.

30. Orton, *Andes and Amazon*, 381; Fernández, *Progreso de Iquitos*, 18, 23–27; Dávila to CGL, June 8, 1868, Comandancia General de Loreto, DML, AMNP.

31. Fernández, *Progreso de Iquitos*, 68–69, 74–75; CGL to Director de Marina, Jan. 25, 1867, Comandancia General de Loreto, Departamento de Marina, situación del departamento, AMNP.

32. Fernández, *Progreso de Iquitos*, 5–12, 52–56; CGL to Director de Marina, Jan. 25, 1867, and enclosures 1–4, Comandancia General de Loreto, Departamento de Marina, situación del departamento, AMNP; see also Romero Pintado, *Historia marítima, 1850–70* 3:122–31. Alzamora's service record, dated July 31, 1873, is in Fojas de servicio de oficiales, A, 1869 a 1877, AMNP.

33. Orton, *Andes and Amazon*, 381–82; Charon, *Estado comercial*, 23; Távara, *Viaje de Lima a Iquitos*, 45–46; Howell to CGL, Sept. 9, 1867 (enclosed with CGL to Director de Marina, Sept.

20, 1867), Comandancia General del DFL, obras, AMNP; Galt to J. M. Cloyd, Mar. 16, 1872, Cloyd Papers.

34. Tucker to Ran, Jan. 13, Feb. 16, Apr. 11, Aug. 16, Nov. 16, 1868, Tucker Papers, Pensacola. Jack and Norris again became sailors of fortune, participating in the ill-fated *Mary Lowell* expedition to Cuba in January and February 1869.

35. Elcorrobarrutia to Tucker, Aug. 23, Oct. 10, 1867, Dirección de Marina, 1866–1867, lc 126, AMNP; Prado to Tucker, Aug. 26, 1867, folder 8, Tucker Papers, ODU.

36. CGL to Director de Marina, Jan. 25, 1867, Comandancia General de Loreto, Departamento de Marina, situación del departamento, AMNP; Fernández, *Progreso de Iquitos*, 35–39.

37. CGL to Director de Marina, Oct. 17, 1867, CHA, Comandancia del DFL, AMNP; CGL to Director de Marina, Dec. 23, 1867 (nos. 151–52), Comandancia General del DFL, 0.1867.4, AHMP; Tucker to Director de Marina, Jan. 31, Aug. 30, 1868, CHA, Comisaria de Marina, AMNP; Charon to CGL, Mar. 20, 1868 (enclosed with CGL to MGM, Mar. 30, 1868), Capitanía del puerto de San Antonio de la Frontera, Comandancia del DFL, AMNP; Faura Gaig, *Ríos de la Amazonia*, 93–96; Mattos, *Diccionário de Loreto*, 83–84, 97–98; Távara, *Viaje de Lima a Iquitos*, 40; Fernández, *Progreso de Iquitos*, 35–39.

38. CGL to Director de Marina, Nov. 19, 1867, Comandancia General de Loreto, vapor "Napo," AMNP; Charon to Tucker, Nov. 17, 1867, and Charon to CGL, Nov. 21, 1867 (both enclosed with CGL to Director de Marina, Nov. 25, 1867), Capitanía del fuerte de San Antonio de la Frontera, Comandancia del DFL, AMNP (note the endorsement on the latter dispatch); Director de Marina to CGL, undated, DFL, 1868–1872, lc 127, AMNP; Charon to CGL, July 12, 1868 (enclosed with CGL to MGM, Oct. 28, 1868), Capitanía del puerto de San Antonio de la Frontera, Comandancia del DFL, AMNP.

39. Galt Diary, 1:296, and Galt's description of "Señora Johnston" in "The performers are," in Galt Diary folder; Herrera, *Leyendas y tradiciones de Loreto*, 323–24. Despite Charon's heroic

302

efforts, Leticia married merchant Alexander Johnston.

40. DeLeon, *Four Years in Rebel Capitals*, 23–24. Family tradition holds that Rochelle named the port for his niece; but, of course, the place had been christened three years before Rochelle reached Peru. See Parramore, *Southampton County*, 195, 261; Nurney, "Two Letitias." The latter item (in folder 39, Tucker Papers, ODU) has a portrait of Letitia Tyler Shands.

41. Werlich, *Peru*, 169–71, 198–99, 201–2.

42. Moreyra Paz-Soldán, *Rouaud y Paz-Soldán*, 18–32; CGL to Director de Marina, Nov. 23, 1866, Comandancia General de Marina del DFL, 0.1866.4, AHMP; CGL to Director de Marina, Dec. 30, 1867, Comandancia General del DFL, 0.1867.4, AHMP; Rochelle, *Tucker*, 76; Paz Soldán, *Atlas*, plates 1, 53–54; Tucker to MGM, June 16, 1868, CHA, Comisaria de Marina, AMNP. The error also had been discovered early in 1867 by the boundary commission, but this apparently was not known until after Tucker left Lima, where the boundary commission's report was published during the second half of 1867 (Rouaud i Paz-Soldán to Carrasco, Feb. 5, 1867, *CDL* 2:330–49).

43. Tucker to MGM, Jan. 31, Aug. 30, 1868, CHA, Comisaria de Marina, AMNP; Tucker to Randy, Aug. 16, 1868, Tucker Papers, Pensacola.

44. U.S. Navy, *American Practical Navigator*, chaps. 1–2; Cotter, *Astronomical and Mathematical Foundations*, 119–71; Romero Pintado, *Historia marítima, 1850–70* 1:78–95.

45. Wertheman, "Coordenadas geográficas," 140, 148; Cotter, *Astronomical and Mathematical Foundations*, 121; Wertheman, *Ríos Perené y Tambo*, 18–19.

46. Wertheman to Junta Central de Ingenieros del Estado, Nov. 7, 1873, in Perú, *Anales del Cuerpo de Ingenieros* 2:214–15. Rochelle, "Geographical Positions," gives the longitude of Iquitos as 73°07'34"W; Faura Gaig, *Ríos de la Amazonia*, 78, shows the same point as 73°14'39"W.

47. Odgers, *Bache*, 154–55; Wertheman, "Coordenadas geográficas," 139;

Wertheman, *Ríos Perené y Tambo*, 18; see also Rouaud i Paz-Soldán to Carrasco, Feb. 5, 1867, *CDL* 3:344–48.

48. Raimondi, *Perú* 3:464.

49. Tucker to MGM, Aug. 30, 1868, CHA, Comisaria de Marina, AMNP; CGL to MGM, Sept. 28, 1868, Comandancia General de Loreto, vapor "Napo," AMNP; lista de revista, Sept. 1868, CHA, AMNP.

50. Tucker, "Extracts from the Diary of a Voyage of Exploration Up the Rivers Ucayali, Tambo and Urubamba," Tucker Papers, Pensacola; Tucker to MGM, Nov. 16, CHA, Comisaria de Marina, AMNP; published version of Tucker's description, *CDL* 2:438–44; report of the *Napo*'s skipper, *CDL* 2:431–37; Stevenson, *Traveller of the Sixties*, 47, 51, 53–54, 56.

51. Tucker to MGM, Nov. 16, 1868, Gutiérrez to Mayor de Ordenes, Nov. 11, 1868, *CDL* 2:442–44, 436; Tucker to MGM, Aug. 30, 1868, CHA, Comisaria de Marina, AMNP; CGL to Director de Marina, Jan. 25, 1867, Comandancia General del Loreto, situación del departamento, AMNP. See also Romero Pintado, *Historia marítima, 1850–70* 3:175–76.

52. Basadre, *Historia* 4:1697, 1705, 1718–19; CGL to MGM, Feb. 21, 1868 (with enclosed manifesto), Comandancia General del DFL, DML, AMNP. A similar declaration followed the 1865 overthrow of Pezet; see Valdizán Gamio, *Historia naval* 3: facing p. 281.

53. Tucker to Randy, Feb. 16, 1868, Tucker Papers, Pensacola; Basadre, *Historia* 4:1705.

54. Diez Canseco to Tucker, June 25, 1868, folder 9, Tucker Papers, ODU.

55. Tucker to MGM, Aug. 30, Nov. 26, 1868, Tucker to CGL, Jan. 15, 1868 (enclosed with CGL to Director de Marina, Jan. 30, 1868), CHA, Comisaria de Marina, AMNP; Tucker to MGM, Jan. 15, 31, Mar. 19, 1869, CHA, 0.1869.4, AHMP; Werlich, *Peru*, 84–85; Diez Canseco to Tucker, June 25, 1868, folder 9, Tucker Papers, ODU. Similar reforms were recommended by Alzamora's chief of staff; see Vargas to MGM, Mar. 2, 1868 (enclosed with La Haza to MGM, Mar. 5, 1868), Comandancia General del DFL, DML, AMNP.

56. Pardo to Tucker, Jan. 21, 1869, Tucker-Randolph Correspondence; *El Comercio*, Mar. 20, 1868, and *El Nacional*, Jan. 2, 1869, clippings in folder 40, Tucker Papers, ODU; Basadre, *Bases documentales* 1:436; Távara, *Viaje de Lima a Iquitos*, 4.

57. MGM to CGL, Mar. 23, Jan. 28, Apr. 28, 1869, DFL, 1868–1872, lc 127, AMNP; MGM, endorsement dated Jan. 28, 1869, on Tucker to MGM, Nov. 26, 1868, CHA, Comisaria de Marina, AMNP; Tucker to Randy, Feb. 16, 1869, Tucker Papers, Pensacola; Tucker to MGM, Mar. 19, 1869, CHA, 0.1869.4, AHMP.

58. Elcorrobarrutia to Tucker, Oct. 10, 1867, Dirección de Marina, 1866–1867, lc 126, AMNP; Tucker to MGM, Jan. 31, 1868, CHA, Comisaria de Marina, AMNP; MGM to CGL, July 4, 1868, DFL, 1868–1872, lc 127, AMNP; L. Prado to Tucker, Mar. 17, 1869, Tucker to Randy, Jan. 13, 1868, Tucker Papers, Pensacola; Pavletich, *Prado*, 59.

Chapter Eight: Tribulations of the Tambo

1. Barrenechea to MGM, June 2, 1869, MRE, 0.1869.2, AHMP; C. Jones to Tucker, July 16, 1869, Tucker to sons, June 30, 1870, Tucker to Randy, Feb. 16, 1869, Tucker Papers, Pensacola. A. Royall Turpin has the spear.

2. The key documents in this voluminous correspondence are Tucker to MGM, Apr. 30, 1869, CHA, 0.1869.4, AHMP; Freyre to MGM, Aug. 26, Sept. 30, 1869, Legación del Perú en los EEUU, 0.1869.3, AHMP; MGM to Ministro de Hacienda, June 2, July 31, 1869, Correspondencia general con los dependencias de Marina, 1868, lc 127, AMNP.

3. Tucker to Freyre, July 14, 1869, Freyre Papers; Freyre to MGM, Oct. 15, Nov. 19, 1869, Legación del Perú en los EEUU de América, 0.1869.3, AHMP; Freyre to MGM, Feb. 21, Apr. 20, 1870, Legación del Perú en EEUU, 0.1870.3, AHMP; Piérola to MGM, Mar. 28, 1870, Ministerio de Hacienda, 0.1870.4, AHMP.

4. Freyre to MGM, Oct. 15, 1869, Legación del Perú en los EEUU de América, 0.1869.3, AHMP; Freyre to MGM, Oct. 28, 1869 (copy enclosed with Freyre to MGM, Feb. 13, 1872), Legación del Perú en EEUU, Expediente del costo del vapor Tambo—y de los viveres, armamentos, instrumentos que se han proporcionado, y de los pasajes dados a los miembros de la Comisión Hidrográfica hasta el Pará (hereafter cited as Expediente Tambo), 0.1872.3, AHMP; Tucker to Pardo, May 16, 1871, Werlich Collection; D. Tyler, *American Clyde*, 14, 26, 28; Pusey & Jones Corp., *Hundred Years A-Building*, 5, 7, 9–10; U.S. House, *Causes of the Reduction of American Tonnage*, 160–63; Bond to Secretary of State, Oct. 3, 1870, USDS, Consular Despatches, Para, T478/3, RG 59, NAUS.

5. MGM to Tucker, Aug. 13, 1869, Correspondencia general de los dependencias de Marina, 1868, lc 127, AMNP; Freyre to MGM, Oct. 15, 1869, Legación del Perú en los EEUU de América, 0.1869.3, AHMP. English and Spanish copies of the contract, dated Oct. 13, 1869, between Tucker and Henry J. Davison, agent for Pusey & Jones, are in Expediente Tambo, 0.1872.3, AHMP; another English copy is in folder 10, Tucker Papers, ODU. A very detailed "Ynventorio del vapor explorador 'Tambo,'" Oct. 18, 1870, accompanies CGL to MGM, Oct. 30, 1870, Comandancia General del Departamento de Loreto, vapor "Tambo," AMNP. For a brief description of the vessel, see "Informe . . . sobre el estado de la flotilla," *CDL* 2:84–85.

6. Freyre to MGM, Oct. 15, 1869, Legación del Perú en los EEUU de América, 0.1869.3, AHMP; Freyre to Tucker, Oct. 18, 1869, Freyre Papers; Freyre to MGM, Oct. 28, 1869, with Balta's endorsement, Expediente Tambo, 0.1872.3, AHMP.

7. Tucker to Freyre, Nov. 11, 1869, Feb. 11, 1870, Expediente Tambo, 0.1872.3, AHMP; Freyre to MGM, Nov. 19, Dec. 3, 21, 1869, Legación del Perú en los EEUU de América, 0.1869.3, AHMP; Freyre to MGM, Feb. 21 (two dispatches), Mar. 4, Apr. 4, 1870, Legación del Perú en EEUU, 0.1870.3, AHMP.

8. Tucker to Freyre, Mar. 26, 1870, Expediente Tambo, 0.1872.3, AHMP; Tucker to Freyre, May 24, 1870, Freyre Papers; "Informe . . . sobre el estado de la flotilla," *CDL* 3:84; Davison to Tucker, June 18, 1870 (copy enclosed with Tucker to Pardo, May 16, 1871), Werlich Collection.

9. Tucker to MGM, Nov. 1, 1869 (two letters), CHA, 0.1869.4, AHMP. The report located here is incomplete. A full version, filed under the same heading, is in 0.1869.1, AHMP.

10. Freyre to Ministro de Relaciones Exteriores, Sept. 30, 1869, extracted in Dorado to MGM, Nov. 18, 1869, MRE, 0.1869.2, AHMP; Tucker to Freyre, Oct. 29, 1869, Freyre Papers; Freyre to MGM, Nov. 19, 1869, misfiled in Legación del Perú en EEUU, 0.1870.3, AHMP; Perú, *Memoria de Guerra, 1870*, 10–11.

11. Tucker to MGM, Mar. 16, July 30, 1869, CHA, 0.1869.4, AHMP; MGM to CGL, Mar. 7, 1870, DFL, 1868–1872, lc 127, AMNP; Freyre to MGM, Apr. 20, 1870 (two letters), Legación del Perú en EEUU, 0.1870.3, AHMP; Tucker to Freyre, May 8, 24, 1870, Freyre Papers.

12. Tucker to MGM, Jan. 3, 1870, Expediente Tambo, 0.1872.3, AHMP.

13. Obituary of Galt from an unidentified newspaper, Veselka Collection; Galt genealogy, typescript, pp. 7–8, Galt Family Papers; M. Galt, "Galt Family of Williamsburg," 259–62.

14. Alumni questionnaires, Francis Land Galt biographical folder, Univ. of Pennsylvania Archives; Tyler to Bell, "Thursday morning," [April 29, 1841], John Tyler Papers; W. Powell, *List of Officers of the Army*, 322; Galt to Craig, Jan. 25, 1861, *ORA*, 1st ser., 1:323; U.S. Navy, *Registers*, 1855–61.

15. Noland to Mother, Mar. 10, 1873, box 3, Noland Family Papers; Galt to Cloyd, Mar. 16, 1872, Cloyd Papers; Carroll, *Staff Officers of the Confederate Army*, 59; Galt to Kell, Oct. 27, 1877, Kell Papers; U.S. Navy, *Register of the Confederate Navy*, 67.

16. Boykin, *Ghost Ship*, 212; Semmes, *Memoirs*, 452–53, 751.

17. Boykin, *Ghost Ship*, 274–75; Sinclair, *Two Years on the* Alabama, 306.

18. Semmes, *Memoirs*, 125, 465–66;

Delaney, *Kell*, 118, 146; Boykin, *Ghost Ship*, 212, 275.

19. Delaney, *Kell*, 161–78; Boykin, *Ghost Ship*, 355–84.

20. Delaney, *Kell*, 181–84; Mallory to Galt, Sept. 26, 1864, Lee to Galt, Oct. 7, 1864, with endorsement, Mitchell to Galt, Nov. 12, 1864, Francis Land Galt folder, ZB File, NHCUS; Sinclair, *Two Years on the* Alabama, 305; *Appomattox Roster*, 450.

21. Galt to Gerhard, Mar. 14, 1866, Society Collection, Historical Society of Pennsylvania; Galt to Kell, Oct. 27, 1877, Kell Papers; newspaper clippings, Veselka Collection. Thomas Galt of Minneapolis has the watch.

22. Norwood High School and College, *Historical Sketch*, 14; idem, *Catalogue*, 15, 18; Tucker to MGM, Jan. 30, 1870, and English and Spanish copies of Galt's contract, Expediente Tambo, 0.1872.3, AHMP.

23. Rochelle, *Tucker*, 10–14; Seager, *And Tyler Too*, 123; Tyler to Mrs. Rochelle, Sept. 14, 1841, Rochelle Papers; Rochelle, *Tucker*, 11; U.S. Navy, *Registers*, 1841–61; Rochelle to Scharf, Jan. 3, 1887, Rochelle folder, ZB File, NHCUS; Taylor, *Broad Pennant*, 400–401.

24. Rochelle to Scharf, Jan. 3, 1887, Rochelle folder, ZB File, NHCUS; Franklin, *Memoirs*, 107; McKinney, *Education in Violence*, 6–7; Mason to Mrs. Rochelle, May 15, 1846, July 10, 1848, Rochelle Papers; Rochelle to Tucker, Sept. 2, 1877, folder 23, Tucker Papers, ODU.

25. Rochelle to Scharf, Jan. 3, 12, 1887, Rochelle folder, ZB File, NHCUS; Rochelle, *Tucker*, 13–15; Rochelle to Mallory, June 8, 1863, Mitchell to Mallory, July 16, 1863, Rochelle Papers; W. Parker, *Recollections*, 350–59.

26. Rochelle to Scharf, Jan. 3, 1887, Rochelle folder, ZB File, NHCUS; Tucker to MGM, Jan. 30, 1871, Comisión Hidrográfica del Perú en Amazonas, 1871, AMNP; Freyre to Rochelle, May 15, 1871, Rochelle to Freyre, May 22, 1871, Rochelle Papers; Freyre to MGM, May 29, 1871, Rochelle-Freyre contract, June 19, 1871 (enclosed with Freyre to MGM, June 29, 1871) Legación del Perú en EEUU, 0.1871.0, AHMP.

27. Paz Soldán to Tucker, Mar. 10,

1870, Tucker to Freyre, Apr. 30, 1870 (with enclosed requisition), Freyre to MGM, May 4, 1870, Henry J. Davison, invoice of June 21, 1870, Expediente Tambo, 0.1872.3, AHMP; Wertheman to Tucker, Mar. 15, 1870, folder 10, Tucker Papers, ODU.

28. Tucker to sons, June 30, 1870, Tucker Papers, Pensacola; Tucker to Ran, Aug. 6, 1870, Tucker-Randolph Correspondence.

29. Freyre to MGM, June 20, 1870, Tucker, receipt for *Tambo* and equipment, Aug. 27, 1870, Expediente Tambo, 0.1872.3, AHMP; Tucker to Ran, Aug. 6, 1870, Tucker-Randolph Correspondence; Galt to Cloyd, Oct. 9, 1870, Cloyd Papers; Tucker to Ran, Aug. 20, 1870, Tucker Papers, Pensacola.

30. Loayza to MGM, Nov. 3, 1870, MRE, 0.1870.3, AHMP; Galt Diary, 1:56, 62, 64–65, 101, 107, 112; Tucker to MGM, Oct. 19, 1870, pp. 2–3, CHAlc.

31. Galt to Cloyd, Oct. 9, 1870, Cloyd Papers; Galt Diary, 1:197–98, 2:1–2, 17.

32. Tucker to CGL, Oct. 12, 17, 18, 1870, Tucker to MGM, Oct. 19, 1870, CHAlc, 1–3; Butt, lista de revista, Oct. 13, 1870, CHA, Comisaria de Marina, AMNP; Wertheman to Tucker, Mar. 15, 1870, folder 10, Tucker Papers, ODU.

33. Carbajal to Prefecto de Loreto, Nov. 1, 1869, Wertheman to Prefecto de Loreto, Nov. 11, 1869, *CDL* 2:466–73, 474–76; Werlich, "Peruvian Montaña," 319–20, 322–23; CGL to MGM, Oct. 30, 1870, CHA, Comisaria de Marina, AMNP; Galt Diary, 2:1.

34. Galt Diary, 2:17; Tucker to MGM, Jan. 29, 1871, *CDL* 3:71–72.

35. Valdizán Gamio, *Historia naval* 4:74–75, identifies the trader as "Romano Guilace." The official reports about this expedition and the Galt Diary do not provide Romano's given name; but he certainly was the "Bartolomé Roma, native of Italy, . . . who had great influence" over the Indians at Sarayacu, as described by José María Chávez, in *CDL* 3:88–89.

36. Galt Diary, 2:26–28, 30, 41, 103, 113; Harris to Smithsonian Institution, June 28, 1937, Galt Diary folder.

37. Galt Diary, 2:16, 29, 33, 35, 50, 52, 82–83, 103, 105, 110, 114, 125–26,

147. A portrait of Major Herrera is in the photo collection at Lima's Museo Antonio Raimondi.

38. Tucker to MGM, Jan. 29, 1871, *CDL* 3:72–75; Raygada to Mayor de Ordenes, Jan. 24, 1871, in Raygada, *Departamento de Loreto*, 41–42; Galt Diary, 2:48, 87, 95, 98, 108, 112–13, 121.

39. Tucker to MGM, Jan. 29, 1871, *CDL* 3:72–74; Tucker to Raygada, Nov. 20, 1870, Jan. 6, 1871, CHAlc, 4–5; Galt Diary, 2:50, 61, 119, 121–22, 125–26, 179 (the latter page has a drawing of the canoe used on this expedition).

40. Distances on the Tambo system calculated from Wertheman, *Ríos Perené y Tambo*, 20; Tucker to MGM, Jan. 29, 1871, *CDL* 3:73. The geographical coordinates reported by the commission are of little help in resolving the problem. The Tambo follows a nearly south–north course here, so all tributaries enter the river at about the same longitude; and the explorers were unable to obtain a good reading of the latitude from solar observations.

41. Tucker to MGM, Jan. 29, 1871, *CDL* 3:73–74; Galt Diary, 2:127–29; Tucker to Ran, May 16, 1871, Tucker Papers, Pensacola.

42. Tucker to Raygada, Jan. 13, 1871, CHAlc, 4; Tucker to MGM, Jan. 29, 1871, *CDL* 3:75, 76; Raygada to Mayor de Ordenes, Jan. 24, 1871, in Raygada, *Departamento de Loreto*, 44; Galt Diary, 2:130–31.

43. Raygada, *Departamento de Loreto*, 3–4; Tucker to MGM, Mar. 16, 1869, CHA, 0.1869.4, AHMP; MGM to Tucker, Sept. 9, 1869 (responding to Tucker's recommendation of Raygada), Raygada to Tucker, May 25, 1870, folders 9, 10, Tucker Papers, ODU. Romero Pintado, *Historia marítima, 1850–70* 3:167–77, discusses Raygada's work as an explorer.

44. Tucker to Pardo, Feb. 16, May 16, 1871, Werlich Collection; Galt Diary, 1:62.

45. Galt Diary, 2:88, 99, 168, 169, 199; Tucker to Pardo, Feb. 16, 1871, Werlich Collection; Rochelle to Tucker, Aug. 16, 1874, folder 19, Tucker Papers, ODU.

46. Tucker to MGM, Jan. 29, 1871, *CDL* 3:76; Raygada to Mayor de Or-

denes, Jan. 24, 1874, in Raygada, *Departamento de Loreto*, 39, 40, 41, 43–44.

47. CGL to MGM, Jan. 31, 1871, Comandancia General del DFL, vapor "Tambo," AMNP; CGL to MGM, Jan. 31, 1871, Apr. 29, 1869 [i.e., 1870], in Raygada, *Departamento de Loreto*, 35, 7.

48. Tucker to Pardo, Mar. 16, 1871, Werlich Collection; Elcorrobarrutia to CGL, June 7, 1868 [i.e., 1867] (enclosed with CGL to MGM, Mar. 30, 1868), CHA, Comisaria de Marina, AMNP.

49. CGL to MGM, Oct. 25, 1874, in Raygada, *Departamento de Loreto*, 8; Galt Diary, 2:152; Fernández, *Progreso de Iquitos*, 29–30.

50. "Cuadro comparativo de las claces, destinos, y sueldos de los jefes oficiales y demás empleados del Departamento Fluvial de Loreto," Jan. 27, 1869, Ministerio de Guerra y Marina, Comisaria General de Loreto, OL500–229, Archivo de Hacienda, AGNP.

51. Karsten, *Naval Aristocracy*, 63, quoting Flag Officer Louis Goldsborough; Tucker to M. Pardo, Mar. 16, 1871, Werlich Collection.

52. CGL to MGM, Apr. 30, 1871, Ministerio de Gobierno—abril, 0.1871.3, AHMP; CGL to MGM, July 31, 1871, CHA, AMNP; MGM to CGL, Mar. 24, 1870, DFL, 1868–1872, lc 127, AMNP; CGL to MGM, May 31, 1870, CHA, Comisaria de Marina, AMNP.

53. CGL to MGM, Mar. 30, 1868, May 31, 1870, CHA, Comisaria de Marina, AMNP; CGL to MGM, Jan. 31, 1871, Comandancia General del Departamento de Loreto, vapor "Tambo," AMNP; Gutiérrez to Mayor de Ordenes, Nov. 11, 1868, *CDL* 2:437. On the Sunday after the commission's return from the second expedition to the Tambo, Tucker and Galt made social calls on both Alzamora and Chief of Staff Enrique Espinar (Galt Diary, 2:141–42).

54. Bond to Secretary of State, Oct. 3, 1870, USDS, Consular Despatches, Para, T478/3, RG 59, NAUS; Tucker to Pardo, Feb. 16, May 16, 1871, Werlich Collection; MGM to CGL, Dec. 19, 1870, DFL, 1868–1872, lc 127, AMNP.

55. Tucker to CGL, Jan. 31, 1871, CHAlc, 6; CGL to Tucker, Feb. 3, 1871

(enclosed with CGL to MGM, July 31, 1871), CHA, AMNP.

56. Galt Diary, 2:159, 162, 164; Tucker to CGL, Feb. 9, CGL to Tucker, Feb. 11, 1871, CHAlc, 16. The rations were restored two days later.

57. Tucker to CGL, Feb. 27, 1871, CHAlc, 18; Galt to Cloyd, Oct. 4, 1870, Cloyd Papers; Galt Diary, 2:161, 162, 166, 169.

58. Galt Diary, 2:164; Tucker to MGM, Mar. 16, 1871 (Spanish original with endorsement), filed with CGL to MGM, Apr. 30, 1871, Ministerio de Gobierno—abril, 0.1871.3, AHMP. An English copy, in Tucker's hand, is in folder 2, Tucker Papers, ODU.

59. Tucker to Pardo, Mar. 16, 1871, Werlich Collection. McCorkle previously had difficulty obtaining his severance pay and passage (Tucker to MGM, Jan. 15, 1869, CHA, 0.1869.4, AHMP).

60. CGL to Tucker, Apr. 19, 1871 (enclosed with CGL to MGM, July 31, 1871), CHA, AMNP; CGL to MGM, Apr. 30, 1871, and enclosed copy, Tucker to CGL, Apr. 20, 1871, Ministerio de Gobierno—abril, 0.1871.3, AHMP.

61. CGL to Tucker, May 15, 1871, folder 2, Tucker Papers, ODU; CGL to MGM, May 31, 1871, Comandancia General del Departamento de Loreto, vapor "Tambo," AMNP; Tucker to Pardo, May 16, 1871, Werlich Collection; Galt Diary, 2:179.

62. Tucker to MGM, May 30, 1871, CHAlc, 22–27; Tucker to Pardo, May 16, 1871, Werlich Collection.

63. MGM to CGL, Apr. 5, 1871, DFL, 1868–1872, lc 127, AMNP; MGM to Tucker, May 4, 1871, folder 2, Tucker Papers, ODU.

64. MGM to CGL, May 10, July 24, 1871, DFL, 1868–1872, lc 127, AMNP; MGM to Tucker, July 19, 1871, folder 11, Tucker Papers, ODU.

65. CGL to MGM, July 31, 1871, CHA, AMNP.

66. Galt Diary, 2:194, 196; Tucker to CGL, July 4, 13, 1871, Tucker to Butt, July 15, 1871, CHAlc, 28, 30, 30–31; CGL to Tucker, July 5, 6, 1871, Tucker to CGL, July 6, 1871, with endorsements, folders 11, 2, Tucker Papers, ODU.

67. Ramírez, passport issued to Tucker, July 16, 1871, with endorsements of port officials, folder 2, Tucker Papers, ODU; Tucker to MGM, Sept. 4, 1871, Tucker, memorandum, Sept. 23, 1871, CHA, AMNP.

68. MGM to CGL, Aug. 2, 1871, DFL, 1868–1872, lc 127, AMNP; Pardo to Tucker, June 10, 1871, *Callao and Lima Gazette*, Nov. 22, 1871, folders 11,

39, Tucker Papers, ODU; Galt Diary, 2:221, 240.

69. MGM to Tucker, Nov. 15, 16, 1871, folder 11, Tucker Papers, ODU; MGM to CGL, Nov. 16, 1871, DFL, 1868–1872, lc 127, AMNP; MGM to Tucker, Nov. 15, 1871 (copy enclosed with CGL to MGM, Feb. 26, 1873, CHA, Comandancia del DFL), AMNP.

70. Galt Diary, 2:255, 221.

Chapter Nine: Perils of the Pichis

1. Freyre to MGM, Dec. 29, 1871, Legación del Perú en EEUU, 0.1871.1, AHMP; Freyre to MGM, Mar. 29, 1872 (two dispatches), ibid., 0.1872.3; Tucker to Ran, Aug. 10, 1872, Tucker Papers, Pensacola.

2. Freyre to MGM, Mar. 29, 1872, Legación del Perú en EEUU, 0.1872.3, AHMP; "Informe . . . sobre la flotilla peruana," *CDL* 2:86–97.

3. Noland, "Peruvian Amazon," 547. This article was extracted from a journal maintained by Noland in Peru; the manuscript original, apparently deposited with the Noland Papers, has been misplaced.

4. Rowlett and Tanner Co., Petersburg, Va., invoice of June 23, 1872, Rochelle Papers; Noland to Pa, Aug. 19, 1872, box 1, Noland Papers; Tucker to CGL, Jan. 27, 1873, Tucker to MGM, Jan. 27, July 25, 1873, CHAlc, 60, 86.

5. Freyre to Tucker, Apr. 30, 1872, folder 12, Tucker Papers, ODU; Freyre to MGM, May 29, 1872, Legación del Perú en EEUU, 0.1872.3, AHMP; copies of Tucker's contracts with Sparrow (Apr. 1, 1872) and Noland (Apr. 10, 1872) enclosed with Lee to Secretary of State, Oct. 13, 1877, USDS, Misc. Letters, M179/495, RG 59, NAUS; U.S. House, *Engineers Corps of the Army*, 8.

6. University of Virginia, *Students*, 132; Walker, *Sparrow*, 40; *DAB*, s.v. "Sparrow, William"; Hayes to Sister, Feb. 5, 1839, Hayes to Mother, Aug.—, 1839, in Hayes, *Diary and Letters* 1:28–29, 36.

7. Obituary from Alexandria, Va., Episcopal High School, *Monthly Chronicle* (Mar. 1916), clipping in T. W. Sparrow file, Student and Alumni Records; University of Virginia, *Students*, 132; Walker, *Sparrow*, 248; Bruce, *University of Virginia* 3:264–84; entries for T. W. Sparrow, Manuscript Confederate Registers, 6:429; 18:478; Alexander and Beringer, *Confederate Congress*, 23; Sparrow to Memminger, Mar. 29, 1862, Kenney to Memminger, Mar. 10, 1862, Heill to [Memminger?], June 9, 1864, and an unidentified fragment recommending Sparrow for a treasury post, in Confederate Papers Relating to Citizens, M346/968, RG 109, NAUS; entry for Thomas W. Sparrow, in Consolidated Index to Compiled Service Records of Confederate Soldiers, M253/450, ibid.; Noland to Ma, Oct. 22, 1872, box 3, Noland Papers.

8. Young, *Berkeleys of Barn Elms*, esp. 54–55, 72–73, 87–89, 110; Couper, *New Market Cadets*, 146–48; Callahan, *List of Officers of the Navy*, 408; Buchanan to Mallory, Mar. 27, 1862, *ORN*, 1st ser., 7:48.

9. Noland to Anderson, Aug. 4, 1904, N. B. Noland alumnus file; W. C. Davis, *Battle of New Market;* Couper, *New Market Cadets*, 146–47; W. C. Powell to Noland, Feb. 2, 1872, C. S. Noland to N. B. Noland, Feb. 2, 1872, box 1, Noland Papers.

10. Noland to Ma, "Thursday night" [Aug. 22–23], Aug. 24, Oct. 8–10, 1872, Noland to Pa, Aug. 19, 1872, box 3, Noland Papers.

11. Noland to Ma, Aug. 24, 30, 1872, Noland to parents, Sept. 6, 1872, Noland to Pa, Sept. 10–Oct. 5, 1872, ibid.

12. Noland to Pa, Sept. 10–Oct. 5, 1872, Noland to Frank, Oct. 6, 1872, Noland to Ma, Oct. 8–10, 22, 1872, ibid.

13. Noland to Pa, Sept. 10–Oct. 5, 1872, Feb. 13, 1873, Noland to Ma, Oct.

22–Nov. 5, 1872, Noland to Mother, Jan. 29, 1873, ibid.; Tucker to Ran, Oct. 6, 1872, Tucker Papers, Pensacola; Ríos, certificate of payment to crew, Nov. 15, 1872, Ríos to Tucker, Nov. 19, 1872, folder 12, Tucker Papers, ODU; Tucker to MGM, Jan. 30, 1873, CHAlc, 62–63.

14. Butt to Rochelle, Nov. 27, 1871, Rochelle Papers; Rochelle to Butt, Nov. 28, 1871; Rochelle to Wertheman, Dec. 16, 1871, Rochelle to CGL, Dec. 20, 1871, CHAlc, 33–34, 35; Rochelle to Brooke, Feb. 16, 1872, Brooke Papers.

15. Galt Diary, 2:240; Malinowski to Tucker, Feb. 27, 1872, folder 18, Tucker Papers, ODU; Rochelle to Meiggs, July 29, 1872, CHAlc, 47–50. A tracing of Malinowski's map, also dated Feb. 27, 1872, is in the R. Douglas Tucker Collection.

16. Galt Diary, 2:167, 176, 248–49; CGL to MGM, Oct. 31, 1872, Comandancia del DFL, DML, AMNP.

17. Basadre, *Historia* 4:1919–45; Galt Diary, 2:185, 187, 206, 209, 222, 239, 249; Espinar to CGL, Sept. 30, 1872, Comandancia del DFL, DML, AMNP.

18. Basadre, *Historia* 4:1973–78; Noland to Pa, Feb. 13, 1873, box 3, Noland Papers; MGM to CGL, Nov. 16, 1871, Feb. 14, 1872, DFL, 1868–1872, lc 127, AMNP; Galt Diary, 2:221–22.

19. Rochelle to Smith, Nov. 4, 1871, June 13, 1872, CHAlc, 33, 44; MGM to CGL, July 2, 1872, DFL, 1868–1872, lc 127, AMNP; Galt Diary, 2:169, 193–94.

20. Tucker to Mesnier, Jan. 22, 1873, Tucker to MGM, Jan. 31, 1873, CHAlc, 58–59, 65–66; Noland to Frank, Oct. 6, 1872, box 3, Noland Papers; Galt Diary, 2:193–94, 199, 222, 255. Galt labeled Mesnier a "Portuguese-Frenchman" in his description of performers at a Mar. 28, 1874 gala, in the Galt Diary folder.

21. MGM to CGL, Oct. 10, 1872, DFL, 1872–1878, lc 146, AMNP; Galt Diary, 2:1, 255, 265.

22. Enrique Carreño, foja de servicio, Feb. 28, 1874, Fojas de servicio de oficiales C, 1871 a 86, AMNP; Galt Diary, 2:263–65; Vicuña MacKenna, *Diez meses* 1:116–17.

23. Tucker to CGL, Jan. 23, 1872, Tucker to MGM, Jan. 30, 1873, CHAlc, 57–58, 62–63. A copy of the survey report is enclosed with CGL to MGM, Jan.

31, 1873, Comandancia General del DFL, vapor "Tambo," AMNP.

24. Tucker to CGL, Feb. 13, 18 (two letters), 1873, CHAlc, 68–69, 70; CGL to Tucker, Feb. 17, 1873 (no. 15, copy marked E), CHA, AMNP; CGL to Tucker, Feb. 18, 1873, CGL, Ynstrucciones que observará el comandante del vapor explorador "Mairo" en el viaje, Feb. 19, 1873, with CGL to MGM, Feb. 26, 1873, CHA, Comandancia del DFL, AMNP.

25. Tucker to MGM, Feb. 28, 1873, CHAlc, 71–73; CGL to MGM, Feb. 26, 1873, CHA, Comandancia del DFL, AMNP. Alzamora's letter of Dec. 31, 1872 (no. 115), cited by Carreño, has not been located; Lima's response is MGM to CGL, Feb. 27, 1873, DFL, 1872–1878, lc 146, AMNP.

26. MGM to CGL, Feb. 27, Apr. 21, 1873, DFL, 1872–1878, lc 146, AMNP.

27. Tucker to MGM, Feb. 28, 1873, Tucker to Captain of the *Mairo*, Feb. 16, 17, 1873, CHAlc, 71–73, 183, 188; Meza to Mayor de Ordenes, July 12, 1873, CHA, Comandancia del DFL, AMNP; Noland, "Peruvian Amazon," 545–48, 577; Noland to Bill, May 6, 1873, box 4, Noland Papers.

28. Galt Diary, 2:266–67; Tucker to MGM, Apr. 10, 1873, Tucker to CGL, Feb. 20, 1873, CHAlc, 81–82, 70–71.

29. Tucker to MGM, Apr. 10, 1873, CHAlc, 81–82; Donayre to Mayor de Ordenes, July 15, 1873, CHA, Comandancia del DFL, AMNP; Noland, "Peruvian Amazon," 546, 579. For the official report of the expedition, see Tucker to MGM, July 31, 1873, *CDL* 3:93–99, a published account copied from CHAlc, 87–95. English copies (dated July 30, 1873) are in CHA, AMNP, and folder 3, Tucker Papers, ODU.

30. Noland, "Peruvian Amazon," 621–22; Noland to Ma, May 19, 1873, box 3, Noland Papers; Galt Diary, 2:274, 279; Tucker to MGM, July 31, 1873, *CDL* 3:95; Donayre to Mayor de Ordenes, July 15, 1873, CHA, Comandancia del DFL, AMNP; Tucker to captain of the *Tambo* [Donayre], Apr. 27, May 14, 15, 1873, CHAlc, 192–91.

31. F. Galt, "Medical Notes on the Pampa del Sacramento," 402; Tucker to MGM, July 31, 1873, *CDL* 3:99. Ro-

chelle's two reports—"Posiciones geográficas" and "Distancias, elevaciones, variaciones magnéticas, y corrientes"— are included with Tucker to MGM, July 30, CHA, 1873, AMNP. Galt's meticulous "Registro meteorológico, marzo-junio, 1873," is in CHA, Comandancia General de Loreto, AMNP, and in folder 33, Tucker Papers, ODU. Galt's general report of the expedition, dated July 17, 1873, was enclosed with Tucker to MGM, July 30, 1873, CHA, AMNP, and published in *CDL* 7:365–73.

32. Noland, "Peruvian Amazon," 622–23; Tucker to MGM, July 31, 1873, *CDL* 3:95; Galt Diary, 2:280–83, 301. The latter page has Galt's sketches of several glyphs at Inca Rock, which clearly are man-made and not the "caprices of nature" suggested in Ortiz, *Pachitea*, 1:371.

33. Tucker to MGM, July 31, 1873, *CDL* 3:95–96; Noland, "Peruvian Amazon," 623, 684–85; Galt Diary, 2:283–87; Tucker to MGM, June 4, 1873, CHAlc, 82–83; Rochelle, *Tucker*, 65–66.

34. The Herrera-yacu is identified as the Chivis in Ortiz, *Pachitea* 1:371, and also by the major's son in Herrera, *Leyendas y tradiciones de Loreto*, 277, opinions probably based on the reports of surveys for the Pichis Trail in the 1890s (see Pérez, "Expedición del río Pichis," *CDL* 3:309). However, the nearly identical latitudes reported by Tucker for Puerto Tucker and Termination Beach on the Herrera-yacu (10°22′55″S and 10°22′33″) support the Azupizu as the Herrera-yacu. Raimondi's large *Mapa del Perú*, plate 17, labels the river "Azupizu or Herrera-Yacu."

35. Tucker to MGM, July 31, 1873, *CDL* 3:96–97; Noland, "Peruvian Amazon," 685–86, 721–22; Rochelle, *Tucker*, 66. The distances traveled during the expedition are given in Rochelle, "Distancias, elevaciones, variaciones magnéticas, y corrientes," enclosed with Tucker to MGM, July 30, 1873, CHA, AMNP.

36. Tucker to MGM, July 31, 1873, *CDL* 3:97–98; Noland, "Peruvian Amazon," 722–23; Galt Diary, 2:287–89; Rochelle, *Tucker*, 67–68.

37. Galt, "Medical Notes on the Pampa del Sacramento," 402–3; Galt Diary, 2:289; Tucker to Ran, July 16, 1873,

Tucker to Ran and Tar, Aug. 16, 1873, Tucker Papers, Pensacola.

38. Noland to Ma, July 9, 1873, box 3, Noland Papers; Galt Diary, 2:289; Noland, "Peruvian Amazon," 781.

39. Tucker to MGM, July 31, 1873, *CDL* 3:98–99. In this published version of Tucker's report, the admiral's Puerto Pardo is shown as "Puerto Prado"; the original English version of the report, dated July 30, 1873, in CHA, AMNP, and an English copy in folder 3, Tucker Papers, ODU, show it as "Port Pardo."

40. Pardo to Tucker, Sept. 18, 1873, and *El Nacional*, Sept. 20, 1873, extracting an article from *El Comercio*, folders 13, 40, Tucker Papers, ODU.

41. Tucker to MGM, July 31, Oct. 26, 1873, Tucker to CGL, July [1]8, 21, Aug. 4, Sept. 10, Sept. 15 (two dispatches), 1873, CHAlc, 87–88, 105, 83–84, 96, 98, 101–2.

42. Tucker to MGM, Sept. 19, Oct. 26, 1873, ibid., 103–4, 105; Rochelle to Tucker, Dec. 10, 1873, folder 19, Tucker Papers, ODU. Tucker combined Rochelle's report and a similar one by Butt for his own report, Tucker to MGM, Dec. 16, 1873, *CDL* 3:100–109. This published version does not have the tables of latitudes and longitudes, distances, and magnetic variations or the "Observaciones de las corrientes" prepared by Rochelle; the omitted documents are in CHA, Comandancia del DFL, AMNP. A paraphrased English version of the document including Rochelle's tables and observations on currents was published as [Perú, Comisión Hidrográfica del Amazonas], "Report of the Hydrographic Commission of Peru on the Amazon River," 357–65.

43. La Torre to Mayor de Ordenes, Oct. 2 (with enclosures, La Torre to Butt, Sept. 25, 1873, Butt to La Torre, Sept. 25, 1873), Oct. 16, 1873, Butt to Tucker, Dec. 10, 1873, CHA, Comandancia del DFL, AMNP. The latter report encloses Butt's "Puntos astronómicos determinados por la comisión exploradora en su viaje abordo de la lancha de vapor 'Mairo' de la Comisión Hidrográfica del Amazonas," a table which has never been published.

44. Tucker to CGL, Oct. 17, 1873, Tucker to Captain of the *Mairo* [La

NOTES

Torre], Oct. 25, 31, 1873, Tucker to MGM, Oct. 26, 1873, CHAlc, 105–6, 185, 184, 105. Many of Wertheman's coordinates were included in Rochelle, "Geographical Positions," 271–74.

45. Butt to Tucker, Dec. 10, 1873, CHA, Comandancia del DFL, AMNP.

46. Rochelle to Tucker, Dec. 10, 1873, Donayre to Tucker, Nov. 21, 1873, Tucker to Donayre, Nov. 21, 1873, folders 19, 3, Tucker Papers, ODU; Tucker to MGM, Dec. 16, 1873, *CDL* 3:101–3.

47. Noland to Mother, Nov. 23–Dec. 17, 1873, box 3, Noland Papers; Pardo to Tucker, Sept. 18, 1873, folder 13, Tucker Papers, ODU; Tucker to MGM, Oct. 27, 1873, CHAlc, 107–8; Tucker to Ran and Tar, Aug. 16, 1873, Tucker Papers, Pensacola.

48. CGL to MGM, July 31, 1873, Donayre to Mayor de Ordenes, July 15, Oct. 12, 1873, CHA, Comandancia del DFL, AMNP; Galt Diary, 2:292–93.

49. CGL to MGM, Aug. 27, 1873 (with enclosures, CGL to Tucker, Aug. 5, Rae to CGL, Aug. 13, CGL to Mayor de Ordenes, Aug. 28 [*sic*], 1873, with en-

dorsement), CHA, Comandancia del DFL, AMNP. The survey report, dated Sept. 29, 1873, accompanies CGL to MGM, Sept. 30, 1873, Comandancia General del DFL, vapor "Tambo," AMNP.

50. Rochelle to Tucker, Aug. 16, March 31, 1874, folder 19, Tucker Papers, ODU. In 1874 and 1875 the *Mairo* was used to explore the Morona, Yavarí, and Napo rivers. The *Tambo* disappears from the documents in 1877. In that same year the impoverished government sold the river fleet (not including the *Tambo*), retaining only the *Mairo* for the Iquitos naval station (Díaz, "Diario de viaje," Oct. 13, 1874, Black to Ministro de Relaciones Exteriores, June 19, 1874, *CDL* 3:120–34, 135–60; Raygada to CGL, Dec. 9, 1875, in Raygada, *Departamento de Loreto*, 45–48; Romero Pintado, *Historia marítima, 1850–1870* 3:238).

51. Tucker to Rochelle, Dec. 16, 1873, folder 13, Tucker Papers, ODU; Tucker to CGL, Dec. 16, 1873 (two letters), Rochelle to MGM, Dec. 27, 1873, CHAlc, 113–14, 118; Tucker to Ran, Jan. 7, 26, Mar. 4, 1874, Tucker Papers, Pensacola.

Chapter Ten: Poker Flat, Peru

1. Kelly and Kelly, *Dancing Diplomats*, 5; Herrera, "Fundación de Iquitos," 108, 117; Orton, "New Exploration of the Amazon," 296; Stevenson, *Traveller of the Sixties*, 70, 40; Noland, "Peruvian Amazon," 781; Perú, *Censo general, 1876* 6:498–504.

2. Charon, *Estado comercial*, 21–22; Noland, "Peruvian Amazon," 781; Alvarado to MGM, Aug. 3, 1872, Prefectura del DFL, 0.1872.5, AHMP; CGL to MGM, Oct. 31, 1872, Comandancia del DFL, DML, AMNP; Riva-Agüero to MGM, Oct. 20, 1873, MRE, 0.1873.3, AHMP.

3. Noland, "Peruvian Amazon," 781; Galt Diary, 2:193–94, 195, 209; Noland to Pa, Feb. 13, 1873, Noland to Mother, Sept. 11, 1873, box 3, Noland Papers.

4. CGL to MGM, Oct. 31, 1872, Comandancia del DFL, DML, AMNP; Carreño, "Memoria . . . sobre el estado en que se halla el Departamento Fluvial de Loreto," Oct. 7, 1876, DML, Comandan-

cia del DFL, AMNP; Galt Diary, 2:253, 293–94; Noland, "Peruvian Amazon," 781.

5. Pardo to Prefecto de Loreto, Aug. 30, 1872, *CDL* 9:410–12; Galt Diary, 2:245.

6. Galt Diary, 2:265, 290, 293, 294; CGL to MGM, Jan. 25, 29, 1873, Comandancia General del DFL, DML, AMNP.

7. Galt Diary, 2:166; CGL to MGM, Jan. 29, Apr. 30, 1873, Comandancia General del DFL, DML, AMNP; CGL to MGM, Oct. 19, 1875, Comandancia del DFL, DML, AMNP.

8. Galt Diary, 2:167, 168, 220–21, 268, 293, 294.

9. Piérola to MGM, Mar. 18, 1870, Ministerio de Hacienda, marzo, 0.1870.4, AHMP; Fernández, *Progreso de Iquitos*, 45–48; documents about the theft of the Moyobamba treasury, in Ministerio de Gobierno, Prefectura de Loreto, 1872, OL509–979, Archivo de Hacienda,

AGNP; Masías to Ministro de Justicia, Apr. 12, 1869, Vargas to Ministro de Justicia, Sept. 17, 1873, Prefectura de Loreto, 1853/1879, RJ126, Archivo de Justicia, AGNP; see also Galt Diary, 2:178, 200, 260.

10. MGM to CGL, Apr. 10, 1872, DFL, 1868–1872, lc 127, AMNP; Galt Diary, 2:185, 264, 268, 290; CGL to MGM, June 1, Jan. 29 (with Medina's endorsement), 1873, Comandancia General del DFL, DML, AMNP.

11. Galt Diary, 2:264, 290, 293, 294; CGL to MGM, June 1, 1873, Comandancia General del DFL, DML, AMNP.

12. CGL to MGM, Apr. 30, 1873, Comandancia General del DFL, DML, AMNP; CGL to MGM, Feb. 19, 1876, Dec. 29, 1874, DML, Comandancia del DFL, AMNP.

13. CGL to MGM, Oct. 9, Nov. 20, 1876, DML, Comandancia del DFL, AMNP.

14. Orton, *Andes and Amazon*, 380; Galt Diary, 2:2, 116, 173, 257, 260; Joseph Beal Steere, letter dated Yurimaguas, Feb. 25, 1872, Steere Papers; Fuentes, *Loreto* 1:188; Palacios Mendiburu, "Estudio sobre la colonización de Loreto," *CDL* 5:260. Naturalist Steere's series of letters about his travels up the Amazon and overland to Lima were published in the *Ann Arbor* [Mich.] *Peninsular Courier and Family Visitant.*

15. Galt Diary, 2:116; Raimondi, *Apuntes sobre Loreto*, 86; Steere letter, Moyobamba, May 10, 1872, Steere Papers; De Kalb, "Social and Intellectual Condition," 114; Galt to Cloyd, Mar. 16, 1872, Cloyd Papers; Kelly and Kelly, *Dancing Diplomats*, 92.

16. Galt Diary, 2:147, 208, 219; San Román, *Perfiles históricos*, 101–2; F. Galt, "Medical Notes on the Upper Amazon," 401; Steere letter, Yurimaguas, Feb. 25, 1872, Steere Papers; Galt to Cloyd, Mar. 16, 1872, Cloyd Papers.

17. Steere letters, Pebas, Jan. 23, and Yurimaguas, Feb. 25, 1872, Steere Papers; Galt Diary, 2:166, 193, 196.

18. Noland to Pa, Nov. 23, 1873, box 3, Noland Papers; Stevenson, *Traveller of the Sixties*, 35, 36–37; Noland, "Peruvian Amazon," 781; Galt Diary, 2:160, 175, 170–71.

19. Noland, "Peruvian Amazon,"

781–82; Fuentes, *Loreto* 1:190; Galt Diary, 2:8, 257, 263; Kelly and Kelly, *Dancing Diplomats*, 98; Steere letter, Moyobamba, May 10, 1872, Steere Papers.

20. Steere letters, Pebas, Jan. 23, and Moyobamba, May 10, 1872, Steere Papers; Stevenson, *Traveller of the Sixties*, 37; Kelly and Kelly, *Dancing Diplomats*, 102.

21. Noland, "Peruvian Amazon," 781, 621; Orton, *Andes and Amazon*, 232; Galt Diary, 2:161.

22. Galt Diary, 2:2, 164; De Kalb, "Iquitos," 432; F. Galt, "Medical Notes on the Upper Amazon," 408; Galt to Cloyd, Oct. 4, 1870, Mar. 16, 1872, Cloyd Papers; Noland to Ma, Jan. 8, 1874, box 3, Noland Papers; Steere letter, Pebas, Jan. 23, 1872, Steere Papers.

23. CGL to MGM, Jan. 27, 1875, Comandancia General del DFL, Mayoría de Ordenes del Departamento Fluvial, AMNP; Noland to Ma, Jan. 8, 1874, box 3, Noland Papers; Galt to Cloyd, Mar. 16, 1872, Cloyd Papers; Galt Diary, 2:171, 200. The Galt Diary, 2:307, lists the rations provided to sailors at Iquitos in February 1873.

24. Galt Diary, 2:207, 290, 143, 199.

25. Ibid., 2:2, 191; Rochelle, *Tucker*, 11; Steere letter, Yurimaguas, Feb. 25, 1872, Steere Papers; CGL to MGM, Sept. 19, 1876, DML, Comandancia del DFL, AMNP.

26. Noland to Mother, July 9, Aug. 17, Sept. 11, 1873, box 3, Noland Papers; Galt Diary, 2:160, 256, 263, 264, 209; Steere letter, Borja, Feb. 20, 1872, Steere Papers.

27. Rochelle to Tucker, Mar. 31, 1874, folder 19, Tucker Papers, ODU; handbill for *Gran concierto en beneficio de la independencia de Cuba que tendrá lugar en Yquitos, marzo 28 de 1874, a las ocho P.M.*, with Galt's comments on the performers, Galt Diary folder.

28. Galt Diary, 2:193–94; Newell to Mayor de Ordenes, Jan. 24, 1870 (with enclosures), Lino Olaria to MGM, Feb. 23, 1870, Prefectura de Loreto, 0.1870.4, AHMP.

29. Galt Diary, 2:215–16; Onffroy de Thoron, *Amérique équatoriale*, title page; Orton, *Andes and Amazon*, 386; Steere letter, Chanuci [*sic*], Mar. 8, 1872, Steere Papers.

30. *Who's Who in America, 1899–1900*, s.v. "Steere, Joseph Beal"; Galt Diary, 2:223; Steere Letter, Yurimaguas, Feb. 25, 1872, Steere Papers.

31. Noland to Mother, Sept. 11, 1873, box 3, Noland Papers; Galt Diary, 2:291–92. Compare the 1870 first edition of Orton, *Andes and Amazon*, 232, with the same page of the third edition (1876).

32. Galt Diary, 2:152, 174; Noland to Ma, Jan. 8, 1874, box 3, Noland Papers; Galt to Cloyd, Oct. 4, 1870, Mar. 16, 1872, Cloyd Papers.

33. Tucker to MGM, Jan. 31, 1873, CHAlc, 66; Noland to Ma, July 9, 1873, box 3, Noland Papers; Galt Diary, 2:266, 191, 290. Copies of Galt's contract, signed July 23, 1873, are in CHAlc, 122–23, and folder 3, Tucker Papers, ODU.

34. Galt Diary, 2:6–7; Tucker to Ran, July 28, 1867, Feb. 16, 1868, Feb. 16, Apr. 16, 1871, Tucker Papers, Pensacola; Noland to Ma, July 9, 1873, box 3, Noland Papers.

35. Noland to Ma, July 9, 1873, box 3, Noland Papers; Mahan to Ashe, Feb. 1–Apr. 12, 1903, Mahan, *Letters* 3:54–55; Galt Diary, 2:200, 201, 208.

36. Rochelle to Smith, Feb. 8, 1872, Rochelle to Butt, Feb. 8, 1872, CHAlc, 37. Herrera, *Leyendas y tradiciones de Loreto*, 327—the only source on the loss of the steamer—confuses the *Cecilia* with the *Alceste*, the vessel Smith apparently obtained to replace his first ship (Galt Diary, 2:209, 218, 291; Steere letter, Yurimaguas, Feb. 25, 1872, Steere Papers; Orton, *Andes and Amazon*, 379).

37. Rochelle to Tucker, Aug. 20, 1872, folder 18, Tucker Papers, ODU; CGL to MGM, July 30, 1873, CHA, Comandancia del DFL, AMNP; Tucker to CGL, Dec. 10, 1873, Tucker to Butt, Dec. 12, 1873, Rochelle to CGL, May 13, 1874, CHAlc, 138–39, 110–11, 177.

38. Steere letter, Yurimaguas, Feb. 25, 1872, Steere Papers; *DAB*, s.v. "Settle, Thomas"; Galt Diary, 2:210; Galt to Cloyd, Mar. 16, 1872, Cloyd Papers.

39. McCorkle to U.S. Consul, Nov. 19, 1867, p. 49, USDS, Post Records, Pará, January 1, 1867–December 31, 1872, RG 84, NAUS.

40. Galt to Thomas, Oct. 27, 1873 (with death certificate of William Dowd), Galt to Thomas, Feb. 28, 1874 (with bap-tismal certificates of Lorena and William Henry Dowd, Jr.), USDS, Post Records, Peru, T724/28, RG 84, NAUS; Larrea, Vapor "Tambo," relación de las novedades, Nov. 15, 1870, CHA, Comisaria de Marina, 1870, AMNP.

41. Galt to Thomas, Oct. 27, 1873, and enclosed death certificate of W. Dowd, USDS, Post Records, Peru, T724/28, RG 84, NAUS.

42. Rochelle to U.S. Consul, Oct. 16, 1873, pp. 55–56, Correspondence of the U.S. Consulate, Pará, Brazil, January 1, 1873–December 31, 1878, USDS, Post Records, Pará, RG 84, NAUS; Galt to Thomas, Oct. 27, 1873, Galt to Thomas, Feb. 28, 1874 (with enclosure, Galt to Thomas ["confidential"], Feb. 28, 1874), Thomas to Galt, Dec. 16, 1873, USDS, Post Records, Peru, T724/28, RG 84, NAUS.

43. DeBoer, "Pillage and Production," 231–46; Galt Diary, 2:131; Noland, "Peruvian Amazon," 548, 723; Galt to Thomas ("confidential"), Feb. 28, 1874 (enclosed with Galt to Thomas, Feb. 28, 1874), USDS, Post Records, Peru, T724/28, RG 84, NAUS.

44. Tucker to Thomas, Apr. 29, 1874, Galt to Thomas, Sept. 30, 1874, USDS, Post Records, Peru, T724/28, RG 84, NAUS; MGM to CGL, July 4, 1874, DFL, 1872–1878, lc 146, AMNP; Rosas to MGM, Aug. 16, 1873, Ministerio de Gobierno, agosto, 0.1873.3, AHMP; CGL to MGM, Oct. 27, 1874, DML, Comandancia del DFL, AMNP.

45. Noland to Ma, Jan. 30, 1874, box 3, Noland Papers; Rochelle to MGM, Dec. 31, 1873, Feb. 28, Mar. 31, Apr. 21, 1874, Rochelle to Sparrow and Noland, Mar. 11, 1874, CHAlc, 120–21, 124–25, 131, 134, 126–27; Noland, "Peruvian Amazon," 782–83.

46. Rochelle to MGM, Apr. 30, 1874, CHAlc, 135–37. The list of maps here is repeated in Freyre to MGM, May 27, 1877 (Consulados de la república en el estrangero, 0.1877.2, AHMP), but added at the bottom is "a plan of the town of Iquitos, drawn on one sheet."

47. Tucker to Ran, Mar. 4, 1874, Pardo to Tucker [Mar. 4, 1874], Tucker Papers, Pensacola; Charon to Tucker, Apr. 19, 20, 1874, folder 14, Tucker Papers, ODU. The preliminary order con-

cerning Wertheman's proposed expedition was issued the same day as Tucker's dinner with the president (MGM to CGL, Mar. 5, 1874, DFL, 1872–1878, lc 146, AMNP).

48. Draft of Tucker's proposal, folder 6, Tucker Papers, ODU; Tucker to Ran, Apr. 14, 1874, Tucker Papers, Pensacola; MGM, supreme decree of Apr. 23, 1874, Decretos supremos, 0.1874.1, AHMP; MGM to Tucker, May 5, 1874, Rochelle Papers.

49. Tucker to MGM, June 11, 1874, copy in folder 14, Tucker Papers, ODU.

50. MGM to CGL, Apr. 4, 1874, DFL, 1872–1878, lc 146, AMNP; García y García, certificate of wages paid Tucker, May 12, 1874, folder 36, Tucker Papers, ODU.

51. Bartlett to Tucker, Nov. 4, 1870, June 10, 1871, Tucker Papers, Pensacola; Rochelle to Tucker, Mar. 31, 1874, folder 19, Tucker Papers, ODU; Rochelle to Mourraille, [Sept. 18, 1874], CHAlc, 171–72; N. B. Noland, "Acct with Admiral Tucker for money advanced at various dates," box 3, Noland Papers.

52. Tucker to MGM, Oct. 24, 1873 (with enclosure, Galt, Noland, Mesnier, Rochelle, Sparrow, and Butt to MGM, Oct. 20, 1873), CGL to MGM, Jan. 26, 1874, CHA, Comandancia del DFL, AMNP; MGM to Tucker, Feb. 5, 1874, Rochelle Papers.

53. Noland to Ma, Jan. 30, June 15, 1874, box 3, Noland Papers; Galt to MGM, Dec. 28, 1873 (enclosed with Rochelle to MGM, Dec. 28, 1873), CHA, AMNP; Lines to Clayton, Oct. 25, 1878, p. 252, USDS, Post Records, Callao-Lima, T781/13, RG 84, NAUS.

54. MGM to Rochelle, Apr. 23, 1874, Rochelle Papers; MGM to CGL, Apr. 23, 1874 (two dispatches), DFL, 1872–1878, lc 146, AMNP; Rochelle to CGL, July 15, 1874, CHAlc, 145.

55. CGL to Rochelle, July 15, 1874 (translation in Rochelle to Tucker, Aug. 16, 1874), folder 19, Tucker Papers, ODU; CGL to MGM, July 27, 1874, CHA, Comandancia del DFL, AMNP; Rochelle to CGL, Aug. 10, 1874, CHAlc, 158–59.

56. MGM to CGL, Apr. 23, 1874, DFL, 1872–1878, lc 146, AMNP.

57. MGM to CGL, Sept. 17, 1874, DFL, 1872–1878, lc 146, AMNP; Rochelle to MGM, July 13, 1874, CHAlc, 146–48; CGL to MGM, July 27, 1874, CHA, Comandancia del DFL, AMNP.

58. Rochelle to CGL, July 15, 17, 1874, Rochelle to MGM, July 16, 31, 1874, CHAlc, 144–45, 145–46, 148–49, 150–53; CGL to Rochelle, July 15, 17, 1874 (translations in Rochelle to Tucker, Aug. 16, 1874), folder 19, Tucker Papers, ODU.

59. Rochelle to MGM, July 31, 1874, Galt, Rochelle, Sparrow, Butt, Mesnier, and Noland to Pardo, July 31, 1874, CHAlc, 150–53, 153–57.

60. MGM to CGL, Sept. 17, 21, Oct. 2, 1874, DFL, 1872–1878, lc 146, AMNP.

61. Rochelle to Tucker, Aug. 16, 1874, folder 19, Tucker Papers, ODU; Mesnier to Rochelle, Aug. 17, 1874, Rochelle to Mayor de Ordenes, Aug. 20, 1874, CHAlc, 161, 160.

62. Rochelle to Tucker, Aug. 16, Mar. 31, 1874, folder 19, Tucker Papers, ODU; Smith to Rochelle, Apr. 28, 1874, Rochelle Papers.

63. Noland to Mother, Aug. 17, 1874, box 3, Noland Papers; Rochelle, Galt, Sparrow, and Noland to Ríos, July 31, 1874, Rochelle to CGL, Sept. 8, 1874, CHAlc, 157, 161–63; CGL to MGM, Sept. 29, 1874, CHA, Comandancia del DFL, AMNP.

64. Rochelle to Galt, Sept. 20, 1874, Galt Diary folder; Hotel do Comercio, Pará, statement of account with Rochelle, Oct. 31–Nov. 6, 1874, Rochelle Papers; Rochelle to MGM, Nov. 12, 1874, CHAlc, 175–76.

65. Rochelle to MGM, Sept. 18, 1874, Rochelle to Mourraille, [Sept. 18, 1874], CHAlc, 167–70, 171–72.

66. Thorneby to Noland, Oct. 20, 1874, Family Letters to Nelson B. Noland, 1874–1882, Noland–Berkeley Papers. In Noland's letters home during the final months in Iquitos, Butt's name is conspicuously absent from those he described as his companions and messmates.

67. Rochelle to Mourraille, [Sept. 18, 1874], CHAlc, 171–72; Rochelle to Galt, Sept. 20, 1874, Galt Diary folder; CGL to MGM, Oct. 27, 1874, DML, Comandancia del DFL, AMNP; CGL to MGM, Sept. 20, 1875 (with enclosures), CHA, Comandancia del DFL, AMNP.

Chapter Eleven: High and Dry

1. Tucker to Ran, June 9, 1874, Tucker Papers, Pensacola; Tucker to MGM, June 11, 1874, S. Van Campen to Tucker, June 11, 1874, American Photo-Lithographic Co. to Tucker, June 11, 1874, folders 4, 14, Tucker Papers, ODU.

2. W. Spaythe & Co. to Tucker, June 25, 1874, Tucker to MGM, July 25, 28, 1874, Tucker to Pardo, July 27, 1874, folders 14, 4, Tucker Papers, ODU.

3. MGM to Tucker, Sept. 10, 18, Nov. 10, 1874, Rochelle Papers; Rochelle to MGM, Sept. 18, 1874, CHAlc, 167–70; Sparrow to "Take Notice Noland," Jan. 25, 1875, Family Letters to N. B. Noland, 1874–1882, Noland–Berkeley Papers; N. B. Noland, undated account with Tucker "for money advanced at various dates," and his statement with Noland to Pa, Dec. 2, 1874 [i.e., 1875], box 3, Noland Papers.

4. Galt to Noland, Jan. 8, 1875, Sparrow to Noland, Jan. 25, 1875, Family Letters to N. B. Noland, 1874–1882, Noland–Berkeley Papers; Wilmont, receipt for suit, Dec. 5, 1874, Rochelle Papers.

5. Rochelle to Tucker, Jan. 18, 23, Mar. 12, 1876, Pardo de Zela to Tucker, June 13, 1876, folders 20, 21, Tucker Papers, ODU.

6. Werlich, *Peru*, 96–97; Capuñay Mimbela, "Historia del presupuesto nacional," 92–93; Pardo de Zela to Tucker, June 13, 1876, folder 21, Tucker Papers, ODU; Perú, *Memoria de Marina, 1876*, 3, 13, 15.

7. Gibbs to Evarts, Apr. 27, 1878, in U.S. Senate, *Claims of the Hydrographic Commission*, p. 4; Rochelle to Tucker, Nov. 21, 1876, folder 21, Tucker Papers, ODU; MGM to Tucker, Jan. 3, 1877 (translation with Rochelle to Tucker, Feb. 6, 1877), Rochelle to Tucker, Feb. 8, 1877, Rochelle Papers.

8. Rochelle to Tucker, Feb. 8, 1877, Rochelle Papers; Pardo [i.e., Prado] to Tucker, Mar. 13, 1877, in Rochelle, *Tucker*, 71; Rochelle to Tucker, Feb. 27, Apr. 10, 1877 (with translation of Bustamante to Tucker, Mar. 13, 1877), folder 22, Tucker Papers, ODU.

9. Rochelle to Tucker, Apr. 10, 17, 1877, Freyre to Tucker, Apr. 25, 1877, Rochelle to Tucker, May 5, 1877, folders 22, 15, 23, Tucker Papers, ODU; Freyre to Tucker, Mar. [i.e., May] 22, 1877, in Rochelle, *Tucker*, 73–79; Freyre to Ministro de Relaciones Exteriores, Nov. 13, 30, 1877 (with enclosed list of maps, signed by R. Alvarez-Calderón, New York, Nov. 13, 1877), Servicio diplomático del Perú, legación en EE. UU. correspondiente a 1877, carpeta 5–3, AGMREP.

10. Rochelle to Tucker, Feb. 8, 1877, Rochelle Papers; Rochelle to Tucker, Apr. 17, 1877, May 5, Aug. 11, Sept. 2, Oct. 7, 1877, Mar. 18, 1878, Jan. 30, 1879, folders 22–24, Tucker Papers, ODU; Tucker to MGM, Apr. 14, 1877, in Perú, *Memoria de Relaciones Exteriores, 1896*, 247; Basadre, *Historia* 5:2239, 2203–4.

11. Tucker to MGM, Oct. 24, 1873 (with petition of Oct. 20, 1873), CGL to MGM, Jan. 26, July 27, 1874, CHA, Comandancia del DFL, AMNP; MGM to Tucker, May 5, 1874, Rochelle Papers; MGM to Tucker, Jan. 7, Aug. 4, 1875, Pardo de Zela, resolution of Jan. 28, 1875, in Perú, *Memoria de Relaciones Exteriores, 1896*, 245–46, 248; Rochelle to Noland, Mar. 12, 1875, box 3, Noland Papers; Rochelle to Tucker, Jan. 18, 1876, folder 20, Tucker Papers, ODU.

12. Pardo [i.e., Prado] to Tucker, Mar. 13, 1877, in Rochelle, *Tucker*, 71; MGM to Tucker, Mar. 13, 1877 (translation with Rochelle to Tucker, Apr. 10, 1877), Rochelle to Tucker, Oct. 7, 1877, folders 22, 23, Tucker Papers, ODU; Tucker to MGM, Apr. 14, 1877, in Perú, *Memoria de Relaciones Exteriores, 1896*, 246–47; Rochelle to Noland, Aug. 18, Nov. 20, 1877, box 3, Noland Papers.

13. CGL to MGM, Jan. 26, 1875 (with enclosures), CGL to MGM, Sept. 20, 1875 (with enclosures), CHA, Comandancia del DFL, AMNP; MGM to CGL, Nov. 9, 1875, Jan. 8, 1876, DFL, 1872–1878, lc 146, AMNP.

14. Noland to Tucker, Dec. 3, 1874, Rochelle to Noland, Mar. 12, 1875, Noland to Pa, Dec. 2, 1874 [i.e., 1875] (with statement), boxes 3, 5, Noland Papers; Tucker to MGM, Apr. 14, 1877, in Perú, *Memoria de Relaciones Exteriores, 1896*, 246–47.

15. Gibbs to Hunter, Feb. 18, 1876, C. S. Noland to Hobson-Hurtado, Apr. 3, 1876, C. S. Noland to N. B. Noland, Apr. 11, 1876 (with enclosure, Galt to C. S. Noland, Apr. 9, 1876), boxes 9, 10, 3, Noland Papers; Gibbs to Ministro de Relaciones Exteriores, July 25, 1876, in Perú, *Memoria de Relaciones Exteriores, 1896*, 249.

16. Noland to Pa, Dec. 2, 1874 [i.e., 1875] (with statement), Noland to Pa, May 15, 1876, boxes 5, 4, Noland Papers.

17. Noland to Pa, Apr. 18, 1876, Rochelle to Noland, Aug. 18, Nov. 20, 1877, Galt to Noland, June 7, 1878, boxes 4, 3, ibid.; Freyre to Rochelle, June 4, 1877, in Perú, *Memoria de Relaciones Exteriores, 1896*, 247–48; Freyre to Tucker, Apr. 25, 1877, Rochelle to Tucker, May 3, 5, 1877, folders 15, 23, Tucker Papers, ODU.

18. Gibbs to Galt, Noland, Rochelle, and Sparrow, Jan. 20, 1877, USDS, Post Records, Peru, T724/47, RG 84, NAUS; Lee to Secretary of State, Oct. 13, 1877, USDS, Misc. Letters, M179/495, RG 59, NAUS; Evarts to Gibbs, Oct. 31, 1877, in U.S. Senate, *Claims of the Hydrographic Commission*, 3–4.

19. MGM to Tucker, Nov. 8, 1878 (translation with Rochelle to Tucker, Jan. 30, 1879), Rochelle to Tucker, Dec. 1, 1882, folder 24, Tucker Papers, ODU; Gibbs to Evarts, Jan. 22, 1879 (with enclosure, Yrigoyen to Gibbs, Jan. 11, 1879), Evarts to Gibbs, Feb. 21, 1879, Evarts to Christiancy, Apr. 28, 1879, in U.S. Senate, *Claims of the Hydrographic Commission*, 6–7.

20. La Haza to Tucker, Oct. 2, 1877, Rochelle Papers; Gibbs to Yrigoyen, July 6, 1878, and Yrigoyen to Gibbs, July 22, 1878 (both enclosed with Gibbs to Evarts, July 24, 1878), in U.S. Senate, *Claims of the Hydrographic Commission*, 5–6; Galt to Noland, June 7, 1878, box 3, Noland Papers.

21. Noland to Ma, Jan. 8, 1874, box 3, Noland Papers; Galt to Kell, Oct. 27, 1877, Kell Papers.

22. Tucker to Ran, Mar. 24, 1875, Tucker Papers, Pensacola; Noland to Pa, Sept. 29, 1875, Dec. 2, 1874 [i.e., 1875] (with statement), Noland to Pa, Apr. 18, May 15, 1876, boxes 5, 4, Noland Papers; Rochelle to Tucker, Dec. 11, 1876, folder

21, Tucker Papers, ODU; Noland to Anderson, Aug. 4, 1904, Noland alumnus file; Mary B. Noland to Werlich, May 5, 1980; *Richmond Evening Journal*, Mar. 3, 1913.

23. Sparrow to Tucker, Jan. 2, 1877, folder 25, Tucker Papers, ODU; U.S. Department of the Interior, *Official Register of the United States, 1879* 2:279 (Sparrow falsely reported his birthplace as Ohio); Selfridge, "Survey of the Amazon," 324, 353–54, 360; Heynen, *Manuscript Charts*, 141; *Boyd's Directory of the District of Columbia, 1896–1913*, s.v. "Sparrow, Thomas W"; Alexandria, Va., Episcopal High School, *Monthly Chronicle* (Mar. 1916), clipping in the Thomas W. Sparrow alumnus file; Jacksonville *Florida Times-Union*, Oct. 2, 1915. Marginal notes to the entry for Sparrow in University of Virginia, *Students*, 132, in the copy at Manuscript Department of the Univ. of Virginia Library show his address as Knoxville, Tenn.

24. Galt to Kell, Oct. 27, 1877, Kell Papers; Rochelle, *Tucker*, 20; Semmes, *Memoirs*, 72; Karsten, *Naval Aristocracy*, 26; Rochelle to Tucker, May 3, 1877, folder 23, Tucker Papers, ODU.

25. Galt to Kell, Oct. 27, 1877, Kell Papers; Rochelle to Tucker, Mar. 12, Dec. 11, 1876, Jan. 1, Feb. 1, Sept. 2, Oct. 7, 1877, Jan. 30, 1879, folders 20–24, Tucker Papers, ODU; Rochelle to Noland, Nov. 20, 1877, box 3, Noland Papers; McCorkle to Brooke, Nov. 11, 1877, Brooke Papers; Galt to Rochelle, Dec. 3, 1888, Rochelle Papers.

26. Tucker to Heth, Oct. 15, 1875, Tucker-Randolph Correspondence; *Petersburg Index-Appeal*, June 15, 1883; Rochelle to Tucker, Mar. 19, Sept. 2, 1877, folders 22, 23, Tucker Papers, ODU; Parker to Rochelle, May 3, 14, 1889, Rochelle Papers; Foster, *Ghosts of the Confederacy*, esp. chap. 4.

27. *Encyclopedia of Southern History*, s.v. "Amnesty"; U.S., *Statutes at Large*, vol. 17, chap. 234, sec. 23, p. 573, vol. 21, chap. 22, p. 557, chap. 99, p. 542; U.S. House, *House Journal*, 50th Cong., 2d sess., 1888–89, pp. 68, 107, 708.

28. *DAB*, s.vv. "Waddell, James Iredell" and "Parker, William Harwar"; W. R. Butt, power of attorney to H. F. Butt, Aug. 26, 1875, and W. R. Butt, "The Loss of the P.M.S.S. 'City of San

Francisco,'" Butt Collection; Sutter to Hunter, May 24, 1877 (with enclosed statement of S. Pérez, May 17, 1877), USDS, Consular Despatches, Acapulco, M143/4, RG 59, NAUS.

29. Butt, "Loss of the 'San Francisco,'" Butt to Fairfield, undated, Butt to Channing, Sept. 27, 1878, Butt to Sallie, Apr. 2, 1882, Butt Collection; Rochelle to Tucker, Mar. 18, 1878, folder 24, Tucker Papers, ODU; Wood to wife, Aug. 14, 1862, Wood Papers; Stewart, *History of Norfolk County*, 500; interview with Marshall W. Butt, Jr., Mar. 28, 1982; Mahan to Ashe, Feb. 1–Apr. 12, 1903, Mahan, *Letters* 3:55.

30. Galt to Kell, Oct. 27, 1877, Kell Papers; Rochelle to Tucker, Jan. 18, Dec. 11, 1876, Oct. 7, 1877, undated draft of Tucker's letter recommending Galt for the quarantine post, folders 20, 21, 23, 6, Tucker Papers, ODU; Galt to Noland, Jan. 8, 1875, Family Letters to N. B. Noland, 1874–1882, Noland–Berkeley Papers; Galt to Noland, June 7, 1878, Mary Noland to Smith, undated, Galt to Noland, Mar. 9, 1880, boxes 3, 11, 10, Noland Papers.

31. Orton, *Andes and Amazon*, 580–614; Galt to Henry, Feb. 3, 10, Mar. 10, 1875, Office of the Secretary (Joseph Henry, Spencer F. Baird), 1863–1879, Incoming Correspondence, RU 26, 144:143, 147, 169, Smithsonian Institution Archives; Henry to Galt, Feb. 8, 14, 1875, Office of the Secretary (Joseph Henry, Spencer F. Baird, Samuel P. Langley), 1865–1891, Outgoing Correspondence, RU 33, 42:277, 333, ibid.

32. Henry to Galt, Oct. 24, 1876, Baird to Galt, Nov. 14, 16, 1886, Outgoing Correspondence, RU 33, 51:305, 199:9, 189, Office of the Secretary, Smithsonian Institution Archives; Galt to Baird, Nov. 4, 1886, Incoming Correspondence, RU 30, box 5, folder 2, ibid.; Galt, "Indians of Peru," 308–15. The material on climate rejected by the Smithsonian was published in Galt, "Meteorological and Sanitary Notes at Iquitos."

33. Galt to Noland, June 7, 1878, box 3, Noland Papers; unidentified newspaper clippings, Veselka Collection; *Atlanta Constitution*, Aug. 5, 1900; Kell, *Recollections*, 291–93.

34. Galt to Kell, Oct. 27, 1877, Kell Papers; Rochelle to Tucker, Feb. 1, 1877,

Mar. 18, 1878, May 5, 1877, folders 22, 24, 23, Tucker Papers, ODU; Galt to C. S. Noland, Apr. 9, 1876 (enclosed with C. S. Noland to N. B. Noland, Apr. 11, 1876), Galt to Noland, Mar. 9, 1880, boxes 3, 10, Noland Papers; unidentified newspaper clippings and photo of Galt with his son, Veselka Collection; Galt genealogy, p. 7, Galt Family Papers.

35. McCorkle to Brooke, Nov. 11, 15, 1877, Brooke Papers; Army of Northern Virginia Association, *Memorial Volume*, 88, 125, 175, 332; U.S. Navy, *Register, 1875*, 4; Rochelle to Kell, Aug. 15, 1881, Kell Papers; U.S. Naval Academy Alumni Association, *Register of Alumni*, p. 2, entry 129.

36. Tucker to Ran, Dec. 20, 1874, Feb. 14, 1875, Feb. 2, 1876, Tucker Papers, Pensacola; Rochelle to Tucker, Jan. 18, 23, Feb. 7, 20, Mar. 12, 1876, Jan. 1, 1877, folders 20, 22, Tucker Papers, ODU.

37. Rochelle to Tucker, Mar. 12, 29, July 14, Nov. 21, 1876, Jan. 1, 9, 1877, folders 20–22, Tucker Papers, ODU.

38. Rochelle to Tucker, Dec. 11, 1876, Jan. 1, Feb. 1, 27, Mar. 19, Apr. 17, May 1, 3, 1877, folders 21–23, ibid.

39. Rochelle to Tucker, Apr. 10, 17, Mar. 19, 1877, folder 22, ibid.

40. Rochelle to Tucker, Jan. 18, July 14, 1876, Feb. 1, Mar. 19, Apr. 17, May 1, Oct. 7, 1877, Mar. 18, 1878, folders 20–24, ibid.

41. Rochelle to Scharf, Jan. 3, 1887, Rochelle folder, ZB File, NHCUS; Rochelle to Tucker, Dec. 11, 1876, Mar. 18, 1878, Feb. 7, 1876, folders 21, 24, 20, Tucker Papers, ODU; Rochelle, *Tucker*, 17.

42. Rochelle, *Tucker*, 79; Edward A. Wyatt IV to Werlich, Nov. 17, 1981; Tucker to Ran, Feb. 2, 1876, Tucker Papers, Pensacola; Rochelle to Tucker, June 18, 1876, folder 21, Tucker Papers, ODU. Tucker's eldest son, John Tarleton ("Jack"), died prematurely on Jan. 26, 1880.

43. Rochelle, *Tucker*, 79; *Petersburg Index-Appeal*, June 13, 15, 16, 1883; *Norfolk Landmark*, June 15, 1883; Genealogy notes, Tucker Papers, Pensacola; *Norfolk Virginian*, June 14, 1883; *Norfolk Landmark*, June 16, 1883; L. A. Marbury, T. Alphonse Jackson, W. Turn-

bull, and N. V. Randolph, inventory and appraisal of the personal estate of John R. Tucker, filed Aug. 31, 1883, Clerk's Office, Hustings Court, Petersburg, Va.

44. Wilson, *Battleships* 1:66–73; Mould Távara, *Távara*, 10–20.

45. Werlich, *Peru*, 106–19; Pavletich, *Prado*, 1–26, 59ff.

46. Herrera, *Leyendas y tradiciones de Loreto*, 276–78; Perú, *Memoria de Guerra y Marina, 1897*, 56; documents in the Timiteo Smith Expediente personal.

47. Rochelle to Tucker, Dec. 1, 1882, folder 24, Tucker Papers, ODU; Galt to Noland, Mar. 9, 1880, box 10, Noland Papers.

48. Rochelle to Noland, Feb. 2, 1885, box 10, Noland Papers; Rochelle to Lee, Feb. 18, 1885 (enclosed with Olney to Shands, Oct. 13, 1896), Galt to Rochelle, July 31, 1888, Rochelle Papers; Bayard to Phelps, Apr. 13, 1885, Buck to Ministro de Relaciones Exteriores, Sept. 16, 1885, in U.S. Senate, *Claims of the Hydrographic Commission*, 8–9; Werlich, *Peru*, 119.

49. Werlich, "Peruvian Montaña," 352–53, 378–79, 381; De Kalb, "Iquitos," 431; "De Kalb, Courtenay," *National Cyclopedia of American Biography* 27:122; Zook, *Zarumilla-Marañón*, 38–39.

50. Zegarra to Ministro de Relaciones Exteriores, July 9, 19, 1888, Comunicaciones de la legación peruana en los Estados Unidos de América a Lima, 1888, carpeta 5–3, AGMREP; Zegarra to Rochelle, July 3, 1888, Rochelle to Randolph Tucker, July 17, 1888, Rochelle Papers.

51. Zegarra to Ministro de Relaciones Exteriores, July 19, Sept. 30, Oct. 31, 1888, Comunicaciones de la legación peruana en los Estados Unidos de América a Lima, 1888, carpeta 5–3, AGMREP. Rochelle's *Tucker* included an appendix, "Notes on the Navigation of the Upper Amazon and Its Tributaries," which Rochelle explained in his preface (dated July 1, 1888) was "added in consequence of letters received asking for information in regard to the navigation of the upper Amazon river and its tributaries."

52. Zegarra to Rochelle, July 20, 1888, Rochelle Papers; Zegarra to Noland, July 22, 1888, and copy of Zegarra

to Galt, July 27, 1888, box 10, Noland Papers.

53. Rochelle to R. Tucker, July 17, 1888, Galt to Rochelle, July 31, 1888, and Noland to Rochelle, July 30, 1888, Buck to Richards, Oct. 24, 1888 (enclosed with Galt to Rochelle, Dec. 3, 1888), Tracy to Shands, Aug. 12, 1889, Rochelle Papers; Galt to Richards, Aug. 15, 1888 (enclosed with Richards to Buck, Sept. 15, 1888), USDS, Post Records, Peru, T724/33, RG 84, NAUS.

54. Adee to Shands, Aug. 30, 1889, Rochelle Papers. The official correspondence pertaining to this phase of the negotiations is in U.S. Senate, *Claims of the Hydrographic Commission*, 9–19.

55. Mattie Tyler to Shands, Jan. 29, 1895, Uhl to Shands, June 7, 1895, Rochelle Papers; McKenzie to Candamo, July 15, 1895 (enclosed with McKenzie to Blaine, July 15, 1895), in U.S. Senate, *Claims of the Hydrographic Commission*, 20.

56. Shands to executor of Tucker estate [N. V. Randolph], June 11, 1895, folder 27, Tucker Papers, ODU; R. Tucker to Shands, June 17, 1895, Noland to Shands, July 9, 1895, and Olney to Shands, Apr. 13, 1896, Rochelle Papers.

57. Noland to Shands, July 9, 1895, Shands to Noland, Oct. 21, 1896, Rochelle Papers; Werlich, *Peru*, 121.

58. U.S. Senate, *Claims of the Hydrographic Commission*, 1–2; Ortiz de Zevallos to McKenzie, Feb. 6, 1896, in Perú, *Memoria de Relaciones Exteriores, 1896*, 252.

59. McKenzie to Candamo, July 15, 1895, in U.S. Senate, *Claims of the Hydrographic Commission*, 20; McKenzie to Olney, Feb. 24, 1896, USDS, Despatches from Peru, T52/55, RG 59, NAUS (due to McKenzie's illness, legation secretary Richard Neill, who had worked on the claim under several U.S. ministers, negotiated with Ortiz); Olney to Shands, Mar. 19, 26, 1896, Rochelle Papers.

60. Shands to R. Tucker, Mar. 30, 1896, folder 27, Tucker Papers, ODU; Olney to Shands, Mar. 26, Apr. 1, 24, 1896, N. V. Randolph, power of attorney to Shands, Apr. 1, 1896 (enclosed with R. Tucker to Shands, Apr. 2, 1896), Rochelle Papers.

61. Olney to Shands, Apr. 13, 1896, copy of Shands to Noland, Oct. 21, 1896, Rockhill to Shands, Oct. 28, 1896 (with enclosure, Lee to Secretary of State, Oct. 9, 1896), Rochelle Papers; Galt to N. V. Randolph, Sept. 2, 1897, folder 31, Tucker Papers, ODU.

62. McKenzie to Olney, Feb. 24, 1896, USDS, Despatches from Peru, T52/55, RG 59, NAUS; Ortiz de Zevallos to McKenzie, July 17, 1896, in Perú, *Memoria de Relaciones Exteriores, 1896,* 253; Ministro de Relaciones Exteriores to Dudley, Dec. 31, 1897, ibid., *1898,* 144–45; Rockhill to Shands, Sept. 28, 1896, Rochelle Papers; Moore, *Digest of International Law* 6:720.

63. Faison, "Report of the Solicitor: Claims of the American Members of the Hydrographic Commission of the Amazon against the Government of Peru," Sept. 25, 1896, typescript, Rochelle Papers. Galt and Sparrow later sent affidavits to the State Department explaining that Tucker had presided over the commission and that he also was due wages. But Peru had fulfilled its agreement with the United States government and was under no further legal obligation; the State Department apparently made no amends for its error. If Tucker's estate did receive compensation, it came through some private and undiscovered agreement with the other claimants (Galt to R. Tucker, Sept. 2, 18, 1897, folders 31, 26, Tucker Papers, ODU; Eguiguren to R. Tucker, Oct. 21, 1897, Rochelle Papers).

Chapter Twelve: Tucker's Tin Can

1. Riva-Agüero to Eguiguren, July 10, 1897, lc de las comunicaciones cursadas entre la cancillería peruana y su legación en los Estados Unidos de América entre 1896 y 1899, tomo 266A, AGMREP.

2. Eguiguren to Adee, Aug. 3, 1897, USDS, Notes from Peruvian Legation, T802/6, RG 59, NAUS; State Department to Eguiguren, Aug. 6, 1897, p. 152, USDS, Notes to Foreign Legations in the United States, M99/79, RG 59, NAUS; Sherman to Eguiguren, Sept. 10, 1897 (enclosed with Eguiguren to Ministro de Relaciones Exteriores, Sept. 18, 1897), Comunicaciones de la Legación del Perú en los Estados Unidos de América dirigidas a Lima, 1897, carpeta 5–3, AGMREP.

3. Galt to N. V. Randolph, Sept. 2, 1897, Galt to R. Tucker, Sept. 8, 1897, folders 31, 26, Tucker Papers, ODU; Eguiguren to Ministro de Relaciones Exteriores, Sept. 8, Oct. 25, 1897, with affidavits of Galt (undated) and Sparrow (Sept. 11, 1897), Comunicaciones de la Legación del Perú en los Estados Unidos de América dirigidas a Lima, 1897, carpeta 5–3, AGMREP; Tucker to CGL, Dec. 10, 1873, CHAlc, 111.

4. Eguiguren to Ministro de Relaciones Exteriores, Oct. 25, 1897 (with enclosures, R. Tucker to Galt, Sept. 6, 1897, M. Freyre to Ministro de Relaciones Exteriores, Nov. 12, 30, 1877, Lee to Sherman, Sept. 21, 1897), Comunicaciones de la Legación del Perú en los Estados Unidos de América dirigidas a Lima, 1897, carpeta 5–3, AGMREP; Rochelle, *Tucker,* 70–71, 73–79; Orton, *Andes and Amazon,* 383. Tucker's notes on agriculture and colonization are in folders 6 and 46, Tucker Papers, ODU.

5. Eguiguren to Ministro de Relaciones Exteriores, Oct. 25, Dec. 8, 1897, Comunicaciones de la Legación del Perú en los Estados Unidos de América dirigidas a Lima, 1897, carpeta 5–3, AGMREP.

6. Freyre to Ministro de Relaciones Exteriores, Nov. 30, 1877 (no. 30), Servicio diplomático del Perú, legación en E.E. U.U. correspondiente a 1877, carpeta 5–3, AGMREP. Lima's Museo Antonio Raimondi has neither these maps nor others of the Hydrographic Commission.

7. Rochelle to Tucker, Sept. 2, 1877, folder 23, Tucker Papers, ODU; Romero Pintado, *Historia Marítima, 1850–70* 3:162.

8. Raygada to Arana, May 26, 1896, in Arana, *De Lima al Amazonas vía Mayro,* 57; Raygada, *Departamento de Loreto,* 5.

9. Basadre, *Historia* 6:2537, 2647; Markham, *History of Peru*, 417, 432. Inquiries to Chile's National Archive, National Library, Foreign Ministry archive, and the Hydrographic Institute of the navy failed to locate Tucker's maps.

10. Wertheman, "Coordenadas geográficas," 139; see also the *Times* (London), July 9, 1884; *El Mercurio*, July 19, 23, 1884.

11. Basadre, *Historia* 7:3323–25; Federico Schwab, "Bibliografía geográfica," 97.

12. Capelo and Pérez, "Memoria sobre la expedición . . . al río Pichis," *CDL* 3:278–304; Ortiz, *Oxapampa* 2:209–43; Perú, *Guía del inmigrante*, 40–45.

13. Contemporary publications with Hydrographic Commission data include Rochelle, "Geographical Positions"; [Perú, Comisión Hidrográfica del Amazonas], "Report of the Hydrographic Commission"; "List of the Principal Latitudes, Longitudes, Magnetic Variations, Barometric Elevations, and Distances Established by the Peruvian Hydrographic Commission, 1873," appendix D of Orton, *Andes and Amazon*, 633–36; Raimondi, *Perú* 3:464–66, 469–70, 475; Paz Soldán, *Diccionario geográfico estadístico*.

14. Rochelle to Rosas, May 30, 1872, Tucker to CGL, Feb. 14, 1873 (two notes), Rochelle to Meiggs, July 29, 1872, CHAlc, 42, 69, 47–50.

15. Medina to Ministro de Gobierno, Apr. 17, 1873, with Wertheman's endorsement, Apr. 21, 1873, CHA, Comandancia del DFL, AMNP; Tucker to CGL, Mar. 2, 1871, Rochelle to CGL, Dec. 20, 1871, Tucker to MGM, Feb. 28, 1873, CHAlc, 19, 35, 73–74; Raimondi, *Perú* 1:66–67. Wertheman likely provided Rochelle with the May 21, 1871, issue of *El Nacional* found in the Rochelle Papers, containing the Swiss engineer's coordinates for many points in Amazonian Peru.

16. Tucker to MGM, June 16, 1868, CHA, Comisaria de Marina, AMNP; Tucker to MGM, Nov. 16, 1868, Jan. 29, 1871, July 31, 1873, *CDL* 2:444, 3:75, 99; Rochelle to MGM, Jan. 31, 1874, CHAlc, 120–21; Rochelle to MGM, Dec. 31, 1873, with Freire's endorsement, CHA, Comandancia del DFL, AMNP.

17. Tooley, *Dictionary of Mapmakers*, 30, credits Babinski with a map "Seas of N. America & Europe, 1869"; the biographical sketch of Babinski in Kochanek, *Polacos en el Perú*, 94–97, notes his geologic maps but not the national map. He explained his project in Babinski to the Junta Central de Ingenieros, July 20, 1874, in Perú, *Anales del Cuerpo de Ingenieros del Perú* 2:381–87.

18. This road map was likely a revision of one Tucker had sent to Lima after reaching Iquitos in October 1867 (MGM to Tucker, Dec. 18, 1867, Dirección de Marina, 1866–1867, lc 126, AMNP).

19. Babinski to Junta Central de Ingenieros, July 20, 1874, in Perú, *Anales del Cuerpo de Ingenieros* 2:381–84; Perú, Cuerpo de Ingenieros y Arquitectos del Estado, *Memoria*, 65, and appended "Mapa del Perú."

20. Wertheman later published two maps of this region. His "Departamento Fluvial von Perú," is plate 12, facing p. 211 in Werthemann, "Aufnahme de Flüsse Paranapura." It shows the Marañón and the lower portion of its southern tributaries from the confluence of the Huallaga to Borja. Wertheman's "Karte eines Teiles de peruanischen de Amazonas," depicting the Department of Amazonas, is plate 1, facing p. 81 in "Bermerkungen su A. Wertheman's Karte."

21. Orton, *Andes and Amazon*, xv, 282–83, 633–36, and appended map; Noland to Mother, Sept. 11, 1873, box 3, Noland Papers; Galt Diary, 2:291–92.

22. Habenicht, "Peruanischen Expeditionen zur Erforschung des oberen Amazonenstroms," 89–91; Habenicht's map, "Der obere lauf des Amazonenstroms und seine peruanischen Nebenflüsse," is plate 5, facing p. 121 in that same volume.

23. Raimondi, *Perú* 3:146, identifies Saint-Cricq but does not mention the publications of "Marcoy." First appearing serially between 1862 and 1867 in *Le Tour du Monde*, a two-volume edition of "Marcoy's" work was published at Paris in 1869; a deluxe English edition is Saint-Cricq, *Travels in South America*. The Ucayali River is shown in plates 3 and 4. Although Habenicht used Orton's map, he seems to have missed Orton's assertion (*Andes and Amazon*, 380n.) that the work of "Marcoy" was "one of the most remarkable impositions on the literary

world" and that the book was based on Castelnau's expedition.

24. Raimondi, *Perú* 3:380–82, 393–97, 438–42, 458–80. The map faces p. 391.

25. Raimondi, *Mapa del Perú*, scale 1:500,000; Balta, *Labor de Raimondi*, 52–55; Raimondi, *Perú* 1:66–67; Stiglich, "Raimondi y la cartografía," 390–91; Schwab, "Bibliografía geográfica," 88, 96; Jochamonitz, "Situación de Antonio Raimondi," 139.

26. Balta, *Labor de Raimondi*, 15, 52.

27. Raimondi, *Perú* 3:571–76; Herrera, *Leyendas y tradiciones de Loreto*, 324–25 (Herrera apparently confuses the dates of death for Charon and Rosas).

28. Raimondi, *Mapa del Perú*, scale 1:500,000, sheet 21; Wertheman, *Ríos Perené y Tambo*.

29. *Crónica* (Lima), Mar. 27, 1921, and several unidentified newspaper clippings in the Ida Werthemann Collection; Steere letter, Chachapoyas, July 16, 1872, Steere Papers; Wertheman,

"Ruinas de la fortaleza de Cuelap," 147–53. Reports of Wertheman's early explorations are in *CDL* 2:465–76, 501–6, 3:12–14, 6:519–22, 7:361–64. Raimondi discussed Wertheman's contributions to Peruvian geography in *Perú* 3:99–100, 409–25, 476–80, 535–39. The latitudes and longitudes determined by the explorer are in Wertheman, "Coordenadas geográficas," 139–48.

30. Newspaper clippings in the Ida Werthemann Collection; Purser, *Metal-Mining in Peru*, 96; Ida Werthemann to Werlich, Sept. 2, 1985.

31. Alumni questionnaires and Galt to "Doctor," Feb. 1, 1911, Galt biographical folder; Galt to Mrs. Kell, Jan. 7, 1911, Kell Papers; unidentified newspaper clippings, Veselka Collection; *New York Times*, Nov. 19, 1915.

32. U.S. Department of the Interior, *Official Register, 1899* 2:379; draft of Mattie R. Tyler to Mr. Devine, May 19, 1905, and miscellaneous documents pertaining to her in box 32, John Tyler, Jr., Papers.

Bibliography

Archives

Much of this book is based on unpublished materials. Several major individual manuscripts and groups of personal papers are included in the alphabetical list below. Among the archival collections consulted in the United States, the most important are conserved at the National Archives in Washington, D.C.; many of these are available on microfilm. I made extensive use of U.S. Navy documents (especially those in Record Groups 24 and 45) and the files of the State Department in Record Groups 59 and 84. The Smithsonian Institution Archives, also in Washington, yielded useful materials, as did the biography (ZB) files in the Early Records Collection of the Naval Historical Center, located in the Washington Navy Yard. The British Foreign Office's General Correspondence for Chile, held at the Public Record Office in London, was consulted on microfilm.

At the Archivo Nacional de Chile, located in Santiago's Biblioteca Nacional, I used the collections pertaining to Benjamín Vicuña MacKenna and, more importantly, the records of the ministries of marine and foreign relations. Foreign ministry documents relating to Peru (and other nations bordering on Chile) are housed permanently in the Archivo del Ministerio de Relaciones Exteriores at the Moneda palace. I was unable to obtain timely permission to search these materials personally during my stay in Santiago, but the ministry later provided photocopies of documents that they deemed pertinent.

Peru's Archivo General de la Nación, housed in the Palacio de Justicia in Lima, holds only those records placed there voluntarily by various agencies. Within the History Section of that depository, the Hacienda (Treasury) and Justice archives had items useful for my research. Far more important for this project, however, were records still conserved by the ministries of foreign relations, war, and marine (the latter two services along with the air force have since been grouped within the Ministry of Defense). The Archivo General of the Ministerio de Relaciones Exteriores is housed in the beautiful eighteenth-century Torre Tagle Palace in central Lima. There I utilized records pertaining to Peru's relations with Chile and the United States. In the same building, several important items also were consulted in the ministry's Archivo de Límites, map library, and general library; the latter collection includes many rare printed works.

The Archivo Histórico Militar del Perú, at the Centro de Estudios Histórico-Militares del Perú in Lima, is the custodian for many of the central files of the old Ministry of War and Marine, which supervised both the army and navy during the nineteenth century. Although a catalog for this collection is being published, this long-term project has not yet progressed to the records for the 1860s and 1870s; thus, the materials consulted for this book are among the depository's unclassified documents. These items are grouped chronologically in folders pertaining to correspondents or subjects; in turn, these files are bundled in numbered packages, with six or more *paquetes* for each year covered by this study. The archive also has many bound copybooks.

The Archivo of the Museo Naval del Perú at Callao, Lima's contiguous port, held the largest corpus of materials (particularly operational records) for my research. The manuscripts in this extensive, well-catalogued collection are filed by year and correspondent or subject. The archive also has numerous copybooks for correspondence between entities within the Ramo de Marina (the navy branch) of the old Ministry of War and Marine.

Other Sources

Alexander, Thomas B., and Richard E. Beringer. *The Anatomy of the Confederate Congress*. Nashville: Vanderbilt Univ. Press, 1972.

Alexandria Daily Advertiser, 1805.

Alexandria Gazette and Daily Advertiser, 1819.

Alexandria Times and District of Columbia Advertiser, 1800.

Allen, Tacitus C. Memoirs. Manuscript Department, William R. Perkins Library, Duke Univ., Durham, N.C.

Allison, David K. "John A. Dahlgren: Innovator in Uniform." In *Captains of the Old Steam Navy: Makers of the American Naval Tradition, 1840–1880*, ed. James C. Bradford, 26–45. Annapolis: Naval Institute Press, 1986.

Anderson, Bern. *By Sea and by River: The Naval History of the Civil War*. New York: Alfred A. Knopf, 1962.

Appleton's Cyclopaedia of American Biography. Ed. James G. Wilson and John Fiske. 6 vols. New York: D. Appleton and Co., 1887–89.

The Appomattox Roster: A List of the Paroles of the Army of Northern Virginia Issued at Appomattox Court House on April 9, 1865. Ed. Robert A. Brock. 1887. Reprint. New York: Antiquarian Press, 1962.

Arana, Benito. *De Lima al Amazonas vía Mayro: Colección de las opiniones mas completas y autorizadas en favor de este vía*. Lima: Imprenta y Librería de San Pedro, 1896.

El Araucano (Santiago), 1866–67.

Army of Northern Virginia Association. Virginia Division. *Army of Northern Virginia Memorial Volume*. Comp. John William Jones. Richmond: J. W. Randolph and English, 1880.

Ashe, Samuel A. "Memories of Annapolis." *South Atlantic Quarterly* 18 (July 1919): 197–210.

Atlanta Constitution, 1900.

Ayers, Mrs. David T. Private collection of materials pertaining to John Randolph Tucker and his family. Richmond, Va.

Babinski, Alejandro. "Mapa del Perú hecho según los documentos del Archivo de la Junta Central de Ingenieros." Scale 1:4,000,000. Appended to Perú. Cuerpo de Ingenieros y Arquitectos del Estado. Junta Central. *Memoria sobre las obras públicas del Perú*. Lima: Imprenta Liberal de El Correo del Perú, 1874.

Balta, José. *La labor de Raimondi*. Lima: Imprenta Torres Aguirre, 1926.

Barreda, Federico L. *El ministro del Perú en los Estados Unidos y su calumniador*. 11 fascicles. Lima: Imprenta de "El Comercio," 1867.

———. Papers. Special Collections, Morris Library, Southern Illinois Univ., Carbondale.

Barron, Samuel. Papers. Manuscript Department, Univ. of Virginia Library, Charlottesville.

Basadre, Jorge. *Historia de la re-*

BIBLIOGRAPHY

pública del Perú. 5th ed., rev., 10 vols. Lima: Ediciones "Historia," 1961.

———. *Introducción a las bases documentales para la* Historia de la república del Perú, *con algunas reflexiones*. 2 vols. Lima: Ediciones P. L. Villanueva, 1971.

Basinger, William S. "Crutchfield's Artillery Brigade." *Southern Historical Society Papers* 25 (1897): 38–44.

"Battle of Sailor's Creek: Part Taken in It by the Savannah Guards." *Southern Historical Society Papers* 24 (1896): 250–54.

Bauer, K. Jack. *Surfboats and Horse Marines: U.S. Naval Operations in the Mexican War, 1846–48*. Annapolis: United States Naval Institute, 1969.

Beauregard, Pierre Gustave Toutant. "Defense of Charleston, South Carolina, in 1862, 1863, and 1864." *North American Review* 142 (May 1886): 419–36.

———. Papers. Manuscript Division, Library of Congress, Washington, D.C.

———. "Torpedo Service in the Harbor and Water Defences of Charleston." *Southern Historical Society Papers* 5 (1878): 145–61.

Beers, Henry Putney. *Guide to the Archives of the Government of the Confederate States of America*. Washington, D.C.: National Archives, 1968.

Benjamin, Park. *The United States Naval Academy*. New York: G. P. Putnam's Sons, 1900.

"Bermerkungen zu A. Wertheman's Karte eines Teiles des peruanischen Departamento de Amazonas." *Zeitschrift der Gesellschaft für erdkunde zu Berlin*. Ed. A. von Danckelman, 81–82. 3d ser., vol. 24. Berlin: Dietrich Reimer, 1889.

Blackford, William W. *War Years with Jeb Stuart*. New York: Charles Scribner's Sons, 1945.

Blake, Thomas B. "The Artillery Brigade at Sailor's Creek." *Confederate Veteran* 28 (June 1920): 213–16.

Boykin, Edward. *Ghost Ship of the Confederacy*. New York: Funk and Wagnalls Co., 1957.

Brodie, Bernard. *Sea Power in the Machine Age*. Princeton, N.J.: Princeton Univ. Press, 1941.

Brooke, George M., Jr. *John M.*

Brooke, Naval Scientist and Educator. Charlottesville: Univ. Press of Virginia, 1980.

Brooke, John Mercer. Papers. Private collection of George M. Brooke, Jr., Lexington, Va.

Bruce, Philip Alexander. *History of the University of Virginia, 1819–1919*. 5 vols. New York: Macmillan Co., 1920–24.

Burr, Robert N. *By Reason or Force: Chile and the Balancing of Power in South America, 1830–1905*. Berkeley and Los Angeles: Univ. of California Press, 1965.

Burton, E. Milby. *The Siege of Charleston, 1861–1865*. Columbia: Univ. of South Carolina Press, 1970.

Butt, Marshall W. *Portsmouth under Four Flags, 1752–1961*. Portsmouth, Va.: Portsmouth Historical Association, 1961.

Butt, Walter Raleigh. Alumnus file. Naval Academy Archives, United States Naval Academy, Annapolis, Md.

———. Papers. Private collection of Marshall W. Butt, Jr., and Brooke Butt Maupin, Portsmouth, Va.

Butts [Butt], Walter Raleigh. "American Officers in the Peruvian Navy." *Californian* 6, no. 31 (July 1882): 147–54.

Calkins, Christopher M. *Thirty-Six Hours before Appomattox: April 6 and 7, 1865*. [Farmville, Va.: Farmville Herald, 1980.]

Callahan, Edward W., ed. *List of Officers of the Navy of the United States and of the Marine Corps, from 1775 to 1900*. 1901. Reprint. New York: Haskell House Publishers, 1969.

Callao and Lima Gazette, 1871.

Capuñay Mimbela, Carlos. "Historia del presupuesto nacional desde 1821 a 1899." Universidad Nacional Mayor de San Marcos, *Revista de la Facultad de Ciéncias Económicas*, no. 23 (Apr. 1942): 67–116.

Catlin, George. *Episodes from Life among the Indians and Last Rambles with 163 Scenes and Portraits by the Artist*. Ed. Marvin C. Ross. Norman: Univ. of Oklahoma Press, 1959.

Charleston Daily Courier, 1862–65.

Charleston Mercury, 1862–65.

BIBLIOGRAPHY

Charon, Manuel. *Estado comercial del Amazonas peruano.* Lima: Impr. de J. F. Solís, 1877.

Chew, Francis Thornton. Reminiscences and Journal. Typescript. Francis Thornton Chew Papers, Southern Historical Collection, Wilson Library, Univ. of North Carolina, Chapel Hill.

Chile. Ministerio de Marina. *Memoria, 1866.* Santiago: Imprenta Nacional, 1866.

Cisneros Sánchez, Máximo. Private manuscript collection. Lima, Peru.

Clayton, William F. "In the Battle of Hampton Roads." *Confederate Veteran* 24 (Oct. 1916): 456–57.

——. *A Narrative of the Confederate States Navy.* Weldon, N.C.: Harrell's Printing House, 1910.

Cloyd, James McGavock. Papers. Virginia Historical Society, Richmond.

El Comercio (Lima), 1868–74.

Confederate States of America. Navy Department. *Register of the Commissioned and Warrant Officers of the Navy of the Confederate States, to January 1, 1863; 1864.* Richmond: Macfarlane and Ferguson, 1862; 1864.

Cortada, James W. "Diplomatic Rivalry between Spain and the United States over Chile and Peru, 1864–1871." *Inter-American Economic Affairs* 27 (Spring 1974): 47–57.

——. *Spain and the American Civil War, 1855–1869.* Transactions of the American Philosophical Society, n.s., vol. 70, pt. 4. Philadelphia, 1980.

Cotter, Charles H. *The Astronomical and Mathematical Foundations of Geography.* New York: American Elsevier Publishing Co., 1966.

Couper, William. *The V.M.I. New Market Cadets: Biographical Sketches of All Members of the Virginia Military Institute Corps of Cadets Who Fought in the Battle of New Market, May 15, 1864.* Charlottesville, Va.: Michie Co., 1933.

Cowley, Charles. *Leaves from a Lawyer's Life Afloat and Ashore.* Lowell, Mass.: Penhallow Printing Co., 1879.

La Crónica (Lima), 1921.

Dahlgren, John Adolphus Bernard. Diary. J. A. B. Dahlgren Papers, George

Arents Research Library, Syracuse Univ., Syracuse, N.Y.

——. Letter Book, 1867. Manuscript Division, New York Public Library, New York.

——. *Maritime International Law.* Ed. Charles Cowley, with a biographical sketch by Madeleine Vinton Dahlgren. Boston: B. B. Russell, 1877.

——. *Memoir of Ulric Dahlgren.* Philadelphia: J. B. Lippincott and Co., 1872.

——. Papers. Manuscript Division, Library of Congress, Washington, D.C.

Dahlgren, Madeleine Vinton. *Memoir of John A. Dahlgren, Rear-Admiral United States Navy.* Boston: James R. Osgood and Co., 1882.

Dalton, Charles, ed. *English Army Lists and Commission Registers, 1661–1714.* 6 vols. London: Francis Edwards, 1960.

Davidson, Hunter. "The Electrical Submarine Mine—1861–65." *Confederate Veteran* 16 (Sept. 1908): 456–59.

——. "Electrical Torpedoes as a System of Defence." *Southern Historical Society Papers* 2 (1878): 1–6.

Davis, Jefferson. *Jefferson Davis, Constitutionalist: His Letters, Papers, and Speeches.* Ed. Dunbar Rowland. 10 vols. Jackson: Mississippi Department of Archives and History, 1923.

——. Papers. Alabama Department of Archives and History, Montgomery.

Davis, William C. *The Battle of New Market.* Garden City, N.Y.: Doubleday, 1975.

——. "The Campaign to Appomattox." *Civil War Times Illustrated* 14 (Apr. 1975): 4–50.

——. *Duel between the First Ironclads.* 2d ed. Baton Rouge: Louisiana State Univ. Press, 1981.

Davis, William Columbus. *The Last Conquistadores: The Spanish Intervention in Peru and Chile, 1863–1866.* Athens: Univ. of Georgia Press, 1950.

DeBoer, Warren R. "Pillage and Production in the Amazon: A View through the Conibo of the Ucayali Basin, Eastern Peru." *World Archaeology* 18 (Oct. 1986): 231–46.

DeKalb, Courtenay. "Iquitos, the

Metropolis of Eastern Peru." *Nation* 50 (May 29, 1890): 431–33.

——. "Social and Intellectual Condition of Eastern Peru." *Harper's New Monthly Magazine* 85 (June 1892): 113–26.

Delaney, Norman C. *John McIntosh Kell of the Raider Alabama.* University, Ala.: Univ. of Alabama Press, 1973.

DeLeon, Thomas C. *Four Years in Rebel Capitals: An Inside View of Life in the Southern Confederacy, from Birth to Death.* Mobile: Gossip Printing Company, 1890.

Diccionario enciclopédico del Perú. Ed. Alberto Tauro. 4 vols. Lima: Editorial Mejía Baca, 1966–75.

Diccionario histórico, biográfico, y bibliográfico de Chile, 1806–1931. Ed. Virgilio Figueroa. 5 vols. Santiago: La Ilustración, 1925–31.

Dictionary of American Biography. Ed. Allen Johnson and Dumas Malone. 21 vols. New York: Charles Scribner's Sons, 1928–37.

Donnelly, Ralph W. *The History of the Confederate States Marine Corps.* Washington, N.C.: by the author, 1976.

Dorris, Jonathan Truman. *Pardon and Amnesty under Lincoln and Johnson.* Chapel Hill: Univ. of North Carolina Press, 1953.

Dozier, Donald M. "Pathfinder of the Amazon." *Virginia Quarterly Review* 23 (Autumn 1947): 554–67.

Drewry, Augustus H. "Drewry's Bluff Fight." *Southern Historical Society Papers* 29 (1901): 284–85.

Dudley, William S. *Going South: U.S. Navy Officer Resignations and Dismissals on the Eve of the Civil War.* Naval Historical Foundation Publication, ser. 2, no. 27. Washington, D.C.: Naval Historical Foundation, 1981.

Du Pont, Samuel Francis. *Samuel Francis Du Pont: A Selection from His Civil War Letters.* Ed. John D. Hayes. 3 vols. Ithaca, N.Y.: Cornell Univ. Press, 1969.

Durkin, Joseph T. *Stephen R. Mallory, Confederate Navy Chief.* Chapel Hill: Univ. of North Carolina Press, 1954.

E. R. F. "Torpedoes." *Fraser's Magazine*, n.s., 5 (Jan.–June 1872): 461–76.

Echenique, José Rufino. *Memorias para la historia del Perú, 1808–1878.* Ed. Félix Denegri Luna. 2 vols. Lima: Ed. Huascarán, 1952.

Edwards, Conley L. "Abstracts of Reports of Aliens, Alexandria County, 1801–1832." *Virginia Genealogist* 24 (Mar.–June 1980): 112–16.

The Encyclopedia of Southern History. Ed. David C. Roller and Robert W. Twyman. Baton Rouge: Louisiana State Univ. Press, 1979.

Encina, Francisco A. *Resumen de la historia de Chile.* 2d ed. 3 vols. Santiago: Zig Zag, 1956.

Ewell, Richard S. *The Making of a Soldier: Letters of General R. S. Ewell.* Ed. Percy Gatling Hamlin. Richmond: Whittet and Shepperson, 1935.

Faura Gaig, Guillermo S. *Los ríos de la Amazonia peruana: Estudio histórico-geográfico, político, y militar de la Amazonia peruana y de su porvenir en el desarrollo socio-económico del Perú.* Lima: Impr. Colegio Militar Leoncio Prado, [1964?].

Fernández, Francisco Emilio. *El progreso del apostadero de Iquitos.* Lima: Imprenta de "El Comercio," 1869.

Forrest, Douglas French. *Odyssey in Gray: A Diary of Confederate Service, 1863–1865.* Ed. William N. Still, Jr. Richmond: Virginia State Library, 1979.

Foster, Gaines M. *Ghosts of the Confederacy: Defeat, the Lost Cause, and the Emergence of the New South, 1865–1913.* New York: Oxford Univ. Press, 1987.

Fragata blindada "Independencia." Copias de los pedidos de la espresada desde el 19 de junio de 1866 hasta el 29 de octubre de 1867. MS 10233. Sala de Investigaciones, Biblioteca Nacional del Perú, Lima.

Franklin, Samuel R. *Memoirs of a Rear-Admiral.* New York: Harper and Brothers, 1898.

Fremantle, Arthur James Lyon. *The Fremantle Diary, Being the Journal of Lieutenant Colonel Arthur James Lyon Fremantle, Coldstream Guards, on His Three Months in the Southern States.* Ed. Walter Lord. Boston: Little, Brown and Co., 1954.

Freyre, Manuel. Papers. Sala de Investigaciones, Biblioteca Nacional del Perú, Lima.

Frothingham, Paul Revere. *Edward Everett, Orator and Statesman.* Boston: Houghton Mifflin Co., 1925.

Fuentes, Hildebrando. *Loreto.* 2 vols. Lima: Imprenta de La Revista, 1908.

Galt, Francis Land. Biographical folder. Univ. of Pennsylvania Archives, Philadelphia.

———. Diary of a Trip to the Headwaters of the Amazon River, 1870–73, 1874. 2 vols. and folder of loose notes, letters, and photos. MS 3975. Microfilm. National Anthropological Archives, National Museum of Natural History, Smithsonian Institution, Washington, D.C.

———. "The Indians of Peru." *Annual Report of the Board of Regents of the Smithsonian Institution, for the Year 1877,* pp. 308–15. Washington, D.C.: GPO, 1878.

———. "Medical Notes on a Trip through the Pampa del Sacramento." *American Journal of the Medical Sciences,* n.s., 67 (Apr. 1874): 396–406.

———. "Medical Notes on the Upper Amazon." *American Journal of the Medical Sciences,* n.s., 64 (Oct. 1872): 395–416.

———. "Medical Notes on the Upper Amazons." Rev. ed. In James Orton, *The Andes and the Amazon; or, Across the Continent of South America.* 3d ed., pp. 580–614. New York: Harper and Brothers, 1876.

———. "Meteorological and Sanitary Notes at Iquitos, Peru." *American Meteorological Journal* 2 (1885–86): 206–7.

———. "Notes on the Climate of the Marañon." *Proceedings of the Royal Geographical Society* 17, no. 2 (1872–73): 130–42.

Galt, Mary M. "Galt Family of Williamsburg." *William and Mary Quarterly Historical Magazine,* 1st ser., 8 (Apr. 1900): 259–62.

Galt Family. Papers. Manuscript Department, Earl Gregg Swem Library, College of William and Mary, Williamsburg, Va.

García y García, José Antonio. *Defenza del Capitán de Fragata D. Aurelio García y García, ex-comandante de la fragata blindada* "Independencia," *pronunciada ante el Consejo de Guerra de Oficiales Generales.* Lima: Imprenta de Aurelio Alfaro y ca., 1867.

Gilman, C. P. "Concerning Battle at Sailor's Creek." *Confederate Veteran* 8 (Oct. 1900): 451.

Glassell, William T. "Torpedo Service in Charleston Harbor." *Confederate Veteran* 25 (Mar. 1917): 113–16.

Gratz Collection. Manuscript Department, Historical Society of Pennsylvania, Philadelphia.

Green [Greene], Samuel Dana. *An Eye-Witness Account of the Battle between the U.S.S.* Monitor *and the C.S.S.* Virginia *(Formerly U.S.S.* Merrimack) *on March 9th, 1862.* [Washington, D.C.: Naval Historical Foundation, n.d.]

Grimball, John Berkeley. Papers. Manuscript Department, William R. Perkins Library, Duke Univ., Durham, N.C.

Habenicht, Herman. "Die peruanischen Expeditionen zur Erforschung des oberen Amazonenstroms und seiner Nebenflüsse." *Petermanns Mittheilungen aus Justus Perthes' geographischer Anstalt* 25 (1879): 89–91.

Hanna, Alfred Jackson, and Kathryn Abbey Hanna. *Confederate Exiles in Venezuela.* Confederate Centennial Studies, no. 15. Tuscaloosa, Ala.: Confederate Publishing Co., 1960.

Hayes, Rutherford Birchard. *Diary and Letters of Rutherford Birchard Hayes, Nineteenth President of the United States.* Ed. Charles Richard Williams. 5 vols. Columbus: Ohio State Archaeological and Historical Society, 1922–26.

Herndon, William Lewis, and Lardner Gibbon. *Exploration of the Valley of the Amazon, Made under the Direction of the Navy Department.* Vol. 1 by Herndon; vol. 2 by Gibbon. Washington, D.C.: Robert Armstrong, 1853–54.

Herrera, Jenaro E. "Fundación de la ciudad de Iquitos." *Boletín de la Sociedad Geográfica de Lima* 23 (Mar. 1908): 102–17.

———. *Leyendas y tradiciones de Loreto.* Biblioteca Loretana. Iquitos: Imprenta "El Oriente," 1918.

Heynen, William J. *U.S. Hydro-*

graphic Office Manuscript Charts in the National Archives, 1838–1909. National Archives Special List 43. Washington, D.C.: National Archives and Records Service, 1978.

Howard, McHenry. *Recollections of a Maryland Confederate Soldier and Staff Officer under Johnston, Jackson, and Lee.* 1914. Reprint. Dayton, Ohio: Morningside Bookshop, 1975.

Jacksonville *Florida Times-Union*, 1915.

Jochamonitz, Alberto. "Situación de Antonio Raimondi en la geografía nacional." *Boletín de la Sociedad Geográfica de Lima* 66, no. 1–4 (1949): 136–51.

Johnson, B. S. "Battle of Sailor's Creek." *Confederate Veteran* 8 (Dec. 1900): 538.

Johnson, Robert Erwin. *Rear Admiral John Rodgers, 1812–1882.* Annapolis: United States Naval Institute, 1967.

Jones, H. L. *Captain Roger Jones of London and Virginia: Some of His Antecedents and Descendants.* Albany, N.Y.: Joel Munsell's Sons, 1891.

Jones, Virgil Carrington. *The Civil War at Sea.* 3 vols. New York: Holt, Rinehart and Winston, 1962.

——. *Eight Hours before Richmond.* New York: Henry Holt and Co., 1957.

Karsten, Peter. *The Naval Aristocracy: The Golden Age of Annapolis and the Emergence of Modern American Navalism.* New York: Free Press, 1972.

Keifer, Joseph Warren. Papers. Manuscript Division, Library of Congress, Washington, D.C.

——. *Slavery and Four Years of War: A Political History of Slavery in the United States Together with a Narrative of the Campaigns and Battles of the Civil War in Which the Author Took Part, 1861–1865.* 2 vols. New York: G. P. Putnam's Sons, 1900.

Kell, John McIntosh. Papers. Manuscript Department, William R. Perkins Library, Duke Univ., Durham, N.C.

——. *Recollections of a Naval Life, Including the Cruise of the Confederate States Steamers "Sumter" and "Alabama."* Washington: Neale Co., 1900.

Kelly, Hank, and Dot Kelly. *The Dancing Diplomats.* Albuquerque: Univ. of New Mexico Press, 1950.

Kennedy, Jean de Chantal. *Isle of Devils: Bermuda under the Somers Island Company, 1609–1685.* London: William Collins Sons and Co., 1971.

Kerr, Winifred Brenton. *Bermuda and the American Revolution, 1760–1783.* Princeton, N.J.: Princeton Univ. Press, 1936.

Kochanek, Kazimierz, ed. *Los Polacos en el Perú.* Trans. Marek Rakower. Lima: Embajada de la República Popular de Polonia en el Perú, 1979.

La Bree, Benjamin, ed. *Campfires of the Confederacy.* Louisville, Ky.: Courier-Journal Job Printing Co., 1898.

Langley, Harold D. *Social Reform in the United States Navy, 1798–1862.* Urbana: Univ. of Illinois Press, 1967.

Larrabure i Correa, Carlos, comp. and ed. *Colección de leyes, decretos, resoluciones, i otros documentos oficiales referentes al Departamento de Loreto, formado de orden supremo.* 18 vols. Lima: Imp. de "La Opinión Nacional," 1905–9.

Lee, George Washington Custis. "Report of General G. W. C. Lee, from the 2d to the 6th of April, 1865." *Southern Historical Society Papers* 13 (1885): 255–57.

Lee, Robert E. Papers. Virginia Historical Society, Richmond.

Lewis, Charles Lee. *Admiral Franklin Buchanan, Fearless Man of Action.* Baltimore: Norman Remington Co., 1929.

Lira Urqueta, Pedro. "La guerra con España en la correspondencia de don Alvaro Covarrubias con don José Ramón Lira." *Boletín de la Academia Chilena de la Historia,* año 25 (2d semester 1958): 149–68.

Lockhart, Paul D. "The Confederate Naval Squadron at Charleston and the Failure of Naval Harbor Defense." *American Neptune* 44 (Fall 1984): 257–75.

Long, John Sherman. "The Gosport Affair." *Journal of Southern History* 23 (May 1957): 155–72.

López Urrutia, Carlos. *Historia de*

la Marina de Chile. Santiago: Editorial Andrés Bello, 1969.

McBride, Robert. *Civil War Ironclads: The Dawn of Naval Armor.* Philadelphia: Chilton Books, 1962.

MacCartney, Clarence Edward. *Mr. Lincoln's Admirals.* New York: Funk and Wagnalls Co., 1956.

McKinney, Francis F. *Education in Violence: The Life of George H. Thomas and the History of the Army of the Cumberland.* Detroit: Wayne State Univ. Press, 1961.

McLain, Minor Horne. "Prison Conditions in Fort Warren, Boston, during the Civil War." Ph.D. diss., Boston Univ., 1955.

Mahan, Alfred Thayer. *Letters and Papers of Alfred Thayer Mahan.* Ed. Robert Seager II and Doris D. Maguire. 3 vols. Annapolis: Naval Institute Press, 1975.

Mahone, William. "On the Road to Appomattox." Ed. William C. Davis. *Civil War Times Illustrated* 9 (Jan. 1971): 42–49.

Mann, Samuel A. "Recollections of Service in the Army of Northern Virginia (August Henry Drewry's Battery of Virginia Artillery) concerning the Defeat of the U.S. Ironclads *Monitor* and *Galena* at Drewry's Bluff, Chesterfield Co., Va., 15 May 1862. Written in 1898." Typescript. Virginia Historical Society, Richmond.

Manuscript Collection. Gilpin Library, Chicago Historical Society, Chicago.

Manuscript Confederate Registers. Virginia State Library and Archives, Richmond.

Manuscript insurance records. Alexandria Library, Alexandria, Va.

Marbury, L. A., Thomas Alphonse Jackson, William Turnbull, and Norman V. Randolph. Inventory and Appraisal of the Personal Estate of John R. Tucker, filed Aug. 31, 1883. Clerk's Office, Hustings Court, Petersburg, Va.

Markham, Clements R. *A History of Peru.* Chicago: Charles H. Sergel, 1892.

Mason, Charles T. Papers. Virginia Historical Society, Richmond.

Mattos, João Wilkens de. *Diccion-*

ário topográphico do Departamento de Loreto, na República do Perú. Pará: Typ. Commércio do Pará, 1874.

Melo, Rosendo. *Historia de la marina del Perú.* 3 vols. Lima: Carlos F. Southwell, 1907; Taller Tip. de "El Auxiliar del Comercio," 1911, 1915.

Melville, Herman. *White-Jacket; or, The World in a Man-of-War.* Ed. H. Hayford, H. Parker, and G. T. Tanselle. Vol. 5 of *The Writings of Herman Melville.* Evanston and Chicago: Northwestern Univ. Press and the Newberry Library, 1970.

El Mercurio (Valparaíso), 1866–67, 1884.

Merli, Frank J., ed. "Alternative to Appomattox: A Virginian's Vision of an Anglo-Confederate Colony on the Amazon, May, 1865." *Virginia Magazine of History and Biography* 94 (Apr. 1986): 210–19.

Minor Family. Papers. Virginia Historical Society, Richmond.

Mitchell, John K. Papers. Virginia Historical Society, Richmond.

Moore, John Bassett. *A Digest of International Law, as Embodied in Diplomatic Discussions, Treaties and Other International Agreements, International Awards, the Decisions of Municipal Courts, and the Writings of Jurists, and Especially in Documents, Published and Unpublished, Issued by Presidents and Secretaries of State of the United States, the Opinions of the Attorneys-General, and the Decisions of the Courts, Federal and State.* 8 vols. Washington, D.C.: GPO, 1906.

Moreyra Paz-Soldán, Manuel. *Manuel Rouaud y Paz Soldán y la exploración al río Yavarí en 1866.* Lima: Talleres Gráficos P. L. Villanueva, 1970.

Morgan, Henry G., Jr. "Education." In *Alexandria: A Towne in Transition.* Ed. John D. Macoll and George J. Stansfield, pp. 89–123. Alexandria, Va.: Alexandria Bicentennial Commission and Alexandria Historical Society, 1977.

Mould Távara, Santiago. *El Doctor Santiago Távara, cirujano mayor del "Huáscar."* Lima: Centro de Estudios Histórico-Militares del Perú, 1951.

El Nacional (Lima), 1866, 1869, 1871, 1873.

National Cyclopedia of American

BIBLIOGRAPHY

Biography. 76 vols. New York: James T. White and Co., 1895–1984.

A Naval Encyclopedia, Comprising a Dictionary of Nautical Words and Phrases, Biographical Notices, and Articles on Naval Art and Science. 1884. Reprint. Detroit: Gale Research Co., 1971.

New York Herald, 1865.

New York Times, 1865–66, 1915.

Niven, John. *Gideon Welles, Lincoln's Secretary of the Navy.* New York: Oxford Univ. Press, 1973.

Noland, Nelson Berkeley. Alumnus file. Special Collections, Library, Virginia Military Institute, Lexington, Va.

———. "The Peruvian Amazon and Its Tributaries: Notes from a Journal of Travel." Pts. 1–6. *Appleton's Journal* 14 (Oct. 30–Dec. 18, 1875): 545–48, 577–79, 621–23, 684–86, 721–24, 780–83.

Noland–Berkeley Family. Papers. MSS 2718-d. Manuscript Department, Univ. of Virginia Library, Charlottesville.

Noland Family. Papers. MSS 2718. Manuscript Department, Univ. of Virginia Library, Charlottesville.

Norfolk Landmark, 1883.

Norfolk Virginian, 1883.

Norwood School. *A Catalogue of Norwood School, Nelson County, Virginia: Session 1868–69.* Baltimore: John Murphy and Co., 1869.

———. *A Historical Sketch of Norwood High School and College, Nelson County, Virginia.* Richmond: Whittet and Shepperson, Printers, 1881.

Núñez, Estuardo. "El Almirante John R. Tucker en el Perú." *Ipna: Organo del Instituto Cultural Peruano-Norteamericano* 19 (May–Aug. 1952): 53–57.

———. "Los viajeros de tierra adentro, 1860–1900." *Journal of Inter-American Studies* 2 (Jan. 1960): 9–44.

Nurney, Daisy. "Two Letitias—A Virginia Beauty and an Amazon Port." *Virginian-Pilot and Norfolk Landmark,* Feb. 26, 1933.

Odgers, Merle M. *Alexander Dallas Bache, Scientist and Educator, 1806–1867.* Philadelphia: Univ. of Pennsylvania Press, 1947.

Onffroy de Thoron, Enrique, viscomte. *Amérique équatoriale.* Paris: Jules Renouard, 1866.

Ortiz, Dionisio. *Oxapampa: Estudio de una provincia de la selva del Perú.* 2 vols. Lima: Imprenta Editorial "San Antonio," [1967].

———. *El Pachitea y el alto Ucayali: Visión histórica de las importantes regiones de la selva peruana.* 2 vols. Lima: Imprenta Editorial "San Antonio," 1974.

Orton, James. *The Andes and the Amazon; or, Across the Continent of South America.* New York: Harper and Brothers, 1870; 3d ed., 1876.

———. "The New Exploration of the Amazon River." *Scientific American,* n.s., 29 (Nov. 8, 1873): 296.

Palma, Ricardo. *Epistolario.* Ed. Augusta Palma and Renée Palma. 2 vols. Lima: Editorial Cultura Antártica, 1949.

———. *Semblanzas.* Ed. Alberto Tauro. Lima: Librería-Editorial Juan Mejía Baca, n.d.

Parker, Foxhall A. *Táctica de escuadras de buques a vapor.* Trans. Domingo Salamanca. Valparaíso: Imprenta de la Patria, 1872.

———. *Táctica naval de las escuadras a vapor.* Trans. and ed. Aurelio García y García. New York: D. Van Nostrand, 1870.

Parker, William Harwar. *Recollections of a Naval Officer, 1841–1865.* New York: Charles Scribner's Sons, 1883.

Parramore, Thomas C. *Southampton County, Virginia.* Charlottesville: Univ. Press of Virginia for the Southampton County Historical Society, 1978.

Paullin, Charles Oscar. "President Lincoln and the Navy." In *Civil War Naval Chronology, 1861–1865,* comp. the Naval History Division, U.S. Navy Department, 6:29–46. Washington, D.C.: GPO, 1971.

Pavletich, Esteban. *Leoncio Prado: Una vida al servicio de la libertad.* 2d ed. Lima: n.p., 1953.

Paz Soldán, Mariano Felipe. *Atlas geográfico del Perú.* Paris: Librería de Fermín Didot Hermanos, Hijos, y ca., 1865.

———. *Diccionario geográfico estadístico del Perú.* Lima: Imprenta del Estado, 1877.

Perry, Milton F. *Infernal Machines: The Story of Confederate Submarine and Mine Warfare*. Baton Rouge: Louisiana State Univ. Press, 1965.

Perú. Comisión Hidrográfica del Amazonas. Exploraciones en el Amazonas y sus tributarios, 1870–1874: Libro copiador de la correspondencia de la Comisión Hidrográfica del Amazonas. Area: Geografía Oriental, LEJ-10–1, Archivo de Límites del Ministerio de Relaciones Exteriores del Perú, Palacio Torre Tagle, Lima.

——. ——. Plano de los ríos Amazonas y Ucayali en el Perú y de sus tributarios por la Comisión Hidrográfica del Amazonas, 1873. Mapoteca del Ministerio de Relaciones Exteriores del Perú, Palacio Torre Tagle, Lima.

——. ——. Plano del río Amazonas del Perú por la Comisión Hidrográfica del Amazonas del Perú, 1874. Sheets 1 and 2. Mapoteca del Ministerio de Relaciones Exteriores del Perú, Palacio Torre Tagle, Lima.

——. ——. "Report of the Hydrographic Commission of Peru on the Amazon River." *Journal of the American Geographical Society of New York* 7 (1875): 357–65.

——. Congreso Constituyente de 1867. *Diario de los debates*. 3 vols. [Lima: n.p., 1867.]

——. Cuerpo de Ingenieros del Perú. *Anales del Cuerpo de Ingenieros del Perú*. 2 vols. Lima: Imprenta del Estado, 1874.

——. Cuerpo de Ingenieros y Arquitectos del Estado. Junta Central. *Memoria sobre las obras públicas del Perú, presentada al supremo gobierno de la república*. Lima: Imprenta Liberal de "El Correo del Perú," 1874.

——. Dirección de Estadística. *Censo general de la república del Perú formado en 1876*. 7 vols. Lima: Imp. del Teatro, 1878.

——. Ministerio de Fomento. *Guía del inmigrante en el Perú: La vía central, zona del Pichis*. Lima: Imprenta del Estado, 1902.

——. Ministerio de Guerra y Marina. *Memoria, 1868; 1897*. Lima: Imprenta de A. Alfaro, 1868; Imprenta de El País, 1897.

——. ——. Ramo de Guerra. *Memoria, 1870*. Lima: Imprenta del Estado, 1870.

——. ——. Ramo de Marina. *Memoria, 1876*. Lima: Imprenta Económica, 1876.

——. Ministerio de Relaciones Exteriores. *Memoria, 1896; 1898*. Lima: Imprenta del País, 1897, 1899.

Petersburg Index-Appeal, 1883.

Powell, Mary G. *The History of Old Alexandria, Virginia, from July 13, 1749, to May 24, 1861*. Richmond: William Byrd Press, 1928.

Powell, William H., comp. *List of Officers of the Army of the United States from 1779 to 1900*. New York: L. R. Hamersley and Co., 1900.

Price, Marcus W. "Four from Bristol." *American Neptune* 17 (Oct. 1957): 249–61.

Purser, W. F. C. *Metal-Mining in Peru, Past and Present*. New York: Praeger Publishers, 1974.

Pusey and Jones Corporation. *A Hundred Years A-Building*. Wilmington, Del.: by the corporation, 1948.

Raimondi, Antonio. *Apuntes sobre la Provincia Litoral de Loreto*. 1862. Ed. Claudio Bravo Morán. Iquitos: Imprenta "El Oriente," 1942.

——. *Mapa del Perú*. Scale 1: 500,000. Sheets 1–11. Paris: Erhard Fres., 1883–90. Sheets 12–32. Lima: Sociedad Geográfica de Lima, 1891–1900.

——. *El Perú*. 3 vols. Lima: Imprenta del Estado, 1874–79.

Randolph, Joseph Williamson. Papers. Virginia Historical Society, Richmond.

Raygada, Eduardo. *El Departamento Fluvial de Loreto*. Lima: Imp. de Torres Aguirre, 1891.

Regal, Alberto. *Castilla constructor: Las obras de ingeniería de Castilla*. Lima: Editorial Ausonia Talleres Gráficos, 1967.

Registro de los despachos transmitidos de palacio a la Comandancia General de Marina desde el 27 de febrero de 1866. MS D4642. Sala de Investigaciones, Biblioteca Nacional del Perú, Lima.

Richmond Daily Dispatch, 1863, 1866.

Richmond Evening Journal, 1913.

Riggs, David F. "The Dahlgren Papers Reconsidered." *Lincoln Herald* 83 (Summer 1981): 658–68.

Robinson, William M., Jr. "Drewry's Bluff: Naval Defense of Richmond." *Civil War History* 7 (June 1961): 167–75.

Rochelle, James Henry. "The Confederate Steamship 'Patrick Henry.'" *Southern Historical Society Papers* 14 (1886): 126–36.

———. "Geographical Positions in the Valley of the Amazon." *Proceedings of the Royal Geographical Society* 16, no. 3 (1872): 271–74.

———. *Life of Rear Admiral John Randolph Tucker, Commander in the Navy of the United States, Captain and Flag-Officer in the Navy of the Confederate States, Rear Admiral in the Navy of the Republic of Peru, and President of the Peruvian Hydrographical Commission of the Amazon, with an Appendix Containing Notes on Navigation of the Upper Amazon River and Its Principal Tributaries, by Captain James Henry Rochelle, and Containing a Biographical Sketch of the Author, and Portraits of Admiral Tucker and Captain Rochelle.* [Edited and introduced by Mattie Rochelle Tyler.] Washington, D.C.: Neale Publishing Co., 1903.

[———.] "A List of the Principal Latitudes, Longitudes, Magnetic Variations, Barometric Elevations, and Distances Established by the Peruvian Hydrographic Commission, 1873." In James Orton, *The Andes and the Amazon*, 3d ed., pp. 633–36. New York: Harper and Brothers, 1876.

———. Papers. Manuscript Department, William R. Perkins Library, Duke Univ., Durham, N.C.

Rodick, Burleigh Cushing. *Appomattox: The Last Campaign.* New York: Philosophical Library, 1965.

Roman, Alfred. *The Military Operations of General Beauregard in the War Between the States, 1861 to 1865.* 2 vols. New York: Harper and Brothers, 1884.

Romero Pintado, Fernando. *Historia marítima del Perú: La república—*

1850 a 1870. 3 vols. Tomo 8 of *Perú.* Comisión para Escribir la Historia Marítima del Perú. *Historia marítima del Perú.* Lima: Instituto de Estudios Histórico-Marítimos del Perú, 1984–85.

Saint-Cricq, Laurent [Paul Marcoy, pseud.]. *Travels in South America.* Trans. Elihu Rich. 2 vols. London: Blackie and Sons, 1875.

San Cristóval, Evaristo. *Manuel Pardo y Lavalle, su vida y su obra.* Lima: Gil Editores, 1945.

Sanford, Daniel B. Letter to "Inquiries and Answers." *Confederate Veteran* 8 (Apr. 1900): 170.

San Román, Jesús Víctor. *Perfiles históricos de la Amazonia peruana.* Lima: Ediciones Paulinas, 1975.

Sass, Herbert Ravenel. "The Story of *Little David.*" *Harper's Monthly Magazine* 186 (May 1943): 620–25.

Schaff, Morris. *The Sunset of the Confederacy.* Boston: John W. Luce and Co., 1912.

Scharf, John Thomas. *History of the Confederate States Navy.* New York: Rogers and Sherwood, 1887.

Schwab, Federico. "La bibliografía geográfica en el Perú." *Fénix* 1 (1st semester 1944): 87–103.

Seager, Robert II. *Alfred Thayer Mahan: The Man and His Letters.* Annapolis: Naval Institute Press, 1977.

———. *And Tyler Too: A Biography of John and Julia Gardiner Tyler.* New York: McGraw-Hill Book Co., 1963.

Selfridge, Thomas O., Jr. "Survey of the Amazon: Report of Commander Thomas O. Selfridge, United States Ship *Enterprise* (3rd Rate), August 1, 1879." In *Annual Report of the Secretary of the Navy on the Operations of the Department for the Year 1879*, pp. 320–71. Washington, D.C.: GPO, 1880.

Semmes, Raphael. "Admiral on Horseback: The Diary of Brigadier General Raphael Semmes, February–May, 1865." Ed. W. Stanley Hoole. *Alabama Review* 28 (Apr. 1975): 129–50.

———. *Memoirs of Service Afloat during the War Between the States.* Baltimore: Kelly, Piet and Co., 1869.

Sevier, Charles Francis. Questionnaire. MS 420. Civil War Veterans' Questionnaires (Confederate), roll 7, Manuscript Division, Tennessee State Library and Archives, Nashville.

Sharrer, G. Terry. "Commerce and Industry." In *Alexandria: A Towne in Transition*, ed. John D. Macoll and George J. Stansfield, pp. 16–38. Alexandria, Va.: Alexandria Bicentennial Commission and Alexandria Historical Society, 1977.

Sherman, Frederick Barreda. *From the Guadalquivir to the Golden Gate by Way of Lima, Baltimore, New York, Newport, Washington, London, Paris, and Cuajiniquilapa*. Mill Valley, Calif.: privately printed by Hall and Smith Co., 1977.

Shingleton, Royce Gordon. *John Taylor Wood: Sea Ghost of the Confederacy*. Athens: Univ. of Georgia Press, 1979.

Sinclair, Arthur. *Two Years on the Alabama*. Boston: Lee and Shepard Publishers, 1895.

Smith, Timiteo. Expediente personal. Expedientes personales, letra S, Archivo Central del Ministerio de Guerra, Lima.

Smythe, Augustine T. Papers. South Caroliniana Library, Univ. of South Carolina, Columbia.

Society Collection. Manuscript Department, Historical Society of Pennsylvania, Philadelphia.

Sotomayor, Rafael. "Viaje de los buques peruanos a Chiloé en 1866." *Revista Chilena de Historia y Geografía* 67 (Oct.–Dec. 1930): 27–42.

Sparrow, Thomas W. Alumnus file. Student and Alumni Records, University Archives, Univ. of Virginia Library, Charlottesville.

Spencer, Warren F. *The Confederate Navy in Europe*. University, Ala.: Univ. of Alabama Press, 1983.

Stampp, Kenneth M. *The Era of Reconstruction, 1865–1877*. New York: Alfred A. Knopf, 1965.

Steere, Joseph Beal. Papers. Bentley Historical Library, Univ. of Michigan, Ann Arbor.

Stevens, Hazard. "The Battle of Sailor's Creek." *Papers of the Military Historical Society of Massachusetts* 6, no. 9 (1907): 437–48.

Stevenson, Frederick James. *A Traveller of the Sixties, Being Extracts from the Diaries Kept by the Late Frederick James Stevenson of His Journeyings and Explorations in Brazil, Peru, Argentina, Patagonia, Chile, and Bolivia, during the Years 1867–1869*. Ed. Douglas Timins. London: Constable and Co., 1929.

Stewart, William H., ed. *History of Norfolk County, Virginia, and Representative Citizens*. Chicago: Biographical Publishing Co., 1902.

Stiglich, Germán. "Raimondi y la cartografía peruana." *Boletín de la Sociedad Geográfica de Lima* 43 (Dec. 1926): 389–91.

Stiles, John C. "Confederate States Navy at Sailor's Creek, Va." *Confederate Veteran* 28 (July 1920): 252.

Stiles, Robert. *Four Years under Marse Robert*. 2d ed. New York: Neale Publishing Co., 1903.

Still, William N., Jr. "Confederate Naval Strategy: The Ironclad." *Journal of Southern History* 27 (Aug. 1961): 330–43.

———. *Iron Afloat: The Story of the Confederate Armorclads*. Nashville: Vanderbilt Univ. Press, 1971.

Storm, Henry. Papers. Manuscript Department, William R. Perkins Library, Duke Univ., Durham, N.C.

Strohm, Robert F. "J. W. Randolph, Bookman *Extraordinaire*." *Virginia Historical Society Occasional Bulletin*, no. 42 (June 1981): 7–11.

Sutherland, Daniel E. "Exiles, Emigrants, and Sojourners: The Post–Civil War Confederate Exodus in Perspective." *Civil War History* 31 (Sept. 1985): 237–56.

Távara, Santiago. *Viaje de Lima a Iquitos*. Lima: Imprenta de "El Comercio," 1868 [1869].

Tavares Bastos, Aureliano C. *O Valle do Amazonas: Estudo sobre a livre navegação do Amazonas, estadística, producções, commercio, questões fiscaes do Valle do Amazonas*. Rio de Janeiro: B. L. Garnier, 1866.

Taylor, Fitch W. *The Broad Pennant; or, A Cruise in the United States Flag Ship of the Gulf Squadron, during the Mexican Difficulties.* New York: Leavitt, Trow and Co., 1848.

Times (London), 1866, 1884.

Tomb, James Harvey. "Confederate Torpedo Boats." *Confederate Veteran* 31 (Feb. 1923): 93–94.

——. "The First Steam Torpedo Boat." *Confederate Veteran* 12 (Mar. 1904): 106.

——. "The Last Obstructions in Charleston Harbor, 1863." *Confederate Veteran* 32 (Mar. 1924): 98–99.

——. Memoirs of Chief Engineer James H. Tomb, C.S.N. Manuscript and typescript. William Victor Tomb and James Harvey Tomb Papers, no. 723, Southern Historical Collection, Library of the Univ. of North Carolina at Chapel Hill.

——. "Naval Operations at Charleston." *Confederate Veteran* 34 (July 1926): 259–60.

——. "Submarines and Torpedo Boats, C.S.N." *Confederate Veteran* 22 (Apr. 1914): 168–69.

Tomb, William Victor, and James Harvey Tomb. Papers. No. 723. Southern Historical Collection, Library of the Univ. of North Carolina at Chapel Hill.

Tooley, Ronald Vere. *Tooley's Dictionary of Mapmakers.* New York: Alan R. Liss, 1979.

Tordich, Charles M. "Franklin Buchanan: Symbol for Two Navies." In *Captains of the Old Steam Navy: Makers of the American Naval Tradition, 1840–1880,* ed. James C. Bradford, pp. 87–112. Annapolis: Naval Institute Press, 1986.

Tschudi, Johann J. von. *Travels in Peru, during the Years 1838–1842.* Trans. Thomasina Ross. New York: George P. Putnam, 1849.

Tucker, John Randolph. Papers. Archives, Library, Old Dominion Univ., Norfolk, Va.

——. Papers. Private collection of John Randolph Tucker, Pensacola, Fla.

Tucker, R. Douglas. Private collection of materials relating to John Randolph Tucker and his family. Ellenboro, N.C.

Tucker, Terry. *Bermuda, Today and Yesterday, 1503–1973.* London: Robert Hale and Co., 1975.

Tucker-Randolph Families. Correspondence. Brock Collection, Henry E. Huntington Library and Art Gallery, San Marino, Calif.

Twentieth Century Biographical Dictionary of Notable Americans. Ed. Rossiter Johnson. 10 vols. Boston: Biographical Society, 1904.

Tyler, David B. *The American Clyde: A History of Iron and Steel Shipbuilding on the Delaware from 1840 to World War I.* [Newark]: Univ. of Delaware Press, 1958.

Tyler, John. Papers. Manuscript Department, Earl Gregg Swem Library, College of William and Mary, Williamsburg, Va.

Tyler, John, Jr. Papers. Manuscript Department, Earl Gregg Swem Library, College of William and Mary, Williamsburg, Va.

United States. Congress. House. *Board of Naval Officers: Letter of the Secretary of the Navy, Communicating, in Answer to a Resolution of the House, Reports of the Board of Officers Ordered to Examine into the Condition of the Navy Yards.* 36th Cong., 1st sess., 1860. Ex. Doc. 34.

——. ——. ——. *Causes of the Reduction of American Tonnage.* 41st Cong., 2d sess., 1870. H. Rept. 28.

——. ——. ——. *Engineers Corps of the Army: Letter from the Secretary of War.* 44th Cong., 1st sess., 1876. H. Ex. Doc. 171.

——. ——. ——. *House Journal.* 50th Cong., 2d sess., 1888–89.

——. ——. ——. *Letter from the Secretary of the Navy, Transmitting, in Compliance with a Resolution of the House, a Copy of the Evidence Taken by the Board of Naval Officers for Investigating the Condition of the Navy Yards.* 36th Cong., 1st sess., 1860. Ex. Doc. 77.

——. ——. ——. *Letter from the Secretary of the Navy, Transmitting the Record of the Court-Martial in the Case of Lieutenant Fabius Stanly, Together with Correspondence Relating Thereto.* 33d Cong., 2d sess., 1853. Ex. Doc. 69.

——. ——. ——. *Letter of the Secretary of the Navy, Transmitting Lists of Clerks Employed in His Office and in the Office of the Navy Commissioners dur-*

ing the Year 1827. 20th Cong., 1st sess., 1826. Doc. 47.

———. ———. ———. Committee on Naval Affairs. *H. H. Doty: Report of the Committee on Naval Affairs, to Whom Was Referred the Petition of H. H. Doty, in Reference to Torpedoes*. 45th Cong., 2d Sess., 1878. Rep. 626.

———. ———. Senate. *Message of the President of the United States, Transmitting, with Accompanying Papers, a Report from the Secretary of State Answering the Resolution of the Senate of January 16, 1896, Addressed to Him, Calling for Information concerning the Claims against Peru of Thomas W. Sparrow, N. B. Noland, and Others, Members of the Commission Known as the Hydrographical Commission of the Amazon, Employed by the Government of Peru, for Compensation for Their Services on Said Commission*. 54th Cong., 1st sess., 1896. Doc. 125.

———. ———. ———. Select Committee. *On the Circumstances Attending the Surrender of the Navy Yard at Pensacola and the Destruction of Property and the Navy Yard at Norfolk and Armory at Harper's Ferry*. 37 Cong., 2d sess., 1862. Com. Rep. 37.

———. Department of the Interior. *Official Register of the United States, Containing a List of the Officers and Employés in the Civil, Military, and Naval Service on the Thirtieth Day of June, 1879; 1899*. 2 vols. each. Washington, D.C.: GPO, 1879; 1899.

———. Naval Academy. *Annual Register of the United States Naval Academy, Annapolis, Maryland, 1859*. Washington, D.C., 1859.

———. Navy Department. *Register of the Commissioned and Warrant Officers of the Navy of the United States, 1834–1875*. Washington, D.C., 1834–75.

———. ———. *Report of the Secretary of the Navy* [1855]. 34th Cong., 1st sess., 1855. H. Ex. Doc. 1.

———. ———. Hydrographic Office. *American Practical Navigator: An Epitome of Navigation, Originally by Nathaniel Bowditch*. Rev. ed. Hydrographic Office Publication no. 9. Washington, D.C.: GPO, 1966.

———. ———. Naval History Division. *Dictionary of American Naval Fighting Ships*. 8 vols. Washington, D.C.: GPO, 1959–76.

———. ———. Office of Naval Records and Library. *Official Records of the Union and Confederate Navies in the War of the Rebellion*. 30 vols. in 2 ser. Washington, D.C.: GPO, 1894–1922.

———. ———. ———. *Register of the Officers of the Confederate States Navy, 1861–1865*. Rev. ed. Washington, D.C.: GPO, 1931.

———. War Department. *List of Staff Officers of the Confederate States Army, 1861–1865*. Comp. John M. Carroll. 1891. Reprint. Mattituck, N.J.: J. M. Carroll and Co., 1983.

———. ———. *The War of the Rebellion: A Compilation of the Official Records of the Union and Confederate Armies*. 130 vols. in 4 ser. Washington, D.C.: GPO, 1880–1901.

United States Naval Academy Alumni Association, Inc. *Register of Alumni Graduates and Former Naval Cadets and Midshipmen, 1845–1977*. Annapolis: by the association, 1977.

University of Virginia. *Students of the University of Virginia: A Semi-Centennial Catalogue, with Brief Biographical Sketches*. Baltimore: Charles Harvey and Co., 1878.

Valdizán Gamio, José. *Historia naval del Perú*. 4 vols. to date. Lima: Ministerio de Marina, Dirección General de Intereses Marítimos, 1980—.

———. *Tradiciones navales peruanas*. Lima: Empresa Gráfica Sanmartí, 1966.

Valle, James E. *Rocks and Shoals: Order and Discipline in the Old Navy, 1800–1861*. Annapolis: Naval Institute Press, 1980.

Varas Velásquez, Miguel, ed. "Algunas cartas y documentos sobre el conflicto hispano-peruano, 1864–1865." *Revista Chilena*, año 12, no. 95–96 (Mar.–Apr. 1928): 171–240.

———. "Algunas cartas y documentos sobre la guerra entre Chile-Perú y España." *Revista Chilena*, año 12, no. 97 (May 1928): 494–549.

Vargas Caballero, Luis Ernesto. "Las adquisiciones navales del Perú en la década 1860–70." *Revista del Instituto de Estudios Histórico-Marítimos del Perú*, no. 1 (1978): 81–95.

Vegas García, Manuel I. *Historia de la marina de guerra del Perú, 1821–1924*. Lima: Imp. "Lux" de E. L. Castro, 1929.

Veloz, Nicholas F., Jr. "Butcher, Baker, Candlestick Maker: The 1810 Census and Personal Property Tax Rolls for Alexandria, Va." Typescript. Alexandria Library, Alexandria, Va., 1978.

Veselka, Elizabeth. Private collection of newspaper clippings and photos pertaining to Francis Land Galt. Englewood, Colo.

Vicuña MacKenna, Benjamín. *Diez meses de misión a los Estados Unidos de América, como ajente confidencial de Chile*. 2 vols. in l. Santiago: Imprenta de La Libertad, 1867.

Virginia. *Proceedings of the Advisory Council of the State of Virginia, April 21–June 19, 1861*. Ed. James I. Robertson, Jr. Richmond: Virginia State Library, 1977.

———. *Proceedings of the Virginia State Convention of 1861*. Ed. George H. Reese. 4 vols. Richmond: Virginia State Library, 1965.

Virginia Miscellaneous Papers. Manuscript Department, William R. Perkins Library, Duke Univ., Durham, N.C.

Wagner de Reyna, Alberto. *Las relaciones diplomáticas entre el Perú y Chile durante el conflicto con España, 1864–1867*. Lima: Ediciones del Sol, 1963.

Walker, Cornelius. *The Life and Correspondence of Rev. William Sparrow, D.D.* Philadelphia: James Hammond, 1876.

Watson, W. A. "The Fighting at Sailor's Creek." *Confederate Veteran* 25 (Oct. 1917): 448–52.

Webber, Richard H., ed. *Monitors of the U.S. Navy, 1861–1937*. U.S. Navy Department, Naval History Division Publication. Washington, D.C.: GPO, 1969.

"The Webb Family of New Kent County." Pts. 1–3. *Virginia Magazine of History and Biography* 25 (Jan.–July 1917): 99–100, 210–12, 330–31.

Webster, Noah. *An American Dictionary of the English Language*. 3d ed., rev. Springfield, Mass.: George and Charles Merriam, 1858.

Welles, Gideon. *Diary of Gideon Welles, Secretary of the Navy under Lincoln and Johnson*. Ed. Edgar T. Welles. 3 vols. Boston: Houghton Mifflin Co., 1911.

Wells, Tom H. *The Confederate Navy: A Study in Organization*. University, Ala.: Univ. of Alabama Press, 1971.

Werlich, David P. "The Conquest and Settlement of the Peruvian Montaña." Ph.D. diss., Univ. of Minnesota, 1968.

———. *Peru: A Short History*. Carbondale: Southern Illinois Univ. Press, 1978.

———. Private collection of manuscripts pertaining to John Randolph Tucker. Carbondale, Ill.

Wertheman, Arturo. "Coordenadas geográficas de algunos puntos de la región oriental del Perú." *Boletín de la Sociedad Geográfica de Lima* 17 (June 1905): 139–48.

———. *Informe de la exploración de los ríos Perené y Tambo, presentado al señor Ministro de Gobierno, Policía, y Obras Públicas*. Lima: Imprenta del Estado, 1877.

———. "Ruinas de la fortaleza de Cuelap." *Boletín de la Sociedad Geográfica de Lima* 2 (1892): 147–53.

Werthemann, Arthur [Arturo Wertheman]. "Aufnahme de Flüsse Paranapura und Cahuapanas im Departamento de Amazonas der Republik Perú." In *Zeitschrift der Gesellschaft für erdkunde zu Berlin*, ed. W. Koner, 3d ser., vol. 15, pp. 210–20. Berlin: Dietrich Reimer, 1880.

Werthemann, Ida. Private collection of newspaper clippings pertaining to Arturo Wertheman. Lima, Peru.

Who's Who in America, 1899–1900. Ed. John W. Leonard. Chicago: A. N. Marquis and Co., 1899.

Wilkinson, Henry C. *The Adventurers of Bermuda: A History of the Island from Its Discovery until the Dissolution of the Somers Island Company in 1684*. London: Oxford Univ. Press, 1958.

———. *Bermuda from Sail to Steam:*

BIBLIOGRAPHY

The History of the Island from 1784 to 1901. 2 vols. London: Oxford Univ. Press, 1973.

——. *Bermuda in the Old Empire: A History of the Island from the Dissolution of the Somers Island Company until the End of the American Revolutionary War, 1684–1784.* London: Oxford Univ. Press, 1950.

Williams, Frances Leigh. *Matthew Fontaine Maury, Scientist of the Sea.* New Brunswick, N.J.: Rutgers Univ. Press, 1963.

Williams, Héctor. *El Vice-Almirante don Juan Williams Rebolledo ante la historia, 1825–1910.* Santiago: Imprenta de Carabineros, n.d.

Williams, T. Harry. *P. G. T. Beauregard: Napoleon in Gray.* Baton Rouge: Louisiana State Univ. Press, 1954.

Williams Rebolledo, Juan. *Guerra del Pacífico: Breve narración histórica de la contienda de Chile y Perú contra España, 1865–1866.* Santiago: Impr. Elzeviriana, 1901.

Wilson, Herbert W. *Battleships in Action.* 2 vols. 1926. Reprint. Grosse Point, Mich.: Scholarly Press, 1969.

Wise, Henry Augustus. Letters. Naval History Collection, New York Historical Society, New York.

——. Papers. Naval Historical Foundation, Manuscript Division, Library of Congress, Washington, D.C.

——. [Harry Gringo, pseud.]. *Scampavias: From Gibel Tarek to Stamboul.* New York: Charles Scribner, 1857.

——. [Harry Gringo, pseud.]. *Tales for the Marines.* Boston: Phillips, Sampson and Co., 1855.

Wood, John Taylor. "The First Fight of Iron-Clads." In *Battles and Leaders of the Civil War.* Ed. Robert U. Johnson and Clarence C. Buel, 1:692–711. 4 vols. New York: Century Co., 1884–87.

——. Papers. No. 2381. Southern Historical Collection, Library of the Univ. of North Carolina at Chapel Hill.

Young, Francis Berkeley. *The Berkeleys of Barn Elms.* 1954. Reprint. Hamden, Conn.: Archon Books, 1964.

Zook, David H. *Zarumilla-Marañón: The Ecuador-Peru Dispute.* New York: Bookman Associates, 1964.

Index

339

INDEX

INDEX

Tucker, John, 1, 2, 3

Tucker, John Randolph: personality of, xii–xiii, 6–7, 12, 13, 50, 51, 52, 88, 96, 97, 116; family background and early years of, 1–3; personal finances and generosity of, 4, 7–8, 75, 88, 93, 143, 195–96, 197, 235–36, 240, 242, 246, 248–49, 257–58, 266, 290 n. 25; physical appearance of, 6–7, 38, 69, 97, 257; love of family, 7–8, 12, 13, 20, 61, 75, 134, 153, 162, 163, 175, 196, 228–29, 241; health of, 9, 10, 96, 182, 210, 214, 215, 255, 257; and religion, 107, 108, 257

—professional qualities, ideas, and contributions of: professionalism, 3, 11, 25, 43, 52, 65–66, 88, 89, 96–97; leadership, 7, 9, 11, 29, 52, 61–63, 68, 71, 72–73, 108; guns, ballistics, and armor, 9, 11, 14, 25, 26, 37, 45, 104, 109, 256, 258; naval training and discipline, 10–11, 13, 26, 60, 62–63, 67–68, 69, 93, 109, 110, 146; naval organization and administration, 13, 61–62, 103–4, 106–7, 109–10; naval strategy and tactics, 27–28, 33, 45, 47–48, 49, 53, 63, 102–3, 105, 109–10; torpedoes, 27, 28, 40, 45, 47–48, 50, 53, 55, 58–59, 63, 65, 104–6, 109, 258; small arms, 167–68

—career of, in United States Navy: with the Mediterranean Squadron, 3–5, 11–12; court-martial of, 4–6; at New York, 5; promotions of, 5, 6, 7, 13; with the Brazil Squadron, 6; at Norfolk, 7, 8, 11, 13, 14, 16–22; cruise to the East Indies, 8–9; with the Home Squadron, 8, 11; in War with Mexico, 9–11; investigates navy yards, 13; summarized, 13, 114–15; and secession crisis, 16; resignation of, 19

—career of, in Virginia and Confederate navies: on the James River, 23, 25–28; at Hampton Roads, 28–33; at Drewry's Bluff, 28, 33–37; raids Charleston blockade, 41–43; assumes command at Charleston, 43–44; and Du Pont's attack, 44–47; employs torpedo boats, 47–50, 53, 55–60; and Morris Island campaign, 52–55; defends Fort Sumter, 53, 55, 60; final months at Charleston, 60–66; and black sailors, 62, 69; commands ashore at Richmond, 67–68; and battle of Sayler's Creek, 68–74, 289 n. 19; imprisoned and paroled, 74–77

—career of, in Peruvian Navy: recruits staff and travels to Peru, 88–94; sojourn in Lima, 95–98; rejected by Peru's officers, 99–101; organizes fleet, 101, 103–7, 109–10; relations with allied officers, 107–9; mutiny against, 112–13; and War of Salutes, 115–28; resignation of, 129–33

—career of, with Hydrographic Commission of the Amazon: enlists members and journeys to Iquitos, 143–48; and Indians, 148, 158, 159, 178–79, 180, 204–5, 207, 209, 210; at Manassas, 152–54, 228; at Leticia, 154–55; explores Yavarí River, 156; explores Ucayali, Tambo, and Urubamba rivers, 158–59; and new government, 160–62; first mission to the United States, 163–75; acquires and equips *Tambo*, 164–67, 174–75; reports on rifles and commercial steamers, 167–68; hires Galt and Rochelle, 168, 172, 174; journey from Pará to Iquitos, 175–76; second expedition to the Ucayali and Tambo rivers, 177–83; feud with Raygada and Alzamora, 183–90; visits Lima, 190–92, 213–15, 233, 234–36; second mission to the United States, 193–96; acquires *Mairo*, 193–94; hires Sparrow and Noland, 194; returns to Iquitos, 196–97; feud with Carreño, 203; expedition to the Pachitea and Pichis rivers, 203–10; surveys Marañón-Amazon and Huallaga rivers, 211–13; life in Iquitos, 228–29; final mission to the United States, 241–44; dissolution of the commission, 244–45; efforts to obtain arrears, 245–46, 248–49

—final years of: dedicates Jackson statue, 251; seeks work with Turks, 255–56; retirement and death of, at Petersburg, 257–58
See also under Alzamora, Federico; Beauregard, Pierre Gustave Toutant; Carreño, Enrique; Pardo y Lavalle, Manuel; Prado, Mariano Ignacio; Williams Rebolledo, Juan; *and* Wise, Henry Augustus

Tucker, John Tarleton, 8; in United States Navy, 16, 22; on the *Patrick Henry*, 27; in the Chilean Navy, 118, 145, 301 n. 18; journey of, to Iquitos, 144, 145, 147, 148; and Manassas, 153; and expedition to Cuba, 302 n. 34

351